WORLD CHRISTIANITY

WORLD CHRISTIANITY

Critical Concepts in Religious Studies

Edited by
Elizabeth Koepping

Volume IV

LONDON AND NEW YORK

First published 2011
by Routledge
2 Park Square, Milton Park, Abingdon, OX14 4RN
Simultaneously published in the USA and Canada
by Routledge
270 Madison Avenue, New York, NY 10016

Routledge is an imprint of the Taylor & Francis Group, an informa business

Editorial material and selection © 2011 Elizabeth Koepping; individual owners retain copyright in their own material

Typeset in Times NR MT by Graphicraft Limited, Hong Kong
Printed and bound in Great Britain by MPG Books Group, UK

All rights reserved. No part of this book may be reprinted or reproduced or utilised in any form or by any electronic, mechanical, or other means, now known or hereafter invented, including photocopying and recording, or in any information storage or retrieval system, without permission in writing from the publishers.

British Library Cataloguing in Publication Data
A catalogue record for this book is available from the British Library

Library of Congress Cataloging-in-Publication Data
World Christianity : critical concepts in religious studies / edited by Elizabeth Koepping.
p. cm.
Includes bibliographical references and index.
ISBN 978-0-415-46827-5 (set) – ISBN 978-0-415-47291-3 (1) –
ISBN 978-0-415-47290-6 (2) – ISBN 978-0-415-47289-0 (3) –
ISBN 978-0-415-47288-3 (4)   1. Christianity.
I. Koepping, Elizabeth.
BR121.3.W67 2010
270.09–dc22
2010006472

ISBN 978-0-415-46827-5 (Set)
ISBN 978-0-415-47288-3 (Volume IV)

Publisher's Note

References within each chapter are as they appear in the original complete work

CONTENTS

VOLUME IV

Acknowledgements ix

Introduction to Volume IV 1

PART 20
Clothed for glory: dress for Christians 11

80 Excerpt from 'Nakedness and clothing in early encounters between Aboriginal people of Central Australia, missionaries and anthropologists' 13
PEGGY BROCK

81 To honor her head: hats as a symbol of women's position in three evangelical churches in Edinburgh, Scotland 25
RUTH BORKER

PART 21
Church within walls 43

82 The immediacy of eternity: time and transformation in a Roman Catholic convent 45
REBECCA J. LESTER

83 Women living between the church and the state: a case study of Catholic women religious in contemporary rural China 68
LI WENWEN

CONTENTS

PART 22
Church beyond walls: the performance of pilgrimage   85

84 Excerpt from 'Pilgrimage and patronage in Brazil: a paradigm for social relations and religious diversity'   87
SIDNEY M. GREENFIELD AND ANTONIO MOURÃO CAVALCANTE

85 Division and demolition at the tomb of a beloved saint: the evolving character of an Orthodox Christian pilgrim centre in India   104
ALEX GATH

86 Performing pilgrimage: Walsingham and the ritual construction of irony   121
SIMON COLEMAN AND JOHN ELSNER

87 Persistent peregrination: from Sun Dance to Catholic pilgrimage among Canadian Prairie Indians   140
ALAN MORINIS

88 Bernard Mizeki: missionary saints and the creation of Christian communities   154
DANA L. ROBERT

89 Excerpt from 'John Wesley slept here: American shrines and American Methodists'   169
THOMAS A. TWEED

PART 23
Performing Christianity   179

90 Catholic hymns of Michigan Indians   181
GERTRUDE PROKOSCH KURATH

91 Uduk faith in a five-note scale: mission music and the spread of the Gospel   191
WENDY JAMES

92 Excerpt from '"Almost persuaded now to believe": Gospel songs in New Zealand evangelical theology and practice'   207
BRYAN D. GILLING

93 Women as religious and political praise singers within African institutions: the case of the CCAP Blantyre Synod and political parties in Malawi   224
CLARA HENDERSON AND LISA GILMAN

CONTENTS

94 Excerpt from 'Dalit theology in Tamil Christian folk music: a transformative liturgy by James Theophilus Appavoo'   242
ZOE C. SHERINIAN

95 Syncretic objects: material culture of syncretism among the Paiwan Catholics, Taiwan   262
CHANG-KWO TAN

96 Introduction to *Christianity in Indian Dance Forms*   280
FRANCIS PETER BARBOZA

PART 24
Issues for Christianity in the twenty-first century   295

97 Beyond Christendom: Protestant–Catholic distinctions in coming global Christianity   297
D. PAUL SULLINS

98 Religion and the awakening of indigenous people in Latin America   316
CRISTIÁN PARKER GUMUCIO

99 Half a century of African Christian theologies: elements of the emerging agenda for the twenty-first century   332
TINYIKO SAM MALULEKE

Index   354

ACKNOWLEDGEMENTS

The publishers would like to thank the following for permission to reprint their material:

Peggy Brock, excerpt from 'Nakedness and Clothing in Early Encounters Between Aboriginal People of Central Australia, Missionaries and Anthropologists', *Journal of Colonialism and Colonial History*, 2007, 8, 1, 1–11. © 2007 Peggy Brock and The Johns Hopkins University Press. Reprinted with permission of The Johns Hopkins University Press.

Elsevier for permission to reprint Rebecca J. Lester, 'The Immediacy of Eternity: Time and Transformation in a Roman Catholic Convent', *Religion*, 2003, 33, 201–219, Copyright Elsevier, 2003.

Li Wenwen for permission to reprint Li Wenwen, 'Women Living between the Church and the State – A Case Study of Catholic Women Religious in Contemporary Rural China', [translated and revised by author 2009]. Originally published in Peter Ng and Wu Xiaoxin (eds), *Christianity and Chinese Society and Culture: The First International Young Scholars Symposium* (Chinese University of Hong Kong, 2003), pp. 359–384.

The University of Wisconsin Press for permission to reprint Sidney M. Greenfield and Antonio Mourão Cavalcante, excerpt from 'Pilgrimage and Patronage in Brazil: A Paradigm for Social Relations and Religious Diversity', *Luso-Brazilian Review*, 2006, 43, 2, 63–89. © 2006 by the Board of Regents of the University of Wisconsin System.

Taylor & Francis Ltd for permission to reprint Alex Gath, 'Division and Demolition at the Tomb of a Beloved Saint: The Evolving Character of an Orthodox Christian Pilgrim Centre in India', *Culture and Religion*, 2000, 1, 2, 171–187. www.informaworld.com

Taylor & Francis Books UK for permission to reprint Simon Coleman and John Elsner, 'Performing Pilgrimage: Walsingham and the Ritual Construction of Irony', in Felicia Hughes-Freeland (ed.), *Ritual, Performance, Media* (Routledge, 1998), pp. 46–65.

ACKNOWLEDGEMENTS

Greenwood Publishing Company Inc., Westport, CT, for permission to reprint Alan Morinis, 'Persistent Peregrination: From Sun Dance to Catholic Pilgrimage among Canadian Prairie Indians', in Alan Morinis (ed.), *Sacred Journeys: The Anthropology of Pilgrimage* [Contributions to the Study of Anthropology, 7] (Greenwood Press, 1992), pp. 101–113.

Dana L. Robert for permission to reprint Dana L. Robert, 'Bernard Mizeki: Missionary Saints and the Creation of Christian Communities', revised by author 2009, originally published in *Yale Divinity School Library Occasional Publication No. 19* (New Haven: Yale Divinity School Library, 2005).

Brill for permission to reprint Thomas A. Tweed, excerpt from 'John Wesley Slept Here: American Shrines and American Methodists', *NUMEN*, 47 2000, 41–42, 45–47, 51–54, 61–64, 66.

Anthropological Quarterly for permission to reprint Gertrude Prokosch Kurath, 'Catholic Hymns of Michigan Indians', *Anthropological Quarterly*, 1957, 30, 2, 31–44.

JASO Occasional Papers for permission to reprint Wendy James, 'Uduk Faith in a Five-Note Scale: Mission Music and the Spread of the Gospel', in Wendy James and Douglas H. Johnson (eds), *Vernacular Christianity: Essays in the Social Anthropology of Religion Presented to Godfrey Lienhardt* (JASO Occasional Papers, 1988), pp. 131–145.

Bryan D. Gilling for permission to reprint Bryan D. Gilling, excerpt from '"Almost Persuaded now to Believe": Gospel Songs in New Zealand Evangelical Theology and Practice', *The Journal of Religious History*, 1995, 19, 1, 92–110.

Clara Henderson and Lisa Gilman for permission to reprint Clara Henderson and Lisa Gilman, 'Women as Religious and Political Praise Singers within African Institutions: The Case of the CCAP Blantyre Synod and Political Parties in Malawi', *Women and Music*, 2004, 8, 22–40.

State University of New York Press for permission to reprint Zoe C. Sherinian, excerpt from 'Dalit Theology in Tamil Christian Folk Music: A Transformative Liturgy by James Theophilus Appavoo', in Selva Raj and Corinne Dempsey (eds), *Popular Christianity in India: Riting between the Lines* [SUNY Series in Hindu Studies], (State University of New York Press, 2002), pp. 233–253. © 2002, State University of New York. All rights reserved.

Sage Publications for permission to reprint Chang-Kwo Tan, 'Syncretic Objects: Material Culture of Syncretism among the Paiwan Catholics, Taiwan', *Journal of Material Culture*, 2002, 7, 2, 167–187.

Elsevier for permission to reprint D. Paul Sullins, 'Beyond Christendom: Protestant–Catholic Distinctions in Coming Global Christianity', *Religion*, 2006, 36, 197–213, Copyright Elsevier, 2006.

ACKNOWLEDGEMENTS

Sage Publications for permission to reprint Cristián Parker Gumucio, 'Religion and the Awakening of Indigenous People in Latin America', *Social Compass*, 2002, 49, 1, 67–81.

Disclaimer

The publishers have made every effort to contact authors/copyright holders of works reprinted in *World Christianity (Critical Concepts in Religious Studies)*. This has not been possible in every case, however, and we would welcome correspondence from those individuals/companies whom we have been unable to trace.

INTRODUCTION TO VOLUME IV

So far in these volumes, we have considered the spreading and embedding of Christianity across the world over the last two thousand years, a process which, while it has gained pace in the last fifty, has not been uniformly effective. The first three volumes set out the initial storyline and subsequent development, interpretation and rewriting by global audiences as well as local and universal ecclesial and liturgical practitioners. The first two parts of Volume I considered *what* Christianity was and is in very broad terms of basic text, context and organization. The subsequent thousand or so pages considered more *where* these Christianities were and *how* they negotiated places and peoples and in the process were almost reborn with new facets, new images and new presentations of multiple selves. Volume III completed the weaving of the basic Christian cloth (replete with snags, double and missing strands and clashing tones) by setting out modern Christian practices and patterns, contextualizing and even inculturating the world over, within the given frame of power, identity, ethnicity, agency, gender, politics and other relevant points of interest.

Given that adherents of living religions express rites and rituals, relationships and reverences continually, regularly or occasionally, it is appropriate that this final volume focuses on living and performing Christianity, taking visible attributes such as dress, prayer, music, material culture, liturgy, convent life and pilgrimage. Uniformity or even inerrancy may well be an expectation for some insiders and an assumption for some with little knowledge of the faith. Yet this is not reflected in reality, the Christian tradition, as all other extra-local faiths, resembling the chameleon as it negotiates, merges with and challenges surface and deep structures of locality. Printing allowed the exact replication of texts, and improvements in transport and communications increasingly enabled more rigorous controls, balanced now to a limited extent by easier access to information through the Web. But negotiation between text and context, including the near-capture of the text by the context, remains the common coin of Christianity in every single locale.

Set liturgy, performance and praxis may appear 'the same', yet locality and internal diversity inscribe difference. Performance studies may suggest that ritual performance powerfully shows the authority of recollection and the creativity of the imagination.[1] If this implies a certain collective homogeneity of intention, even of belief, among those attending such powerful performances, we should be cautious, for little or nothing about actual belief or intention beyond the fact of the act can be imputed to hymn singing, prayer, liturgical dance, robes or pilgrimages. Recollecting as part of looking forward in imaginings may well be redemptive; established ritual may be oppressive or liberating. Meeting for prayer or worship involves a process which may be intensely contested on theological, political or personal grounds. The performance of ritual can thus dramatize conflicting discourses within one faith tradition, embracing differences of ethnicity, caste, class, gender and indeed of theology (given normal internal differences in a congregation, together with incomers from other faiths or denominations), thereby creating unintended transformations.

Part 20: Clothed for glory: dress for Christians

It is not uncommon for religions to decide upon specific dress codes either for the everyday life of all identifying as adherents or for the performance of specific rituals.[2] Outward markers may be those enjoined on members, such as the headcover for women expected by St Paul (unbound hair at that time being a statement of sexual interest or even availability) and the pattern of naked heads for male laity, covered arms and thighs for women, and modest clothing for both males and females, current in some churches, which avoids drawing the gaze of the opposite sex to breasts or genitals.[3] There are also order-specific habits worn by monks and nuns, black suits and white shirts for male Mormon missionaries, and uniforms worn by ranking women in parts of Africa for church and at times beyond its walls.

Those performing the liturgy or taking a service, gathering or rally also present in certain ways. The many-layered costly garb of the Orthodox, Roman Catholic and Anglican priest will show status – deacon, priest or Bishop – by the draping of certain items; a stage in the church cycle – purple or green; or the significance of certain days – red for martyrs, white for major festivals. Protestant ministers use a simpler form, mainly black and white with at most a colour-coded narrow stole. Pentecostal, Evangelical non-liturgical, and locally initiated church leaders wear a suit, collar and tie, or local robes. It is arguable whether 'dressing down' obscures the actual power of the suited preacher, who gets to choose the readings and hymns at will: officiants in firmly liturgical traditions[4] have to stick to and preach on set readings. Special clothing is said to be a theological statement that robed ones merely *perform* rather than *direct* the ritual, their personality or character being irrelevant: this may be contested.

Brock's article on the vexed issue of the introduction of clothes for the normally naked as an essential practice for proper Christians (Chapter 80) usefully shows Lutheran missionaries eventually accepting that while clothes may be accepted dress in the church place, nakedness was also proper dress in the camp.[5] In this regard, Lutherans showed more respect for Aboriginal decisions on dress, derived not just from association with the mission but with cattle station and other work done for whites, than did some later anthropologists and government officials.[6]

Equally emblematic, and making clear theological and biblical statements in the process, is the wearing of hats by Christian women in 1970s Edinburgh. Borker (Chapter 81) chose three Evangelical churches: a large Baptist congregation, and two small churches, Open Brethren and Seventh Day Adventist. She finds Seventh Day Adventist hat use reflects the actual position of women, which is more nuanced than the Brethren and Baptist taboo on their speaking in church. Women saw donning a hat or not as related to subordination, either within a spiritually interdependent or a spiritually unequal relationship; as related to dignity and modesty in not attracting the gaze of others; and also as a base both for power and reverence for God. Hats were thus used strategically to mark status or worth within their own or in regard to other congregations.

Part 21: Church within walls

Outsiders may well assume walls keep the world at bay for those committed to a life of poverty, chastity and obedience in enclosed convents or monasteries. Yet those within feel they are involved in a different way, being for the world but not in it in their life of prayer and contemplation. Such set-aside places have existed since the first Orthodox monasteries in Sinai as places of prayer, of learning and for the copying of liturgical or biblical texts, for advice and often health care and education for those in the area. Some orders were founded for religious to mix in society, starting with the thirteenth-century Franciscans and Poor Clares; since Vatican II, more have moved outside the cloister. Certain orders remain firmly enclosed, as is the case with certain Orthodox, Roman Catholic, Anglican and Lutheran nuns and monks who, while more usually beyond the walls, have still retained contemplative orders in all parts of the world. Anthropological studies of convents and nuns have increased in recent years, from the early work of Drid Williams in an enclosed English convent[7] and that of Sister Mary Aquina[8] in Central Africa to the cross-continent research of Gertrud Hüwelmeier.[9]

Lutkehaus in Volume II (Chapter 36) discussed one group of German nuns in New Guinea linked to the anthropologically refined Society of the Divine Word order, publishers of *Anthropos*. But while nuns offered a vital gender balance in the nineteenth-century mission field, given a male clergy, they, like the priests, were initially all from EuroAmerica. Yet there were clusters of people who had taken personal or somewhat less binding vows, such as the 'dedicated virgins' of eighteenth-century China who appeared in Volume I, and Volume II's Melanesian Brotherhood begun by Codrington in nineteenth-century Oceania, who were almost if not entirely made up of and run by people of the place.

The two contemporary uncloistered groups discussed in these papers by anthropologists are respectively from Mexico and China. The first focuses on one aspect of the initiation period, the rearranging of personal history into a new narrative of self, and the second on the way the nuns do their job in the world despite the difficulties deriving from their male colleagues, who feel themselves superior. Yet both texts, especially the second dealing with mature nuns, make clear the agency, autonomy and decision-making powers of these women.

Writing of the spiritual and ritual preparations made by young nuns before their vows, Lester (Chapter 82) explains their view of the Call to religious life as being not (or not just) a discrete event of deciding, training and taking vows but a developing process which, the postulants expect, will last their whole lives of working for gender and social justice in Mexico. This offers a useful parallel to conversion. There may be a discernible ritual point of testimony, reception and final personal commitment whether the convert is an ascribed member being reborn or a new entrant. Yet there is also a lifetime process of completing what the convert may (and the nun will) wish to be a close tie to God.

Li (Chapter 83) writes of Chinese nuns who are totally involved in running key parts of Roman Catholic church life in Shaanxi province, China; she is especially interested in the power relations between the sisters and the state, the sisters and the priests. They live an independent life, less restricted, says one, than are nuns in Italy, being much influenced by growing gender equality in China. They are also unwilling to maintain attitudes towards non-Christians held by the Church, mixing easily as between equals. Like Chia's laity in Volume I, Li's nuns think and act independently within what outsiders may wrongly assume to be a rigid institution.

Part 22: Church beyond walls: making a pilgrimage

A pilgrimage in the context of religion is embarked upon with more forethought and set-aside time than a stroll to Sunday service. It is a specific and often arduous journey to a place estimated by pilgrims to be linked to or imbued with the sacred. This may arise through connections to a 'good' person, an ecclesiastical or secular event, the relic of one declared locally and perhaps more widely to be a saint, or the divine manifested through a vision or visitation. Commonly, more than one element is involved. A site attracting pilgrims from far and wide may be 'validated' by the appropriate church authority. In the past as now, validation at the highest level could be financially beneficial – hence the occasional purloining of a saint's bones from the next town in late medieval Italy.

Yet the site did not need to be authorized, nor indeed need the particular tradition approve of anything like a pilgrimage or the formal creation of saints, to be well used by those whose 'chain of memory' causes them to regard a visit as beneficial. This may be to give thanks or fulfil a vow to the figure honoured there, on salvific or healing grounds. Others focus on the journey itself, as an extended liminal moment of divine communitas[10] or just an enjoyable expedition. Whether in communion with other pilgrims or as solitary seekers, a pilgrimage can be a performance of 'church beyond walls'. As such, the actual structure and process will vary according to time, place, context and intention.

Greenfield and Cavalcante's focus on Roman Catholic pilgrimage and the cult of saints in Brazil is placed into the local pattern of patron–client relations and thus of power and control (Chapter 84). Yet pilgrims who save for five years to make the arduous trip to fulfil a vow are also empowered by their set-aside experience. Power and control, indeed outright contest, occur in south India as well as Brazil, and in a Syrian Orthodox context at the tomb of a saint. Indeed, Gath's paper (Chapter 85) makes clear that the contest continued throughout the twentieth century.

'The ritual construction of irony' is the subtitle of Coleman and Elsner's paper on an Anglican pilgrimage in eastern England (Chapter 86). Formal though High-Church Anglican liturgy is, the Walsingham site allows pilgrims to 'mix and match' their own ritual response within the site, but also outwith the shrine in what, as one priest said, shows an overlap between church and a fairground. Pilgrimages in early Christianity frequently reused old sacred sites, attributing certain saints to the place through a vision, a story of succour, a miraculous healing. Morinis details this same process in the plains of Canada (Chapter 87), where Roman Catholics, largely of Plains Indian origin, recreate the summer ceremonial gathering of their previous tradition in Roman Catholic cladding.

Robert (Chapter 88) describes this same 'creation of a saint' in Zimbabwe and the associated pilgrimage in honour of Bernard Mizeki, the 'Apostle of the Shona' people, killed apparently for his faith in 1896 amid the occupation of the then Southern Rhodesia. Some thirty years after his martyrdom, the site began to be specially revered: 18,000 people now attend each year. The event is not uncontested, less for reasons such as those shown by Gath than because of a struggle over both interpretation and performance between laity and clergy.

'John Wesley slept here' is not exactly a salvific pilgrimage to a saint in an institutionally authorized sense of the term but, showing the way both the Methodist church and members have used it, Tweed presents an illuminating account of how people create a site of pilgrimage by their visits (Chapter 89). Pilgrimages to Martin Luther King sites also clearly fall into the same category of saints in the making (effectively so regarded by the Episcopal Church of America) as that of Mizeki, though, as Wendell Hines wrote, 'It is easier to build monuments than to make a better world'.[11]

INTRODUCTION TO VOLUME IV

Part 23: Performing Christianity

Moving towards the end of this last volume, it is time to show how seeing, hearing, moving, thinking, smelling, singing are variously used when people relate to God in ways prescribed by or practised in Christian tradition. Praying is invited by or responds to any of these tools, yet, as (ideally) an internal dialogue with God, prayer is essentially independent of symbols such as Cross, sanctuary screen or vestments, choir anthems, hymns, drums and praise songs, dancing, processing or censing. Though it may be said or sung aloud following a precisely set liturgy, some of which go back two thousand years, or done freely for as long as the Spirit moves the person praying, at another level prayer is invisible and personal, and that in all contexts of Christian worship, both public and private. Relating to God in community (for a religious praying in a cell, a person about to sleep, is still in community with fellow religious and God) may be the prime 'work of faith' from which should follow the fruits of faith in daily care for others. The more accessible elements contributing to that end, hymns, praise songs, dance and constructed symbols, are therefore presented in these readings.

The music of Christianity, the songs, hymns, chants and sung psalms, is, apart from the figure of Jesus, church buildings and clerical dress, perhaps what is most immediately associated with the faith. While hymns are more a Protestant than a Catholic expression of belief, our starting point for ancient hymnody is Kurath's 1950s exploration of hymns among Catholic Alagonquin Indians (Chapter 90). Assisted by translations of Jesuit fathers of the seventeenth century, the Algonquin sang hymns according to the style and sound of their own prayer songs, later adding an Austrian and German flavour after the manner of priests from those countries. Hymns were an even more important element in the popularization of and conversion to Christianity among the Uduk people in twentieth-century Sudan, James (Chapter 91) showing the missionary preference for doctrinally unambiguous texts which spread the basic and often repetitive message using the Uduk five-note scale: she cites the three different styles of hymn used over the years. Gilling (Chapter 92) looks at the differing way evangelicals in New Zealand used hymns and choruses in the six mass American-inspired rallies of the twentieth century. As with the Uduk, the words were simple and memorable, the tunes catchy, though Gilling notes the changes in theology reflected in the words over the century, the Second Coming and Christ the Victor (along with the singer as victor) gaining strength. Henderson and Gilman (Chapter 93) show the way in which Presbyterian women in Malawi sing praise both in church and in political meetings, the style (and often content) doing service in both contexts – just as the women's subordination is present in both. Such praise songs also include dancing, and the group organizing them is responsible for pastoral and social work within the congregation. Sherinian's chapter on Tamil Christianity (Chapter 94) shows the link between music and theology in liturgical compositions of Appavoo, part of his 'liberative indigenisation through Dalit folk music'. Dalit Christians of Tamil Nadu are suborned not only through their despised status in the wider Indian society but also through finely honed rank-ordering within churches.

Within a church the altar is commonly the focus, and Tan (Chapter 95) looks at an altar cross in a Catholic aboriginal church of Taiwan, in which Christ resembles an ancestral chief on a ritual house. Taking up the topic of syncretism and bricolage, he discusses the sculptor of the Taiwan cross, a female catechist, as a 'syncretic subject' carving her two-fold identity, and that of most viewers, in wood. She, and other carvers of this growing school, encountered the art of ancestors in the Catholic Church, enabling them to speak the Gospel with their own hands and eyes.

Yet such approaches are not unproblematic. The final paper, on speaking the gospel story through Indian dance, by the Roman Catholic priest Francis Barboza (Chapter 96), was a risky enterprise, not least because, as he says, he was accused of 'bringing paganism into churches . . . with his half-naked dancing'. One difference, and it is important, between his liturgical dancing and that of Malawi women is that his refers to the socio-historical context of only a small part of the potential audience of Christians in India, 80 per cent of whom are Dalit, with no relation to the Vedic system on which the dance is based other than as its victims. It is a salutary caution against 'contextualizing' from outwith the unit.

Part 24: Issues for Christianity in the twenty-first century

At the start of the twenty-first century, most people, groups and churches identifying as Christian still hold in common those key points with which Volume I began. All hold the Bible as important; but are continued and alternate revelations such as that of Joseph Smith or new Japanese founders seen as specious or sublime? Is it the inerrant and unchanging word of God, or a text for all time which is reinterpreted in each time? Prosperity Gospels may assert there is 'enough for all'; but are Christians, who make up almost half the world's people, prepared to tackle the ecological and socio-political changes implicit in that view? Almost all Christians hold the Trinity in common; but what does this mean theologically and in worship for adherents of each church, within and across contexts? This is not a divergence between North, South, East or West, richer or poorer, Orthodox, Pentecostal, Catholic or Protestant, but one based on individual religiosity and experience, class, caste, gender, rural or urban residence, education, global experience (gained by migrant labour as well as business class flights), as well as denomination. And denomination is little guide to belief, in part because moving may mean changing churches if being in touch with the 'spiritual forces of the place' is seen as more important than staying within boundaries derived more from historical human failings than divine decree. A varied denominational history is not sloughed off like last year's fashion. Moreover, developments in ecumenism as well as post-denominational churches in China and the education of a mobile laity make the future uncertain.

Sullins (Chapter 97) takes issue with Philip Jenkins's *The Next Christendom*, in which the latter demolished Old Christendom with swift sweeps of the brush,[12] showing that with the shifting centre of gravity, the global South, will take the pre-eminent position in Christianity as 'the New Christendom'. Sullins points out that by 2050, on current estimates, close to half the world's Roman Catholic population will be Latino broadly defined, and half of the world's Protestants African, with an increasing proportion from Asia. He shows the necessity of building arguments with the greatest care, a job he asserts Jenkins, who largely ignored (or arguably misinterpreted) Roman Catholic material, failed to do adequately, being blinkered by his own agenda. It is unfortunate that in *his* efforts to include Catholicism Sullins himself effectively ignores Orthodoxy; both writers ignore the maintenance of Euro-American economic and ecclesial power, priestly celibacy and women's roles.

In the first volume, Passi (Chapter 2) wrote of his Christian–Torres Straits view of the world and Razafindrakoto and Holter (Chapter 9) of the Malagasy non-Christian use of the Bible; such weft-threads, contested, revised, rejected and smoothed down, weave into the long warp-threads of Christianity in specific times and places. Here, Gumucio (Chapter 98) lays out other aspects of ethnic identity and the affirmation of memory in Latin America which relate to the visible and less visible world yet without doffing the cap to Rome, Canterbury, Seoul, Geneva, Athens, Dallas or any centre of Christian power other than the local. In setting out this strand, he sagely reviews Christian history in Latin America in its complexity as he investigates the status of shamans, ending with the comment that '[in the twenty-first century] religion will form a part of the process of the recovery of an indigenous identity, menaced by the processes of globalization'.

The final reading, by the South African theologian Maluleke (Chapter 99), gives both a reprise and a preview of African theologies for the twenty-first century. Given that the philosophy, purpose and praxis of Christianity are what localized theology and praxis addresses, his paper serves as a useful reminder that any religious studies, anthropology or sociology of religion approach which ignores theology as 'biased church-speak' falls into a methodological and intellectual mire. He pays attention to five issues: theologies of the African-initiated churches; Charismatic/Evangelical theology; translation theologies; African feminist/womanist theologies; and theologies of reconstruction. With his plea for a more thorough biblical hermeneutics from localized African viewpoints, we return to whence we began, with locality expressed in those Atlanta Baptists, and all other peoples and places set out in these volumes.

INTRODUCTION TO VOLUME IV

Notes

1 R. Schechner, *The Future of Ritual*, New York: Routledge, 1993; and R. Schechner and W. Appel, *By Means of Performance*, Cambridge: Cambridge University Press, 1990.
2 See A. Lurie, *The Language of Clothes*, London: Bloomsbury, 1992.
3 See 'Gold and Cholis: Indian Christian Sartorial Style', in E. Kent, *Converting Women*, Oxford: Oxford University Press, 2004.
4 For male clerics as cross-dressers, see Gisela Völger and Karin von Welck, *Männerbünde: zur Rolle des Mannes im Kulturvergleich*, Cologne: Rautenstrauch-Joest-Museums für Völkerkunde, 1990. Clerical dress is based on fourth-century (non-Christian) Roman fashion.
5 Langdon describes Peruvian Christians who, expected to wear 'fitting clothes' after conversion, designed their own version based more on their dress than that of the missionaries. E. J. Langdon, 'Sinoa Clothing and Adornment, or You Are What You Wear', in J. Cardwell and R. A. Schwartz (eds) *The Fabric of Culture: The Anthropology of Clothing and Adornment*, The Hague: Mouton, 1979.
6 The 'trousers or skirts for Tongan pastors' issue, discussed in Volume I, similarly cautioned the innocent reader not to assume there is an 'obviously right' answer.
7 Drid Williams, 'The Brides of Christ', in S. Ardener (ed.) *Perceiving Women*, London: Wiley, 1975.
8 G. Hüwelmeier, *Närrinnen Gottes: Lebenswelt von Ordensfrauen*, Münster: Waxman, 2004.
9 A. Simpson, 'Personhood and Self in Catholic Formation in Zambia', *Journal of Religion in Africa*, 33/4, 2003.
10 V. Turner. *The Ritual Process*, Chicago: Adine, 1969, gave a focus for pilgrimage studies.
11 Quoted in S.W. Hoffman, 'Holy Martin: The Overlooked Canonization of Dr. Martin Luther King Jr.', *Religion and American Culture: A Journal of Interpretation* 10/2, 2000: 141.
12 Also see Robert D. Woodberry and Timothy S. Shah in 'The Pioneering Protestants', *Journal of Democracy*, 15/2, 2004, for a useful discussion of democracy and Christianity.

Part 20

CLOTHED FOR GLORY: DRESS FOR CHRISTIANS

Excerpt from
'NAKEDNESS AND CLOTHING IN EARLY ENCOUNTERS BETWEEN ABORIGINAL PEOPLE OF CENTRAL AUSTRALIA, MISSIONARIES AND ANTHROPOLOGISTS'

Peggy Brock

Source: *Journal of Colonialism and Colonial History*, 8(1) (2007), 1–11.

The body and how it is covered and decorated is an important signifier within any society. Physical adornments communicate a wide range of information including age, status, gender and relative affluence. Members of a community have no difficulty reading each others appearance, but when members of two different societies come together in close physical proximity, it is not only their languages which are mutually incomprehensible, but their customs, values and morality which are often reflected in what they wear, how they treat their hair and other physical indicators, 'In many early cross-cultural encounters ... it seems dress served to bewilder or mislead rather than inform.[1] In this article I investigate early encounters between Aboriginal people in central Australia and two waves of missionaries who came to their lands, the first in the late 1870s and the second in the 1930s, and the perceptions of bodily adornment by the two sides of these encounters. By the 1930s anthropological ideas of pristine cultures and the 'authentic' Aborigine had changed the views of missionaries and other settler officials responsible for Aboriginal administration, yet the field notes of anthropologists who visited central Australia suggest that their cultural relativism was not very thoroughgoing.[2] Missionaries and anthropologists had clear ideas about whether Aboriginal bodies should be clothed or naked and tried to impose these views on Aboriginal people without consulting them over their own preferences. The evidence suggests that Aboriginal people were attracted to clothing and sought it out, but experimented with garments in ways which both missionaries and anthropologists found disconcerting resulting in tensions between Aboriginal people and missionaries over when and how clothes should be worn.

Central Australia is a vast, largely arid area encompassing the southern part of present day Northern Territory, northern South Australia and the arid interior of Western Australia. It was, and still is, a thinly populated territory. Several Aboriginal language groups occupied the region organised into small kin-based food gathering units which moved over large distances between scarce water sources to find seasonal food, coming together from time to time for ceremonial and other activities when environmental conditions allowed. Because of the harsh climate this region was one of the last to be colonised by Euro-Australians. Lutheran missionaries were among vanguard of settlers. Their mission station, Hermannsburg, gradually attracted local Arrernte people and then people from further west. By the 1930s the Lutherans were trying to discourage this eastward movement to Hermannsburg by establishing outstations. At the same time the Presbyterians (now the Uniting Church of Australia) concerned about the impact of uncontrolled contacts between Pitjantjatjara and Yankunytjatjara people and Ero-Australians to the south west of Hermannsburg in northern South Australia founded Ernabella mission in the Musgrave Ranges in 1937.[3] [. . .]

A group of ordained and lay Lutheran missionaries arrived on the banks of the Finke River in central Australia in June 1877 after a long journey of 19 months from the German settlement in the Barossa Valley in southern South Australia. They immediately set out to build a settlement for themselves to which they hoped to attract the local Arrernte people, 'The native people among whom we were to work left us in peace for the time being. So books, pen and paper could also have a spell . . . We made use of axe, saw and hammer [to start building Hermannsburg mission].'[4] It took two months for the first Arrernte men to appear at the encampment. They were described as vigorous and stately. The missionaries offered them a shirt and some food. As more men began to visit the small settlement some element of trust was established. The Arrernte men even allowed their moustaches to be shaved by the missionaries althouth they were very protective of their beards and whiskers.[5]

The only Arrernte report we have of these early encounters is the autobiographical account of Moses Tjalkabota dictated in the 1950s when he was an old man. He was a boy, possibly four or five years old when the missionaries first appeared on Arrernte lands. Many retrospective stories of first encounters by Aboriginal narrators, as we shall see, emphasis nakedness as an indicator of pre-contact society, but Tjalkabota does not describe his people as naked. He discusses an easy life of hunting and gathering, playing games and learning from the adults in his family. Girls and boys were taught appropriate gendered behaviours. The old women told the girls, 'Girls you must sit side on when men are present. Don't sit the wrong way, that is front on.'[6] Lack of clothing did not preclude modesty among the Arrernte, although Protestants from Europe habituated to fully covered bodies could not recognise the modesty of unclothed bodies.

Tjalkabota recalled the first description of Europeans which attempted to make them explicable, 'Some *inkawoberara* men have come, that is, men with boots whose feet cannot be seen.'[7] Tjalkabota also mentions, as do so many descriptions of first sightings of Europeans by Aboriginal people, that the Arrernte thought the 'white men were black men who had died, and then returned as spirits to the place where they had died long ago.'[8] In his memories of his early childhood Tjalkabota recalls the Arrernte noted that the strangers' feet were covered, and that their skin colour indicated they were not human, but the spirits of the dead returning. Arrernte associated things worn on the feet (not covering them on the top, but on the sole) with *kurdaitcha*, a magical enemy presence intent on retributive killing. The *kurdaitcha* shoes, made of emu feathers and tied to the foot with human hair string, were thought to enable the *kurdaitcha* to appear and then disappear without a trace.[9] Tjalkabota relates such an incident that frightened him and his family group when two unknown Aboriginal men visited them,

> In the middle of the night those two men did not make a fire, and did not make a place to sleep. . . .
> Then they returned to their home.
> They had put on feather-shoes, so we were not able to see their tracks. . . .
> The women said, 'Our enemies have spied out this place. We really must go back.'

Similarly the missionary party which arrived on Arrernte lands was a mysterious and threatening presence. The missionaries' appearance associated them with death, and their shoes with an unspecified menace.

Some time later Tjalkabota's father, Tjita, and some other men went to the settlement and began teaching the missionaries the Arrernte language. Tjita returned with a sheep's head and a goat's head for the family to eat, and shirt and trousers. 'The people said, "This is a different skin."'[10] Eventually the young Tjalkabota was allowed to visit the mission,

> Schwartz [a missionary] said, "Boy you are thin and covered with ashes. Come to me." . . . he gave me clothing. He gave me water to have a wash. I gave myself a really good wash, and then he gave me a towel to dry myself. Then he also gave me some sheep meat. Then he also gave me a blanket. Taking all this, I went back to camp. I thought to myself, "What a big present." And I was very happy.[11]

On longer acquaintance with the missionaries the clothes and blankets were sought out by the Arrernte. By the 1890s missionary Carl Strehlow candidly acknowledged that Arrernte people came to Hermannsburg and put up with Christian instruction because they wanted *mana* (bread) and *mantara* (clothing).[12]

In the Euro-Australian's mind clothes were associated with cleanliness, and Aboriginal people were perceived to be dirty. Arrernte generally covered themselves with grease (often emu fat) and sometimes red ochre, which had a practical as well as aesthetic purpose, protecting the skin from becoming dry and cracking in the hot and dry conditions of central Australia. Washing the body as well as wearing clothes were important aspects of overcoming the nakedness of the Arrernte. Changing hairstyles was another aspect of making people's bodies ready to accept Christ the Saviour and participate in useful work. Then new skills had to be learnt, at least by the women, to care for clothes. It was easiest to regulate and teach children. They could be washed before school, and the girls were taught how to wash, make and mend clothes as part of their training on the mission. But there was no way of compelling people to stay at the settlement, and for many years people came and went as they pleased. Tjalkabota's story illustrates this mobile lifestyle. He would attend the school at Hermannsburg for a while and then leave with his parents or grandparents to travel back to their favoured locality, Laprapuntja on Ellery Creek, or other locations. Sometimes Tjalkabota helped the missionaries shepherd sheep, but eventually a missionary would come looking for him and he would return to Hermannsburg, be given clothes and attend school.[13]

Tjalkabota describes one occasion on which missionary and Arrernte attitudes regarding bodily decoration came into direct conflict. Men and women were preparing for a ceremony close to the mission buildings. When missionary A. H. Kempe realised what they were doing, he with three of his associates attacked the participants, grabbing the decorations out of their hair. The women wailed, but the older men avoided the attack and continued with their dancing. The next morning the men appeared during morning prayers still naked with their bodies painted. This was an obvious challenge to the missionaries and their teaching – a battle over the hearts and minds of the children,

> Mr. Schwartz asked, 'Where are your clothes?'
> 'Our clothes are in the camp,' the men replied.
> 'Why haven't you put them on?'
> But they said, 'Everybody has to first of all see the markings of the men's tjurunga [sacred markings].
> The women, the young girls, the children all have to see it.'
> 'First go put your clothes on, then come and have something to eat.'
> '*Jakai*, are we being called evil? We are *iliara* [initiated] men.' Then they put their clothes on and came back. They were given food to eat.[14]

Later the Arrernte became more discrete about their cultural and religious activities, and the missionaries learnt not to see activities that might be a challenge to their authority. In 1898 Mounted Constable C. E. Cowle wrote to the anthropologist Baldwin Spencer after a visit to Hermannsburg,

> You should see the state of affairs there and without being prejudiced, honestly they [the missionaries] only hear of the things that are done by the Natives who do not happen to be persona grata with the scholars – the others they rig out and shield in every way and, when anything does occur, they pretend not to know who has done it – fancy psalm singing all day and then dancing all night with the others in the Creek.[15]

Clothing and the use of blankets for warmth were quickly adopted by many Arrernte in the mundane parts of their lives, but were dispensed with during their sacred activities. Clothing and bodily decoration were a marker of religious adherence, whether traditional or Christian. After Tjalkabota was baptised, he visited his father off the mission. He and Tjika had a tense conversation over the meaning of baptism. Tjalkabota told his father he wore 'good white clothes . . . good trousers' as well as a belt and handkerchief. Tjika apparently had observed the baptisms from afar. He pointed out that while his son had 'received good clothes. I received many *tjurunga* decorations' from the old men during initiation rites. Tjika interpreted baptismal clothing as representing a rite of passage parallel to an Arrernte man's initiation into manhood and adult knowledge. He did not perceive himself as naked or unclothed but decorated with significant indicators of his status.

While the wearing of what the missionaries (and other Euro-Australians) regarded as appropriate dress was gradually learned, it was much more difficult to manage clothing in what the missionaries regarded as an appropriate manner. Clothes turned to rags and became dirty. At the settlement there were facilities to wash and mend clothes, but away from the mission clothes were either discarded or soon became ruined.

The missionaries were still worrying about the maintenance of clothing fifty years after Arrernte were first introduced to European attire. In the 1920s the mission developed separate clothing policies for the Arrernte living permanently at Hermannsburg, and the people who visited the station from the desert regions further west, who the missionaries referred to as Loritja.[16] The Arrente by this time had been in contact with Euro-Australians for decades at Hermannsburg, on surrounding cattle stations (ranches), in the small township of Alice Springs, at mining camps and along the newly constructed railway line. These people were familiar with, maybe one could say habituated to, European clothing, but were not able to access it other than through periodic distributions at the mission or governmentrun food ration depots. They still had difficulties managing clothes in ways which accorded with the standards of Euro-Australian society. The teacher H. Heinrich who was temporarily in charge of Hermannsburg in the early 1920s wrote about his frustrations over supplying clothing. He had experimented with giving the children loin cloths rather than clothes which they wore through so quickly, but found that if their clothes were removed they dressed themselves in men's and women's clothes instead. He warned the women that next time they needed clothes, they would have to have short skirts to save on cloth. He bemoaned earlier policies under which the Arrernte had learned to wear clothes, rather than loin cloths. So when 37 'naked blacks' arrived at Hermannsburg from the west Heinrich invited them to attend church issuing the men with loin cloths for the occasion, rather than the full kit of clothes.[17] Two and half years later he was still voicing his exasperation, particularly over trying to keep the children and old people respectably dressed. He complained that the silk and crepe de chin clothes sent from the south were not suitable and were worn through in a week, and that the Mission Board should send thicker material or he would no longer take responsibility for maintaining the clothing of the Arrernte.[18]

In 1929 members of a scientific expedition visiting Hermannsburg took up the idea of replacing European clothing with loin cloths or shorts as a health measure to reduce head and body lice. The scientists apparently had no regard for the fifty year history of European clothing in the region. Nor did they consider how Arrernte might feel as they were relegated to an outward status of unclean and semi-naked.[19]

It would be quite misleading to assume that Arrernte people were only responding to mission expectations or dictates in their adoption of European clothing. Off the mission station Arrernte encountered increasing numbers of Euro-Australians, mainly men, who came to central Australia. The Arrernte became the chief labor source in the region. Those who were employed were often issued clothes, along with food rations, in lieu of wages.[20] Yet even within the constraints of the mission settlement, and before other strangers populated Arrernte land, it is clear that Arrernte were not just attracted by European foods, but by access to clothes and blankets. What is less clear is why they wanted what must have been cumbersome and difficult to manage appurtenances. In winter they may have appreciated the additional warmth, and younger people, as with most innovations, were quicker to acquire a liking for clothes than the older generation. Clothes were passed on from one individual to another, but there is little indication as to the basis of this sharing or exchange. As clothing was a new commodity, it would have been adapted to established reciprocal relationships. Spencer noted that garments might be worn by a man one day, his wife the next, and a friend another day, which suggests clothing did not have gender or status associations.[21] The missionaries were as frustrated by this redistribution of clothes as they were by Arrernte propensity to share rations and other food amongst themselves. From the missionary perspective they issued food and clothing to the deserving, that is those who worked or attended school, but these resources inevitably found their way to the undeserving – the 'loafers' who refused to engage in productive activities.[22]

People who attended church services at Hermannsburg were expected to come not only clothed, but neat and clean. There were special clothes worn for baptism, so clothes may have acquired some religious significance, just as the discarding of clothes continued to be a necessary part of Arrernte ceremonies which occurred away from the watchful eyes of the missionaries.[23] There was, no doubt, a gendered response to the wearing of clothes, although it is not well documented at Hermannsburg. [. . .] I will consider changing attitudes among the Lutheran missionaries who were contacting Aboriginal people west of the settled areas; and the documented views of anthropologists who visited central Australia in the 1930s and 1940s.

In the 1930s and 1940s there was an upsurge in mission activity in central Australia. Little Flower Catholic Mission was established in Alice Springs in 1935. It was relocated several times, finally moving 90 kilometres southeast of Alice Springs in 1953.[24] In the early 1930s Lutheran missionary, F. W. Albrecht, and the Hermannsburg Arrernte started making trips out to the west to Haast's Bluff, Pikilji (Vaughan Springs), Ilpili and Potati. For the first time the mission attempted to establish an ongoing itinerant evangelism by leaving Hermannsburg Arrernte evangelists at key locations near water sources with several weeks' rations to tide them over until they were able to contact local people and support themselves. This experiment failed, but it was the beginning of a movement to set up mission outstations.[25] The attitudes of the Lutheran missionaries had changed dramatically since the late nineteenth century. Albrecht believed that the people remote from Euro-Australian settlements would survive best if they remained on their own land, maintaining themselves by hunting and gathering, as they moved around their country. He strongly discouraged people from the Ehrenberg, Krichauff and Petermann Ranges and places inbetween from coming to Hermannsburg. But after the first failed attempt to send Hermannsburg-born evangelists to live off the land, they were set up in one location, initially near Haast's Bluff, with enough rations to maintain themselves. Albrecht quickly realised that the evangelists would be under enormous pressure to share their access to food and clothes with the local people who established camps nearby. He arranged regular visits to the outstation to replenish food rations and clothes.

The clothing policy for these western peoples was much less prescriptive than that of the first two generations of missionaries at Hermannsburg. At Haast's Bluff and later Areyonga there was no compulsion to wear clothes, although people were not prevented from acquiring clothes if they wished. If they came into the settlement or attended church services the men were issued with loin cloths.[26] Albrecht met Dr Charles Duguid and the Rev Munro from the Presbyterian church at Haast's Bluff in 1936 as they started a joint four-week expedition to survey Aboriginal people further west. As the

Presbyterians arrived, '100 natives, mostly naked [were] singing heartily' the hymn "Die Gnade unseres Herrn Jesu Christi." '[27] Pastor S. O. Gross visited Haast's Bluff in December 1941, the year a ration depot was established there and noted the range of bodily decoration,

> Some of the people ... are quite well-dressed, others are in rags, and the rest are naked; some however had just returned from a corroboree and were in their red-ochre corroboree paint.[28]

The non-judgmental tone of these reports is very different from that of the first and second generation of Lutheran missionaries at Hermannsburg who had attacked men in ceremonial (un)dress.

The anthropologist C. P. Mountford who visited Haast's Bluff the following year confirmed Gross's observation. Mountford's photographs of the Arrernte evangelist, Titus, preaching to a group of people show some unclad, and others fully clothed – the men in stockmen's outfits of shirt, pants and hats, and the women in dresses.

But Mountford, who criticised the assimilationist pressures of missions, was rather ambivalent in his attitudes to clothing. His field diary is peppered with photographs of naked Aboriginal men and women set against rocky gorges, digging for yams and other 'traditional' activities. These were posed and did not represent the reality of Aboriginal life observed by Mountford. While staying at the Jay Creek ration depot he planned to photograph some men at Standley Chasm. He had chosen four Ngalia men recently arrived from the west as 'models', but the police had raided their camp and confiscated their spears and spear throwers. Mountford observed, 'a native without these is awkward as a lady without her handbag,' so he scoured the camp for replacements.[29] He referred to another of his models as 'a happy obliging soul ... He acts as my model usually without complaint, although he makes a mild protest if the wind is cold. I always protect him as much as possible for I think he has worn clothes for some time, and much of his natural protection is gone.'[30] He rewarded a young woman who performed a witchetty grub and yam ceremony for him with a new dress,

> This poor lady, a woman about 20, had only the merest apology of a rag about her middle ... when I finally showed her the reward, she was so overcome with joy and surprise, that, except for a look of great pleasure on her face, she did not make a gesture. But I saw her tears well up in the corners of her eyes and slowly run down her cheeks.
>
> I left, but I could not help thinking how much she or any other woman, black or white, in rags must desire pretty frocks. – and their chance of getting them practically nil, except she could get to Alice Springs, and gather money through prostitution.'[31]

Mountford believed he was documenting an Aboriginal world that had already disappeared, which he had to reconstruct through these subterfuges. But his attitudes are more conflicted than that. He could imagine the Aboriginal women he met having the same desires as his wife and other women he knew. But there any similarity with middle class white women ended. Aboriginal women could only cloth themselves by selling their naked bodies. This fantasy seems to ignore the regular distributions of clothing by mission and government as part of their rationing regimes. Mountford's photographs show Aboriginal women at Haast's Bluff fully attired in dresses, presumably not gained by prostituting themselves in Alice Springs. His view of men's spears as accessories, rather than weapons feminises them. Spears have no function but signal the primitive and ineffectual Aboriginal man, who is no longer a hunter nor yet a civilised working man.

Mountford's conception of Arrernte men as neither fully savage nor fully civilised was challenged by the water colourist, Albert Namatjira.[32] Mountford was amazed to find that this great artist who became recognised nationally and internationally was living like all the other Arrernte, 'in a low windbreak of boughs and a smouldering fire, a spear and spearthrower and portions of cooked kangaroo lying on the leaves of the break' with several wonderful watercolours also lying there wrapped in oil cloth. He fervently hoped that Namatjira would never realise what a great artist he was as that would corrupt him, and feared that if someone took Namatjira to the cities it would be 'his ruination'. Mountford had trouble reconciling Namatjira's great gift as an artist painting in a European genre with a person living like a 'native' (fully clothed). He was even more astonished when Namatjira the man who could paint better than many Europeans offered to draw a tjurunga pattern of his own totemic area,

> What a thing to see. The man on the one hand drawing the most primitive art in the world, and on the other producing work which equals that of the most modern. One would scarcely think it possible to have both in one man especially as the legend that he drew in the primitive symbols was his own inherited from his mother. – the story of the creation times, when his mythical ancestor created the natural features that he drew for me.[33]

Nine years earlier in 1933 another anthropologist, Norman Tindale, accompanied by Dr Cecil Hackett, visited Ernabella cattle station (not yet a mission station) on their way to the Mann Ranges to record what they considered a still functioning Aboriginal society and culture. On the first night at Ernabella they witnessed an *inma* (dance) in which 'Fifty naked savages singing lustily, linked by a common bond of song was a most impressive sight.'[34] Tindale, like Mountford, judged degree of 'civilisation' by appearance. The people at Ernabella whom he identified as 'Pitjanjatara' are 'quite uncivilised,' except two men. One of these had been in jail for cattle stealing and had become 'cheeky'; the other had been attached to a Euro-Australian's camp 'and wears half a shirt and one sock. All the others are free from dress. They keep themselves well greased with red ochre. Their hair is in a long bun at the back & serves as a repository for flints (adze stones) wooden hair pegs etc.'[35] A few days later Tindale confirmed his first impressions,

> Neither sex wears any clothing. An occasional individual wears a fur string belt; men wear a head band. The women wear their hair tied up in front and the ends turned in.[36]

The savage – civilised continuum suggested by Tindale in these remarks is pejorative with no analytical utility. Both Mountford's and Tindale's journal entries suggest these anthropologists were far from the objective, open minded participant observers of classic cultural anthropology. Both men are quick to base judgements of cultural authenticity on very superficial observations of people's appearance. Aboriginal people steeped in their age-old culture are naked with a few bodily decorations. Even the adoption of a few rags could corrupt the unadulterated 'savage', as could superficial contact with Euro-Australians. Despite both men recording complex social and cultural data in their expeditions to central Australia, they reflected attitudes of the wider Australian society labelling these intricate social networks and rich ceremonial life as primitive and savage. [. . .]

Notes

1 Michael Sturma, 'Dressing, Undressing, and Early European Contact in Australia and Tahiti' *Pacific Studies* 21 (3) (September 1998): 87–104, 87.
2 Paige Raibmon in her study of colonial encounters on the northwest coast of America in the late nineteenth century suggests that authenticity 'is a powerful and shifting set of ideas that worked in a variety of ways toward a variety of ends', rather than a 'stable yardstick against which to measure the "real thing."' Paige Raibmon, *Authentic Indians. Episodes of Encounter from the Late-Nineteenth-Cetury Northwest Coast* Durham and London: Duke University Press, 2005, 3.
3 Sitirani Kerin, '"Doctor Do-Good?" Charles Duguid and Aboriginal Politics, 1930s–1970s' Australian National University PhD, 2005.
4 P. A. Scherer, *From Joiner's Bench to Pulpit* (Adelaide: Lutheran Publishing House, 1973), 12.
5 Sherer, 66–67.
6 Moses Tjalkabota in PA Albrecht, *From Mission to Church. 1877–2002 Finke River Mission* (Adelaide: Open Book Publishers, 2002), Appendix, 239. This account was given in Arrernte to the missionary F.W. Albrecht and the typescript translated by P.A. Albrecht.
7 Tjalkabota, 242.
8 Tjalkabota, 242.
9 Spencer, Baldwin, *Wanderings in Wild Australia*, vol I (London: Macmillan, 1928), 259–261.

10 Tjalkabota, 243.
11 Tjalkabota, 244.
12 C. Strehlow to Friends of the Mission, 6 September 1899, 16 A 2/2, Lutheran Archives, Adelaide, South Australia (hereafter LA).
13 eg Tjalkabota, 244, 245, 249.
14 Tjalkabota, 246–247.
15 John Mulvaney with. A. Petch and H. Morphy (ed) *From the Frontier. Outback Letters to Baldwin Spencer* (Sydney: Allen and Unwin, 2000), 105.
16 Loritja was a term adopted from the Arrernte to describe neighbouring peoples, which the peoples so described found offensive.
17 H. Heinrich to J.J. Stolz 1 February 1923 'Correspondence with mission station 1923' 16 B 1/2, LA.
18 H. Heinrich to J.J. Stolz 9 October 1925 'Correspondence with mission station 1925' 16 A 5/6, LA.
19 There is a long colonial history of dressing colonial subjects in outfits which distinguish them from the settler society. An excellent discussion of the meaning of clothing to German missionaries, including at a Hermannsburg mission can be found in Kirsten Ruether, 'Heated Debates Over Crinolines: European Clothing on Nineteenth-Century Lutheran Missions Stations in the Transvaal', *Journal of Southern African Studies*, vol 8, no. 2 (2002): 359–378.
20 Tim Rowse, *White Flour, White Power: From Rations to Citizenship in Central Australia* (Melbourne: Cambridge University Press, 1998).
21 Rowse, quoting Baldwin Spencer [1896, 40] in a chapter titled 'Rationing the Inexplicable', 22–23. Maybe what was inexplicable was the Arrernte use of introduced goods.
22 Eg Strehlow to Friends of Mission, 12 December 1905 published in *Kirchen und Missions Zeitung*, 10 January 1906, 11–12; Strehlow to Stolz, 29 March 1921, 16 A0/1 folder "1922 (21)", LA; Albrecht to Riedel, 7 September 1927, Box 16 A5/6, folder "1927" LA (all documents translated from German by J. Van Gent).
23 Clothing as an important mark of religious adherence has been noted in many parts of the missionised world eg see Norman Etherington, 'Outward and Visible Signs of Conversion in Nineteenth Century Kwazulu-Natal' *Journal of Religion in Africa* vol 32, no. 4 (2002), 422–439, 435–436.
24 Rowse, 73, 77, 92.
25 Albrecht in Leske, 51.
26 H. Heinrich to J.J. Stolz 11 November 1923 "Correspondence with mission station 1923" 16 B 1/2, LA; *Lutheran Herald*, 27 March 1933, 106–107. No mention is made of women, presumably because these were all-male parties who initially visited the station.
27 *Lutheran Herald*, 4 January 1937, 11.
28 S. O. Gross to Mission Friends *Lutheran Herald*, 6 June 1942, 184. Ted Abbott was a mixed descent Arrernte man in charge of ration distribution and discipline at the depot.
29 C. P. Mountford Diary June–July 1942 Journey to Haasts Bluff, Alice Springs and Hermannsburg, Mountford-Sheard Collection, Archival Heritage Collections, State Library of South Australia, 61.
30 Mountford Diary, 231, 316.
31 Mountford Diary, 321. See Rowse for a discussion of Euro-Australian views of Aboriginal men and women trading women's sexuality for material gain.
32 Albert Namatjira was a renowned Aboriginal artist painting in a western influenced genre. See Jane Hardy, J. V. S Megaw and M. Ruth Megaw eds, *The heritage*

of namatjira: the watercolourists of Central Australia Port Melbourne: William Heinemann, 1992.
33 Mountford, 225, 227.
34 N. B. Tindale Journal of Expedition to the Mann Ranges 1933, 29 May 1933, South Australian Museum (SAM), 13.
35 Tindale, 30 May 1933, 25.
36 Tindale, 2 June 1933, 35.

81

TO HONOR HER HEAD

Hats as a symbol of women's position in three evangelical churches in Edinburgh, Scotland

Ruth Borker

Source: Judith Hoch-Smith and Anita Spring (eds), *Women in Ritual and Symbolic Roles*, New York: Plenum Press, 1978, pp. 55–73.

1. Introduction

The position of women in evangelical churches is determined by a number of interweaving factors, the most important of which is the Bible. Although these churches are often regarded as highly male-dominated because of the supposed unambiguous nature of the Biblical texts, I hope to show here that in fact the very absoluteness of the Biblical standard and the ambiguity of meaning built into it generate a marked flexibility in meaning that permits a variety of symbolic strategies by both men and women with important implications for women's position. In this chapter I will demonstrate this semantic flexibility through an in-depth analysis of the meaning of a key symbol of women's position in three Edinburgh churches: the wearing of hats.

The theoretical framework I am using here draws upon work in two major approaches in anthropology: symbolic analysis and the ethnography of communication. Two currents within symbolic analysis are particularly relevant: (1) the focus on the nature of symbols (e.g., Turner 1967) and types of symbols (e.g., Ortner 1973; Harris 1977), and (2) the focus on the use of symbols by individuals in particular social situations (e.g., Turner 1964; Deshen 1970). These are paralleled by two relevant concerns in the ethnography of communication with its concentration on speech: (1) the focus on the structure of the communicative system and the impact of this structure on what is communicated (e.g., Marks 1974; Levy 1973) and (2) the ways individuals employ their communicative repertoires and actually operate within the structure of the system (e.g., Gumperz 1971). Using this framework I will be examining the constraints influencing an individual's interpretation of symbols and the symbolic strategies an individual employs in communicating his or her religious belief and experience as framed in those symbols.

In order to do this I have made a distinction between two general types of meaning: core and situational. By core I mean that constant set of meanings that exists in the "abstract"; it is the background meaning people keep in their heads and bring to bear in interpreting any specific usage. I am here using the word *core* much as a linguist would use the word *referential* or *dictionary* in speaking of word meaning. By situational meaning, on the other hand, I mean those aspects of meaning involved in a specific use of a symbol in a specific time and place. A major element in this meaning is often the particularization of the core meaning. What is of interest is how this particularization is shaped by the social, experiential, and personal constraints operating in the situation itself.

Before examining these two sets of meanings for hats, it is necessary to briefly look at the social position of women in the churches, which is an important element in the symbol's meaning. The Biblical basis for core meanings and these meanings themselves will then be examined, followed by a consideration of a number of specific situations and the meanings involved in them with a focus on individual strategies of interpretation and usage.

The three churches studied were an extremely large Baptist church (in fact the largest in Britain, membership about 900), a small and elderly Open Brethren assembly (membership about 45), and a small Seventh Day Adventist church (membership about 50). Each of these churches is evangelical, by which I mean that their members believe in the truth of the Bible as God's word to man and they believe the purpose of the church on earth is to spread the gospel message—that man is basically a creature of sin, incapable of "saving" himself, and bound for hell and that salvation is only possible by spiritual rebirth through the personal acceptance of the atoning sacrifice of Jesus Christ on the cross, recognizing that "Christ died for *my* sins." It should be noted that the salvation message is the same for men and women. All three share this common evangelical understanding of the New Testament, such that differences between them can most fruitfully be seen as variations on a single theme. These differences are not on a single dimension, such as strictness to laxity, but rather result from differences in emphasis on multiple dimensions within an overarching framework (cf. Borker 1974 for a fuller discussion of the similarities and differences in their interpretation of the gospel).

The social position of women in the churches is an extremely complex one, both in response to and conducive of the semantic complexity discussed below. Although on the surface women seem to be placed in a subordinate position, in most churches women's position is not as simple as it appears.

Looking at the official level of church organization, women are seemingly excluded from positions of authority. In the Brethren, which in many ways is the most extreme in differentiating a member's role by sex, women are not allowed to be elders (there are no ministers) and in fact women are not allowed to speak when men are present. Despite the fact that they maintain they practice the "priesthood of all believers," in practice only male members participate in the meetings as they feel led by the Holy Spirit to do so, while the women worship in silence. However, women are completely in charge of the Women's Meeting, which is one of the primary evangelistic activities of the church, and the speakers are frequently women. In addition, women are Sunday school teachers (although not Bible class teachers dealing with the older children) and girls receive the same rigorous Bible training as boys. In the Baptist church women are not allowed to preach or teach from the pulpit, but they can otherwise participate in meetings. As in the Brethren, women are not allowed to be elders (or ministers). The Women's Meeting, which is primarily directed to church members, is headed by the pastor's wife and again the speakers may be women. The Adventists, in contrast to both, permit women considerable participation in the church organization. Although they as yet have no women pastors, women can speak in church and hold a variety of positions of authority, e.g., head of the Sabbath school and church treasurer. In all the denominations women can be missionaries, where they are frequently in the position of teaching and even preaching to men and are always serving as official representatives of their churches.

Women's influence is not completely exhausted by these official positions. Frequently women exercise considerable informal authority through their husbands or fathers, and some older women by virtue of their long Christian service and experience wield considerable influence on their own. Even in situations in which women are restricted in actual participation, hymns written by women are read and sung and generally used for spiritual edification.[1] Finally, there is considerable variation in belief among the members of the various churches as to the proper role of women and this leads to a certain amount of situational variation in their actual participation depending upon the persons present.

2. The Biblical basis of meaning

As is always the case with evangelical Christians, the meaning of hats is first looked for in the Bible. However, as the Bible is a complex system of interlocking multivocal symbols, words with a multiplicity of meanings, the meaning of hats is by no means unambiguous. For evangelicals the Bible is not just a book of words but rather The Book consisting of the Living Word, and as such one of its primary characteristics is that through the Holy Spirit it speaks to different individuals as is appropriate for them in their particular situations.[2] The Bible thus provides both a general and universal truth and a full guide for action and belief for each individual.

In discussing the Bible the Baptist minister wrote, "The Bible alone must be our authority in all matters of faith and conduct; ... what the Bible says must be the deciding factor in any decision that has to be made; ... every opinion must be examined in the light of what the Bible says" (Prime 1967). Elsewhere the same minister presented these general principles for Bible study: "Know the background of the passages which you study. Watch the context (verses before and after the passage considered). Use Scripture to explain Scripture. Remember the Bible is God's Word. Ask for the help of the Holy Spirit" (Prime 1972). On this last point he went on to elaborate: "The Holy Spirit, who caused the Scriptures to be written, is given to every Christian to teach and to instruct him in the things of God.... Spiritual understanding, thank God, is not a matter of intellectual ability but rather a matter of submissive wills and minds bowing before God as the Scriptures are studied, and being taught by the Holy Spirit" (Prime 1972).

There are four passages in the Pauline epistles that are central for evangelical Christians in determining the meaning of hats and the position of women. The first of these passages deals explicitly with the question of head coverings, while the others, which deal more generally with the role of women, are often cited in attempting to explain the first.[3] Because of their importance I shall quote each in full. All quotes are from the Authorized, or King James, Version of the Bible. The first and most important is I Corinthians 11:1–16, in which Paul writes:

> [1]Be ye followers of me, even as I also am of Christ. [2]Now I praise you, brethren, that ye remember me in all things, and keep the ordinances, as I delivered them to you. [3]But I would have you know, that the head of every man is Christ; and the head of the woman is the man; and the head of Christ is God. [4]Every man praying or prophesying, having his head covered, dishonoureth his head. [5]But every woman that prayeth or prophesieth with her head uncovered dishonoureth her head: for that is even all one as if she were shaven. [6]For if the woman be not covered let her also be shorn: but if it be a shame for a woman to be shorn or shaven, let her be covered. [7]For a man indeed ought not to cover his head, forasmuch as he is the image and glory of God: but the woman is the glory of the man. [8]For the man is not of the woman but the woman for the man. [9]Neither was the man created for the woman; but the woman for the man. [10]For this cause ought the woman to have power on her head because of the angels. [11]Nevertheless neither is the man without the woman, neither the woman without the man, in the Lord. [12]For as the woman is of the man, even so is the man also by the woman; but all things of God. [13]Judge ye in yourselves: is it comely that a woman pray unto God uncovered? [14]Doth not even nature itself teach you, that, if a man have long hair, it is a shame unto him? [15]But if a woman have long hair, it is a glory to her: for her hair is given to her for a covering. [16]But if any seem to be contentious, we have no such custom, neither the churches of God.

Later in the same letter, Paul states in I Corinthians 14:34–35:

> [34]Let your women keep silence in the churches: for it is not permitted unto them to speak; but they are commanded to be under obedience, as also saith the law. [35]And if they will learn any thing, let them ask their husbands at home: for it is a shame for women to speak in the church.

Then in I Timothy 2:8–15 Paul writes:

> [8]I will therefore that men pray every where, lifting up holy hands, without wrath and doubting. [9]In like manner also, that women adorn themselves in modest apparel, with shamefacedness and sobriety; not with braided hair, or gold, or pearls, or costly array: [10]But (which becometh women professing godliness) with good works. [11]Let the woman learn in silence with all subjection. [12]But I suffer not a woman to teach, nor to usurp authority over the man, but to be in silence. [13]For Adam was first formed, then Eve. [14]And Adam was not deceived, but the woman being deceived was in the transgression. [15]Notwithstanding she shall be saved in childbearing, if they continue in faith and charity and holiness with sobriety.

The last text is of a somewhat different nature. It is very short and, contrary to the others, denies rather than asserts the distinction between men and women. This is Galatians 3:28, which reads:

> There is neither Jew nor Greek, there is neither bond nor free, there is neither male nor female: for ye are all one in Christ Jesus.

While these are not the only verses relevant to the question of hats and the position of women, they are primary in the minds of church members and are sufficient to spell out the core meanings of the wearing of hats.[4]

3. Core meanings

In my discussion with them, church members drew out three principal meanings of the wearing of hats from these passages: (1) subordination, (2) dignity or modesty, and (3) formality. I have called these Biblical meanings core in the sense that unless a Christian can base his argument on Biblical citations, he has no argument. Thus when in interviews I asked the direct question "What does the wearing of hats mean?" I was answered either with an explicit or implicit reference to these or other Biblical passages. The point is that for these evangelicals a question about the meaning of hats called for a response explicitly in terms of the Bible. Biblical citations form a necessary framework in which particular meaning will be framed, much as the "dictionary" meaning of a word gives focus to its usage in a particular situation. Like dictionary meanings, these Biblical core meanings are generally agreed upon—in fact, all individuals I interviewed gave one or more of these meanings and no others.

3.1. Subordination

The dominant meaning of hats for most church members is the subordination of the woman to the man, both within the church and in the home. This relationship between the sexes is summarized for most in Paul's statement: "The head of every man is Christ; and the head of the woman is the man"; i.e., as man is to God, woman is to man. There are two different models used by church members in conceptualizing this relationship of subordination, each based on linking I Cor. 11 with other verses in the Bible.

For some, subordination is a result of the need for order and does not imply inferiority. It refers to a "surface" difference in function (i.e., a difference in what they do but not in what they are). The usual analogy made is with the Trinity: while the Spirit is subordinate to the Son and the Son to the Father, all are equal. This model for subordination is the result of an explicit linking of I Cor. 11 with Gal. 3:28. If there is "no male nor female in Christ," Paul could only be referring to a surface distinction resulting from the need for order in Corinthians. Essentially this is the model of social difference and interdependence implied in the Durkheimian notion of organic solidarity.

For others, however, the important illuminating passage is I Tim. and the subordination of women is interpreted as a function of their spiritual weakness as shown in the fall of Eve. This is essentially a model of spiritual inequality. In it the role of the woman is restricted and separated from that of the man as a consequence of her lower and to some extent polluting nature. This theme is commonly discussed in the anthropology of the symbolism of women (e.g., Ortner 1974).

3.2. Dignity

The second core meaning of hats is that of dignity or modesty and to some extent it mediates between the other two, subordination and formality. It is primarily concerned with woman's position in society, a position to some extent derived from her subordinate relationship to man. A basic element is that a woman's quiet acceptance of her "proper" position creates for her a power or authority. To some extent church members make an equation between wearing a hat as "honoring her head" (i.e., the man) and as "having power on her head." In fact only through her fulfillment of her proper role can a woman exercise authority from God and so influence others toward God, as seen in Peter's advice to wives of non-Christians (I Peter 3:1–2). Conversely, not to accept this position implies immodesty and shame. An important element in dignity–modesty is the nonassertion of self that is demonstrated in covering one's head as opposed to the brazenness and immodesty in adorning oneself and one's head with gold, pearls, and braided hair that women are warned against. Part of wearing a hat is that "women are instructed not to call attention to themselves or to dress so as to cause someone to stumble." There is a connection made between a woman's modesty and her godly influence, especially on men. The principle involved is essentially that of "honor and shame" as has been discussed for the Mediterranean (e.g., duBoulay 1974).

3.3. Formality

The final meaning of hats is primarily concerned not with the relationship between men and women but with that between humans and God. While the need to exhibit formality is supported Biblically by quoting the equation of God and king, the fact that *hats* on women express this formality is traditional. Until recently in Scotland, hats were a normal part of women's apparel, especially when "dressing up." Thus it indicated the formality of an occasion, while not wearing one indicated informality, and for some Christians not to wear a hat to church was irreverent in that it failed to define the situation with sufficient respect. As one informant summarized it, "Head coverings are associated with reverence, even if the principle is not there in black and white."

That the equation of formality and hats is cultural is clearly seen in the insistence by many evangelicals on hats as opposed to other coverings, e.g., scarves. A woman in the Brethren, struck by what she felt was the absurdity of this confusing of Biblical and cultural elements, used to tell me jokingly that one day she was going to wear a wig and not a hat just to get people's reactions.

These three core meanings of wearing a hat provide a basis for agreement among church members, but because of their ambiguity they also provide a basis for disagreement. Agreement results from the shared view that the Bible is the primary referent of meaning, the fact that this Biblical meaning can be expressed in a number of key words and phrases (e.g., *subordination, dignity, modesty, formality*), and the assumption that agreement over phrases is the same as agreement over meaning. Disagreement results from the fact that the meanings of these words and phrases are in fact ambiguous. This real ambiguity in meaning that may exist behind the apparent agreement can be of crucial importance in the attributing of meaning in particular situations, as will be discussed below.

4. Situational meanings

In this section I will be looking at a number of specific situations that demonstrate how particular meanings emerge from this framework of core meanings, by examining how individuals "select" meanings to fit the situation and even change them by "playing" with the system. Three types of variations in situational meaning of hats will be considered: (1) variations between churches, (2) variations in strategies and meanings in a particular church setting, and (3) variations in the strategies and meanings for a single individual from one setting to another. In the first category I will compare churches as well as examine how the meaning attributed to hats marks off one church from another. In the second, I will be contrasting two Bible studies, one in the Baptist and one in the Adventist church. In the third I will be examining the strategies of women in the Baptist and Brethren groups in actually wearing or not wearing hats to different meetings at their churches.

In looking at the variation between the churches, the subordination of women is clearly the dominant meaning. Among the Adventists, where women come closest to sharing an equal official position with men and many question the modern relevance of women's subordination, only a few older women wear hats and it is never brought up as an issue.[5] Among the Baptists, with their intermediate position on the role of women in the church, there is a corresponding intermediate position with regard to the wearing of hats and people both for and against wearing hats express concern over the problem. Among the Brethren, with their position of very restricted participation for women in the assembly, the wearing of hats is mandatory for women members.

Although subordination is the most relevant meaning in the context of interchurch variation, there is significant variation between men and women within each church regarding the appropriate model for understanding this. In the Brethren, men tend to hold the "spiritual inequality" interpretation of subordination while women tend toward that of "social difference." In the Baptist church, on the other hand, the reverse is true. Men tend to hold the "difference" interpretation, while women tend toward that of "inequality." This is related to the different experience of the sexes within and between the churches resulting from differences in the social organization of sex roles (Borker 1976) and it produces a striking difference between the churches in the self-conceptions of women. Brethren women, who have a strong sense of the different spheres and functions for men and women, with no sense that these imply inferiority, exhibit considerably more self-confidence than do women in the Baptist church, who often view their position as a result of their spiritual weakness. Here we can see a dramatic indication of the impact of social experience in framing the meaning of Biblical symbols and the importance of sexual separation in women's religious self-concepts (cf. Fallers and Fallers 1976).

The interchurch variation has resulted in hats having a boundary-marking function in distinguishing members of different churches. Grace Harris (1977) has made a distinction between inward- and outward-looking symbols that is useful for discussing this boundary-marking process. An inward symbol is one that serves as a rallying or unifying symbol for the people within a particular group, while an outward symbol is one that marks one group off from others; it "stands" for the group. Hats for the Brethren have taken on both these functions as the wearing of hats has declined in other churches. As an inward symbol it signifies to the Brethren, both men and women, their adherence to the Bible, to God's way. Hats have come to represent for them their doctrinal purity, as opposed to other churches that are willing to give in to the standards of the secular world. Hats thus mark the boundary between the assemblies and the other evangelical churches.

At the same time hats serve as an outward symbol of the Brethren to many Baptists. For the Baptists, hats signify the Brethren tendency to be like the Pharisees, overemphasizing outward form at the cost of the inward *meaning* of the individual's relationship to God. To use de Saussure's terms, they feel the Brethren are giving more importance to the signifier than to the signified. They feel the Brethren position has resulted in driving women from the church,[6] that they "strained for the gnat and swallowed the camel," as one informant put it. Given the situation within the Baptist church, with its division over this issue and the resulting need to de-emphasize it (see below), it is not surprising Baptists should see the Brethren in this light.

Moving from general differences between the churches to specific church settings, it is illuminating to contrast the interpretation of hats in similar settings in two different churches. The setting, that of a Bible study, presents certain situational constraints that are the same for both cases. Yet the meanings selected are very different due to other situational factors, in this case the differences between the churches in the consensus of interpretation and in the social position of women in each of the churches. The first of these studies I will discuss in some detail as an illustration of the processes involved in determining core meanings and applying them to a situation.

The pastor of the Baptist church devoted one of the regular Thursday evening Bible study classes to an examination of I Cor. 11:1–16. He had chosen the topic of women and hats in response to a missionary's query on the subject and the attendance was extremely high (200+, as opposed to a usual 125), reflecting the degree of interest in the topic.

In order to understand the strategy he employed in this study it is necessary to keep in mind a number of factors about the Baptist church. One such factor was size. With a membership of 900, many members did not know one another personally and so were forced to rely largely on outward signs in making judgments about each other. The large size also increased the importance of the pastor, whom all knew and who, despite his comparatively short tenure at the church, knew almost everyone in the congregation at least by name. Thus he served to link together the entire membership.

A second important factor was the minimum of doctrinal consensus required of members of Baptist churches in Scotland. In order to become a member one only needed to have undergone conversion and believer's baptism: to have experienced a personal acceptance of Jesus as savior and to have been baptized by immersion after a profession of faith. It was therefore important for the operation of the church that other doctrinal issues did not emerge as sources of conflict and factionalism within the church, something about which the pastor would be particularly concerned. This danger of factionalism was particularly marked due to the church's size, which in itself led to the formation of subgroups within the church.

The wearing of hats and the position of women was one such source of potential conflict, being an issue over which there was wide variation in interpretation and in the translation of belief into action. The most striking aspect of this variation was the almost universal wearing of hats by older women, the equally universal absence of hats on young women, and the split among the women in their 30s and 40s. It should be mentioned here that comparatively few of the young people (between the ages of 16 and 27) went to the evening Bible study as they had their own Young People's Meeting, including Bible study, on Wednesday. Thus the audience at the meeting was somewhat biased in favor of hat-wearers. The pastor in this meeting employed a symbolic strategy explicitly concerned with influencing others toward a particular set of meanings and actions that he felt was the correct interpretation for the *church*.

The pastor laid out four steps in approaching the passage: (1) "understanding the passage," i.e. a verse-by-verse examination aimed at determining core meanings, (2) examining the context and background of the passage, (3) working out the principles involved, and (4) applying the principles. Although separating these steps in theory, in actually going over the passage the pastor tended to stress the principles being expressed as well as putting the chapter in context. This was partly a result of the difficulty in trying to isolate core from situational meaning and partly a result of his overall strategy.

The format of this first and major step in the study was to read each verse and then discuss its meaning. Essential to this step was the assumption that word meanings are basically unambiguous and so one could determine *the* meaning of a sentence or verse. He began with v.1–2, which he interpreted as Paul's setting the issue in its proper perspective as a nonfundamental of the Christian faith.[7] This in fact constituted a major part of his strategy of interpretation and presentation. This strategy was twofold in purpose: (1) to downplay the importance of the issue, thereby eliminating it as a legitimate basis for doctrinal division in the church, and (2) to influence others toward a particular and rather conservative interpretation he regarded as correct. He did this by stressing "general principles," upon which all should supposedly agree, while not setting categorical translations of these into action.

The first and for him most important of these principles was that of subordination stated in v.3. Using the analogy of the Trinity, he distinguished subordination from inferiority,[8] a confusion he felt was often made in modern society. The next four verses were then seen as a further statement of this subordination principle, which generated an opposition between men and women, but one of a restricted nature. He felt men were only more like God in that they could exercise authority, whereas women could not, and that in fact being the "glory of the man" provided the woman with dignity through being served and protected from danger by her husband, to whom such behavior was "instinctive." Thus he introduced early the focus of his interpretation of v.10 and by doing so further emphasized it.

His analysis was as follows: Women should acknowledge their proper relationship to men, though he felt Paul did not want to "encourage extremes"; head coverings are a clear symbol of this subordination but, conversely, as such they are also a symbol of women's authority, i.e., a woman with a proper sense of her dignity exercises "authority under her husband." He felt the angels referred to (v.10) were guardian angels who are concerned that "we do right" and who set an example for women by veiling their faces before God. In his framework, v.11–12 became an extension of another principle, that of complementarity, and another warning against an extreme position. In his words, "One's relation to Christ affects all others, Paul is not saying anything to detract from the basic equality of the sexes; God is not creating rivalry but complementarity." In concluding the pastor went on to discuss the three verses on hair and to stress that v.16 again warned against making this a major issue in the church.

The context in which he placed the passage again fit with his playing down of the problem for the modern church.[9] He pointed out the special problem of the Corinthian church, located in a city renowned for its immorality and one where women uncovered in public were regarded as morally loose. He elaborated on this by explaining the meaning of veils in Middle Eastern society, stressing that veils symbolically made a woman invisible. He made it quite clear that the word for covering used in Greek clearly referred to veils, that Corinth's cultural background was very different from that of modern Edinburgh, and that hats in Edinburgh were not equivalent to veils in Corinth. Although he here presented the foundations for the interpretation that these passages apply only to Corinth, he never suggested this as a possible interpretation. His acknowledgment of this context did, however, temper any criticism that might be leveled against such an interpretation.

Given the structure of his interpretation thus far, the principles and applications flowed quite naturally. The primary principle was that of subordination of woman to man and "this should find expression in Christian worship," although this was difficult "in our culture, which has almost no way of expressing subordination." Second, he felt women should be marked by modesty and the Christian should be "sensitive" to what is regarded as "right" in his society, reiterating that hats were not veils. From the point of view of someone interested in the position of women, it is worth noting that here he did not expand on the principle of complementarity.

In discussing the application of these principles he began with a statement of another issue entirely—that of the position of women in the church—by pointing out he had refused to allow the wife of a missionary (who had led one Sunday morning service) to give the children's address because "women should not teach when men are present." He in fact strengthened this point by acknowledging that others might disagree with him and warning that if they did it must be "on the basis of Scripture and not prejudice." The reason for this seeming digression is clear in terms of his overall strategy. To avoid potential conflict he had presented himself as taking the most reasonable position with regard to the passage's meaning. Throughout the study he had presented his as the most reasonable interpretation, avoiding extremes in either direction, and to do this he had throughout presented aspects of both positions, usually favoring the conservative more strongly. Here he was stating his agreement with one major aspect of the conservative application of the complex of verses on women before rejecting another—that women *must* wear hats. Rather he suggested each woman should consult her husband and then follow his wishes, thus expressing the principle of subordination. It was a perfect solution, as it meant that a woman could express subordination both by wearing and not wearing a hat and it posited no "blame" on a husband for either favoring or not favoring a wife's hat wearing. Essentially, it said any agreement reached between a husband and wife was okay.

The pastor accomplished a number of objectives through this strategy. Given his position of influence, he successfully managed to head off any attempts to press this as an issue and provided a framework in which it became impossible to know a woman's interpretation of the passage from whether or not she wore a hat. In addition, he presented his interpretation in such a way—by avoiding literalism and stressing underlying principles—that it appeared the most reasonable view and as such was impossible to invalidate or even to seriously question. Finally, he provided a framework in which both the conservative and other views could be incorporated as Biblical and thereby avoided alienating either camp. Perhaps one sign of his success is that informants I spoke with always thought the pastor agreed with them no matter how different their views were from each other.

I would like to contrast briefly this Bible study with a much shorter one dealing with I Corinthians 14 that occurred in the young people's meeting of the Adventist church. Here the church context was completely different. The Adventists did not make a major distinction between the roles of men and women in the church. To begin with, the minister in charge of the meeting asked one of the young women to read v.33–36 and to comment on them.

This in itself set forth part of his own interpretation and strategy as it involved having a woman speak. After the woman's suggestion that Paul seemed to oppose women preaching, he, as well as another minister attending, went on to suggest a number of contextual interpretations for the verses, all of which restricted their application to the present, e.g., that this was a cultural carry-over from before becoming Christians, that it referred to the particular moral situation in Corinth, that as the chapter dealt with the health of the church the verses might be a warning addressed to some specific women in Corinth who were causing disruptions by asserting themselves and asking foolish questions in church. The entire thrust of interpretation was toward particularizing the meaning to Corinth. The minister even went so far as to jokingly mention that some scholars had cast doubt on the authenticity of these verses, feeling they might have been added by a medieval scribe. This was not presented as a serious interpretation (in fact it would be horrifying as such to an evangelical) but rather served to emphasize the general strategy of particularization and to imply a danger in attempting to apply them rigidly today. This strategy resulted from the general lack of relevance seen for the church of any of the core meanings associated with this entire complex of passages. In particular, women were not perceived as subordinate within the church and to some extent could not be, as the church itself was founded by a woman, Mrs. Ellen G. White.

The differences in these two strategies of attributing meaning are not a matter of crass calculation, of only seeing what one wants to, but largely stem from very real differences in situations that in fact generate different meanings. I have here been able to suggest only some of these situational factors, such as degree of consensus among church members, the official position of women within the church organization, and differences in church history.

Individuals employ symbolic strategies across church settings as well as within a single setting. I would like now to examine the types of strategies women in the Baptist and Brethren churches use in different settings and the ways in which different core meanings are made relevant for the individual in this context.

The women in the Baptist church for whom hats are most problematical are the middle-aged. For the older women there is a correspondence between their interpretation of Biblical meaning and their behavior, both religious and secular. For them hats represent subordination and formality, which are required in both the secular and religious domains. Not only do they always wear hats to church, many of the older women wear hats whenever they leave their homes. For the young women, on the other hand, a correspondence also exists, but their interpretation and behavior are different. Within their cultural framework hats express formality, and within their general religious framework formality in worship is de-emphasized and hats are not worn. Rather than stressing that church is a place to meet with God the king, as do the older women, they stress meeting with God as friend, a situation demanding informality or at least a feeling of being "comfortable," which would not exist if hats were worn.

Neither situation holds for the middle-aged. They were raised believing that women wear hats to church and that not wearing a hat is a sin. They related to me that with the change in Scottish culture they no longer have a "conviction" that wearing hats is necessarily a God-ordained universal as opposed to a man-made tradition. At the same time they are ambivalent as to whether one's relationship to God as king or friend should dominate. For these women, hats have often been a significant factor in their reevaluation of their concept of sin and of their relationship to God. The extent and depth of the meaning of hats for them were quite clear to me in their discussions. They would often speak at length about the process by which they gave up wearing hats or the "compromises" they had reached. In many cases women had in effect rank-ordered services according to their degree of "sacredness" or solemnity (which in turn warranted a corresponding degree of formality) by setting up a continuum of meetings in which they would or would not wear hats. In essence, they had made formality the dominant meaning involved in actually wearing hats in particular situations.

For some of these women the additional factor of not "offending one's brother" entered into their decisions, especially for those who were wives of deacons and elders. Sometimes this factor provided a solution to their dilemma. Although they no longer felt not wearing a hat was sinful in itself, they still found it hard to overcome the feeling it was wrong. This provided them with a good Biblical reason for continuing to wear hats but avoided a firm commitment to particular meanings for the symbol itself.

Whereas, among the Baptists, the ability of women to "manipulate" the system or to express themselves within the system emerges from lack of consensus in the church and from the nature of hats as multivocal symbols with many different alternative meanings, among the Brethren, the ability of women to use hats "strategically" comes from the very rigidity of the equation of form and meaning in which hats are multivocal symbols that mean many things at once. This potential for the strategic use of hats in the Brethren context is best illustrated by an examination of a case of a young woman who attended services at the assembly but did not wear a hat.

This woman was raised in a Brethren assembly and regularly came to most church services with her mother, who was a member. She had undergone a conversion experience in her teens and was accepted as a Christian by most church members, but she was not asked to join the church because she would not wear a hat. The point is that despite the clear equation between hat wearing and being a female member of the assembly—in fact, because of this fixed equation—the position of this one woman was totally ambiguous. There was no way of determining from her actions her attitudes toward the church and church doctrine. There was no way of determining whether she wasn't a church member simply because she did not want to wear a hat or because she did not want to be a church member as well. The rigidity of the rule protected her from ever being asked about her religious beliefs.

5. Conclusion

In this discussion I have been considering the conception of women's position in one important variant of Western Christian culture—evangelical Protestantism. I have done this by examining in depth the meaning of one central symbol of the position of women—the wearing of hats to church. To discern and understand these meanings I have made a distinction between core meanings, with their Biblical basis, and situational meanings, in which the Biblical core is understood in terms of one's experience and the social situation in which one is placed.

Core meanings are those agreed-upon meanings that are drawn from the Bible and that provide a basic frame for situational meanings. Three such core meanings of hats are dominant: subordination, dignity or modesty, and formality. Two of these, subordination and dignity, relate to general themes in studies done on cultural conceptions of women, in particular the examination of notions of power, pollution, modesty, honor, and shame. The third meaning, on the other hand, relates to the general issue of the relationship between humans and their divinities. I have tried to show that it is distorting and misleading to stop the analysis at the level of core meanings. These meanings are in many ways ambiguous and are only given substance through the use of the symbol in particular situations, which themselves generate fields of potential meaning.

After looking at general differences between the churches in the meanings they attribute to hats, I focused on the strategies different individuals used in particular situations to communicate particular interpretations of the meaning of hats. Specifically, I discussed how two pastors, concerned primarily with the need of harmony in their churches, employed symbolic strategies aimed not so much at expressing a particular conception of women's position as at creating consensus among church members, both male and female. Also I discussed how women among the Baptists and the Brethren used symbolic strategies for a variety of purposes: to express their relationship to God, to indicate membership or nonmembership in a church, to communicate a particular conception of their position in the church, and to express the nature of the relationship between wives and husbands. I have tried to demonstrate throughout this analysis that understanding the meaning of hats as a symbol of women's position involves the examination not only of women as objects whose nature and position are defined by fixed cultural conventions, but also of women as part of the social arena of pastors and other individuals interpreting these symbols, and finally of women as social actors in their own right defining cultural realities through their strategic use of hats as symbols.

Acknowledgments

I would like to thank John Gumperz, Jane Monnig Atkinson, and my husband, Daniel Maltz, for their comments on an earlier version of this article. It is based on research conducted in Edinburgh from September 1972 to October 1973.

Notes

1. Even in the most conservative Brethren assemblies where women cannot sing solos during gospel services, hymns written by women will be read and sung. The "contradiction" involved in keeping a woman from speaking while others speak her words was first pointed out to me by a member of the Brethren.
2. Ann Kibbey Levy (1973) has presented a detailed study of the Puritan understanding of how the Holy Spirit speaks through the Bible to individuals that shows many similarities to the understanding of this by evangelicals that I found (Borker 1974).
3. Christians will use a wide variety of verses to illuminate other verses and this provides for an almost endless source of variation in the meaning that may be given to a particular verse.
4. The meanings of hats and hair are closely connected for many evangelicals. In recent years a number of general studies on the symbolic importance of hair have appeared, e.g., Leach's study of magical hair, Hallpike's on social hair, and Firth's on the relation of public and private meanings of hair. In this discussion I am concerned not with the search for universal meanings in symbols such as hair or coverings but rather with the meanings a symbol has for a particular group of people in particular situations.
5. An important factor in the Adventist attitude toward hats is the strong influence of the American church, where hats became of little significance years ago. American influence is quite marked both in terms of members of the Edinburgh church going to American Adventist meetings and institutions and in terms of the number of American church members visiting the Edinburgh church. For example, the minister in charge of the young people's meeting when I did my research was an American who was in Edinburgh to get a Ph.D. in theology.
6. Baptists often gave the example of Brethren assemblies that posted signs saying women without hats would not be admitted and explained that this violated two fundamental principles of the evangelical message, in that it meant judging women on the basis of behavior and keeping women who needed to hear the gospel from in fact hearing it.
7. These two verses need not have been included as part of the complex of verses. The chapter divisions in the Bible are arbitrary, i.e., the Bible was written in verses and books but these were not originally divided into chapters. Thus it was an individual decision on the pastor's part that these verses "went with" the others. This again provides for another possible range of variations in the meaning of the Bible passages themselves, the definition of immediate context.
8. He is thus here favoring the social difference as opposed to the spiritual inequality model of subordination.
9. He had in fact started, the process of contextualization at the very beginning of the meeting as a whole, by using as his introductory Bible reading (such a reading is given at the beginning of all meetings in the Baptist church) the passage from Acts dealing with Paul's visit to Corinth (Acts 18:1–17).

References

Borker, Ruth A. 1974. Presenting the Gospel: Religious communication and expressive strategies in three evangelical churches in Edinburgh, Scotland. Ph.D. dissertation, University of California, Berkeley.

Borker, Ruth A. 1976. Strategies of activity and passivity: Women in evangelical churches. Paper presented at the annual meeting of the American Anthropological Association, Washington, D.C.

Deshen, Shlomo. 1970. On religious change: The situational analysis of symbolic action. *Comparative Studies in Society and History* 12:260–274.

duBoulay, Juliet. 1974. *Portrait of a Greek Mountain Village.* New York: Oxford University Press.

Fallers, Lloyd and Margaret Fallers. 1976. Sex and role in Edremit. In J. G. Peristiany (ed.), *Mediterranean Family Structures.* Cambridge: Cambridge University Press.

Gumperz, John. 1971. *Language in Social Groups.* Stanford: Stanford University Press.

Harris, Grace. 1977. Inward-looking and outward-looking symbols. In A. Bharati (ed.), *The Realm of the Extra-Human: Ideas and Actions.* Chicago: Aldine.

Levy, Ann Kibbey. 1973. Puritan beliefs about language and speech. Paper presented at the annual meeting of the American Anthropological Association, New Orleans.

Marks, Morton A. 1974. Uncovering ritual structures in Afro-American music. In I. Zaretsky and M. Leone (eds.), *Religious Movements in Contemporary America.* Princeton: Princeton University Press.

Ortner, Sherry B. 1973. On key symbols. *American Anthropologist* 75:1338–1346.

Ortner, Sherry B. 1974. Is female to male as nature is to culture? In M. Z. Rosaldo and L. Lamphere (eds.), *Woman, Culture and Society.* Stanford: Stanford University Press.

Prime, Derek. 1967. *Questions on the Christian Faith Answered from the Bible.* London: Hodder and Stoughton.

Prime, Derek. 1972. *Methods and Means of Bible Study.* Mimeo.

Turner, Victor W. 1964. An Ndembu doctor in practice. In A. Kiev (ed.), *Magic, Faith, and Healing.* New York: Free Press.

Turner, Victor W. 1967. *The Forest of Symbols: Aspects of Ndembu Ritual.* Ithaca and London: Cornell University Press.

Part 21

CHURCH WITHIN WALLS

82

THE IMMEDIACY OF ETERNITY

Time and transformation in a Roman Catholic convent

Rebecca J. Lester

Source: *Religion*, 33 (2003), 201–19.

One of the most striking things about life in a Roman Catholic convent is that every second counts. Not in the ways most of us are used to: rushing from meeting to meeting, trying to meet grant and conference deadlines, struggling to balance career with family. In our hyper-rush culture, we have learned to guard our time closely. It is, after all, *our* time—it belongs to us. We get indignant if someone wastes it or imposes on it without our consent, because once our time has been wasted, it can't be recouped. It is a limited, expendable resource, and in a very real sense our time is a commodity. The less we have of it—the more it is in demand—the more it is worth.

Time in the convent is conceptualized somewhat differently. Time isn't money for the Sisters, but it *is* precious. It's precious precisely because it does *not* belong to us but to God. Indeed, extracting oneself from this 'worldly' temporal plane and relinquishing this false sense of time ownership is one of the first and often one of the hardest tasks young women must master when they enter the nunnery. They must come to understand that this illusory perception of time significantly hinders the experience of God, since it privileges human management of time and agency over the divine orchestration of human existence. The ideal in the nunnery, then, is what Spinoza characterizes as 'liv[ing] under the aspect of eternity' (Spinoza, 1910 [1677]) —that is, to experience time in its genuine, eternal fullness, rather than as filtered through human distinctions.

This article is about how coming to inhabit a new phenomenology of time functions as a key element in the religious training of young women entering a convent in Mexico. Specifically, I suggest that learning to navigate two temporal frames—to, in effect, *read the self* across both contexts simultaneously—helps to affect a change in subjectivity for these women as they progress through their first stage of Religious Formation. The new nuns learn to construct an understanding of their selves as continuous across different temporal spheres, alongside (and perhaps *in spite of*) certain experiences of discontinuity that are purposefully imposed by the nunnery such as separating from one's family and wearing the convent uniform instead of street clothes. In other words, a fundamental part of the formation process is learning how to negotiate these tensions between continuity and discontinuity, and developing an experience of self that embraces both. In developing this argument, I consider what happens in the convent as both reminiscent of and characteristically different from millenarian and fundamentalist forms of Christianity.

The broader project from which this essay is drawn is concerned with the specifics of this larger developmental process, which hinges on certain intersections of gender, religion, and modernity in the Postulants' own understandings of their transformation. I argue that the process is composed of seven contingent stages that facilitate the working through of a collection of metaphysical problematics of the self—problematics which are explicitly associated in the Congregation's philosophy with larger social and political concerns. These seven stages are Brokenness, Belonging, Containment, Regimentation, Internal Critique, Surrender, and Recollection. The present essay is concerned with the final stage in this process—the re-collecting and rearranging of one's personal history into a new narrative of self that is based in a dual temporality through which that self is read and experienced.

The time(s) of our lives: negotiating temporalities

The commodification and personalization of time as a possession, and the ways we learn to barter with it in our everyday relationships, is one of the key elements many theorists—including Habermas (1987), Harvey (1990), Gergen (2000), and Giddens (1991)—point to when distinguishing so-called 'modern' and 'postmodern' ways of being from more 'traditional' forms. In the crudest and simplest of terms, we can say that this temporality of modernity is standardized, linear and progressive. It becomes a private possession, something under our personal control. This is contrasted to the more fluid, cyclical and inter-referential models of time reckoning associated within more traditional contexts, such as within bounded religious communities.

This difference in temporal framing has commonly been described by scholars of religion as 'profane' or 'ordinary' human time versus 'sacred' or 'mythic' religious time (see Berger, 1990; Bloch, 1977; Eliade, 1959; Otto, 1958). These two temporal systems can and do operate simultaneously within cultures or groups, overlapping and intersecting in complex ways. And people often look to religious experts for guidance in how to effectively and legitimately manage these two accountings of time. Religious practitioners themselves must become skilled in navigating between sacred and profane times. Scholars from Durkheim (1995 [1915]) to Levi-Strauss (1963) to Weber (1963) to Turner (1967) to Csordas (1997) have worked to document the complexities of this process.

Recently, some ethnographic material seems to suggest that this distinction between sacred and profane (or cyclial and linear) time not only is *not* helpful in some cases, but may, in fact, lead us to significantly misunderstand the beliefs, practices, and experiences of the people with whom we work. Robbins, for example, takes up these issues in his work with the Urapmin of Papua New Guinea, who, following a Christian Revival movement in 1977, consider themselves to be a Christian group and actively anticipate Jesus' imminent return (Robbins, 2001:532). Robbins presents the problematic of the Urapmin expecting 'the end' to come at any moment, while at the same time continuing with mundane daily tasks that seem to contradict this expectation, such as planting food for the next harvest. Such 'everyday millenarianism', Robbins argues—where people simultaneously expect the end of the world as they know it and continue to invest meaningfully in the continuation of that world—is not unique to the Urapmin but appears throughout history and in many different contexts (Robbins, 2001:526), suggesting that there is more to such apparently internally inconsistent beliefs than meets the eye. Indeed, the perception of a fundamental contradiction in these practices comes, Robbins says, not from the beliefs themselves, but from our own cultural models of time, which are so naturalized within social scientific theories of human behavior and experience that they impair our abilities to understand alternative models of temporality as legitimate.

As noted, traditional Western notions of temporality hold that time is infinite, linear, continuous, and irreversible. There is, according to this model, a past, which is 'behind' us and potentially knowable. There is also a present, within which we go about the business of living. And there is a future, which may not be predictable in the strict sense but which is believed to follow more or less logically from the present, so that contingencies can largely be anticipated and planned for. But Robbins notes that for the Urapmin, as with other millenarian groups (see, for example, Ammerman, 1987; Boone, 1989; Boyer, 1992; Brummett, 1991; Harding, 1994, 2000; Thrupp, 1970; Weber, 1987; Wuthnow and Lawson, 1994), time not only begins, but also ends and then perhaps begins again (Robbins, 2001:530). In this way, time is punctuated with a series of discontinuities or ruptures, with the future not necessarily following predictably or logically from the past. The effect, Robbins argues, is an orientation to time that is radically different from traditional western understandings. Extending the kind of model Robbins constructs, we can say that if time is discontinuous, cyclical, and even reversible, expectations of an imminent end-of-days are not necessarily delegitimated by attending to what we might view as 'future oriented' tasks such as storing food for the winter and planning a wedding. When 'future' and 'past' are no longer vectors heading off in opposite directions but are bent and woven together, the relationships between 'beginnings' and 'endings' is no longer necessarily oppositional.

The formulation of time in the convent, like that among the Urapmin described by Robbins, is not easily parceled out into 'sacred' and 'profane' time, or even 'linear' and 'cyclical' time, but is understood as being simultaneously linear, cyclical, progressive, *and* regressive. But unlike the Urapmin and other millenarian groups, the focus in the convent is on the *continuity* of time rather than on its discontinuity. Specifically, although ruptures, breaks, and discontinuity are believed to be important and necessary components of self-discovery in the convent, they are understood to be *subjective reorientations* to an otherwise continuous and meaningful temporal system.

For example, the experience of rupture or discontinuity a girl experiences when she first leaves home and comes to live in the convent is acknowledged and validated as personally painful but is then quickly reframed as a parallel to the experience Mary must have had when she left her family to marry Joseph. The newcomer learns that God has chosen her, just as he chose Mary, for a special purpose. Her feeling of disjuncture, then, is recast as simply the growing pains of recognizing her true calling, which God had set out for her since the beginning of time. Gradually, this continual naming of such experiences of rupture and discontinuity in conjunction with their reframing as spiritually and temporally continuous with God's plan for her persuades the new nun to move toward an alternate experience of self. She learns how to navigate between temporal realities and, with increasing skill, to use this process instrumentally to achieve a change in the subjective experience of the self. In this way, I suggest that coming to inhabit a new phenomenology of time helps the new nuns I worked with to integrate and personalize the various elements of Religious Formation they encountered over the course of the first year.

Religious (trans)formation

I spent eighteen months with an incoming group of Postulants in an active-life congregation of Roman Catholic nuns in the city of Puebla, Mexico. I wanted to get a feel for what goes on emotionally, psychologically, and spiritually with these young women as they try to decide if they should pledge themselves, body and soul, to Christ for all eternity. From my readings of historical accounts of convent life, I expected to find fasting nuns who wished to escape their bodies, disciplined women who saw their materiality as an impediment to saintliness and who felt the clear and constant call of God. But what I found was something else.

I was surprised to learn that the sense of 'the call' is usually far from clear to these women as they enter the nunnery. They have a general feeling that

God wants them there, but they are unsure, nervous, and acutely aware that something besides God could be propelling them toward the Religious Life. Challenging, questioning, and refining these feelings of Religious Vocation is a lengthy and difficult process, and it is one that requires careful guidance and care by those who have gone through it themselves.

In their first year, the Postulants are mentored through a shift in self-interpretation that serves as the foundation for their subsequent religious training. They learn to incorporate into their daily experience a new story of who they are and what their purpose is—one that reorders and restructures their understandings of their own personal histories, while at the same time situating these new understandings within a temporal frame that is different from that on the 'outside'. By the end of this first stage of training, the Postulants had learned to reframe their experiences of The Call to the Religious Life not as a discrete event but as a *developmental process* that spans their whole lives.

The congregation

The congregation I worked with was established in Mexico in 1885 by Father Juan Diego de Muro y Cuesta.[1] Born in 1851, he was heir to the War of Independence from Spain and the Mexican-American War. He was also witness to a no-holds-barred project of modernization and the resulting social and economic upheaval that eventually led Mexico to bloody revolution in 1910. He saw the emergence of a new social class, a disenfranchised urban poor, who seemed to be left behind in the march of progress. Father Muro founded the Congregation—which he called The Siervas, or Servants—with the specific mission of helping this poor, forgotten, and suffering group of people to reclaim their 'traditional' (Mexican) values and dignify themselves as human beings against the 'dehumanizing' and 'evil' effects of modernization. He directed his critique at what we might call the *subjectivity* produced and cultivated through the forces of industrial capitalism and modernization and bolstered by the Protestant ethic. This modern subjectivity took on an added dimension for Father Muro when viewed through his particular theological lens. It assumed a gender.

Father Muro came to locate the decay of Mexican values and identity with mothers who had been 'masculinized' by capitalist development. He also believed that young women are, by the grace of God, the only possible saviors of a world in crisis, and a concern for the 'proper' formation of young women came to eclipse the other works of the Congregation. In the founder's understanding, this non-modern subjectivity—this particular way of knowing, experiencing, being in, and relating to the world—is purposefully and undeniably female, Mexican and Catholic, as defined *against* the 'masculine' and 'Protestant' values perceived to be foundational to American-style 'modernity'.

Today, almost 100 years after his death, the Sisters believe their founder's mission to have radically new importance as Mexico grapples with the contravening tensions of globalization on the one hand and the preservation of a sense of national and cultural integrity on the other. They view their mission as nuns as nothing less than providing a moral compass by which Mexicans can see their way through the perils posed by these social and cultural conflicts. And they set out to do this by inhabiting an alternative orientation to the world as Brides of Christ and Mothers of the Poor. The process of Religious Formation is designed to cultivate in newcomers to the convent the attitudes and dispositions necessary for the development of this internal constellation.

Formation, then, involves not merely a spiritual commitment but a political and social one. Women who enter the Congregation with only a vague sense of Vocation must come to believe that God wants them in this particular congregation, at this particular time, to engage actively these particular issues. During the first year of training, the Postulants slowly begin to master the tools and techniques necessary for this transformation.

Religious vocation as a story of the self

To understand how this works, we need to look at the experience of Religious Vocation ('the call' to the Religious Life) not just as a spiritual or psychological event but as a *story of the self*—a 'narrative identity' in Ricoeur's (1992) sense of the term, a cohesive account of the self that follows a particular trajectory and that is intelligible only in retrospect. Narrative identity in this sense is not necessarily a consciously devised presentation of self, though this may sometimes be the case. Rather, Ricoeur suggests that it is a function of trying to make sense of two radically different experiences of self—the diverse experiences we have of ourselves at different points in our lives ('selfhood') and the sense that there is some essential kernel of self that can be traced through these various permutations ('sameness'). He argues that our subjective sense of who we are is continually produced and reproduced through a dialectical relationship between these modes of experience. What narrative identity does, then, is to provide an arena for the integration of these different temporal modes of self-experience in a way that has meaning in a particular context. For Ricoeur, this story of the self is primarily an explanatory exercise for making sense of 'how did I get here' (wherever 'here' is for the narrator) that reflects multiple layers of experience and interpretation. As the 'here' changes, the story, too, is altered to accommodate the new direction. This narrative implicitly appeals to a certain kind of temporal organization (Ricoeur, 1985). Time is understood to unfold along a linear trajectory, with the present firmly ensconced between the past (known) and the future (imagined).

But in the convent, we see something a little different. Newcomers are guided in how to tell a new story of themselves—to construct a particular type of linear, narrative identity that resituates all life experience, past, present *and future*, within a temporal framework that favors the *circularity* of time and draws meaning from it. The essential elements of one's human life story are worked into a larger narrative with a different temporal frame of reference. This new temporal lens is both timeless and cyclical: it enfolds both the notion of eternity (that time and existence have no beginning and no end) and of the shaping of time according to certain meaningful patterns, which find expression in various religious beliefs and observances. Just as Moses led the Jews out of bondage in Egypt and into the Promised Land, for example, so it is believed that Jesus lead the faithful out of the bondage of sin and into Eternal Life. The lambs' blood on the Jews' doorpost caused the Angel of Death to pass over their homes, just as Jesus' blood—as the Lamb of God—protects his followers from sin and therefore from death. Sinful, disobedient, carnal Eve brought about the Fall of humankind, but this Fall is repaired by the obedience and chastity of a woman who herself is free of original sin. There is, in other words, a cycling and overlapping through time, repeated and varied enactments of key themes such as bondage and freedom, sin and redemption.

These cross-temporal correlates—and many, many others—are woven into the celebrations that make up the Liturgical year, which begins with the Annunciation to Mary, continues through Jesus' birth at Christmas, and culminates with his crucifixion and resurrection at Easter. The entire year is structured to parallel the life, death, and resurrection of Jesus, which itself is understood to parallel the creation, fall, and redemption of humankind. The rhythm of convent life is modeled on this cycle on various levels, with the days of the month, the progression of the week, and even the hours of the day organized to replicate this pattern. It is within this temporal frame that the Postulants learn to understand their Vocations and their decisions to enter the nunnery not simply as one young woman's desire to unite with Jesus but as part of an awesome, divine plan of salvation.

So how might this happen? As noted, most of the Postulants were initially unsure if they had really been called by God. They anxiously looked for any sign—no matter how small—that their Vocation was genuine. The Postulants learn, in fact, that it is certainly possible to *have* a genuine Vocation and not know it, or to believe falsely that one has been called to the Religious Life when this isn't the case. They tended to view Vocation as something they did or didn't have, and it was not clear to them how to tell the difference. They are wary of their own senses of calling, and rely on outside validation from their superiors as to whether or not their experiences were 'real.' As Carlota (a 19-year-old Postulant) told me, 'I just wanted someone to tell me, "Yes, you have a Vocation", or, "No you don't"'. 'But it's not that easy. No one can tell you for sure if you have a Vocation or not. This is between you and Christ.'

One way the Postulants begin to engage critically their motivations for joining the convent is by learning new ways of thinking about themselves as flesh-and-blood actors within the material world, while at the same time continually (re)interpreting their embodied experience as evidencing important things about their spiritual state. They must come to situate and reinterpret their mundane daily activities within both 'worldly' (linear) time *and* 'sacred' (eternal, cyclical) time, and to attach meaning to their actions that bridges both domains.

The ritualization of everyday life

The crux here seems to be development of an alternate experience of daily practice as ritual activity, or what we might call a *dual movement* with regards to action, time, and experience. Specifically, daily life in the convent becomes an arena for the negotiating of these temporal frames by simultaneously regulating the Sisters' every waking and sleeping moment *and* highlighting the illusory nature of these temporal distinctions.

We can understand this approach more clearly if we think of the convent as a ritual space, in Bell's (1992) sense of the term, which operates with its own game rules and generates its own ritual activities and meanings. The protective and isolative nature of the convent creates a bounded realm of sacred experience, where daily life becomes alive with the presence of the otherworldly. For the believer, the power of God is palpable and infuses every aspect of the Sisters' lives. The Sisters are never 'outside' of ritual, in the anthropological sense of the term. They feel that they are constantly communicating with the divine in a powerful and direct way, whether in the chapel praying or doing the laundry. In this way, everyday activities take on new meaning and new significances. Washing the floor, for example, is no longer simply utilitarian. It is a tribute to God and a test of one's Vocation. Peeling vegetables and preparing meals is not merely a duty but a manifestation of humility and enlightened servility. Studying for courses is an act of gratitude to God for one's intellect. Bathing is a reminder of one's pledged purity of both body and spirit. Eating reminds one of the frailty of the flesh and the eternal nourishment of the soul to be had in heaven.

In other words, the Postulants are guided in how to experience their every action, no matter how small, as an articulation of their spiritual relationship with God, and as an opportunity for them to feel his presence and follow his will. As opposed to the outside world, where the drudgeries and chores involved in keeping things running are often seen as distractions or burdens which draw us away from 'quality time' or 'down time' these tasks become for the nuns a means of experiencing God on a deeply intimate level. As Amelia (a 22-year-old Postulant) told me, 'I used to hate to do chores when I lived at home. I'd do them if I had to, but I resented it because they got in the way. I wanted to go hang out with my friends or do something fun. But we learn here that washing the pots and pans and things can be a way of praying, a way of loving God. It's still not exactly what I'd call "fun", but if you offer your work up to God, it's a way of being with him and showing him how much you love him. It can actually be a beautiful experience.' In other words, the recasting of daily activities as drawing their significances from a sacred temporal reference *as well as* a mundane one, allows the Sisters to engage them as tools in their personal and spiritual transformation. Learning how to analyze their inclinations and actions along these lines—and to internalize them as the Word of God—is the primary skill the Postulants must master during that first year.

Reading the future in the past

But this altered relationship to in-the-world action is not limited to the confines of the nunnery, or even to the here and now. After all, the present, as James (1950) characterizes it, is 'specious'. It contains part of the past as well as part of the future. Our 'selves' involve judgments about past events and experiences as articulated through actions and emotions in our present and are given meaning through our imaginings of what our future selves will be like. The Postulants learn not only how to monitor their present behaviors and inclinations but also how to project these interpretations into the past. And it is here that the question of temporality most explicitly leans on the subjective experience of self.

The Postulants are taught that, if they really do have a Vocation to the Religious Life, it is because God has chosen them specifically for this path before they were born. In fact, they are told, God selected them to be his Brides since *the dawn of creation* and wants them to fulfill this Vocation regardless of their weaknesses, faults and personal histories.

If a woman believes she has been called to Christ from beginning of creation, this means that, whether she realized it or not, each and every thing that she has done or experienced since her birth occurred in the context of that calling. Whether she realized it or not, God had chosen her to become his bride and was gently guiding her toward this path. And whether she realized it or not, God was communicating with her—and she with him—even as she went about her daily business. It didn't matter if her family wasn't religious or if she didn't start going to church until she was thirteen. It didn't matter that she went through a rebellious stage and would sneak out of the house to meet her boyfriend. It didn't matter that she had planned to go to veterinary school and spent her afternoons at the vet hospital instead of at catechism. The Postulants learn that spiritual communion with God not only is possible but can be *pervasive* in our daily lives, if we cultivate it. 'There are so many things in my life I didn't give any importance to', Carmen (a 29-year-old Postulant) told me, 'but now I can see that it was the Lord trying to get my attention. Good thing for me the Lord is patient!'

In the course of their first year in the convent, then, the Postulants are guided in reconceptualizing their whole lives as a series of events indicating a divinely directed transformation, a progressive unfolding of self in particular image. This self is eternal, yet embodied in the here and now. It has been singled out by God for special grace but risks eternal damnation by virtue of its incarnation in human flesh. It is an agent in the world and is endowed with free will, yet is constantly guided and persuaded by God in ways beyond its awareness.

And they learn to view their bodies as the domain of negotiation between these temporal frames, a negotiation that proceeds in fleshy, concrete ways. In a May retreat on the Virgin Mary, for example, one month before they were to enter the Novitiate, Mother Veronica observed to the group that the ten months of the Postulancy are like the months of pregnancy—that the Postulants were, in a very real spiritual sense, gestating Jesus in their own wombs. They had become, in other words, simultaneously the daughters, brides, *and* mothers of Christ, orienting toward a spiritual rather than a physical model of female reproduction. Learning to construct a meaningful narrative of self that embraces—rather than denies—such paradoxes as they develop and change over time sits at the heart of the transformation these women undergo in their first year.

To see how these issues play out, let us look closely at narratives related to me by three of the Postulants, describing their understandings of 'the Call' and their own processes in answering it. These accounts are transcribed from taped interactions.

Vocation narratives

Abby, age 19

My Vocation emerged when I was four years old. Yes, four years old. I didn't do much about it at the time, of course. I do remember playing nun with my friends, tying a towel around my head like a veil. But I did all the normal things—I played, went to school, got into trouble. When I was in middle school I joined a group called Youth Missionary League. They're dedicated to going on missions, where you go outside of the country and missionize. Everything about the group is dedicated to missions. But for young people. And, well, that's how I started to get a little more involved in religious things, because of this group. I was enamored with the idea of working on missions—I really think it's so important, working with the poor.

Eventually, I went on my first mission. We don't start off going to faraway places like Africa. Eventually, you can get there. But we start closer to home. There are so many people right here in the State of Puebla that need help! So I started out in *el campo* here in Puebla. And ay, no! It's amazingly beautiful, because the people are so simple. But they are *so poor*, so poor—materially as well as spiritually. And you say to yourself, 'And me, having everything!' Because I didn't lack anything—the love and care of my parents, everything. I had everything. And I thought, 'Ay, no, my God! I have to do something, no?' But I didn't realize that God was asking something of me. No, at this point it was nothing more than, 'Ay! I have to do something! I have to do something!' But I had no idea what.

So I started to go on more missions, I traveled a lot, went out of the region. I met young people from all over Mexico. And I kept liking it more and more. And I got to know priests and some foreigners who came from Peru and missionaries who came from all over and told us their experiences as missionaries and everything. Ah! I loved it!

And eventually, I said to myself, 'Well, it's time, to do something, no?' But I was very, very afraid. So I thought, 'Ay, no, no, no. How?' I thought, if God is asking me to do something, then yes! But I didn't know *where* or *when* or anything. So I decided, 'Well, I'm going to start to investigate my possibilities. I'm going to start to look for what I want to do.'

So I started to look. I went to retreats, I got to know various congregations. I got to know people called 'laicos comprometidos'—lay people who take vows similar to ours but who live wholly in the world. And I evaluated it all. I would say to myself, 'This one is good, this one no, no WAY on that one.' And I did this for a long time, for almost two years. During this time, I continued with my normal life. I kept going out with my boyfriend and everything. But I kept this other side private, knowing I was looking for something more.

Finally, one day I said, 'Enough! I've had enough!' Even with everything I had I wasn't satisfied. Not anymore! Something was missing. *Something.* But something *spiritual*, something very, very profound. Not something superficial. And this is when I went to a conference in Monterrey. And it was *beautiful*, beautiful, because it is there that my vocation started to become clear to me. And I said, 'That's it. The religious life. That is where God wants me. And I want to give myself to him completely. OK.'

So then I began to investigate. Sometimes I would think, 'A nun? What am I thinking?' But it's true—I kept coming back to the feeling that *yes*, there was something, something telling me that I was to become a nun. I was surprised, because I had always envisioned being a missionary. But there was something not quite complete about that for me. I didn't quite find what I was looking for. But when I *did* find it, I thought, "Well, here it is! *Here* it is! Absolutely, positively, here it is.'

And, well, I met the Siervas. My parents' house is close to the Novitiate, and my little brothers and sisters go to the Sierva's preschool. But all that is relatively new, so I hadn't spent much time there myself. But I started to visit, and before I knew it was going by almost every day, staying and talking with the Sisters. Finally, I decided to attend the vocational retreats, and it was there that I decided it was time to enter. I thought about entering with the Sisters of Guadalupe, but in the end, it was the Siervas that felt right to me.

And thanks be to God that I'm here! I entered the Postulancy. It hurts so much to let go of everything outside. Yes, it hurts. But it something that goes away eventually. It's that you're full of the things of the world, and you have to let them go. But when you come to the religious life, all of this starts to leave you, leave you, leave you. You scrub everything out, and then new things come, like grace, like the love of God. It's when you feel *universal* love that you know. And when you realize that you've been filled with it, you say, 'Ay! No, no no, no! It can't be!' But it is. You can't believe it because it's so beautiful because you are so happy! And outside you can be happy ... but only in *parts*. You're kind of half-way happy. You feel happy and you live in the moment, but inside, no. Here in the convent you know what true happiness is. You give everything to others and you think, 'I'm exhausted, but I'm happy! And the more I give, the more I receive! And in the end, I'm going to receive the ultimate prize—eternal life!' Well, anyway, this is what happened to me. I would say to myself, 'I exist because of the love of God. Everything I do is for the love of God.'

Yes, I'm here inside a convent, and perhaps I should think, 'No! I'm incarcerated!' But it's something, I don't know. People on the outside view it differently. They think, 'how can you stand being incarcerated?' I'm not incarcerated! I feel *free*. *Free*. Absolutely free. There are so many things I've let go of, worldly things that were weighing me down. And now I feel so *light*, as we say. Free.

Celeste, age 19

My Vocation . . . well, I feel it began when I was small, since I was very young. More than anything, when I was young I dreamed of becoming a priest and of giving mass [laughs]. I told my parents I wanted to be a nun, and finally, when I was nine years old, my parents sent me to stay at Father Muro's school. It was hard, because I was only nine years old, and the other girls there were fifteen, sixteen. I was bored, and I missed my mom a lot. But I really was curious about what the Sisters did—there was something about it that kept calling my attention. When I was at school, I missed my mom. But when I was home, I would miss the Sisters and the school and couldn't wait to go back.

This was the first stage of my Vocation—first wanting to be a priest, and then at the school. But at this age, one doesn't understand, no? As I got older, into middle school, I began to help at the retreats—youth retreats, seminary retreats, retreats for all the congregations in the city. And I became even more curious. I really liked the atmosphere, everyone laughing, everyone treating one another with friendship.

So it was in middle school that I started to look more seriously, trying to discover if I was really meant for the Religious Life or not. I knew I liked it a lot. I felt very satisfied in the retreats, and it was never the same leaving a retreat and returning to the world, to school, sports—the things I did on the outside that didn't fill me up, didn't satisfy me. And I realize this, that each time I went to the retreats, I felt full, complete.

I spoke with Mother Josephine, the Vocations Director, about this, and told her I thought I might want to enter the Religious Life. She was supportive, but told me I was much too young to decide yet, that I should take at least three years, finish school, and then see where God wanted me. I was disappointed, but she was right.

Something else happened on that particular retreat that changed things. When I was little, I suffered two rape attempts. This really influenced how I thought about things. At the time, I didn't know how to think about what had happened. During that retreat, one of my friends told me that something similar had happened to her. Because it had happened to me, too, I was able to tell her, 'Don't worry—I've overcome it, you can, too.' But in truth, remembering what had happened to me hurt a lot—it uncovered something in me, and afterwards I didn't want to have anything to do with nuns or vocation or anything. No thank you. I decided it wasn't for me.

When I returned to school it was very difficult, no? Because I had decided I didn't want that life. I closed myself off to it. I stopped going to mass, I didn't like going to school. But I did keep going to retreats. I think even then something inside me knew that I would come back to God.

Anyway, I finished middle school, went on to high school. And all the while, I felt this kind of disequilibrium, as if I was trying to figure out who I was and what I wanted to do with my life. I guess this is normal at this age—we all try to figure out our personalities. And not just whether we are aggressive or sensitive. I started to feel drawn again to the Religious Life. But still, those two rape attempts affected me. As I got more involved in religious things, my spiritual director pointed out to me that maybe I was looking for some sort of compensation, some kind of affective compensation in the religious life for what had happened to me. So I started questioning myself all over again. What if it was true? If that's what was motivating me, she said, then I shouldn't enter the Religious Life.

So I threw myself into sports. Sports get out all the negative energy, you know? I played a lot of sports, and I spent a lot of time writing and reading, trying to figure out what I really wanted and why. I got interested in psychology and philosophy, and threw myself into my studies. I did this until my last year of high school, and then I had to decide if I was going to have a career or what I was going to choose to do.

But, then, I had my boyfriend, and he could always support me [laughs]. My boyfriend was very important to me because it was a way for me to test myself, to see if I really was looking for compensation for what had happened to me, if I really could redo my life so to speak. Because after something like that happens to you, you feel like dirt, and you don't even know sometimes if you're really alive or not. That's how I felt. So for me, having my boyfriend was very important. And I was very upfront with him. I told him, 'I want to be a nun.' I don't think he believed me, but he accompanied me on retreats.

At school, I had a spiritual director and went to confession every week. I also had an academic advisor (the psychology teacher). We received communion every day, and this was very helpful to me. And through all of this, I always felt . . . I had this *inquietud* here inside, no? And I still felt that the Lord was calling me. I felt it more strongly every day.

I went to more and more retreats. I broke up with my boyfriend. But Mother Josephine thought I should wait longer. I was impatient, so I went and joined another congregation. I felt the call so strongly, you know? And I wanted to turn myself over completely to God. So I entered with the Dominicans. My parents didn't approve at all. I was there for a week. Just a week. I was miserable. I couldn't eat. I couldn't sleep. I got sick. I remember crying and crying, thinking that I just couldn't stay in that congregation. The sisters we so kind to me, but I knew it wasn't right.

But I still felt that the Lord was really calling me. So I went back *again* to Mother Josephine, and I told her, 'I feel that the Lord is calling me.' 'Fine, come back to the retreats,' she told me. So I went through the vocational retreats again. I went to visit one of the Sierva's houses in Huajuapan. Mother Josephine thought this would be a good way to see if I really wanted to enter.

I loved the experience in Huajuapan, and when I returned, I wanted to give myself to the Lord more than ever. Not so much for the work itself, but to really *give* myself to the Lord.

Oh, the day I entered the Congregation I was so happy!! Ayyyyy! For me it was . . . well, all of us were so excited! And in here, I really began to see how I feel about things. You truly surrender yourself to God, and I love it. The Postulancy has been a really beautiful experience for me. The only thing you carry with you is the Call. You renounce yourself, join with your Sisters. So many things you used to think were important just don't matter anymore. Outside, in the world, you limit yourself. But not anymore. And what's more, you know what you're committing to here, no? So if sometimes you feel discouraged, you can think, 'Well, the Lord is with me. What do I have to fear?' And here you continue to clarify your Vocation, because here you realize that you can be a contemplative in action, right?

And you become aware of your miseries. It's as if the Lord is saying to you, 'Do not worry, I am with you, be at peace.' For example, here you know that every act you do is an act for the love of God. And I love this. Because every step you take, every word you say is something very special—everything you do is out of love for God. And if your forget something, this is because you're lacking Love. For example, if I forget to chop the fruit for lunch, this is a lack of love. So everything must be done for the love of God.

. . . But as I was saying, the rape attempts in my childhood marked my life, and so even today I wonder, 'Am I doing this as a compensation?' I'm happy here—who wouldn't be happy being close to the Lord in a place like this? It is beautiful, beautiful. But you start to wonder, 'Is this really where God wants me?' Not just whether or not it's where I want to be, but if it's where *God* wants me to be. You have to make yourself completely available to God—what the Lord wants, I want. It's like what Mother Veronica told us, 'I don't want the outcome to be more or less or better than what He wants.' So one should be docile, try to see everything with eyes of faith.

So this is how I've come to think about everything that's happened to me. And it's helped me a lot. You remember that Father Muro says that to live with the poor it is first necessary to *become like* the poor? Well, because of what I've been through, I can help young girls that have had similar experiences. And who better to help someone who's traumatized, than someone who has been through trauma herself, like me? How can you understand their experience unless you've been through it yourself? But coming through a trauma is one thing. Coming through it and being able to help someone else is a different thing all together. I think the Religious Life is helping me know how to do this.

Each Vocation is very particular. The Lord takes hold of each of us in a special way. Frankly, this whole experience in the convent has fascinated me. Everything just fills me up. It is a beautiful, beautiful thing to abandon yourself into the hands of God.

Amelia, age 22

Well, my Vocation began when I was very young. Ever since I can remember, since I had the use of reason, I used to tell my aunts that I wanted to stay with them: they were cloistered nuns. So whenever we would go visit them, I would always tell them that I wanted to stay with them, that I didn't want to leave. Well, they would laugh and tell me that I just had to grow up, and then I could go there.

That's how it was. In my childhood it was always that way. I made my first Communion. I was so excited! My aunt made my little dress for my first communion. It was so pretty. She made my dress for my *quinienera*, also.

But when I got to be fifteen years old, I . . . well, actually, it was from when I was about twelve years old, I no longer wanted to enter a congregation, that is, to be a nun. I hung out at school and with my friends (I usually played with boys rather than girls). And that's how I spent my time. The funny thing is that whenever my friends would make me angry or something, I would tell them that I was going to enter a convent. I would always tell them this as way of getting out of a problem or out of anger or something.

I remember that on one occasion we were playing, and they left. They were gone for an hour, and I was waiting for them. They didn't come. So I got really mad and I told them . . . well, they came to see me at my house and they said to me, 'Why didn't you wait for us?' And I said, 'I did wait for you, but then I left.' 'But why?' they asked. And I said, 'I shouldn't spend too much time out of my house because I'm going to enter a convent!' So from that point on I felt that, how should I put it? After I had gone something like four years without mentioning the convent, I started talking about it again. It was during this time that I started to say a lot that I was going to enter a convent. And from there this idea practically never left me. Always, in different situations, this idea would come to me. It was constant.

So I went to high school. I didn't like it. I left. But always with this idea that I would someday become a nun. But, how should I put it? It was if had hadn't yet assimilated it, or rather, like there was something inside that said, 'You are going to be a nun, you have to be a nun, you can be a nun.' But I would say, 'No, I don't want to.' It's difficult to explain because it's a feeling that moves you, a kind of an inclination, but at the same time you yourself refuse it, reject it. It's like . . . it's like your spirit, no? Your spirit calls you one way—let's say, to perfection. It wants you to attend to this. But you, you say no, because it requires sacrifices, it will be too hard. In other words, renunciation. So with the simple word 'nun,' I said, 'no, no!'

I was out of school for three years. And then some musicians came to town and asked me, 'Don't you think you might want to study music?' And I did. So they took me to see Father Bruno, and I went back to school so I could study music.

For the next three years I went on missions with the school, and I liked it more and more. I talked to the director about becoming a nun, but he said he thought I was more excited about the music than about the religious aspect of the missions. So on that third mission, he didn't let me play any music at all, but made me stay in the chapel the whole time. I hated it.

I finished school. I didn't like being at home and started to look for a band to play with. And then—who knows what got into me—I went to talk with a priest who was about to be ordained. And I told him *everything*—all my *inquietudes*, what had been happening, how I had experienced my Vocation. And he told me, 'Well, look. I don't know many congregations. But of the few I know, and from what you've told me, I think you'd fit well with the Siervas.' He gave me their address and told me to go talk to Mother Josephine.

But I didn't go see her. He gave me the address in December, and it wasn't until the following Easter that I thought about it again. Easter was coming, and I knew I didn't want to just stay home. So I decided I would go somewhere, but I didn't know where to go. That's when I dug out the address of Mother Josephine—I figured she would know of somewhere to go. I expected her to be big and fat, at least sixty years old or so. To me, all nuns were like that.

The curious thing is that I arrived at the central office of the diocese— that was the address the father had given me. But when I got there, well, I'm a little timid, so when the secretary said Mother Josephine wasn't there,

I didn't tell her whether I was going to wait or leave. I just kind of sat in a chair. When she realized I was still there, it had been four hours! I was waiting there four hours to see this Mother Josephine. 'I'll call Mother Josephine right now,' the secretary told me, and she did. She told her that there was a girl who had been waiting to see her for four hours. Mother Josephine told her to put me in a taxi and send me to the Central House right away. I arrived at the Central House and met Mother Josephine. She was nothing like what I had expected. We talked for a long time, and she told me I should attend the Vocational retreats.

After this, I started attending the Aspirant retreats. I spent some time at one of the Congregation's houses. I was trying to decide what to do. I couldn't decide if I wanted to enter the convent or enroll in the university. I talked to Mother Josephine. 'Look, it's your decision,' she told me. 'Enter the congregation or enter the university. But if you enter the university, you should stay until you've finished. Understand? No dropping out early.' It was interesting, though. Because as soon as she said, 'Choose the congregation or your career', I thought *'the congregation!'*

This was at the beginning of August. I went home and told my mom what I wanted to do. 'Are you sure?' she asked. 'Yes!' I told her. So I got all my papers together quickly. I think I was the last one to turn in my application letter. And then one day they called me on the phone. I answered, and Mother Josephine said, 'Amelia, guess what?' 'What, Mother?' I asked. And she said, 'They accepted you.' And I just stood there for a minute. 'What?' I asked. And she said, 'Yes! They've accepted you into the Congregation!' And I started to laugh. I couldn't believe it. 'Now what do I do?' I thought. I didn't have any of the clothes I needed, nothing. But I got my things together, and I entered.

When I entered the Congregation, I thought, 'Well, let's see what happens.' I had only been here two weeks when Mother Veronica wheeled out the piano, and I played it. She told me she thought I should continue studying music, and I was thrilled. I always thought that when I became a nun I would have to say goodbye to music, goodbye to everything. But now that I'm here, the Congregation teaches us that the Lord works through us in all sorts of ways, and that music is one way He works through me. So for me this is something, how shall I say it? A very nice surprise. Because bit by bit—there are so many things that I experienced before and now that I'm here . . . there are so many surprises that come, that now I see that this is my place. This is my place! And not before, not later, but right here in this moment.

There are so many things. Our charism is that of reparation, and our patron saints here are the same ones that were mine outside! There are so many coincidences! I have always had a special devotion to Saint Joseph and to the Sacred Heart and to the Virgin. And they have all that here as well. There are so many things that it's a little bit spooky. And you're not doing anything—it just happens. Sometimes you feel like a boat, drifting here and there, almost turning over in the storm. But from somewhere outside, the Lord guides you, saying, 'Over here, come this way.' And everything that happens to you helps to reaffirm this. To be more generous in your *entrega* [surrender/sacrifice] and everything. And although we're not always perfect, we always try to get there, no?

As we can see, in recounting their Vocations, Abby, Celeste, and Amelia go back through their lives, giving significance to things in ways they themselves admit they hadn't before (Amelia not wanting to leave convent, Abby playing nun, Celeste playing priest). They resituate these elements within a larger trajectory, a story that takes 'the call' as something that existed throughout their lives, whether or not they were aware of it. They talk about their Vocations as the gradual realization of their true place in the world. This realization did not come in a flash of insight, though (as in Celeste's case) it was sometimes punctuated by specific, identifiable events. Rather, the recognition of Vocation was for these women more a gradual accumulation of feelings, with lots of fits and starts and doubts along the way. Throughout this process, the constant motivating force they all describe is the deeply felt sense that something wasn't right, that something crucial and fundamental was missing in their lives. Each of these women sought out alternative ways to be happy (Abby with her boyfriend, Amelia with her music, Celeste with sports). But despite a superficial satisfaction, they all describe an eventual realization that the void they felt was only met through their spirituality. And not just any spirituality, but rather an all-embracing, all-engulfing sense of intimacy with God.

Over time, and through different ways, each of these women came to understand her feelings of emptiness in the 'outside world' as the call to enter to Religious Life. But more than this, they came to understand this call as directing them to the Siervas in particular. In separate conversations, Abby, Celeste, and Amelia (along with many of the other Postulants) told me that they had originally planned to enter with another order—the Dominicans, the Franciscans, the Paulinas. Some of them actually spent time in other congregations before leaving and seeking out the Siervas. All talked about the focus on cultural integrity and social justice—the reclamation of women and the affirmation of Mexican values—as being key things about the Congregation that appealed to them, though most of the Postulants did not become truly acquainted with this dimension of the Congregation's teachings until after they had entered. Like the sense of Vocation, then, the Postulants learned to read these political commitments back through their lives, giving new meanings to their experiences as specifically preparing them for the life of a Sierva.

Celeste's story is perhaps the most explicit in terms of the reinterpretation of past experiences through an altered framework in the 'recollecting' of

Vocation. She talks about the trauma she suffered as a child, a victim of two separate rape attempts by different individuals. She acknowledges—both in this particular narrative and in many other conversations we had about these events—that they shook her to the core. She told me that she lost faith in God for a long time after the second attack. 'I thought, 'How could there be a God who lets things like this happen?' And I know I'm not the only one—it happens to girls all the time. I just couldn't imagine a God who would permit that.' It is perhaps striking, then, that by the end of her first year in the convent, Celeste had come to see her traumatic experiences as, ironically, one of the ways God had worked through her. She does not in any sense believe God 'wanted' her to be traumatized, or that it was necessarily part of His plan for her that she be raped. Rather, she told me, she feels now that he did *permit* the attacks to take place. Not to punish her for some kind of personal failing, as she has sometimes thought in the past, but rather, as she explained it to me, because he knew she had the strength and the character to 'handle it,' to transform her experiences into something that would help others.

She sees her calling to the Siervas in particular as relating to this in a specific way. 'Father Muro talked about the exploitation and abuse of women,' she told me one day as we walked in the convent garden. 'He believed that this comes from a devaluing of women, from not valuing women for the special qualities that they have *as women* in this world—the care, the tenderness, the *entrega* we give to others. He believed strongly in the *regeneration* of women, of helping women to know their own worth so that they can perform the roles God assigned to them. I think what I went through gave me a special kind of understanding about what he meant.'

We can see, then, how the Postulants learn to incorporate into their daily experience a new story of who they are and what their purpose is that reorders and restructures their understandings of their own personal histories, while at the same time situating these new understandings within a temporal frame that is different yet not wholly separable from that on the 'outside'. They learn to tell new stories of their lives that are more than a simple recountings of facts and that move back and forth between temporal frames—between 'worldly' and 'eternal' domains of reference—overlaying them, drawing correspondences and parallels. This shift in self-interpretation serves as the foundation for their subsequent religious training by teaching them to experience their own bodies—their working, praying, eating, studying, playing, cleaning bodies—as the domain of negotiation between temporal worlds.

Evangelizing the self: (un)certainty and the temporal contours of salvation

At least in part, then, this transformation in the convent seems to hinge on a rhetorical reformulation of the self similar to what Harding describes in her exploration of American evangelicalism (Harding, 2000). In considering the persuasiveness of fundamentalist Baptist rhetoric, Harding characterizes conversion (being 'born again' or 'saved') as 'an inner transformation which quickens the supernatural imagination as it places new believers within the central storied sequence of the Christian Bible' and develops in the newly faithful 'the wherewithal to narrate one's life in Christian terms' (Harding, 2000:34). Specifically, she argues that the language and performances of fundamentalist Baptist gospel teaching work as a rhetoric of conversion, (re)constituting both the speaker and the listener through the language of salvation. Over time, Harding maintains, the newly saved come to adopt new Bible-based interpretive practices that enable them to conceptualize and experience their own lives, as well as current political and social events, in radically new terms (Harding, 2000:34–35).

This reframing of one's life story within Fundamentalist Baptist discourse is similar to what I observed in the convent, as the Postulants learned to reinterpret and reexperience their selves across both 'worldly' and 'sacred' temporal frames simultaneously. But there are some important differences between these two groups. Here, I will consider only the two that most directly lean on questions of temporality and the experience of religious transformation.

First, though both groups are Christian, the 'point' of conversion is not the same in each. In the Baptist context, the direct aim and consequence of conversion is salvation, which is predicated on being 'born again' through a new baptism in the Holy Spirit. It is, in other words, a future-directed process built around the kinds of ruptures and discontinuities Robbins (2001) describes as characteristically millenarian. Such elements as achieving a *new birth*, preparing for the *second coming* of Christ, becoming saved before the *impending apocalypse* effectively construct the experience of rupture as, perhaps paradoxically, part of the progressive path towards salvation. In the convent, however, salvation is understood to be granted in one's baptism in infancy. There is, then, no need to be 'born again'; rather, one is called to comply with the original baptismal sacrament, to recommit to a covenant already made between the person and God. Consequently, conversion in the convent is not geared toward achieving an elusive salvation since one is already saved, but rather toward submitting one's personal will to that of God.

Following from this, conversion enfolds a different sort of process in the two groups. In the Baptist context, where 'conversion' means being born again through a new baptism by the Holy Spirit and the ensuring of salvation, it is taken as an absolute certainty that God wants the conversion of all people, that everyone can be 'saved,' and that this is the ultimate goal for all participants. Conversion, then, follows a predictable path, with the 'success' of the conversion process measured in large part by the certainty that one has found salvation in Jesus, Hence the importance of the kinds of rhetorical strategies and performances described by Harding. In the convent, however, the process of conversion has an uncertain outcome. For the nuns, conversion depends not on specific supernatural events or on public evidence of personal salvation, but rather comes through the gradual *process* of learning to relinquish the self and submit one's personal will to that of God, whatever that is determined to be. This means that a woman must be open to the possibility that God is not calling her to the Religious Life and that she should leave the convent all together.

Conversion in the convent, then, is not about moving along the kind of predictable, linear model of development with a clear and certain end point that Harding describes among fundamentalist Baptists (which, I would argue, holds true despite the rhetorical emphasis on rupture and circularity) but rather about *letting go* of this certainty and opening the self to God. In other words, what may seem to be consistent forms of rhetoric and practice across different Christian groups can in fact enfold radically different understandings of the subject and his or her relationship to both the mundane world and to the divine.

Concluding thoughts

To sum up: I suggest that the experience of navigating two temporal frames in the convent leads to fundamental changes in the three key areas:

1 The Postulants learn to recognize the existence of two temporal systems, one that constructs time as a personal possession and one that recognizes time as belonging only to God, and to value the former as illusory and the latter as genuine.
2 They become increasingly adept at navigating these two arenas through the reframing of daily practice as ritual acts. In this way, the worldly notion of time as a limited commodity that can be wasted or maximized loses its hold, and the distinction between mundane and sacred time (ideally) falls away.
3 This recasting of mundane activities is projected back over the life course, and past events and experiences are reinterpreted as articulations of one's Vocation. This reinterpretation then permits a young woman to construct a coherent narrative of her life that validates her decision to enter the convent as inevitable.

Successful Formation, then, relies on the resituating of the story of self within this new temporal reference—not only in the way Ricoeur suggests, where the narrative identity mediates between immediate and continuous experiences of self, but in a way that rests on an particular understanding of time, action, and agency in a context in which, for the Sisters, there *is* an ultimate Truth.

The ideas presented here constitute just one small piece of what the Postulants told me of their experiences of Vocation and the changes they were undergoing during their first year of religious training. But these issues of temporality and self-understanding highlight, I think, some of the complexities of thinking through the issues of subjectivity and personal transformation within the context of religious or spiritual commitment. Though, as I have noted, they share some important parallels with other Christian groups such as the Urapmin of New Guinea and American Evangelicals, the Catholic sisters I worked with engage questions of temporality and the self in ways that not only differ doctrinally from these Protestant models but also carry additional significances within the modern Mexican context. This would seem to suggest that one concern of a nascent 'anthropology of Christianity' should be the ways in which local (re)formulations of 'history' and 'culture' articulate (or perhaps resist) religious models of time, agency, and salvation, and how individual people learn to make sense of their own lives within these systems.

One way to understand the 'work' of religion in its various permutations, then, might be to see it as an arena of *becoming*, that is, of developing a permissible and valued self in a given context. Religious systems invest culturally shaped categories of legitimate/illegitimate identities with moral force, provide believers with the tools for integrating the key elements of these identities into (or removing them from) their subjective experiences of themselves and the world, and detail clear and solid signs for knowing if the project of self-transformation is working. For the Sisters, this comes, at least in part, in the acceptance of a new narrative of the self that casts them not only as young women struggling to find purpose in their lives but also as Brides of Christ from the beginning of creation to the end of time.

Note

1 All names used are pseudonyms.

References

Ammerman, N. T., 1987. Bible Believers: Fundamentalists in the Modern World. Rutgers University Press, New Brunswick, NJ.
Bell, C., 1992. Ritual Theory, Ritual Practice. Oxford University Press, New York.
Berger, P. L., 1990. The Sacred Canopy: Elements of a Sociological Theory of Religion. Anchor Books, Garden City, NY.
Bloch, M., 1977. The past and the present in the present. Man (n.s.) 12, 278–92.
Boone, K. C., 1989. The Bible Tells them So: The Discourse of Protestant Fundamentalism. State University of New York Press, Albany.
Boyer, P., 1992. When Time Shall Be No More: Prophecy Belief in Modern American Culture. Harvard University Press, Cambridge, MA.
Brummett, B., 1991. Contemporary Apocalyptic Rhetoric. Praeger, New York.
Csordas, T. J., 1997. The Sacred Self: A Cultural Phenomenology of Charismatic Healing. University of California Press, Berkeley.

Durkheim, E., 1995. The Elementary Forms of the Religious Life. Free Press, New York. Original edition 1915.
Eliade, M., 1959. The Sacred and the Profane: The Nature of Religion. Harcourt, Brace, New York.
Gergen, K., 2000. The Saturated Self: Dilemmas of Identity in Modern Life. Basic Books, New York.
Giddens, A., 1991. Modernity and Self-Identity: Self and Society in the Late Modern Age. Stanford University Press, Palo Alto, CA.
Habermas, J., 1987. The Philosophical Discourse of Modernity: Twelve Lectures. MIT Press, Cambridge, MA.
Harding, S., 1994. Imagining the last days: the politics of apocalyptic language. In: Marty, M. E., Appleby, R. S. (Eds.), Accounting for Fundamentalism: The Dynamic Character of Movements. University of Chicago Press, Chicago, pp. 57–78.
Harding, S., 2000. The Book of Jerry Falwell: Fundamentalist Language and Politics. Princeton University Press, Princeton, NJ.
Harvey, D., 1990. The Condition of Postmodernity. Blackwell Publishers, Cambridge, MA.
James, W., 1950. The Principles of Psychology. Dover Publications, New York. Original edition 1890.
Levi-Strauss, C., 1963, Structural Anthropology. 1. Basic Books, New York.
Otto, R., 1958. The Idea of the Holy. Oxford University Press, New York.
Ricoeur, P., 1985. Time and Narrative, Vol. 3. McLaughlin, L., Pellauer, D. trans. University of Chicago Press, Chicago.
Ricoeur, P., 1992. Oneself as Another. Blamey, K. trans. University of Chicago Press, Chicago.
Robbins, J., 2001. Secrecy and the sense of an ending: narrative, time, and everyday Millenarianism in Papua New Guinea and in Christian fundamentalism. Comparative Studies in Society and History 43, 525–51.
Spinoza, B., 1910. Treatise on the correction of the understanding (tractatus de intellectus emendatione) and on the way in which it may be directed towards a true knowledge of things. In: Boyle, A. trans. (Ed.), Spinoza's Ethics and 'De intellectus emendatione'. Dent, London; Dutton, New York, pp. 225–236. Original edition 1677.
Thrupp, S. L. (Ed.), 1970. Millennial Dreams in Action: Studies in Revolutionary Religious Movements. Schocken, New York.
Turner, V., 1967. The Forest of Symbols. Cornell University Press, Ithaca, NY.
Weber, M., 1963. The Sociology of Religion Beacon. Press, Boston.
Weber, T. P., 1987. Living in the Shadow of the Second Coming: American Premillennialism, 1875–1982. University of Chicago Press, Chicago. Enlarged edition.
Wuthnow, R., Lawson, M. P., 1994. Sources of Christian fundamentalism in the United States. In: Marty, M. E., Appelby, S. R. (Eds.), Accounting for Fundamentalisms: The Dynamic Character of Movements. University of Chicago Press, Chicago, pp. 18–56.

83

WOMEN LIVING BETWEEN THE CHURCH AND THE STATE

A case study of Catholic women religious in contemporary rural China

Li Wenwen

Source: originally published in Peter Ng and Wu Xiaoxin (eds), *Christianity and Chinese Society and Culture: The First International Young Scholars Symposium*, Hong Kong: Chinese University of Hong Kong, 2003, pp. 359–84; translated and revised by author, 2009.

Discussions concerning the strained relations between the Chinese state and the Roman Catholic Church usually remain at an ideological level, rarely examining the day-to-day experience of Chinese Christians, the majority of whom are female rural residents. Historical studies stressed relations between western missionaries and the Chinese elite (Bays 1996); some focus on a specific religious community (Wiest 1988), institution (Graham 1995) or historical event and movement. Studies of both politics and theology stress that relations between two apparent monoliths are couched in terms of either domination and oppression (Vree 1976; Treadgold 1979) or contextualization (Whyte 1987: 21).[1] While historical studies may touch on gender issues, political or theological ones scarcely say a word, ignoring the fact that at grassroots level women outnumber men in daily religious life. In reality, the Chinese Catholics live in a more delicate and ambiguous relation between Church and State, formal Church hierarchy and volunteer Church community, as well as orthodox Church teaching and local religious practice. This paper sets out the lives and thoughts of a group of rural women who have chosen to belong to a Catholic religious order in the underground Fengxiang diocese. Using concrete cases, this focus allows me to investigate the power relationship between the sisters and the State, as well as the sisters and the priests. In so doing, I demonstrate a process of negotiation of gender ideologies provided by Christianity and Chinese society both vertically (through time) and horizontally (through social interaction), and this process in turn impacts on the complex transformation in gender practice within the Chinese church.

The Catholic community in Shaanxi Province

Shaanxi Province is an inland province along the middle reaches of the Yellow River and a gateway to northwest China. Since the third century BC, Shaanxi, with its capital Xi'an, has been the political, economic, and cultural heart of China, that is, for more than one thousand years. The province has an area of 205,600 square kilometers, a population of approximately 36 million, of whom 67 percent live in the rural area. Because the area is rich in historical heritage and distinctive folk culture, tourism is one of the major industries in Shaanxi. Despite its abundant cultural deposit and long history of agriculture, Shaanxi is poorer materially than the southeast or coastal areas. Converted by Jesuits after 1640, by 1900 Shaanxi had 37,000 Catholics and it now has an estimated 2.8 million Catholics, 9 bishops, over 160 priests (including 44 underground priests who are not recognized by the government), 550 Sisters, 226 churches, five seminaries, and three religious communities of sisters scattered in eight dioceses.

Catholics usually live together in a village, known as Catholic Village, and grow wheat and corn, sesame and fruit. Young women often work in temporary contract work in the town or city, while wives are the major agricultural labor force, further contributing to the household income by raising livestock, via household-based enterprises, as well as taking care of the children. They support the church by paying tithing once a year, in this case wheat, during the harvest season from July to August, and generally more than the stipulated amount, 5 kilos per head. Tithing is called grain of the fourth regulation, *SiguiLiang* (四規糧), a variation form of the Four Regulations in the Catholic Church, financially helping the Church according to capability. Since the relaxation of religious policy in 1979, funds for the reconstruction of churches are accumulated mainly from local Catholics; as one Catholic told me, "before building our own houses, we would like to build the church first." Church attendance for morning and evening prayers is good, and the church is packed during Sunday Mass. Men and women sit separately on two sides of the church. Women and old people are the majority; men working in the city usually return to the village on the "Four Big Feasts" according to the Catholic calendar: Christmas, Easter, Assumption of Our Lady, and Pentecost. During the busiest harvest season, priests relax the ban on and penalties for Sunday work, as they do for a Catholic building his own house. The cult of Mary prevails here, the rosary being one of the favorite prayers in the village. In some churches built before the middle of the 1990s, the picture of Mary is in the middle of the altar, while the cross with the crucified Jesus is at the right or left. Besides the liturgical Catholic prayers, villagers pray for rain in times of drought, and pray for sunshine in periods of long consecutive rainy days.

Most marriages in the village take place between Catholics. If not, those wishing to marry would be required to convert, and before holding the wedding ceremony and banquet the marriage is ratified in a sacrament during the Mass by a priest. In recent years, cases of divorce appear and are increasing. While the divorced person is not allowed to receive the sacraments according to the Catholic doctrine, he/she may continue attending the Mass in the church. Though officially forbidden, the baptism of newborn babies is tolerated tacitly by the local government as an ethnic tradition rather than a religious ritual. Many children participate in the church rituals: Girls love chanting and lead readings, while boys fight to be altar boys. All are fluent in reciting long prayers in classical Chinese, learning them by rote at home and in the church. Catholic funerals and the other rituals around the dead are important constituents of life in the village. What distinguishes Catholic from non-Catholic rituals is that there is no burning of incense sticks and mocking of paper money, nor offerings of food. These are the rituals of "ancestor worship" that were the main objects of the Rites Controversy. However, the Catholics do kowtow to the casket, which is also among the objects of the Rites Controversy. Generally ceremonies are held at home: Priests, sisters, relatives, friends, and neighbors are invited to pray for the dead to rise to heaven. The third anniversary is considered the turning point from a sad ceremony to a happy one, with firecrackers in the middle of the Mass as a symbol of celebrating. The church is a place of entertainment for the Catholics. Many of the villages used to have a men's orchestra in the church. But with the men leaving the villages to work outside, women's orchestras took over. The orchestra plays during the Mass, especially on Feast days, and sometimes is invited to play in funerals as well. The instruments vary from violin, trumpet, saxophone and drum to traditional Chinese ones, such as flute, accordion, fiddle and Sheng, a traditional reed-pipe wind instrument. The Catholic women, mostly young wives, practice with enthusiasm.

Life in the Catholic villages, on one hand, is integrated into a context of the national economic, social, and political system. Economically villagers have to earn a living as an ordinary peasant, socially they have to accept the one-child policy, and politically they are under a Communist regime. However, on the other hand, a distinctive calendar and worldview have been constituted, which make the peasants feel themselves to be participating in a majestic cosmos. And such a village produces a number of vocations to the priesthood or sisterhood.

The Congregation of Sisters

S congregation, initially founded in 1923, was renewed in 1980. From 1980 to 1993, it was growing rapidly, more than two hundred women having joined, and only a few dropped out. Now it is the biggest of the sixty Religious Congregations of Sisters in China. The community is an independent body with its own top decision-making institution: six committee members plus one Mother Superior, elected by all the professed sisters once every six years. There were in 2001 307 members, including 211 with perpetual and 81 with temporary vows, 9 novices, and 6 postulants. The congregation is composed of about sixty groups scattered in five dioceses. Each group has to earn its living, by running medical clinics or kindergartens, making clothing and vestments, painting pictures and making sculptures for the church. Retaining its living expenses of 300 RMB per year for clothing and other needs, they should send the rest of the income to their motherhouse for the whole administrative operation. Living conditions vary greatly from diocese to diocese, area to area, and church to church. Generally, the sisters lead a very simple life in the village and have great difficulty in making ends meet.[2]

Almost all the members of the congregation come from rural areas with a strong Catholic atmosphere. However, a vocation is not simply a product of one's family environment but must be actively cultivated by the believer. The influence of family, parents, relatives, friends, and community combines with an internalized faith mixed with a mysterious experience of a calling or a liberating gift from God. All these elements have great influence on her subsequent vocation. Giving a specific reason for her choice is difficult, most citing a point appropriate for her position at that moment, which leads to multiple responses in one individual. These may include: Experience with sisters, who pray the breviary, play the accordion and sing chants, appeared "nice and special" to the young girls in the village; an alternative to marriage seen as "unfair for women" or (taught by mothers and sisters) "a terrible state, for husbands are unkind toward their wives"; failure to pass the entrance examination to the university, which may be facilitated later at home or abroad by the community; failure to find a marriage partner; influence from family members, it being an ideal in Catholic villages to have a sibling pair of priest and sister who support each other, financially and in daily life; being the middle child or youngest child in a big family.

The relation of Chinese clergy with Western Church and Chinese State

When the Communist government established the Chinese Catholic Patriotic Association to oversee the Catholic Church in the 1950s, most clergy chose to resist the government because they were trained to believe that loyalty to the Vatican was essential to the Catholic faith. Today, whether they belong to an official church or an underground church, most priests still adhere to a view which sees the Church as a centrally ordered hierarchy, rather than a community, and the Pope as an absolute authority, rather than as the head of the Church (Madsen 1999: 28–48). For example, in many churches in

Shaanxi, several bishops still maintain and encourage the custom of kissing the ring of the bishop, and to the belief this will bring Catholics blessings and indulgences. One advantage of 'universal hierarchy' for priests is the regular flow of financial aid from the West, enabling them to build churches and establish businesses. One outcome in Shaanxi was irregularity among Church hierarchy and pervasive corruption; another is that the control of the schism between government-recognized official church and underground church is mainly conducted by priests, who become the major target of attack and control by the government. This variously affects religious women's scope and freedom to work.

Between Chinese sisters and Western Church

The Society of the Sacred Heart of Jesus has long been less controlled by foreign sisters or by Rome than were or are male religious or female international congregations, whose rules and constitutions, adapted from those of the Western groups, were Western in style and in spirit,[3] sometimes leading native sisters to the conclusion that Chinese ways were inferior to Western (Wiest 1988: 251). In contrast, the sisters of the Society of the Sacred Heart of Jesus were free to live in villages, forming small groups of three or four, working in the manner of the Christian Virgins. This self-supporting and self-sufficient tradition has continued up to this day and influenced the way the sisters build their community. For example, while the wearing of trousers is not permitted in many congregations in China and elsewhere, in China sisters seldom wear skirts that expose their legs and are inconvenient for their daily work in the village. One sister described how, when she first arrived in Italy, she wore trousers to attend the Sunday Mass. Her supervisor, an Italian sister, was shocked and soon ordered two sets of dresses for her. Though she accepted this custom during her two-year stay in Italy, on her return to China all the sisters decided to reform their formal-use Western-style habits, explaining that "We are designing a new habit that is suitable for our title as a Catholic sister, and for our identity as Chinese, and one which is convenient to wear everyday."

Though every year a few sisters are sent to study abroad with the aid of the Western Church, the religious formation is carried out almost totally by the native sisters. The formator in the novitiate, a sister in her late thirties who has received three-year training on psychology in a college in Xi'an and further one-month training on spirituality in Hong Kong, is playing an important role in the congregation. She is responsible for the courses of religious studies, such as the Bible, the Three Vow,[4] the Constitution of the congregation, and spirituality. The remaining courses, such as manual work, music, and English, are run by the novices themselves. There are always voices from the Western Church that the quality of religious formation in China needs to be upgraded, and the Chinese sisters also show great interest in the formation and training provided by the Western Congregations of Sisters. However, the Chinese sisters do not blindly follow teaching from overseas, retaining a certain scepticism. For example, one sister describes a class she attended thus: "One morning, when the class begins, the sister [from Taiwan] criticized us for our lack of energy and for not looking like young people, but she has seldom eaten together with us, because she cannot get used to our meals. And she has hardly tried to understand our difficulty in making ends meet. How can she blame us for lack of energy?" Another sister says, "The priest [from Hong Kong] prepares in advance what he is going to talk about in the class, and never tries to adjust his teaching materials according to our levels and our needs. I don't like to follow this way. When I teach catechism before the villagers, I always pay attention to their response, and change my topic to be better acceptable by them." It is evident that the faith of Chinese women religious is rooted in rural society. In some old Catholic villages, the lay Catholics have a long tradition of taking care of the sisters' life, by sending agriculture products to the sisters, waiving the electricity and water fee for the sisters, affiliating their medical clinic with the one of the sisters, so as to help the sisters to lead a stable life in order to better serve the people. Before being a Catholic woman religious, a sister is first a rural Chinese woman. The knowledge about being a Catholic sister imparted from the West may do her good, but it cannot cover her whole living experience in the village.

Between the sisters and the State

Confronted with the internal split of the government-recognized official church and the underground church that is mainly conducted by the priests, the sisters of the Society of the Sacred Heart of Jesus try to keep a neutral stance. They express that "We are neither official, nor underground" to show their political disengagement. The sisters manifested their reluctance to be involved in the male-dominated political conflict by pointing out that many priests pay too much attention to politics, and thus deviate from the original principle of the Church: "Some priests are busy with arguing who is right, and who is wrong. What they are trying to do is to draw the Catholics onto themselves, not onto God." However, notwithstanding their detached self-consciousness, the sisters are inevitably entangled in the complex political reality. In general, the congregation is viewed as an official religious order due to the location of its motherhouse just beside the "official" Cathedral of Xi'an. As a result, the community working in the underground Fengxiang Diocese is discriminated against by the bishop, which in the sister's words is unfair to them.

In fact, much evidence suggests that the sisters have taken a political stance without even realizing it. They are careful not to be involved with the government. When required to be present at political meetings organized by the religious bureau, they show passive resistance, by hiding in the room or by going out, or by sending two elder sisters of eighty years of age to attend. They send sisters to study abroad in Italy and the Philippines through informal and interpersonal relationships, for example, which may circumvent government rules.

The attitude toward the government can be seen from the kindergartens, one of the recent vital enterprises for the sisters in the village. The setting up of kindergartens stems from the new needs of the rural society. With the decrease in the number of children in each family as both a product of the implementation of the one-child policy and the transformation of the consciousness of children, rural residents become more aware of the importance and necessity of early education as a transitional period to prepare for the elementary schools, from getting used to community life to learning some basic skills for study, such as how to hold a pencil. Preschools are usually privately owned, and the education informal.

Sisters, with much formal training in child education, can readily gain permits from local government, although the latter is not always happy with the sisters' work in education. According to the fundamental religious policies, no religious institution in China may be involved in education. In quite a few areas, kindergartens run by the sisters are restricted or supervised by the government, and the curriculum is carefully scrutinized. The sisters are fully aware of the situation and take care not to draw too much attention from the government, as the following case indicates:

> It was a Thursday afternoon in a small and poorly equipped kindergarten with more than ten kids run by two sisters in Village Y. The next day, September 14th was a holy day for the local Catholics to make a pilgrimage to a sacred mountain "Cross Hill," sanctioned by the Pope as early as 1770. When the class was over, the sister told the kids that tomorrow, Friday, would be a holiday, and they needn't come until the next Monday. Half of the kids are from non-Catholic families in the village. Taking the kids home, the sisters happened to meet the lay leader of the parish. The experienced Catholic man admonished the sisters not to close the kindergarten for the sake of the pilgrimage because half of the kids are not Catholic. The sisters agreed and one of them decided to remain the next day. "I will go to call the kids one by one tomorrow. It is true that a consecutive three-day holiday is too long, and will give a bad impression to the non-Catholic parents," a sister said with a sad tone. Later, when I discussed this with other sisters elsewhere, all agreed that, "she should have given up the pilgrimage."

While constraints clearly exist, nuns do have more freedom of action than priests, though this may derive not so much from female piety as from a differentiation of the roles proper to men and to women grounded in the cultural heritage of both Christianity and China. In both gender structures, women's position is understood as domestic, and therefore sisters who wield no power in ecclesiastical institutions and hierarchy are not worth serious concern. This may well explain a comparatively tolerant attitude of the government toward the sisters. Limits placed on female authority within the church actually enable sisters to exercise their own power in the wider context of rural society, which transforms the church from a self-enclosed world into a more open space for non-Catholics as well.

Between the sisters and the priests

Currently the Congregation runs altogether forty-three clinics as its primary source of income. Twelve were set up by the sisters, and the rest with the help of a priest or laity. In the former case, one-third of the income should be remitted to the church, and in the latter, two-thirds. Recently, the sisters found themselves facing keen competition from more and more newly opened clinics in the village. The sisters are seeking new enterprises that are both suitable for them and able to adapt to the changing rural society. In Village T, the sisters recently started a new business of machine embroidering to make tablecloths and curtains. Two sisters worked in a factory for two years to learn the necessary skills. They have bought new machines and are preparing themselves for the new business. They showed me the products they designed, and expect me to help them with PR. One said to me, "We sisters should secure our position in society, for that, we should gain economic strength."

Now women religious become more than ever conscious of their own dignity, their rights, and their equality with men both inside the Church and in the society, for whom the idea that rural Catholic sisters would claim and win social position for themselves, not to mention setting up their own business, was as unimaginable as the change is unpalatable to priests, most of whom advocate a traditional Christian perspective of women as confined in a domestic category. Despite their great effort to remain self-supporting and self-sustaining in a rapidly changing environment, the sisters face pressure and meddling not only from the government, but also from within the church, particularly from the priests, and the most controversial issue often concerns money:

> Four sisters live in a clinic in Village Q. A kindergarten was in preparation when I arrived in August. A poster concerning admission to the kindergarten was put up at the gate of the church: "Kindergarten for children from three to five years old. 80 RMB/Term. Classes include Chinese, Mathematics, English, Pinying (Alphabetic system of Chinese writing), Painting, Dance and Physical Education."

There is one resident priest in his late thirties serving this parish, who objects to the establishment of the kindergarten. He has two concerns; one is that the kindergarten would lessen the sisters' work in the church, such as the maintenance and cleaning of the chapel, visiting the sick, helping the priests with various rituals and ceremonies. Another worry is that there is no precedent for a kindergarten in this diocese, and he is not willing to be the first one. Upon these objections, the sister said: "It doesn't matter if he supports us or not, if only he doesn't obstruct our way, that's OK. We invest money, and prepare the textbooks, toys, and furniture. We can manage everything by ourselves." The kindergarten at last opened in the beginning of the new term as planned.

Another case is that of a more cooperative priest:

Five sisters live in Village D and run a clinic, a kindergarten, and a tailor shop. One resident priest is serving the parish, and the church owns a grocery shop run by lay people. The kindergarten started last year. One sister is mainly in charge of about twenty children. The tuition is 75 RMB per term including the textbooks and a handmade jacket. The timetable is from 8:00 to 11:30, 14:30 to 17:00. Usually the kids go home to have lunch, but at the request of the parents kids can also eat with the sisters at 1 RMB per meal. The kindergarten is well decorated and painted, and this was totally completed by the sisters themselves. The kindergarten has gained great support from the priest and the lay people since the phase of the construction of the building. And the furniture was paid for by the lay organization. "If we sisters can manage to be self-sustaining, it will reduce the economic burden on the priest and laity, so they are willing to support us," said one sister.

Yet the fact is that if the kindergarten is set up with the help of the priest any income must be divided between the sisters and the priests: covert or overt disputes between priest and sister are common. Among the five dioceses the sisters serve, only in Xi'an diocese do the sisters get living expenses for their maintenance of the church and catechist work for the diocese: 100 RMB for sisters living in the city, and 60 RMB for those in the countryside. The salary of the priests recently increased, but they strongly opposed raising the salary of the sisters. True to the lack of esteem for 'women's work' (Truman 1996: 35), the sisters' work in the parish, such as maintaining the sanctuary and the church in good condition, teaching catechism, and preparing for feasts, becomes invisible, and thus justifiably underpaid; the public ritual work of the priests, being "real work," is fully paid.

Another point is that priests cling to an image of women religious in the Church as dependent on the men—an image which was brought by the missionaries four centuries ago. A typical demonstration of this concept is that some priests express their favoritism towards Christian Virgins, who still exist in a few Catholic villages, rather than the sisters, who have a strong backup as an autonomous community. And it is obvious that the priests are also deeply influenced by the unequal and unbalanced gender relations inherent in contemporary Chinese rural society, where the women do not have rights comparable to men within their communities in terms of access to or management of resources.

Though complaints are frequently heard from the sisters that the priest is greedy and dominant, the sisters hardly find any effective way to resist. Moreover, they themselves are sometimes trapped in the traditional view that they are inferior to the priests. For example, in village Q a group of sisters built a new three-floor building for living in and opening up a kindergarten. "Some priests went to complain to the bishop that we sisters could live in a new building, while the resident priest of the village still lived in an old one," one sister told me; "even we sisters ourselves feel ashamed to move into such a new building [laugh]. We are used to be under the priests in every area."

Having rejected motherhood for themselves, the sisters incorporate the care of and for children, Christian and non-Christian, into their daily lives: "Contact with the children may help us live our life of the three vows. Children may greatly relieve the feeling of loneliness which may occur in the religious life." This provocative comment suggests how these rural Chinese Catholic women religious perceive their sexuality and gender roles.

> The sisters have a close relationship with the children in Village T, which has a population of 2600 and is 90 percent Catholic. It seems natural that middle school students living nearby drop into the convent and borrow something like a badminton racket. Every Saturday afternoon, the children come to visit the sisters, singing and studying English. On Sundays, they play ping pong or chess with the sisters.
>
> Every summer, more than two hundred children, divided into seven or eight classes, attend the three-week summer school, a variation of Sunday school, which becomes the major work for the sisters during the summer. The schedule of summer school is arranged according to the life rhythms in the countryside, 7:00–9:00 in the morning, and 4:00–6:00 in the afternoon, followed by the Mass. In the morning, sisters give classes on religion, as well as supplementary education, such as mathematics or English, which are very popular and attract many non-Catholic children to join. The afternoons are for chanting.

This concept of the role of women resonates with the Chinese traditional ethos. As taught in the class on the three vows in the convent, "For a sister, the vow of chastity also indicates a kind of maternal love, attentiveness, and thoughtfulness unique to women. Therefore, our service in the church is very different from that of the priests. We do small things, such as taking care of the kids, and keeping the church clean."

All sisters are required to follow the vow of obedience in their religious life, which means submitting oneself to God, the Church hierarchy, and religious superiors. The center of this vow is to abandon one's free will. In traditional Catholic teaching, true freedom comes from obedience. To be free is not to do whatever one wants but to follow the will of God. And the will of God is known through the authoritative teachings of the Church hierarchy. The Catholic idea of obedience is not completely at odds with China's traditional philosophy. Particularly in the context of the Chinese Catholic Church, the concept of obedience is inevitably linked to the idea of loyalty. "The vow of obedience" is translated in Chinese as "to listen to orders (*tingming*, 聽命)," which indicates a basic model of social behavior continued throughout the centuries in China, where filial piety takes first place, followed by loyalty to the sovereign, and conjugal affection. This traditional sense of obedience makes it difficult for Chinese women and men religious to distinguish between being open to God and simply following the orders of authority and supervisor.

For example, in one parish with two young resident priests in their thirties, after the Mass the sister clears up the altar and prepares for the next day. Since there are no cabinets to hang up the vestments, the sister has to fold them carefully so that they are ready for the priest to just stretch his arms out and wear them. To my surprise, the sister said, "This has become a custom; if we sisters do not do it, the priest will get angry." Actually the two priests are competent and have a good reputation among the villagers. Like other rural priests, besides the sacraments they take care of many other matters related to the everyday life in the village, such as drilling wells and setting up water distribution networks. However, they have never noticed that they have relegated sisters to an inferior position.

In the West, many religious call into question the above traditional understanding of obedience; they suggest that obedience should be based on consensus achieved by dialogue and listening. However, this new concept of obedience in the Catholic Church has not yet reached the Chinese sisters, who seem to have found their source of empowerment in the context of Chinese society rather than Western Catholic 'dialogue and listening' innovations. In fact, though the promise of "gender equality" made by the Chinese socialist revolution to women, and especially by the May Fourth Movement, has not been fulfilled, and the road to liberation for Chinese women as a whole still stretches far ahead, since the 1990s Chinese women, especially those in well-developed cities or suburban villages with easier access to a free-market economy, have been enjoying an unprecedented improvement in their status. Women are becoming valued members of the workforce, sharing leadership positions in companies, earning as much as their husbands or brothers, and gaining more opportunities to receive higher education. The Catholic women religious are not blind to these transformations related to women; they have a more open and accommodating attitude toward the non-Catholic world, including secular gender equality as a part of the Communist philosophy. They do not hesitate to embrace these social changes and make them a resource for seeking a new interpretation of obedience rooted in their faith.

Three issues seem crucial. First, the sisters, increasingly aware of the gap in their education compared with priests and the wider society, are studying hard to upgrade their educational level, an enthusiasm not shared by priests. Each year the congregation sends twenty or thirty sisters to study and be trained in programs considered useful for the development of the community, such as computers, English, medicine or preschool education. There is some anxiety about giving an affiliate, not yet a formal member of the community, a chance to study, but the following opinion seems to gain the upper hand:

> If we sisters don't study, we will be easily sifted out by the rapidly developing society. And it is more efficient to study when one is young, and after the process of taking vows the sister will be at least in her late twenties or early thirties, so that it will be hard for her to absorb the knowledge. And in the long run, even if she leaves, the candidate won't forget that the Church has cultivated her. You see, seminarians that were forced to leave the Church during the Cultural Revolution all work for the Church now. Of course, we have to be careful and choose those that are reliable.

Second, sisters know they are indispensable to both lay people and priests. More and more priests are forced to admit that without the sisters their work is inconvenient and sometimes impossible, in particular because the primary targets of evangelizing are women. When priests are busy performing the sacraments, the sisters spend considerable time in the countryside and in the mountain areas spreading the Gospel, teaching catechism, and visiting the sick.

Third, the sisters have far more opportunities to get in touch with non-Catholics through their work in clinics, tailor shops, and kindergartens. And they are developing their own ministry creatively from a distinctive women's point of view.

> During Lent, we sisters held a workshop for the Catholic women in Village T. We feel that the Church doesn't really play an important

role in the everyday life of the laity. The priest usually requires people to make specific prayers so many times a day. That misleads people to regard praying as a task; if you finish the quota of that day, you will be saved. Life and faith are disjointed. Catholics still fight with their neighbors; conflicts remain between the mother-in-law and the young wife. Our workshop focused on how to live the faith in the daily life. It was held three times for one week in about one month. This year, eighty women in the village have attended the workshop.

Here is the story of another sister who is enthusiastic in evangelization:

> I dropped out of high school to give way to my younger brother, who was expected to become a priest. He didn't become a priest, but I entered the religious life [laugh]. I love my evangelizing work. I have been sent to study education psychology for two years in a college in Xi'an. I am good at teaching Bible and catechism. I have organized Bible study groups in many villages. At Christmas, I arrange shows with the lay people, dances, plays, comic dialog, traditional Chinese opera; the content is all around the Church and the Bible. Most people attending the show are women of twenty to forty years old.
>
> In the rural village, the major obstacle of evangelization is the conflict with the popular customs of offering food or incinerating paper money for the dead. For example, there once was a woman who almost changed her mind the moment before baptism; she said that her deceased father complained to her, in a dream the night before the baptism, that he was so cold and had nothing to wear. I persuaded her that it was just her illusion, and her father also would have the possibility to be saved through Mass and praying. But I am wondering why we have to forbid these rituals. I regard them just as expressions of filial piety, not superstition. I have asked the opinion of the bishop, and he told me that it could be allowed in the beginning, but should be confessed. You don't think this ridiculous?

The sisters do not simply choose to listen to orders; instead, they start challenging the absolute authority of the bishop and priests.

Rethink gender in Chinese Christianity

Let us rethink gender in the Chinese Catholic Church by focusing on the everyday experience of the Catholic women religious. As previously discussed, most of the studies on Chinese Christianity have been over-intellectual and heavily text-oriented, putting predominant emphasis on the official response or the responses of Chinese intellectuals to Christianity, while peasants have appeared as merely historical objects. By focusing on the day-to-day reality of the rural women religious, I intend to avoid a unitary image and discourse on the Church people and their reality, showing rather the realms in which women are free to negotiate their gender role and to achieve their own ends.

The life of the women religious has been examined from three dimensions: their relation with the Western Church, with the Communist State, and with the priests. The concept of "equality of the sexes," legitimated and propagandized as a national policy, has provided varying degrees of support for women to change their lives; however, it also results in the problem of "women's heavy double burden." Moreover, the capacity of the policy to effect change in the countryside has been limited. In such circumstances, to choose a celibate life provided by Christianity serves as an alternative lifestyle for some rural women. It permits them to be free of marriage and seek professional careers outside of the family: their "family" becomes the community of faith in which they develop their abilities freely. However, in reality, the hierarchical/patriarchal dimension of Christianity has been preserved in the Catholic Church and results in a gender-differentiated institution and Church hierarchy which appears to subordinate women to this gendered system. Though their power is in part controlled and diminished by males, it would be too hasty, however, to infer the male dominance in the Church, for nuns are also active agents and subjects. Clearly the gender role of the women religious is in a process of constant negotiation and constitution. It would be futile to say the status of the Catholic women religious is low (or high), for the status of rural women religious in Shaanxi changes according to the context: their relation with the State, with Chinese society, and with the priests, as well with the local Catholics.

First, the rural women religious are active in embracing the social changes concerning the improvement of female status in secular Chinese society. In their attempts to subvert patriarchy, the women religious do not directly confront the problem of gender discrimination; rather, they implicitly accept the proposition in some respects, such as the fact that with regard to formal education and access to economic resources, women are at a disadvantage compared with men. They place their emphasis on improving their lives to overcome their weaknesses. This is a realistic approach under conditions of entrenched patriarchy in the rural Chinese Church. In practice, they proceed with their business or send young sisters to colleges to receive higher education regardless of the objections or criticism from priests.

A sister regards herself as a Chinese rural woman before being a Catholic woman religious. This self-identity affects the relation of the sisters with the Western Church. We have seen that in contrast to the dependency of the priests spiritually and financially on the Western-centered Church hierarchy, the sisters are subordinated neither to foreign sisters nor Western customs. This shows itself in their daily clothes and religious habits. It is also manifested in their attitudes toward formation and training from overseas. Though a sister has chosen a renounced life and left the home of her birth, she remains an integral part of the rural society.

Another realm available to women to negotiate and make changes is their distinct relation with the State. There is little doubt that women have been excluded from the political sphere by both the clergy and the government. This in turn leaves more room for the sisters to seek their professional goals, in contrast to the activities of the priests, which are restricted and limited by the stringent control and supervision of the government. In this process, the sisters are fully aware of the restraint due to the political environment and try to avoid any direct symbolic confrontation with the government, while evolving an enclosed church to a more open space including non-Catholics, in which process they may be more important than priests. It can be said that this distinct flexibility directly results in reducing the amount of political meddling in normal church activities, and indirectly helps the priests to survive in the dominant regime and regulations. As a Catholic puts it, "In a parish, there could be no priests, but never no sisters."

One problem is left: What distinguishes the women religious from the other rural women? We should not forget that it is the religious faith that determines the way they live their everyday life in a manifold web of social relations. This faith is not only something that leads the women to make an initial step out of the "received" model of women located in the dominant structure. It is also something that helped the women to survive and persist throughout the difficult years during the Cultural Revolution. The "faith," as a lived and shared reality, on the one hand leads the women to subordinate themselves to the gendered system inherent in Christianity; on the other hand, it transcends the boundary of nation, culture, and sex, and functions as a powerful resource for these Chinese women to achieve their ends.

Notes

1 But see Entenmann (1996) for early Chinese Virgins; and for the influence of women's education on individual women or groups at the turn of the twentieth century, see Kwok (1996), Ross (1996), Liu and Kelly (1996).
2 In China, sisters take a vow of poverty, while most of the priests, being diocesan, do not. A diocesan priest serves one diocese for his entire priesthood and lives alone. Religious priests serve the church under a religious superior and live with others in community. Since there are few male religious orders in China now, the majority of the priests in China are financially diocesan priests, who eat meals in Catholic homes in turn without any payment, and earn their living by performing various sacraments, such as in funerals, ceremonies for the dead, weddings, special prayers in the Mass. Shaanxi priests commonly own a motorbike and a mobile phone.
3 See a historical study on Maryknoll in China, 1918–1955, by Wiest (1988).
4 The sisters' religious life is characterized by the three vows of poverty, chastity, and obedience, by which the religious handle the three dynamics of human life: sexuality and relationships, material goods and ownership, freedom and power.

Bibliography

Adkins, L. (1995) *Gendered Work: Sexuality, Family and the Labour Market*, Buckingham: Open University.

Bays, D. H. (1996) *Christianity in China: From the Eighteenth Century to the Present*, Stanford, CA: Stanford University Press.

Entenmann, R. E. (1996) "Christian Virgins in Eighteenth-Century Sichuan," in D. H. Bays (ed.) *Christianity in China: From the Eighteenth Century to the Present*, Stanford, CA: Stanford University Press.

Graham, G. (1995) *Gender, Culture and Christianity: American Protestant Mission Schools in China 1880–1930*, New York: Peter Lang.

Judd, E. R. (1994) *Gender and Power in Rural North China*, Stanford, CA: Stanford University Press.

——. (1999) "Rural Women in Reform Era China," *Chinese Sociology & Anthropology* 31(2).

Kwok, Pui-lan (1996) "Chinese Women and Protestant Christianity at the Turn of the Twentieth Century," in D. H. Bays (ed.) *Christianity in China: From the Eighteenth Century to the Present*, Stanford, CA: Stanford University Press.

Liu, J. and Kelly, D. P. (1996) "'An Oasis in a Heathen Land': St. Hilda's School for Girls, Wuchang, 1928–1936," in D. H. Bays (ed.) *Christianity in China: From the Eighteenth Century to the Present*, Stanford, CA: Stanford University Press.

Losada, I. (1999) *New Habits: Today's Women Who Choose to Become Nuns*, London: Hodder & Stoughton.

Madsen, R. (1999) *China's Catholics: Tragedy and Hope in an Emerging Civil Society*, Berkeley: University of California Press.

Ross, H. A. (1996) "'Cradle of Female Talent': The McTyeire Home and School," in D. H. Bays (ed.) *Christianity in China: From the Eighteenth Century to the Present*, Stanford, CA: Stanford University Press.

Tang, Edmond and Wiest, J. P. (1993) *The Catholic Church in Modern China: Perspectives*, Maryknoll, NY: Orbis Books.

Treadgold, D. W. (1979) "Introduction," in Sergei Bulgakov, *Karl Marx as a Religious Type: His Relation to the Religion of Anthropotheism of L. Feuerbach*, trans. Luba Barna, Belmont, MA: Nordland.

Truman, C. (1996) "Paid Work in Women's Lives; Continuity and Change," in T. Cossleff, A. Easton, and P. Summerfield (eds.) *Christianity in Women, Power and Resistance: An Introduction to Women's Studies*, Buckingham: Open University Press.

Vree, D. (1976) *On Synthesizing Marxism and Christianity*, New York: Wiley.

Whyte, B. (1987) *Unfinished Encounter: China and Christianity*, London: Fount.

Wiest, J. P. (1988) *Maryknoll in China: A History, 1918–1955*, Maryknoll, NY: Orbis Books.

Journals

Guide to Catholic Church in China 1997, Singapore: China Catholic Communication.

Tripod, 1995–2000, Hong Kong: Holy Spirit Study Center.

Asian Focus, September 29, November 10, 2000, Hong Kong: The Union of Catholic Asian News (UCAN).

Part 22

CHURCH BEYOND WALLS: THE PERFORMANCE OF PILGRIMAGE

84

Excerpt from
'PILGRIMAGE AND PATRONAGE IN BRAZIL
A paradigm for social relations and religious diversity'

Sidney M. Greenfield and Antonio Mourão Cavalcante

Source: *Luso-Brazilian Review*, 43(2) (2006), 63–89.

Introduction

In a paper on pilgrimage to the shrine of Bom Jesus da Lapa in the state of Bahia, Daniel Gross lamented more than three decades ago, "Pilgrimages have been largely neglected in the ethnographic literature, not only in Brazil and Latin America but in other areas where they occur frequently" (Gross 1971: 129). While some valuable studies of the subject have been published in the intervening years,[1] this important aspect of what Brazilian scholars refer to as "popular" Catholicism is still inadequately documented and insufficiently examined.

In the years since Gross conducted his research, Brazilian society has changed greatly. The population has almost doubled with most of the growth occurring in the urban areas; the economy has been industrialized; and the society and its citizens have been subjected to the onslaughts of modernization and globalization.[2] Research on religion has reflected these economic and demographic changes; recent studies are concerned with the Afro-Brazilian and Spiritist groups and rapidly expanding evangelicals all prevalent primarily in the ever-growing urban centers. Less attention has been paid to the traditionally rural pilgrimages and the cult of the saints of which it is a part.

Subjected to new theoretical influences studies of pilgrimage have moved away from Gross' concern with social structure to other issues.[3] Gross saw pilgrimage in terms of the model of patronage and clientage still accepted at the time as characteristic of social relations in Brazilian society. He concluded his 1971 paper saying "... pilgrimage provides ideological support for the system by projecting earthly relationships into the sacred sphere in which people act out debt paying as ritual" (Gross 1971: 129).

Worship and the paying of *promessas* correspond to the fealty and labor which a client owes to his superior. The saint, like a paternalistic patron, has enormous powers of decision over his client. Both may choose to heal or not to heal; often they hold life-and-death power over a client. They are under no earthly constraint to accede to the client's wishes except for *noblesse oblige*. If a patron or a saint fails to fulfill a request, there is no appeal to a higher power possible (Gross 1971: 145).

Our objective in this paper is to return to what Gross had focused on: social structure and more specifically relations of patronage and clientage.[4] Part I describes a pilgrimage to a shrine for *São Francisco* (St. Francis of Assisi) also in the Brazilian northeast conducted over a period of years beginning more than a decade after Gross did his work. Examining the data will lead us to conclude, as he did, that patronage is the dominant pattern of relations evidenced in the interaction between worshipper and the supernatural. It also provides the symbolic imagery for patterns of interaction between those with power and control in this world and those without.[5] [...] beliefs and ritual practices, since the supernatural entities of each are offered to help humans with their problems in exchange for devotion, the model still can be applied.

We refer to the ritual participants as *potential* devotees because in these new faiths, as in the older worship of the saints, acts of devotion and veneration follow from rather than precede the completion of an exchange between an individual in search of help and the supernatural. That is, the living do not necessarily participate in rituals and perform behaviors commonly thought of as religious and devotional until after they receive what they had requested from the supernatural in an initial encounter.

The analysis will enable us to: 1) better integrate the study of pilgrimage, the cult of the saints and "popular" Catholicism into the literature on the contemporary "popular" religions; 2) conclude that pilgrimage may be viewed as the paradigm for modeling social relations; and 3) propose a revised framework for understanding Brazilian religion and symbolic life and their relation to the social organization of the society.

Part I

A pilgrimage to the shrine of St. Francis in Canindé

When the driver suddenly applied the breaks to the rickety old truck while making the sharp right turn onto the traffic congested road marked Canindé, Maria de Fátima Batista[6] braced herself on the backless bench she had occupied for much of the previous four days. She was almost there. Her dream was about to be realized.

It all began some five years earlier when Fátima, an agricultural laborer almost thirty years old, fell from a cart badly hurting her leg. Though taken to a doctor, several weeks after treatment the swelling was still there and the pain had grown worse. Unable to return to work in the fields and having difficulty caring for her husband, house and children, Fátima realized that her problem was serious. Not knowing what else to do, she sought the help of *São Francisco* (St. Francis), the powerful holy being she had heard so much about.

While it was true she had barely been inside a church for years, and was not, by any measure, a religious person, her plight was such that the idea of turning to the supernatural seemed a viable option. The woman prayed with great fervor to the saint, promising that if cured she would visit his shrine in Canindé where she would light candles, attend mass, take confession, walk the stations of the cross and dress in a *mortalha*, a brown habit similar to the one he wore in life. As an additional expression of her lowliness, dependence and humility in the face of this important heavenly figure, she added that if healed she would cut off her beautiful waist length black hair that was so admired by friends and relatives.

In the weeks to follow Fátima's leg improved and gradually she was able to resume her normal activities. A month later she was back at work. Soon thereafter the pain disappeared completely. Thrilled with the "miraculous" recovery, Fátima told her cousin what had occurred. The other woman offered to accompany her to fulfill the vow. Maria Laura's own visit to Canindé, she reminisced, had been the high point of her life and returning, though requiring great sacrifice, would bestow untold pleasure.

Seu Antônio, who freighted goods in the region, put benches without backs and a precarious cover on his truck each year on the anniversary of the saint's birthday and carried passengers to Canindé for the festival. The *pau-de-arara*, as such trucks are called, accommodated some 60 to 70 pilgrims. When Laura learned the cost, she estimated the amount of money the two would need for food and other items to sustain them during the ten-day trip. The women realized that the journey would cost considerably more than they had and it might be several years before they would be able to accumulate enough disposable income to go. But they also knew that St. Francis would understand and wait patiently as long as necessary to receive what was owed to him by Fátima.

Four years later, after saving tiny amounts periodically from their wages and selling several of the small animals their families raised, the women had enough money. Six months before the festival they contacted Sr. Antonio and reserved two places on his truck. The night before it was to leave, amid joyous retellings of their own experiences by friends and relatives, the two women carefully packed food, a small stove, their hammocks, clothes and the wood carving of a leg that Francisco, Fátima's mate, had made for her to deposit at the shrine as a votive offering attesting to the miracle cure by the saint. Other companions, unable to make the trip this time, asked them to carry small gifts to the shrine. At six AM the following morning the women arrived by mule cart to meet the truck at the designated place in the small municipality of Regeneração in the interior of the northeastern Brazilian state of Piauí. Joining the other passengers, they were at last on their way.

For the next four days the travelers bounced uncomfortably across the dry, barren moonscape known as the *sertão*, a semi-desert the size of France and Spain. There had been no rain that year, or the previous one. The riverbeds were dry and the few plants that managed to sprout withered quickly due to the lack of water. The livestock already showed the signs of danger and more than a few carcasses were strewn along the roadside. For the remainder of the trip the driver stopped the truck only for the passengers to prepare and eat meals, relieve themselves, rest in the late afternoon heat and sleep at night. He went through the towns and settlements along the way, but five flat tires had delayed their arrival at the destination.

Fátima was not consciously aware of it, but she had become part of the pilgrimage tradition in Christianity that stretched back well over two millennia. The moment she boarded the truck, she had separated herself from her normal, every day social reality and entered what Victor Turner called a liminal state (Turner 1969: 96). The Brazilian agricultural laborer was "betwixt and between social worlds."[7] While it is true that pleasantries were exchanged with their fellow passengers, there was no significant interaction with any of them during the trip. The cousins had not known any of the other travelers when they departed and the same was true when they returned to Regeneração. No anti-structure was formed and no *cummunitas*, as Turner maintains occurred with pilgrims to the Marian shrines he studied (Turner and Turner 1978). Interaction was to be primarily between each individual and the saint. No social transformation in the lives of the pilgrims was to happen.

Christian pilgrimage: a magico-religious complex

Pilgrimage has its roots in Greco-Roman and Hebrew practices. Visiting sacred places did not become important in Christianity itself until after the fall of the Roman Empire, long after Constantine had made it the imperial religion. While its importance declined, (mostly) in (western) Europe after the Reformation when the forms and meaning of the practice were changed, it was still a vital element in the Roman Catholicism of the inhabitants of the Iberian peninsula when, in the late fifteenth and early sixteenth centuries, they embarked on the conquest and colonization of the rest of the planet and specifically, for our purposes, the Western Hemisphere. For Brazil, pilgrimage was to be a central feature of the Christianity imposed by the Portuguese.

A pilgrimage is not an isolated event or activity and cannot be fully understood as such.[8] In its preReformation, or medieval form it is part of a complex of understandings central to which is a belief in and a reverence for saints, supernatural beings who at one time are believed to have lived as mortals on earth. "Reborn" and elevated to everlasting life in heaven by an all-powerful creator God postulated to have control over all aspects of the universe, including the destinies of those on earth, they are believed, as a "friends of God," to be able to act as intermediaries with Him on behalf of supplicants on earth. As Wilson (1983: 23) has phrased a position proclaimed in the official theology of the Church, ". . . saint(s) might be seen as advocates pleading causes before a stern judge, as mediators, as go-betweens, as intriguers or wire-pullers at the court of Heaven. . . ."[9].

Humans pray to the saints using words in which they petition their help with material as well as spiritual problems. Attaining supernatural intervention in our (material) world is referred to as a miracle. Miracles, as Augustine of Hippo was so influential in maintaining, "were signs of God's power and proof of the sanctity of those in whose name they were wrought" (Woodward 1990: 62). Saints may be invoked at any time and in any place, but their help is most likely to be obtained if a request is made at their tomb. Pilgrimage is a visit to the shrine of a saint where a powerful and mystical religious intensity is believed to be present.

The saints are assumed to be sympathetic to human suffering and generally disposed to assist (potential) devotees because they once had lived on earth. To increase the probability of obtaining the saint's intercession, a petitioner invariably will make a vow[10] promising in exchange for the requested assistance to visit the saint's shrine. As further incentive he may promise to have masses said, light candles and perform acts of penance. A material representation of the miracle, or a letter attesting to it, also may be included in a vow and deposited as a votive offering at the shrine as testimony of the saint's abilities and accomplishments.

As Queiroz (1973: 86) observes, "the relationship between a saint and a devotee is one of reciprocity, or better of *Dou ut des*: I give to receive something in exchange." For it to work and the petitioner to be successful, he must be familiar with the saint, his likes and dislikes, his preferred forms of treatment, and include them in the vow in a way that will make the saint obligated to reciprocate the offer.

Vows to the saints are made conditionally. They do not have to be fulfilled (discharged) unless and until the petitioner obtains what has been requested and only then is there an obligation to make the pilgrimage and perform all the devotional and other acts promised in the vow.

The cult of the saints and pilgrimage in Brazil

Christianity was brought to the lands that were to become Brazil by representatives of the Portuguese Crown and the Church as part of the discovery, conquest and founding of the New World colony; it was to be the official religion until the establishment of the Republic at the end of the nineteenth century.[11] Christian practice in Brazil, as Freyre (1964) and others (Azzi 1978) have reminded us, was mostly a private matter. Individuals, many of them the founders of the great houses (families) established around the production of sugar cane, the mining of gold and diamonds and other economic boom activities, had their own domestic shrines and chapels. Shrines also were built in out of the way places in gratitude to a specific saint or the Virgin for some good fortune obtained there that was believed to have been the result of an intercession in response to a prayer.

Priests, who always were in short supply in the colony, said masses, performed baptisms, weddings, funerals, and taught the catechism to slaves and other dependents when they were available, but most of the "religious" activity practiced in Brazil over the centuries was a personal dynamic between a "believer" and a saint at a private shrine. As Bastide (1951: 346) observed some time ago, popular religious worship in Brazil is turned more toward the saints and the Virgin than to God.

The saints venerated during the early part of the colonial period in Brazil were those brought from the Old World and listed in the official Church calendar. The pau-de-arara carrying Maria da Fátima and her fellow pilgrims from Regeração was on its way to one of them, the shrine to St. Francis which is located in the municipality of Canindé in the state of Ceará. St. Francis (of Assisi) is known by the inhabitants of this part of Brazil as *São Francisco das Chagas*, St. Francis of the wounds.[12]

Canindé is a municipality of 2,883 square kilometers located at the edge of the sertão about 100 kilometers from the Atlantic coast. It is approximately 4 degrees south of the equator. The average temperature is 75 degrees Fahrenheit, but since there are few clouds and little rain, by late in the day it gets much hotter. In good years rains fall between January and June (winter). In the 1980s, when this study was begun, its official population was in the neighborhood of 60,000, with fewer than 20,000 of them living in the town center that, as in all Brazil, is called by the same name as the municipality. Approximately one million people visit the town and its shrine each year during the ten days of the festival.

The shrine to St. Francis in Canindé is believed to have been the fruit of the efforts of Francisco Xavier de Medeiros, a Portuguese sergeant major traveling in the area in the late eighteenth century who, for reasons not reported, wished to build a chapel on the banks of the Canindé river in honor of the saint after whom he had been named. He is said to have written to the three brothers who owned the land asking them to donate it as patrimony for a church. When they refused, the supernatural intervention that has come to be associated with the site is reported to have begun. One of the brothers took sick and died shortly thereafter. Then, following a brief illness, a second brother also died. When the third brother took ill, he immediately made the donation Medeiros had requested. He is reported to have recovered as mysteriously as he had become ill and his brothers had died (Greenfield 1990: 3).

When construction was delayed due to one of the periodic droughts that plague this part of the country, a statue of the saint was brought to the site. Reports began to circulate about the sick or injured recovering "miraculously." People from surrounding neighborhoods began visiting the statue. Those "blessed" left gifts and the first church was constructed. Additional donations made over the years were applied to build the numerous additions. Today a large basilica stands in an area near the river and forms the geographic and symbolic center of the municipality. Most public and commercial buildings are situated to the north of it, across from the *praça*, or square. From the square the streets radiate out in all directions with those with more substantial buildings closest to the basilica and the poorer ones stretching out and up the incline to the urban periphery where there are a few repair shops and marginal commercial establishments—such as tire repair shops, Afro-Brazilian religious centers and brothels.

During the period of the festival, Canindé appears as a series of concentric circles. At its center is the basilica where the sacred activities take place. Just outside it, along the river, is the grotto of *Nossa Senhora de Lourdes*, where pilgrims go to wash, drink the "holy water" and fill containers to carry home with them to be shared by friends and relatives unable to make the trip. Water from the grotto is believed to have miraculous curing properties.

Between the basilica and the stalls where statues and other religious memorabilia are sold is an area where unofficial religious activities are performed. These include a museum owned and operated by the Franciscan brothers and a zoological garden. Nearby are the *lambe-lambes*, photographers who snap pictures of pilgrims dressed in their brown habits holding their votive offerings standing next to a cardboard cutout of the saint. Beyond the zone of religious commerce is a secular one where food, beverages (both hard and soft), and most mass-produced items available throughout Brazil may be purchased. Next are games of chance, pool tables, and an amusement park with a huge Ferris wheel, other rides and forms of entertainment. Finally there are bars, dance halls and *vai quem quer* (Go Whoever Wishes), as the local houses of prostitution are picturesquely called. We move from the sacred to the profane both symbolically and geographically (Cavalcante 1987: 6).

Preparing for the pilgrims

Starting about six weeks before the official mass that opens the annual festival on September 24th, the Franciscan brothers make ready the simple shelters called *abrigos* that will house many of the pilgrims unable to afford space in hotels and private dwellings. They will set up and clean makeshift lavatories, places to bathe, and facilities on which travelers like Fatima and Laura will be able to cook the food they bring to Canindé.

The town merchants prepare their shops making room for items ordered specifically for the occasion. Townspeople, and residents of neighboring municipalities seeking to earn extra money, set up stalls and booths using poles, scraps of wood and old pieces of cardboard brought in by truck from Fortaleza, the state capital and main commercial center some 90 kilometers distant.

When the trucks arrive, crosses, rosaries, pictures and statues of St. Francis, the Virgin and other saints appear. Merchandize including foods, beverages, clothing, ribbons, toys and the numerous items of plastic manufactured in São Paulo that are to be found in most market places throughout the country are unloaded and await the pilgrims arrival.

Many of the residents who have family homes in the nearby rural hinterland rent their primary dwellings to more affluent visitors for the period of the festival. Some only will make rooms available. Still others will set up stalls to sell food and beverages, or to run games of chance to earn extra income. Most people who live in or near Canindé depend on what they earn during the festival to sustain them throughout the year.

Paying a promessa *at the shrine of St. Francis in Canindé*

When the truck from Regeneração turned off the pot hole filled, weather beaten old road on which it had crossed the backlands onto the new paved highway that led into Canindé, it joined with the numerous other paus-de-arara bringing pilgrims from all over the Brazilian northeastern. The slow moving lanes contained buses rented especially for the occasion, private automobiles, animal drawn vehicles and pilgrims on horses and donkeys. Some arrived on bicycles with still others making the journey, often as payment of a vow, on foot. While most of the travelers to the shrine were from Ceará and neighboring states, smaller numbers came from as far away as São Paulo and Rio de Janeiro and a handful of individuals from Europe and North America.

The majority were agricultural laborers, domestic servants, or unemployed. Of some two thousand people interviewed in the 1980s, one third reported having neither land nor homes of their own, but rather lived as sharecroppers on properties belonging to large estates. Half reported moving regularly in the hope of finding better living conditions (Barreto 1986: 3). Although primarily poor, as are the vast majority of Brazilians, all social classes and racial and ethnic categories are represented in Canindé during the festival. The number of men and women are approximately equal and small numbers of children frequently accompany their parents.

The first stop made by the truck carrying Maria de Fátima was at one of the abrigos (shelters) prepared by the Franciscan brothers and located close to the basilica. Finding space available there, the occupants of the truck hung their hammocks on hooks, stored the food and other items they brought with them and changed their clothing. Then, although it was late in the afternoon and they had not eaten since early morning, the two women left for the basilica. They passed a photographer and Fátima stopped to wait on a line to have her photograph taken standing next to a cutout representation of the saint. She was now wearing the typical brown habit of St. Francis and holding the votive offering her husband had made. A half hour later the women, still on their way to the basilica, entered the *sala de milagres*, a large room on whose walls are hung thousands of pictures of pilgrims and the material representations of the miracles conferred on them by the saint. Fatima placed one copy of the Polaroid picture just taken of her on the wall. The second she would keep and place next to her bed at home. She walked across the room to deposit her *ex-voto* (votive offering), thus completing another part of the bargain she made to the saint. The large container, filled with thousands of carvings placed there by other pilgrims, was so high that Fátima had to climb a stepladder and then stretch to reach the top of the pile. While some of the items in the container were beautifully hand carved pieces of art commissioned in fulfillment of a vow, others were made of balsa wood, local bamboo, clay or cloth crudely fashioned by a grateful pilgrim.

Near the sala de milagres Fátima and Laura entered a small room where a beautician stood sheering the hair of an elderly woman. Clarice Magalhães de Sousa, wearing a brown habit that masked her middle class status, had traveled with her husband, a lawyer who worked for a bank, by bus from the capital of the state of Rio Grande do Norte several hundred miles away. For their stay in Canindé the Sousas had rented a room with bed and a bath; and they took their meals in restaurants where they ate eggs with their coffee for breakfast and meat and vegetables with the rice and beans for lunch and dinner. Clarice had been diagnosed some years previously as having breast cancer. She prayed to St. Francis, promising him that if he helped her she would make the pilgrimage to Canindé, attend mass, take confession and light candles at his shrine, and if she were cured, she would cut off her shoulder-length hair. Certainly the educated and sophisticated Sousas knew that her recovery should be attributed to modern medical science, but could it not also be that it was the intercession by the saint? Like so many Brazilians, Clarice had made a vow, a bargain with the saint before undertaking treatment. She had paid what she owed to the doctors when she received their bills. Now she was paying her debt to the saint.

Brazilians, if they have the means, generally seek medical treatment when they are hurt or take sick or they may go to a large and diverse number of alternative healers. But many pray to saints believing that surgery, medications and other treatments work, but only when there also is aid from the supernatural.

A young woman from João Pessoa, capital of the neighboring state of Paraíba, stood nervously in front of Fátima. The previous year Angela had been too vain to part with her long, beautiful locks in spite of having promised to cut them. When her severe headaches returned, even worse than before, she was ready to give the saint his due. This year she would complete her obligation.

> "Do you think that St. Francis will forgive you?" we asked her.
> "Yes he will," she responded, "because he has forgiven more than this. I have faith, I believe that he will."

It was now Fátima's turn to cut her hair and she was filled with feelings of both sadness and gratitude. Of course her beautiful hair would be missed, but it felt good to be completing her vow to St. Francis. When the beautician finished, Fátima took the bag in which the cuttings were placed and, like Angela before her, and others to come later, returned to the sala de milagres to place it on top of the ever-growing pile of ex-votos. Having completed this very personal and emotional part of her *promessa*, she joined her cousin and the two returned to the abrigo to start the fire on which they would cook the rice and beans that would be their dinner. Several hours later, exhilarated but exhausted, and feeling safe in their hammocks, they finally went to sleep.

The festival was already alive with activities when they awoke at dawn the next morning. A line of people were patiently waiting for the lavatories and bathing facilities. Their breakfast, consisting only of coffee, laced with ample amounts of sugar, had to wait until the fire they lit became hot enough to boil the water. Drinking hurriedly, the cousins quickly trotted off once again to the basilica. As they entered the courtyard on their way to the church office to inquire about masses and confession, they came upon Pedro, a young man from Fortaleza who had made the ninety-kilometer trip on his bicycle. He was now circling the church on his knees. His mother had a problem with her left leg. She had gone to the doctor, but even with surgery, bone grafts and a cast, she almost lost her leg. "It was very serious, but now she was well thanks to God and St. Francis." The son had prayed to the saint on his mother's behalf, promising that if she were cured, he would make the pilgrimage and walk around the courtyard on his knees, not once, but twice. Completing his second turn, he said that he felt well and pleased, though it had been difficult and he was tired and sore. His mother had recovered and he was fulfilling his debt to the saint who had cured her. He would now be able to return home satisfied and in peace.

At the small Church office a volunteer provided Fátima and Laura with a schedule of masses. When asked the date of her last confession, Fátima replied that it had been more than 10 years. She was instructed to attend a preparation class and forty-five minutes later, after the class was over, the two women took their places on a line that stretched the length of the basilica to wait their turn to enter the confessional booth. After acknowledging their sins, they returned to the abrigo to prepare and eat the rice and beans that would be their lunch. It was early afternoon when they finished cleaning and storing their possessions. Finally it was their opportunity to attend a mass and they excitedly rushed off to the basilica. Following the service, they joined with others to walk the Stations of the Cross. The symbolic representation of the route taken by Jesus through Jerusalem to Calvary is laid out on a wide, tree-lined avenue that runs from just outside the basilica to a second church on a rise at the northern end of the town.

When Fátima bent to pick up a rock from a pile along the road that she would place on her head to increase her penance, she accidentally bumped into Sérgio, a young man who also was reaching for one of the rocks. He had made the trip on foot from Fortaleza where he was studying at the university. Sérgio had twice failed the *vestibular*, the standardized examination all Brazilians must pass to gain university admission. Before trying for the third time he made a vow to St. Francis. Now a freshman studying computer science, the grateful pilgrim was fulfilling his debt for the help received from his supernatural benefactor.

There was not a cloud in the sky, the temperature soared under the tropical sun, and the ad hoc groups of strangers, with a common purpose, proceeded solemnly along the avenue changing rocks at each station. After they reached the second church, the two women drank a cup of water they had purchased from a girl sitting on the roadside. The young entrepreneur had filled a bucket at a standpipe and in the afternoon heat was doing a brisk business.

The two cousins proceeded to the museum where they gazed at the dazzling jewels and garments used by the Franciscan brothers in their services. Wandering next through the stalls they admired the many items, religious and secular, few of which they could afford to purchase. They did buy some things commissioned by friends and relatives, plus one or two small souvenirs for their mates and children. Exhausted, they returned to the abrigo to wash, use the lavatory, rest and start preparing for their evening meal of rice and beans. The secular festival, with its games of chance and other entertainments, enticed them, but as women traveling alone, they passed up the bars, dancing establishments and other high points available to men. Returning to the abrigo at about 9 PM, they were too excited to sleep and instead sat for several hours chatting and sharing the pleasure they were experiencing.

Laura and Fátima were awakened the following morning by the sunlight and noises of the street. The now familiar routine of long lines for the use of the lavatory and baths, succeeded by the making of a fire to heat their meager breakfast of sweetened coffee was this day followed by walking to the grotto of *Nossa Senhora de Lourdes* where they washed in its curative waters. They drank and filled the plastic containers they brought with them that they would bring back to Regeneração for friends and relatives.

The Franciscan monastery, where hundreds of pilgrims formed a line in the courtyard waiting to see and spend a few minutes with a life-sized statue of St Francis just outside the door, was the next adventure. Fátima's turn came after one hour's wait. Like the others before her, she conversed aloud with the saint in a low voice. First expressing her gratitude, she soon confided several very personal matters, as she might do with her cousin or best friend and requested help with additional problems. An emotional Laura then quickly led her into a small room off the entryway to the monastery where a group of pilgrims stood trying to peek through the door of an inner room. A rumor was circulating that St. Francis, himself, was inside and alive. In fact, he had never died. The Franciscan brothers reportedly were said to be holding the saint as a prisoner unwilling to share him and keeping him "for themselves." When the wait proved fruitless, the two women, frustrated and disappointed, walked back to the abrigo to begin once more the task of making their rice and beans. After eating and taking a short rest, they wandered off, this time to the zoological gardens where they spent the next few hours looking at the animals, most of which they had never seen before. They giggled and laughed as they went from cage to cage, commenting on the magnificent colors of some of the birds and the strange postures assumed by other animals. Their favorite, and that of most visitors, were the monkeys, in front of whose cage they stood enthralled until the middle of the afternoon. As the time for them to depart Canindé approached, they rapidly walked back to the abrigo, collected their few belongings and placed them aboard the waiting truck. Shortly thereafter they were on the road to Regeneração. During the next four days, as they sat together on the crowded, uncomfortable truck as it bounced across the rugged interior roads of the sertao, the women shared with each other their feelings about what they had experienced. They were as seemingly oblivious of their fellow travelers as the others were of them. When they arrived home they repeated what they had said to each other to the members of their immediate families, other relatives and close friends.

Pilgrimage and healing

The vast majority of the visitors to the shrine of St. Francis in Canindé like most of their coreligionists who visit pilgrimage shrines elsewhere, are there to thank the saint and to discharge the obligation incurred to him for helping them to recover from an illness or injury. In a study conducted in the late 1950s, Father Joly, for example, found that 80 percent of the pilgrims to Canindé were there because they had been ill (Hooneart 1987: 5).

In another study done almost three decades later—conducted between 1984 and 1988—Professor Adalberto Barreto and his students in the Department of Social Medicine of the Federal University of Ceará collected more than 80,000 ex-votos and examined and classified them. More than 86 percent represented parts of the body that had "malfunctioned." Of these, almost five thousand showed wounds, cuts or openings in the skin, 2,350 more were protuberances indicating edemas or growths, 1,400 represented deformities of the skin and other dermatological problems, 800 were breaks and fractures while another 325 represented deformities that had been "made right" (Barreto n.d.). Fewer than 14 percent were of objects unrelated to illness and healing.

The pilgrims we interviewed rarely used terms such as illness or disease. They spoke instead of impediments, like a pain in the back, leg, or head, or the inability to walk that prevented them from functioning normally. Their assumption was that their suffering had been caused by God to punish them for the commission of a sin (Zaluar 1983: 84). In traditional Catholic theology the saints may be invoked to intercede with God on behalf of such victims. In Brazil, according to Leers (1977: 85), the saints are attributed a degree of autonomy that enables them to operate in the material world in direct response to appeals by the living. He suggests that this may be interpreted as God delegating to the saints the ability to regularly redress grievances and help sufferers.

A promessa, according to Azevedo (1968:177) "... consists of a ... ritualism ... in which ... individual and collective acts ... are expected to have ... efficacy in pleasing the 'saints,' inclining them to reply favorably to the appeals of their devotees in cases of difficulty and crisis." From the perspective of the devotee, Oliveira adds, "The saints represent all of the possible supernatural allies the faithful can count on to gain happiness in this life and the other, and a source of permanent supernatural power that can be invoked to obtain solutions to the problems of this world" (quoted in Rolim 1976: 147). They are like rich godfathers, "who are in the world of the poor to distribute favors and the recipients of prayers, candles, payments of promises, processions, songs and fireworks" (Leers 1977: 84).

This presence of a non-human force in the life of the people indicates a closeness, an almost familiarity between the saints and their devotees. We could say that the saints penetrate the lives of those who worship them, entering into their problems, sharing their urgent needs, their domestic life, their business affairs, their marriages, and their love affairs. ... Everything is known between the saint and his worshipper (Rolim 1976: 159).

With respect to Canindé, Cavalcante (1987), echoing Gross, adds:

> The relationship between the pilgrim and God reproduces the relationship between poor men and authority in that they always must have an intermediary. Just as the resident of a neighborhood gets to the mayor through the councilman, the pilgrim gets to God through St. Francis.

The saint then may be viewed as the pilgrim's protector, as can be a politician, a *fazendeiro* (landowner), or a godparent in the material world who helps those in need confront the hostility of nature and civil society. In times of difficulty, recourse to the saint for help "is a part of daily life of man in the Brazilian northeast" (Barreto 1986: 2).

Pilgrimage and modernity

The pilgrimage described above and exchanges between worshippers and saints are not vestigial cultural leftovers found in a backward part of a national society that will disappear with further modernization. Active shrines to saints are found all over Brazil, from the northeast and distant Amazon to the industrialized urban centers of Rio de Janeiro and São Paulo. As in Canindé, people are making vows and visiting shrines to fulfill them more than ever before in Brazilian history. Furthermore, new saints are being created regularly to whose shrines new generations of Brazilians are flocking. This is a continuation of the old, still vital, Catholic tradition of the faithful venerating admired and respected local figures who when they die are believed to be elevated to heaven where they can continue helping their fellows back on earth. The official church may never learn of, let alone acknowledge, these "popular" saints, many of who were medical doctors in life (see for example Cavalcante and Greenfield 2003). As word spreads, ever-greater numbers come to their graves, or shrines to venerate them and discharge debts made in the process of invoking the help of these new supernatural patrons and protectors. [. . .]

[. . .] Whether this is understood as "projecting earthly relationships into the sacred sphere in which people act out debt paying" as cultural materialist Gross (1971: 129) proposed, or as the projection of spiritual relationships into the secular sphere as others would contend, the point is that the range of religions presently competing for followers in the urban Brazilian religious marketplace organize relationships between their members and potential converts and the supernatural in terms of patron-client exchanges reinforcing in ritual this most important system of relationships. Given their significance, students of Brazilian culture and society should show greater awareness of the intimate tie between religion and social structure and specifically that between ritual practice and relations of patronage and clientage.

Notes

1 As, for example the especially valuable *Os Cavalheiros do Bom Jesus* by Rubem Fernandes (1986) and *O Sertão das Romarias* by Carlos Steil (1996). See also King (2005) and the other chapters in the *Pilgrimage and Healing* volume edited by Dubisch and Winkelman (2005).
2 Reflecting this reality, most studies of Brazilian society during the past several decades have focused on the changes that have been and are continuously

taking place. While we fully recognize the importance of the major upheavals and transformations occurring, and do not question their significant impact on the society and the lives of its members, our interest here is not on what is new or changing, but rather on continuities in traditional cultural patterns. As anthropologists, our concern is with both continuity and change in cultural practices in society. Here our purpose is to show that relations of patronage and clientage that have long characterized social relations in Brazil have not disappeared as a result of all the changes taking place, but rather have been incorporated, at times in modified form, as part of the change, in the new, alternative religions that are competing with once hegemonic Roman Catholicism in the Brazilian religious marketplace. For the most part this is a point that has not been examined in the literature on these religions.

3 See, for example, Turner (1967, 1969, 1974; Turner and Turner 1978) with his focus on performance and the application of Van Gennip's model of transition, and the criticism by Eade and Sallnow and collaborators (1991) who emphasize competing discourses.

4 We do this not because we think the other issues are not important and worthy of study, but because social relations in Brazil are still poorly understood and that in his analysis, Gross had taken significant steps towards their clarification.

5 Portions of the description of the pilgrimage to Canindé presented in Part I are taken from *Pilgrimage and Healing in Northeast Brazil* by Sidney M. Greenfield and Antonio Mourão Cavalcante from *Pilgrimage and Healing* by Jill Dubisch and Michael Winkelman, editors. © 2005 The Arizona Board of Regents. Reprinted by permission of the University of Arizona Press.

6 Maria de Fátima Batista is not an actual person. We have combined the stories of several informants into this fictitious individual to facilitate telling the story. Other characters also are composites of real people.

7 Interesting insights into Arnold van Gennep's (1960) phase model of transitions by individuals and groups into new social positions and categories used by Turner as the basis for his examination of pilgrimage may be obtained by refraining it in terms of Thom's mathematical model of catastrophe theory (Thom 1975, 1983).

8 It is unfortunate that in what is still perhaps the most important anthropological book on the subject, Victor and Edith Turner's *Image and Pilgrimage in Christian Culture* (1978), did just that when they applied van Gennep's model of transition to focus on the implications of the liminal experience of visitors to some of the major shrines of Christendom. Their contribution to anthropological thinking removed pilgrimage from the cult of the saints that had been (and still is) its context doing a disservice to the reader who might not have been familiar with pilgrimage in its ancient and medieval form.

9 All of the metaphors were used.

10 "One feature, above all," writes Sanchis (1983: 266), "characterizes the devotion paid to [the] saints, . . . , and it is also a distinguishing feature not only of the [pilgrimage] festival but of popular religion generally, and that is the vow."

11 Sixty-seven years after national independence in 1822.

12 This is to differentiate him in the minds of his Brazilian followers from the Italian saint, thereby making him their own.

Bibliography

Azevedo, Thales de. "Popular Catholicism in Brazil." *Portugal and Brazil in Transition.* Raymond Sayers, ed. Minneapolis: University of Minnesota Press, 1968. 175–178.

Azzi, Riolando. *O catolicismo popular no Brasil*. Petrópolis, RJ: Editora Vozes, 1978.
Barreto, Adalberto de Paula. "A romaria e a doença." Paper presented at the Meetings of the Latin American Studies Association, Boston, MA. 1986.
——. "Ex:Votos: Os milagres dos santos," unpublished manuscript.
Bastide, Roger. "Religion and the Church in Brazil." *Brazil: Portrait of Half a Continent.* T. L. Smith & A. Marchant, eds. New York: The Dryden Press, 1951.
Cavalcante, Antonio Mourão. "As Festas da Festa." *Diário de Notícias*, October 11 1987.
Cavalcante, Antonio Mourão and Sidney M. Greenfield. *Argeu: A construção de um santo popular.* Fortaleza, Br.: Editora UFC, 2003.
Dubisch, Jill and Michael Winkelman, eds. *Pilgrimage and Healing.* Tucson (AZ): The University of Arizona Press, 2005.
Eade, J. and M. J. Sallnow, eds. *Contesting the Sacred: The Anthropology of Christian Pilgrimage.* London and New York: Routledge, 1991.
Fernandes, Rubem C. *Os Cavaleiros do Bom Jesus.* Rio de Janeiro: Brasiliense, 1982.
Greenfield, Sidney M. "The Pragmatics of Conversion in the Brazilian Religious MarketPlace." in Dwight B. Heath, ed. *Contemporary Culture and Society in Latin America*, Prospect Heights(IL): Waveland Press, 2002. 490–96.
——. "Turner and Anti-Turner in the Image of Christian Pilgrimage in Brazil." *Anthropology of Consciousness.* 1.3–4 (1990): 1–8.
——. "Domestic Crises, Schools, and Patron Clientage in Southeastern Minas Gerais" *Brazil: Anthropological Perspectives.* M. Margolis & W. Carter, eds. New York: Columbia University Press, 1979. 362–378.
——. "Patronage, Politics and the Articulation of Local Community and National Society in Pre-1968 Brazil." *Journal of Inter-American Studies and World Affairs.* 19.2 (1977): 139–172.
——. "Charwomen, Cesspools and Road Building: An Examination of Patronage, Clientage and Political Power in Southeastern Minas." *Structure and Process in Latin America: Patronage, Clientage and Power Systems*, A. Strickon & S. M. Greenfield, eds. Albuquerque (NM): The University of New Mexico Press, 1972. 71–100.
Greenfield, Sidney M. and Antonio Mourão Cavalcante. "Pilgrimage and Healing in Northeast Brazil: A Culturalbiological Explanation." *Pilgrimage and Healing*, Jill Dubisch and Michael Winkelman, eds. Tucson (AZ): The University of Arizona Press, 2005. 3–24.
Gross, Daniel. "Factionalism and Local Level Politics in Rural Brazil." *Journal of Anthropological Research.* 29.2 (1973): 123–144.
——. "Ritual and Conformity: A Religious Pilgrimage to Northeastern Brazil." *Ethnology.* X.2 (1971): 129–148.
Hooneart, Eduardo. "A teologia das romarias." *Diário do Nordeste*, 11 October 1987.
King, C. Lindsey. "Pilgrimage, Promises, and Ex-Votos: Ingredients for Healing in Northeast Brazil." *Pilgrimage and Healing*, Jill Dubisch and Michael Winkelman, eds. Tucson (AZ): The University of Arizona Press, 205. 49–68.
Klass, Morton. *Mind over Mind: The Anthropology and Psychology of Spirit Possession.* Lanham (MD): Rowman & Littlefield, 2003.
Leers, Bernadino. *Catolocismo popular e mundo rural.* Petrópolis, R.J.: Editora Vozes, 1977.

Queiroz, M. E. P. de. *O campesinato brasileiro*. Petrópolis, R.J.: Editora Vozes, 1973.
Radcliffe-Brown, A. R. "On Social Structure." In *Structure and Function in Primitive Society: Essays and Addresses*. Glencoe (IL): The Free Press, 1952. 188–204. First printed in *Journal of the Royal Anthropological Institute* 70, No. 1 (1940).
Rolim, Francisco C. "Condicionamentos sociais do catolocismo popular." *Revista Eclesiastica Brasileira*. 36 (1976): Fasc. 141.
Sanchis, Pierre. "The Portuguese 'Romarias'." *Saints and Their Cults: Studies in Religious Sociology, Folklore and History*, Stephen Wilson, ed. Cambridge: Cambridge University Press, 1983. 261–289.
Steil, Carlos. *Sertão da romarias*. Petrópolis: Vozes, 1996.
Thom, R. *Mathematical Models of Morphogenesis*. New York: Wiley, 1983.
——. *Structural Stability and Morphogenesis*. New York: Addison-Wesley, 1972.
Turner, Victor. *Dramas, Fields and Metaphors: Symbolic Action in Human Society*. Ithaca, NY: Cornell University Press, 1974.
——. *The Ritual Process; Structure and Anti-Structure*. Chicago: Aldine, 1969.
——. *The Forest of Symbols*. Ithaca, NY: Cornell University Press, 1967.
Turner, Victor and Edith. *Image and Pilgrimage in Christian Culture*. New York: Columbia University Press, 1978.
van Gennep. Arnold. *The Rites of Passage*. London: Routledge and Kegan Paul, 1960. Original 1908.
Wilson, Stephen, ed. *Saints and Their Cults: Studies in Religious Sociology*. Cambridge: Cambridge University Press, 1983.
Woodward, Kenneth L. *Making Saints: How the Catholic Church Determines Who Becomes a Saint, Who Doesn't, and Why*. New York: Simon and Schuster, 1990.
Zaluar, Alba. *Os homens de Deus: Um estudo dos santos e das festas no Catolicismo popular*. Rio de Janeiro: Zahar Editores, 1983.

85

DIVISION AND DEMOLITION AT THE TOMB OF A BELOVED SAINT

The evolving character of an Orthodox Christian pilgrim centre in India

Alex Gath

Source: *Culture and Religion*, 1(2) (2000), 171–87.

> The paper explores some reasons for changes affecting a popular Orthodox Christian pilgrim centre in Kerala, South India. These changes have become apparent both in the style of conducting the pilgrimage and in the organisation of the site itself. They have occurred in the context of an ongoing ecclesiastical dispute which has divided Christians in Kerala throughout this century, creating a division which itself follows schisms and disputes in previous centuries. As a result there is rivalry between pilgrim centres of varying allegiance and also between different styles of worship, especially since the rise of charismatic movements. All of this has occurred against a background of increased politicisation of pilgrimage, and religion in general, in India. This has led to some concern that Christianity can be considered a 'foreign' religion, with attempts by Orthodox Christians to refute such a claim.

There is a holy river in South Central Kerala, in the southernmost part of India, called the Pampa River. It descends from mountains on the eastern side of Kerala state, flowing close to Sabarimala, a Hindu pilgrim centre of immense popularity. Downstream it passes famous Hindu temples at Aranmula and Changannur, before turning north to merge with Vembanad Lake. This is a large lake on Kerala's west side, stretching through a large section of Kerala's backwater country before reaching the ocean near Cochin. Beyond Changannur, the river divides for a short distance to form an island called Parumala. This has become one of the most important Christian pilgrim centres in a state richly endowed with sacred Christian sites.

At Parumala, there is located the tomb of Mar Gregorios, who is venerated by the Orthodox section of Kerala's Christians. He is their one local, Kerala born saint. He is revered as an outstanding holy man by many Christians and non-Christians alike. Throughout the year, pilgrims visit the site in order to pray and make offerings at the tomb. Towards the end of the rainy season each year, there is a flood of visiting pilgrims, arriving to commemorate the saint's death anniversary in early November. They arrive from all directions, often walking long distances, to pay their respects to the holy man of Parumala. The character and significance of the pilgrimage has developed throughout this century, especially in recent years. This paper will trace some of the reasons for this.

The historical background

Mar Gregorios of Parumala was born in 1848 at Mulanthuruthy near Cochin. As a boy he was called Kochu Ipeora. He came from a priestly family, and was educated by his uncle who was a noted scholar of the ancient Syriac liturgical traditions of Kerala. At the age of ten he was ordained as a Deacon and at the age of eighteen he became a Priest. By the time he was twenty-eight, the Metropolitan (senior most cleric of the Orthodox hierarchy in Kerala) had decided that he should be the man to create a new seminary. He should develop a place of learning and prayer in the southern part of the state. He was elevated to the rank of Bishop, with the title Geevarghese Mar Gregorios. The consecration was performed by the Syrian Orthodox Patriarch of Antioch who was visiting India at the time; the Patriarch was acknowledged as the supreme head of the Orthodox Church in Kerala (Thomas 1977:18).

Mar Gregorios moved south to take up residence at Parumala. It was at that time a lonely island, said to be haunted and visited by criminal gangs. In time, however, Mar Gregorios established an active seminary around a chapel, with a large shed for teaching and dining. The Bishop and his pupils lived in rigorous and frugal manner. It was said that the seminary was often at the point of running out of food provisions, but Mar Gregorios would simply say 'tomorrow will take care of itself' (S. Thomas 1977:21). Many people sought out the Bishop to ask for advice and blessings. Stories began to circulate concerning healings, for example from smallpox, and other miracles associated with the intervention of Mar Gregorios. He established, in addition, a reputation as a man of peace and gentle conciliation in a turbulent time for the Church in Kerala.

The nineteenth century was a period of upheaval and dispute for many of Kerala's Christians as a result of conflicts which had their roots in the early part of the colonial period. This ancient community, according to tradition established by St Thomas in the first century, was certainly thriving for many centuries before the colonial period. Its liturgy and traditions derived from the Syriac-cultural region of the Middle East, and were sustained by frequent arrival of clerics and traders from that area. In 1599 the Portuguese effected, by coercion, the incorporation of the Syrian Christian community of India into the Roman Catholic fold. However, in the middle part of the seventeenth century, a substantial section of the Christians broke the tie with Rome, and re-established the Syrian traditions (Babu Paul 1993:33). Ever since there has been a rivalry between Catholics and 'Jacobites'—Orthodox Christians siding with the Syrian Patriarch of Antioch. In addition, there have been further divisions and struggles for positions of leadership within each group.

In 1789, much of the northern half of Kerala fell under the control of Tippu Sultan, the Muslim ruler of Mysore. This necessitated a hasty removal of the headquarters of Jacobite Christians from Ankamali, north-east of Cochin, to Kottayam further to the south. The Mysorean invasion also precipitated the intervention of the British, who thereby became the effective power in the region (Bayly 1989:281). The British authorities were anxious to provide practical assistance to the Jacobites. With grants of cash and land, and with the help of British missionaries of the Church Missionary Society (i.e. Anglicans), the facilities of the Jacobites were improved, especially with the establishment of a seminary at Kottayam.

Despite the promising beginning, relations between Jacobites and some successor British missionaries became strained. The latter were considered to favour excessive reform of the theology and traditions of the Kerala Christians, perhaps with a view to bringing them into the Anglican fold. Undermining either the cherished 'Syrian-ness' of the church or key features of its theology would have been resented. At a synod at Mavelikara in 1836, relations were broken off between the Jacobites and the Protestant missionaries (Daniel 1986:152).

This did not end the problems of the Jacobites. Whilst some of their numbers broke away to form a Syrian-dominated section within the Anglican Church (now part of the Church of South India), others remained but maintained hopes of reforming liturgy and theology from within. By the 1870s the rift within the Jacobite community was such that there were two rival Metropolitans, each claiming to be the legitimate head of the Kerala hierarchy. One led a pro-reform party, favouring changes to bring belief and practices in line with Protestant teaching, whilst the other led the opposing, conservative section. It was the pro-reform party, with British support, which came to control the seminary at Kottayam. For this reason the conservative Metropolitan asked Mar Gregorios to establish a seminary at

Parumala for training priests in the (conservative) Orthodox traditions (S. Thomas 1977:19).

There was a long struggle between the reform and conservative sections, with endless litigation to determine which side should legitimately control the property of the Church. Eventually, the reformers were forced to surrender property, including the Kottayam seminary, and establish themselves as a separate church, the Mar Thoma Church, in 1886. It remains the principal Syrian Protestant denomination. There were also some new Protestant movements, often centring around charismatic, ostensibly prophetic individuals, and these posed some threat by attracting members from the Jacobite community. Throughout, Mar Gregorios stood firmly for maintaining the theology and the established sacraments of the Church including the veneration of saints, especially St Mary.

The training of priests was transferred back to Kottayam from Parumala. As a result, Mar Gregorios was able to take an interest in other aspects of education. He helped to establish English medium schools, for example the one at Thiruvella near Parumala which now bears his name. Throughout this period Mar Gregorios was regularly consulted by the Metropolitan and other senior clerics. It was said that nobody was inclined to oppose him in meetings, such was his natural authority and fair-mindedness.

Towards the end of the rainy season of 1902, Mar Gregorios fell ill. He deteriorated despite the attentions of physicians. Concerned friends and admirers rushed to visit him, hearing of the seriousness of the situation. Many of the priests who had been his pupils came to Parumala. But after a few days, following the administering of the Last Rites, he passed away and was buried on the island. Many of the friends and admirers continued to return to his burial site, not just at the customary occasions of commemoration. The Metropolitan was noted as a frequent visitor, continuing to consult Mar Gregorios through prayer and meditation at Parumala. The date of his actual demise, 2nd November, each year brought large crowds of visitors. A larger church and pilgrim centre were built to accommodate them.

The divisions of the twentieth century

The twentieth century did not bring peace to the Jacobite community. It was again split into two opposing factions. Although the reformers had left, there now arose problems over the authority of the Patriarch of Antioch. The Patriarchs had long resided at Mardin, in Turkey, and required recognition from the Turkish government in order to hold office. In 1906, one Patriarch was derecognised and, probably after some political manipulation, a successor was enthroned. At first, the latter was accepted by Jacobites in Kerala. However, whilst on an extended visit to India between 1909 and 1911, he quarrelled with the Metropolitan (at this time a former pupil of Mar Gregorios of Parumala) over their respective powers.

The disagreement between the two prelates escalated, until the Patriarch excommunicated the Metropolitan. The latter responded to this by arranging for the enthronement of a Catholicos, a local head for the Kerala Church, to have powers effectively equivalent to those of the Patriarch. The Catholicate was formally established by the former, deposed Patriarch, whom the Metropolitan invited to Kerala claiming that he still retained legitimacy. In earlier centuries in the history of the Syrian Church in the Middle East, a Catholicos had sometimes presided over areas which were inaccessible to the Patriarch. In twentieth century Kerala, the Catholicos was henceforth able to consecrate Metropolitans and allocate dioceses—he was, in effect, the head of an autonomous Church, with the Patriarch merely a figurehead.

Neither the Patriarch who had excommunicated the Metropolitan, nor any of his successors, would accept the Catholicate. As a result, there were once again two rival figures king the allegiance of the Jacobites—the Patriarch and the Catholicos—each leading a large group of supporters. The Catholicos was based at Kottayam, whereas the followers of the Patriarch, now led by a Metropolitan of their own, were strong around the old headquarters of the Church at Ankamali (Daniel 1986:218).

Throughout the twentieth century, the Kerala Christians who maintain Orthodox theology and Antiochene liturgical traditions have been divided between two bitterly opposed factions. They have come to operate, virtually, as two separate churches owing allegiance either to Patriarch (henceforth 'Jacobites') or Catholicos (henceforth 'Orthodox'). There was a period of peace in the 1960s—a rapprochement between Patriarch and Catholicos—but it collapsed in the 1970s. Since then, the division has been as bitter as ever, with two separate, parallel hierarchies vying for the allegiance of the community, and the right to be considered the legitimate Orthodox Church of Kerala. We will see shortly that the Orthodox (pro-Catholicos) side has developed an evolving notion of their identity as Kerala's legitimate, Orthodox Church. Parumala and its pilgrimage play a significant, if somewhat ambiguous, role in this.

Both Jacobite and Orthodox Christians revere Parumala Mar Gregorios (Visvanathan 1993:64–5). After all, he lived before the current dispute arose, and had long been regarded as a holy man by many Christians and others. He is the most beloved figure of recent Jacobite/Orthodox history. He is held to be the only saint to have emerged from within their own community. Whilst saints of the early church, St Mary, St Thomas, St George etc., are widely venerated, as are a number of prelates who hailed from the Middle East and were buried in Kerala, none of these originated from India. There is no comparable figure to Mar Gregorios, in whose name churches, shrines, schools, hospitals and so forth are often founded.

A portrait of Mar Gregorios hangs on the wall of almost every Jacobite/Orthodox home. Usually there are other devotional pictures as well, but it is the standard portrait of the Parumala saint, with his long beard and bishop's robes, holding a crozier and ornamental cross and with head slightly raised, eyes staring into the distance, which marks out a home as Jacobite/Orthodox. Furthermore, both sides like to claim Mar Gregorios as one of their own—on their side in the present dispute. The Jacobites point out that he was personally close to the Patriarch during his lifetime; it was the latter who elevated him to the episcopacy. For the Catholicos side, it is commented that it was his pupil and close follower Geevarghese Vattaseril who created the Catholicate, and others of his pupils subsequently held that position. Beyond such disagreements, however, all are agreed that Mar Gregorios can be held to transcend the bitterness and animosity of the dispute. People often comment that he was a model of holiness and dispassionate judgement, in contrast to the scheming worldliness which is said, by opponents, to characterise leading partisans of the opposing side. Stories circulate concerning aggressive or underhand action by supporters of each group, in contrast to the accounts of miraculous deeds and gentle, ascetic behaviour of Mar Gregorios (Visvanathan 1993:65).

The status of Parumala—and its rivals

The Parumala pilgrim centre is under the direct control of the Catholicos, the head of the Orthodox section. In common with the main seminary, the residence of the Catholicos, and the Church headquarters which are located in Kottayam, it is administered centrally by the Catholicate. It does not comprise parish or diocesan property which might be subject to local and inter-party dispute. Elsewhere there are important churches and properties which are disputed between the two sides. An important example is a seminary at Alwaye, to the north-east of Cochin, in which a leading Jacobite Bishop lies buried. By contrast, Parumala is unequivocally in the hands of the Orthodox—to the chagrin of Jacobites, many of whom visit it nonetheless. The fact that this key site is under the Orthodox is critical for them, because other famous pilgrim centres, such as Manjinikara, Kothamangalam and North Paravur belong to the Jacobites. These latter churches, however, contain tombs of Middle Eastern prelates, whose significance for the Orthodox is now unclear because their relations with contemporary Middle Eastern equivalents, especially the Antiochene Patriarch himself, are strained.

It is worth noting that the aforementioned Manjinikara lies not far from Parumala. It is the most important pilgrim centre of the Jacobites. The tomb of a former Patriarch of Antioch, the only one buried in Kerala, is located here. He passed away during a visit to Kerala in 1932, whilst attempting to establish some peace in the church. Within a short time, his burial place became a major pilgrim centre, perhaps, in part, because Parumala belonged to 'the other side'. Manjinikara parallels Parumala in several respects. It has been used as a small monastery at which young men could be trained for the priesthood in accordance with Jacobite tradition. For many years, the instruction was supervised by a Middle Eastern Bishop who acted as a delegate for the Patriarch. The current resident Bishop is a native of Kerala, although he was himself trained in the Middle East. The site is directly under the control of the Patriarch and therefore it is distinct from other parish or diocesan property.

It is especially significant that the pilgrimage to Manjinikara, ever since the Patriarch's demise and especially since the recent intensification of the Church dispute in the 1970s, has achieved formidable success. With the persistence of the split, the motivation of Jacobites to make the Manjinikara pilgrimage, in the most visible possible manner, seems to have increased. Every February they proceed in their thousands to the Patriarch's tomb, especially visible as they march along the Main Central Road of the state, accompanied by decorated chariots carrying portraits of the Patriarch and singing songs proclaiming loyalty to Antioch. The Manjinikara pilgrimage is, one might say, a 'rival show'—and an immensely popular one. The Jacobites walking en route to the tomb are especially conspicuous at Kottayam, the headquarters of the Orthodox side, and also at Thiruvella near to Parumala. Each year, this pilgrimage grows in size, evidently strengthening the commitment of many to the Patriarchy and raising the prominence of Jacobites within the wider society. Many stories are told concerning blessings received by pilgrims following prayers and offerings at the tomb. This particular Patriarch, Mar Ignatius Elias III, has been declared a saint by the current Syrian Orthodox hierarchy, thus permitting churches, shrines and other institutions to be named in his honour, as they have been for Mar Gregorios. All Jacobite households will display a portrait of Mar Ignatius as well as one of Mar Gregorios.[1]

The significance of the Manjinikara pilgrimage is not lost on the Orthodox side. Considerations of prestige demand that Parumala is not outshone. But it is not only Jacobite pilgrim centres which are rival sites to Parumala. There are also important locations of Catholic and Protestant worship. These are not necessarily pilgrim centres in the same sense. Usually there is no tomb and often no particular object as the focus of worship. Frequently it is a charismatic style of worship which is the principal attraction. This may focus on the charisma of particular priests, their apparent gifts of healing in particular, although at other times the emotionally charged worship does not centre around any specific individual. There are well-known locations for large scale worship meetings of this kind; a number of them are close to Parumala. For any individual interested in visiting a centre of Christian worship, whether for healing, spiritual-emotional experience or simply out of curiosity, such places add to the range of possible choices. For conservatively-minded Orthodox, they threaten to attract the allegiance of some of their own people, whilst redirecting enthusiasm, money offerings—and therefore prestige—which could flow towards Parumala.

The theology of intercession, and the new charismatics

One of the most important features of Orthodox theology is its emphasis upon intercessionary prayer (Kadavil Paul Ramban 1973:38). The faithful are encouraged to pray to saints in order that the latter may intercede on their behalf, by praying themselves to God about the supplicant's concerns. Ordinary people are held to be sinful; for this reason the prayers of very holy people, famous saints and leaders of the Church, are thought to carry particular weight, enhancing the efficacy of the prayers offered by devotees. In addition, there is a widespread sense that ordinary worldly concerns are more appropriately taken to saintly, but thoroughly *human* figures who can readily sympathise with them. In a unique fashion, St Mary is held to possess particular sympathy for our human concerns and frailties, although, as Christ's mother, she is thought closer to God than any other human person (Daniel 1992:118).

The theology of intercessionary prayer permits the possibility of addressing human and this-worldly concerns within religious practice, according to some to an excessive degree. Prayers to the saints are considered especially effective when in the presence of a tomb or relic. They often take the form of requests for practical assistance in the concerns of life. For this practice, saints are generally considered approachable and sympathetic, whilst, by contrast, there is often a certain remoteness in the conception of God. This leads to a situation in which some argue that cults of the saints dominate popular religious practice to the exclusion of the 'vertical' dimension, the relationship of people with God. This is a concern expressed by some Orthodox as well as Protestant clergy. It is as though the relationship with God is considered a lofty concern beyond the understanding or worthiness of ordinary people.

For Jacobites/Orthodox, there are standard prayers, regularly recited, for the saints in both the daily prayer cycle and the mass. This reinforces the emphasis upon intercession, in addition to the practice of private prayer. The whole phenomenon is, of course, encouraged by the ubiquitous devotional portraits resembling icons (Paulos Mar Gregorios 1986:39), stories about miracles and other deeds, and the festivals and days of commemoration. The central importance of intercession, both conceptually and emotionally, is one of the principal forces underlying theological conservatism, that is to say, the hostility towards the reformers of previous years and towards new Protestant churches currently. In fact, the emphasis upon intercession ensures a certain congruity at the level of popular practice between both Orthodoxy and Catholicism on the one hand and at least some Hindu worship on the other. They all feature multiple, more or less human, representatives of the sphere of divinity, who are capable of granting blessings to devotees and who are associated with particular holy sites and standard forms of offering and ritual performance. This is one reason why Christian pilgrim centres are popular with many Hindus.[2]

Catholic theology also emphasises intercession, although there are some differences with Orthodoxy. There is no veneration of statues for the latter; instead it is usually the tombs which are the focal point. In general, the systematic investigation of claims concerning sainthood, a formal inquiry which may lead to canonisation, is not characteristic of the Orthodox. Consequently, for the latter the emphasis lies almost entirely upon local popular tradition and stories which circulate concerning miracles and blessings granted, pointing to the saintly status of a departed person. Such stories are central to the tradition concerning Parumala Mar Gregorios, although, unusually for a recent figure, he has been officially declared a saint by both Patriarch and Catholicos groups. These differences between Orthodox and Catholic practice, although notable, are overshadowed by differences created by the rise to prominence of charismatic worship within the Catholic Church. It is this ecstatic style of worship, often associated with healing ministry, which is considered by many Orthodox to comprise the alien face of contemporary Catholicism and a potent threat.

The new charismatic cults are well-known, well-funded and immensely popular. They attract individuals seeking specific types of help, as well as those looking for a more emotional worship experience (D'Netto 1985). They threaten to divert attention and energy of Orthodox Christians, if not lead them away altogether. Of course some of these groups are controversial within their own Catholic or Protestant Church, but this does not prevent their evident success. There arises, therefore, the question of what would comprise an appropriate response by the Orthodox. Some leading figures within the community advocate the development of more expressive and modern forms of worship in their own churches. They argue that the ancient liturgy and prayers have diminished appeal, especially for younger members today. However, there is probably a limit to how far innovations would be acceptable to the community in general. There are religious conferences and other meetings which include some worship which is broadly of this type. However, it is possible that the appeal of rival cults reflects, in part, disillusionment with ecclesiastical authority. If this is leading some individuals to favour the apparently more informal or democratic structures of new Protestant churches, it would be little affected by modifying styles of worship. It is notable that informal 'house groups' and other neighbourhood networks are popular occasions for prayer and evangelism. It is also significant that some Hindu organisations, such as the RSS (Rashtriya Swayame-sevak Sangh) aim to encourage a more militant style of Hinduism to counteract the influence of such Christian groups. This leads to some hardening of religious boundaries, with some Hindus more reluctant to participate in Christian pilgrimage.

Instead of imitating rival groups, mimicking a reformed theology or style of worship, many within the Orthodox community argue that they must enhance their existing strengths. One of these is the high repute of some of their important pilgrim centres, especially Parumala. Here it is of central significance that Mar Gregorios is a well-loved, local and recent figure. He is accessible to a degree which surpasses most other saints. As a consequence of this, active steps have been taken to encourage and elaborate pilgrimage to this site. Well-organised pilgrimages are now arranged which set out, often by walking, for Parumala from all directions. Such groups, if carefully organised, can be well-publicised before departure and carefully managed throughout the whole event, with arrangements for feeding and accommodating the pilgrims. People are encouraged to bring their friends, in the knowledge that the event will not require too much preparation on their part. For those who enjoy voluntary work for the Church, it is an occasion to help out, perhaps with the associated honour of carrying a cross or flag in a prominent position within the pilgrimage party.

The evolving character of the pilgrimages

We should look briefly at the character of the walking pilgrimges. They are a powerful experience. They demand exertion over at least one day, often longer, and a complete break from regular daily routine. They have a unique quality of their own, with long hours of walking punctuated by stops for prayers and frequent speeches, usually concerning the holiness of the saint. The pilgrimage parties look impressive, with long lines of participants marching down Kerala's roads, always accompanied by the decorated chariots carrying portraits of the saint. They powerfully express the commitment of the devotees, with the rhythmic, somewhat repetitive songs, constantly proclaiming the virtues of Mar Gregorios. It is a performance which has been perfected, perhaps, by the Jacobites in their long march to Manjinikara. Now, many of the Orthodox pilgrims to Parumala approach the journey in a similar way.

The pilgrimage should be a time of abstinence—no meat, no liquor, no sex—during which attention can be given over fully to contemplating the saint, and the example he has set. Pilgrimage can, in fact, be said to fit into the regular cycle of 'Lents'. These are periods of fasting and prayer, of varying length, which occur throughout the Orthodox year, not just before Easter. In this way, the pilgrimage performs a spiritual function fully consistent with the traditional patterns of Church practice, but in a way which attracts young participants, especially young men, for whom it is also a challenge and a chance to be away from home with their peers. The pilgrimages have, therefore, been especially encouraged amongst the youth and student organisations of the Catholicos side, especially in the last decade. Participants in the pilgrimages experience a vivid, memorable form of devotion, which is related to, but distinct from, regular church worship. In addition, they display a loyalty to their group, which can amount to a show of strength which draws attention to the ownership of (and strength of commitment towards) the holy site by their community.[3] A statement is made which responds to the rising popularity of other pilgrim centres and cults, including the organised pilgrimages of the Patriarch side. By contrast, Patriarch supporters do not usually participate in organised pilgrimages to Parumala, since the site is controlled by the other side. They may visit the church, but probably at quiet times, outside of the main pilgrimage period.

The pilgrimage journey in which I participated, in November 1995, was particularly special because it travelled from Mulanthuruthy, the birthplace of Mar Gregorios, southwards to Parumala. In a way, the journey symbolised the span of the saint's holy life. It took three days. Throughout, there was constant repetition of his name in the simple, but engaging devotional songs. The entire process often acquired a rhythmic, almost hypnotic quality, although this would be interrupted by stops for much needed rest and refreshment. Because it was the late part of the rainy season, there were some heavy downpours, including one at the end as we neared our final destination. The overnight accommodation was simple, pilgrims stretching out on the floor of a school or church. For this reason the pilgrimage was, unusually, restricted to men only—facilities were considered too cramped and limited for the mixing of both sexes.

Our arrival at Parumala was dramatic. There were enormous crowds, with thousands of pilgrims arriving from other directions. The rain was falling hard, so people hurried the final yards, weaving through the crowds and souvenir stalls, mostly huddling beneath black umbrellas. At last the coloured-light decorations could be seen on the church. There was a final circumambulation of the church, mainly to permit a preceding party to vacate the area around the tomb, and then, finally, we entered and stood at the holy spot itself. The tomb is at ground level, with, on one side, people jostling to light candles to be placed by it. On the other side, a huge portrait of Mar Gregorios hangs above the tomb. Standing facing the picture, the priest of our party began to sing the prayers for the saint, with a powerful intensity and vigour. This performance concludes the journey, whilst also offering a chance for individuals to connect it, through private prayer, with the particular issues and anxieties of their life. It is the conviction that prayers said here are answered which motivates so many to undertake the pilgrimage, and provides a basis for further stories about healings and other miracles.

The 'Indianness' of Indian Orthodoxy and the ambiguous status of Parumala

It has become increasingly common for members of the pro-Catholicos Orthodox community to refer to their group as the 'Indian Orthodox Church' (e.g. Paulos Mar Gregorios 1982). In this way, they assert their autonomy, implying that they are independent of, and equal in status to, the Syrian, Armenian and other Orthodox churches. This self-understanding enables them to emphasise the 'Indianness' of their Church. They argue that Christianity is a religion of India as much as anywhere else by virtue of having existed there, according to tradition, from the time of the earliest establishment of the faith. Specifically, 52 CE. is the traditional date of the arrival of St Thomas in India (see myths in Houtart and Lemercinier 1981:29–32). Furthermore, the ancient Indian Christianity, they would imply, is more genuinely maintained by themselves in India than by those other churches which are subject to foreign control. This argument is one of the most emotive ways in which the Orthodox distance themselves from the Jacobites, sometimes referring to principal figures of their side as 'freedom fighters', the phrase used for participants in the struggle for independence from Britain (e.g. Foreword by K. M. Tharakan in Samuel 1986). Likewise, Catholics and many Protestants are said to be subject to foreign domination, receiving funds and missionaries from overseas.

Claiming to represent authentic, and 'free', Indian Christianity is a powerful means of dissuading any shift of allegiance by their own people, and could persuade some Jacobites to join them. An extremely important point here is that the argument parallels, and in some degree responds to, accusations levelled by some sections of militant Hinduism. According to the latter, both Christianity and Islam are foreign religions, possibly controlled by the 'foreign hand', that is to say, by international organisations which can promote their own agendas, perhaps to the detriment of Indian culture. Those Christians who label themselves 'Indian Orthodox' can be said to imply that this point has some validity, at least for Jacobites, Catholics and Protestants. They would assert, however, that they represent fully Indian Christianity, a tradition so ancient that it demonstrates that the faith belongs to India as much as elsewhere (see essays in M.K. Kuriakose 1988).

As a matter of fact, similar claims to the above are announced by members of the Mar Thoma Church, the Protestant group which separated from the Jacobites in the nineteenth century (Alexander Mar Thoma 1985:114). Orthodox Christians would probably say that the Mar Thomites were too much influenced by the British, even though they are now independent. Significantly, somewhat similar claims can be advanced by Muslims in Kerala, whose community was established by visiting traders in the very earliest days of their religion, long before Islam entered India by force.

There are a number of important respects in which the evolving ecclesiastical self-understanding of the Orthodox affects the Parumala pilgrimage. This occasion can be seen to be one of the most notable contexts within which the credentials of the Orthodox community to comprise a thoroughly Indian Church are displayed. After all, thousands of pilgrims, Christian and non-Christian alike, come to venerate a saint who was born, and passed away, in Kerala. As a local figure, Mar Gregorios is distinct from most of the saints venerated by Christians. Furthermore, he had a reputation for being concerned for the welfare of people of all castes and social backgrounds. It is notable, also, that Parumala lies close to Niranam, a church also belonging to the Orthodox, which is famous as one of seven churches traditionally said to have been founded by St Thomas himself, and therefore associated with the beginnings of Christianity on the subcontinent.

In November 1995, at the time of my own pilgrimage to Parumala, a BJP politician of national prominence visited, and had an audience with the Catholicos there. The BJP (Bharatiya Janata Party) is considered close to the organisations of vigorous (perhaps 'militant') Hinduism. It propagates a message incorporating a type of Indian nationalism wherein 'Indian' often seems to be equated with 'Hindu'. It was reported in the press that the BJP politician observed the proceedings at Parumala, after which the Catholicos impressed upon him the view that Christianity is a fully Indian religion. There was, presumably, the implication that the so-called Indian Orthodox exemplify this at least as well as any other group. It was a meeting which strikingly illustrates the general politicisation of pilgrimage. Politicians are routinely invited to address crowds at pilgrim centres, especially, as in this case, near the time of a general election. The encounter conveys some concern on the part of the Catholicos to publicly clarify the position of the BJP and a desire to encourage them to adopt a friendly stance towards Christians. Critically it also suggests that an autonomous Indian Church might be best suited to advance the interests of Indian Christians in such a context. Where better to publicise this point than at the pilgrimage for its own, cherished Indian saint?[4]

The fact of increased politicisation of pilgrimage, and the possible need for rapprochement between Christians and at least some Hindus, had earlier been brought to the fore in Kerala by the Nilackal problem. The dispute which this engendered would have been seen as an important part of the background to the visit by the BJP politician. At Nilackal, a site in the mountains within the same district as Parumala, there had been, according to tradition, another church founded by St Thomas. In 1983, a cross was found which indicated, it was said, the site of the original church. It was proposed to build a new church there, which was to be an ecumenical Christian centre, jointly maintained by the main Christian Churches. However, Nilackal lies within the traditional kingdom of Sri Ayyappan which surrounds the temple at Sabarimala, the most important Hindu pilgrim centre of the area. It was said that it would be offensive for the Hindu deity and his devotees to have a Christian church built at the proposed site. The Christian Churches united in their desire to honour St Thomas, whilst many Hindus were united in their opposition (Vaidyanathan 1992:186–7).

The disagreement became a tense dispute which threatened serious confrontation between the two communities. The Nilackal problem came to be referred to as 'Kerala's Ayodhya'—a reference to the subsequently far more violent dispute over the Babri Masjid in Northern India. Fortunately, for Nilackal a compromise was struck. A plot of land was found some distance away, upon which the Christians agreed to build their pilgrim centre. Memories of this problem would have been readily recalled by those hearing about the meeting of the Catholicos and the BJP politician. The Nilackal issue is still discussed, albeit in fairly muted tones. The Catholicos could hold, perhaps, that it was a gesture of magnanimity on his part to meet a politician of that party at the most important Orthodox pilgrim centre. From the point of view of the politician, showing respect to the Catholicos and the pilgrim centre could be advantageous in a state with many Christian voters, some of whom might consider voting BJP given very strong disillusionment with the Congress Party. It remains to be seen how relations between the BJP and the Christian communities will progress, and how far the 'Indianness' of the Orthodox will be developed by the Catholicos and his followers.

Demolition at Parumala

With regard to the rivalry between Parumala and other pilgrim centres, it is significant that, at the time of my pilgrimage in 1995, the site had a rather melancholy character. This was because the old church had been demolished to make way for a larger, modern one. Fortunately, I had visited the old church a number of times previously. It was certainly rather small for the huge crowds visiting at busy times, but, although only a portion of the structure was part of the original church constructed by Mar Gregorios, it was well liked by visitors and locals. It was decided that a larger church was needed to handle the enormous crowds, a development which parallels schemes for expanding and 'improving' facilities at many pilgrim centres. These constructions are thought to encourage yet more pilgrims and enhance the prestige of the sites. Such developments have occurred at other notable locations such as Sabarimala (Hindu), Manjinikara (Jacobite), Bharananganam (Catholic) and many others.[5]

There are obvious advantages to schemes for upgrading facilities at pilgrim centres. Nonetheless, they are certainly not universally welcomed. Many pilgrims regret them, and say that they spoil the character of the sites. They are too modern or ugly; they put too much stress on convenience, it is said. In the case of Parumala, as far as I could tell, most Orthodox Christians of the vicinity and many other visitors disliked the plan. Many locals would have grown used to visiting the old church both for mass and life-cycle rituals. But, as mentioned, it is not a parish church but is under the direct control of the Catholicate, so that local people were effectively powerless to stop the alteration.

It should be said that the holiest parts of the Parumala site, the tomb and main altar area, are to be preserved and incorporated into the new structure. However, this fact did not prevent disquiet amongst ordinary pilgrims and devotees. Such changes would be unlikely to occur at Niranam, for example, a parish church hallowed for its association with St

Thomas. Developments of this kind would also be unlikely at, for example, Mulanthuruthy where the local Jacobites who control it would jealously guard their right to determine its management, whether this was challenged by local Orthodox (who are permitted occasional access to the church) or even senior Jacobites. The recent changes at the Parumala site seem almost to exalt in its direct control by the Catholicate, in contrast to Jacobite or other locations, even in the face of some regret by local, loyal Orthodox devotees. There is, perhaps, a triumphalism in this display of control over the site. It is also a bid to boost the Orthodox Church's general prestige by building an especially large church, which can credibly rival all the other pilgrim sites and religious meeting centres in Kerala.

The modern character of the new church—it is circular in shape—might provide some impetus for innovations in the style of worship to be conducted within it. Already, in some Orthodox services, laity are now allowed to lead the congregation in intercessionary prayer, a practice which is standard in many Protestant Churches. In general, however, attitudes towards the format for worship remain conservative, especially amongst the hierarchy. As regards the church structure itself, some of the negative sentiments that are sometimes expressed may dissipate once the new church is finished. In the meantime, the demolition of the old church, whilst perfectly legitimate given the established control of Parumala, is a striking reminder of the fact that disagreement ofteru arises over the management of pilgrim centres (Eade and Sallnow 1991).[6] Disagreements about maintaining holy centres regularly occur in Kerala, as much as throughout India and elsewhere.

Conclusion

There have been vigorous efforts by Orthodox Christians in Kerala to elaborate and popularise pilgrimages to Parumala. As the burial site of a fairly recent, local-born saint, Parumala comprises an appropriate pilgrim centre for a display of commitment by those Orthodox Christians who favour greater autonomy for the Church in India. Rival Jacobites, who favour close ties with the Syrian Patriarchy, have achieved notable success in promoting their own pilgrimages to the tomb of a former Patriarch who was buried in Kerala. For the pro-autonomy Orthodox, the organised walking pilgrimages to Parumala provide an opportunity to participate in a community event, displaying loyalty to their side, whilst at the same time praying about their personal concerns in the context of a demanding, but experientially powerful, religious performance.

The Parumala site is being redeveloped, with the construction of a large new church. This enhances the prestige of the pilgrim centre in a situation of rivalry with other sites, whether the Jacobite tombs or the increasingly popular venues for charismatic-style worship, both Catholic and Protestant. The style of worship of the Orthodox shows some signs of modification in response to this competition, but it remains to be seen how far this will develop.

The Parumala cult has acquired some increased political significance because it can be held that the cult of a local Indian saint, maintained by an ancient and autonomous Indian Church, helps to undermine claims that Christianity is a 'foreign' religion. Such a charge might be heard from some sections of militant Hinduism. It is notable that a well-publicised meeting was held at Parumala between the Catholicos, head of the pro-autonomy Orthodox, and a leading BJP politician, at the time of my own pilgrimage.

The reason for the success of the organised walking pilgrimages is that participants gain a sense of full involvement in the process, whilst displaying a commitment which is conspicuously visible to all the communities which are passed through along the route. These aspects of the pilgrimage experience have been explored by me at length elsewhere (Gath 1997). In the present context, we should emphasise that, for the Orthodox group which controls the pilgrim centre, the cult of Mar Gregorios—widely considered one of the most approachable, well-loved saints of Kerala—is an immensely valuable asset in its struggles with rival Christian groups and beyond, in the wider sphere of contemporary politics.

Notes

1. See Gath (1997) for ethnography of Manjinikara and other Jacobite pilgrimages. It is clear that pilgrim centres need to be studied in the context of a 'field' of possible locations to which a prospective worshipper might be attracted.
2. Another possible reason is syncretism—that is to say, the cult might show a blending of Hindu and Christian features in either ritual or popular legend. However, this is much more evident in the cults of ancient saints, for example St. George, than in the veneration of modern saints such as Mar Gregorios.
3. Experiential aspects of Christian pilgrimage in Kerala are discussed by me in Gath (1997). Issues such as enhanced social bonding—Turnerian 'communitas'—and the bodily character of religious experience during pilgrimage are considered there. These themes are explored for an important Hindu pilgrimage in Kerala in Gath (2000). See also Turner and Turner (1978), and on related issues see Simon Coleman in this volume.
4. On the BJP in Kerala, including some discussion of Christian attiudes towards it, see Chiriyankandath (1998). It should be mentioned the Syrian Christians have rarely engaged in proselytisation, so there is relatively little tension around the issue of conversion.
5. On Bharananganam see Corinne Dempsey in this volume.
6. One often hears the view that these disputes are really over money—who is to benefit from offerings made at the pilgrim centre. Whilst this is undoubtedly important, the differences in opinion over what counts as appropriate worship, and who has legitimate authority, clearly are of concern to many people.

References

Alexander Mar Thoma, Metropolitan. 1985. *The Mar Thoma Church: Heritage and Mission*, Thiruvalla.

Babu Paul, D. 1993. *The Syrian Orthodox Christians of St Thomas*, Trivandrum: T.P. Mathew (2nd ed).

Bayly, S. 1989. *Saints, Goddesses and Kings: Muslims and Christians in South Indian Society 1700–1900*, Cambridge University Press.

Chiriyankandath, J. 1988. *Bounded Nationalism: Kerala and the Social and regional limits of Hindutva.*', in *The BJP and the Compulsions of politics in India* ed. T B Hansen and C Jaffrelot. Oxford University Press.

Daniel, D. 1986. *The Orthodox Church of India* (2nd edition), New Delhi: R. David.

———. 1992. *Blessed Virgin Mariam*. New Delhi: R. David.

D'Netto, T. B. (ed.). 1985. *Jesus Heals: Guidelines for Ministry in the Catholic Charismatic Renewal*. Bombay.

Eade, J. and Sallnow, M. J. (eds) 1991. *Contesting the Sacred. The Anthropology of Christian Pilgrimage*. London: Routledge & Kegan Paul.

Gath, A. D. H. 1997. *Varieties of Pilgrimage Experience: Religious Journeying in Central Kerala*, PhD Dissertation, University of Edinburgh.

———. 2000. *Social Learning, Poitics and Memory on the Road to Sivagiri*. Paper presented to European association of Social anthropologists (pilgrimage panel) Krakow, July 2000.

Houtart, F. and Lermercinier, G. 1981. *Genesis and Institutionalization of the Indian Catholicism*. Louvain-la-Neuve.

Kadavil Paul Ramban. 1973. *The Orthodox Syrian Church: Its Religion and Philosophy*. Puthenruz: K V Pathrose.

M. K. Kuriakose (ed) 1988. *Orthodox Identity in India. Essays in honour of V. C. Samuel*. Bangalore.

Paulos Mar Gregorios. 1982. *The Indian Orthodox Church: An Overview*. Kottayam: Sophia Publications.

———. 1986. *The Joy of Freedom: Eastern Worship and Modern Man*. Madras: Christian Literature Society.

Tharakan, K. M. 1986. Foreword in *Truth Triumphs: Life and Achievements of Metropolitan Mar Dionysius VI*. V. C. Samuel, Kottayam: CMS Press.

Thomas, S. 1977. *Behold A Saint: The Life and Times of Parumala Mar Gregorios*, New Delhi.

Turner V. and Turner E. 1978. *Image and Pilgrimage in Christian Culture*. New York: Columbia University Press.

Vaidyanathan, K. R. 1992. *Pilgrimage to Sabari*, Bombay: Bharatiya Vidya Bhavan.

Visvanathan, S. 1993. *The Christians of Kerala: History, Belief and Ritual among the Yakoha*, Madras: Oxford University Press.

86

PERFORMING PILGRIMAGE
Walsingham and the ritual construction of irony

Simon Coleman and John Elsner

Source: Felicia Hughes-Freeland (ed.), *Ritual, Performance, Media*, London: Routledge, 1998, pp. 46–65.

Introduction: pilgrimage as performance

> Walsingham is like a huge icon. It's almost like a Christian theme park, in which we set out the wares and then allow people to make of it what they will. And I think there's something about that which is very therapeutic: that they'll make the stations of the cross; they'll just come and sit in the shrine; they'll sit in the gardens; they'll go and light candles; they'll sit in the Holy House and just look at the image; they'll go for a walk up to the parish church; they'll go and visit the Orthodox chapel or they'll go and buy things in the shops to take home. All of that I think is very, very significant, because it's the best kind of spiritual direction, which actually allows a pilgrim to find his or her own way in what God offers. . . . And I think we just make available these resources, and people use them as they find best.

These are the words, spoken in an interview, of a priest at the Anglican shrine of Walsingham, north Norfolk. They indicate some of the elements he considers key to the performance of a successful pilgrimage: the sense, for instance, that a pilgrim must find a spiritual direction not only on the way to a sacred shrine, but also within the environs of the sacred space; the conviction, as well, that ritualized 'browsing', far from representing an heretical evasion of fixed liturgical structures, will have divinely sanctioned and therapeutic – even performative – effects.

Such attitudes might initially seem surprising because they come from a source hardly known for its encouragement of liturgical innovation. The Anglican shrine at Walsingham has the reputation within ecclesiastical circles of being a defender of old-style, High-Church principles, indicated as much by its continuation of unashamedly 'smells and bells' styles of ritual as by its apparently firm opposition to the ordination of women. In this chapter, however, we wish to argue that the priest has nevertheless identified an important aspect of much contemporary pilgrimage to Walsingham. We propose to examine the relationship between carrying out pilgrimage rituals and the cultivation of creativity in performance by exploring the ways in which many visitors to the site use Christian tradition and liturgy less as sources of fixed legitimacy than as flexible symbolic means or resources through which to ritualize social relations.

Some pilgrimages to both the Anglican and the Roman Catholic shrines at Walsingham can be described as 'official' and 'controlled' in the sense that they involve organized journeys, usually arranged by a given parish, to the sacred sites of a single religious tradition. Many visitors, however (including some who come on supposedly collectively co-ordinated pilgrimages), act as self-conscious spiritual bricoleurs, constructing their own paths through the numerous sacred foci of the village. The shrines of both main religious groups in the village encode implicit narrative versions of the Walsingham tradition in their spaces and liturgies, yet such narratives can be subverted by pilgrims as they cut and paste their way through the village, experimenting with a variety of religious genres without necessarily endorsing any single one of them. In practice, Walsingham – or rather 'the Walsingham experience' – offers a continuum of ritualized performances: at one end lies the potential for full and deliberate submission to liturgical order; at the other a self-conscious cultivation of pilgrimage as innovation is evident, in which ritual improvisation is invested with a form of sacramental irony.

We contend that the power of many of the more innovative examples of pilgrimage we examine lies in the self-aware transformation of traditional liturgy into performances that simultaneously genuflect towards conventional ritual forms and yet subvert those forms in the very act of genuflection. In the process, the boundaries of ritual action are shifted and expanded. People may create sacralized performances incorporating the pubs, gift-, souvenir- and tea-shops and even the nearby seaside in their pilgrimages, or draw canonical texts and liturgy into dialogue with personal, often overtly secular images and practices taken from everyday life, the imagination, literature, films and theatre. In these instances, ritual is not merely submitted to determination by history and evaluation by participants through being performed (cf. Schieffelin 1995); it is actively accommodated to personal preferences before it is even staged.

Walsingham therefore acts as a physical 'medium' for pilgrimage, offering various spaces for the enactment of rituals. However, as a holy site the village is not so much a single place as a roughly defined set of activities broadly contained within a permeable temporal and spatial frame. Such activities involve shifting fields of social relations that can move over periods of hours or days around sometimes interlocking, sometimes separate arenas of action. During a pilgrimage, a person can experience a number of sites or liturgies with varying combinations of friends, partners or kin, and then return in future years to repeat a similar process.

In some of the following, then, we shall move far from the view of ritual constructing a coercive formality that links particular events into a pre-existing order (cf. Bloch 1974). Where pilgrims become authors or self-conscious orchestrators of their own pilgrimages, the degree to which they are forced into submission by established liturgical orders is greatly reduced. The pilgrimages described here raise complex issues regarding the relationship between constraint and creativity (cf. Hastrup and Gore, both this volume). While pilgrimage is turned into a kind of 'play' in many cases, casual tourists as well as pilgrims may also come to see themselves as engaging in activities that transcend purely self-indulgent leisure. Furthermore, even improvised performances are not usually created *de novo*, since they are defined by simultaneously echoing and altering conventional forms.

It should be clear by now that we view the performance of ritual as involving much more than the mere replication of a given liturgical script. Rather, in the case of Walsingham it can frequently be seen as a strategic deployment of symbolic resources. Performance in this sense comes close to Bell's definition of the process of ritualization as 'a way of acting that is designed and orchestrated to distinguish and privilege what is being done in comparison to other, usually more quotidian, activities' (1992: 74). The virtue of this definition is that it does not presume to specify universal, necessary features of sacred or secular activity, but rather stresses the idea of differentiating – by whatever means – one form of action or behaviour from another. Adapting Bell's notion of ritualization, one can argue that ritual performances carried out by pilgrims act semiotically to create a sense of 'difference' in relation to whatever other actions they wish to invoke and transcend. Many parishes do not come to Walsingham in order to engage in novel forms of ritual *per se*. Instead, their pilgrimage enables them to carry out their normal forms of worship in a particularly authoritative context. To celebrate Mass or carry out the stations of the cross at a national shrine – and moreover one where unknown others are seen to be doing the same – therefore gives such actions a significance they would not have in a local church. Their ritual action as pilgrims is defined not merely in relation to everyday life, but also in comparison to other ritual in a more 'workaday' context. For others, the playful 'misuse' of conventional liturgical forms is a form of ritualization of ritual, in the sense that it is an active transformation of Anglo-Catholic or Roman Catholic liturgy, a metacommentary on religious orthodoxy that signals association with, but also distance from, such orthodoxy.

Walsingham as a genre of pilgrimage

Our characterization of ritual performance at Walsingham has implications for analyses of pilgrimage as a whole. Broadly Durkheimian perspectives see the phenomenon as a ritual means of integrating disparate sections of society (e.g. Wolf 1958). Others have characterized pilgrimages as legitimating oppressive ideologies (e.g. Gross 1971). The Turners (1978) famously proposed that pilgrimage provides a ritual means of reversing conventional social structures, not least through the generation of states of 'communitas', though critics have viewed their work as expressing more of a religious ideal than a sociological reality (e.g. Sallnow 1981, Coleman and Eisner 1995). Recently, Eade and Sallnow (1991) have attempted to distance themselves from the alleged determinism of Durkheimian, Marxist or Turnerian analyses. Their thesis is that a deconstruction of the fetishized notion of an autonomously powerful holy place is necessary. Rather, pilgrimage should be seen as involving:

> an arena for competing religious and secular discourses, for both the official co-optation and non-official recovery of religious meanings, for conflict between orthodoxies, sects, and confessional groups, for drives towards consensus and communitas, and for countermovements towards separateness and division.
>
> (Eade and Sallnow 1991: 2)

Eade and Sallnow's position is a powerful one, avoiding the dangers of essentializing pilgrimage and its constituent elements. However, we contend that they do not give sufficient weight to the infinitely modulated nuances in performing pilgrimage which are evident in many of the ritual forms we discuss. For Eade and Sallnow, apparent holiness lies in the emptiness of shrines, with the latters' universalism 'ultimately constituted not by a unification of discourses but rather by the capacity of a cult to entertain and respond to a plurality' (1991: 15). We agree on the issue of multiple discourses, but would stress that in another, important sense, the 'religious void' is in fact full. It is full in the way that the 'empty space' of a theatre is full – crowded with material props, holy objects and reminiscences of other holy sites; crowded with pilgrims who may even be reaffirming the sanctity of the site not least through performances of ritual.

Walsingham, then, can be understood as an 'empty space' in the theatrical sense proposed by Peter Brook (1968) (cf. Hastrup, this volume). The sacred site is a particular kind of dramatic arena in which an overdetermination of material resources is offered to pilgrims, providing props with which to enact their own play – whether this means wholesale participation in the range of 'official' activities on offer, ironic reflection on such activities, or private rituals whose value is defined by their personal significance to the actors. The sanctity of Walsingham as England's prime Marian shrine lies in the constant interaction of its complex topography and rich material culture with different scripts endlessly performed by different groups of pilgrims.[1]

The idea that a sacred site like Walsingham may effectively be a stage, well equipped for certain kinds of performance which its pilgrims come to enact, resonates with recent discussions of the museum in western culture. Carol Duncan argues (1995: 7–20) that art museums are sites imbued with sanctity through their architectural forms, their shrine-like displays and the elevated levels of aesthetic contemplation many visitors expect to attain there. They are thus liminal spaces in which visitors indulge in particular forms of ritual which involve both watching the 'play' of objects put on by the curators and constructing their own performances of interpretation, in which: 'people continually "misread" or scramble or resist the museum's cues to some extent; or they actively invent, consciously or unconsciously, their own programs according to all the historical or psychological accidents of who they are' (1995: 13).

Where the pilgrimage site is more radical than both museum and theatre is in its provision of a much more active space for 'misreading'. While misunderstandings of and resistance to an official or established narrative in the theatre or the museum tend to lie in the area of the interpretation of a series of givens (a play's script or a museum display), in Walsingham the potential for such resistance is actively encouraged in the spaces provided for personal pilgrimages. What the official liturgies and topography of the site provide – apart from an establishment script for those who want it – is precisely a series of cues to be missed, a great number of props to be played with, a formal structure of ritual to be ironized.

Setting the scene: Walsingham as a stage

The stage

Little Walsingham, a small and picturesque village in Norfolk, is an extraordinarily rich venue for the interactive and processional theatre of pilgrimage. At the heart (both of the village and of the pilgrimage, physically and conceptually) lies an absent centre: the ruins of a medieval Augustinian priory destroyed in the Reformation in 1538. This ruin, set in the grounds of a privately owned minor stately home, is open to tourists.[2] It is also the probable site of the original 'Holy House' of Walsingham, built according to legend in Anglo-Saxon times in response to a vision of the Virgin granted to an aristocratic woman named Richeldis. The structure was supposed to represent, in accordance with the wishes of the Virgin, an exact copy of the house Jesus occupied in Nazareth, and as a result Walsingham is sometimes called 'England's Nazareth'. In the sixteenth century, the Holy House and its medieval statue of the Virgin formed a principal target of iconoclasts.

Directly to the north of the priory ruins is the Anglican shrine, a privately owned and administered centre of Anglo-Catholicism which moved there in 1931 from the parish church. The shrine is not only the spiritual centre of

Anglo-Catholic pilgrimage to Walsingham, it is also its functional heart, offering hospices, dining facilities and a social centre for pilgrims. Its church is built over what appears to be a Saxon well, the only monument in Walsingham to date back to the legendary period of Richeldis and her vision.[3] However, the *pièce de résistance* is a rebuilt Holy House placed within the church, whose fabric is in part composed of stones gathered from monasteries destroyed in the Reformation. This building houses the Anglican replica of the statue of Our Lady of Walsingham.

Beside the Roman Catholic parish church on the south side of the village is a hospice and pilgrim bureau. These organizations provide accommodation, food and a social centre for visitors whose pilgrimage focuses not on the village but on the Slipper Chapel and Chapel of Reconciliation at the Roman Catholic shrine, situated about a mile outside the village to the south. The Slipper Chapel is a fourteenth-century building which was once (probably) a stopping-off point for medieval pilgrims to Walsingham, but is now owned by the Roman Catholics and houses their replica of the medieval statue of Our Lady.

Between the shrines, in particular along the High Street and around the Village Pump, are ranged a string of souvenir shops, pubs and tea-rooms. These offer a treasure trove of sacred knick-knacks: Virgins that glow in the dark, icons and statues, postcards with religious themes and other souvenirs. The shops help to orchestrate a spatial dynamics in which they indicate that the 'truly' holy spots – the shrines, the ruins – are yet to be approached. They provide acceptable spaces of apparent secularity within the process of modern Walsingham pilgrimage, as opposed to other kinds of secular space like the housing estate to the north-west of the village which is divorced from the pilgrimage complex and which provides a mostly invisible backdrop to the conventional staging of ritual performance.

The sets and props

Some material 'props' upon which pilgrims' performances can focus are familiar features of Christian ritual – such as the stations of the cross available at both shrines. Others are more unusual or at least flamboyant by the standards of English worship. These include the many offertories, relics, sacred objects and votives which clutter the space of the Anglican church. The two polychrome replica statues of Our Lady of Walsingham kept in the Slipper Chapel and in the Holy House clearly mark the most conventionally sacred spots of their respective settings. Before these images, both imitations of an original, medieval image, and housed in buildings with the maximum of medieval resonance, pilgrims often pray in private as well as celebrating Mass.

Both shrines also offer visitors numerous other opportunities to engage physically with the site. The Slipper Chapel and the Holy House encourage pilgrims to light candles, and both include areas to collect holy water to take home or drink on the spot. The places are to be interacted with and not merely viewed, even if the visitor's knowledge, commitment and/or liturgical competence are somewhat limited. Thus, below is a piece of dialogue overheard by one of the authors in the village museum. Two tourists question a guide, apparently regarding Anglican and Roman Catholic sites as undifferentiatedly sacred sources of a pilgrimage 'souvenir':

TOURIST: How do we get to the church?
GUIDE: Which one?
TOURIST: The one with the holy water.
GUIDE: You get holy water at both the Anglican and the Catholic churches.
TOURIST: Which is the nearest?

Dimensions of performance

As we shall see, some pilgrims play with sacred boundaries in ways rather more skilful and self-conscious than the tourists mentioned above. We argue that a useful way to characterize variations in attitude and performance is along a dimension indicating distance from perceived orthodoxy in liturgical practice. The variations we have observed have been suggested to us as a result both of accompanying pilgrims round the shrines and talking to them either informally during their stays in Walsingham or in recorded interviews, often away from the villager.[4]

Canonical enactments

Perhaps the 'ideal type' of the conventional pilgrimage to both Anglo- and Roman Catholic shrines is provided by the annual, parish-based visit. These are often carried out over a given weekend and consist of a number of generally invariant elements: a series of Masses; carrying out the stations of the cross; a procession incorporating the Virgin or Host; confession and prayers for intercession. In the Anglican shrine, pilgrims will also be sprinkled with holy water from the Saxon well. Such pilgrimages are ideally to be experienced collectively by a group of people who are likely to know each other well during their everyday lives, who tend to come to the site at the same time each year. As one Anglican pilgrim put it, describing how her parish would be leaving Walsingham the next day, but would already be anticipating its return:

> Quarter to two tomorrow afternoon, we all assemble around the Holy House and we have our prayers of departure which is very sad. . . . But we always say – right, next year.

In such cases, coming to Walsingham provides more than a sense of stability, however. It also invests the activities of the parish with translocal significance – and one that can only be provided by a national pilgrimage site. A Roman Catholic resident of the village, who has also been engaged in the work of the Anglican shrine, notes:

> A lot of parishes look to Walsingham. It's a great experience for them because they come from a parish where possibly not very many people go to church, and maybe they feel it's a bit of a struggle to keep what they feel is important going there. . . . When they come on their annual pilgrimage, it's great because a whole lot of them go; there's a programme laid on. . . . Then they go down to the parish church Mass on a Sunday, and the church is bursting with people, and they suddenly think, my goodness this is wonderful, you know? Now we can go back and hang on.

For Anglo-Catholics in particular, the sense of collective validation that pilgrimage can bring is important, given that they are likely to perceive themselves as a beleaguered minority within the contemporary Anglican church. However, for both Anglo- and Roman Catholics, various ritualized means of linking their own parish indexically with the site exist. Candles may be lit in remembrance of people or groups back home, or the names of particular people invoked during the recitation of 'Hail Marys'. The performance of stations of the cross at both shrines links a parish not only with a national centre of faith, of course, but also with a biblical narrative which is both recalled and enacted. At such times, a priest might use short homilies spoken at each station to reflect upon matters related to the local parish or particular members of his congregation. This sense of the need to use performance as a method of investing 'everyday' religious practice with wider significance is described by an Anglican priest (himself a regular visitor throughout his career, with a variety of parishes), who states:

> Well I think why people like coming here, and . . . people [from my parish] have been coming 40–50 years, is that it's both unlike home, in the sense that Walsingham is a village not a bit like [industrial town in the north of England], but on the other hand the religion is something which fits. There are so many things I suppose which people take for granted, or don't see the point of at home. You come here and it begins to fall into place. . . . After a while you realise that what you do back [home] in say a church that was built at the end of the last century has been going on in some of these churches for seven or eight centuries, and it makes you feel that you are part of something which is more than . . . just local, just the way we do it, just the way people have been doing it in my lifetime.

In this description, echoed by other pilgrims to Walsingham, we see the idea of a parish observing itself performing pilgrimage in a highly charged liturgical context, and coming therefore to see itself in transcendent terms. Part of the power of the visit comes from the way local and national forms of worship parallel or 'fit' each other. It is also the case, however, that for some pilgrims Walsingham is a place to be seen by others – to demonstrate to the church and the world that one has chosen to go to such a sacred centre. This element of demonstration takes on an element of defiance among Anglo-Catholics who go to the more controversial Anglican shrine, and is made explicit on days of the Anglican national pilgrimage, when those processing through the streets have to run the gauntlet of evangelical Protestants who stand in the centre of the village and accuse them of idolatry.

Conventional parish pilgrimages vary in the extent to which they incorporate wall-to-wall liturgy. Some fill every moment of the day with sacred activities. Others explicitly incorporate periods of leisure, although such periods of fun, while seen as a necessary part of the experience, tend to be kept separate from strictly liturgical activities. One middle-aged Anglican woman, Beryl, states:

> The essence of a good pilgrimage in my eyes . . . is that . . . you can involve the reverence of the shrine . . . [but also include, at other moments] . . . the fun that we have. I mean this afternoon I organized a walk, and there were eighteen of us went on this walk even in the rain. And we went up to St Peter's in the fields, went in there, and . . . looked at the architecture and everything, and then we walked up to the National Trust Craft Centre, had coffee there, and then walked on the old road back into Little Walsingham. . . . And it was wonderful.

Apart from stressing that the 'fun' is complementary to rather than mixed with the liturgy, as well as mentioning that her definition of pilgrimage has received 'official' approval, Beryl also takes care to note the large numbers who went on the outing, implying as she does elsewhere that collective action during the trip provides an important indication of group solidarity. Her commitment to the pilgrimage as involving periods of serious, even solemn moments that are orchestrated by the shrine and its officials is also indicated by the following description of how she felt when she first entered the Anglican shrine and Holy House:

> Absolute awe. A very old priest friend of mine . . . met me at the gate there, and he said, right, this is your first time, come on in. And he took me into that Holy House, and I think every candle was lit, and I just stood there, in awe, and I felt enveloped, completely, and that's all I can say. And I felt this was my, you know, place.

Beryl expresses eloquently sentiments that are evident in other parish pilgrims' accounts, in which Walsingham is valued less as a liminoid opportunity to play with identity (cf. Turner 1982) than as a means of locating self-identity and ritual performance within a wider, amplified liturgical frame. As one Anglican priest put it, describing his first visit to the national pilgrimage, what was striking about the pilgrimage experience was its scale and intensity as much as the form of worship:

> I think I would say that while I was mesmerized of course by seeing hundreds of priests . . . and you know bishops concelebrating and all that – it was marvellous, it was everything a genuflectious youth would want. Benediction given simultaneously in three places: I was beside myself with excitement!

The importance of physical confirmations of faith should not be underestimated in a branch of Christianity that stresses the sacramental means of achieving grace. For many Anglo-Catholics, Walsingham achieves a kind of holiness precisely because it provides the correct material background to performances of pilgrimage. Thus, one middle-aged man who has actually retired and come to live near Walsingham describes how the beauty and liturgical perfection of Walsingham led, at least in his memory, to a focusing on the village that required few other distractions: 'I mean, we used to come to Walsingham for donkey's years every year and never move out while we were there. We'd have a week and we'd never go out of Walsingham.'

Both the couple described above and many who go on formal parish pilgrimages attempt to locate themselves as exactly as possible, theologically and spatially, within a particular religious tradition. Indeed, a priest who currently works at the Anglican shrine referred in an interview to the difficulties involved in persuading visiting parishes to allow him to be experimental with liturgy. Each performance is to be like a 'token' replicating an original 'type' (cf. Lewis 1980), while descriptions of their experiences by such pilgrims tend strongly to affirm the idea that a 'communitas'-like solidarity is generated among those who go.[5] The literal and metaphorical location of the self within tradition allows the performance of pilgrimage to act for some like a form of restricted ritual code, an embodiment of collective belonging to particular forms of religious authority and stability.

Performing irony

Many other dimensions of participation than those described above exist, and they involve a much more complex attitude towards engagement in canonical ritual forms.[6] A number of pilgrims, *pace* Rappaport (1974: 31), may regard participation in pilgrimage to Walsingham as implying something less than a public acceptance of liturgical order. Instead, participation can imply to the self and even to some of one's fellow pilgrims a form of ironic engagement that comes close to parody.[7] One trainee priest noted:

> I think it's really great, I love it. I mean it's not, lock stock and barrel my cup of tea, but that colour and commitment and enthusiasm are really wonderful. Yes it is quite vulgar, extremely vulgar in places, but I mean fairgrounds are vulgar, and I think there's a great deal of overlap between Walsingham and a fairground.

If for some pilgrims, such as those examined in the previous section, it is necessary to distinguish the fun part of the pilgrimage from its serious side, here the ludic aspect of the experience is incorporated *into* the interpretation and positive evaluation of pilgrimage liturgy. What is evoked here is less a sense of awe and more one of wry amusement in an unconscious echo of the shrine priest who referred to Walsingham as a Christian theme park. This pilgrim described himself as a loner, and moreover one not particularly wedded to Anglo-Catholicism. His engagement with the shrine had little to do with the articulation of group identity and much more with a form of self-realization. He described the experience of going to Walsingham – itself an unusual event for him – as 'a point of departure if you like rather than something that I sought and wanted to immerse myself in', and indeed at one point he actually left the village to engage in a 'slightly strange caper in the Norfolk countryside one night', involving a visit with a friend to a night club. Significantly, however, such an act was regarded only partially as a rebellion against the formality of shrine liturgy; in another sense he saw himself as acting perfectly within the spirit (as well as the temporal frame) of pilgrimage, engaging in an intense if not conventionally sacred experience with a chosen companion in a context very different to that of his quotidian existence. Another pilgrim referred, in the same vein, to a walk he had taken with a companion along a nearby beach. Such an event, during which the two had talked in ways they would never have done at home, was the high point of his visit to 'Walsingham'.

The description of Walsingham as vulgar is strikingly common among certain interviewees. Yet it is usually not intended as a simple criticism of the site, but is more an acceptance of the appropriateness of vulgarity in the set-apart context of a pilgrimage. This appropriateness seems to lie in the playful aspect it lends to ritual performance. Here is another reflection on the pilgrimage experience, again from a young man very involved in the Church of England:

> I think the whole idea of it being a sort of religious holiday is important, that you can go and do . . . things you wouldn't normally do in church. You can cross yourself hugely, and genuflect at every available shrine, and you can do sort of High Church stuff, get a feeling for it in a way that you can't elsewhere.

The pilgrim does not see his religious identity as essentially bound up with High Anglicanism. Rather, the pilgrimage allows him to engage temporarily in forms of 'ritual excess'. His viewing of the experience as somehow less serious than normal ritual is reinforced by his perception that the pilgrimage mixes sacred and secular genres of performance:

> It's very theatrical. . . . There is in it something quite self-conscious. . . . I can't take it too seriously. . . . It's two-dimensional in the way that camp is often two-dimensional. . . . It's in good bad taste. . . . You know, you can enjoy it and enter into it, but you never need take it too seriously. But I do know that people do take it seriously.

Or again, describing being sprinkled at the Anglican shrine:

> It was quite moving. . . . There was a man taking photographs of us as we went through the well . . . and I felt that was a bit out of order really. . . . But that's part of the whole two-dimensional thing about it. I mean you're at a moment of great intimacy and spiritual intensity and there's this flash. And I think there's something about that, about Walsingham, that's sort of consonant with that.

In one sense, this pilgrim's perception of what he is doing is similar to that of the 'parish' pilgrims, in that going to Walsingham encourages a certain degree of self-consciousness whereby he is forced to consider whether he 'fits' within the religious tradition on offer. He is, however, far from feeling the need to engage conventionally in canonical forms of worship; rather, his involvement seems akin to watching himself as he passes through a hall of distorting mirrors, each presenting him with an image of himself that is an amusing self-parody. Ritual here seems to be about a temporary dwelling in an alternative role, a means of experiencing the world of a liturgical 'other' without permanently crossing the boundaries into that world. The young man is actually rather surprised when a part of the liturgy proves to be emotionally charged. Other pilgrims express this ambivalence at the way Walsingham combines affect with spectacle by comparing it to the experience of inhabiting, for a brief period, a fictional, Chaucerian world of conviviality and self-conscious spirituality.

Similar attitudes are evident in comments on the tourist/pilgrim shops in Walsingham. The question is easily raised whether the shops are selling portable embodiments of the charisma of the place or knick-knacks, valued not least because their tastelessness has a ludic if not ludicrous quality, like a stick of rock bought from a seaside resort. Such purchases express the ambiguity of the whole experience for some – they are fun, but not the kind of thing one would indulge in at home. In this sense, the very fact that people feel free to buy goods from religious traditions other than their own is also significant: a number of interviewees have bought icons even though they are not Orthodox, for instance, implying that they feel free to experiment with other religious genres without necessarily being seen entirely to endorse them.

The ludic element of pilgrimage need not be expressed through a revelling in vulgarity, however. Instead, the mixture of genres – secular and sacred, theatrical and liturgical – made available on pilgrimage can be exploited with rather more gravity. One Roman Catholic pilgrim, for instance, talked of a weekend visit with a group of fellow theology students, most of them Anglican. She described a performance of the stations of the cross put on by two of her party, who had previously been drama students:

> This particular weekend it had been snowing, and I think it had snowed the day before and there was ice and still a bit of snow around. ... And [the people who were arranging the pilgrimage] organized these stations of the cross all around the streets and country lanes. ... And ... instead of having visual markers as you would do in the gardens, they acted out the scenes of the stations without announcing them first. ... I thought 'Oh, this is a bit different from hot, dusty Palestine. ... It's going to be a bit funny walking around all these slushy, cold, Norfolk country lanes, pretending that we're dying of the heat in Jerusalem.' But what they actually did was cleverly use the conditions we were actually in – the cold, the damp, and snow – to make the points, to incorporate them into the devotions. And there was one point ... on the corner of the road. ... The man who ... was playing the part of Jesus – he was only wearing shirtsleeves ... and he fell over in the mud, and just got covered. ... And he got up and angrily said 'Oh, I've had enough of this, I'm not going on with it ...' And everybody was just terribly awkward and thinking 'Oh no, what's going to happen next?' And just as he was saying this, one of the students who was standing in the crowd of us ... he just walked out of the group standing there, and took off his coat ... and put it on him, and suddenly we all realised that was Simon of Cyrene taking the cross. ... It was extraordinarily effective.

This example refers to a collective experience, as the boundaries between drama, liturgy and 'real life' are skilfully broken down. The effectiveness of the performance seems to lie in its geographical and liturgical variations on standard enactments of the stations. Convention is made to refer indexically to the unique group of pilgrims present – a group that may never gather again in the same way, unlike the parishes described earlier. Most strikingly, of course, the boundaries between performance and audience are transgressed through an action that appears out of place, but is then reassimilated within sacred narrative, as the identity of Simon of Cyrene is established. The device of making the audience/participants feel that the actors have come out of character has an effect very different to usual notions of the way ritual works: it explicitly incorporates the unexpected. The result is not so much irony as 'serious' play.

One can re-examine this analysis in the light of Peacock's (1990) argument, developed partially in relation to primitive Baptists, but also supposedly the general traditions of western salvation religions, that the notion of performing the sacred is almost an oxymoron. For Peacock, to perform is a sign of inauthenticity, an indication of the triumph of stylized form over meaning. What is going on in the theatrical performance of the stations of the cross is admittedly a partial denial of the legitimacy of fixed ritual located in the conventional spaces of Walsingham. Yet the ritual is very far from the conscious denial of dramatic form and cultivation of spontaneity characteristic of, say, primitive Baptism. In one sense the ritual focuses attention on itself as performance, an activity staged for the group clearly different from anything done before or since, but explicitly modelled on and parallel with following the stations of the cross. The enactment of the stations thus presents an ambiguous Janus-face to convention: it takes place at one remove from the Anglican or Roman Catholic site geographically and liturgically, yet is sufficiently close to be encompassed by the space and time of a pilgrimage to Walsingham. It would not have been the same if it had been staged one winter afternoon in the London districts of Islington or Putney. The event thereby remains faithful (albeit probably unwittingly) to one tradition at Walsingham, that of transformation through a kind of semi-replication – a practice we have also seen in the various versions of the Holy House, or multiple images of the Virgin. After all, Walsingham itself – 'England's Nazareth' – has made its name as an East Anglian appropriation and transformation of a place in Palestine: the village provides not merely a flexible stage for pilgrimage performances, but also easy if vicarious access to a mythically charged, biblical landscape.

The kind of performance being described here is therefore a little different from the revelling in campness described earlier. Both forms of play provide ways of distancing oneself from convention, but to be camp is merely to exaggerate the traditional forms of liturgy, whereas this performance actually recreates liturgy. Interestingly, the latter, perhaps because it is so much more personalized in form, seems largely devoid of irony – extraordinarily effective rather than two-dimensional fun.

Neither set of attitudes is revolutionary, however, in the sense of implementing a permanent transformation of official pilgrimage liturgy: rather, both actually require the presence of canonical forms as symbols and actions against which to define themselves. Such canonical forms are useful resources, therefore, but are not to be taken as the only divinely sanctioned means to achieve powerful religious experiences. Indeed, it seems significant that so many of those interviewed even regarded the original legend of Mary sending a message to Richeldis, or the early history of the site, as essentially irrelevant to the site's importance for them. The significance of pilgrimages for more 'playful' visitors lies in its ability to become a cipher for the cultivation of powerful personal or group experiences. Like 'parish' pilgrims, they see Walsingham as providing an arena for the consolidation of social relationships. However, they are less concerned with the collective affirmation of commonality in belief, faith and practice, and more interested in a celebration of idiosyncratic, perhaps temporary social formations (such as the particular group of Anglican and Roman Catholic theology students mentioned above, or relationships between just two people) or even in the cultivation of entirely personalized experiences.

Thus both kinds of pilgrim are likely to agree that Walsingham acts, as one interviewee put it, like a 'pressure cooker' for human relationships, but their forms of sociality and, often, frames of ritual performance are likely to differ. One pilgrim, a deaconess who is opposed to the shrine's opposition to women priests, noted how she had spent much of her time meditating on her own in the Holy House; only towards the end of her interview did she actually remember that her pilgrimage group had included not only personal friends, but also an entire parish from south London, so little an impact had the latter made on her memory of her visit. She also stated of the site:

> I have a sneaking suspicion that Walsingham is probably like Scottish culture and Celtic Christianity. They're both inventions of the nineteenth century.... I don't think it matters. I think it expresses something we want to express and can express through that place.... It would be false to say this is something we've inherited unchanged from the medieval period. Actually, we've invented it for ourselves.

Such a statement, especially from a member of the clergy, would probably seem puzzling to her fellow pilgrims from south London. Yet it states eloquently the idea predominant among some visitors that pilgrimage derives its value from being constantly reinvented in performance rather than becoming a fetishized container of fixed structures of authority.

Concluding remarks

Hastrup notes that 'whenever we orientate ourselves in place, we actively constitute a space' (1994: 225). In this chapter, we have traced some of the ways in which various pilgrims to Walsingham use ostensibly the same site to constitute very different spaces for performance. 'Canonical' and 'ironic' forms of pilgrimage present alternative ways to incarnate symbolic action:

in one, the individual and group attempt a perfect replication of sacramental liturgy; in the other, ritual practices are modified either through exaggeration or through more active types of transformation. Very broadly, it might be said that canonical ritual performance is partially about the self-conscious location of the particular (a certain group of pilgrims) in the general (the authorized rituals of a nationally renowned site of Christian worship). On the other hand much ironic ritual performance is about making the general (the liturgical forms offered by the shrines) adapt to and accommodate itself to the particular demands and experimental whims of the group or individual.

While the presence of irony implies a degree of deliberately cultivated fun as well as a mixing of performance genres, it should not be assumed that the presence of entertainment and theatre necessarily implies a lack of performative efficacy. For some of the pilgrims we discuss, certain rituals only become effective when invested with a certain playfulness and distance from conventional forms, while liturgy as well as drama are only valued in so far as they can provide effective means through which to express personal meanings or ritualize particular social formations. Schechner (1993: 27) has noted how play, as a western category, has often been tainted by implications of unreality, duplicity and inconsequentiality. Like him, we argue that it can, however, be valued by some performers of ritual precisely because of its provisionality, its ability to experiment with alternative forms of identity and action. Handelman (1990: 63–6) also discusses play in relation to ritual, linking it with qualities of indeterminacy and process. Again, in some ironic pilgrimages we see how ambivalence as to the status and value of conventional liturgy is translated into performances moving between genres of the conventionally sacred and secular, the predictable and unpredictable, the newly created and the traditionally inherited.

Of course, pilgrimage is likely to provide fertile ground for any researcher interested in the role of play in ritual, given that as a rite of passage it tends to incorporate ludic elements. However, our paper attempts to separate out particular context- and culture-bound aspects of the ludic in pilgrimage ritual. What is striking about canonical pilgrims is the way they regard much of what they do at Walsingham as an earnest reassertion of orthodoxy. In a national context where Anglo-Catholicism in particular, but also Christian commitment in general, are relatively peripheral activities on an everyday level, going to Walsingham provides the opportunity to take a holiday from being liturgically and spiritually marginal, in the company of an unusually high concentration of like-minded others. The playful aspects of such pilgrimage thus tend to be sharply separated from the serious business of engaging in powerfully charged liturgy. When viewed in the light of such attitudes, ironic pilgrims – somewhat ironically – seem almost more conventional as pilgrims given their Chaucerian stress on secular fun combined with spiritual devotions.

Our distinction between the canonical and the ironic has some resonances with Turner's (1982) differentiation between liminal and liminoid realms of experience. Walsingham offers to certain pilgrims something of the obligatory, corporate, cyclical elements of the liminal, in both its celebration of the official liturgical year and its incorporation of regular annual visits by parish groups. It also provides space for more obviously optative, liminoid and even commoditized forms of liturgical as well as touristic freedom. The distinction can also be phrased in relation to Walsingham in terms of an ideal-typical contrast between 'tradition' (which, even if 'invented', sets a value on a supposed continuity with the past) and 'heritage', a consumer-friendly, postmodern pastiche of styles (cf. Chaney 1994). Along with other contemporary ritual forms (cf. Boissevain 1992, Crain 1992), pilgrimages to Walsingham are partially supported and revived by the practices of a modernity shading into postmodernity, such as the cultivation of leisure, consumption and the commercialized 'staging' of culture, and are thereby sometimes transformed into objects of play, displaced from conventional temporal or liturgical frames.

Pilgrims to Walsingham are not the only contemporary participants in ritual forms to use irony and/or pastiche consciously in order to cultivate personally meaningful experiences and performances. Bowman (1993), for instance, describes how Glastonbury, itself a pilgrimage site, provides a kind of multivalent, shifting, spiritual service industry for its many Christian and New Age visitors. Luhrmann (1989) argues that part of the attraction of pagan movements lies in their capacity to allow practitioners to combine religious traditions in novel, often deliberately theatrical combinations, in order to create an imaginatively satisfying link with the past. An examination of ritual performance at Walsingham may thus lead into much wider, comparative considerations of the role of the personal and the institutional, the innovative and the apparently fixed, in the simultaneous enactment and transformation of cultural forms.

Notes

1 As Brook points out, the outstanding term in French for watching a play is 'assister' – a creative collaboration of performers and their audience (1968: 155–6). To an extent much greater than with a theatre audience, pilgrims to Walsingham write their own scripts and perform their own ritual plays, which may or may not intersect with official ceremonial.
2 Processions to the priory ruins on major pilgrimage days attract thousands of visitors.
3 The Orthodox are actually granted a small space in an upper room of the Anglican shrine church.
4 It can be argued that the narrative reconstruction of a performance is very different to the performance itself. However, as noted, we have combined interviews with observation of and participation within rituals. In addition, interviews give us access to points of performance that pilgrims feel to have been especially significant.

5 One of us was present when a parishioner and a priest attempted to explain the significance of Walsingham. The parishioner, having described the perfection of the place and her parish's annual pilgrimage there, was clearly both discomfited and annoyed when her own parish priest proceeded to describe the generational differences between pilgrims and expressed his opinion that a number of previous administrators and guardians of the Anglican shrine were slightly lunatic.

6 Some similarities should become evident with the notions of restricted versus elaborated codes in ritual (developed by Douglas (1973), drawing on Bernstein's (1965) work on language). Canonical performances are 'restricted' in the sense that they assume that all participants will be party to the same essential assumptions about the nature of their faith. Ironic performances are more geared to the articulation of unique experiences within the performance of ritual itself. It is tempting to claim, in line with the Bernstein/Douglas argument, that differences in ritual can be related to class differences between ritual performers at Walsingham. Undoubtedly, 'parish' pilgrimages tend to have a large number of working-class participants, whilst the more innovative or ironic forms of participation we describe have often come from more clearly middle-class sources. However, rigid distinctions along these lines should be avoided, not least as the same person may engage in both forms of pilgrimage at different times in her or his life.

7 The terms 'canonical' and 'ironic' are used by the authors, rather than pilgrims themselves. They are intended to indicate one – but not the only – dimension of contrast between styles of performing pilgrimage at Walsingham. By its very nature, the category of 'ironic' pilgrims is extremely internally heterogeneous.

References

Bell, C. (1992) *Ritual Theory, Ritual Practice*, Oxford: Oxford University Press.

Bernstein, B. (1965) 'A socio-linguistic approach to social learning', in J. Gould (ed.) *Penguin Survey of the Social Sciences*, London: Penguin.

Bloch, M. (1974) 'Symbol, song, dance and features of articulation: is religion an extreme form of traditional authority?', *European Journal of Sociology*, 15: 55–81.

Boissevain, J. (ed.) (1992) *Revitalizing European Rituals*, London: Routledge.

Bowman, M. (1993) 'Drawn to Glastonbury', in I. Reader and T. Walter (eds) *Pilgrimage in Popular Culture*, London: Macmillan.

Brook, P. (1968) *The Empty Space*, Harmondsworth: Penguin.

Chaney, D. (1994) *The Cultural Turn: Scene-Setting Essays on Contemporary Cultural History*, London: Routledge.

Coleman, S. and Eisner, J. (1995) *Pilgrimage: Sacred Travel and Sacred Space in the World Religions*, London: British Museum Press, Cambridge MA: Harvard University Press.

Crain, M. (1992) 'Pilgrims, "yuppies", and media men: the transformation of an Andalusian pilgrimage', in J. Boissevain (ed.) *Revitalizing European Rituals*, London: Routledge.

Douglas, M. (1973) *Natural Symbols: Explorations in Cosmology*, London: Barrie and Jenkins.

Duncan, C. (1995) *Civilizing Rituals: Inside Public Art Museums*, London: Routledge.

Eade, J. and Sallnow, M. (eds) (1991) *Contesting the Sacred: The Anthropology of Christian Pilgrimage*, London: Routledge.

Gross, D. (1971) 'Ritual and conformity: a religious pilgrimage to northeastern Brazil', *Ethnology*, 10: 129–48.
Handelman, D. (1990) *Models and Mirrors: Towards an Anthropology of Public Events*, Cambridge: Cambridge University Press.
Hastrup, K. (1994) 'Anthropological knowledge incorporated: discussion', in K. Hastrup and P. Hervik (eds) *Social Experience and Anthropological Knowledge*, London: Routledge.
Lewis, G. (1980) *Day of Shining Red: An Essay on Understanding Ritual*, Cambridge: Cambridge University Press.
Luhrmann, T. M. (1989) *Persuasions of the Witch's Craft: Ritual Magic and Witchcraft in Present-Day England*, Oxford: Blackwell.
Peacock, J. L. (1990) 'Ethnographic notes on sacred and profane performance', in R. Schechner and W. Appel (eds) *By Means of Performance: Intercultural Studies of Theatre and Ritual*, Cambridge: Cambridge University Press.
Rappaport, R. (1974) 'Obvious aspects of ritual', *Cambridge Anthropology*, 2(1): 3–69.
Sallnow, M. (1981) 'Communitas reconsidered: the sociology of Andean pilgrimage', *Man*, n.s., 16: 163–82.
Schechner, R. (1993) *The Future of Ritual: Writings on Culture and Performance*, London: Routledge.
Schieffelin, E. (1995) 'On failure and performance', in C. Laderman and M. Roseman (eds), *The Performance of Healing*, London: Routledge.
Turner, V. W. (1982) 'Liminal to liminoid, in play, flow and ritual: an essay in comparative symbology', in *From Ritual to Theatre: The Human Seriousness of Play*, New York: PAJ Publications.
—— and Turner, E. (1978) *Image and Pilgrimage in Christian Culture: Anthropological Perspectives*, Oxford: Blackwell.
Wolf, E. (1958) 'The Virgin of Guadelupe: a Mexican national symbol', *Journal of American Folklore*, 71 (1): 34–9.

87

PERSISTENT PEREGRINATION

From Sun Dance to Catholic pilgrimage among Canadian Prairie Indians

Alan Morinis

Source: Alan Morinis (ed.), *Sacred Journeys: The Anthropology of Pilgrimage* (Contributions to the Study of Anthropology, 7), New York: Greenwood Press, 1992, pp. 101–13.

The cultural contents of pilgrimage centers and practices tend to be highly malleable, changing in reflection of the social and cultural trends within the field of the pilgrimage. In contrast, traditions of sacred journeying and ceremonial gathering tend to be remarkably enduring, although the ostensible purposes, end-goals, and practices undertaken show enormous variation, even within cultures and within single pilgrimages over time. This contention is borne out by tracing the persistence of pilgrimage practice through eras of social and cultural upheaval. The revival of sacred journeys of the Maoris (Chapter 12) reflects this phenomenon. The following chapter provides a classic example of this type. The Plains Indians of Canada in the nineteenth century developed an extensive ceremonial life that had as a main pillar a tradition of ritual gatherings. The colonial incursions, made especially devastating by the destruction of the buffalo herds in the early 1880s, led to the abandonment of these annual "Sun Dances". Within only a few years, however, the tribes began to gather once again, only now for a Catholic pilgrimage to a mission shrine. There are today about a dozen such shrines patronized by Plains Indians. The popularity of these pilgrimages is due in no small measure to the tradition of summer ceremonial gathering practiced until only one hundred years ago by the pagan ancestors of today's devout Catholics. Although this persistence of pilgrimage has never before been documented on the Canadian Plains, it is well known in Latin America, where (unlike in the Canadian case) contemporary Catholic shrines stand on sites of pre-Columbian sacred places.

In 1887, while on home leave in his native Brittany from his missionary station in northern Alberta, Father Jean-Marie Lestanc paid a visit to the famous shrine of Ste-Anne d'Auray. His prayers at the shrine were rewarded by a vision of Ste. Anne herself, who called on him to establish a shrine in her honor in his remote Canadian mission territory. The priest hurried back to Canada and threw himself into the construction work. The shrine he built received its first group of seventy-one pilgrims in 1889 (Drouin 1973: 52).

Father Lestanc was a member of the Oblates of Mary Immaculate, a missionary order that has established itself in western Canada and works among Indians and Metis. The first mission station west of Manitoba had been established in 1884 at a lake called Manitou Sakahigan by the Woodland Cree, in whose territory it lay. The founding priest, Father Thibault, who renamed the lake as Lac Ste.-Anne (the original meaning of the Cree name was "spirit lake," although the missionaries translated it as Devil's Lake), was not himself an Oblate, but his famous successor Father Albert Lacombe in 1855 became a novitiate of that order (cf. Hughes 1911; Breton 1955). From that date to the present Lac Ste.-Anne has been under the administration of the Oblates. It was at Lac Ste.-Anne that Father Lestanc established his promised shrine in 1887.

In the past century about fifteen Catholic shrines have been founded on the Canadian Prairies. Although both Indians and non-Indians visit these shrines on their summer celebration days, Indian pilgrims overwhelmingly predominate. Even Lac Ste.-Anne, which is visited by many non-Indians and which until 1971 reserved separate days for Indian and White pilgrims, is today much more heavily attended by Indians. In this chapter I seek reasons to account for the rise and popularity of these pilgrimages among a people that has only been Catholic for one hundred years. My contentions are two: (1) these pilgrimages were established at an historical moment when traditional Indian summer gatherings had been recently abandoned, leaving a gaping cultural void into which the new religion stepped, and (2) the new gatherings performed and continue to perform many of the social and cultural functions of the pre-missionary summer assemblies that were the high point of the social calendar among all Prairie Indian tribes. The contemporary pilgrimages are functional extensions of the traditional gatherings that had, in another cultural era, become central social events of great significance to the Plains Indian tribes. It is this transmutation of the pilgrimage traditions that I call persistent peregrination.

Pilgrimage is a practice defined by its structure—the journey to the sacred place—and not by the content of symbols, meaning, rituals, and so on, that fills in the structure. Pilgrimages tend to persist through cultural change because the structure can continue to exist while accommodating new, even radically different cultural contents. We can find examples from around the world where pilgrimages have undergone transformation with every succeeding cultural generation but have nevertheless remained popular because people continue to seek out the salving ideal that stands beyond space and time in the sacred place. What is considered "sacred" or "ideal" will change with time, but that these qualities are accessible in special locations situated beyond the sphere of everyday life—the basic belief underlying all pilgrimage systems—continues to motivate journeys to sacred places. So long as the character of God is malleable, the same sites or an enduring tradition of sacred journeying can continue to serve pilgrims' goals throughout history.

Pre-missionary summer gatherings

The Indians of the Plains are known to have obtained horses by the eighteenth century at the latest (Wissler 1914). This acquisition transformed subsistence foragers into extraordinarily capable buffalo hunters. An era of abundance followed, and with abundance came a florescence of culture.

All of the buffalo-hunting peoples of the Plains celebrated an elaborate annual pageant that was the high point of the social calendar. In summer the buffalo herds converged because of the abundance of pasture, and in consequence all of the dispersed bands of hunters and gatherers could come together in a full assembly of the tribe. This gathering, known in the literature as the Sun Dance, after the sun-gazing rituals performed by the Oglala Sioux, showed a good deal of ritual variation from tribe to tribe among the twenty groups that practiced the annual gathering (Wissler 1918; Spier 1921). I will deal briefly with two of the cultural groups that concern us in the next section: the Cree and the Blackfoot.

David Mandelbaum says of the Plains Cree Sun Dance: "Late in June or early July the scattered sections of a band, or even several bands, converged to the preappointed places where the ceremony was to be held. The great encampment might hold together for two weeks or even longer, if there were buffalo herds in the vicinity" (1940: 203–4). The focus of the dance was the individual who pledged to undergo austerities and often self-inflicted tortures in fulfillment of a vow. The entire event involved much prescribed ritual and could last several weeks: "This occasion was the outstanding event of the ceremonial calendar. Large encampments, often of several bands, gathered in June or July to participate. It was a time for a great spurt of social activity; other dances were held; gambling and games went on continually; it was the ideal period for courtship" (Mandelbaum 1940: 265).

Other reports on the Cree Sun Dance are similar (e.g., Skinner 1914). Pliny Goddard cites a report concerning the Cree in Saskatchewan: "The sun dance marks the yearly gathering of people whom the exigencies of life compel to spend the fall and winter in isolation, and it is looked forward to as such. The young make and the old renew acquaintances, and it is a general holiday" (1919: 307).

Of the Sun Dance among the Blackfoot, John McLean says, 'The most important sacred festival of the Blackfeet is the Sun-Dance" (1887–1888: 231).

He goes on to describe the religious rituals that took place in the midsummer gatherings of an estimated 2,000 people that he observed.

Clark Wissler also comments on the importance of the Sun Dance to the Blackfoot. "In winter," he observes, "the tribes scattered out, usually two to five bands in a camp, often miles apart" (1918: 268). At the approach of summer, messengers would go out to tell the bands where the summer gathering would be held, and with the coming of summer they would assemble in one large camp circle: "The camp circle is intimately associated with the sun dance" (268). Wissler concludes, "The sun dance was for the Blackfoot a true tribal festival, or demonstration of ceremonial functions, in which practically every important ritual owner and organization had a place" (229).

George Dorsey predicted in 1910 that "with the disappearance of tribal organizations and tribal interests, there is no doubt of the ultimate doom of the Sun Dance" (1910: 649–52). Dorsey did not foresee the enduring strength of tribal identity, which has kept the Sun Dance alive into the present (cf. Dusenberry 1962; Liberty 1980). Nor did he anticipate the transmutation of the summer tribal gathering into an intertribal pilgrimage, in reflection of a new pan-Indian identity, involving Christian elements and a new set of Indian interests beyond the tribal.

Catholic pilgrimages of the Prairie tribes

Little research has been done on the Catholic shrines that are dotted across the Canadian Prairies. In 1983 I attended the largest and longest of these gatherings, at Lac Ste.-Anne.[1] Data on other pilgrimages, although scanty, are available and were examined in the archives of the Oblate Fathers in Edmonton.[2] I will concentrate almost exclusively on the case of Lac Ste.-Anne. Map 1 shows the names and locations of the twelve most important of the contemporary Prairie Indian pilgrimages.

The pilgrimage to Lac Ste.-Anne was founded in 1889 at a time when the Indian tribes of the Plains were under great physical and cultural stress. The preceding decade had seen the complete extermination of the buffalo herds that had been the central pillar of the peoples' way of life (1877–1880), the encroachment of the railways and White settlers, epidemics (one outbreak of smallpox around this time caused over 3,000 deaths in a population estimated to be 26,000), the signing of the treaties (1876 and 1877), the Riel uprising and subsequent suppression (1885), along with other wars and skirmishes, and the devastation bred or at least exacerbated by the increasing flow of the alcohol trade. These simultaneous pressures brought the culture of the Indian tribes to the edge of total collapse, a situation in which any and all support was welcome. The missionary fathers, who had been working among the Plains Indians since the 1840s and who had already achieved a good measure of support from the tribes and their leaders, loomed large as a steadfast group of friends on whom the Indians could lean.

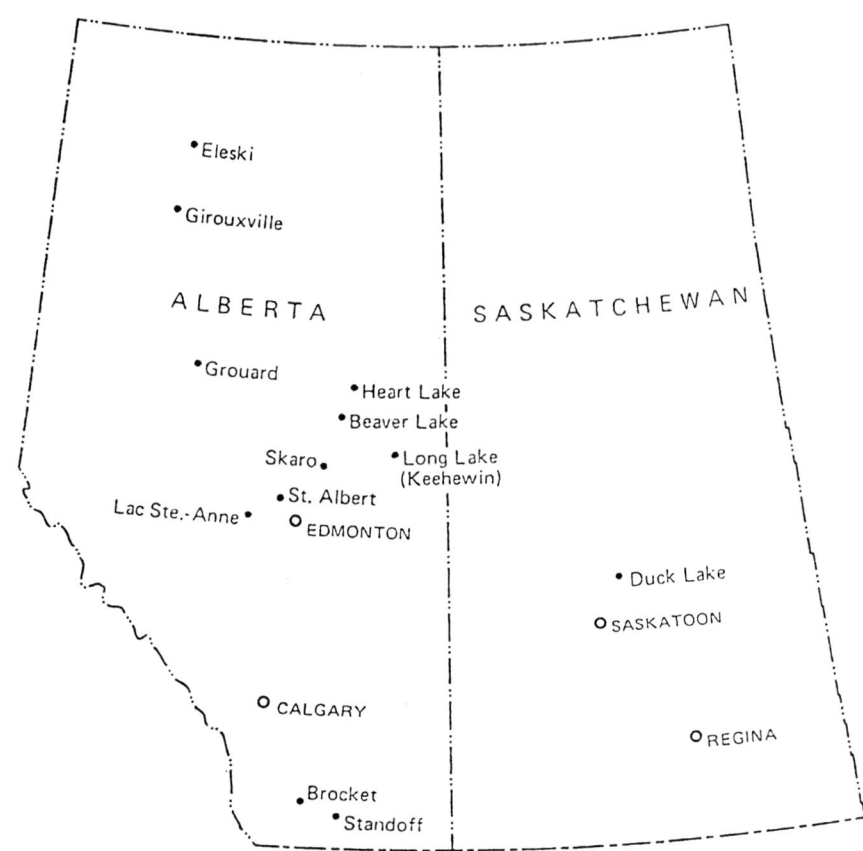

Map 1 Indian pilgrimages on the Canadian Prairies.

The priests had been doctoring, teaching, preaching, marrying, and burying the Indians for forty years before they were called upon to be allies at a time of near-total devastation.

The mission at Lac Ste.-Anne, established in 1844, was the first mission west of Manitoba. At the time of the founding of the pilgrimage it had begun to go into eclipse, but the centre was reinvigorated by the new attraction of the shrine. The official story of the origin of the shrine, as mentioned above, tells of an instruction given by Ste. Anne in a vision had by a missionary. The pilgrims themselves tell different stories. The most common tale of the origin of the shrine that I was told during the 1983 pilgrimage was that in the 1880s a tremendous grass fire swept the Prairies and drove people and animals to flight. When the fleeing people reached the mission station at Lac Ste.-Anne, the priest led them in prayer, and subsequently rain fell, extinguishing the fire. It is said that rain is expected during the pilgrimage and is welcome.

The first pilgrimage, in 1889, attracted 71 pilgrims. By 1891 over 400 pilgrims attended. Numbers reached 1,200 in 1906, 4,000 in 1927, and 20,000 in 1982. A relic of Ste. Anne was obtained in 1896, and after this was destroyed in a fire in 1928, another was obtained. There are presently two. The large, modern shrine building was constructed in 1979.

The shrine building is the focal point of the physical arrangements at Lac Ste.-Anne. It is a large structure, open on three sides, with seating for 3,000. The closed side protects the altar and a large statue of Ste. Anne and her daughter Mary. A rustic quality has been given by building the facing and back of the altar of split logs. To each side of the altar hang banners depicting Indian images such as a tipi and pipe, bearing slogans such as "God Sent His Son to Pitch His Tent With Us" and "I Long for God as a Deer Longs for Cool Water."

The shrine is encircled by small huts, each depicting a scene from Christ's ascent to the Crucifixion. During the days of the pilgrimage priests sit and hear confession in these huts. On the last night, a procession is made of this Way of the Cross. A statue of Ste. Anne stands near the front gate to the shrine territory. Many pilgrims arriving or departing stop at this statue, touch one hand to its feet, lower their heads, and pray silentiy.

The remainder of the mission land is hay-field, leading down to the lakeside. This hay is cut just before the pilgrimage, and for a period of a week before the event, early travelers are arriving and pitching camp in the fields. Old photos of the pilgrimage show tipis, tents, and wagons. Today's encampment is of trailers, recreational vehicles, campers, and tents.

The largest contingent of Indians at the gathering is Cree from Saskatchewan, Alberta, the Northwest Territories, and the northern American states. Next in number are the Chipewyan, followed by the Blackfoot and Dogrib. Although the shrine is located immediately adjacent to the territory and reserves of the Stoney, these people do not attend the pilgrimage because they were missionized by Protestants. In 1983 confession was heard in English, French, Cree, and Chipewyan, and sermons were preached in these languages plus Blackfoot. The Dogrib people from the northern center of Fort Rae have been attending the pilgrimage only for the last few years, and their language is not used in public ceremonies. Other Catholic tribes, such as the Blood and the Peigan, were few at Lac Ste.-Anne because of the occurrence of a pilgrimage at Brocket, Alberta, closer to their reserves. There may, as well, be some legacy of the traditional hostilities that plagued relations between the Cree and members of the Blackfoot Confederacy.

The ritual of the pilgrimage is structured to represent a version of the human life cycle, over a twenty-four hour period. Although pilgrims have been arriving for a week previously and have been camped in large numbers on Sunday and Monday, the ritual of the pilgrimage begins Tuesday afternoon. Previous to this point there have only been mass in the shrine and the blessing of objects by priests. On Tuesday afternoon the pilgrimage proper is initiated by a local bishop who leads a procession down to the lake for a blessing of the waters. In his sermon he invokes the many practical and symbolic roles played by water, but he stresses the role of water in baptism. He calls upon the gathered crowd to renew its vows of baptism and begins the pilgrimage with an invocation of a new spiritual birth.

In small groups people, fully clothed, wade into the lake. Some go in only to a shallow depth, but others walk out along the gently sloping lake bed to reach a submerged rock, which is believed to have imprinted on it the footprints of Ste. Anne. The more devout or those wanting a special intercession from Ste. Anne submerge up to the neck and remain in the water for up to half an hour. On the shore men and women chant the hymn to Ste. Anne in Cree and set a meditative mood for the immersion. As this mood passes, bathers begin to return to shore, bringing with them bottles that have been filled with the blessed lake water and reedy lake grass that will be kept and burned as needed, to invoke this powerful moment of the pilgrimage.

Lac Ste.-Anne's shrine has developed a reputation for miraculous cures. At least thirty such cures have been recorded in the *Codex Historicus* (Drouin 1973: 89–91). Bathing in the lake is considered to be an especially efficacious means to bring about a miraculous cure, and so many of the bathers who go deepest and remain longest, especially those congregated around Ste. Anne's underwater rock, are in need of curing. One young man I observed had been brought from Horse Lake, Saskatchewan, to bathe in the hopes of being cured of paralysis that he had suffered in a snowmobiling accident the previous winter.

It would seem that bathing fully clothed, as the pilgrims do, serves to distinguish this act of ritual immersion from ordinary playful or functional uses of water. Many symbolic interpretations could be ventured to explain the attraction of bathing in clothes at this ceremony, but since none was provided by participants themselves, these interpretations would be only speculative.

Wednesday there are regular masses in the shrine, as well as special benedictions for the sick. On the front wall of the shrine hang several canes and crutches made of hand-hewn tree branches and reportedly left behind by healed pilgrims. The collection of canes and crutches is reported to have been much larger, but many were destroyed in the fire of 1928.

With the setting of the sun comes the next special event, the procession of the Way of the Cross. A priest leads a crowd of several thousand on a re-creation of the final journey of Christ to his Crucifixion. At each station, the event is told and a moral concerning steadfastness, effort, generosity, and other Christian virtues is extracted. The procession completes the stations, then proceeds to the cemetery, where the final sermon—on death and the return to God, in His "Happy Hunting Ground," the priest said—is delivered. As the final streaks of light fade into the darkness of night, the pilgrimage closes. It has led participants from a symbolic rebirth through re-baptism, through a microcosmic lifespan in re-creation of the journey of Christ, to a final resting of the body in the graveyard and the risen soul in heaven.

In 1983 the later part of this last night was given over to a Tea Dance, held around a fire just beyond the circle of light cast by the shrine. The drums were beaten and songs were sung by the least acculturated of the Indians—the Dogribs—but participants included members of all the attending tribes. As well, a number of younger priests, who are not averse to participating in Indian ceremonies such as the pipe initiation and the sweat lodge, joined in the early morning shuffling circle of dancers.

Throughout the pilgrimage it was plain that the two traditions represented—the Catholic and the Plains Indian—were two streams that at points converged, at others merged, and at still others diverged. The bathing in the lake, for example, is a point of convergence, since it brings together some pre-missionary aspects of Indian culture with Catholic symbolism. The bathing in the lake is easily assimilated to the Catholic baptism, but the fact that this lake was known as "Spirit Lake" before being renamed by the missionaries suggests that it was held in some reverence in the pre-contact period. Contemporary informants, including some of the priests, hold this view. Convergence is also to be noted in the practice of collecting lake grass, a modification of the traditionally valued sweet grass, during the ritual of re-baptism.

Another point of convergence took place during the Tea Dance. Although during the blessing of the lake the Catholic tradition ruled dominant, the Tea Dance saw the Indian tradition dominant and the priests joining in. The new generation of missionary priests is not averse to participating in Indian cultural events, even of a religious kind, that previous generations of priests would have branded heathen and tried to stamp out. Many of these so-called "buckskin priests" have adopted moccasins and beaded hide jackets and even tanned hide shawls as part of their ritual vestments. One priest attending the pilgrimage wore blue jeans, moccasins, and a buckskin jacket, regularly attended the sweat lodge in his territory, and had recently taken initiation as a pipeholder in the local religious society.

Points of merger were to be seen during the mass. Here Catholic and Indian traditions had merged to create a distinct, synthetic Plains Indian Catholicism in which the two traditions were inextricably intermingled. In sermons, the terms God and Manitou were used interchangeably. From my discussions with both priests and pilgrims I got the impression that the object of the evident devotion of the pilgrims was neither the White man's God nor Manitou but, rather, a single entity with whom they felt comfortable, who was supreme, and who was thus both God and Manitou.

A major point of divergence was to be seen in the conceptions held about the gathering. As evidenced in their sermons, the priests saw this ceremonial as a religious pilgrimage in the Catholic mold. There was much talk about morality, salvation, and the extraordinary benefits to be reaped from having visited a shrine in a year Pope John Paul II had declared a Holy Year. It was obvious when one looked at the crowd, however, that the gathering was at least multipurpose and that, undoubtedly for some, it was not at all religious. Besides the rituals associated with the pilgrimage to the shrine, the following activities and functions were significant aspects of the assembly:

- *Social interaction* For many pilgrims, a primary focus of the gathering was the opportunity to meet with family and friends who might not be encountered at any other time of the year. Even while mass was in progress, many campsites were full of people and their visitors, discussing every aspect of life. Although some young people were evidently devout, many others were completely oblivious to the religious nature of the pilgrimage. For them the occasion was an opportunity for courting, sporting, and social displays.
- *Trading* The gathering was attended by a trader. Pilgrims expected him to be there and brought with them tanned hides and furs to sell. In addition, behind the shrine and over a small stream that separated church land from private property, a fairly large marketplace had been set up for the duration of the pilgrimage. Small, decorative jewelry, pocket-knives, hats, and especially very cheap, used clothing were for sale, along with the odds and ends of a garage or rummage sale.
- *Information exchange* Conversation was constant, and so the gathering created an opportunity for an update on current information of all kinds. Important topics ranged from jobs and income tax to life passages (who died and who was born) and community politics. Considering that the Indian communities are scattered over the large territories of the Prairies, a major gathering will be an occasion for the exchange of all sorts of important personal and social information.
- *Relaxation/holiday* Many of the visitors were regularly employed and had scheduled their annual holidays to be able to attend the pilgrimage. This recreational aspect of the gathering was itself a feature of the social interaction, trading, and information exchange that took place.

These functions of the pilgrimage gathering are, in large measure, reminiscent of the functions performed among the Plains tribes by the annual Sun Dance assemblies. In pilgrimage we find the persistence of the tradition of gathering, as relics and saints have become heir to the Sun Dance poles and lodges as the focus for the personal and social activities of the midsummer meetings. Although some of the functions of the Sun Dance gatherings have been assumed by secular pow-wows, as pointed out by Koozma Tarasoff (1980: 22), the religious core of the pilgrimages makes them the more logical inheritor of the Sun Dance tradition. Pilgrimages can perform the social functions but also provide the religious and spiritual aspects that were an integral part of the Sun Dances. It is probable that pow-wows are now more popular among Protestant Indians, although there is no reason the social aspects of powwows should not appeal to Catholic Indians as well.

Persistent peregrination

In an early article on the remarkable recurrence of what he called ceremonialism among North American Indian tribes, R. H. Lowie reached the conclusion that the ostensible reasons for ceremonies, such as the Kwakiuu potlatch and the Plains Sun Dance, have little connection to the ultimate purpose of the rites. He concluded that ceremony itself, rather than its manifest purpose, such as success in battle or initiation, is the raison d'etre of the events: "We regard its very performance as self-sufficient, as gratifying certain specific non-utilitarian demands of the community. View it not as a primitive religion, or as a primitive attempt to coerce the forces of nature, but as a free show, and the mystification ceases: ceremonialism is recognized as existing for ceremonialism's sake" (1915: 255–56).

This conclusion is overly reductionist, but it does point to the fact that in the Plains cultural area, between groups and within the same group at different eras, great variety was permitted in the composition of ritual gatherings. While the ostensible purpose for gathering should not be dismissed so easily and totally as Lowie makes out, among Plains Indian tribes ceremonial gathering itself was a recurrent social practice in which the content varied considerably to reflect the needs and influences of the particular culture at that moment in its development. Gathering itself was an important feature of the cultural tradition; it was the focal point in the annual cycle of assembly and dispersion that dominated the life pattern of the Plains tribes.

The extermination of the buffalo, combined with the encroaching population and increasingly restrictive regulations of the Europeans (such as pass laws), brought about the temporary end of gathering in the late nineteenth century and so eliminated the crucial hinge of the annual ritual and social cycles. This change opened up a gap in the psycho-cultural environment, the magnitude of which is difficult to conceive, and the dislocation, anxiety, and suffering that inevitably followed the demise of this pillar of the social universe are difficult to imagine. When the opportunity soon arose again—now for a mid-summer Catholic pilgrimage—there was little hesitation to seize the chance. True, the ostensible purpose for gathering was at odds with the Sun Dance or other traditional ceremonials, but times had changed once again, and the acceptance of a new ceremonial content to the gatherings did not present a major obstacle to participation.

Since the Prairie Indians have adopted the practice of pilgrimage, these annual gatherings have taken over from the Sun Dance the role of the focal social assembly, where many non-ritual social functions take place. Of special note is the fact that the pilgrimages, like the Sun Dance gatherings before them, are the meeting-places for a dispersed population and so are the stage for all manners of highly valued social interaction. Without minimizing the importance of the mass and the other Catholic performances at Lac Ste.-Anne, it was clear that chitchat, gossip, romancing, complaining, instructing, and other sorts of everyday social communication took up a great deal of the pilgrims' time and were surely an important aspect of the pilgrimage, as they had been of the Sun Dances. The importance of this function of the gathering is underlined when we remember that it was likely only on this occasion of all the year that families, friends, and acquaintances would rendezvous from their remote reserves and settlements scattered over the vast territory of the Prairies. Clearly there has been cultural change since the days of the Sun Dance, but there is structural continuity as well.

A major difference to be noted between pre-missionary and post-missionary summer gatherings is that the former were almost exclusively tribal and the latter are mostly intertribal. Goddard (1919: 305) notes that the Cree Sun Dance he observed in the early twentieth century was attended by representatives of other tribes, but this was no longer the traditional situation. Already in this case, and even more so in the intertribal Catholic pilgrimages, the constitution of the assembly has changed to reflect the new identity and interests of contemporary Canadian Indians. Exclusively tribal identity has been complemented by a broader concept of pan-Indian identity, within which tribal boundaries still have some—reduced—importance. These boundaries are reinforced by linguistic and cultural differences but are crosscut by other allegiances, such as the ties to the church. Pilgrimages today can be tribal—as in the case of the pilgrimage to the shrine at Standoff, which is exclusively patronized by the Blood—but tend, under the influence of the church, to be intertribal. Here we find that the composition of the assemblage has altered to reflect changing personal and group allegiances, but once again these changes have not disturbed the continuity of the tradition of the mid-summer social gathering.

In some important ways the cultural content of Prairie pilgrimages is similar to what went on in the Sun Dances. Both lay stress on the importance of vows undertaken by individual participants. As is typical of Catholic pilgrimages, many pilgrims come to the shrine to initiate or fulfill vows to Ste. Anne, as intercessor with her grandson Jesus. Although this practice is a common feature of the Catholic tradition, it was also a central feature of the Sun Dance. Mandelbaum notes, "The dance was initiated in fulfillment of a vow" (1940: 265). During my visit to Lac Ste.-Anne I encountered a woman who had walked all the way to the shrine from her home reserve in Saskatchewan province in fulfillment of a promise made to Ste. Anne when her son was very ill.

Both Sun Dance and pilgrimage are concerned with rain, as evidenced in the most commonly heard legend of the origin of the Lac Ste.-Anne pilgrimage as told by the pilgrims themselves and noted as well in the ethnographic record on the Sun Dance. Goddard, writing about the Sun Dance of the Alberta

Cree, remarks, "It seems to be held in part for the purpose of inducing rain" (1919: 306). Mandelbaum says of the Cree Sun Dance: "Prayers for rain were a salient feature of every Sun dance. The pledger continually exhorted his supernaturals to bring on a storm and used every magical device in his power to secure that result" (1940: 270).

There are also cases of continuity in ritual performances. For example, many pilgrims to Lac Ste.-Anne brought objects that they wanted to have blessed by the priests. Besides rosaries and other standard Catholic paraphernalia, pilgrims had wild herbs and traditional medicines for blessing. It was a common feature of the Sun Dance, too, that objects would be brought to receive the blessing of the person undertaking the vow of austerity.

While these manifest continuities from pre- to post-missionary summer gatherings should not be dismissed (it has, after all, been only one hundred years since the first pilgrimages were founded), it is at the level of social functions that the greatest and, to my mind, most significant continuity is to be found.

The case of Prairie Indian pilgrimages is not an isolated instance of persistent peregrination. Catholic missionaries in Latin America and India have taken over indigenous shrines, which they converted to Catholic shrines and to which people continued to come. A similar transformation can be noted in the case of the Arabian tribes that adopted Islam and, with it, pilgrimage to Mecca, which they had been visiting as a sacred place in pre-Islamic times.

It seems that the institution of pilgrimage has a great capacity to endure through the upheavals and shifts of cultural change. The reason, I suggest, lies in the structure of pilgrimage. Although it appears at first sight that the most significant aspect of a pilgrimage is the shrine deity that draws the crowds to the centre, in most cases the character of this deity is malleable. People journey to a place that enshrines some trace of a cultural ideal, usually the greatest ideal, styled God. If the ideological construction of this ideal is malleable, then the ideal will continually change to reflect changing culture, and the pilgrimage will remain popular. Pilgrimage shrines that are conceptually inflexible will retain favor so long as the ideals they house are popular and likely for some time thereafter because traditions die hard (they may even become identified as sites where the ideal past is to be encountered), but eventually they are likely to fade in public esteem as they fall out of step with current ideals and values. It could be said that it is to forestall decline that the gods of the centers are left open to reinterpretation, and because this does happen commonly, pilgrimages tend to be highly persistent practices.

In historical perspective it is clear that an enduring pilgrimage tradition emphasizes the structure of the performance over the contents. At any given moment, the specific contents of the pilgrimage institution, as constituted at that time, will undoubtedly be uppermost in the minds of participants, but it is the persistence of journeying to, and gathering at, shrines, rather than the changing characters of their occupants, that accounts for the endurance of a pilgrimage tradition, over time and through successive eras of cultural change. The stress in understanding pilgrimage then falls on ritual journeys and gatherings rather than on the sacred place itself.

This emphasis is especially pertinent in the case of Plains Indian ritual gatherings, since the actual locations of the Catholic pilgrimages do not coincide with Sun Dance sites (which themselves shifted from year to year). This variation, along with the radical changes brought about by the missionary colonization of Plains Indian culture, has not destroyed the underlying cultural template for ritual journeys and gatherings, which continue to be practiced with altering content into the present. Peregrination is the essence of pilgrimage. In this case peregrination persists through the sweeping transformations that have refashioned Plains Indian culture over the last century because the personal and group satisfactions gained from sacred journeys and ritual gatherings are largely independent of the ideational content of the institutions.

Notes

1 This field trip was made possible by a travel grant from the Canadian Plains Research Centre, Regina, Saskatchewan. I express my gratitude for this support.
2 I would like to express my thanks to Father E. O. Drouin, O.M.I., Archivist of the Oblates in Edmonton, for his invaluable assistance and guidance in this research. My appreciation and thanks go as well to Fr. P.-A. Hudon and Fr. J. M. Lizee for their time and cooperation.

References

Breton, Paul Emile
   1995   *The Big Chief of the Prairies*. Edmonton: Palm.
Dorsey, George A.
   1910   The Sun Dance. In *Handbook of American Indians North of Mexico*. F. W. Hodge (ed.). Bureau of American Ethnology, Bulletin 30, pp. 649–52.
Drouin, E. O.
   1973   *Lac Ste.-Anne Sakahigan*. Edmonton: Editions de l'ermitage.
Dusenberry, Verne
   1962   *The Montana Cree: A Study in Religious Persistence*. Stockholm: Almqvist and Wiksell.
Goddard, Pliny Earle
   1919   Notes on the Sun Dance of the Cree in Alberta. *Anthropological Papers of the American Museum of Natural History*, 16, pp. 295–310.
Hughes, Katherine
   1911   *Father Lacombe: The Black Robe Voyageur*. Toronto: William Briggs.
Lowie, R. H.
   1915   Ceremonialism in North America. In *Anthropology in North America*. F. Boas et. al. (eds.). New York: G. E. Stechart, pp. 229–58.

Skinner, Alanson
   1914   The Sun-Dance of the Plains-Cree. *Anthropological Papers of the American Museum of Natural History*, 16:4, pp. 283–94.

Spier, Leslie
   1921   The Sun Dance of the Plains Indians: Its Development and Diffusion. *Anthropological Papers of the American Museum of Natural History*, 16:7, pp. 451–527.

Tarasoff, Koozma J.
   1980   *Persistent Ceremonialism: The Plains Cree and Salteaux*. Ottawa: National Museum of Man.

Wissler, Clark
   1914   Influence of the Horse in the Development of Plains Culture. *American Anthropologist*, 16:1, pp. 1–25.

Wissler, Clark
   1918   The Sun Dance of the Blackfoot Indians. *Anthropological Papers of the American Museum of Natural History*, 16, pp. 223–70.

88

BERNARD MIZEKI

Missionary saints and the creation of Christian communities

Dana L. Robert

Source: originally published in *Yale Divinity School Library Occasional Publication No. 19*, New Haven, CT: Yale Divinity School Library, 2005; revised by author, 2009.

For mission historians, one of the most interesting problems in a people's identification with Christianity is the role of the missionary. Past generations of historians crafted "big man" theories of mission history.[1] Although there are theological benefits to the "big man" approach, to fixate on the missionary over-simplifies a complex historical process: it fails to do justice to the community whose worldview evolves in response to both internal needs and external influences. Yet to ignore, downplay, or caricature the foreign missionary as a tool of imperialists is not the answer. In notable instances, particular cross-cultural messengers embodied the dialogue that occurs between the universal intent of the Christian faith and a local community. As anthropologists have increasingly noted, "translocal and putatively foreign agents" are themselves important in the production of locality.[2]

The Anglican Bernard Mizeki, the "Apostle of the MaShona," illustrates the paradox of the missionary outsider becoming the consummate insider. Communal mythification of Mizeki exemplified the Christianization process itself. Simultaneously, the process of Christianization shaped people's commitment to their missionary saint. Bernard Mizeki represented the ability of particular communities both to deepen local identities, and to solidify commitment to a world religion. The meanings attached to the missionary by the receptive community are crucial to understanding the missionary founder's role in the gradual process of communal Christian identification. Through this case study I argue that the meaning vested in the missionary over time by the Christian community is often more significant than the details of his or her life. The communal mythification process itself is what distinguishes an ordinary missionary from a "missionary saint."[3]

To take one well-known example, St. Patrick, born a Briton, an uneducated former slave and self-appointed ambassador, was transformed into the patron saint of Ireland. His persistence and spiritual power became the source of legends, as admiring biographers attributed to him miracles and struggles against druid priests, as well as credited him with the ultimate success of Christianity over paganism, as symbolized by the snakes he allegedly expelled from the Emerald Isle. Various representations of Patrick show him battling snakes, or holding a shamrock to symbolize his teachings about the Trinity, or reading and writing. According to a seventh-century life of Patrick, St. Patrick's "breastplate," a *lorica*, or "words of power" for protection against evil forces, purportedly turned him into a deer to escape from a druid king. Later generations believed that reciting the prayer would protect them from evil for twenty-four hours.[4]

In the early Middle Ages, "pilgrimage merged insensibly into mission."[5] The Christianization process of the Irish involved not only religious specialists, but ordinary people who undertook pilgrimages to places overflowing with the spiritual power of Patrick himself. One ancient holy site that was transformed into a destination for Christian pilgrims was the Croagh Patrick, a conical-shaped mountain near Westport, County Mayo. This holy mountain still sees 25,000 pilgrims visiting on "Reek" Sunday each July. According to tradition, Patrick undertook a forty-day Lenten fast there in 441. He prayed, saw visions, and was comforted by divine messengers who assured him Ireland would one day be Christian.[6] Roman Catholic authority over Irish Christianity was also confirmed in popular consciousness by the tradition that Patrick had learned of the consecration of Pope Leo the Great while he was on the mountain. He immediately sent word of his obeisance to the pope and was rewarded by the gift of holy relics from Rome. After blessing the people, and insuring that no snakes could remain in Ireland, Patrick descended the mountain and celebrated Easter with his followers.

The legends of Croagh Patrick are significant not because they are necessarily true in an historical sense, but because they demonstrate how Irish druidism was transformed and fulfilled by Christianity in the name of Patrick. The snake is an embodiment of traditional divinities in many cultures. In these stories from lives of Patrick written several hundred years after his death, Patrick's ministry transforms the pagan holy mountain into a Christian one, drives away a symbol of pagan divinity, suffuses the mountain with holy power and miracles, and also links Irish Christianity to Roman Catholicism. The continued presence of European pilgrims at Croagh Patrick, as well as other sites such as Patrick's purgatory, Lough Derg, an island in a lake in County Donegal, affirms both Irish Christian identity and unity with the rest of Catholic Europe.[7]

Patrick's stature grew in tandem with the shaping of Irish national identity. Patrick the man left two poorly written but passionate documents. Patrick the saint embodied a unified Irish people who paradoxically—and perhaps unreflectively—took their place as part of a multi-cultural and global religious family, which shared in theory, if not in practice, a universal ethic of love and justice under one God. The deeper paradox of St. Patrick's Day is that in celebrating the particularity of Irish identity, it also commemorates their incorporation into a multi-cultural vision of universal community.

Bernard Mizeki, "Apostle to the Shona"

In June of 1996, an estimated 20,000 people gathered in Marondera, Zimbabwe, to commemorate the 100th anniversary of the martyrdom of Bernard Mizeki, an Anglican catechist. Billed as the largest gathering of Anglicans on the continent, the annual Mizeki pilgrimage is also the only regular meeting of the entire Central Africa Province of the Anglican Church. Bishops, priests, and members of indigenous religious communities, Mothers' Unions, laymen from Bernard Mizeki guilds, and ordinary Christians come regularly from Zimbabwe, Zambia, Mozambique, South Africa, and Botswana, as well as occasional delegations from as far away as the United States. At the Centennial Celebration, the Archbishop of Canterbury laid a wreath at Mizeki's shrine. Mizeki's transformation from "native house boy,"[8] to "native teacher,"[9] to "missionary martyr," to "Apostle of the Mashona," and now to "saint" whose feast day is marked June 18 on the Anglican calendar,[10] is a metaphor for the growing self-confidence and identity of Anglican Christians in South Central Africa during the twentieth century.

Bernard Mizeki was born in 1861. His birth name was Mamiyeri Mizeka Gwambe. He was a Shangaan[11] who grew up near the Bay of Inhambane in what became Mozambique. As a young teen curious about the world, he sailed to Cape Town. Around age twenty, with some fellow migrants, he began attending a night school run by a German missionary woman under the aegis of the Cowley Fathers, a young high church Anglican monastic community that sent missionaries to the Cape Colony. Under the influence of Fräulein von Blomberg, Barns struggled with his reading and writing, but he was fascinated by instruction on Scripture and the rudiments of Christianity. Said his teacher, "in everything concerning religion he was always the first and best pupil."[12] Taking the name Bernard, in 1886 he was one of the first group of seven baptized by triune immersion, by the Cowley Fathers in Cape Town, after which he became a mission worker with the Fathers.

After the Berlin Conference of 1884–5, European governments divided the continent into spheres of influence: Rhodes obtained the mineral rights over the vast territory controlled by the Ndebele King Lobengula. At the same time, increased interest in world evangelization was drawing half a dozen Christian denominations to the unevangelized regions of South Central Africa. The struggle for influence in Mashonaland, and the church's uneasy relationship with the European adventurers and settlers who founded Rhodesia, is captured by the comment of missionary David Carnegie in 1889 to the London Missionary Society: "Gold and the gospel are fighting for the mastery, and I fear gold will win."[13]

As part of the race for Rhodesia, Bernard Mizeki was one of several "native catechists" who accompanied Anglican Bishop George Wyndham Hamilton Knight-Bruce on a boat from South Africa to Portuguese East Africa, and then inland to the newly erected Episcopal diocese of Mashonaland in 1891.[14] Already in 1888, Knight-Bruce, then Bishop of Bloemfontein in South Africa, had walked through Mashonaland and negotiated with King Lobengula in hopes of someday being allowed to open missions among the Shona.[15] The Shona had been subjugated and treated as a slave class by the Ndebele since 1840, when Shaka's lieutenant Mzilikazi had invaded and subjected them to a scorched-earth policy. Knight-Bruce opposed the Rudd concession that granted Mashonaland to Cecil Rhodes in exchange for weapons for Lobengula. The bishop negotiated with Shona chiefs to allow missions in their territories. Thus Bernard Mizeki, born in Mozambique, minimally educated in South Africa, and with little knowledge of either the Shona people or their language, was settled in the territory of Chief Mangwende. The only other catechist who could stand the isolated life and remain faithful to the missionary vision, Frank Ziqubu, settled in the territory of Chief Makoni.

Mizeki's ministry among the Shona lasted five years. In that time he proved himself the best linguist of the Anglicans in Rhodesia, mastering Shona within a year. Ultimately he came to know eight African languages, as well as English, Dutch, Portuguese, and some French, Greek, and Latin. In his mission work he itinerated among villagers, led the daily offices of the church, kept a successful garden that included vegetables and flowers, and taught children. One of his attractions for the people was his musical ability; he gave singing lessons and taught hymns. He had a charismatic personality and was liked by both white colonists and Mangwende's people. The senior wife of Chief Mangwende became his special patron, and many royal women were attracted to the mission.[16] In 1895, an itinerant Anglican priest married Bernard to an unbaptized Shona woman, Mutwa, an adopted granddaughter of Chief Mangwende. In that year, Bernard worked in a translation team, putting prayers and Bible portions into Shona.

As Bernard grew more confident in his understanding of Shona customs, he increasingly challenged the work of *ngangas*, the traditional diviner/healers. Through prayer, he opposed their animal sacrifices for healing. He rescued twins and opposed the punishment of witches. He participated in vaccination campaigns and supported western medicine. In religious instruction, he tried to teach the people that *Mwari* was a loving God who listened to people and met their personal needs.[17] As Mizeki gained influence, around 1894 he received permission to found a settlement at a sacred grove on a stream-fed mountain. Bernard removed some of the sacred trees and planted a large garden and experimental wheat crop. He protected his garden from the traditional spirits by carving crosses into trees around its perimeter. These spiritual and economic challenges to the traditional spirit mediums—opposing their healing practices, desecrating a sacred grove, using crosses to fence off the movement of ancestors across the land, and drawing followers to the new ways—proved to be fatal when in 1896 the Shona rebelled against the British.

With the founding of Rhodesia in 1893, it became apparent that the British had come to stay. Although the Shona had been brutally subjugated by the Ndebele, they nevertheless saw the British defeat of Lobengula as a deeper challenge to their way of life, especially when Rhodesia imposed such things as a hut tax, disease control, and the branding of cattle. Incorporation into the colonial economy gave the advantage to modernizers like Mizeki, who had salaries and access to western commodities. Led by traditionalist spirit mediums and a series of directives from the high god in the Matopo Hills, the Ndebele revolted against the British and the Shona soon followed.[18] As the uprising began, Mizeki was warned to leave his mission and take refuge in a safer location. But with a pregnant wife, and as benefactor of his small village, Mizeki wrote, "Mangwende's people are suffering. The Bishop has put me here and told me to remain. Until the bishop returns, here I must stay. I cannot leave my people now in a time of such darkness."[19] After midnight on June 18, 1896, three of Chief Mangwende's male relatives came to the mission, stabbed Bernard with a spear, and left him for dead.[20] Mizeki managed to crawl to the nearby stream of water and wash his wounds. His wife Mutwa and another woman went to his hut to gather blankets and make him some gruel. As they later testified, when they walked back up the mountain, they saw a blinding white light and heard a noise like many birds' wings where Bernard lay.[21] When they looked again, he had disappeared and his body was never found. One month later, his closest student, John Kapuya, accepted baptism as the first Shona convert of the Anglican mission.

Because Cecil Rhodes gave mission lands to the Anglican Church, Mangwende's territory remained under Anglican control after the suppression of the rebellion. In 1899, a white Anglican priest returned to the site of Mizeki's mission and built a small school for boys. Sometime in the early twentieth century, Father Ernest Simpson tentatively identified the site of the martyrdom, painted a cross there, and held an annual service on June 18. Then in 1933, Father Edwin Crane found the floor of a hut underneath collapsed ruins that some elderly people identified as the location of Mizeki's hut. Over this place of martyrdom, Crane built a circular shrine, with an altar, elevated above the original mud floor. On June 21, 1938, about a thousand Africans and a hundred Europeans celebrated a high mass at the dedication of the shrine. In 1946, for the fiftieth anniversary of Mizeki's martyrdom, six hundred persons attended, including two bishops and many clergy, and a message was read from the Governor of Rhodesia. Two thousand communicants participated, including Mizeki's widow and daughter as guests of honor.

Africans outnumbered Europeans as participants, but the formal communion celebration marking the Mizeki anniversary remained under the control of white bishops and clergymen well into the mid-twentieth century. The Cowley Fathers promoted his cult wherever they did mission work. White prelates sang his praises as an exemplary convert, who in traveling the road from convert to martyr remained faithful to his missionary calling. Although Mizeki's faithfulness to the Shona people was heralded as the reason for why he was considered a martyr, his popularity among white Anglicans remained assured because he had also been faithful to them. He had maintained deep friendships with white colonists and priests, and he remained where the bishop had placed him. In the views of historians Terence Ranger and Janet Hodgson, the Mizeki site was promoted as part of an early twentieth-century pilgrimage strategy to create "a new mystical geography" that would cement African loyalty to Anglicanism. From a white Rhodesian perspective, the non-racial shrine "could be used to foster loyalty to cross and crown. Mizeki thus became the prototype Christian colonial citizen."[22]

The white Archbishop of the new Province of Central Africa first visited the shrine in 1960 and acted as celebrant and preacher with the white Bishop of Mashonaland. The diocese authorized an official biography of Mizeki, which was published in 1966 as *Mashonaland Martyr* by Jean Farrant. By the time of the book's publication, memorials to Mizeki in South Africa, Rhodesia, Botswana, and Swaziland included half a dozen stained-glass windows, two reliquaries, several murals and carvings, half a dozen churches and schools bearing his name, and the inclusion of his name on the Anglican provincial calendars of South and Central Africa.

But the nationalist struggles of the 1960s and 1970s undercut the neatly defined colonial appropriation of Mizeki. In 1961 Rhodesian Bishop Cecil Alderson reinterpreted Mizeki as a prophet, a "forerunner of the African nationalist intellectual."[23] In a concession to Shona theologies of ancestral intervention, Alderson by the mid-1960s was also arguing that African belief in the intervention of ancestors was consistent with Christian beliefs in the intervention of the saints on behalf of the living. Mizeki's path to symbolic sainthood during the 1960s was not simple, however. As civil war broke out in Rhodesia, Mizeki could no longer serve as an effective symbol of non-racialism. To Father Salathiel Madziyire, keeper of the shrine in the 1970s, the Mizeki shrine was primarily a symbol of cultural nationalism. But to many who were fighting for freedom from the white Smith regime, Mizeki remained a colonial collaborator. As the bloody Rhodesian civil war continued through the 1970s, participation in the Mizeki pilgrimage shrank precipitously.[24] During *chimurenga*, interpretations of Mizeki were as fractured as his followers.

Mizeki after colonialism

By the 1960s, with decolonization in full swing throughout Africa, both churches and states lurched unevenly toward indigenous control. Anglicanism was beginning the post-war growth that would roughly double its numbers from 1960 to about eighty million in the year 2000. The decolonization of the Mizeki cult occurred in tandem with the growth of Christianity in southern Africa. In the late 1960s, black Anglican migrants working in South Africa felt excluded from ordinary churches and began attending Methodist, Zionist, and parachurch gatherings that allowed them to express their cultures in prayer, song, and revivalistic worship styles. With the dedication of a largely migrant church in Paarl to Bernard Mizeki in 1973, the Bernard Mizeki Guild was established for Anglican laymen who sought a more intense, African-style worship life, including all-night prayer vigils, healing, and sharing of dreams.

Ironically, even as Mizeki was considered a colonial collaborator by revolutionaries in Rhodesia, his reputation as a symbol of African resistance was spreading in South Africa. Composed largely of Xhosa-speaking migrant workers, Bernard Mizeki Guilds spread across South Africa.[25] Laymen wore purple waistcoats, a special badge, and danced with staves. Anglican migrant workers could identify with Bernard Mizeki as a fellow migrant who sacrificed himself for Christ. By linking lay piety to the name of Bernard Mizeki, Anglicanism was also able to slow defections to the Methodists or the Zionists. Members of Bernard Mizeki Guilds aspired to make the annual pilgrimage to the Mizeki festival.

After the end of *chimurenga* with the establishment of the country Zimbabwe in 1980, the Mizeki pilgrimage entered a period of rapid growth. The formal Eucharistic celebration on Saturday morning of the annual pilgrimage transitioned from white to black Episcopal leadership. But the deeper contextualization of the Mizeki pilgrimage occurred at the informal, lay level. In the growing popular appropriation of Bernard Mizeki, his meaning became Africanized alongside a deepening of Anglican unity. The high popularity of the pilgrimage can be seen as continuous with Shona traditions of pilgrimages to the burial places of chiefs in the mountains.[26] Since such gatherings also affirmed the ties of people with the land, the postcolonial "mystical geography" of the Mizeki pilgrimage celebrated black indigenous control of Zimbabwe. When the Archbishop of Canterbury laid a wreath on his shrine at the centennial pilgrimage in 1996, it was not to honor a faithful colonial retainer, but to honor as Anglican martyr "a simple catechist in Mashonaland who died for his witness for justice."[27]

Descriptions of pilgrimages from the late 1990s into the early twenty-first century reveal multiple layers of African Anglican identity expressed in the celebration of Bernard Mizeki. Lay people arrive in the thousands on buses and trucks from South Africa, Zambia, Malawi, Mozambique, Bostwana, and of course Zimbabwe for the weekend nearest the martyrdom anniversary of June 18. Recalled Fr. Stephen Gendall, who led an annual delegation of thirty from his parish:

> I can never forget the experience of coming around the final corner on the strip road and seeing our destination: the black hillside with the glow of scattered wood fires. As we drew closer we could make out people walking, dancing and singing, or huddled by their fires. Before we knew it we were in the midst of the thousands of pilgrims. The singing was loud and drums were beating; the mountainside was alive with worship to God.[28]

Pilgrims camp out from Thursday until Sunday of the Mizeki pilgrimage weekend. Mothers' Union members, in their distinctive blue and white uniforms, surround the shrine, where they sing hymns and preach. Younger people, camping farther from the shrine, mingle with each other, singing praise choruses, dancing, and eating. People cook their food on wood fires and huddle near them on the cold winter nights. In the spirit of an old-fashioned camp meeting or an all-night *pungwe* meeting, people sing, dance, pray, and exhort throughout the night.[29] The Bishops and high-ranking clergy are nowhere to be seen, as they are housed in hotels and cottages. On Friday occur the annual provincial meetings of religious communities, and on Friday evening a choir competition from various church choirs.[30] To Lin and Liz Parsons, American Episcopal missionaries who attended the pilgrimage in the early 2000s, the most impressive aspect of the celebration is the vibrancy of the singing.[31]

For the clergy and bishops, the central ritual of the Mizeki weekend is the two-hour long Saturday morning communion service, with choral accompaniment. A giant procession, in full regalia, builds up in rank, beginning with members of religious communities, then diocesan deacons, priests, bishops, and finally the Archbishop of Central Africa. The bishop from Mozambique, who has been participating since 1986, carries a large cross brought from there, as if to remind everyone that Mizeki was a Mozambican. Clerical authority is evident in that subdeacons and laity are left out of the procession, even though Mizeki himself was a lay catechist. With archbishop as celebrant, and bishops as concelebrants, the liturgy is conducted in all the main languages of the province. The multiplicity of languages underscores the broadening and unifying significance of Mizeki for the Province, for in earlier years the liturgy was conducted in English and Shona. After the priests distribute communion to the thousands in attendance, the key clerics process out after the "Go in peace" (*Nunc dimittis*).

After the hierarchy withdraws, the people's celebration begins. Popular leaders like Reverend Lazarus Muyambi, founder of the Zimbabwe Spiritual Healing and Manger Centre at St. Agnes Mission in Gokwe, Zimbabwe, and members of his religious community, begin healing people. Because healing services are not typically held during Anglican services in the province, and because Fr. Muyambi performs exorcisms, his work and that of others like him remains controversial among bishops and diocesan priests.[32] But for thousands of lay people, Mizeki is interpreted as a healer full of spiritual power and they have come to be healed. As Fr. Muyambi and leaders from Mothers' Unions conduct healings around the shrine, thousands begin walking up the holy mountain to the stream in which Mizeki washed his wounds. A penitential climb made in prayerful silence is the heart of the pilgrimage to those who have come for healing.[33] They queue in long lines to dip containers into the stream to take home the holy water, believed to have healing powers.[34]

Farther up the mountain is the rocky cave from which Mizeki allegedly disappeared. A tree split by lightning and grown back together helps mark the spot.[35] People tear off bark from tender saplings, and then tie their bark string around the several larger trees at the sacred rock. They pray, confess their sins, and beg Bernard to intervene with God on their behalf. They feel Bernard's mystical presence on the holy mountain. The mixture of traditional religious beliefs with Christianity is evident in the ascent of the mountain, which is a holy grove according to Shona traditional religion. Since chiefs were traditionally buried in high mountain caves, marked by holy groves, there is a deeper continuity with Shona tradition in the climb to the cave than in the communion service at the shrine itself. Many taboos originate in the spirit of traditional religion: pilgrims are not allowed to dip up water with a black pot, or to bathe in the water. Reminiscent of Croagh Patrick, people believe that no snakes can live on the mountain.[36] In Shona traditional religion the snake is a sacred animal that can embody ancestors or spirits, or be a witch's familiar.[37] The sacred grove itself is still respected by the people, as they bring in their own wood for cooking fires and do not fell the trees on the holy mountain. They do pocket leaves and soil to take home for medicine, however. According to the Reverend Gift Makwasha, a Zimbabwean diocesan priest, Mizeki would not have approved of the incursion of traditional beliefs into Anglicanism, as he himself felled trees in the sacred grove in order to plant his crops.[38]

Reflecting the basis of popular religion in oral cultures, traditions grow and change during the pilgrimage. One such tradition is that every year a lamb makes its way from the mountain and passes through the gathered people. The word ripples through the crowd that the lamb has passed.[39] Another tradition that emerged in the late 1990s was that every year someone will die at the pilgrimage and go straight to heaven. Since so many people come to be healed, it is probably natural that sickly and vulnerable people are at risk in the crowds. It is believed that the spirit of Bernard takes somebody to itself in revenge for his murder, and that person becomes a martyr.[40]

On Saturday afternoon, a dramatization of the life of Bernard Mizeki takes place at the shrine. Performed by charismatic Anglicans who tend to oppose traditional religion, the play shows Mizeki's work as healer, catechist, and one who loved the Shona people by refusing to leave them. It pits Mizeki, a violator of traditional taboos, against traditional *ngangas* and forces of evil ancestors. In the play Mizeki wears a clerical collar even though he was actually a layman. One of the killers is depicted as a *nganga*—another bit of theatrical license. In the play the ancestors decree that Mizeki be destroyed in order to save their land. After the stabbing, Mizeki prophesies that one day Anglicans will fill the mountain. His disappearance in a flash of light, witnessed by the women, reminds worshipers of the resurrection of Jesus Christ, or the disappearance of Elijah.

The dramatization of Mizeki's life becomes for the observers a ritualized way of reconciling the dissonance they might feel between traditional religion and Christianity. Although the *ngangas* and ancestors are seen as responsible for Bernard's death, in the end the religion of Jesus Christ overcomes the traditional religion. Traditional religion has power, but Christianity is more powerful. Mizeki's prophecy of the growth of Anglicanism, enough to fill the mountain, is fulfilled in the presence of the people at the pilgrimage. The sacred grove is retained on the holy mountain, but now under the ultimate power of the Christian God. Through Bernard Mizeki, traditional religion is fulfilled rather than displaced by Christianity.[41] Or as expert in Shona religion M. L. Daneel would say, Christianity transforms traditional religion without obliterating it.

On Saturday night, people remain awake. In the flickering light of hundreds of small fires, they sing, pray, give testimonies, and speak in tongues. The uncontrolled noise and spiritual wrestling are not supervised or led by the clergy. Then on Sunday morning is the final Eucharist, served by local priests. People get on their buses and trucks and go home on Sunday afternoons. Pilgrims feel that their spiritual devotion has increased, their sense of unity as African Anglicans across ethnic and national boundaries has deepened, and they return to their ordinary lives inspired and perhaps healed of the problems that make life difficult.

Contested interpretations of Mizeki today

The transformation of Bernard Mizeki into a multi-ethnic people's "saint," or an Anglican "ancestor" for the provinces of Central and South Africa, is neither complete nor uncontested. As recently as 2004, a writer calling himself Murairidzi, meaning Teacher or Guardian, wrote an article in the Zimbabwean *Sunday Mirror* entitled "Saints Who Have Hands Tainted with Blood." Claiming to be a spirit medium for the "Great Spirit," the author accused outsiders of destroying the Shona "culturally and spiritually" and Mizeki of being their agent, "whose scorn was even more arrogant than that of the whites." Whites had "miseducated" Mizeki and "stolen his mind and soul in Cape Town" so that "he could not tell the difference between the white man's culture and God's word." Rather than a saint or martyr worthy of an annual pilgrimage, the author argues, Mizeki was a traitor who deserved to have his head crushed like a viper.[42]

It is hard to know simply from the above-cited article the extent to which Shona traditionalists might be resisting the Mizeki pilgrimage at a grassroots level. The seizure of white-owned farms and businesses in the early 2000s was billed by some as the "third *chimurenga*," and the anti-colonial rhetoric of the liberation struggle was revived in government quarters. Yet even amid crippling fuel and food shortages, economic collapse, and an 80 percent unemployment rate, 18,000 persons participated in the Mizeki pilgrimage in 2005.[43] Clearly the popular affection for Mizeki rejects attempts to repoliticize the pilgrimage or to pit a post-colonial Anglicanism against Zimbabwean national identity.

Most public tensions over the meaning of Mizeki are played out not between traditionalists and Christians, but between the clergy's continued appropriation of Mizeki as a source of their own power, and the lay people's interpretation.[44] For ordained clerics and linguistically limited western visitors, the formal liturgy is the core of the pilgrimage. After their ritual performance on Saturday morning, bishops get into their vehicles and drive back to their hotels. The "cultured despisers" look down on or ignore the popular exercises.

But the people fight back, not only by maintaining their unscripted customs, but by objecting when people disturb their spiritual equilibrium by politicizing the festival. People grumbled when in 1999 the five Zimbabwean bishops stood at the shrine and read a joint statement against political violence.[45] Then in 2003, forty parishioners from the Cathedral of St. Mary's and All Saints in Harare attended the pilgrimage to demonstrate against their Bishop Nolbert Kunonga for actively supporting the destructive economic and social policies of the dictator President Robert Mugabe. Said one of the protestors:

> Our bishop continues to tell Zimbabweans that we have mended our differences but he continues to preach hatred. His politics has destroyed our once good church. The bishop has continued to attend ruling party and government functions, abandoning his spiritual role, home and hospital visits, church services and even the burial of parishioners which he is being paid for.[46]

Despite the merit of the parishioners' grievances against a bishop who has been banned by the European Union for his support for the Mugabe regime, others decried the politicization of the Mizeki pilgrimage. Even so, participants in the pilgrimage criticized church officials for ostensibly collecting millions of dollars from pilgrims but not providing them with toilets or safe drinking water.

In addition to tensions between laity and clergy, and between groups of lay people at the pilgrimage, clerics also fight among themselves for control of the Mizeki name. Although the Anglican African bishops promote the shrine as a symbol of unity for the Province of Central Africa,[47] and they gather there for the consecration of bishops and other provincial tasks, disputes among the Zimbabwean Anglican bishops can spill over into control of the shrine. No doubt money and power are at stake for the hierarchs, despite their general disdain for the popular aspects of the pilgrimage. Bishops' tussles over the control of Mizeki's shrine are reminiscent of the 1100s, when the Archbishops of Armagh claimed Patrick's chapel on Croagh Patrick because "they were his successors," but the Archbishops of Tuam claimed it because it was located in their dioceses.[48]

Perhaps the most fascinating aspect of the Africanization of Bernard Mizeki is how he is evoked to undergird both local ethnicities, and the catholicity of an Anglican version of Christianity that spreads beyond tribe and nation. To Shona pilgrims, Mizeki is a Zimbabwean. He is the founder of their church, better known than his white sponsor Bishop Knight-Bruce. He married a Shona woman related to a chief, and he refused to leave his Shona people to save his life. He chose to become a Shona. To Mozambicans, Mizeki is a compatriot born and bred among them who deserves praise for his great deeds. South Africans take credit for having converted, trained, and sent him out, and for having organized the powerful Mizeki Guilds. Yet the plural national affiliations of Mizeki compose the united identity of South Central African Anglicanism, and point beyond it to the realities of Christianity as a global religion.

African Christian unity has supplanted the symbolic role Mizeki played early in the twentieth century as a loyal catechist and reconciler between the black colonized and the white colonizers. In the same way that legends of St. Patrick signaled both Irish identity and participation in the multi-ethnic Catholicism of the crumbling Roman Empire, so does the Mizeki *cultus* reinforce both African identity and the multi-ethnic Anglicanism of the former British Empire.

Notes

1 See, for example, such classics as James Thayer Addison, *The Medieval Missionary. A Study of the Conversion of Northern Europe A.D. 500–1300* (New York: IMC, 1936); Stephen Neill, *A History of Christian Missions* (New York: Penguin Books, 1964).
2 Andrew Orta, *Catechizing Culture*, New York: Columbia University Press, 2005, p. 11.
3 The process of becoming a Roman Catholic saint is a formal one requiring several major steps over many years, including testimonies of miracles performed

by the saint after his or her death. In Catholicism, therefore, formal sainthood is not even possible based on the mere "facts" of a person's earthly life. Although Anglicans do not have a formal canonization process, noteworthy individuals have been embraced as popular saints. Their feast days appear on official calendars, and an informal iconography gradually takes shape. Whether formal or informal, the concept of sainthood requires communal assent over many years.

4 Jacqueline Borsje, "Druids, Deer and 'Words of Power': Coming to Terms with Evil in Medieval Ireland," p. 12, unpublished paper delivered at the conference on "Religion and Evil," Amsterdam, March 18, 2005.

5 Richard Fletcher, *The Barbarian Conversion*, Berkeley: University of California Press, 1999, p. 94.

6 Robert C. Broderick (ed.) *Catholic Encyclopedia* (Nashville: T. Nelson, 1987), s.v. "Croagh Patrick."

7 The function of Christian pilgrimage in creating different types of community was analyzed by Victor and Edith Turner in their groundbreaking study *Image and Pilgrimage in Christian Culture: Anthropological Perspectives* (Oxford: Blackwell Publishers, 1978). For a helpful overview of recent anthropological theories regarding pilgrimages, see John Eade, "Introduction to the Illinois Paperback," in *Contesting the Sacred: The Anthropology of Christian Pilgrimage*, ed John Eade and Michael J. Sallnow (Urbana and Chicago: University of Illinois Press, 2000), pp. ix–xxvii.

8 "Long before he was called to join the white-robed army of martyrs, he had filled a place in the white-robed army of house-boys. He stands for modern Africa." Fr. Osmund Victor, quoted in Jean Farrant, *Mashonaland Martyr: Bernard Mizeki and the Pioneer Church* (Cape Town: Oxford University Press, 1966), p. xxv.

9 Bishop G. W. H. Knight Bruce, *Memories of Mashonaland* (London: Edward Arnold, 1895), pp. 88–9.

10 Bishop C. W. Alderson, "Foreword," in Farrant, *Mashonaland Martyr*, p. ix.

11 The Shangaan, who live in Mozambique and Zimbabwe, are an offshoot of the Zulu.

12 Quoted in Farrant, *Mashonaland Martyr*, p. 23.

13 David Carnegie, quoted in *Gold and the Gospel in Mashonaland 1888, being the journals of the Mashonaland Mission of Bishop Knight-Bruce, and the Concession Journey of Charles Dunell Rudd*, ed. Constance E. Fripp and V. W. Hiller (London: Chatto & Windus, 1949), p. v.

14 On the importance of migrant workers in the evangelization of Mozambique in the 1800s, see Patrick Harries, "Christianity in Black and White: The Establishment of Protestant Churches in Southern Mozambique," *Lusotopie* (1998): 317–33.

15 See Knight-Bruce's journal in *Gold and the Gospel*.

16 On Mizeki's ministry, see Farrant, *Mashonaland Martyr*, pp. 118–42.

17 *Mwari* is the name of the Shona high god, whose central oracle resides in the Matopo Hills. M. L. Daneel, *The God of the Matopo Hills—an Essay on the Mwari Cult in Rhodesia* (The Hague: Mouton, 1970).

18 The classic account of the first *chimurenga* is Terence O. Ranger, *Revolt in Southern Rhodesia, 1896–7: A Study in African Resistance* (London: Heinemann, 1967).

19 Mizeki, quoted in Farrant, *Mashonaland Martyr*, pp. 208–9.

20 For a helpful overview of the theme of resistance to domination in African history, see Klaas van Walraven and Jon Abbink, "Rethinking Resistance in

African History: An Introduction," in *Rethinking Resistance: Revolt and Violence in African History*, ed. van Walraven and Abbink (Leiden: Brill, 2003).
21 According to Terence Ranger, the first written account of the story of the "strange and unaccountable light" was recorded by Archdeacon Foster in 1909. Terence Ranger, "Taking Hold of the Land: Holy Places and Pilgrimages in Twentieth-Century Zimbabwe," *Past and Present* 117 (1987): 177.
22 Janet Hodgson, "Ecclesial Communities of the Excluded," in *African Christian Outreach: Vol. II The Mission Churches*, ed. Dana L. Robert (Pretoria: SAMS, 2003), p. 134.
23 Ranger, "Holy Places and Pilgrimages," p. 190.
24 Ibid., 190–2.
25 Hodgson, "Ecclesial Communities," p. 135.
26 Ranger, "Taking Hold of the Land," 163.
27 Archbishop Rowan Williams, "Sermon in Odibo, Namibia, January 30, 2000," Anglican Communion News Service 2011, February 7, 2000.
28 Stephen Gendall, "A Bernard Mizeki Pilgrimage," *The Bridge* (June 2005): 8.
29 On night meetings as an enduring feature in Zimbabwean spirituality, see Titus L. Presler, *Transfigured Night: Mission and Culture in Zimbabwe's Vigil Movement* (Pretoria: Unisa Press, 1999).
30 The choir competition has in recent years been suspended as being too competitive and not in the spirit of Mizeki. Fr. John Kaoma, interview by author, May 16, 2005, Boston, Massachusetts.
31 Lin and Liz Parsons, interview by author, August 31, 2005, Somerville, Massachusetts.
32 See Tabona Shoko, "Mainline Church Healing in Zimbabwe: Two Case Studies," in Dana L. Robert (ed.) *African Christian Outreach*, Pretoria: South African Missiological Society, 2003, pp. 208–35.
33 Fr. Gift Makwasha, interview by author, May 26, 2005, Boston, Massachusetts.
34 Bishop Tawonezvi notes that bishops do not encourage the popular aspects of the pilgrimage such as collecting bottles of "holy water." Bishop Godfrey Tawonezvi, interview by author, August 1, 2005, Masvingo, Zimbabwe.
35 See the online reflection on the pilgrimage by Ethan, "The E-report from Windhoek," http://apgar.net/chillye/windhoek/html.
36 Kaoma interview.
37 On Shona symbolism in African traditional religion, and its significance for African Christianity, see the extensive studies by M. L. Daneel, *Old and New in Southern Shona Independent Churches, Vols. 1–3* (The Hague: Mouton, 1971–89).
38 Makwasha interview.
39 Kaoma interview.
40 Makwasha interview. I wish to thank John Kaoma and Gift Makwasha for their assistance in constructing the basic outline of the Mizeki pilgrimages.
41 "Fulfilment theory" is a major way in which mainline Protestant missionaries have conceptualized the relationship between Christianity and non-Christian religions since the late 1800s. See Kenneth Cracknell, *Justice, Courtesy, and Love: Theologians and Missionaries Encountering World Religions, 1846–1914* (London: Epworth, 1995).
42 Murairidzi, "Saints Who Have Hands Tainted with Blood," *Sunday Mirror*, May 30, 2004, www.africaonline.co.zw/mirror/stage/archive/040530/weekend19934.html.
43 Tawonezvi interview.
44 For a detailed study of similar tensions between popular pilgrimage and clerical hierarchy in southern African Anglicanism, see Janet Hodgson, "Mantsopa: Popular Religion and the Anglican Church in South Africa," in *Frontiers of African*

Christianity: Essays in Honour of Inus Daneel, ed. G. Cuthbertson, H. Pretorius, and D. Robert (Pretoria: Unisa Press, 2003), pp. 210–35.
45 Kaoma interview.
46 Precious Shumba, "Anglican Flock Stages Demo against Kunonga," *Daily News*, 16 June, 2003, http://www.zimbabwesituation.com/jun16a_2003.html#link7.
47 Tawonezvi interview.
48 Broderick, *Catholic Encyclopedia*, s.v. "Croagh Patrick."

89

Excerpt from
'JOHN WESLEY SLEPT HERE
American shrines and American Methodists'

Thomas A. Tweed

Source: *NUMEN*, 47 (2000), 41–2, 45–7, 51–4, 61–4, 66.

On a winter morning in 1736 Methodism's founder John Wesley first stepped on American soil. He landed on uninhabited Cockspur Island, just off the Savannah coast, and there on a small hill the British religious leader fell to his knees to give thanks for a safe journey. Today Methodist pilgrims make journeys of their own to that spot — to recall Wesley's landing and return to Methodist origins. To officially recognize the site's sacrality, in 1976 the United Methodist Church named John Wesley's American Parish, which includes Cockspur Island and six other Savannah sites, the nineteenth "national Methodist shrine."

The denomination's use of the term *shrine* to mark this sacred place might seem odd. Methodists, after all, don't have shrines — or at least most scholars of religion have presupposed that. Catholics have shrines, the standard view goes, and so do Buddhists, Jains, Hindus, and Muslims. But most Protestants seem to eschew round-trip journeys to sacred sites.[1]

There is some truth in this view, and Protestant suspicions about shrines and pilgrimage have roots that extend to the Reformation, when reformers and their followers challenged the alleged abuses of Roman Catholic practice. In this Protestant view, establishing shrines and promoting pilgrimage risks endorsing the Catholic sacramental worldview with its mistaken, even morally dangerous, collapse of the distinction between the sacred and the secular. To designate a site as sacred, and venerate persons or objects there, muddles Protestants' understanding of God's relation to the world. It distracts from the authentic sources of religious authority and power: sacred scripture and religious experience. As shrines venerate saints and celebrate miracles they open the door to papist superstition. In short, they risk idolatry.

In this essay I begin by defining and classifying shrines, surveying a wide range of sacred sites in the United States. Then I challenge the assumptions about Protestants and pilgrimage. Focusing on the United Methodists, I argue that while the spiritual descendants of John and Charles Wesley do not consecrate all types of sacred sites or endorse all pilgrimage practices, commemorative shrines play a role in American Methodist piety. If I am right, Protestants, and American Methodists in particular, are less anomalous in the history of religion than most scholars have assumed. [. . .]

[. . .] Most religious traditions have pilgrimage sites, but the meanings and functions of those shrines vary widely. We can classify the variety of shrines in several ways.

Shrines can be classified, first, by religious tradition. So using this apparently straightforward scheme, we could note that El Santuario de Chimayó in New Mexico, currently one of the most frequently visited Catholic pilgrimage sites in the United States, is a Christian shrine. However, sometimes classifying shrines by religious affiliation can be more difficult. Some sites inscribe multiple religious influences, and self-consciously ecumenical sacred spaces claim to venerate multiple traditions, as with the 1986 Light of Truth Universal Shrine at Satchidananda Ashram in Virginia. And classifying shrines by religious affiliation is problematic because that method overlooks quasi-religious sites. Some places that claim secular status nonetheless share some of the standard features of shrines, for example, nationalistic spaces like the Washington Monument and tourist destinations like Cooperstown's Baseball Hall of Fame.[4]

Shrines also can be classified geographically since they vary in placement and scope. Although there are very few of these in the United States, some shrines, such as Lourdes in France and Muhammed's tomb in Saudi Arabia, become international sites, drawing pilgrims from many nations. Others are national as saints — for example, St. James in Spain and Our Lady of Guadalupe in Mexico — become entwined with the nation's history and identity. Regional shrines attract devotees from a few counties or states, while local shrines draw visitors from a single town or city. Narrowing the scope still more, some shrines decorate pathways or mark the boundary between domestic and civic space, as with Afro-Cuban yard shrines in Miami. Homes become sacred, too, as devotees place images and artifacts associated with holy persons on bedroom walls or living room altars. And recent technological innovations, especially the internet, have made some shrines even less spatially fixed: web pages allow cyberpilgrims to email prayers, check schedules, and take virtual tours.[5]

Finally, shrines also can be classified by their origin and function, even if most sites share features of several types. *Commemorative shrines* recall the site of key historical or mythological events (e.g., a founder's vision or the world's creation), and pilgrims recount historical narratives or sacred myths about the deeds done there as they perform rituals that memorialize holy persons or transport followers to religiously significant times or places. Some American Indian sacred sites, for example, are commemorative: several mountains in New Mexico and Arizona mark places where the Pueblo, Hopi, and Navajo peoples first were told to settle or first established their spiritual relationships with bear, deer, and eagle. *Miraculous shrines*, a second type, mark the site of miraculous interventions or sacred encounters, such as apparitions and healings. Many shrines acquire a reputation for their healing powers. The holy dirt at El Santuario de Chimayó, for example, draws Latino pilgrims who believe it has the power to heal body and soul, and those who are transformed leave notes or crutches to signal their thanks. Sometimes shrines also originate because followers find or acquire relics, objects considered sacred because of their association with holy persons (*built or found-object shrines*), or because devotees want to give thanks that an individual or group was saved from some crisis or catastrophe (*ex voto shrines*). Other shrines are self-consciously constructed on sites that do not recall historical events, mark miraculous interventions, house ancient relics, or thank a deity. Some of these, *imitative shrines*, replicate images and architecture from older sites elsewhere, as with the many American Catholic sites whose design mirrors European pilgrim centers like Lourdes and as with American Hindu centers like Pittsburgh's Sri Venkateswara Temple, which recalls one of the most sacred sites in South India, the hilltop shrine of Tirupati. Other self-consciously created pilgrimage sites, *identity shrines*, celebrate saints or deities that mark ethnic, religious, or national identity. These shrines have been especially important to first and second generation immigrants, as they make sense of themselves in the new American cultural context.[6] [. . .]

Protestant pilgrims and shrines: the American Methodist case

[. . .] One religious tradition is noticeably absent from this brief survey: Protestants. There has been little research on shrines and pilgrimage in the United States, and of the few studies that have appeared none explicitly and systematically considers Protestant pilgrimage practice. The presumption, as I indicated at the start, is that Protestants do not have shrines or make pilgrimages. And it is true that few American Protestant denominations have used the terms *shrine* and *pilgrimage* to describe their revered places or their religious practice, and many Protestants have felt uneasy about the Catholic preoccupation with pilgrimage centers. For some Protestants, talk about shrines or pilgrimage signals that the speaker has been seduced by dangerously sensual Catholic culture. However, while round-trip religious journeys have been less central for Protestant piety than for Catholic devotion, America's children of the Reformation are less anomalous in this regard than many have assumed. Focusing on white U.S. Methodists in the twentieth century, I suggest that these mainline Protestants have sacralized sites and made religious journeys.

In most ways, they have done so despite their Methodist heritage, not because of it. The denomination's founder, John Wesley, sometimes offered qualified admiration for Catholic persons and practices. For instance, he praised Thomas à Kempis's *Imitation of Christ* in his journals and letters. And sometimes, as in his more eirenical 1749 *Letter to a Roman Catholic*, Wesley restrained his criticism of Catholics. More typically, as in *Popery Calmly Considered* and *A Caution against Bigotry*, he let loose a flurry of condemnations. Consider the latter sermon, delivered in 1750, where he described the Roman Catholic Church as "in many respects anti-scriptural and anti-Christian: a Church which we believe to be utterly false and erroneous in her doctrines, as well as dangerously wrong in her practice, guilty of gross superstition as well as idolatry . . ." Wesley found idolatry in many things Catholic — including the office of the papacy and the doctrine of transubstantiation. Yet, as one Methodist historian has argued, the founder saw idolatry "especially in the cult of images, in what he perceived to be the worship of the Virgin Mary, and in the offering of prayers to the saints." And, of course, these idolatrous paraliturgical practices flourished at Catholic shrines. For Wesley and other leading Methodists, then, Catholic pilgrimage culture — with its enshrining of images and petitioning of intercessors — was misguided.[11]

Homaging their heritage, and especially the longstanding suspicion of Catholic sacramentalism, Methodists have distanced themselves from some — although not all — shrines and pilgrimage. Yet to understand Methodist practice it is important to be precise about the nature and classification of shrines. To use my labels, then, U.S. Methodists usually have not established miraculous shrines, found-object shrines, or ex voto shrines, and they have consecrated imitative shrines only in the loosest sense of the term. Methodists fail to found these types of shrines, in part, because they continue to affirm the Wesleyan critique of Catholic images and saints, but the Reformation doctrine of a limited age of miracles also has shaped their practice. As one historian of Christianity has noted, the Reformers held that "miracles were essential for both the revelation of the Bible and the establishment of the Christian church, but after the completion of the scripture they ceased to occur." Applying this principle (which held among most English-speaking Protestants until 1930 and continued to have influence after that), if there are no more miracles, there can be no more miracle shrines established at the site of sacred healings and supernatural interventions. In turn, there can be no ex voto shrines built to express thanks for those interventions. Further, because Methodists wanted to distinguish themselves from the Catholic practice of enshrining saints, they did not develop a strong tradition of relic preservation or veneration. One Methodist divinity school exhibits John Wesley's death mask; another preserves George Whitfield's thumb and displays pieces of Wesley's coat. Yet with the possible exception of the World Methodist Building at Lake Junaluska, North Carolina, which one prominent Methodist historian playfully called "the Methodist Disneyland," the United Methodist Church has not encouraged popular reverence for those items or established a pilgrimage center to house them. In this sense, the presuppositions about Methodists, and other Protestants, are correct: they have rejected most kinds of shrines.[12]

American Methodists, however, have not eschewed all types of shrines: they have identified and visited *commemorative* shrines, sites that recall key historical events and transport pilgrims to religiously significant times. And these function as *identity* shrines since, for many Methodists, collective identity emerges from historical consciousness. As historian Russell Richey has argued persuasively, "Methodists have consistently turned to history when called upon to say who they were, to state purposes, to define themselves." This appeal to history first emerged from the practice of sharing conversion narratives, and it took root in the teaching and example of Methodism's founder, John Wesley, and its most influential American leader, Francis Asbury. Wesley advised his preachers to keep a journal, and he followed his own advice by preserving a personal record for over sixty years. Asbury had a similar historical impulse: as early as 1780 Asbury wrote in his *Journal* that he had been "collecting all the minutes of our Conferences in America to assist me in a brief history of the Methodists." And since 1787, *The Book of Discipline*, the regularly updated summary of Methodist doctrine and practice, has opened with an historical preface. In that central text and in other contexts, when Methodists have been asked to explain who they are, they often have told stories about their denomination's past. For this reason, it is not surprising that U.S. Methodists would consecrate commemorative shrines. That practice is an extension of their longstanding inclination toward historical self-consciousness. And their commemorative shrines, like the *Book of Discipline's* historical prefaces, construct collective identity by linking adherents with a sacred heritage.[13] [. . .]

[. . .] John Wesley's American Parish, and the thirty-seven other commemorative shrines, attract contemporary Methodist pilgrims, although it is impossible to know exactly how many since the denomination does not keep such records. But my research indicates that most locales annually attract at least several thousand pilgrims, much less than most U.S. Catholic shrines but more than most scholars might have guessed. The administrator at Philadelphia's St. George's Church, the oldest Methodist house of worship in continual use in America and the site of Asbury's first American sermon, reports that the church draws approximately 3,000 to 4,000 pilgrims each year. Records of Trinity United Methodist Church, one of the seven sites connected with John Wesley's American Parish in Savannah, suggest that locale drew more than 5,000 visitors between January and September in 1997. Tour registrations show that those Methodist pilgrims came from thirty-seven states and fourteen foreign countries. Other sites report similar figures. Lovely Lane Museum in Baltimore is near the site where Lovely Lane

Chapel stood. There in 1784 the chapel hosted the famous Christmas Conference where the new denomination, the Methodist Episcopal Church, was born, and where John Wesley's emissary consecrated Francis Asbury as "general superintendent" of the Methodists in America. The Baltimore museum reports 4,000 annual visitors, and more take the self-guided tour of the nearby Robert Strawbridge House.[23]

Shrine or landmark? Methodism's dual impulses

Mention of the Lovely Lane Museum and the Robert Strawbridge House raises vividly an issue that American Methodists have faced in recent decades: Since the most widely known and religiously resonant terms for spiritual journeys and sacred places carry unwanted Catholic associations, how should Methodists understand and describe their own inclination to identify and visit holy sites? For more than four decades American Methodists officially designated hundreds of pilgrimage centers, and regularly used the word *shrine* to describe the most venerated sites. However, while reaffirming their commitment to identifying and visiting historically significant places, in 1993 the Shrines and Landmarks Committee began to consider a change in the terms they used. The Minutes for the 17 September meeting indicate that the members considered "Lasley's memorandum." After attending an earlier meeting where members had expressed worries about the "confusions" introduced by the term *shrine*, the Reverend Joseph W. Lasley wrote a letter to the committee's chair. "I got to thinking that we could call them 'heritage landmarks,' and I was surprised to find that my letter was distributed to others there, and it was approved at the next meeting." That memorandum did not include any specific mention of the Catholic issue, but he and several other members present "voiced concerns" about that. Lasley wanted the change in terminology, he later reported, "because the shrines we had were not the same as those in the Roman Catholic tradition. There are no bones or saints at our shrines . . ." Others agreed. In 1995, at a full session of the Commission, the change was proposed. It won approval, and next year the advance edition of the *Daily Christian Advocate*, which appeared before the 1996 General Conference, printed the Commission on Archives and History's proposal to replace "historic shrines" with "heritage landmarks." That petition was approved, and the terminological changes now appear in the denomination's *Book of Discipline*.[24]

The shift in language has altered little, either among the Commission members or Methodist pilgrims. The Commission continues to consider proposals from local sites that want special recognition, and some Methodist laypeople continue to make round-trip journeys to places that capture denominational memory and create shared identity. And they continue to take home mementos, as pilgrims always have done: from postcards and pamphlets to Francis Asbury coffee mugs and John Wesley porcelain busts.

Nonetheless, most changes in language encode desires and convey meanings, and this one reveals the complexity of Methodist attitudes about sacred places. Consider, for example, the response to this change among caretakers of Baltimore's Lovely Lane Museum and Robert Strawbridge *House*. The Commission's 1998 list of American Methodism's thirty-eight most venerated places describes the residence of Strawbridge, one of America's pioneer Methodist preachers, as "the Robert Strawbridge Log House." However, challenging the authority of the Commission on Archives and History, and the mandates of the 1996 *Book of Discipline*, local Methodist caretakers of Strawbridge's Baltimore residence continue to call it a *shrine*. One of those caretakers is the Reverend Edwin Schell, executive secretary of the regional Methodist historical society and former member of the Commission on Archives and History, who debated the name change at the 1995 meeting. Schell recalled that "one of the brothers argued that the word *shrine* made people think of Catholic shrines, and so we should change the term." Schell dissented. For Schell, the change of language was very unfortunate. He prefers *shrine* and rejects *landmark* because "the new language makes it a more secular designation." The Methodist minister wants to signal that the site is holy. Undeterred by the prescriptions of the national organization, then, Schell and others at the Lovely Lane Museum resist the change: "We still call the Robert Strawbridge Shrine by that name."[25] [...]

[...] Because of that enduring suspicion, United Methodists consecrate only commemorative sites, historical locales that help Methodists explain themselves to themselves. And since Protestant identity always has involved *protest*ing — defining self in opposition to the other, namely Roman Catholicism — Methodist sacred sites and pilgrimage practices continue to avoid any explicit association with the "idolatry" that Wesley condemned. There is no evidence that any Methodist pilgrim to John Wesley's American Parish has prayed to Wesley for a miraculous cure and then left crutches by the altar to signal her gratitude for the founder's supernatural intercession. In the Reverend Lasley words, "there are no bones or saints at our shrines."

However, that does not mean that Methodists, or all other Protestants, are as spiritually distinctive as believers imagine or scholars presuppose. Whether John Wesley's American Parish, St. George's Church, and Lovely Lane Museum are called "heritage landmarks" or "historic shrines," for a small but significant proportion of Methodists they function like traditional pilgrimage centers, and spiritually motivated round-trip travel remains a notable feature of contemporary Methodist piety. In this sense, United Methodists share much more with other people of faith than *The Book of Discipline's* recently secularized language indicates. They have something in common with other American pilgrims — even white-clad U.S. Muslims circumambulating the Ka'aba in Mecca and Latino Catholics fingering holy dirt at El Santuario de Chimayó. However the General Conference elects to describe the sites or the journeys, American Methodists continue to make pilgrimages and consecrate shrines — even if they also continue to mark the boundaries between their faith and others.

Notes

1 The only scholarly volume dedicated exclusively to U.S. shrines and pilgrimage is G. Rinschede and S. M. Bhardwaj, eds., *Pilgrimage in the United States, Geographia Religionum*, vol. 5 (Berlin: Dietrich Reimer Verlag, 1990). It includes three chapters on Catholic shrines, two on quasi-religious sites, and one each on Sikh, Mormon, and Hindu shrines. None of the chapters focuses on Protestant sacred sites. The same pattern holds in guidebooks that claim comprehensiveness: Colin Wilson, *The Atlas of Holy Places and Sacred Sites* (New York: D.K. Publishers, 1996); and Paul Lambourne Higgins, *Pilgrimages USA: A Guide to Holy Places of the United States for Today's Traveler* (Englewood Cliffs, N.J.: Prentice Hall, 1985).

4 On Chimayó, see Ramón A. Gutiérrez, "El Santuario de Chimayó: A Syncretic Shrine in New Mexico," in Ramón A. Gutiérrez and Geneviève Fabre, *Feasts and Celebrations in North American Ethnic Communities* (Albuquerque: University of New Mexico Press, 1995), 71–86. On the Light of Truth Universal Shrine, see Thomas A. Tweed and Stephen Prothero, eds., *Asian Religions in America: A Documentary History* (New York and Oxford: Oxford University Press, 1999), 253–57. On quasi-religious sites in the United States and elsewhere, see Ian Reader and Tony Walter, eds., *Pilgrimage in Popular Culture* (London: Macmillan, 1993).

5 On Cuban yard shrines in Miami, see James R. Curtis, "Miami's Little Havana: Yard Shrines, Cult Religion, and Landscape," *Journal of Cultural Geography* 1 (Fall/Winter 1980): 1–15. For an example of a webpage that promises cyberpilgrims a "virtual tour" see www.nationalshrine.com., the site sponsored by the National Shrine of the Immaculate Conception in Washington, D.C.

6 On Sri Venkatesvara Temple, see Fred W. Clothey, *Rhythm and Intent: Ritual Studies from South India* (Madras: Blackie and Son, 1983), 164–200. Examples of identity shrines include Marian centers for Polish Catholics in Doylestown, Pennsylvania, and for Cuban Catholics in Miami. See Gabriel Lorenc, *American Czestochowa* (Doylestown, Penn.: National Shrine of Our Lady of Czestochowa, 1989); and Thomas A. Tweed, *Our Lady of the Exile: Diasporic Religion at a Cuban Catholic Shrine in Miami* (New York and Oxford: Oxford University Press, 1997). Among the recent books on the quasi-religious dimensions of fan devotion at Elvis Presley's former home see Erika Doss, *Elvis Culture: Fans, Faith, and Image* (Lawrence: University Press of Kansas, 1999).

11 On Wesley's attitudes toward Catholicism, see David Butler, *Methodists and Papists: John Wesley and the Catholic Church in the Eighteenth Century* (London: Darton, Longman, and Todd, 1995). The passage from Wesley's sermon *A Caution against Bigotry* is quoted in that work (xiii). The historian quoted on the cult of images is also Butler: *Methodists and Papists*, 158. It is interesting to note that some of John Wesley's early critics condemned his views by comparing them with those of the Roman Catholic Church. In this view, both Methodists and Catholics were guilty of "enthusiasm." For example, see [George Lavington], *The Enthusiasm of Methodists and Papists Compar'd* (London: J. and P. Knapton, 1749). Wesley, annoyed by the comparison, responded. See John Telford, ed., *John Wesley's Letters*, vol. 3 (London: Epworth Press, 1931), 258ff.

12 Robert Bruce Mullin, *Miracles and the Modern Religious Imagination* (New Haven: Yale University Press, 1996), 1. The exhibit that includes one of four copies

of Wesley's death mask is "John Wesley: Death and Remembrance, 1791–1991," Duke Divinity School Library, Duke University, Durham, North Carolina. On Wesley's coat and Whitfield's thumb, see Colleen McDannell's analysis of Drew University's Methodist Archives in *Material Christianity* (New Haven: Yale University Press, 1995), 42–45. The reference to "Methodist Disneyland" surfaced in a telephone interview with K. R., a prominent and informed Methodist historian, 4 November 1998. Official Methodist documents even have used the term *relic* to describe the artifacts housed at Lake Junaluska. For example, *The Book of Discipline of the United Methodist Church: 1968* (Nashville: The Methodist Publishing House, 1968), 445.

13 Russell E. Richey, "History as Bearer of Denominational Identity," in Russell E. Richey Kenneth E. Rowe, and Jean Miller Schmidt, eds., Perspectives on American Methodism: Interpretive Essays (Nashville: Kingswood Books, 1993), 496. Asbury's journal was quoted in Edwin Schell History of Northeastern Jurisdictional Historical Concerns (n. p: Northeastern Jurisdictional Commission on Archives and History, United Methodist Church, 1976), 1.

23 I invited site administrators to estimate annual visitors and searched available printed records. This method is flawed, of course, but it yielded the best figures available. The estimate from St. George's Church came from Brian McCloskey, church administrator, telephone interview, 3 November 1998. The estimate for Trinity United Methodist Church, a part of John Wesley's American Parish, came from the Reverend Ralph Bailey, "Composite Report of 1997 Activities," Trinity United Methodist Church, Savannah. Georgia, page 6. The figures for Lovely Lane Museum and the Robert Strawbridge House are from: telephone interview, the Reverend Edwin Schell, 3 November 1998. These estimates of visitors suggest both that Methodists do value pilgrimage, but they also confirm presuppositions that Catholics cherish it even more. As one cultural geographer has calculated, many Catholic shrines in the United States draw hundreds of thousands of annual visitors. On feast days or holy days, some Catholic sites attract more pilgrims in a single day than some Methodist locales draw in a year. See Gisbert Rinschede, "Catholic Pilgrimage Places in the United States," in Rinschede and Bhardwaj, eds., *Pilgrimage in the United States*, 63–136.

24 *Daily Christian Advocate*, Advance Edition I, The United Methodist Church General Conference 1996, vol. 1 (Nashville: The General Conference of the United Methodist Church, 1996), 907. *Book of Discipline: 1996*, 582–83. According to General Commission on Archives and History records available to the public, the issue of the name change for historic shrines first arose 17 September 1993, during a plenary session of the committee in charge of Shrines and Landmarks. The following year, at the annual meeting, the Shrines and Landmarks Committee reported that they would be ready to present a change to *The Book of Discipline* at the next general meeting. In 1995, at a full session of the Commission, the disciplinary change was suggested. Minutes, Shrines and Landmarks Committee, 17 September 1993, Methodist Archives, Drew University, Madison, New Jersey. Minutes, Plenary Session, General Commission on Archives and History, 25 August 1995, Methodist Archives, Drew University, Madison, New Jersey. Because the records do not describe the origin of the name change or preserve the ensuing debate, I turned to oral history. I quote here from an interview: Telephone interview, the Reverend Joseph W. Lasley, 10 November 1998.

25 The General Commission on Archives and History, "The Heritage Landmarks of United Methodism, 1997–2000," typescript, Methodist Archives, Drew University, Madison, New Jersey. The minutes available to researchers do not suggest any clear reason for the change in terminology.

Part 23

PERFORMING CHRISTIANITY

90

CATHOLIC HYMNS OF MICHIGAN INDIANS

Gertrude Prokosch Kurath

Source: *Anthropological Quarterly*, 30(2) (1957), 31–44.

In the rush to preserve the native cultural fragments of the American Indian, ethnologists and musicologists have tended to neglect or scorn semi-Christian aspects. Lately the students of ethnology have awakened to the importance of culture mixtures termed acculturation, but musicians lag behind. To my knowledge only Willard Rhodes is aware of the rich fund of Indian hymnody. During my four years of work among the Algonquian Indians of Michigan[1] I would have been blind and deaf to escape this type of music, for it plays a profound role in the lives of these Christian Indians.

Three centuries after their sight of the first blackrobe missionary they color their Christianity with pagan fragments, but they have effectively submerged this paganism. A generation ago all of the Catholics celebrated semi-pagan feasts on Catholic holidays and sang perplexing hymns in their native language. Now only the older people know the hymns, confined to wakes and family feasts. In the Upper Peninsula the feasts have all but disappeared but in the Lower Peninsula they survive among the Ottawa of Little Traverse Bay, L'Arbre Croche of the French. This scenic Ottawa metropolis, settled as a mission in 1742, still extends from Cross Village on Lake Michigan to Petoskey.

The calendar of family feasts begins with the New-Year-Epiphany celebration, which is complimented by a return called Tabandang. It now omits Corpus Christi and other former summer festivals and skips to the Ghost Suppers after November 1. A child's Naming Ceremony and a wake can come at any time. Other celebrations as Christmas, birthdays, weddings, etc. are typically European. Just as the weekly Sunday services, they contain the same liturgies and hymns as in white churches. (Communication, Jane Ettawageshik).

The bilingual Algonquians sing by heart, in unison, usually a cappella, occasionally with piano accompaniment. For the texts they have to consult battered heirlooms, hymnals printed a century ago without the melodies. The arrangement of these hymnals shows how the Anamie-nagamonan (prayer songs) were adapted to every event in the Catholic calendar and to every act of worship. They were devised for Kitchi-ogimagijigak (New Year), Eukaristiwin (Eucharist), Tchibaigijigad (All Souls' Day), Niba-anamiegijigad (Christmas), for eulogies to Jesus and the Blessed Virgin, Kitchitwa Marie. Any can be adapted to a wake.

Whereas the Ottawa share texts with the Ojibwa near Sault Ste. Marie, Nahma on Lake Michigan, Baraga on Lake Superior and other Upper Peninsula settlements, they sing other tunes. Sometimes they use entirely different melodies, sometimes variants of the same tune. Versions vary between adjacent locations as Burt Lake and L'Arbre Croche, and even between individuals. This has been remarked by the Ottawa themselves and by a friend of the Indians and hymn collector, the Jesuit priest Fr. Paul Prud'homme.

This variation, which is a characteristic of folk music as well as of nineteenth century hymn singing practices, is interesting in itself. It also plays a part in unravelling the development which has been forgotten even by the oldest Indians and by the most assiduous prelates.

° °
°

Two typical hymns, recorded by David Kenosha and Susan Shagonaby, were formerly intended for Christmas (Ex. 1) and for the Blessed Virgin Mary (Ex. 2). Their central ideas, as translated by Fred Ettawageshik, are much akin.

Ex. 1.
Kakina minawasida   All let us make merry
Ki mino nondagemin: He was pleased to hear us:
Kinawind gi-ondji-nigi,   For us he was reborn,
Kije-manito Ogwissan.   The Holy Spirit's Son.
Chorus.
Ogwissan, Ogwissan   The Son, the Son,
Kije-manito Ogwissan.   The Holy Spirit's Son.

Ex. 2.
Kagenig Kije-manito   Always, Holy Spirit,
Kigi-bisagiig, Marie;   She loved you, Mary;
Bwa mashi ondadissiyan   Before you were born
Ki gi-makwenimig.   He thought of you who are a virgin.
Chorus.
Gagangowiian   You who are a virgin
Marie eninijiminang,   Mary who is like us,
Gwanatchiwiian,   Who is beautiful,
Nadamawishinam.   Help us.

CATHOLIC HYMNS OF MICHIGAN INDIANS

Both hymns, as also all others, have many more verses, pressing the native language into European metre.

That is to say, it looks like European metre and song pattern. The examples are in regular 4/4 and 3/4 time, respectively, marked off into groups of four measures, which cluster into two parts, with B as chorus. The only departure from this regularity is the Chorus of Ex. 2, with phrases of seven, six, and three measures. The printed melody, despite variations, has a similar phrasing. For Ex. 1 the book brings two quite different tunes.[3] All are in a major diatonic scale, with rising and falling contour.

The first question is the relationship of these qualities to the typical patterns of native songs known to a few singers. Ex. 3 is the first phrase of an Eagle

Dance song by David Kenosha, Ex. 4 is one verse of a Deer Song by Thomas Shalifoe. Every song should be rendered four times, the sacred number of the Algonquians. Metre and phrasing of both songs are orderly but not cut-and-dried. Ex. 4 resembles Ex. 1 in the sequential recurrence of a theme consisting of even quarter and eighth notes. But the sequences of the hymns rise and fall; in all native songs they descend. Thus Ex. 2, which starts on its highest note, is quite unlike the animal songs, what with its many ups and downs.

There are other differences. The native songs are accompanied by a duple drum beat and adhere to a strict tempo, while the hymns, sung a cappella, may be rubato especially at the end. The native songs are rendered with a light, staccato touch, the hymns heavy and legato.

The most striking differences are apparent in the scales. The native songs have compact pentatonic scales with the tonic at the bottom. The hymns dispose their diatonic scales both sides of the tonic, Ex. 2 even dangling an octave below. They are here tabulated in ascending order, notwithstanding the descending native contour. The "gaps" in the pentatonic scales bypass all semitones. Ex. 3 omits the third, hence any affiliations with our major or minor.

```
Ex. 1            5̲ 6̲ 7̲ 1 2 3 4 5
Ex. 2    2 3 4 5̲ 6̲ 7̲ 1 2 3 4 5
Ex. 3                1 2    4 5 6
Ex. 4                1    3 4 5   7 8
```

The texts and their ideology show even greater contrasts. The hymns are addressed to Mary and her Son, the native songs to the eagle, the supernatural thunder spirit, and to the clan totem, the sacred deer ancestor. The short, repetitious word phrases mean:

Ex. 3
Bineshiwok togoshonok   Wasa bionjipawok
The birds are coming   From far away they arrive

Ex. 4
Mano mano dimadja   Wawashkeshe n'dodem
Let, let him go   The deer, my pal (totem)

How did the Indians manage to accept a song type so different from their native repertoire, which to this day remains in a separate compartment? For lack of any memory of the transition, the explanation must be pried out of the few early documents, particularly out of the *Jesuit Relations,* the reports written by the early missionaries for their superiors. Here is a brief reconstruction of the history.

In the wilderness around the Great Lakes the Blackrobes or Jesuit missionaries followed hard on the heels of the first explorers. They found a people whose religion consisted mainly in singing to the beating of drums. They sang in worship, recreation, and suffering.[4] To the priests the religion appeared as superstition and the music as lacking in sweet harmony. Yet their approach was not entirely condemnatory. Many of the nature spirits were pronounced demons, but Jesus replaced the sun symbol, Mother Mary doubled for beloved Nokomis, grandmother Earth, and the cross replaced the prayer stick in thanksgiving sacrifices and the grave post with the upside-down image of the totem.[5] Above all, hymns were taught to the children and through them to the adults. By 1644 Huron converts were enthusiastic over Christmas hymns[6] and soon afterwards were harmonizing them in four voices.[7] The native drum and flageolet found a counterpart in drum and fife music by French soldiers for the blessing of the bread.[8]

By 1672 the French Jesuits had made another diplomatic move in learning the native languages and translating the hymns into these tongues. Said Fr. Druillettes, pastor of the mission at Ste. Marie du Sault,

"They are assiduous in saying their prayers in the Church . . . and take pleasure in chanting beautiful hymns in their language."[9]

All of the many references are to plainsong, to Pange Lingua for the Sunday before Lent and Palm Sunday, the Magnificat, Te Deum, Miserere, Gloria Patri,[10] and at a large intertribal council at the Sault the Vexilla and Exaudiat.[11] Fr. Pierre Cholenec specified the 8th mode used in chanting a hymn to the Virgin.[12] In 1671 Fr. Louis André told of responsorial rendering of these chants at Manitulin Island, northern Lake Huron.

"No sooner had I begun to have these sung in the Chapel, accompanied by a sweet-toned flute . . . than they all came in crowds . . . so that . . I let only the girls enter the Chapel . . . thus we sang in two choruses, those without responding to those within."[13]

The influence of this excellent musician and apt popularizer reached from Manitulin all across the Upper Peninsula to the Menomini Indians near Green Bay of present Wisconsin. His round trip concluded in Canada, after a year (1682) in St. Ignace. A description of his activities in the *Jesuit Relations* summarizes his approach, and also brings up two interesting points, that he had the children learn French airs and that he himself composed songs.

"The reason why he was so eagerly sought was found in certain spiritual songs that he was wont to have the children sing to French airs, which pleased these Savages extremely . . . This success . . made him resolve to assail the men through the children, and to combat idolatry with souls of extreme innocence. In short, he composed songs against the superstitions that we have mentioned, and against the vices most opposed to Christianity; and after teaching the children to sing them to the accompaniment of a sweet toned flute, he went everywhere with these little Savage musicians, to declare war on Jugglers, Dreamers, and those who had several wives . . ."[14]

Perhaps they sang melodies like those in *Jesus Wegwissian*, which enlists Jesus and Mary against the powers of darkness, though to-day the descendants use neither antiphony nor flute accompaniment. The text books name *Ave maris stella* as the air to these words. One of the versions which appears in the music book is indeed derived from *Ave maris*, though 1) in Ex. 5 is in the Aeolian or rather Hypo-Aeolian, minor mode, that is, the 8th (plagal) ecclesiastical mode; while 2) is in the Ionian mode, our major diatonic.[15] Is the former the chant to the Virgin mentioned by Fr. Cholenec? Is the latter a modification by Fr. André or a mutation by the Indians in the course of centuries? Or is the third tune 3) the composition by Fr. André, or a derivation therefrom? This last, recorded by Thomas Shalifoe of Baraga, has been handed down from his half-French, half-Indian ancestors (his name is a corruption of Charlevoix). The tune, the most beautiful one in my collection, is in the Dorian mode.[16] The Dorian mode persists in older French (and other European) folksongs, as in the French-Canadian voyageur song *V'la le bon vent*.[17] Verses 1 and 4 emphasize the ideas of allegiance to Jesus and Mary and abhorence of dark (pagan) powers.

1. Jesus wegwissiian   Jesus who art the son
   Mojag gaie bekish   Forever may you
   Gagigangowiian   Take care of me
   Kiminowinigo.   So I will be happy.
4. Marie, abiskon   Marie, deliver
   Neta-betadidjig   The sinners,
   Wassenemaw gaie   Remove indeed
   Tebikadisidjig.   The powers of darkness.

A similar problem involves the tunes to *Sagitoda Jesus wiiaw*, a hymn for Corpus Christi and the Eucharist. The text, to be sung "Sur l'air *Pange Lingua*," paraphrases the Latin original.

Sagitoda Jesus wiiaw   Let us cherish Jesus' body
Ketchitwawendawadinig;   It is holy;
O miskwim manadjitoda,   His blood, let us glorify it,
Gasiginan apinassind,   He poured it when he was killed,
Kigisiginamagonan.   He poured it for us.

Ex. 6, 1) and 2) reproduce the first two phrases of *Pange Lingua*, the plainchant, and the older version of *Sagitoda,* both in the Phrygian or 3rd mode.[18] The L'Arbre Croche melody, 3), recorded by Kenosha, is equally removed from native song and plainchant. In the same major diatonic scale as Ex. 2, it has a more rigid form: a binary structure of four-measure phrases in march time, and a theme that rises sequentially in A and A^1 and descends in B and B^1. Its structure, phrasing, and very theme vividly recall the Austrian national anthem, composed by Joseph Haydn in 1797, "Gott erhalte Franz den Kaiser", taken over later on by Germany for "Deutschland, Deutschland über alles."[19]

This is not the only hymn of L'Arbre Croche with an Austrian flavor. A hymn of thanksgiving, recorded by Jane Ettawageshik at a New Year feast of the Kishigos, appears as a legitimate variant of a folkdance known in Austria and Bavaria as "Siebenschritt" and in Czechoslovakia as "Four Steps". One need only compare the B part in Ex. 7, 1), with the second half of 2) Siebenschritt, 3) Four Steps,[20] and—4) Humperdinck's folkderived "Brüderlein, komm' tanz' mit mir!" The dance tunes are twice as fast as the hymn. Their ideology is quite different. The hymn says—

Gijigong anjenidog,	In heaven the angels
Wi-manadjiada	Let us honor him,
Jesus kijadisid	Jesus is charitable
Mojag migwetch inada.	Always thanks you say to him.
Chorus	
Mamoya wamada,	Let us thank him,
Jesus egwashimining,	Jesus who saves us,
Mamoya wamada	Let us thank him
Meno-jaweniminang.	Who is good, merciful to us.

[...] The transition from plainchant to French folk melody began in the seventeenth century. One can only suppose that this process continued through the eighteenth century, with inevitable changes. The *Jesuit Relations* dwindled and were not replaced by similarly accurate documents. In some areas the priests withdrew temporarily. But intense missionization resumed in the nineteenth century. The story of L'Arbre Croche Catholicism gives a plausible reason for a shift to Austrian folk songs, for it tells of a series of Austrian and German prelates, both Jesuit and Franciscan, from 1831 to 1889—Fr. Friedrich Baraga, the sympathetic Fr. Francis Pierz, Fr. Ignatius Mrak, compatriot of Baraga, Fr. Seraphim Zorn, Fr. Louis Sifferath, and the energetic Prussian Franciscan, Fr. Bernard Weikamp.[21] The most important figure was Baraga, a Slovene, native of Carniola, who spent only 1831–1833 in L'Arbre Croche, but often returned during his ministrations in the Upper Peninsula, his founding of the mission at Baraga, and his functions as Bishop of Marquette and Sault Ste. Marie. Though not the first missionary to print hymn books,[22] nor the first to learn the native languages and translate, he was the first to write a grammar, to advocate reading in the languages, and to widely popularize the hymns. His name is on many a battered title page.

It is very likely that he introduced folk tunes and anthems from his native land, which have persevered side by side with previous tunes. Though his activities were centered in the Upper Peninsula, they did not oust French influences of French prelates. At L'Arbre Croche the new Austrian tradition became firmly established under his successors. Till recently this tradition extended to the teaching of German in the convent school at Cross Village, so that Kenosha and his age mates speak German.

This localization of Austrian influence would account for much of the difference between the L'Arbre Croche and the more conservative Upper Peninsula, with its remnants of plainsong and its French tunes.

A search for more definite identification has led me to the perusal of dozens of folk song volumes and to the pestering of many a musicologist, all sympathetic but puzzled. It led me to a detour between Nahma and St. Ignace in a pouring rain to consult the colorful friend of the Indian, Fr. Prud'homme at the mission of St. Isaac Jogues outside Sault Ste Marie. Fr. Prud'homme had observed the French and Austrian folk song origins and supposed that somewhere the prototypes must be in print. A worthy successor to André and Baraga, he has covered the Upper Peninsula, has been concerned with the Indians and their music, and has worried little about origins.

○   ○
○

Not all of the hymn tunes float in a three-century-old haze. Some are quite identifiable. In all locations a Christmas hymn is sung to the very same *Adeste Fideles* that resounds in our schools and churches. Even the words are as accurately translated as possible: "Enamiaieg (you who pray), Onaningwendamog, Ambe (rejoice, come)." It is so exact that it offers no challenge.

A hymn to the Virgin is set to the tune we know as "America," which was composed in 1743 by Henry Carey for "God Save the King," was fitted in 1781 to the Austrian "Heil, Kaiser Josef" and in 1793 to the German "Heil Dir im Siegerkranz."[23] There are other settings to the words, heard from two Ottawas, Whitney Albert of the Lower Peninsula and Margaret Lambert of the Upper Peninsula; but "America" is the favorite both in the printed music[24] and in the recording by Kenosha.

The text, which officially calls for "Sur l'air *Nous vous invoquons tons*", can be translated as follows—

Wenidjanissimiiang	Treat us like your children
Genawenimiiang	Take care of us
Gwanatch Marie;	Gracious Mary;
Ganodamawishinam	Speak for us
Kinwegimigoian	We love you like our own mother
Jawenimishinam	Have mercy on us
Gwanatch Marie.	Gracious Mary.

Kenosha identified the tune as our national anthem. Nevertheless he digresses from the norm, expands some of the measures to 4/4 time instead of the correct 3/4. Such metric change, not uncommon among older Indian hymn singers, has two implications.

In the first place, it suggests perseverance of the Indian feel for metrical flexibility. Fifty years ago the oldtimers sang their hymns with many Indian mannerisms, such as slurs, pulsations, and an "Indian throat".[25] The youngsters of that era have all but shed these mannerisms, even in their native songs, but in both categories they show little concern for set time signatures.

In the second place, the slight deviations from a wellknown tune indicate possibilities of larger changes in more obscure melodies. As already mentioned, individual and local variations prevail in folk song. These hymns have all the earmarks of folk music. Since the time of Baraga they have inevitably changed. Perhaps identifiable at that time as Austrian folk songs, they have become transformed. Since the time of André the changes must have been even greater. The only tunes to resist such changes are the established and long printed chants and hymns of the church.

One would like to predict a picturesque future for the hymnody, under modern influences and with a new generation. But there can be no future. The new generation shows no interest in the native languages or traditions. Some exceptional youngsters chime in when the hymns are sung during intermission at public shows termed powwows. Already tossed from the church to the family gathering, the Ottawa hymns may continue for a short while as secular entertainment, alongside the once religious native songs. But they are rapidly disappearing. With them will vanish an interesting transitional stage, a blend of native and European art and custom.

Notes

1 Field work from 1953–1956 was supported by grants from the Michigan Academy of Science and the American Philosophical Society.
2 Père Paul Prud'homme and Père Desautels, *Anamie-Nagamonan*, Nipigon, Ontario, 1931.
3 *ibid.*, p. 174.
4 Edna Kenton, *The Jesuit Relations*, New York, 1925, pp. 58–9.
5 Henry R. Schoolcraft, *Information Respecting the Indian Tribes of the United States*, Philadelphia, 1852, pp. 49 and 60.
6 Reuben G. Thwaites, *The Jesuit Relations and Allied Documents*, 73 Vols., Cleveland, 1896–1901, Vol. 25, pp. 113 and 211.
7 *ibid.*, Vol. 28, p. 249.
8 *ibid.*, Vol. 45, p. 131.
9 *ibid.*, Vol. 57, p. 207.
10 *ibid.*, Vol. 48, p. 231.
11 *ibid.*, Vol. 55, pp. 107 ff. (report by Claude Allouez).
12 *ibid.*, Vol. 60, p. 283.
13 *ibid.*, Vol. 55, p. 147.
14 *ibid.*, Vol. 56, pp. 129 ff.

15 Prud'homme and Desautels, *op. cit.*, p. 329 (no. 251) and p. 179 (no. 139), respectively.
16 Ethnic Folkways, New York, *op. cit.*, Side A, Band 3.
17 Marius Barbeau, *Alouette*, Montreal, 1946, p. 38.
18 Prud'homme and Desautels, *op cit.*, p. 319 (no. 243) and p. 146 (no. 112).
19 Clemens Schmalstich, *Das Deutsche Volkslied*, Berlin, n. d., p. 81.
20 Anna Schley Duggan, *Folk Dances of European Countries*, New York, 1948, pp. 57 and 103.
21 Mary Belle Shurtleff, *Old Arbre Croche*, Cross Village, 1940. pp. 24–30. In a personal communication, Fr. Martin Gusinde remarked that the influence of Austrian Jesuits and Franciscans in North America was generally underestimated.
22 The Clements Library at the University of Michigan has a hymn book printed in 1830, with the title page bearing the name of "Dejean Macate Okonoye" (Dejean Blackrobe).
23 Schmalstich, *op. cit.*, p. 88.
24 Prud'homme and Desautels, *op. cit.*, p. 230 (no. 175).
25 Frederick R. Barton, *American Primitive Music*, New York, 1909, pp. 136–37.

91

UDUK FAITH IN A FIVE-NOTE SCALE
Mission music and the spread of the Gospel

Wendy James

Source: Wendy James and Douglas H. Johnson (eds), *Vernacular Christianity: Essays in the Social Anthropology of Religion Presented to Godfrey Lienhardt*, JASO Occasional Papers, 1988, pp. 131–45.

Conversations with the old lady Umpa remain a vivid memory from my first weeks of fieldwork among the Uduk in the 1960s.[1] She decided to keep a kindly eye on me from the start, helped me to housekeep, introduced me to others and explained as well as she could what was going on. I found her company reassuring, though she was sometimes a little over-zealous in her defence of my privacy against visitors from neighbouring hamlets. Loyal and enthusiastic in defending the 'traditional' culture of the Uduk villages, Umpa nevertheless treated me to occasional speeches on the Day of Judgement. Opening her arms wide over the imagined crowd of chosen ones, she would sweep them up as if to Heaven, peering down over her shoulder at those abandoned to the fires below. She loved the drama of the scene, and her anxiety about it was real. But she was in no sense a Christian. The gusto of the portrayal belied a sober caution about the claims of the local evangelical mission and stubborn doubt about its motives. She refused to become a 'person of Jesus' and had only rarely been to the sermons preached at Chali church. But like many others in the outlying villages, she had picked up some elements of Christian dogma from the hymns which had been spread, almost as popular folk-songs, by the younger people who came and went freely between the mission and the countryside. Familiar as so many villagers were with these new tunes, but without the background to make morally intelligible the stark messages they often brought, she would snort that *she* didn't wish to be snatched up in the air, nor dumped in the fire either.

Such disturbing ideas easily circulated far beyond the limits of 'mission education' or 'Christian belief' in the conventional sense. Older people were perhaps particularly sensitive to the images of death, destruction and separation prominent in much evangelical teaching. Like Umpa, many of them personally remembered the slave-raiding disturbances and wholesale flight of the late nineteenth century. Images of the Day of Judgement were of a kind to command attention and provoke worry among many who were otherwise not attracted to the mission. This, however, is only one aspect of the more general and very interesting question of the way in which partial and highly selective elements of that supposed entity, 'Christianity', may spread beyond the confines of formal teaching and the controlled transmission of belief and practice. Orthodox instruction, at least of the Protestant variety, requires the authority of biblical exegesis and the discipline of literacy. But there are more infectious ways in which 'religion' can apparently spread, among them the singing of mnemonic lyrics to attractive tunes.

The Sudan Interior Mission (SIM), even today recognized as an organization of extreme fundamentalist views and old-style methods, began work among the Uduk in 1938. This was a remote area, close to the Ethiopian border and in a belt of country administered alternately from the north and the south of the Sudan during the present century. As an apparently very 'primitive' group, the Uduk were of little interest to the government but had a special appeal to the evangelical (and mainly American) missionaries of the SIM.[2] Their work was interrupted during the Second World War because of hostilities on the Ethiopian frontier, but by the mid-1950s they had built up a flourishing mission station and Christian village around it. Political troubles assailed them after the independence of the Sudan in 1956, and by 1964 the foreign missionaries at Chali, in accordance with government policy, had been deported. However, 'Christianity' of a kind continued to flourish among the Uduk after their departure, and by the early 1980s a large proportion of the Uduk were claiming some degree of affiliation to the church. The new expansion of 'faith' was largely in the hands of indigenous personnel; it broke free of the rigid disciplinary codes of the old mission station; and it was carried into the countryside partly on a wave of song, music and practical activity like building chapels and clearing football fields.

I have written in *The Listening Ebony* on the problems of scripture translation into Uduk, which entails grappling with the 'difficult' language of the Revised Standard Version and following its difficulty as far as possible in the new rendering.[3] Commentaries abound on the generally knotty matters of such translation, as well as, of course, on the equally problematic 'untranslation' or unscrambling of the sources which have gone to make up the Bible as we know it in the first place. Variant readings and definitions may claim authority, and ambiguity and many-layered meanings are anticipated as of the essence. It is even accepted in modern scholarship that meanings embedded in the scriptures from their earlier language-contexts can emerge when translation is carried into a vernacular like Uduk, while remaining obscure in modern English. The production of scriptures in a language like

Uduk is thus fully recognized to be hazardous, and success to be relative. But problems of this kind, which have surely troubled translators even of fundamentalist faith and a literal approach to the Bible, are happily left behind in the making of a vernacular hymn-book.

In the matter of composing new 'songs of praise' or even making free translations from existing models, those dilemmas of obscurity and ambiguity which make mission teaching so difficult can be set aside. One can present a definitive view of God, Satan, humankind, and their interrelation. Each hymn can have a specific and limited theme, spelled out and repeated without too much interference from the complexities of scripture (or even the competing messages of other hymns). Songs praising the Lord, while vivid and compact, like the lyrics of the tele-ad need not qualify as good poetry or metaphor to be effective. Phrases are brief, in a telegraphic rather than a poetic sense, and (especially in missionary versions) often pedagogic or imperative in tone. The words can be those of advocacy, of the hard sell and the stark choice. After all, hymns are explicitly what human language is offering, at its very best offering to God, and in no sense what the Word of God is handing down to mere mortals. Although older hymns may acquire through long use a hallowed patina, they never become *sacred* texts in the same sense as the scriptures and very rarely in the Protestant context become regarded as *sacred* music. (It is debatable, of course, whether the Uduk, not a 'sacred'-minded people, have properly appreciated the difference between the words of the Bible and the texts of the hymn-book in this respect.) A mission hymnal evokes no expectation of mystery in the meaning of the lyrics, and indeed it seems that an opportunity to acclaim the elements of faith in joyful, concise and direct terms was welcomed by Protestant missionaries as a practical way of getting the Christian message across.

While the love of God may here 'gladden' the heart and the power of Satan 'threaten' and 'destroy', there is little place for the opaque complexities of joy or for the darker ambivalence of faith itself in such a celebration. While disturbingly qualified emotion may permeate the psalms of David, or even *Hymns Ancient & Modern*, it is happily absent from those Baptist hymnals which have been a major source for SIM translations. For reasons of this kind, the rendering of evangelical hymns into a language like Uduk, or the composition of fresh lyrics, is easy for one of optimistic faith. At the same time, the bare and culturally shallow language of the resulting texts is open to all kinds of misunderstandings, and to none.

Hymns are sung by the Uduk today as one of several styles of popular song throughout a belt of countryside where Christianity's hold by any standard is tenuous. 'Songs of Jesus' are popular not so much because of what they actually say, but *because they are sung.* In the context of evangelism among the Uduk, these songs are virtually the only medium for the non-verbal transmission of Christian ways. Uduk are strongly oriented to musical expression in the various secular and ritual activities of village life, and song, melody and rhythm play a significant part in the most popular ritual and divinatory cults they have adopted from their neighbours. For example, at the festivals and rites of the Order of Ebony Diviners, they happily sing a range of songs in the Jum Jum language (quite unrelated to theirs). Community singing of these songs is a part of the day's activities, as is instrumental playing and dancing. The fact that a good proportion of the singers do not understand the words of the Jum Jum songs does not matter.

Words themselves, I have suggested in *The Listening Ebony*, do not 'do things' for the Uduk; their world does not lend itself to easy verbal interpretation by informant or ethnographer, nor can words as such easily redefine it. In contrast, the project of changing the Uduk world by verbal means, by statements of belief, confessions, acceptance of Jesus and so on, was precisely the task of the SIM as they saw it. Composing the words of the hymns was a part of that project, and those words were intended quite literally to define aspects of the new belief for the Uduk, to reinforce the language of sermons and Bible classes, and indeed to explain in basic terms what the Bible teaches. In some cases the aim has been true, and a striking message has come through in the vernacular; in other cases the vernacular message is clear though not necessarily what was intended; and in yet others, the Uduk words (though individually true coinage) fail to cohere. In most cases those metaphorical overtones assuredly present for the missionary translators have not been transmitted. Godfrey Lienhardt has illuminated his discussion of the missionary enterprise in the Dinka context by introducing the notion of linguistic parallax: that is, a shift in the sense of words resulting from a different external perspective. He has suggested that missionaries have lent new meaning to Dinka religious language not by altering the sense of individual words, but by creating from a fresh perspective new patterns of association between words.[4] This process is evident also in the Uduk case and is illustrated with the clarity of near-caricature in the corpus of song texts.

Neologisms stand out like beacons in the context of hymn lyrics, as, of course, do arbitrarily imported religious words. Malcolm Forsberg, one of the early Chali missionaries, has written of their first attempt at a hymn in Uduk, before they had arrived at a decision as to what to call God. The result, set to the tune of 'We Praise Thee, O God, for the Son of Thy Love', looked like this (with my translation opposite):

God diid imis   God is above
God diid imis   God is above
Akim bidi yuka Yesus. His child is called Jesus.

Forsberg commented, 'We taught the people to sing it, but it did not sound quite right', and his wife observed that the English word 'God' sounded terribly out of place in the Uduk hymn.[5]

Some of the hymns later incorporated in the church hymnal *Mii ma Kaniisa Dhala Awarkaŋ Gway*[6] nevertheless incorporate foreign terms, such as *halleluya* in the following example, Hymn 4, where the poetry is much reduced by comparison with the original model used for the tune of 'Praise Ye the Lord, the Almighty; the King of Creation':

Hallelu, hallelu, hallelu, halleluya,	Halleluja . . .
Taka Arumgimis mo ma.	Praise God.
Hallelu, hallelu, hallelu, halleluya,	Halleluja . . .
Taka Arumgimis mo ma.	Praise God.
Taka Arumgimis ma, halleluya.	Praise God, halleluja.
. . .	. . .
Taka Arumgimis mo ma.	Praise God.

Arumgimis, 'the spirit which is in the sky', was the neologism eventually adopted for 'God', a made-up compound reifying into a Being Set Above the very general and diffuse *arum*, or spirit of bodily life on earth. In the new form it was inextricable from the authority claimed by the missionaries for themselves and on behalf of the written texts they produced; outside the Christian community, it had the very specific connotation of the particular *arum* of the mission station, a power not without its own perceived ambiguities. *Tak*, in this hymn and elsewhere used for 'praise', is not, as far as I know, used of any kind of *arum* in the villages, but rather of the respect due to chiefs, important guests and so forth. *Hallelu, halleluya* cannot be rendered into everyday Uduk usage; indeed, it could not be translated into an everyday idiom even in English, as the expression belongs to a distinct genre of religious discourse. Such a genre is itself lacking in the dominantly colloquial discourse of Uduk, and the singing of these syllables, while no doubt conveying a sense of holiness to a listening missionary, cannot as yet (if ever) have that aura for the ordinary Uduk singer. The bald content of this song, the words taken alone, bears no comparison with the original and seems to me to fail as a newly constructed pattern or innovative association. The vernacular does not even pick up the rhythm of the melody and is awkward to sing.

A few hymns were sung in English, such as 'Go, Tell it on the Mountain', quite popular in the mission days and still sung today. The robust rhythm of words and tune together in this case seems to have assured the song's popularity. A few Arabic-language hymns were introduced at Chali from other Protestant churches of the Sudan, and some of these are still sung. But on the whole, the body of hymns sung during the heyday of the mission at Chali in the 1950s were drawn from the growing corpus of Uduk-language lyrics, and it is these which have successfully spread into the countryside today. Hymns in the Uduk mission context tended to have a New Testament focus and were called *gway ma Yesus*, songs of Jesus.

The 92 Uduk-language lyrics in the hymnal fall into three categories. The first includes straight translations of texts, set to their existing tunes. Some of these are to be found in, for example, *Hymns Ancient & Modern*, and others are from the American evangelical tradition. Many of the latter may be found in a recent collection, the *Gospel Singer's Wordbook*,[7] and where I refer to English-language models below, I have taken them from this American source. The second category includes those set to an existing Western tune, but with a fresh lyric bearing little or no reference to any textual model. Finally, in the third category are those hymns with both brand-new words and fresh melody, likely to appeal more directly to the Uduk ear than the standard churchy tunes we know. I might just mention here a certain indigenization of even the most familiar; a visitor's ear cannot at first always recognize a well-known hymn tune when rendered into a five-note scale with harmony in fourths throughout.

1. Translated hymns

The direct translation method works quite well for those hymns where the content is simple, narrative or descriptive rather than theological or metaphorical in intent. A good example would be 'Away in a Manger' (No. 14 in the hymnal), where I sense no areas of difficulty or ambiguity in the transposition of meaning. The baby asleep in the animal shed, on the dry grass, not crying, the baby who is Jesus, whom I love and whom I ask to stay with me until the dawn, is carried over into Uduk without any difficulty. Other carols seem to work well also, for example 'O Come all Ye Faithful' (No. 15), 'While Shepherds Watched' (No. 17), 'Silent Night' (No. 18), 'O Little Town of Bethlehem' (No. 19).

The method of more or less direct translation sometimes, however, runs into difficulties because of the sensitivities of the social and political context in which the missionaries were working. Here and there a literal translation has been prudently avoided, as in the rendering of 'Onward Christian Soldiers' (No. 76). The 'soldiers' of this example, which could appear provocative in the Sudanese context, make no appearance. Instead, the call is to 'people of the Church', or 'people of Jesus', to advance and to overcome with success, though not actually as if war. I should note here too that, presumably because of political sensitivities, an important element in the Negro spirituals of the United States has not been carried through. The great cry for freedom, for temporal release from bondage as an analogue and even accompaniment of spiritual freedom, has been muted; there are no songs in the Uduk hymnal on the lines of the famous 'Go Down Moses': 'When Israel was in Egypt's land / Let my people go. / Oppressed so hard they could not stand, / Let my people go. / . . . O let us all from bondage flee; / And let us all in Christ be free. / . . . We need not always weep and mourn; / And wear these slavery chains forlorn.' These cries are too close to underlying truths of historical feeling for appropriate inclusion in the context of the Chali mission, throughout its brief life on a political precipice. But the general sentiment was there, and found other expression.

It is, of course, in the area of theological and philosophical language that close textual translation encounters the thorniest areas of difficulty and is obliged to reconstruct verbal definitions and accounts of the world. Very often, a problem has been evaded by rendering original expressions of an abstract or ethereal kind in tangible, experiential form.

Consider what happens, for example, in this case, the first verse of 'My Faith Looks up to Thee' (No. 69). The verse reads in the original, 'My faith looks up to Thee, / Thou lamb of Calvary, / Savior divine! / Now hear me while I pray; / Take all my guilt away. / O let me from this day be wholly Thine.' The vernacular, with my close translation back, reads as follows:

Em pem hil 'kup ki le,	My eyes look up to you,
Ka'bal ma Arumgimis,	Sheep of God,
Manwoth ahal.	The one who saves me.
Cikaal mon'tho e le.	Listen to me, the praising of you.
Kali miim pem 'peni 'bal.	Take my deeds away from me.
Ahal mina jim pini	I shall be yours
'Baar mo.	All of me.

The abstractions of *faith* and of *guilt* have gone. The first has become eyesight (which is indeed in the Uduk view involved in understanding, in comprehending) and the second deeds, by implication bad deeds, which transposes an inner state to external and accountable actions. It is true that *'tho* is regularly used in mission discourse for pray or prayer, but I do not think that the vernacular term distinguishes between the notion of communicating with a *divine* being and merely *praising* a human being. The 'Savior' is no longer explicitly 'divine', and indeed that notion would be difficult to translate into pre-Christian Uduk discourse, except as one possessed or risen from the dead. That is why I have not carried through in the re-translation the religious implications of 'Thine' as against 'yours'. In other ways the attempt at direct translation produces awkwardnesses: for example, the completeness of 'wholly Thine' has been reduced to the completeness of 'my self, all of me' being yours. Nor do I believe that the lamb of Calvary, rewritten as the sheep of God, carries through the overtones of biblical sacrifice that it should, for although animals are killed for various rituals by the Uduk, these acts are not part of a theocentric ritual system.[8]

Compare, in the following English original 'Let Jesus Come into Your Heart', the way in which the image of a tempest *inside* a person, presumably signifying internal confusion, doubt and turmoil, has become a storm *outside* in the process of translation into Uduk and back again into English. Quelling an outside storm is indeed a sign of spiritual potency for the Uduk:

and this is understood as a physical 'reality' of effect and is not intended as psychological metaphor, as in the case of the model:

> If you are tired of the load of your sin
> Let Jesus come into your heart
> If you desire a new life to begin,
> Let Jesus, &c.
>
>> Just now, your doubting give o'er;
>> Just now, reject Him no more.
>> Just now, throw open the door;
>> Let Jesus, &c.
>
> If 'tis for purity now that you sigh . . .
> Fountains for cleansing are flowing near by. . . .
>
> If there's a tempest your voice cannot still . . .
> If there's a void this world can never fill. . . .

Corresponding verses of Hymn 49 read as follows (I should explain that the liver is regarded as the seat of the emotions, the stomach that of reason; when using these anatomical terms in this figurative sense, I give them an initial capital letter):

Wa<u>k</u>kil le wukina is gom miinthus,	If you are weary because of bad-deeds,
Dhalka Yesus yayi'd leya du.	Let Jesus come to your Liver.
Wa<u>k</u>kil le ŋap <u>t</u>el miin this 'pen shwanel,	If you want to begin a new way-of-doing-things today,
Dhalka Yesus yayi'd leya du.	Let Jesus, &c.
Shwanel da<u>k</u>i gwo shil 'ku<u>p</u>.	Today leave bad talk alone.
Dhalki a'di ki ush mo.	Do not reject him.
Shwanel yi<u>p</u>a campur ki <u>k</u>any.	Today throw the door open.
Dhalka Yesus yayi'd leya du.	Let Jesus, &c.
Wa<u>k</u>kil le ŋa<u>p</u>ana dun dheleli'd . . .	If you wish to have a cleansed Liver . . .
Abas ma Yesus kasha'd mmolam le. . . .	The blood of Jesus flows to wash you. . . .
Wa<u>k</u>kil <u>p</u>unthar mola le kar ki shwam . . .	If you cannot keep the storm quiet . . .
Wa<u>k</u>kil mombushuru'd mol ma 'cesh 'tu'd. . . .	If the earth cannot fill the empty place. . . .

In other cases, the general theme has been appropriated with a given tune but the lyric somewhat adapted. This has often meant a reduction of significance and scale, a stripping of poetry and richness to leave a bare slogan. This has happened, for example, with the American folk hymn 'Were you there?' The original model reads, 'Were you there when they crucified my Lord? / Were you there when they crucified my Lord? Oh, / Sometimes it causes me to / Tremble, tremble, tremble. / Were you there when they crucified my Lord? / Were you there when they nailed Him to the tree? ... / Were you there when they laid him in the tomb?' The Uduk hymn composed to this tune, retaining only a tenuous link with the inspiration of the original, begins as follows and continues in much the same vein: 'Jesus died on a wooden cross / Jesus died on a wooden cross / Jesus died just over there / Died in our area / Jesus died on a wooden cross.'

The effect of making allusions more concrete is sometimes to give a more tangible, bodily existence to God, Satan and so forth, than was necessarily intended in the English originals. This can be seen, for example, in the third verse of Hymn 8 (tune: 'A Mighty Fortress') which conjures up the spirits of the earth and the Leader of Darkness. The model reads, 'And though this world with devils filled, / Should threaten to undo us; / We will not fear, for God hath willed / His truth to triumph through us. / The prince of darkness grim, / We tremble not for him / His rage we can endure, / For lo! his doom is sure, / One little word shall fell him.' Here the Uduk conception of the earth as the resting-place of the shades of the dead (*aruma 'cesh*) is made to serve for the 'devils' and their prince (an arrangement which follows conveniently from the translators situating God in the sky above). The Uduk, with translation back, goes as follows:

Bahila rum 'cesh 'tu'di mo mo	Behold the *aruma 'cesh* filling the place
Mmomuri shwaa 'cesh ki sho'k mo.	About to spread everywhere.
Arumgimis lilki is k̲om bana	God is guiding our living
Gwoŋ ganam piti ye mii 'bal mo.	His true words are victorious for ever.
Tap̲a mondhurumi'd,	Chief of the Darkness,
Usha ana mmodee	We refuse to fear him
Abumburush piti,	His dodging attacks,
Mina ana 'dim 'kup̲.	We will resist.
Ari gwoŋ 'del mish kum a'di mo.	One small word will overcome him.[9]

2. New lyrics to old tunes

In the second category of hymns, an existing Western tune has been used, but the message is very freely composed in Uduk. There may be a correspondence of sorts, or merely a general inspiration. But in some cases there is no link between the old and new texts. This is true in the case of the new words to the song 'Old-time Religion': "Tis the old-time religion / ... And it's good enough for me. / It was good for our mothers, / ... It has served our fathers, / It will do when I'm dying.' The old words would obviously convey quite the wrong message, and so a fresh ditty has been set to the tune. The result, Hymn 31 in the Uduk book, is popular and sung with gusto. The rhythm goes down well, and this must be the reason for its popularity; for although the words do seem to swing with the tune, they have become a string of statements and instructions, with the feel not of the heart but of the schoolroom:

Yan moŋ'kokile ki sulel . . .	This is life everlasting . . .
Mmomisha Arumgimis.	To understand [= see] God.
A'di ta'da Yesus ganal . . .	He is the true Jesus . . .
A'di be, jasi a'di 'del.	He is, just he alone.
Yan moŋ'kokile ki sulel . . .	This is life everlasting . . .
Mmomish Yesus si'dal.	To know [= see] Jesus too.
A'di wu'd mo iwoth ana . . .	He died to save us . . .
Wu'd ki cwany'cithan dhul.	Died on a wooden cross.
Gami gwo ma Yesus is mo . . .	Believe in [the word of] Jesus . . .
Dhali um minu woth mo be.	And you will all be saved.

In the vernacular hymns patterned only loosely on available models, crucial emphases are easily given. The next example vividly evokes Satan, as a bad *arum*, of course, having formerly 'seized' the believer, with the ideophonic expression *ki nyeŋ!*—conjuring in the mind a tight grasp. The expression for having been unhappy, and later, being happy in the Stomach with Jesus, are perfectly ordinary everyday expressions; but the notion of the Word entering the Liver is emotionally striking and powerful in the Uduk idiom. The notion of Jesus himself actually being there in the Liver is very potent indeed. An immediately understandable interpretation of hearing a call from Jesus would be that it came in a dream, but I do not know if this meaning is intended here, in Hymn 67:

Setaan bu'thki ahal ki nyeŋ,	Satan held me firmly gripped,
Bwam pem shilaa ki ski.	My Stomach was very bad.
Ayuk ma Yesus cikkikal,	The call of Jesus I then heard,
Gwo wurki ahal adu.	The Word entered my Liver.
Ayuk ma Yesus yukgal 'twal,	The call of Jesus I answered to,
Abas piti wothki ahal.	His blood saved me.
Miinthus kalkina a'di 'bal,	Bad actions [= sin] he has taken as a burden,
'Borkikal bwa mo a Yesus.	I am happy now in Jesus.
Miinthus dhalkikal ki sulel,	Sin I have left for ever,
Yesus karaal ki 'kus.	Jesus set me free.
Ca'bkal ki 'borel e Yesus,	I am sitting very well with Jesus,
A'di di'da dum pem.	He is there in my Liver.

Hil ka Seṯaan ki ṯocaal 'kus,	And if Satan bothers me,
Migal gusa Yesus.	I will run to Jesus.
Anyor caaca gom a'di di'd,	Great anger for him [viz. Satan] there is [in Jesus],
A'di ki la gus mo.	He will soon flee away.

In the next example, Hymn 9, there is an interesting interchange between using the expression *gwo* (word or words) for a story and for the Word, which can 'change the Liver', 'pierce the Liver', a novel image in Uduk and an arresting one. The Word, or the story, the teachings, the instructions, of Jesus (all are possible readings) are quite appropriately to be kept in the Stomach (committed to memory, made permanent knowledge), making one happy there. Nevertheless, although elegant and suggestive in its own way, the making of a *being* out of 'words' stretches the Uduk imagination almost too far:

Gwo ma Yesus ta gwoŋ ganal,	The story of Jesus is the truth,
Ta gwo jin di ki e.	It is the living Word [lit., a story which is alive].
Jamul p̱iyi'd jin waki a'di,	There is no other which is like it,
Ta gwo jin di ki shel.	It is a story quite unique.
Gwom 'boro'd, Gwo 'kunyu'd,	The Word is good, the Word is sweet,
Gwo mom'bi'th, Gwo monyca.	Word of strength, Word of greatness.
Gwo jin midi diki p̱i mo,	The Word which will never disappear,
Midi di kan ki sulel.	It will be for ever.
Gwo ma Yesus to gwo miimer,	The story of Jesus is a story to wonder at,
Ta gwo mmolaḵa du.	A story to change the Liver.
Jamul p̱iyi'd mokar ki e kan,	There is no other to keep you alive like this,
Ta gwo jin di ki shel.	It is a story quite unique.
Gwo ma Yesus ta gwon thoson,	The story of Jesus is a tale of good instruction,
Ta gwo mmoṯor miinthus.	It is a story which tells us about sin.
Jamul p̱iyi'd mosukaal du kan,	No other can pierce my Liver like this [= to move me emotionally],
Ta gwo jin di ki shel.	It is a story quite unique.
Gwo ma Yesus ta gwoŋ gam is,	The story of Jesus is a story of belief,
Ta gwo mom'bi'th caaca.	A story of great strength.
Jamul p̱iyi'd jin p̱i miinthus e,	There is no other to overcome sin,
Ta gwo jin di ki shel.	It is a story quite unique.
Gwo ma Yesus ta gwo malas,	The story of Jesus is one of comfort,
Ta gwo mmodhu e bwa.	It is a story to keep in the Stomach [= to remember].

Jamul piyi'd mo'boraal	There is no other to make me so happy
bwa kan,	[lit., good in the Stomach],
Ta gwo jin di ki shel.	It is a story quite unique.

In the next example, we look directly to the expected bodily resurrection of all believers and to the Second Coming. Those whose Liver is good and clean are bright and shining. This image goes so far from ordinary understanding that it must retain a 'foreign' feel even for the believer. Hymn 43 reads as follows:

Ki a'di pu'dki'd, ki a'di pu'dki'd,	When he arrives, when he arrives,
Mmotul uni is mo,	To gather them together,
Kun dhelelin mo ki jarol,	They who are clean and bright,
Kun ena a'di mo.	Those whom he loves.
Waka cul e mon'thamo	Like a morning star
Mmokar mo ki jarol,	To keep the place bright,
Uni kushi mo ki bany bany	They are white and shining
Kun woth ma Yesus.	Those saved by Jesus.
A'di tulki'd, a'di tulki'd	He gathers up, he gathers up
Gom Bampal e Mis mo	For the Land on High
Kun dhelelin, kun 'bor ma du,	Those clean ones, those of good Liver,
Kun ena a'di mo.	Those whom he loves.
Ushi uci, ushi uci,	Little children, little children,
Kun en Manwan 'bal,	Whom the Redeemer loves,
Ta kun dhelelin mo eya du,	Are those clean in the Liver,
Kun ena a'di mo.	Those whom he loves.

The theme is continued in several other hymns, and the negative side of the next Coming is not ignored. In Hymn 37 (tune: 'How Firm a Foundation'), which here begins 'Jesus has gone to his home in the sky, / He will come back. / He will descend with a great cry', the last two verses read in translation back:

Um gun dar ka bas ma Yesus,	Those of you without the blood of Jesus,
Um nonkunu mo mo be.	You will be barred.
Jasa nyor ma Arumgimis midi	Just the anger of God
Ca'ba po um 'baar mo be.	Will remain upon you all.
Kana, ciki gwo ma Yesus,	Listen, hear the word of Jesus,
Dhali hayi a'di e,	And obey him,
Haala cim yan mishu yisa,	Because that day is not known,
A'di 'disha'dish mo be.	It is very close.

The note of schoolroom warning is unmistakable. Perhaps this was what had first struck Umpa and lasted in her memory beyond the contrived linguistic innovations of the new theology.

3. New songs

The fresh compositions, made for the Uduk context with their own words and tunes, are often simple to the point of sounding like slogans. Hymn 34 plays upon only three lines: 'From the grave, Jesus appeared. / The grave could not keep him. / He overcame death.' This is a minimal and powerful statement of the message of the resurrection and touches a deep chord in the existing Uduk world. Like the following example, Hymn 36, it is not a translation but a new composition:

Yesus midi yayul . . .	Jesus is coming . . .
Yesus midi yayul dokle.	Jesus is coming again.
A'di midi yayul . . .	He is coming . . .
A'di midi yayul bwaa rak.	He is coming from out of the clouds.
Yesus midi yayul . . .	Jesus is coming . . .
Yesus midi yayul yuk kum piti.	Jesus is coming to call his people.
Kun iikin mina bwa 'bor . . .	Those who go will be happy . . .
Kun iikin mina bwa 'bor ki sulel.	Those who go will be happy for ever.
Kum bocon mini ko . . .	Those who remain will cry . . .
Kum bocon mini ko gom a'di.	Those who remain will cry for him.

This hymn, produced especially for the Uduk congregation at Chali, like several others presses the key theme of the Second Coming, when the faithful will be taken up to Heaven. The plight of the rest is explicit. The notion of a final judgement and authoritative separation of the good and the bad lies behind the disciplinarian tone of a few other hymns in which a severe God demands obedience. The following example, Hymn 45, is particularly threatening, and in so far as it demands to know if the believer's name is 'written in the book' it is almost too strongly suggestive of the powerful authority of government, court and police:

Gwon dwall ma Arumgimis di'd.	God's judgement exists.
Ana 'baar mina dosh a'di bwambor. . . .	All of us will stand before it. . . .
Gwo mina a'di dwall gom miim bana. . . .	He will give judgement on our acts. . . .
Uni gun 'kona gwayi bwa ma warkal	Those who have their names in the book
Wothkunu mo be. . . .	Will be saved. . . .

Uni gun dar ki gwayi bwa ma warkal	Those who do not have their names in the book
Ṭagu o'd mo be. . . .	Will be thrown in the fire. . . .
Gway pini mane? Gway pini mane?	Where is your name? Where is your name?
'Kwaru mo 'taa? 'Kwaru mo 'taa?	Is it written? Is it written?

The reference to the book or paper (*warka*, the Arabic term) was no doubt intended by the missionary teachers to be taken *metaphorically*. However, a metaphorical book is more than the ordinary Uduk could be expected to assume, given the emphasis on *the book* and all it meant in a literal sense in the mission context. Of course, having one's name in the book was also, and is still, unavoidably linked with matters of administration, and hence the threat of not having one's name in the book carries far more worrying overtones for the non-literate villager than can have been really intended by those who introduced the hymn.

And yet, in spite of these grave problems of verbal translation and composition in the making of Uduk hymns, their performance has played a key part in holding together the Christian community and tradition after the departure of foreign missionaries and in the subsequent expansion of Christian activity to the countryside. During the song session I held during a revisit in 1983 to Waḵa'cesh, an area six miles from Chali where there had been no Christian activities during the heyday of the mission, I was offered mainly 'songs of Jesus'. Most of these were from the collection in the hymnal, though in every case belonging to my categories 2 and 3 above. That is, they were not the literal translations but lyrics composed afresh in the Uduk tongue either to existing tunes or to new ones. A couple more of the hymns were clearly of the same 1950s vintage but were not included in the printed hymnal. In addition, there were a couple of new ones, said to have been recently composed. The words were of impeccable lineage, but the melody was distinctly more lively than many of the original collection. In the new context of Christian revival, the old genre was alive and well, due perhaps to its musical rather than its textual side.

Of course, the awkwardness of the verbal translation of a hymn, or the putting together of words in unfamiliar ways to make one, is highlighted when the text is put down on a page in black and white. It is not the primary purpose of hymns to be read, or even understood as words alone. They are for musical performance, for singing, especially community singing. This side of Christian hymns was thoroughly understood and largely accepted by the Uduk. The significance of verbal discourse as such was limited in pre-Christian Uduk social and formal ritual life, but by contrast the place of music and song, dance and bodily gesture, was very important. Hunting rituals, rites of passage, ceremonies of those cults devoted to healing, all were rich in songs, music and movement, and in addition there was a range of secular styles of music and dance. On this level, we can guess that the practice of hymn-singing was a key element in the establishment of a Christian community at Chali in the heyday of the mission, as it certainly was later in the spread of Christian ways across the countryside.

The SIM, at least a generation ago, was not disposed to encourage the people to contribute from their own musical and singing tradition to the hymns of the church. Only now are a few brand-new songs of Jesus making an appearance, sung to the lyre in the old style. Jon Arensen reports that he found a very different situation among the Murle, further to the south but also in the Sudan-Ethiopia border region. The American Presbyterian Mission worked among the Murle only from about the mid-1950s to 1963, and they did not produce a formal hymnal. After the first Sudanese civil war (1955–72), when the Summer Institute of Linguistics arrived to carry out language work, some hymns were introduced for the first time. During the next decade the singing of Christian songs spread, and many new ones were being created informally in the Murle musical tradition, often antiphonal in form. Arensen tells me that during his work with the Summer Institute in the early 1980s, he arranged for a girl to make notes of these songs, and within a week she had made a collection of 250. The musical contribution of the Murle seems to indicate a real responsiveness to what the mission there was offering, and it is Arensen's opinion that in general, only hymns which are in an indigenous musical mode will really succeed. On this criterion, those elements of Christian belief which have apparently been dispersed through song among the Uduk villages sit very lightly.

Postscript

Since this essay was completed, I have received news that as a result of the new civil war which broke out in the Sudan in mid-1983, Uduk country has been visited by fresh devastation. During 1987, forces of the Sudan People's Liberation Army pushed northwards along the Ethiopian border into Blue Nile Province, at one point taking and holding the town of Kurmuk. The retaliatory actions and reprisals of the national armed forces in the Kurmuk district included their burning of sixteen small village churches and chapels in the Uduk area (though, I understand, not Chali church itself). Many of the people have fled. The accompanying photograph shows the village chapel of Waka'cesh with some of its congregation in May 1983. This is one of the chapels reported burned by the army in 1987.

Notes

1 From December 1965, fieldwork, supported by the University of Khartoum, was carried out in various periods until June 1969. A subsequent brief visit was made

in 1983. A general account of the Uduk may be found in my book, *Kwanim Pa: The Making of the Uduk People. An Ethnographic Study of Survival in the Sudan Ethiopian Borderlands*, Oxford: Clarendon Press 1979.
2. L. M. P. and N. Sanderson, *Education, Religion and Politics in Southern Sudan 1899–1964*, London: Ithaca Press 1981, esp. pp. 240–1.
3. See my book, *The Listening Ebony: Moral Knowledge, Religion, and Power among the Uduk of Sudan*, Oxford: Clarendon Press 1988.
4. R. G. Lienhardt, 'The Dinka and Catholicism', in J. Davis (ed.), *Religious Organization and Religious Experience*, London and New York: Academic Press 1982 (ASA Monographs, no. 21), pp. 81–95.
5. Malcolm Forsberg, *Land Beyond the Nile*, New York: Harper 1958, p. 157.
6. *Mii ma Ḵaniisa Dhala Awarkaŋ* Gway, Chali: Sudan Interior Mission 1963. Throughout this essay I follow the orthography established by the SIM, which employs an apostrophe to indicate implosion or explosion in the consonant it precedes, underlining to indicate aspiration, and the oblique stroke to represent a glottal stop. Tones ate not marked.
7. Linda R. Beddoe, *Gospel Singer's Wordbook*, New York: Oak Publications 1984.
8. For a study of the pitfalls of using sacrificial terminology in Africa, see Patricia M. Holden, 'Aspects of Sacrifice in the African Ethnographic Literature', University of Oxford: MLitt. Thesis 1984.
9. Stephen Missa Dhunya helped me with the translation of this and also of Hymns 9, 43 and 67 below.

92

Excerpt from
'"ALMOST PERSUADED NOW TO BELIEVE"
Gospel songs in New Zealand evangelical theology and practice'

Bryan D. Gilling

Source: *Journal of Religious History*, 19(1) (1995), 92–110.

The music used during religious events has often been overlooked by scholars more concerned with the spoken word as representative of the the beliefs held by the participants. This is a particularly tempting trap when studying a phenomenon like a mass evangelistic crusade, where one man (and it is virtually always a man) forms the focus for an entire event. His words and deeds are both easier to determine and study, and he seems so important.

However, an American historian has observed that 'Protestantism, when all is said and done, is more adequately represented by its hymns and prayers than by its textbooks'[1] — and, we might well add, than by the public utterances of a relative handful of individual preachers. British sociologist David Martin asserts that 'the hymn is the most central item in the religion of Britain'.[2] The nature of what the ordinary attenders believe and feel may be more accurately discerned from the aspect of worship in which they participate actively: congregational singing.

The importance of music in the creation and maintenance of religious belief and practice has been confirmed in several recent scholarly studies. The title of one is particularly suggestive: '"I Want to be Like Jesus": The Self-Denning Power of Evangelical Hymnody'.[3] In that article the author argues for the crucial influence songs and hymns have, both on the intellectual level in forming theology and on a more emotional and practical level in moulding expressions of piety.

In New Zealand, specifically, American mass evangelists have come and gone. They have attracted tens of thousands to hear them. But when, after only a few days, they have left, their most perceptible ongoing legacy has been in the music bequeathed to the New Zealand churches. Each of these missions came with its own distinctive style of music, and in the case of the first two, its own music leader, who was nearly as great an attraction as the evangelist. By studying that music and the methods of its use observers can gain some insights into the conduct of evangelistic missions attempting to harvest 'decisions for Jesus'. Also, this shows ways they can both influence and reflect the theological climate in which they operate. Finally, by comparing the different styles and content of the missions' music it becomes apparent that there have been shifts in theological fashions throughout the century. This change is apparent despite the fact that these missions are held amongst people who seek a religion which remains constant, unchanging — the 'old time religion' which had been 'good for Paul and Silas' and sundry other worthies. We shall seek here to discern some of those changes in evangelical theology and methodology and thus to reveal alterations in the understanding and expression of Christianity in New Zealand through the twentieth century.

New Zealand has been visited by six mass evangelistic missions. Conveniently enough, they can be grouped in three pairs through the twentieth century. The first pair were at the beginning of the century, before the First World War. In 1902 Reuben Archer Torrey, soon to be a leader of the fundamentalist movement, toured the country from Wellington south. Ten years later, in 1912 and 1913, one of his colleagues, J. Wilbur Chapman, carried out a much more extensive mission, lasting several months and travelling from one end of the country to the other.[4] The music leader for both of these missions was Charles McCallon Alexander, compiler of the durable *Alexander's Hymns*.[5] Then in the middle of the century Billy Graham made two fleeting visits, fitted around visits to Australia, one in 1959 and the second in 1969. As song leader and music expert he brought Cliff Barrows who produced his own, much smaller, hymnbook. A third pair of virtually simultaneous but discrete missions were run in 1987. The first was held by former Billy Graham associate Leighton Ford in the southern part of the country; the second by Argentinian Luis Palau in the northern areas. Neither of these brought his own music specialist or distinctive hymnbook, relying instead upon local organizers to provide for these facets of the mission.[6]

I

The music of the two earlier missions was a major feature in a way not repeated in any subsequent campaign. This was chiefly because of the personality and ability of their music leader, Charles Alexander.[7] He was a graduate of the Moody Bible Institute in Chicago, recently founded by D. L. Moody. While there he had been a student of R. A. Torrey, whom he now accompanied.

Charles Alexander had a definite agenda for his songleading and his music clearly reflected his intentions: to prepare the audience psychologically for the following speaker by welding them together in one large, comfortable and happy family. He had earlier made those intentions clear to a colleague in what was almost a programmatic statement:

> The first thing I like to do is by some method to produce a homelike atmosphere among the people in the audience. One must make them forget that they are in a set service. I try to do nothing undignified or eccentric, but endeavour to induce such a feeling as you have in a company of friends gathered around a fireside at home . . .[8]

This was precisely how he proceeded seven years later when in New Zealand. The homelike atmosphere was induced with a series of jolly, even triumphalist, choruses comprised of simple, often repetitive, lyrics set to catchy, easily acquired tunes. His songleading technique was that of the hearty family fireside sing-along. One example was provided by the *Evening Post* as he dealt with the first Wellington audience:

> You tell me you can't sing; I don't believe you. Anyone who has got a mouth can sing this song . . . Everyone who is good-looking sings. Now ladies, now men, come down off your dignity and dig. It's a nice little rattle-bang air, as you hear.[9]

This 'nice little rattle-bang air' was 'The Old Time Religion'. He also insisted that 'a leader must be a leader. He will certainly fail if he does not make up his mind that he is going to conquer the audience before he sits down. People like to follow when they have a leader.'[10]

And lead he certainly did. One observer noted: 'As a leader, his sway over a chorus is phenomenal . . . People who can't sing and know they can't sing open their mouths and do sing when his ringing "Folks, wake up there!" rouses them from their lethargy.'[11] The same Wellington critic observed how the simplistically winsome gospel choruses were transformed by Alexander's presentation so that they became a powerful expression of group emotion, and that this phenomenon overruled more cerebral theological evaluation. The critic wrote:

> The leader is a magician who takes commonplace Gospel music — mere rubbish it might be thought — and changes it into gems of song by his exquisite interpretation of sentiment . . . The heart is

> greater than the head. Pure sentiment transcends the principles of musical criticism. And thus it is that Mr Alexander can transmute even the odds and ends of harmony into religious classics.[12]

This could involve embarrassment of individuals — all in good fun, of course — as in one case in Dunedin.

> But Mr Alexander is never easily satisfied, and his searching eye detected several who were not joining in. 'That's absolutely unallowable in this place,' he exclaimed abruptly, with the old delicious American accent. 'You've got to sing or go home. You know that.' The audience smiled, but they took him at his word all the same, and joined in with renewed vigour. 'Infidelity never wrote any songs,' he remarked pointedly . . .[13] [. . .]

[. . .] If these accounts give some idea of the method of using the music as an evangelistic tool, there were also clues to its theological effects — shaping the ideas of the participants. The musical style, lowbrow and 'popular', was calculated to do just this. As one commentator said:

> Nobody, of course, says that the songs are going to rank with 'Jesus, Lover of My Soul", 'Rock of Ages', and other classics; but they serve their purpose; they convey a message; like all new things, they catch the ear and lodge in the memory.[18]

The intention was that they could be recalled and hummed long after the preached word had passed out of mind. The choruses contained many phrases which the continual repetition and 'hummable' tunes made readily memorable, such as "God will take care of you', 'Oh yes he cares, I know He cares', and 'He will keep you from falling'. Alexander's aim was consciously to assist these phrases and their associated ideas to become firmly fixed in the audiences' minds. He was questioned about the frequency of their repetition: '"You hit us often in the same place." "Yes, I'm drilling a hole," was his reply'.[19]

What, then, were the messages being conveyed in Alexander's music? First, there were those which directly encouraged — sometimes almost bullied — hearers into responding to the evangelist's appeal. One example will suffice. This song browbeat the hearer into compliance with the urgency of the need for decision.

> You must do something with Jesus,
> You must do something tonight!
> You must decide this great question:
> You must do something tonight!

> No neutral ground must be taken.
> You must do something tonight!
> You must be *for* or *against* Him:
> You must do something to-night!
>
> You must do something with Jesus,
> You must do something tonight!
> Will you reject? or will you accept?
> You must do something tonight![20]

Then, if one could resist that, there were those songs which tugged at the hearers' heartstrings, intended to stir up emotion to the extent that they could melt any resolve to resist.

> Somebody's here with an aching heart,
> No rest and no peace within;
> Somebody's here and the teardrops start,
> As God convicts of sin.
>
> Jesus will give you rest,
> Jesus will give you rest;
> Turn from your sin, call now on Him,
> For Jesus will give you rest.[21]

In addition to music which was calculated simply to enhance the evangelistic appeal of the meeting, much of the material used conveyed distinct social messages. One frequently repeated theme in both the music and preaching was of the Christian home from which the prodigal child had strayed. Strangely, though, the image was not the biblical one of the anxious father. Instead the pious mother had completely supplanted the patriarch. Fathers appeared seldom and then usually in the preaching where they were called to forsake drink and immorality and return to the home. The music used the appeal of this saintly mother to attract those errant offspring. [. . .]

[. . .] Moving to theology, we find that there is an assumption made of the audience's knowledge and acceptance of the central tenets of evangelical theology. A key doctrine for evangelical Christians is the view of Jesus' death as a substitutionary atonement for human sins, yet in Alexander's songs there was little direct explication of that death, rather the concentration was upon the benefits available for the believer. For example, a very popular song, 'There's Power in the Blood', despite its title and the constant repetition of the phrase, revelled solely in personal benefits derived from the believer's appropriation and application of that power, rather than in its origin.

> Would you be free from your burden of sin?
> There's power in the blood, power in the blood;

> Would you o'er evil a victory win?
> There's wonderful power in the blood.
>
> Would you be free from your passion and pride? . . .
>
> Would you be whiter, much whiter than snow? . . .
>
> Would you do service for Jesus your King? . . .[23]

Jesus himself was continually referred to as 'the / my / our / Saviour', but the mechanics of the soteriological process were not gone into. The term 'Saviour' lost many of its theological implications — it was not even linked in a direct way with the believer's individual conversion decision. Rather, 'the Saviour' was portrayed as a consoling, guiding, encouraging and protecting companion,[24] 'this Friend so dear',[25] and 'the lowly Jesus' whose quality of friendship is uniquely holy, meek, steadfast and generous.[26] The work of Christ thus appeared largely in terms of the consolation of the believer in this life. This differs substantially from the traditional emphasis in evangelical theology on Christ's atoning death on the cross and on his roles as the sinner's advocate before God and as eschatological Judge. These songs portrayed a much milder, sweeter Victorian vision of religious life with a featherbed Christ cushioning the believer from the impact of this-worldly adversities. Even when praising the loving, self-giving nature of Christ, the concentration remained fixed firmly on the advantages accruing 'for me'. [. . .]

[. . .] With the Chapman mission in 1912–13, many of the same themes and emphases were retained by Alexander, although expressed in a largely new repertoire. A major study of the use of songs in nineteenth-century revivalism notes the tendency which we have observed here, the replacement of hymns dealing directly with doctrine with songs telling a story or giving a testimony, paralleling the preacher's anecdotes.[30] When Deity was addressed, earlier expression of direct praise and thanks had been replaced with soft, pleading supplication. Many songs had no audience at all, but were merely personal 'testimony', as if the singers were witnesses on Jesus' behalf before a hostile jury, as in, for example, 'I Love to Tell the Story' — which never actually does — and 'He Lifted Me' which recounts the lifting of the sinner 'to a higher plane'.[31] The New Zealand situation in which these songs were employed and so readily accepted was one still closely tied to and influenced by its colonial origins, but receptive to the missioners for a variety of reasons. At one end of the ecclesiastical spectrum were the attitudes which formed what one historian has characterized as 'mahogany religion', seeking respectability and standing in the still-raw settler society.[32] At the other was a growing swell of revivalism and pietism, again largely imported. It was influenced by recent arrivals such as the Brethren, Seventh-day Adventists and the Salvation Army, and also by the evangelists of the rapidly accepted Keswick movement who had been operating in the country for at least a decade.³³ New Zealand Keswick conventions were first held in 1901 and spread throughout the country over the next several decades. The Holiness themes of full surrender and personal piety were thus already familiar to many.

New Zealand evangelicals also followed closely their British counterparts in the centrality of conversionism, activism, biblicism and crucicentrism.³⁴ All of these elements they found in the Torrey and Chapman missions and could sing about in Alexander's gospel songs. In the context of the new debates over Darwinism and theological Liberalism many sought comfort and solace in the 'old-time religion' of the missions, but likewise the widespread atmosphere of doctrinal irenicism and cooperation abroad in these enterprises would have been appreciated by those who sought a rapprochement with new developments.³⁵ They could still frequently seek the 'deeper life' in their piety and pleasure in their worship-going without challenging their intellectual integrity. For all of these reasons and more, then, Alexander's sing-along songs were effective and popular.

II

There was a gap of nearly half a century before the next major mass evangelistic venture in New Zealand, the coming of Billy Graham in 1959. In the interim, New Zealand had been exposed to the new American-style fundamentalism, but its evangelicals found the movement wanting, at least in charity and winsomeness. Attempts had been made to foster some such development, but had mostly proved fruitless.³⁶ Revivalism, though, had become the standard evangelistic methodology amongst such groups with dozens of practitioners, mostly British, itinerating through the country. New para-church agencies proliferated, such as the Open Air Campaigners and the youth and university organizations associated with Scripture Union and the Bible Class movement. The New Zealand Bible Training Institute and its journal, *The Reaper*, had been founded to foster this expression of Christianity, and the Keswick camps flourished in many places. Although Barthian neo-orthodoxy won a number of clerical followers, few New Zealand Christians received much exposure to most aspects of critical theology.

Through the 1950s church attendances were rising. The Presbyterians, for example, increased their attendance at public worship by nearly 16 per cent and their communicant membership by 19 per cent between 1955 and 1959.³⁷ When Graham arrived in 1959, therefore, it was to an environment largely supportive of and sympathetic to both his methods and message. This was the end of the golden weather; when he returned in 1969 New Zealand churches had been rocked by *Honest to God*, anti-Americanism resulting from the Vietnam War, the anti-authoritarianism of the new youth, a move to the political and theological left by the National Council of Churches, and a highly publicised heresy trial amongst the Presbyterians.

The music for these 'crusades' (as these events were now called) was not led by a charismatic person of the individual stature of Charles Alexander. [...]

[...] The selection contained a higher proportion of standard hymns replacing many of the sentimental and topical entries.[39] A prominent theological theme was the substitutionary atonement of Jesus, central to evangelicalism, but largely avoided by Alexander. 'For God So Loved the World' was a musical adaptation of John iii.16, in which God's love was described wholly in terms of Christ's death and millennial return.[40] The attraction and efficacy of 'The Old Rugged Cross' was hymned, as was the 'Power in the Blood' again.[41] The gory Victorian imagery remained, too, in the clear spelling-out of the doctrine in 'Nothing but the Blood':

> What can wash away my sin?
> Nothing but the blood of Jesus;
> What can make me whole again?
> Nothing but the blood of Jesus.
>
> For my pardon this I see...
> For my cleansing this my plea...
> Nothing can for sin atone...
> Naught of good that I have done...
>
> Oh! precious is the flow
> That makes me white as snow;
> No other fount I know,
> Nothing but the blood of Jesus.[42]

There was still no other view of the atonement celebrated and little of any other doctrine, even of the person or work of Christ. Unlike Alexander's book, there was little scope for a topical index. As another hymn put it:

> My hope is built on nothing less
> Than Jesus' blood and righteousness...
> His oath, His covenant, His blood,
> Support me in the whelming flood...[43]

This hope was one theme which had not been clearly defined in the earlier missions, but which was now. The Second Coming of Christ, including full eschatological judgment, was presumed.

> When He shall come with trumpet sound,
> O may I then in Him be found;
> Dressed in His righteousness alone,
> Faultless to stand before the throne.[44]

The concept appeared in other hymns, too. It might have been in terms of the Christian's confidence of ultimate acquittal — 'I'll go with Him thro' the judgments'[45] — or it might have been expressed in what seems a physical, even astronautical, new world:

> Soon He's coming back to welcome me
> Far beyond the starry sky;
> I shall wing my flight to worlds unknown,
> I shall reign with Him on high.[46]

The version of eschatology espoused was clearly that of dispensationalism, with its expectation of a potentially immediate End, and the sudden 'Rapture' or snatching-away of believers. 'Is It the Crowning Day?' began by asserting that 'Jesus may come today' and 'I may go home today'.[47] Another song awaited the time 'When the trumpet of the Lord shall sound, and time shall be no more', and 'When His chosen ones shall gather to their home beyond the skies', again in a very physical heaven.[48] The doctrine was most clearly expressed in 'It Is Well With My Soul':

> And, Lord, haste the day when the faith shall be sight,
> The clouds be rolled back as a scroll,
> The trump shall resound and the Lord shall descend,
> 'Even so' — it is well with my soul.[49]

This view of eschatology differs from what many, probably most, Evangelicals in New Zealand would have held at the turn of the century. Then, in the flush of European imperialism, most espoused postmillennialism. This view anticipated the irresistible advance of Christian civilization until the whole world was converted; Jesus could then return to the Church Triumphant. However, the First World War revealed this dream to be ephemeral; so-called Christian civilization had not progressed beyond mass slaughter and destruction. So, many Evangelicals turned to the more pessimistic dispensationalism which saw the world descending further and further into godlessness until the coming of the Antichrist and the rescue of the Church. [...]

[...] The theology of the Graham crusade hymnbook, then, revealed a concentration on only a few themes, particularly on Christ's substitutionary atonement and Second Coming, which was portrayed in dispensationalist terms. The atonement doctrine was central to the evangelical theology and the evangelistic call to sinners to repent and accept Christ as 'their personal Saviour', the individual accepting his work on their behalf. The prospect of Christ's imminent return added urgency to that call. Graham's hymnody, then, appears to have been an agent for the conserving and reinforcing of the distinctives of evangelical theology, but remaining untainted by fundamentalist belligerence. In 1959 this may have been the peaceable stroking of the complacent, well-fed Protestant body of churches. By 1969 it was to restore confidence and the shattered nerves of many theologically conservative Christians.

III

By 1969, as conservative Christianity became increasingly separated from the *Zeitgeist* of the mid-twentieth century, Graham and his colleagues were faced with a dilemma. On the one hand was the requirement for conservatism: having to retain songs and hymns which were well-known and comfortable to his audiences and which would maintain the atmosphere of unity and the unchanging nature of the evangelical gospel. On the other hand was the often antithetical requirement to stay abreast of the times, moving with the new cultural and musical styles. In 1969 the Graham crusade had opted for a retention of the same style of music as Alexander had used, but the two missions of 1987 moved much more towards contemporary styles.

These contemporary styles were most strongly influenced by two factors emergent since mid-century. As had occurred elsewhere, New Zealand Christians had begun to write music, both songs and hymns, in more modern idioms, occasionally even incorporating Maori or Polynesian elements, broadening the range of material available. More visibly, New Zealand churches had been influenced powerfully from the late 1960s by the Pentecostal and charismatic movements.[52] Spurning traditional hymnals, they, too, had produced much of their own music, nearly all in the form of short choruses which comprised a separate corpus of New Zealand church music. They had, too, revolutionized how that music was played, popularizing diversity in instrumental accompaniment and styles of worship leading.

In the 1987 missions the hymnbooks of the earlier eras had been replaced by single, give-away sheets usually comprising short songs, sometimes only a verse long. The professional songleaders had given way to local music directors in each centre. The music appeared to be much more of a pale adjunct to the personality of the preacher than it had been earlier in the century. These personalities and the way in which the two missions were conducted reveals the dichotomy which now existed within conservative Christianity in New Zealand.

The mission of Leighton Ford, Billy Graham's brother-in-law and former associate, attempted to strike a stylistic balance. The music used was selected by New Zealanders Guy Jansen and Ross Pilkinton, mostly from a recent New Zealand hymnbook, *Servant Songs*. In their selection of twenty-two, six were older hymns, four of which had been used in the 1969 crusade. The remainder were largely contemporary songs, several written in New Zealand. Thought had been given to inclusiveness: the usual 'Brother, let me be your servant . . .' was altered to 'Will you let me be . . .'; one song was in Samoan, while another song and one verse of 'Guide Me O Thou Great Jehovah' were in Maori. The songs' themes were mixed but remained largely within the pietistic emphases of the earlier missions and traditional Evangelicalism. Praise of Jesus featured, though often obliquely, as in the lines:

> Magnify, come glorify Christ Jesus the King.
>
> Ev'ry knee shall bow, ev'ry tongue confess
> That Jesus Christ is Lord.[53]

The whole Trinity was worshipped in 'Holy, Holy, Holy, Lord God Almighty', and reference was made to the resurrection of Christ in 'Alleluia, Alleluia, give thanks to the risen Lord'.[54] But beyond these were more sobering references to the cross, such as 'When I Survey the Wondrous Cross' and

> We worship Jesus' great majesty
> Who thro' His love gave everything.
> We stand before Him now washed and free
> Because He died on Calvary.[55]

The large bulk of the Ford songs were pietistic in emphasis rather than either doctrinal or of directly evangelistic use. Only one song even came close to being the response to an appeal, but it applied equally well to the rededication of believers' lives to God, and even to some form of mystical union:

> Jesus take me as I am
> I can come no other way
> Take me deeper into You
> Make my flesh life melt away
> Make me like a precious stone
> Crystal clear and finely honed
> Life of Jesus shining through
> Giving glory back to You.[56]

Mostly, the songs were worshipful and exhortations to worship, including several based on scriptural texts of comfort and encouragement. Others acknowledged human sinfulness and shortcomings and sought God's mercy, forgiveness and restoration, such as the the song in Maori, 'Tama Ngakau Marie' which asked the 'Tama a t'Atua [Son of God]' to 'love us', 'take away our sins' and 'undo these evil ties which bind us'.[57] Uniquely, the 'Servant Song' was directed not to deity but humanity, the singers offering to be servants, companions, empathizers and rejoicers with the hearers, the ultimate object being to 'be as Christ to you'. It thus emphasized practical response to and manifestation of the relationship enjoyed with God.

The Leighton Ford mission songs thus reflected many of the characteristics and emphases of Ford's evangelistic approach. They included a substantial traditional element, familiar to evangelicals for decades, and, theologically, several of the central elements of evangelical worship, particularly of Jesus' ministry and crucifixion. The tone of many of the songs was joyful, yet reverent and not merely thoughtlessly happy, again focusing on praise and thanks to the godhead rather than dwelling on the personal benefits of being a Christian. And there was recognition of the need for ongoing divine action in the singer's life and for that life to be put to the service of both God and humanity — echoing the 'hope in action' theme of the mission. The compilers of the collection seemed to have captured well the essence of the mission and the best aspects of the evangelical background from which it sprang.

The music of the Palau mission, on the other hand, promoted a noticeably different theology and Christian experiential base from Ford's and from those of the earlier missions. Again there was no professional songleader and a double-sided sheet with twenty-one songs on it was used. Of those twenty-one, only three were of a hymn type: 'Blessed Assurance', 'Amazing Grace' and 'How Great thou Art'. The rest were a selection of short choruses taken (without acknowledgement) from the *Scripture in Song* songbooks widely used in theologically conservative churches in New Zealand, especially those associated with the charismatic and Pentecostal movements. The three older hymns, too, are among the few retained in use in such churches.

This music selection, therefore, indicated some of the shift which had taken place in the mass evangelist's constituency. Whereas people from most denominations would at least have known the popular hymns in the Graham books, to many from the 'mainline' denominations, used only to hymnals, the Palau mission songs would have been unfamiliar. The fact that the choruses formed 85 per cent of the the mission's music suggests at least two things: that the organizers had some conditioning towards short, popular, theologically superficial songs, and/or that they had an expectation that the large majority of the audience would be composed of attenders at the sorts of churches which used that material.

Without exception, the songs were upbeat and triumphalist, having a single focus with no internal development. They omitted the pietistic, prayerful emphasis of such Graham crusade selections as 'Guide Me, O Thou Great Jehovah', 'The Lord's My Shepherd' or 'Rock of Ages'. Instead, the Palau songs fell into two categories. The first category comprised usually oblique praise to Jesus (virtually none mentioned other members of the Trinity). These included:

> O how I love Jesus (repeat 2x)
> Because He first loved me.
>
> To me He is so wonderful (repeat 2x)
> Because He first loved me.[58] [. . .]

[. . .] Others such as 'Majesty, worship His majesty' and 'You are the King of Glory' did put that injunction into effect.[60] Apart from one verse of 'How Great Thou Art' there was no direct reference to Jesus' earthly ministry, teaching, suffering or death. At most, the few indirect references were softened by association with a concentration on pleasant results for the believer:

> With His blood He has saved me
> With His power He has raised me.
>
> Yes I'm a conqueror, reigning with him
> Secure as the blood of Jesus
> Cleanses me within.[61]

The Jesus thus presented had little in common with the 'Man of Sorrows' sung of in the Graham meetings, he who suffered on "The Old Rugged Cross' which was 'the emblem of suff'ring and shame'.

The second group of songs used in Palau's Mission Waikato were celebrations of the believer's blessings resulting from beings a Christian. Since 'this is the day that the Lord hath made', they sang 'let us rejoice and be glad in it'. They told one another to 'rejoice in the Lord always', because 'we are one in the bonds of love'.[62] The Christian Church appeared only as an all-conquering, triumphant army, as God was apparently saying

> For I'm building a people of power
> And I'm making a people of praise
> That will move through this land
> By My Spirit
> And will glorify my precious name.[63]

This army fought using the name of Jesus as a magically omnipotent weapon against devilish forces of evil. [. . .]

[. . .] The atmosphere anticipated in the selection of music was reinforced by the style of congregational worship. In Hamilton, for example, there appeared to be a high proportion of charismatic and Pentecostal believers in the audience and the singing was directed in a boisterous, cheerleading fashion by the master of ceremonies, the Rev. Jim Williams, a local Assemblies of God minister.[67]

There was, then, despite their contemporaneity, a vast difference in musical style between the Ford and Palau missions. The Ford music was as broad in theme, approach and musical style as could have been expected within a single-sheet limit, while the Palau music was narrow theologically and stylistically. The Ford music expressed most key evangelical soteriological and Christological doctrines and developed them to result in imperatives to improvements in both piety and society.

The Palau music, though, lacked any substantial doctrinal content, even regarding the actual work of Christ. In addition, its celebration sought no response in singers' lives: the whole thrust was back to introverted, passive reception of divine blessings. Where earlier hymn writers had fled to places of refuge and leant on the everlasting arms for support, the 1987 version was to reign with Jesus, to be seated in heavenly places with him and to gain victory over demonic forces by standing on the name of Jesus. Unlike the music of the Ford campaign, this change reflected strongly the new position of influence held in many New Zealand churches by the Pentecostal and charismatic movements, and their intrinsically triumphalist, experiential nature was here promulgated at the expense of accustomed evangelical doctrinal emphases.

IV

The compilations of hymns and songs we have discussed have demonstrated themes and concerns generated by their varying historical contexts.

In the early period, Alexander relied heavily on the nineteenth-century gospel song style and the theology reflected the Holiness movement of the time in its concern for personal piety, full surrender and the like. The presentation of the family, especially the pious mother, was unique among these missions, having disappeared by mid-century. Jesus appeared as the divine friend and there were at least oblique references to his substitutionary atonement. A concern for the music to assist the evangelistic appeal was evident in both the choice of persuasive songs and the use of the music.

By contrast, the lesser importance of music to the Graham crusade organization was obvious. The theology was much the same as earlier, the substitutionary atonement being much in evidence. Perhaps it was still as important to the audience as it had been in creating fellow-feeling and in reaffirming common dedication to the faith, but reports from that time gave no indication of substantial musical influence in the meetings. The common faith, though, had begun to change, at least in its expression, with less emotionalism and less use of the Holiness movement's motif of surrender to God.

The centrality of music had faded still further by 1987. It was not presented by an imported specialist and again none of the reports thought it significant enough to comment on. Ford's music retained many of the emphases of Graham's era, but with a few new elements, especially in the acknowledgment of other cultural groups and the use of more modern folk-style hymns. Palau's music, though, showed few of the traditional evangelical concerns. The focus was on triumphalist personal experience, with even Christ, especially when considered as suffering Saviour, being subordinated to this self-centredness. The fact that this style of music and leading were of local origin demonstrated the extent of Pentecostal influence in contemporary New Zealand conservative Christianity.

Fashions have changed in New Zealand's churches, even amongst those who endeavour to adhere to and propagate an unchanging 'old-time religion'. The style has changed from a Victorian, home-style sing-along to more impersonal meetings in sports stadiums with massed choirs — perhaps indicating a change in role for the audience from congregation towards observers of entertainment. Emotionalism was initially favoured, then largely eliminated, in the more clinical Graham meetings, only to return in a new form with Palau. The emotions engendered, though, changed from mawkish sentimentality to effusive heartiness.

Beneath the medium, the theological message, too, has changed. Little of the Palau music drew one towards making the full surrender upon which Torrey, Chapman and Alexander were so keen. This reflected the passing of the influence of the Keswick conventions in favour of the Full Gospel Businessmen's Association and Women's Aglow meetings, with the abandonment by the Pentecostals of their aspects of their Holiness roots. Christ as the suffering Lamb of God seemed to have lost his attraction, to be replaced by Christ the Victor; no longer was he (or the Christian) a 'loser', only winners were allowed. Musically this was reflected in the omission of the songs concentrating on the atoning death in favour of those which celebrated power, strength and obvious success. Although this has long been a strand within Evangelicalism,[68] such an overwhelming obsession was a novelty and seems to suggest a slipping away, even denial, of the evangelical centre ground which has been a feature of New Zealand Christianity. [. . .]

[. . .] The music of these evangelistic missions reveals that the beliefs of many New Zealand Christians in and about Jesus, and the reasons for those beliefs, seem to have changed substantially during this century.

Notes

1 Robert McAfee Brown, *The Spirit of Protestantism*, New York 1975, p. xxi. Quoted in Dale A. Johnson, 'Is This the Lord's Song? Pedagogy and Polemic in Modern English Hymns', *Historical Magazine of the Protestant Episcopal Church*, Vol. 48, 1979, p. 196.
2 David Martin, *A Sociology of English Religion*, London 1967, p. 88. Quoted in Johnson, 'Lord's Song', p. 196.
3 Mary G. De Jong, '"I Want to be Like Jesus": The Self-Defining Power of Evangelical Hymnody', *Journal of the American Academy of Religion*, Vol. 54, 1986. See also the historical study, Sandra S. Sizer, *Gospel Hymns and Social Religion: The Rhetoric of Nineteenth-Century Revivalism*, Philadelphia 1978.
4 Bryan D. Gilling, 'Fundamentalism and Full Surrender: The Message of the 1902 R. A. Torrey Mission in New Zealand', *Lucas*, No. 14, December 1992, and

'Revivalism as Renewal: J. Wilbur Chapman in New Zealand, 1912–1913', *American Presbyterians/Journal of Presbyterian History*, Vol. 70, No. 2, 1992.

5 *Alexander's Hymns No. 3*, Charles M. Alexander (ed.), London and Edinburgh n.d. [Hereafter referred to as *AH*] Smaller editions were used for both of these earlier missions, but as these could not be located, references have been made to this edition. At least thirty of the forty-four songs used in 1902 and nearly all of the 1912–13 songs were included in the third edition.

6 Bryan D. Gilling, ' "Back to the Simplicities of Religion": The 1959 Billy Graham Crusade in New Zealand and Its Precursors', *Journal of Religious History*, Vol. 17, No. 2, 1992, and 'Mass Evangelistic Theology and Methodology and the 1987 Luis Palau Mission to Auckland', *Transformation*, Vol. 8, No. 1, 1991.

7 Helen C. Alexander and J. Kennedy Maclean, *Charles M. Alexander: A Romance of Song and Soul-Winning*, London n.d.

8 Quoted in George T. B. Davis, *Torrey and Alexander: The Story of a World-Wide Revival*, New York 1905, pp. 239–41.

9 *Evening Post*, 29 August 1902.

10 Davis, *Torrey and Alexander*, p. 241.

11 *Evening Post*, 3 September 1902.

12 *Evening Post*, 3 September 1902.

13 *Otago Daily Times*, 21 March 1912.

18 *New Zealand Methodist Times*, Vol. 2, No. 26, 20 April 1912.

19 *New Zealand Methodist Times*, Vol. 3, No. 1, 4 May 1912.

20 *AH*, No. 18, vv.1, 2, chorus.

21 *AH*, No. 124. v.1, chorus.

23 *AH*, No. 169, vv.1–4.

24 'The Saviour with Me', *AH*, No. 218.

25 'Old Jordan's Waves I do not Fear', *AH*, No. 28.

26 "No, Not One!' *AH*, No. 206.

30 Sizer, *Gospel Hymns*. Chapman, following his mentor D. L. Moody, was famous for his use of sentimental anecdotes.

31 *AH*, No. 21.

32 Peter J. Lineham, *New Zealanders and the Methodist Evangel*, Auckland 1983, p. 10.

33 Edward C. Willard, *What God Hath Wrought*, London 1891, and *The Same Lord*, London 1893.

34 David W. Bebbington, "The Gospel in the Nineteenth Century', *Vox Evangelica*, Vol. 13, 1983.

35 John Stenhouse, ' "The Wretched Gorilla Damnification of Humanity": The "Battle" between Science and Religion over Evolution in Nineteenth-Century New Zealand', *New Zealand Journal of History*, Vol. 18, 1984.

36 Allan K. Davidson, 'A Protesting Presbyterian: The Reverend P. B. Fraser and New Zealand Presbyterianism, 1892–1940', *Journal of Religious History*, Vol. 14, 1986; Bryan D. Gilling, 'Contending for the Faith: *The Contender* and Militant Fundamentalism in Mid-Twentieth Century New Zealand', in *Be Ye Separate: Fundamentalism and the New Zealand Experience*, Bryan D. Gilling (ed.), Hamilton 1992.

37 Annual *Proceedings of the General Assembly of the Presbyterian Church in New Zealand*.

39 Still not enough, though, for some critics. An Anglican columnist lamented inaccurately that none of the great hymns of the faith was used for even such a conspicuously interdenominational occasion, overlooking, amongst others, 'Praise to the Lord, the Almighty', 'Love Divine, All Loves Excelling', 'A Mighty

Fortress Is Our God', 'Join All the Glorious Names' and 'Amazing Grace', *Church and People*, Vol. 14, No. 4, May 1959, p. 6.
40 *Billy Graham Crusade Songs*, compiled by Cliff Barrows, Sydney 1958, No. 62. [Hereafter referred to as *CS*].
41 *CS*, Nos 9, 25.
42 *CS*, No. 32.
43 *CS*, No. 30.
44 *CS*, No. 30.
45 *CS*, No. 65.
46 *CS*, No. 20.
47 *CS*, No. 45.
48 *CS*, No. 48.
49 *CS*, No. 44.
52 For example, Peter J. Lineham, 'Tongues Must Cease: The Brethren and the Charismatic Movement in New Zealand', *Christian Brethren Research Journal*, Vol. 34, November 1983; Colin Brown, 'How Significant is the Charismatic Movement?' in *Religion in New Zealand Society*, Brian Colless and Peter Donovan (eds), 2nd edn, Palmerston North 1985.
53 'Leighton Ford 1987 New Zealand Missions Songsheet,' unpublished printed sheet [Hereafter referred to as LFNZMS], Mission Christchurch Office, 332 Cashel Street, Christchurch, Nos 4, 17.
54 LFNZMS, Nos 10, 1.
55 LFNZMS, Nos 7, 13.
56 LFNZMS, No. 12.
57 LFNZMS, No. 5.
58 'Complimentary Song Sheet', Luis Palau Waikato Mission 18–22 March 1987, unpublished song sheet [Hereafter referred to as LPCSS], No. 4.
60 LPCSS, Nos 12, 17.
61 LPCSS, Nos 5, 18.
62 LPCSS, Nos 1, 6, 8.
63 LPCSS, No. 15.
67 Author's personal observation, Luis Palau mission meeting, Hamilton, 22 March 1987. For example, Williams led the crowd in a cheer for Jesus: 'Give me a J! Give me an E! . . .'
68 See, for example, Douglas W. Frank, *Less Than Conquerors: How Evangelicals Entered the Twentieth Century*, Grand Rapids 1986. pp. 103–66.

WOMEN AS RELIGIOUS AND POLITICAL PRAISE SINGERS WITHIN AFRICAN INSTITUTIONS

The case of the CCAP Blantyre Synod and political parties in Malawi

Clara Henderson and Lisa Gilman

Source: *Women and Music*, 8 (2004), 22–40.

This collaboration between the folklorist Lisa Gilman and the ethnomusicologist Clara Henderson explores the roles played by women in two types of institutions in Malawi: on the one hand, political parties, and on the other, Blantyre Synod of the Church of Central Africa Presbyterian (CCAP), a member of the largest protestant denomination in the country. Both the three dominant political parties and the Presbyterian churches have women's wings whose activities include the singing of praise songs and dancing at all-female as well as public events, a custom rooted in community cultural practices that contribute to an Africanization or localization of these Western-style institutions. Most formal institutions in Malawi, be they governmental or political, church or educational, are based on European models—a legacy of colonialism and a result of the globalization of cultural and political systems that has marked the last century and continues into the new one. From the time of colonialism to the present, men have integrated more readily into emergent Western structures, whereas the majority of women have tended to remain more rooted in traditional cultural practices (Johnson-Odim and Strobel 1999, xxxv; Martin 1994, 413, 419). In both real and symbolic ways, women are frequently relied upon to sustain the country's connection to and groundedness in what is often labeled "African" or "traditional" ways of doing things, while men have been expected to Westernize and move the country into the new "modern" or "Western" world.

The social and political situation in contemporary Malawi is one in which participation and identification with the "West" or the "modern" is generally linked with success, power, and prestige. Within formal church and political institutions, for example, those people who wield the most power come from the country's social, economic, and political elite and thus usually have high levels of education, speak English, live in urban areas, have access to "company" cars, and so on. Conversely, the majority of the population in Malawi (approximately 88 percent) is more closely linked in their activities and in public discourse to the "traditional" or "African" ways of life; they tend to have little formal schooling, and they struggle to sustain themselves at very low economic levels, relying mostly on subsistence-based agriculture (Lwanda 1996, 19; Mvula and Kakhongwa 1997).[1] The association of women in church and political institutions with African or local ways of doing things therefore implicitly places women at least symbolically in gendered roles in which they have less access to resources and positions of power.

This article grows out of our interest in detailing the similarities of women's performances in these distinct institutions, both of which are central to social, political, and religious life in Malawi. We begin by comparing and contrasting some of the features (dress, movement, and singing) of women's performances in each type of institution in order to demonstrate the gendering that occurs within both. We then examine the organizational structures through which women perform and explore some functions that these performances play both in individuals' lives and in the furthering of the organizations' goals. Our analysis reveals that though women performers play central roles in both types of institutions, they (as well as the specific activity of their singing and dancing) are frequently placed in peripheral roles within their organizations, and women who perform often have fewer opportunities than do their male counterparts to participate in the decision-making bodies and power structures of these institutions. [. . .]

[. . .]

Introduction to the Mvano and women's wings of political parties

Mvano, meaning "mutual agreement," is the name of the women's guilds that are the backbone of many church activities within Blantyre Synod of the CCAP. Blantyre Synod's membership is close to one million, and its constituency encompasses the entire southern region of Malawi, including Ntcheu district. Mvano have groups in each of the synod's 320 congregations and the three to eight prayer houses (satellite churches) connected to each congregation. Depending on the size of individual churches, Mvano groups vary from twenty to more than one thousand members.[3] Distinguished by their black-and-white uniforms worn on special occasions, Mvano are an integral part of every church function and activity, from funerals and pastoral visiting to evangelism campaigns and the opening of new churches. During most of the year Mvano meet once per week for Bible study and practical lessons ranging from nutrition to women and the law. In the area of Christian music, Mvano are particularly noted for their distinctive compositions and performance style. It is at their weekly meetings and at larger gatherings with local and regional Mvano groups that the Mvano create and exchange music in the form of instructional songs, choir songs, and dance songs, to name a few. Their dance songs are primarily performed among Mvano women within the domain of their own meetings. When the Mvano dance publicly at formal church functions, it is frequently at the periphery of these events, with the exception of evangelism campaigns or the occasional special church service. Of the different genres of their music, the Mvano dance songs are the focus in this paper.

Similar to the women's guilds within the CCAP, the three dominant political parties, the ruling United Democratic Front (UDF), the Malawi Congress Party (MCP), and the Alliance for Democracy (AFORD), have women's wings with female leadership and members.[4] The women's wings exist to integrate women from all parts of the country into the structure and activities of the party. In addition to spreading messages from parties' leadership and organizing women to vote, the women's wings are also the structures through which women are coordinated to be the praise singers and dancers for the party. Each party's women's wing holds regular meetings throughout the country on a regular basis, and women party members are an ever-present feature of all party events, from political rallies to private presidential functions. They attend these events ideally draped in party fabric, position themselves in visually salient positions, dance spontaneously during the course of the event, perform rehearsed dances during specified entertainment sections, and sing songs that praise the party and its politicians and castigate its opponents.

Performance

A glance at a typical political rally or a large synod function immediately highlights the gendering of real and symbolic roles filled by men and women. These gendered differences extend beyond local ideas about masculinity and femininity and into the realm of cultural identification. As mentioned in the introduction, the participation of women members, exemplified in dress, dancing, and singing, is associated in local discourse with local (African) cultural practices, while men's activities are associated with "Western" (European/ American) ones. At most rallies, for example, party leaders, who are mostly male and important figures in the locale in which the event takes place, wear Western-style clothing, sit in chairs, and participate by displaying party symbols on T-shirts or buttons, initiating slogans, and making speeches. Active women party members, by contrast, usually wear "African" clothing, sit on the ground in the audience space, and participate by singing songs of praise for their parties and dancing "traditional" dances during scheduled entertainment segments as well as spontaneously during the course of the events.

At large synod functions, attended by a number of church dignitaries, male clergy wear white clerical collars, dark clerical shirts, and suits under black Geneva preaching gowns. Like their male colleagues, female clergy wear white clerical collars and black preaching gowns, and some choose to distinguish themselves with colorful preaching stoles and head scarves (*dukus*), clerical shirts, and skirts made from "African" material. Both male and female clergy sit on elevated platforms at the front of the church or hall in which the event is taking place and participate by sharing in leading the order of service, reading the scripture, and saying prayers. On these occasions male clergy who are elected synod officials are usually the ones who preach. Mvano women, wearing "African" clothing, sit in the congregation in designated areas at the front of the church. They participate by welcoming church dignitaries with singing and dancing at the beginning of the function and at designated times throughout the proceedings, sometimes spontaneously ululating and breaking into song when moments in the program inspire them to do so. As illustrated in the scenarios above, the stylistic features of women's dress, dancing, and singing implicitly position women as the symbolic embodiment of local/"African" cultural and social identities.

Standardized clothing plays a significant role in Malawian society, as illustrated in the school uniforms worn by students in both the private and public educational system, and in the tradition of female wedding guests' wearing outfits sewn from the same cloth design chosen by the bride (Perani and Wolff 1999; Martin 1995). Both women party members and Mvano clothe their bodies with distinctive fabric and uniforms that distinguish their groups from others within Malawian society. Their unique clothing plays an important role in serving as a vehicle of self-expression for making political and religious statements, and the ceremonious covering of their dancing bodies colorfully complements the messages of their praise songs. The clothing styles worn by these women conform to local categorizations of "African" as opposed to Western dress. The *chitenje*/blouse combination is often referred to as the national dress or traditional wear. This contrasts with what is commonly worn by men. Typical male dress consists of trousers, shirt, and closed-toe shoes. Men in leadership positions ideally wear suits and ties.[5]

Each political party has its own cloth whose dominant color is the identifying color of the political party: bright yellow for UDF, blue for AFORD, and green for MCP. The fabric is usually decorated with the party's acronym and its kinetic symbol. Sometimes referred to as "national dress," the uniforms fashioned from this material consist of a *chitenje* (a two meter rectangular piece of cloth) wrapped around the hips to form a full-length skirtlike outer covering, a short-sleeved blouse, and a headpiece, all made from the same fabric. Those who do not have a uniform wear similar clothing made from assorted materials.

Women's church groups throughout Malawi are also identifiable by their uniforms. The Blantyre Synod Mvano uniform consists of a black skirt that, in their words, means "we are living in a dark and sinful world"; a white long-sleeved blouse testifying "we have accepted Christ as our light"; a white head scarf signifying "we are striving ahead in light"; a white belt "to strengthen us for the journey"; and a badge depicting an open Bible and a cross together with the letters "CCAP" (GJB 1998). The Mvano uniform is consecrated at a special religious ceremony and is therefore considered sacred. The wearing of the uniform carries with it the responsibility of representing Christ and the church. Consequently, the Mvano wear their uniforms only on specific designated occasions, for example, during Holy Communion, evangelism campaigns, and special church services or Mvano gatherings; when preaching; when visiting the sick, bereaved, and needy; and during funerals, to name a few.[6]

Women in both organizations sometimes wear cloth commemorating special occasions. The styles in which this cloth is sewn fit the general category of "national dress," though each woman also displays her individuality in the unique design of her sleeves or the distinctive pattern of her skirt and headpiece. For example, in 1998, when Mvano were celebrating fifty years of their formal establishment within the church, they held a number of events to which they wore outfits made of specially designed cloth they had commissioned for the celebration. Similarly, the ruling UDF party on occasion commissions cloth to commemorate special events, such as the president's wedding or the millennium celebrations. Women wear these outfits at the events for which they are designed and then at subsequent political or religious functions.

The dancing styles of the Mvano and the women party members differ significantly, yet the similarities are again notable. The dancing of both groups has its roots in a common type of female dancing in this part of Africa. Many ethnic groups in Malawi have similar female dance forms characterized by the circle formation in which women dancers move counterclockwise. Most Malawians categorize these dances as "traditional dances" or "magule a makolo athu" (dances of our ancestors). These dances are distinguished from other musical and dance practices, such as the singing of translated European hymns or popular music genres that are understood as originating from imported forms.

Political dancers from a given locale draw directly from the dance forms of the ethnic group(s) in their area, frequently calling their dance styles by their local names. Malawians often refer to political dances with the name of the female circle dance typical in the region. However, women's political dancing usually displays a mixture of different dance styles, largely as a result of the constant intermixing of dancers from different regions during Dr. Banda's rule (see Kerr 1998). As women from different cultural groups performed together and observed the dances of their compatriots from other regions, they naturally influenced each other's styles. The resultant interaction gave rise to the creation of new steps and the complication of existing forms. Though each dance has its own unique features, a woman familiar with one style can easily join a group dancing a related form and perform adequately.

Similarly, the Mvano draw on the different southern region traditions when creating their dances. Because each woman brings her own style to Mvano dancing, the resultant dance patterns reflect combinations of various cultural groups. In their dancing the Mvano may periodically reference movements from well-known traditional dances, but they do not link the general style of their dancing to a specific traditional dance. For both groups the circle formation is the prime organizing factor for the majority of their dances, facilitating and providing the configuration and shape for the creation of their movements and praise singing.

Often, when the women's wings of political parties are dancing at a rally, two or three male drummers enter the performance space first and begin drumming. Presently women party members enter, usually in a single or double column, quickly moving into a circle formation while performing synchronized dance steps in concert with the drum patterns. When large groups of women are dancing, the entrance patterns are frequently more complex, with leaders facing each entering column and dancing them into the circle, where they proceed to form complex spirals and concentric circle patterns, commonly ending in a more simple circle formation. Once they are in a circle formation, they move in a counterclockwise direction, maintaining their synchronized steps and gestures.

A tremendous variety of movements are performed at political functions, each with its own distinctive style. Many of these dances involve intricate dance steps with an emphasis on hip and buttock movements that intertwine with the drum patterns. Performers sometimes stop singing for short periods of time while they focus on the interlocking of their dance steps with the drum. Arms and hips swing together from side to side, and dancers may occasionally turn inward to face the center of the circle. Dance steps usually vary for each new song, though the steps for each piece generally consist of alternating repeated foot patterns. For example, in a *chiwoda* song, the right foot may move back and forth, marking out three consecutive beats, followed by a brief alternating right and left foot pattern, and then switch to the left foot to repeat the same three-beat pattern on the opposite side. Distinctive arm, hip, and buttock movements usually synchronize with their feet and the drumming. A signaled change by the song leader can initiate a shift in the dance steps, with the first pattern repeated a number of times before it moves to the left side again. On further direction from the song leader the dance can shift once more to another alternating foot pattern in which the singers rhythmically move side to side as they sink closer to the ground, their torsos and arms moving forward and backward.

When the Mvano dance counterclockwise in their circle, they use various combinations of synchronized dance steps, graphic gestures, drama, and hand clapping to enhance the messages of their songs. For their dance songs, the Mvano tend not to use the style of the complex foot patterns like those of *chiwoda*. Instead, as they begin forming a circle in preparation for singing and dancing, one of the most common steps the Mvano establish alternates from the right foot to the left foot, marking out a pulse as their arms and hips sway from side to side and they move counterclockwise. With each forward movement of their feet, their torsos rock upward and downward, marking out another pulse that falls between each foot movement. Another basic dance pattern involves moving around the circle at a faster speed with the alternating left and right feet marking out each pulse in double time. With this simple basic pattern as a foundation, the Mvano use various tactics to dramatize the messages of their songs such as direction changes, syncopated three-beat foot patterns on key words, and arm and hip movements together with rhythmic syllables (vocables) imitating the nailing of Jesus to the cross, to name a few. For example, they may accentuate their song's message by doubling the speed of their foot pattern, moving quickly to the center of the circle, or clapping on an accented word and beat before returning to their basic formation. At other times they may incorporate graphic gestures and demonstrative body movements into their dance to illustrate a biblical story. For the story of Ezekiel and the valley of dry bones, for example, at one point in the dance they imitate the bones coming to life by facing into the circle, moving rhythmically from side to side, and bumping each other's shoulders as they sing an onomatopoeic text.

Both Mvano and political dancers adapt their performance styles to specific contexts. When welcoming and seeing off political figures at airports, for example, political dancers alter their basic dance formation from that of a moving circle to static rows. Standing in one place, dancers move their feet and bodies, simulating the steps that would normally propel them around the circle. Similarly, within the space limitations of a church building, Mvano dance songs can be accommodated by eliminating the circle formation:

> It is not a requirement to make a circle [when dancing in the church]. People can start singing and dancing while they are standing in a row ... you can dance according to the space you have.... In other churches you can make a circle and dance at the front because they have room, but if they don't have room then you must use the space you have. (Kapuma 1994)

Most song texts performed by both Mvano and political dancers fit into the larger category of praise poetry, a genre common throughout sub-Saharan

Africa and also categorized locally as "traditional" or "African." Praise songs are characterized by lyrics that glorify or uphold a single individual, often commemorating her or his actions, events in life, and personality and achievements (see Vail and White 1991; Berger 1999; Cope 1968; Finnegan 1976, 111–18; Opland 1983; Schapera 1965). Mvano songs praise God and Jesus Christ and encourage Mvano groups and church members, while political songs uphold individuals or politicians, exuding praise for their personal qualities and achievements and thanking them for what they have accomplished for the community, political party, or nation. [. . .]

[. . .] Apart from drawing on the dance steps of the different cultural groups represented in many of their guilds, the Mvano also draw on the song traditions and languages represented in the southern region. To accommodate the various women represented, a Mvano group will often sing the same song in Yao, Lomwe, and Chichewa, three of the dominant languages spoken in the southern region. When the Mvano perform their dance songs, apart from singing well-known church choruses and songs with Mvano-composed texts, they also transform the texts and melodies of translated European hymns. The same hymn can be transformed and altered in numerous ways, with each resultant hymn having its own distinct character and dance movements. [. . .]

[. . .] One example of a song that is currently sung with altered text by both the Mvano and women's party associations is described below. The same tune and general rhythmic structure of the song is retained by both organizations, but each group has reinterpreted its text and performance style. The Mvano refer to this song as, "O Saina" (Oh, Sign). They have been singing it for over fifteen years, and some claim that it originated from a wedding song that focuses on the bride and groom signing the register during their marriage ceremony. In the Mvano version, the theme of signing is related to joining the Christian faith and linking themselves to the word of God. Swaying back and forth, with a fast-paced alternating left and right foot pattern undergirding the dance, the act of signing with their hands is rhythmically mimed by the Mvano as they change their dance pattern to perform a quick three-step movement that mirrors the tempo of the text at the end of selected phrases. The song leader mentions the names of different Mvano groups present, beckoning them to "sign today." The responding refrain sung by the other women focuses on the text "O Saina," (Oh Sign) until they join together to urge each other not to engage in gossip but to adhere to the word of God.

"O Saina" (Oh, Sign), as sung by Mvano women from Mulanje Presbytery

Leader: *Azimayi a Matemba, lero*   *Women of Matemba, today*
All: *O Saina!*   Oh Sign!

Leader:	*Azimayi a Matemba, lero*	Women of Matemba, today
All:	O Saina!	Oh Sign!
Leader:	*A Matemba mutosaina*	Women of Matemba, You sign
All:	O Saina!	Oh Sign!
Leader:	*Inde musaina mawu a Mulungu*	Yes, you will sign the Word of God
All:	O Saina!	Oh Sign!
	Mayi wa Matemba O saina	Woman of Matemba, Oh sign!
	Lero lino mutosaina, O saina!	This day you sign, Oh sign!
	Ife miseche sitifuna, O saina,	We don't want gossip, Oh sign!
	Koma timafuna mawu a Mulungu, O saina,	But we want the Word of God, Oh sign!

Chichewa and Chilomwe languages, Mvano Meeting, Malowa CCAP, 8 November 1988 [. . .]

[. . .]

Organizational structure

Mvano women and women party members who perform are organized through the women's sections of their respective institutions, whose overall structure as well as the positioning of women again bear striking similarities. Both types of associations are configured nationally into a pyramid structure. At the pinnacle of each political party is the national executive committee. Each party is divided into the three administrative regions of the government (northern, central, and southern), which are further broken into districts, then divided into areas, which are finally broken down into branches. A branch, the smallest division, can comprise one or more villages in a rural area or one or more neighborhoods in an urban center. Blantyre Synod is one of five synods under the administration and general secretariat of a general synod of the CCAP. Two of the other synods are in the central and northern regions of Malawi, and the remaining two are in Zimbabwe and Zambia. Organized according to the Presbyterian system of government, each synod oversees the activities of its presbyteries, which in turn oversee the activities of congregations and their prayer houses (satellite congregations). For both types of organizations, leaders and members at higher levels monitor the activities and give directives to those at lower levels.

Within these pyramid structures of both the political parties and Blantyre Synod, the women's bodies are suborgans of the larger organization. In the case of the political parties, the dominant organization is called the main body, which subsumes two subsidiary bodies, the women's wing and the youth wing. The main body of each party oversees all party activities and is dominated by, though not exclusive to, men. At each level within the pyramid structure are committees of the women's wings, which provide formalized leadership. At each level—national, regional, district, area, and branch—there is a chairman, vice-chairman, secretary, vice-secretary, treasurer, vice-treasurer, and committee members for each party committee (main body, women's wing, and youth wing). Those in executive positions of the women's wings are responsible for coordinating and overseeing the activities of all the women party members in the country. Leaders at each subsequent level are responsible for overseeing women at their levels, thus facilitating constant communication and coordination of activities between the national and local.

Similarly, in Blantyre Synod a main administrative body of elected officials oversees a number of departments, including the Women's Desk and Chigodi Women's Centre, whose activities are supervised by the synod-level Women's Work Committee. One of the tasks of the administrator of the Women's Desk is to organize and coordinate Mvano activities together with the salaried women's coordinators in each of the synod's fourteen presbyteries. Each Mvano group has a leader, or *mtsogoleri*, who heads a tenmember committee (treasurer, secretary, *et al.*) Because each congregation may have three to eight prayer houses attached to it, an elected *oyendera* (one who runs the organization) works with the *mtsogoleri* of each prayer house Mvano group in overseeing Mvano activities within that particular congregation. This model is also found in the other synods of the CCAP within Malawi.

There is a significant difference in the types of women who are members of each type of organization. Mvano members belong to a broad spectrum of the society, mirroring the makeup of the general population. Rural and urban, rich and poor, educated and lesser educated all participate. In the case of political parties, though people in all sectors of Malawian society are members of political parties, almost all women who are actively involved in the women's wings, with the exception of those in leadership positions in the national and some at the regional levels, belong to the poor majority. Reasons for the preponderance of poor women actively involved in party activities have to do primarily with material incentives provided by the party leadership (see Gilman 2001).

Many women involved in political organizations are also involved in church organizations. Though we have yet to conduct adequate research to ascertain the frequency with which this occurs, we have each encountered numbers of individuals involved with both. For example, Gilman asked women who regularly attended party meetings whether they were members or held leadership positions in other types of organizations. Most mentioned that they were also involved in the women's sections of their respective churches. Henderson similarly noted women who attend Mvano events wearing political cloth and knows individual women who have prominent roles in a political party and are also respected Mvano members. On the local level, those who are involved both in a political party and a church women's organization may have similar roles in each. For example, the branch secretary of a political party might also be the secretary in her congregation's women's guild. Or a song leader or composer in one might have the same position in the other.

In both types of organizations, women have a great deal of autonomy, and women members are responsible for making decisions within their bodies. All, however, work within and are subordinate to the larger organizational structures, which are dominated by men. In Blantyre Synod, for example, women did not become voting members of their local congregational sessions until 1980, when the ordination of the first women elected to be church elders took place. These female elders are church leaders outside of their membership in Mvano, though they are also expected to be members of Mvano. Not until 1995 were salaried full-time women's presbytery coordinators granted the right to vote in the highest courts of the church, and not until 2001 was the first woman ordained to the Ministry of Word and Sacrament. In the political parties, there are some women who hold leadership positions in the main bodies of political parties or even as parliamentarians, though these are few and far between (Mvula and Kakhongwa 1997, 30). Leaders of the women's wings do attend the meetings of the main bodies at the levels at which they lead as representatives of the women's wings. At the national and regional levels, the leaders of the women's wings are in important positions within the party because mobilizing women and increasing the support base is a priority. Sometimes, a female leader of the women's wing can also have a leadership position in the main body of the political party. For example, at the time of writing, Barbara Momba was the regional chairman of the League of Women of the MCP in the southern region as well as the regional secretary for the main body. As the regional secretary, she was subordinate to the regional chairman and vice-chairman, both of whom were male. Despite these leadership opportunities, the positions and activities of the women's wings are accorded less status and prestige than are those of the main body.

The meeting schedule and activities of the Mvano are much more formalized than are those of political parties. Congregational Mvano groups meet once a week from March through October and once a month during the planting and harvesting season, from November through February. These meetings alternate between Bible studies and visiting the sick, bereaved, and needy. Their meetings usually consist of various combinations of prayers, testimonies, memory verses, studying the Bible and their own study guide (*Bukhu la Mvano*), sewing, handcrafts, and learning about contemporary social issues that affect women, as well as the singing of hymns and their dance songs (see Women's Work Committee of Blantyre Synod CCAP 1993). A number of congregational groups get together at the presbytery level for extended training classes that meet less frequently. It is at their meetings that Mvano singing and dancing plays a significant role in the women's interaction. The regularity of meetings for political parties varies between political parties and in different locales. Ideally, women members at a given level meet on a regular basis. In Blantyre, a political center, for example, women at the branch levels of the UDF party met once a week during 2000, while in more rural areas meetings might take place every two weeks, every month, or only when there was a special event or issue that made a meeting necessary. At these business meetings, dues are sometimes collected, party directives are spread, upcoming events are announced, and logistics for attending events are coordinated. Meetings usually end with rehearsals during which women learn new songs and moves and perfect existing ones in preparation for forthcoming events.

Function

Mvano and women political dancers play important roles in maintaining their organizations' vitality and in attracting members, as well as in fulfilling more personal goals of individual political and spiritual expression and empowerment. Because of inherent differences in the types of organizations being discussed, the roles played by the women's sections differ, though again the similarities are striking. The CCAP is a religious institution that exists to care for the spiritual, material, and physical well-being of its members, to work toward building just and equitable relationships within church and society, and to engage in charitable works within the community. Political parties, on the other hand, exist to establish a broad support base so that politicians and political hopefuls can promote their policies and ultimately hold leadership positions within the state. A significant difference between the two is the question of who benefits from women's participation. In the case of political parties, despite rhetoric about the importance of integrating women into the political arena, women's wings exist largely to help mostly male party leaders achieve their goals. To achieve their goals of winning or maintaining parliamentary seats or the presidency, political leaders need to attract a large support base, disseminate their symbols and messages, and appear as though they enjoy widespread support. Through their singing and dancing at public events, women help political parties achieve these goals. Though the personal goals of women committed to a political party may include helping that party gain support, women for the most part are not pursuing their individual goals through their party activities.

The Blantyre Synod, on the other hand, exists ostensibly to draw people into Christian beliefs and practices in order to enrich their Christian lives and encourage them to influence society by becoming more responsible and caring citizens within their communities. Mvano members are involved in formal proselytizing activities through their own activities and formally organized evangelism campaigns aimed at attracting others to become Christians, which in effect increases the membership of their church. Their singing and dancing plays a significant role in these activities.

Though women play a similar role of evangelizing for the church or disseminating propaganda for political parties, there is a significant difference in how and why this happens. In the political sphere, the role women play as avenues for the dissemination of party symbols and messages is probably their most important contribution. Women's participation is oriented toward others, as they perform to aid in achieving the goals of those who wield more power and authority in their parties. Conversely, Mvano's role in evangelizing is only one dimension of their participation in church activities. The ultimate goal of the Mvano is not to serve the interest of their church leaders but to serve each other and members of their church and society by assisting them in their Christian development and fulfillment. Their attempts to draw new members into the church is an attempt not to help someone else wield power but to enable others to join the Christian faith, which is seen as subsequently benefiting the new members, not the Mvano organization or church leaders as such.

Women members are often the most effective at attracting other women into both types of organizations. In addition to sharing with their friends the experiences they have and the benefits they have gained from their membership, the activity of singing and dancing attracts members, as this is an activity enjoyed by many women in Malawi. As one member of the Mvano said, "I know women who joined [Mvano] because they liked our singing and dancing" (Silamoyo 1994). Similarly, many women join in political party dance rehearsals that take place in their locales because it is enjoyable, and then they subsequently attend rallies and ultimately become active members in parties.

Women's singing and dancing also helps to attract people of both sexes to public events. Numbers of people interviewed, for example, explained that people would not attend political rallies if it were not for the entertainment component. One member of AFORD called the dancing "the bait" that draws people to the rally. Once there, politicians can try to influence them politically, or as one MCP parliamentary candidate put it:

> To bring more people to go to your meetings, you are going to drum, perform some dances. And then when you are halfway with the dances, then you can stop and put in a political speech and say, "Okay, dancing will continue." In so doing, people tend to stay on, [thinking,] "Okay, after his speech, which anyway I'm not interested in, but later on I will watch the dances." (Anonymous 1999)

Similarly, Mvano whom we interviewed explained that some people come to church because of the singing. Once they are there, they are more likely to be influenced spiritually: "We sing songs to encourage others to follow Jesus and to bring backsliders back . . . some come to church because of it" (Namwali 1994).

Though we have been emphasizing that women in political parties serve primarily the interests of party leaders, at the same time, individual women who participate do gain something; otherwise, the institution could not exist on a voluntary basis. Some of the benefits enjoyed by women in political parties are similar to those enjoyed by Mvano. Both types of associations provide a sense of community for their members. Women meet other women at meetings and events, and women within organizations help one another in times of need. Attending the meetings and events of both the church and political parties also provides women with alternate activities to those of their day-to-day lives. Women interviewed in both types of organizations articulated that sometimes they like to go to meetings simply because it is better than staying at home. Both the Mvano and women party members sometimes have opportunities to travel to other countries and other regions of Malawi to participate in regional, national, or international events, something they would otherwise rarely be able to do. Women in both groups have opportunities to hold leadership positions, gain higher status recognition, receive special training, and develop new skills from their participation (see Phiri 1997, 74). Some women see the Mvano as a place of refuge, a place to go and gain support at times of need. Both organizations provide women with various opportunities for self-expression whether it is about political or religious convictions. The degree to which both the Mvano and political party members express themselves is limited, however, in that they are expected to express what is positive for their parties and their church. Though many women claim to have nothing but positive feelings about their parties, churches, and leaders during interviews, subsequent conversations revealed a range of feelings, which are rarely if ever expressed through song texts.

* * *

This introduction to women as singers and dancers of praise within Malawi's major political parties and within Blantyre Synod of the CCAP brings to the fore the important roles women's organizations play in undergirding and strengthening the institutions to which they are attached. It also reveals interesting intersections of cross-influencing musical and dance expressions between women in religious and political spheres that are dynamic, intelligent, and creative, and at the same time vital in bringing others into the church or in securing votes for political parties. The contributions made by women are recognized and valued by those in their organizations, as is indicated by the attention paid to ensuring women's participation and, in the case of Blantyre Synod, to investing in the leadership training of women. At the same time, however, an implicit hierarchy in the structures of both types of institutions situates most women in less advantageous positions than those of their male counterparts. For example, men dominate the overarching organizations, which are the centers of power for both the synod and the political parties. Conversely, the women's organizations are subsidiary to these male-dominated groups, and most women's contributions are channeled through them. The structures of both the synod and the political parties, therefore, institutionalize women's peripheral roles within the larger organizations. It ensures that the majority of women will continue to be funneled into the women's groups and that the overarching organizations will remain primarily male domains, continuing a system in which mostly men enjoy positions in the centers of power.

In addition to women's being institutionally subordinated within these organizations, some of women's most salient activities, notably their service, dress, singing, and dancing, also work to situate them symbolically in lower-status positions vis-à-vis their male counterparts. Here we return to the ideas introduced at the beginning of this article: local musical and dance practices are usually categorized as "African" or "traditional" ways of doing things, and women's performances function essentially to "Africanize" these Western-style organizations. The integration of local cultural practices into Western-style institutions should ideally contribute to the development of Malawian institutions that integrate both Western and local idioms, ideologies, and social and political structures. The problem arises, however, when different values are placed on what is considered "African" and "Western": what is labeled "Western" is almost always associated with higher status and prestige. If women are relied upon to be the purveyors of the local or "African," it follows that women's activities are also inevitably associated with less status and prestige. One only has to attend a political rally to understand the gross discrepancies in prestige and status accorded men and women in these contexts. Ranking party males wearing suits and ties customarily sit in chairs in front of a throng of women seated on the ground wearing "African dress" who occasionally burst into singing and dancing. Likewise, within the CCAP, the Mvano's Africanized European hymns, as expressed in some of their dance songs, are frequently taken for granted and are not placed on a par with church hymns that follow Scottish Presbyterian tradition. At church worship services or special functions that customarily use hymns and an order of service from the Scottish Presbyterian tradition, the Mvano typically perform their dance songs outside the church building, before and after the central event, and peripherally to the main activities. An exception to this practice would be on those specific occasions where male clergy or elders who are in control of the function invite the Mvano to perform their dance songs during a worship service. In the course of these formal church ceremonies, therefore, it is men, responsible for following Presbyterian practices and procedures as handed down by the Church of Scotland, who decide to what extent to include Malawian expressions of

Christianity as they are articulated in Mvano dance songs. Because the inclusion of Mvano dance songs in this way is more the exception than the rule, Mvano and their Africanized dance songs could be seen as having lower status and recognition at these events than the Scottish Presbyterian order of service and hymns favored by some male officials whose responsibility it is to uphold Scottish Presbyterian tradition.[8]

This institutionalization of women in subsidiary and more traditional roles is especially relevant within the context of contemporary Malawi, where gender issues have become a central topic in political discussions, media debates, strategic planning, and development projects. Many prominent voices in the political and religious arena claim a commitment to improving gender equity, yet the organizations from which these voices come remain structurally disadvantageous to women. The question, then, is whether the positive changes advocated for women can feasibly take place without structural changes to dominant political, social, economic, and religious institutions. [. . .]

Notes

1 We are not suggesting the existence of a reified, unambiguous Western/African dichotomy. Rather, we are addressing how different types of social practices are identified and valued by Malawians when they classify something as either "African" or "Western."
3 For information on the history and development of the Mvano organization and of women's leadership within the CCAP, see Chingota 1999 and Henderson forthcoming.
4 Since the time of research, a new political party, the National Democratic Alliance (NDA), has emerged as a fourth dominant party.
5 These gendered ideas about clothing and their relation to Western versus African divisions were institutionalized under President Banda, who, coincidentally, was an elder in the CCAP. The constitution during his rule specified that women could not wear trousers and had to wear skirts or dresses that extended well below the knee. Men, on the other hand, could not wear shorts and were instructed to wear long trousers and shirts. The outfit described both for contemporary female political dancers and for Mvano on special occasions was termed "national dress" for women during Banda's era.
6 Mvano wear their uniforms only at funerals of full-communicant church members who were in good standing with the CCAP. The deceased must have been baptized and have had her or his wedding blessed in the church. Once the elders and ministers confirm that the deceased meets the necessary requirements, the Mvano are free to wear their uniforms and participate fully in the funeral.
8 This issue is complicated. Henderson personally knows male ministers and elders who outwardly enjoy Mvano singing and dancing and who express their appreciation for the Mvano's Africanization processes within the context of church ceremonies that follow Scottish Presbyterian tradition. Our point here, however, is that, outside the Mvano's own domain, the power both to include Africanized Mvano dance songs within Westernized church ceremonies and to grant them official recognition still lies with the men who continue to hold the positions of power and status within church structures and who ultimately make decisions about whom to include in the main program of these church ceremonies.

Bibliography

Anonymous. 1999. MCP group interview. 29 March.
Berger, Iris. 1999. "Women in East and Southern Africa." In *Women in Sub-Saharan Africa*, edited by Iris Berger and E. Frances White, 5-62. Bloomington: Indiana University Press.
Chimombo, Steve, and Moira Chimombo. 1996. *The Culture of Democracy: Language, Literature, the Arts, and Politics in Malawi, 1992-1994*. Limbe, Malawi: WASI.
Chingota, Felix. 1999. "The Case of Blantyre Synod, Malawi." *Reformed World* 49(1):3-21.
Cope, Trevor. 1968. *Izibongo Praise Poems*. Collected by James Stuart, translated by Daniel Malcolm. Oxford: Clarendon Press.
Finnegan, Ruth. 1976. *Oral Literature in Africa*. Oxford: Oxford University Press.
Gilman, Lisa. 2001. "Purchasing Praise: Women, Dancing, and Patronage in Malawi Party Politics." *Africa Today* 48(4):43-64.
GJB. 1998. "Golden Jubilee Celebrations, 1948-1998: Fifty Years of Women's Guild Existence in Blantyre Synod." Unpublished ms. (English).
Graham, Scott. 1999. Personal communication. 26 January.
Henderson, Clara. Forthcoming. *Rolling Away the Stone: The Africanisation of Christian Music by Presbyterian Mvano Women in Southern Malawi*. Blantyre, Malawi: Christian Literature Association in Malawi.
Jiya, Daina. 1994. Personal communication. 8 June.
Kapuma, Gertrude. 1994. Personal communication (Chichewa and English). 15 July.
——. 1995. Personal communication (Chichewa and English). 15 March.
Kerr, David. 1998. *Dance, Media, Entertainment, and Popular Theater in East Africa*. Bayreuth African Studies 43.
Lwanda, John Lloyd Chipembere. 1996. *Promises, Power, Politics, and Poverty: Democratic Transition in Malawi, 1961-1999*. Glasgow: Dudu Nsomba.
Martin, Phyllis. 1994. "Contesting Clothes in Colonial Brazzaville." *Journal of African History* 35:401-26.
——. 1995. *Leisure and Society in Colonial Brazzaville*. Cambridge: Cambridge University Press.
Mvula, Peter M., and Paul Kakhongwa. 1997. *Beyond Inequalities: Women in Malawi*. Zomba, Malawi: Centre for Social Research.
Namwali, Lizzie. 1994. Personal communication (Chichewa). 21 June.
Ncozana, Silas. 1986. "Mvano and Evangelism in the Synod of Blantyre." *Africa Theological Journal* 15(3):183-87.
——. 1994. Personal communication. 15 July.
Nyirenda, Elizabeth, AFORD member. 1999. Personal communication. 4 September.
Opland, Jeff. 1983. *Xhosa Oral Poetry: Aspects of a Black South African Tradition*. Cambridge: Cambridge University Press.
Perani, Judith, and Norma H. Wolff. 1999. *Cloth, Dress, and Art Patronage in Africa*. Oxford: Berg.
Phiri, Isabel Apawo. 1996. "Marching Suspended and Stoned: Christian Women in Malawi, 1995." In *God, People, and Power in Malawi: Democratization in Theological Perspective*, edited by Kenneth R. Ross. Blantyre, Malawi: Christian Literature Association of Malawi.

———. 1997. *Women, Presbyterianism, and Patriarchy: Religious Experiences of Chewa Women in Central Malawi.* Blantyre, Malawi: Christian Literature Association of Malawi.

Schapera, I. 1965. *Praise Poems of Tswana Chiefs.* Oxford: Clarendon Press.

Short, Philip. 1974. *Banda.* London: Routledge & Kegan Paul.

Silamoyo, Bena. 1994. Personal communication (Chichewa). 2 July.

Spencer, Anne M. 1982. *In Praise of Heroes: Contemporary African Commemorative Cloth.* Newark NJ: Newark Museum.

Vail, Leroy, and Landeg White. 1991. *Power and the Praise Poem: Southern African Voices in History.* Charlottesville: University Press of Virginia.

Women's Work Committee of Blantyre Synod CCAP [Bungwe la Ntchito za Amayi, Blantyre Synod CCAP]. 1993. *Bukhu la Mvano* [The Mvano Study Guide]. N.p.

94

Excerpt from
'DALIT THEOLOGY IN TAMIL CHRISTIAN FOLK MUSIC
A transformative liturgy by James Theophilus Appavoo'

Zoe C. Sherinian

Source: Selva Raj and Corinne Dempsey (eds), *Popular Christianity in India: Riting Between the Lines*, SUNY Series in Hindu Studies, New York: State University of New York Press, 2002, pp. 233–53.

vānattila vāṛuhiṛa pettavarē sāmi–om
The divine one, our parent living in heaven,
pēr veḷaṅga vēṇuñcāmi viḍutalai varavēṇum
Let the meaning of your name be understood as 'let there be freedom!'
ottumayā oru olaiyil sēndu tiṛrum sōṛu
Give us daily the 'oru olai' food that is shared
nittanittam keḍaikkaṇumē pettavarē sāmi
In unity O, divine parent.

In this spoken (*pēccu*) Tamil folk version of the Lord's Prayer, the Dalit[1] composer/theologian Theophilus Appavoo proclaims the meaning of God's name as freedom (*viḍutalai*) thereby defining Christianity and Christian indigenization as the action of liberation.[2] His strategy of Christian indigenization is to re/construct a valued cultural status for low-caste Christians (and non-Christians) by reclaiming their folk music and rural culture for use in Christian liturgy. Appavoo's theological strategy suggests that Christian indigenization of music necessitates use of a musical system, as well as religious and cultural content, that allows for a recreative process of adaptation and manipulation for Dalit people's own liberative theological and social use.

Christian theology in India has multiple manifestations that reflect the cultural diversity of Christians and ultimately the diversity of Christianities. Dalit theology is one of several forms of indigenous Christian theologies expressed through music, a phenomenon of religious transmission that has existed in Tamil Nadu since its first contact with Christian missionaries as early as 1535. Christian music used by Tamils today is a complex mixture of European, American, Brahmanical, Indian cinematic, and Dalit flavors that have been sautéed in the oil of cultural contact over four hundred years to create not one, but a variety of musical and socio-religious styles: Western, Carnatic (indigenous classical), light (film or popular music), and folk. The most dynamic manifestations of Tamil Christian indigenization today continue to be the creation and transmission of Tamil theological perspectives through indigenous music; Dalit Christian theology has found its voice in folk music.

This essay presents a case study of Reverend James Theophilus Appavoo, a Protestant Dalit composer/theologian of the Church of South India (CSI), who has created a musical theology of liberation. Appavoo is one of the most influential and prolific Christian composer/theologians in Tamil Nadu today. He not only communicates a Dalit theology through sermons and written treatises but, as I will demonstrate, he musically actualizes and disseminates it through songs and liturgies—a significant strategy within the field of Dalit theology.[3]

The term "Dalit" reached Tamil Christian theologians and Christian activists by the mid-1980s and led to the development of a body of literature on Dalit theology. The earliest theological/academic use of the term Dalit in south India was at U.T.C. (United Theological College) Bangalore in April 1981 by A. P. Nirmal. Kottapalli Wilson used it in 1982 in his *The Twice Alienated Culture of Dalit Christians.* The CSI Bishop M. Azariah first brought the term to an international forum in 1984 to raise international Christian concern about the contemporary problems of Dalits. One of the most striking problems for Christian Dalits is that the government does not afford them the same degree of compensation (quotas in government jobs and educational seats) as "Hindu" Dalits because of their religion. In 1994 Bishop Azariah led the march to Delhi to fight for compensatory rights —affirmative action and quotas in education and government jobs—for Christian Dalits equal to those offered to "Hindu" Dalits.

Caste differentiation and prejudice continues to be practiced in the Protestant Churches, while its meaning has been recontextualized within the Christian subculture. My informants claimed that today caste distinctions affected elections for bishops, church pastorate committees, and Student Christian Movement leaders, as well as job preferences in Christian institutions, admission into choirs, seminary selection and financial support, decisions about whether one would invite another Christian into their house for a meal, and individual choice of music.

Dalit Christian music attempts to address oppressions that particularly plague the lives of Christian and non-Christian Dalits in villages. "Untouchables" are still given tea in differentiated tumblers at village tea stalls and forced to draw water from wells away from those near the upper-caste houses. Dalit women in many villages carry water daily from government wells, often a good distance from their *ceris* (colonies). Basic infrastructure services like access to clean water, electricity, and phones are often denied or delayed in Dalit communities. Dalit men and women are most often employed as manual laborers in construction or agriculture. In urban areas Dalits are assigned the menial jobs of cleaning toilets and removing garbage.

The composer Theophilus Appavoo is of the ex-untouchable Paraiyar caste;[4] however, unlike the majority of Christian and non-Christian Paraiyars who are landless agricultural laborers, his family has lived in urban areas (Vellore and Cuddalore in Arcot district) for the past four generations, benefiting from middle-class employment and Christian education.[5] His musical journey began with his family who performed and highly valued Carnatic music—a phenomenon among some lower-caste families that reflects their musical Sanskritization. By reflecting on his experience of casteism in urban churches as a boy, and observing oppressive caste practices in rural areas as a priest, Appavoo has developed a theoretical critique of the hegemonic cultural values transmitted and reinforced through indigenized Christian Carnatic music used among a primarily lower-caste Protestant Christian community.[6]

Appavoo teaches at the Tamil Nadu Theological Seminary (TTS) in Madurai, a Protestant seminary with a rich musical environment where theology has become "singable" in multiple styles (Thangaraj 1990, 109–18). Within this environment, the folk music composed by Appavoo stands out not only for its beauty, rhythmic vitality, and theologically powerful lyrics, but also for the way it has generated excitement and inspiration among the pastoral and lay communities. While doing fieldwork (1993–94), I observed the transmission network generated by TTS. Students, faculty, and lay people learned, recomposed, and ultimately became carriers of Appavoo's message through his songs. As a "student" in this community, I too was moved not only by his message, but also by his theo-musicological position that folk music is the form of Tamil Christian music with the greatest potential to empower and liberate Dalits from caste and economic oppression.

Appavoo's theological purpose is to change the values of this world that divide people, bringing to fruition what he understands as the "kingdom values" of love, equality, and justice between all in this world today, not exclusively in heaven or at some indefinite time in the future. Appavoo never advocates conversion to the institution of Christianity, but to these "kingdom values." He works toward socially empowering the oppressed regardless of religion and changing the values of those who oppress, especially those Christians who continue to practice casteism. He believes that this goal requires radical action on all social and cultural levels.⁷ He advocates beginning this process with the practice of poor people eating communally: practicing *oru olai* (literally "one pot"), a daily "Eucharistic" lifestyle of sharing food and the labor necessary for its production. *Oru olai*, then, is modeled on the communal labor and eating practices of the Indian joint family and used by many Dalit communities during festivals. It is also in tune with the values and practices of the early Church community.

Because Appavoo believes Christianity should be a means for social liberation, he theorizes that Christian indigenization of music should involve the use of local music and cultural perspectives. The adjective "Christian" is an essential defining characteristic of the musical, theological, and social method he has undertaken to create indigenized Tamil Christian music. He distinguishes between "Christian indigenization," which he understands as a method of liberation for the economically and socially oppressed, and "indigenized Christianity," which in India historically reflects the methods of Sanskritization, colonialization, Westernization, and translation. To "indigenize" Tamil Christian music necessitates reversing the hegemonic dominance that Brahmanical and Western cultural/musical forms and lyrical content have had on Christian music.⁸ Because at least 75 percent of Tamil Christians come from the Dalit and Sudra castes, and a majority live in rural villages, Appavoo argues that folk music is the most meaningful and liberative due to its content and language, its participatory nature, and because it is easily transmitted to these people.⁹

Whether indigenization as cultural synthesis is destructive or constructive depends on its motivating purpose and the power dynamics between outside "missionaries" and indigenous people, and among indigenous groups. Appavoo asserts that if the purpose of synthesis is to destroy or replace the egalitarian nature of local religions, it is neither positive nor liberative. He maintains that Western missionaries destroyed the empowering practices of local religions by labeling them "devil worship" and, with rare exception, only chose to indigenize Christianity using the religious content of Brahmanical Hinduism.¹⁰ In contrast, "Christian indigenization," according to Appavoo, is liberative in instances when 1) people reflect on and include their experience in the music, 2) they develop self-esteem by proudly reclaiming folk Dalit culture and identity, 3) they resist the tendency to internalize the hegemonic Brahmanical and Western cultures, and 4) they struggle together (in ritual, action, and performance) against multiple oppressions.

In Tamil village religions, empowerment occurs through transphysical rituals of "possession" by the *sāmi* (deity). The village deity possessing or "coming upon" a villager allows even the weakest members of the community to gain power both physically and emotionally. Emotions such as anger and fear are not pacified but rather channeled into action. The key to inducing this possession is the power of *parai* drumming.¹¹ Yet, the *parai*, and the drummers who play it, are more commonly thought of as polluting by upper castes because the drum is a necessary ritual accompaniment for upper-caste funerals.[12] Appavoo's most radical act of musical indigenization has been to bring the *parai* and its driving syncopated rhythms into a Christian liturgy that reclaims it as valuable and worthy rather than associates it with pollution (considering it *kōccai* or denigrated). Through reclaiming the content and form of folk culture, Appavoo similarly reclaims Dalit status as nonpolluting and esteemed.

The use of the folk form in the Tamil Church and in the larger hegemonic culture in which anything "folk" is considered to be degraded, represents significant subversive protest and marks an important first step in Appavoo's goal for a Dalit cultural revolution.[13] Folk music for Appavoo is music that is economically and socially accessible, draws on community skills, is potentially recreative, treated as unauthored, and orally learned. It uses spoken language and a musical syntax with which poor and oppressed people are facile. He furthermore reclaims rural musical moods, instruments, stylistic devices, agricultural metaphors, and elements of Dalit religions and politics. Appavoo has discovered through his own work with Tamil villagers that a message of Christian liberation is not as easily and powerfully spread through other "indigenized" Christian styles such as classical south Indian (Carnatic), Western hymnody, and some popular (film style) Tamil Christian musics. As communication mediums, these styles are oppressive to poor Dalit Christians because they reflect the culture and values of the higher-caste/class defined society, and moreover are rarely pedagogically accessible.[14] For example, Appavoo argues that transmission of Carnatic music is inherently limited and difficult; it is an individual art that does not facilitate community participation, unity, or protest to change society; and it cannot encode anger effectively but instead pacifies. The key to the difficulty of its transmission is its nature as a performance art controlled by class and caste elites.[15] Appavoo contends that if the message of a song has meaning to Dalits, if it is politically and spiritually empowering, it will spread quickly (Appavoo 1993, 75). If it is not meaningful, its message and style will either be changed to become powerful, or it will die a natural death from lack of use.

History and context of indigenized Tamil Christian music

Since the early sixteenth century, music has played a primary role in the process of indigenization and the expression of each "new" mode of Tamil Christianity in its specific historical context. Translation and vernacularization of the Christian message into Tamil dialects and musical styles were central to the conversion process. Throughout this history, language and musical style continued to be markers of local identity as well as cultural and aesthetic values. Music became a means for theological transmission, while particular styles of music transmitted the aesthetic and social values associated with Sanskritization, Westernization and Dalitization. Music then became a means for expressing and transmitting indigenized theology as well as contextualizing Tamil Christian identities.

As local and foreign players changed throughout history, so did the dynamics and complexity of indigenization.[16] Beginning in the eighteenth century, different denominationally-based mission societies were involved with different Tamil groups—divided by caste, class, geography, and theological identity—creating a variety of indigenized Christianities in Tamil Nadu. The dynamics between missionaries and native groups took on specific qualities of power and valuation. Several factors played a role in creating these dynamics including the religio-cultural ideology of each mission society, the reasons for conversion and indigenization of each local Tamil group, as well as the influence of individual culture brokers. These social dynamics were in turn expressed through the resulting indigenous styles of music; particularly through the dynamics of linguistic and stylistic transmission, the values and cultural perspectives encoded in each style, and the degree of empowerment and passivity associated with each.

Although the Tamil Christian population today is relatively small—three million or 5.81 percent of the total state population (Grafe 1990, 2)—the support for the use of one music style over another often reflects the historically constructed identities and theological stances of particular Tamil Christian subgroups (Sherinian 1998, 193–291).[17] A brief description of the historical relationships between these social and musical categories will help to illuminate the context in which Appavoo has created his folk music liturgy and the meaning of its indigenization and reception.

Tamil Protestant Christian music can be divided into three major categories: Western hymns sung in European languages, Western hymns translated into Sanskritized Tamil, and indigenous classical, folk, and popular songs. Protestant missionaries brought their hymnody and instruments with them to India, musical representations of both their theology and cultural baggage. Most urban Christians learned this repertoire. Some lower-caste Christians have continued to use English-language hymns accompanied by organ and four-part harmony as a symbol of class mobility and an expression of agency against local elites. They associate themselves with colonial powers and Westernization in an attempt to shed the stigma of untouchability. Yet in the process of musical adaptation, they internalize the foreign and elite cultural ideology, rejecting Tamil village culture as "heathen" and "degraded."

Western hymns translated in the eighteenth century into highly Sanskritized Tamil, called *pāmālai* and *ñanappāṭṭu*, retained their English or German tunes and meters, rendering them meaningless to most Tamils. *Pāmālai* continues as the hegemonic music genre sanctioned by priests and lay officials in contemporary urban CSI and Lutheran churches, particularly by those concerned with maintaining the cultural values, Western aesthetics, and liturgical traditions inherited by the missionaries.

247

Indigenous Christian music sung in the vernacular, using local musical styles, poetic forms, and instruments, express culturally contextualized Christian hermeneutics as well as social hierarchies. Caste division among Christians played a core role in the process of indigenizing Christianity.[18] Caste distinction, then, manifests itself not only in daily relationships between Tamil Christians, but also in theology, liturgy, and music. Upper-caste identity has been most strongly encoded in classical indigenous song styles. The Catholic missionaries in the seventeenth century constructed an indigenized Christianity culturally and musically identified with Brahmins in hopes that conversion of these social/religious elites would lead to a trickle-down effect on the lower-castes. The Roman Jesuit missionary, Robert de Nobili, who worked with Brahmins in Madurai from 1606, did not consider the Christian principle that all people are equal before God to be contradictory to the social hierarchy of caste (Thekkedath 1982, 214).

The Lutheran missionaries at Tranquebar and Tanjore in the eighteenth century accommodated the upper-caste Vellala's determination to retain caste and their indigenous theology of pluralism.[19] They allowed for caste separation in seating and reception of Communion. As part of this accommodation, they also embraced the Carnatic Christian compositions of the famous Vellala (upper-caste) Christian composer/poet Vedanayagam Sastriar as the primary source for indigenized Tamil Christian music. Over 100 of Vedanayagam Sastriar's Christian *kīrtanai*, a three-part song form using classical Indian modes and time cycles, were compiled into the first Tamil Hymnal in 1853 by the American Congregational missionary Edward Webb.[20] The missionaries then disseminated the *kīrtanai* to the rural lower-caste Christian population who had minimal previous exposure to this elite form. This resulted in indigenization as Sanskritization, or elite cultural "Hinduization," for lower-caste village Christians who continue to use *kīrtanai* as their primary liturgical song genre.

Many of the Protestant missionaries since the nineteenth century have worked hard to eliminate caste identity distinctions, often requiring their upper- and lower-caste converts to sit together at love feasts.[21] Most did not, however, recognize the upper-caste and class values encoded in Carnatic music. Instead, missionaries, along with upper-caste elite Tamil Protestants, continued to support Carnatic music as the only form of indigenized Tamil Christian music considered acceptable for church liturgy.[22] Furthermore, because of the early establishment of caste practices by the Lutheran Vellalas and postindependence power struggles within the Protestant (CSI and Lutheran) Churches, caste has remained a category of identification and hierarchical social differentiation within the Tamil Christian communities.

In postindependence India, middle-class educated Tamil Christians, many of them theologians, combined elements of Carnatic music and de-Sanskritized or *sen* (pure) Tamil to create songs and liturgies, called *tamil isai vari pāṭṭu*.[23] While these replace the Hindu theological content and Sanskritized Tamil of the *kīrtanai* with a progressive Tamil Christian theology, the language and poetic metaphors of literary Tamil continue to reflect the values and cultural experiences of middle- and upper-class, highly educated Tamil Christians. Literary Tamil remains inaccessible to, and unreflective of, the lower-class members of the lower-castes. Furthermore, the musical performance is even more classicized than the contemporary *kīrtanai*: the message is more liberating, but the linguistic and musical medium of transmission remains elite.

Since the 1950s, indigenous Christian popular or light music, which fuses elements of Western pop music with Indian folk and light classical music, is often used by Tamil evangelists. However, it has faced official Church resistance because its style is too closely associated with secular themes in films. Many liberation theologians also feel light music pacifies people because its tunes and rhythms are used to attract masses of poorer people, yet it fails to address the issue of social oppression. Evangelists ask the people to have faith in order to find salvation in heaven, a message that helps maintain the status quo in a culture that is dominated by the ideology of caste karma.

The development of a Tamil Christian music that both addresses the social needs of poor village Dalits, the majority of Protestant Christians, and transmits a liberative message in a musical style that positively reflects their values and cultural traditions, was not created until the 1980s.[24] Appavoo and others who create folk-based music question earlier assumptions about the superiority of Western and elite Indian musical values by reviving pre-Christian village traditions, combining them with local hermeneutics perceived as parallel to early Christian or Jewish social contexts and Gospel ideologies. Activists and common people use Dalit Christian music to alleviate the religious stigma of pollution, to fight against the social and internal psychological oppression of discrimination, and to reconstruct their economic and political status. The following musical and linguistic analysis describes how Appavoo reclaims the content and form of folk culture as a powerful and valuable tool of Dalit liberation in Tamil Christian liturgy.

Liberative indigenization through folk music in Appavoo's "Worship in Folk Music"

Appavoo's "Worship in Folk Music" (*girāmiya isai vaṛi pād*) is one of several CSI Tamil music liturgies or *Tamil Isai Vaṛi Pāṭṭu* (TIVP).[25] Since the 1950s, six of these fully sung liturgies have been composed in classical Carnatic style using Sanskritized or high literary Tamil. Appavoo composed his Tamil folk, spoken language version in 1994 in order to (re)indigenize the content and musical style of the TIVP to include metaphors, stylistic and performance devices, and cultural and religious values of rural Tamil life. Appavoo also intended to formally introduce folk music and spoken language into the CSI churches; thus he translated the language of the traditional CSI order from high literary written to pan-regional spoken Tamil.

Appavoo communicates his theology both in lyrical content and musical medium. While the transmission of the message through the lyrics is of primary importance, the values at the core of his theology, universal family, *oru olai*, and the strategy of reversal are contained within the system of folk music sound and performance. The corporate worship values of unity and sharing are encoded in call-and-response techniques, community participation in leading the service, and transformative empowerment through musical and theological recreation.

Appavoo seeks to create an unalienating participatory liturgical context, where the message is primarily communicated through the heart and emotions. This is signified musically through mood and rhythm, which he believes are the key structural elements to the transformative power of folk music. The lyrics help create the musical moods through painting nostalgic rural images and through emotional shock engendered by using "unrefined" language.[26] Appavoo also consciously draws on linguistic accents of spoken Tamil to create dramatic emotional responses in performance.

The three primary theological metaphors Appavoo constructs in his village liturgy are God as bigendered parent of one universal family, the Eucharist as *oru olai* (shared communal eating), and God as farmer (the strategy of reversal). They all address issues of unity as the means for a change in values and action against oppression. Appavoo believes that God has provided everything people need to live. He views the source of human problems as located not in God, but in the Church, the larger social structure, and Dalits themselves who do not worship as a unified group or universal family. According to Appavoo the essential action of being in one universal family is to share food communally; indeed he advocates this as the proper way of worshipping God.[27]

In the "universal family" all people are siblings born of the same parent's (*pettavarē*) womb.[28] There is no separation of people based on class, private ownership, or gender differences. Appavoo uses Galatians 3:28 as the biblical foundation for this tenet. He preaches that, "If you are in one family then [as in Christ] there is no difference between . . . man or woman, between slave and master."[29] There is no caste difference; no person is separated from the family table because he/she is considered unclean. There is also no separation between those who "have been saved" and those who have not nor between Christians and non-Christians.

Through exposure to the Dalit people's material reality, Appavoo realized that the Eucharist needs to be a daily living practice of communal eating and shared labor that liberates people from social and economic injustice. When discussing I Corinthians 10:22 in a rural theological education class ("We who are many are one body, for we all partake of the one bread"), a Dalit village girl asked Appavoo what he had eaten for breakfast. He replied "*idlies*"—a middle-class breakfast of steamed rice cakes and curry. She stated that she had had *kañji* the poor peoples' breakfast of rice gruel, and that her neighbor had had nothing (Appavoo 1992, 7). This encounter signified for Appavoo the reality that everyone does not literally partake in *one* food. Economic and social classes eat different foods, and some are not able to eat at all. Appavoo feels strongly that this analysis from the perspective of the most marginalized in Indian society, a Dalit girl, "questioned all the theological arguments over issues such as transubstantiation, consubstantiation, and memorable feast. Eucharist became *oru olai*, [the] common food of the Universal family" (Appavoo 1993, xxviii).

Appavoo advocates several "reversals": of values, of social hierarchy, of the paradigms with which hegemonic institutions interpret the Bible, of the concepts of inauspiciousness, cleanliness and purity, and of the metaphors used to understand Jesus and God. Appavoo's strategy of reversal is expressed most powerfully through reclaiming the use of folk music as a legitimate source for indigenized Christian liturgy in his *girāmiya isai varipāḍu*. He uses instruments such as the *parai*, vernacular language, melodies, rhythms and folk-music genres commonly thought of by middle-class pastoral and lay leaders as the degraded cultural antithesis of classical Carnatic music or Western hymnody.

Appavoo's biblical grounding for his theology of reversal lies in the metaphor of the kingdom of God. He follows Jesus' strategy of "using the language of paradox and reversal to shatter the conventional wisdom of his time" (Borg 1994, 80–81). The interpretation of Jesus' actions as efforts to benefit primarily the poor and oppressed challenge traditional Indian and Western interpretations that value private property and money over human relationships, and reverse the hierarchies of class, caste, and gender. Appavoo intends to reverse the metaphor of Jesus as *raja* (king), which has been common in Tamil liturgy for over 250 years. Instead, he portrays God as a farmer (*vevasāyi*) or a working-class political leader who rides a working animal, the donkey. Both reclaim a positive status for Dalit subjects. Appavoo also attempts to reverse the patriarchal ideology of Western Christianity by interpreting the qualities of God as both masculine and feminine.

Analysis of James Theophilus Appavoo's "Worship in Folk Music"

The invocation at the beginning of Appavoo's village music liturgy, *Girāmiya Isai Varipāḍu*, mirrors the Tamil village religious tradition of invoking *sāmi* (God), announcing that all community disputes have been settled, and all the people have gathered in unity. The Adoration (Greetings and Praise) is extended to clearly define and reclaim God in the local agricultural and social context. The Repentance and Absolution draw on the folk lament style of *oppari*. Although the content and style have been redirected toward a village perspective, the Creed, Preparation of the Meal, Blessing the Meal, Lord's

Prayer, and the Final Blessing all follow the CSI form very closely. All of the sections of the liturgy are usually sung except the Gospel readings and the sermon. However, Appavoo often replaces the formal spoken sermon with a street theater style skit that involves members of the congregation. Appavoo also consciously undermines the sanctioned priest/congregation hierarchy by involving the congregation in a call-and-response format with a rotating lead singer during the blessing of Communion traditionally sung only by the priest.

The penultimate section between Communion and the Final Blessing allows anyone from the congregation to pray publicly. It functions similarly to intercession prayers normally placed after the Creed and also provides an opportunity for community and individual expression typical of Dalit religions and many rural Christian congregations.

Greetings and Praise of God, *Sāmiya Vaṇaṅguṟadu*

Section 1
pettavarē olagattai paḍaiccavarē -ammayappā
O, parent who created the world, mamma/papa.
attaṉaikkum āṇḍavarē ompādam vaṇakkam
Lord of everything, we bow at your feet.
mūttavarē mīṭṭeḍukka vandavarē -kaṉṉimari
O, the eldest one who has come to redeem us.
petteḍutta pālagarē ompādam vaṇakkam
O, child of Virgin Mary, we bow at your feet.
suttattiru āviyarē sūriyarē -ottumaye
O, the Holy Spirit, the sun.
kattuttarum vāttiyārē ompādam vaṇakkam
The one who teaches us solidarity, we bow at your feet.

Section 2
āttukkuḷḷa ūttu taṇṇi sāmiyaruḷ nādā–pāva
You are the spring in the river, O divine one, gracious lord!
ūttai pōkkum jīvataṇṇi sāmiyaruḷ nāda.
The living water that cleans the filth of sin, O divine one, gracious lord!
sutta neyyi poṅga sōṟu sāmiyaruḷ nāda–pasiye
You are the pure *ghee pongal* rice, O divine one, gracious lord!
nittam pōkkum jīvasōṟu sāmiyaruḷ nāda.
The living rice that removes hunger every day, O divine one, gracious lord!
kāttula nī teṉṉaṅkāttu sāmiyaruḷ nāda–olaham
You are the breeze from the coconut grove, O divine one, gracious lord!
mottattukkum vīsum kāttu sāmiyaruḷ nāda.
That blows for all the world, O divine one, gracious lord!

Section 3
muttipōṉa sorakkā nāṅga sāmiyaruḷ nāda–oḍacci
We are the over-ripe vegetable, the *sorakkā*, O divine one, gracious lord!
vitteḍuttu vedappavaru nī sāmiyaruḷ nāda.
You are the one who breaks the gourd, removes the seeds and plants them!
neruñcimuḷḷu neṭañca nelam sāmiyaruḷ nāda–ēṅga
We are the land full of *nerinji* thorns, O divine one, gracious lord!
neñcaikkoṭṭi kaḷaiyeḍuppavar nīyē aruḷ nāda
You are the one who plows our hearts and removes the weeds, O divine one, gracious lord!

Section 4
karugippōṉa kāṇappayiru sāmiyaruḷ nāda–adai
We are the wilted *kāṇai* plant, O divine one, gracious lord!
tuḷukkavaikkum vevasāyi nī sāmiyaruḷ nāda
You are the farmer who makes it sprout, O divine one, gracious lord!
viruttiyillā paruttikkāḍu sāmiyaruḷ nāda–adai
We are the cotton fields that do not yield, O divine one, gracious lord!
veḷaya vaikkum vevasāyi nī sāmiyaruḷ nāda.
You are the farmer who makes them grow, O divine one, gracious lord!
ēreḍuttu vantavarē sāmiyaruḷ nāda–oṅga
O you who took up the plow and came, O divine one, gracious lord!
pēreḍuttu pōtṟi seyyirōm sāmiyaruḷ nāda.
So we take your name and praise you, O divine one, gracious lord!

Interpretation of the greetings and praise

The Greetings and Praise consists of four sections, each delineated by a change in musical mood, exploring joy and sadness, particularly through changes in tempo. Section one of the "Greetings and Praise" demonstrates how Appavoo uses music to articulate the core aspects of his indigenized theology. Using the same melody to describe the Holy Trinity (and their essential nature as equals or "three-in-one"), Appavoo outlines his theology of the universal family, characterizing God as the bigendered parent (*pettavarē*) and Jesus as the elder brother (*muttavar*) and son of Mary. Then, with a driving vocal and instrumental unity he describes the Holy Spirit, the sun, as a teacher of solidarity.

The second phrase of each melodic couplet musically defines the quality of each aspect of the Trinity by emphasizing the following words with *oṭṭuccol* syncopated accents at the end of the line: 1) *ammaiyappa*,[30] mother/father lord of everything; 2) *kaṉṉimari*, Virgin Mary; and 3) *ottumaya*, the one who gives and teaches solidarity. *Kaṉṉimari*, or Virgin Mary, is constructed from Appavoo's feminist standpoint as the independent bearer of salvation. Jesus was conceived independently of a male's help; furthermore, there would be no salvation without Mary's consent to the angel Gabriel's request and her willingness to risk social ostracism as an unmarried pregnant woman.[31] Rhyme patterns throughout become mnemonic devices in the folk transmission system that help people to remember the words and thus transmit the ideas easily.

Section two of the "Greetings and Praise" introduces a happy, excited mood both melodically and rhythmically. Its lyrics combine Christian, Tamil, Dalit, and rural metaphors to create a positive and hopeful indigenous perspective on the gracious gifts of *sāmi*, the divine one. In the first of three choruses, God is defined as "the spring in the river, the living water that washes off (or 'removes') the filth of sin."[32] Through rural symbols Appavoo calls on Christian Dalits to return to the life force of the land, to its rural simplicity and beauty, to wash off the filth of sins (like classism and internalized casteism), and to reclaim rural Dalit identity as clean. Appavoo attempts to reach the minds and hearts of the middle-class urban Dalit who has left behind the village and everything associated with it.

The second stanza continues this theme of rural purity, yet focuses more on culture. He presents the metaphor *sāmi* (or Christ), the living Eucharist, as "the pure *ghee pongal* rice, the living rice that removes hunger every day." *Pongal* is the Tamil harvest festival named for the sweet *pongal* rice that is cooked in a pot and boiled over to represent the promise of good fortune in the coming year. In a village context the *pongal* is cooked and shared communally. This metaphor is the basis for Appavoo's understanding of Eucharist as *oru olai*. By describing the *pongal* rice as pure *ghee* [*nei*], Appavoo again attacks the myth of lower-caste culture as impure, replacing it with an emphasis on the rich delicacy and ritual purity of *ghee* (clarified butter).

In the Tamil context, the Western concept of the Eucharist as living bread is indigenized as the living rice that removes the daily hunger of poverty. Going beyond the simple cultural substitution of rice for bread to create an oppositional Dalit construction, Appavoo consciously uses the often denigrated vernacular term *sōru* for rice instead of the more literary or Brahmanic *sādam*. He reclaims the auspiciousness of Dalit culture and subverts the Brahmanic hegemony by fusing *sōru* with the more Sanskritic *jiva* (living) in a blasphemous marriage of the Brahmanical and Outcast as the primary Christian symbol of God: the Eucharist given with grace.

In this second section, the word *pōhhum* is used in two contexts: the daily removal of hunger, *pasiya nittam pōhhum*, and the removal or cleansing of the filth of sin, *pāva ūttai pōhhum*. The double use reinforced by their articulation with the same melody ties these two ideas together in the practice of *oru olai*. Appavoo advocates that if people of different communities eat together communally every day, no one will go hungry. Moreover, through this radical action they will undermine participation in the "sins" of caste separation and private property.

In the third stanza, Appavoo returns his congregation to a peaceful pastoral scene where they can feel the breeze from the coconut grove given freely as the grace of God and available for all to enjoy. He reminds us that God has already given people everything they need in nature, in contrast to the inequalities of modern urban life, with its material necessities like fans, which are available only to those who can afford electricity.[33] Section two of the "Greetings and Praise" focuses on "re-claiming" Appavoo's strategy of indigenization for the liberation of Dalits. God and God's grace are represented as rural beauty and natural auspiciousness in order to reassociate village life as positive. Appavoo's focus on food in this section represents the centrality of Jesus' radical action in table fellowship and highlights the perspectives and concerns of poor Dalit people.

In sections three and four of the "Greetings and Praise," rural hardships of rot, pain, heat, and infertility are not romanticized but in fact starkly spelled out as metaphors for humans who have made mistakes; this theme is encoded musically with melodic tension. Each couplet contrasts poignant rural images with positive images of God's grace as the nurturing *vevasāyi* (gender neutral "farmer") who plows, sows, and grows new life, bringing redemption and forgiveness for human mistakes and resolving the (social and musical) tension of painful misfortune. Appavoo reflected in a 1994 interview on the Dalit farmer as a metaphor for the divine: "I'm moved by that metaphor. I was really happy that I got that metaphor because we have only been thinking of God as father, the patriarchal father, only as king, the aggressive dominant king. *Vevasāyi* is a term that is used for both man and woman."[34]

The lyrics in section three ask the congregates to ponder their own sins. Accordingly, Appavoo slows the tempo back to the original and uses a 6/8 meter to express an interior "depressed mood," as one would reflect upon what has been left undone. The first couplet of section three reflects upon people's sins with the line "we are the overripe *sorakkā*." *Sorakkā* is a gourdlike vegetable that becomes inedible when overripe. It is also thought by some, particularly Brahmins, to be an inauspicious vegetable.[35] Farmers do not, however, waste or throw away the overripe *sorakkā*; they either dry its shell and use it to hold water, or break the shell to get seeds for the next generation of plants. The message of this metaphor is that, like the next generation of seeds, God sees our potential and has use for us even when we appear rotten to others or ourselves. Appavoo also described the overripe *sorakkā* as a symbol for the third and fourth generation of Christians who have left the village, and have become "soft" (passive, rotten, and corrupted by materialism, selfishness, and individuality) middle-class people. They have lost the taste for *sorakkā*, or village culture, and for liberating protest. In a tone of hopeful faith, the verse asks God to break our shells and "make us seeds to grow new *sorakkā*."[36]

The second couplet describes the land that grows *nerinji* (thorn weeds) because it lies fallow or is left uncultivated. If these thorns pierce the skin, they can be very painful. Furthermore, in Tamil literature this landscape carries negative symbolism. In Appavoo's liturgical context, God the farmer plows away the pain from our hearts, removing the harmful weeds. The phrase *karugippōṉa*, when applied to a plant, means that it has wilted or been burned by the sun. *Kāṇappayir* is a type of legume that needs very little water to grow, and thus does not wilt easily. If the *kāṇappayir* does wilt, as Appavoo describes in section four, the sun must be very hot. Such extreme heat is a metaphor for people's sins which lead to social oppression: people are hot with sin like the intense sun that wilts the *kāṇappayir* plant. But God, as farmer, gives grace to make the people sprout again.

The fifth and final couplet ends the "Greetings and Praise" section on a fully positive tone musically and lyrically. This time the two phrases do not contrast the sins of the people with the saving actions of God, but reverse the order of focus. The salvation of Jesus is described first by evoking the sacrifice of the Dalit farmer who takes up the plow (the cross) for all others. The people follow, taking up the name of Christ as liberator to praise him. The substitution of the Dalit plow for Jesus' cross, accompanied by powerful folk singing and playing in unison, fully indigenizes Christian faith and worship in the sacrifices and joy of Dalit culture. God is not only with Dalits, but *is* Dalit.

Indigenized Tamil Christianity, therefore, only becomes "Christian" if it is indigenized into a cultural medium that liberates the poor and oppressed (i.e., Dalits) through claiming them as valuable, auspicious, and worthy. In Tamil Nadu, in order for the Untouchables to be liberated, their cultural resources must also be liberated from hegemonic associations of inferiority, degradation, and inauspiciousness. Appavoo's *Girāmiya Isai Varipāḍu* intends to induce spiritual, cultural, and psychological liberation in a Tamil Christian liturgical setting. This is achieved by drawing on the transformative aspects of folk culture including the transphysical power of *parai* drumming and rhythms, community participation, the emotional power invoked by folk language, metaphor and melodic devices, and a folk transmission system that allows for theological recomposition as indigenization.

Reception and conclusion

The reception to Appavoo's "Worship in Folk Music" since its composition in 1994 has been positive, if slow. Several of his former students have adapted the liturgy to their own local contexts by making the language more regionally colloquial. As priests, a larger number of Appavoo's students have also been inspired to attempt an occasional practice of *oru olai* (communal eating) among their village congregations. By pooling financial and labor resources to share the ritual of eating in *oru olai*, many Dalit villagers have seen the possibility of unity, hope, and social change. Before Tamil Dalits can organize for structural, economic, and socio-political change, it is necessary to break the psychological barriers that prevent them from believing change is possible. The experience of *oru olai* in practice and as symbolized in the ritual and music of Appavoo's "Worship in Folk Music" appears to help inspire social change among these Dalit Christians who have been touched by his musical theology.

Since 1999 the Tamil Nadu Theological Seminary has been actively reviving rural congregations that have had little pastoral attention in years. To this end, they are introducing Appavoo's folk music liturgy and the practice of *oru olai* as the primary mode of worship instead of the orders of service in the CSI prayer book and hymnal.[37] The liturgy has thus gained official institutional sanction to be propagated among the rural people who may benefit from it the most.

The greatest challenge for Appavoo will be to reach middle-class and urban people, for folk music represents everything the lower-caste Christians in these communities have attempted to leave—poverty, caste identity, and an oppressive village context. Appavoo recognizes that social change for Dalits requires a cultural reeducation process at all levels of the Protestant Churches in Tamil Nadu that positively revalues folk culture and recognizes its necessity as the foundation for indigenized music and theology. The tools for reclaiming, recreating, and transmitting Tamil folk music and theology are within this "Worship in Folk Music" (*Girāmiya Isai Varipāḍu*) liturgy. Appavoo's strategy is to begin by transmitting the liturgy to seminary students and rural people. If his musical theology is in fact liberating it will find meaning among the people who need to re/claim and transform their cultural esteem and value in the Church and in the greater Tamil society.

Notes

1 Dalit literally means broken or oppressed, taken from the Sanskrit root *dal*. It is the self-selected term that many people formerly called outcastes, Untouchables, or Harijans, call themselves particularly in the context of oppositional politics. It was first created in the early 1970s by the Dalit Panthers and other organizations based in Maharastra who claimed it as an expression of cultural pride and a rejection of oppression (Joshi 1986, 3).
2 These verses are from a larger liturgy called *girāmiya isai varipāḍu* (literally 'village music worship'). For a full analysis of Appavoo's songs, liturgy, and music history, see my dissertation in ethnomusicology entitled "The Indigenization of Tamil Christian Music: Folk Music as a Liberative Transmission System."
3 Dalit theology addresses the social and spiritual needs of Untouchables, as well as the lower castes, the economically disenfranchised, and women.
4 Untouchability was legally abolished in the Indian constitution in 1950. People from the Paraiyar community are categorized as a "scheduled caste," which allows for some compensatory rights through government quotas in jobs and education.
5 Since the early twentieth century, more Christian Dalits have become middle class, although the number is relatively small (20 percent of the population at the most).

6 Dalits make up 70 percent of the CSI and Lutheran churches in Tamil Nadu (Kambar Manickam personal communication, August 1994). Although 80 percent of this population still lives in rural settings, until recently the needs, values, and cultural perspectives of middle-class urbanites have dominated the focus of ministry, ministerial training, and liturgy.

7 Appavoo's conception of total liberation is articulated through his EPSIPEGS system. EPSIPEGS—*E*conomic, *P*olitical, *S*ocial, *I*deological, *P*sychological, *E*nvironmental, *G*ender-based, *S*piritual—is an acronym for a holistic analysis of oppression in India.

8 The idea of reversing the hegemonic dominance of Brahmanical cultural elements in Tamil music (as well as gender and caste inequity) occurred in The Dravidian Movement between 1949 and 1972. Many Christians joined the Dravidian political parties, which had a significant influence on indigenized Christian music and literature. This movement articulated a positive Tamil identity through literary and linguistic study, Tamil Isai (music), and the de-Sanskritization of Tamil (Ryerson 1988, i). Although it contributed to self-respect among Dalits that had begun in the mass-conversion movements of the 1910s and continued under Ambedkar in the 1930s, it failed to speak to the economic grievances of the poor outcastes.

9 Appavoo (1993, 30), notes that 72 percent of total female agricultural labor in Tamil Nadu is Dalit, and 80 percent of Christian Dalits are landless. Furthermore, 80 percent of Dalits live below the poverty line.

10 Lower-caste scholars and activists have argued that Dalit religions are distinct from Hinduism. See Ilaiah 1994, and Appavoo 1994 in Massey.

11 The *parai* is a frame drum (small) played with the hands or (large) played with two thin sticks.

12 In the process of funeral performance, Paraiyar (pariah) drummers inherently repollute themselves by being associated with the pollution of the dead body and by having to touch the body in order to pick up coins thrown to them as payment.

13 Upper-caste elite and Westernized (neo-Victorian and popular) cultural values define cultural hegemony in the Protestant Tamil Christian Church today. In the greater Tamil culture the aesthetic values of upper-caste Brahmanical art forms devalue folk culture as *kōccai* (slang or vulgar), polluting, and not serious, but mere entertainment (see the theorist P. Sambamurthy 1984, 140–41, 105). Appavoo (1986, 13) challenges the discourse arguing for a lack of a purpose in folk music, insisting that its defining characteristic is purposeful adoption and dissemination connected with the social, economic, political, and cultural life of the folk.

14 Ethnomusicologists argue that social and musical structures are often homologous (Feld 1984, 383–409). By embracing upper-caste/class values that differentiate elite culture as pure and more refined than lower-caste folk culture, Dalits internalize this depravation.

15 J. T. Appavoo, speech given at the People's Music Festival, Tanjore, January 30, 1994.

16 I model my theories of indigenization in the Tamil context on Steven Kaplan's (1995) work on indigenized Christianity in Africa.

17 Christians make up approximately 2.5 percent of the total population of India today. Tamil Nadu is the state with the third largest percentage of Christians.

18 I have identified three major Tamil Protestant caste groups, Paraiyars, Nadars, and Vellalas, and several minor groups. See Sherinian (1998, 23–26) for a list of minor Christian castes. Also see Elder for an earlier list of Christian castes in Madurai.

19 When the Anglican Calvinist missionaries later attempted in the 1820s to eliminate the caste divisions that the Vellalas had incorporated in the eighteenth

century as acceptable practice in Tamil Lutheran Protestantism, these new missionaries struck at the heart of what Hudson (2000, 180) theorizes as an indigenous theology of pluralism. That is, all Christian people are unified by a common faith in Jesus expressed by the congregation as united prayer and love for each other; but they live, eat, and sit separately.
20 See letter from E. Webb (1853), ABCFM collection, Houghton Library, Harvard University and *The Missionary Herald*, 1854, New York: ABCFM. The Lutheran missionary C. F. Schwartz mentored Vedanayagam Sastriar from the time he was a boy (Sherinian 1998, 76–78).
21 Mid-nineteenth century American Congregational missionaries (ABCFM) required the new converts to give up their caste by participating in "love feasts." This meant a readiness to eat "under proper circumstances with any Christians of any caste, and to treat them with respect, hospitality, and other acts of kindness" (Chandler 1912, 141. Also see S. Manickam 1993 and J. C. B. Webster 1992).
22 *Kīrtanai* along with *pāmālai* continue to form the core of the Tamil hymnal.
23 This development within the Christian subculture reflected the larger regional Dravidian Tamil Isai (music) movement. It was also one of the earliest examples of a large body of indigenized repertoire having been composed without the influence or oversight of missionaries.
24 Christian castes defined today as Dalit in Tamil Nadu include Paraiyars, Pallars, and Chakliyars. The fishing communities like the Paravars and Mukkuvars are also considered by some to be Dalit; most of the Christians among them are Catholic.
25 Appavoo's liturgy uses spelling that reflects spoken Tamil pronunciation.
26 Nostalgia for rural landscape and village culture is aimed towards middle-class urban Dalits who have fled the village, and all its negative associations, physically and psychologically.
27 J. T. Appavoo, Interview, Madurai, July 1, 1994.
28 Appavoo understands the Christian God as both mother and father, feminine and masculine. Here *pettavarē*, literally means "parent who bore me," signifying the maternal womb.
29 J. T. Appavoo, Interview, Madurai, July 1, 1994.
30 Here *ammaiyappa* (*amma*—mother, *appa*—father, as one word) is separated from the other words with a syncopated rhythmic accent and articulated with a pulsating series of high melodic notes which then slide down into the beginning of the next line.
31 J. T. Appavoo, Lecture, Nagarcoil, September 20, 1994.
32 The word for sin in this passage is *ūttai*, which literally means foul-smelling (body) waste, (Kriya Dictionary 1992, 164). Thus the metaphor of cleaning the sin is appropriate here.
33 J. T. Appavoo, Interview, Madurai, August 18, 1994.
34 J. T. Appavoo, Interview, Madurai, August 18, 1994.
35 Paper given by Radhika Iyer, Conference on Religion in South India, Toronto, June 14, 1997.
36 J. T. Appavoo, Interview, Madurai, August 18, 1994.
37 D. Carr, Interview, Madurai.

References

Appavoo, James Theophilus. 1986. *Folk Lore for Change*. Madurai: Tamil Nadu Theological Seminary.

———. 1992. "*Oru Olai*: The Vision and Its Potential for Dalit Liberation." Unpublished paper.

———. 1993. "Communication for Dalit Liberation: A Search for an Appropriate Communication Model." Master of Theology thesis. University of Edinburgh.

———. 1994. "Dalit Religion." In *Indigenous People: Dalits. Dalit Issues in Today's Theological Debate*, ed. James Massey, 111–21. Delhi: ISPCK.

Borg, Marcus. 1994. *Meeting Jesus Again for the First Time: The Historical Jesus and the Heart of Contemporary Faith.* New York: Harper Collins.

Chandler, John S. 1912. *Seventy-Five Years in the Madura Mission: A History of the Mission in South India Under ABCFM.* Madurai: American Madura Mission.

Elder, Joseph Walter. 1954. "Caste in the Churches of South India in Madurai." Masters thesis proposal, Oberlin College.

Feld, Steven. 1984. "Sound Structure as Social Structure" *Ethnomusicology* 28, no. 3: 383–409.

Grafe, Hugald. 1990. *History of Christianity in India.* Vol. 4, part 2. *Tamilnadu in the Nineteenth and Twentieth Centuries.* Bangalore: Church History Association of India.

Hudson, D. Dennis. 2000. *Protestant Origins in India: Tamil Evangelical Christians, 1706–1835.* Grand Rapids, Mich.: William B. Erdsman Pub.

Ilaiah, Kancha. 1994. *Why I Am Not a Hindu: A Sudra Critique of Hindutva Philosophy, Culture and Political Economy.* Bombay: Samya.

Joshi, Barbara R., ed. 1986. *Untouchable!: Voices of the Dalit Liberation Movement.* London: Zed Books.

Kaplan, Steven, ed. 1995. *Indigenous Responses to Western Christianity.* New York: New York University Press.

Kriya Dictionary of Contemporary Tamil [Kriyāviṉ Tarkālat Tamiḷ Akarāti]. 1992. ed. S. Ramakrishnan. Madras: Government of India, Department of Education.

Manickam, S. 1993. *Slavery in the Tamil Country.* 2nd edition. Madras: Christian Literature Society.

Massey, James. 1994. *Indigenous People: Dalits. Dalit Issues in Today's Theological Debate.* Delhi: ISPCK.

Nirmal, Arvind. P., ed. n.d. *Towards a Common Dalit Ideology.* Madras: Gurukul Lutheran Theological College.

Ryerson, Charles. 1988. *Regionalism and Religion: The Tamil Renaissance and Popular Hinduism.* Madras: Christian Literature Society.

Sambamurthy, P. 1984 [1952]. *A Dictionary of South Indian Music and Musicians.* 3 vols. Reprint. Madras: Indian Music Publishing House.

Sherinian, Zoe. 1998. "The Indigenization of Tamil Christian Music: Folk Music as a Liberative Transmission System." Ph.D. Dissertation. Wesleyan University.

Thangaraj, Thomas. 1990. "Toward a Singable Theology." In *Venturing Into Life: The Story of the Tamil Nadu Theological Seminary*, ed. Samuel Amirtham and C. R. W. David, 109–18. Madurai: Tamil Nadu Theological Seminary.

Thekkedath, Joseph. 1982. *History of Christianity in India.* Vol. 2. *From the Middle of the Sixteenth to the End of the Seventeenth Century (1542–1700).* Bangalore: The Church History Association of India.

Webb, Edward. 1853. Letter #440 from the Archives Collection of The American Board of Commissioners for Foreign Missions. Houghton Library, Harvard University, Cambridge, Mass.

———. 1854. Letter published in the *The Missionary Hearld.* New York: The American Board of Commissioners for Foreign Missions.

———. 1875. *Christian Lyrics for Public and Social Worship.* (5th Ed.) Revised by G. T. Washburn. Nagarcoil: Madras Tract and Book Society.

Webster, John C. B. 1992. *A History of the Dalit Christians in India.* San Francisco: Mellen Research University Press.

Wilson, Kottapalli. 1982. *The Twice Alienated Culture of Dalit Christians.* Hyderabad: Booklinks.

95

SYNCRETIC OBJECTS

Material culture of syncretism among the Paiwan Catholics, Taiwan

Chang-Kwo Tan

Source: *Journal of Material Culture*, 7(2) (2002), 167–87.

It has often been said that Christianity is a world religion with many local faces, such as African Christianity and Pacific Christianity. The interaction of Christianity and local traditions is of particular concern for anthropologists and historians of religion. In the domain of material culture, this interaction has been considered in two different yet related directions: first, how local people appropriate Christian objects of foreign origin in their specific, culturally informed ways; and second, how local converts express their Christian faith through local symbolism and material culture. The first direction can be exemplified by Toren's (1988) study of how Fijian Christians appropriate the reproduction of 'The Last Supper' tapestries. These objects were imported from Lebanon where Fijians had served in the UN peacekeeping force. Toren points out that the Fijian notion of tradition is not a fixed, immutable past, but processual and mutable. The images of communal feast and spatial relations between Jesus and his 12 disciples in 'the Last Supper' are perceived by Fijians as an instantiation of Fijian tradition of chiefship and *kava* rituals. In this way, Fijians are able to see 'The Last Supper' as a revelation of the inherent Christianity of the Fijian people's past, and use it to construct 'The Fijian way'.

The second direction is my main interest here, which is triggered by a piece of wood carving in the Tjaubar Catholic Church of the Paiwan. This piece is called by local Catholics 'The Paiwan Cross'.

The image of Christ on this cross is not a familiar one (a dying white man with two outstretched hands and a slim and twisted body); instead, the body of Christ on this cross looks robust and straight like a trunk, and the two raised hands look like a victorious gesture. This imagery resembles the imagery of a chiefly ancestor on the central post of a traditional ritual house.

We can notice that this object is characterized by a mixture of indigenous religious and Christian symbolism. As we will see, this mixture is not an arbitrary juxtaposition, but a careful design by a local Catholic transmitting important messages, either religious, or cultural, or both. These objects can be usefully understood as syncretic.

In its broadest sense, 'syncretism' can be defined as 'the combination of elements from two or more different religious traditions within a specified frame' (Stewart, 1999: 58; see also Stewart and Shaw, 1994: 10). Syncretism should be distinguished from *bricolage*. According to Stewart and Shaw, the former is 'the formation of new cultural forms from bits and pieces of cultural practice of diverse origins' (1994: 10), whereas the latter should be 'limited to the domain of religious and ritual phenomena' (1994: 10). Basically, my usage of 'syncretism' here follows their suggestion, and I am interested in the combination and interaction of elements of the Paiwan indigenous religion and Catholicism which are historically different. The former is perceived as 'ancient customs' passed down from their ancestors, while the latter was brought in by foreign missionaries no more than 50 years ago.

Furthermore, Stewart and Shaw redefine the central issue in the study of syncretism as the politics of religious synthesis. They rightly point out that all religions have composite origins and are continually reconstructed through an ongoing process of synthesis and erasure, so simply identifying a tradition as 'syncretic' does not add much to our knowledge. Instead of treating syncretism as a category we should 'focus upon *process* of religious synthesis and upon *discourse* of syncretism. This necessarily involves attending to the workings of power and agency' (Stewart and Shaw, 1994: 7, emphasis in original). Recently, Orta's (1999) study among the catechists of Aymara Indians in Bolivia takes up this issue and turns to focus on the field of body politics. Aymara catechists are often seen as cultural brokers between Catholic missionaries and Andean traditions and communities. In the discourse of missionaries, the bodies of Aymara catechists are characterized as inert indices of a hybrid history. By contrast, Aymara catechists understand their bodies as a dynamic rather than an inert core; more precisely, their bodies are vehicles of an unfolding process of engagement with a complex world. Through the positioned practices anchored on their bodies, Aymara catechists combine dual cultures as their coherent lived worlds.

The main argument Orta advances is that Aymara catechists are far from passive victims of hybrid cultures; rather, they are 'syncretic subjects', who place the locus of their agency on their bodies. His notion of 'syncretic subjects' is directly relevant to the Paiwan ethnography of catechists. Tjinuai is an influential Paiwan catechist in the Tjaubar Catholic Church, and also a researcher of Paiwan traditional rituals. Her double involvement in the church ministry and the study of tradition leads us to consider her as a 'syncretic subject'. What is special about Tjinuai, as I will show, is that she constructs her identity through designing devotional objects, such as 'The Paiwan

Cross', in which symbols of Christianity and indigenous religion are mixed and novel meanings are generated. In this way, the syncretic subjectivity of Tjinuai receives objective expression in this object. I suggest we can call such object a 'syncretic object'.

The mutual relationship of syncretic subjects and syncretic objects is the main concern in this article. I will argue that the becoming of syncretic subjects is bound up with the social and historical process of the production of syncretic objects. Moreover, I am interested in how syncretic subjects can exert their influence on the audience (believers or non-believers) via the artworks they design or make. To address this issue I will follow the lead of Gell (1998) in *Art and Agency* and discuss the social agency of syncretic objects through the example of the Paiwan Cross.

Tradition and Catholicism in Tjaubar

The Paiwan are one of nine ethnic groups of aborigines in Taiwan.[1] Today there are about 70,000 Paiwan inhabiting 80 villages in the southern end of Taiwan. The Tjaubar village, where I conducted fieldwork over the period of 1997–8, is located in the mountains near the Southeast coast. Tjaubar is one of a few Paiwan villages where traditional authorities are still highly respected in the public life. There are three chiefly houses which are concerned with keeping their status by preserving traditional religion. In a total population of 228 households and 1220 people, only a few Protestant households (about 30) are resistant to the authority of chiefs. The Tjaubar Catholic Church claims to have believers of 375 people and 81 households; almost one third the population of Tjaubar. Most Catholics are either tolerant of or followers of traditional religion.

Paiwan traditional religion is characterized by the belief in the existence of many kinds of spirits (*tsemas*), including natural deities, ancestral spirits, souls of the recent deceased, and ghosts. Amongst all these spirits, ancestors (*vuvu*) are the most important in the social life, and the Paiwan have developed a social-religious institution of ancestor worship.[2] Paiwan ancestor worship is bound up with the house.[3] Each house has its own ancestral altar (*umaqan*), while beyond a single house, several houses can be connected through siblingship, and all siblings born in the same house worship their common ancestors. If some siblings have been married out, they are obliged to return to their 'original house' (*tjumaq*) to join the worship hosted by 'the firstborn heir' (*vusam*). At the community level, the chiefly house is the center for the worship of the founding ancestors. In a village with several chiefly houses like Tjaubar, the center of worship is the ritual house belonging to the paramount chief (Tan, 2001).

We can take the Patjalinuk, the present paramount chiefly house in Tjaubar, as an example. The Patjalinuk owns a ritual house for the collective worship.[4]

We can see several sacred objects. Besides several pieces of pottery behind the girl, the central post is one of the most important. On the post, we can see two figures of relief carvings: a human and a two-headed snake. Both images are associated with ancestral origin. People who see the Patjalinuk as their original house come here to make offerings. The Patjalinuk chiefly house is thereby a 'centered worship community' (Errington, 1987: 406),[5] in which the living chief is the embodiment of ancestral origin, and sacred objects are the objectification of this origin. Moreover, the Patjalinuk always attempts to expand itself as the all encompassing center of ancestor worship in the village.

For early missionaries, this institution of chieftainship was perceived as an obstacle to their evangelical project. Catholic missionary activity in the Tjaubar village was launched by two Reverends from the Swiss Bethlehem Mission Society (SMB) in 1955. They collected money from Swiss Catholics to build the first church, dedicated in 1958, made of wood and concrete. Villagers were in need at that time, and relief goods drew them to the church. Otherwise villagers were afraid of going, because the church was built on a taboo site where a woman had died of a miscarriage. Some local politicians supported the work of the Catholic Church, because missionaries brought in medical services for the community. Education was also a crucial channel of evangelization.

The early image of the Catholic Church was bound up with relief goods, medical services, and educational opportunities. It became an index of 'progress', which constituted a challenge to traditional leaders. Missionaries were intolerant of indigenous magico-religious practices, and launched a campaign of abolishing indigenous sacrifices and 'idolatry'. In the 1960s, missionaries had several disputes with chiefs over the timing of millet reaping. Chiefs ordered, according to the custom, that villagers could reap only after harvest rites had been performed. Catholics were reluctant to obey because they worried about the damage from typhoons and field mice. This conflict could not be settled between two sides until the police intervened. Also, missionaries and local catechists confiscated wooden spoons and joint cups with carved images of snakes and human heads from churchgoers' houses and burnt them all on the river bank.

The Second Vatican Council (1962–5) had great impacts on transforming the attitude of foreign missionaries toward local customs from confrontation to acceptance.[6] Indigenization or inculturation became a dominant trend among the Catholic Church all over the world. In the case of Tjaubar, Reverend Hans Egli of SMB, serving since 1979, was the one who contributed most to indigenizing the liturgy. As a well-trained linguist, he learned Paiwan quickly and used it in the mass alongside Japanese for the benefit of the older congregation. He was absorbed in studying local language and folklore, and translated a part of the New Testament into Paiwan. He paid respect to local customs and shamans' work, and was sympathetic to the villagers' view that the mass and indigenous animal sacrifices were not only compatible but also complementary. His practices and attitudes strongly influenced Tjinuai, who was a catechist and his research assistant at that time. She was encouraged to study her mother tongue and to understand traditional rituals and art. She was also inspired to bridge the boundary between Catholicism and traditional religion by making friends with chiefs and shamans.

The existence of a viable and expansive chieftainship is a social condition which local Catholics have to live with and learn how to adapt. The material culture of chieftainship, such as the carving on the central posts, is a resource which Catholics appropriate in their making of syncretic objects. I now turn to look at the art of carving from both within the frame of Paiwan society and without.

Carving in two frames

In his study of Australian Aboriginal art, Morphy (1991) uses the concept of 'frame' to analyze the meaning of artworks in an intercultural context.[7] He analyzes the Yolngu art from the frame of the Yolngu world and that of the European-Australian world. Morphy also points out the same object can occur in many different frames within a culture. The major focus of this article is the interaction of two intracultural frames: the Paiwan traditional world, and the Paiwan Catholic world, in the field of defining the meaning of unconventional forms of carving such as the Paiwan Cross. However, before we move on to discuss this topic, I would like to sketch the interaction at intercultural level: the Paiwan world and Japanese-Taiwanese world. This knowledge is helpful for our understanding of why local Catholics wanted to acquire carvings to decorate their church, and how a local Catholic, Sapari, found his path to become a professional carver.

Carving is called *ventsik* in Paiwan. In it narrowest sense, *ventsik* refers to 'lines and strips'. It extends to refer to figures, drawings, designs, and any objects with these attributes, such as tattooing, embroidery, painting, and carving. Modern writing is also called *ventsik* by the Paiwan. The ensemble of *ventsik* constitutes what we call the Paiwan visual artwork. Before Japanese colonialism (1895), the ownership of *ventsik* was associated with aristocratic prestige (*veseng*). In the case of carving, only chiefs and their close relatives could possess carvings to decorate their houses, and only aristocrats could enjoy the leisure time to carry out carving. Chiefs controlled the production, circulation and consumption of carvings, and they could grant this prestige to those who wanted to climb up the social hierarchy by establishing alliances with chiefly houses.

Carving was a process of magical production bound up with ritual regulations and cosmological concerns. Most carvings were part of the fabric of the house. If we visited a pre-colonial chiefly house, we would firstly see a stone post with carved human-like figures and snakes in the front yard. On the outer walls there were figures of human heads, snakes, deers, and boars. On the eave-beam, similar figures reappeared alternately in a horizontal series. Finally, we would see a central post of two to three meters high, with a human-like figure surrounded by a pair of one-hundred-pace-snakes (*vurung*, to be discussed later).

Though Japanese colonial government defined aborigines as 'savages' due to their custom of headhunting, colonial scholars rather appreciated the Paiwan carvings as the representative of Taiwanese indigenous art and placed them alongside 'primitive art' of the Oceania (see Hsu, 1991). These scholars collected carvings and made systematic investigation. Later on some institutes for training aborigines to make indigenous art objects were established in lowland towns, and talented Paiwan were encouraged to participate. As a result, some new categories of carvings emerged, including three-dimensional human figures and realist figures, which were produced as souvenirs for the Japanese.

Near the end of colonialism (1945), the economic situation of chiefly houses began to decline because the Japanese government forbade them to collect tributes from commoners. Poverty forced some chiefly houses to sell their heirlooms of carvings for survival, and they gradually lost the control of production and consumption of carvings. At about the same time began the collection of 'ethnic art' by official institutions, personal collectors, and antique dealers. They established three categories of collection: pre-colonial antique carvings, carvings produced in colonial period, and carving produced by newly emergent carvers. The market of 'primitive art' formed around the 1970s, and the increasing demand led some Han Chinese to copy Paiwan carvings for sale.

For the Paiwan themselves, the high amount of sales of carvings to the outside world generated a great sense of loss among chiefs and aristocrats. This sense has stimulated a desire to buy new carvings to replace the old ones once they regained enough money. Besides, many commoners who have achieved economic and social success are acquiring 'traditional-style' carvings to display their wealth and elevate their status. They imitate old chiefly houses and use newly produced carvings to decorate their modern houses.

Moreover, under the recent national cultural policy which encourages the preservation of local traditions, Paiwan carving is recognized as 'cultural heritage'. An environment has been created for carvers to acquire funding more easily and have more chances of participating in exhibitions. In some Paiwan elementary schools, carving has been set as part of the curriculum for transmitting skill and knowledge to the next generation. Both the external and the internal demand have encouraged more part-time carvers to become full-time professionals.

The Tjaubar Catholic Church also contributes in part to the increase in demand for carvings, the revival of the tradition of carving, and the training of professional carvers. In the following section I will look at the history of the design and creation of new carvings whose form is the synthesis of traditional images and Christian images, and the mutually constituted process of the emergence and growth of syncretic subjects.

The making of syncretic objects and syncretic subjects

The Paiwan Cross, placed in the visual center of the church, can be seen by the devotees immediately after they enter the church and face the altar. The production of this cross was initiated by a church restoration project. In 1980, the church building had decayed considerably, and the roof was almost gone due to typhoon damage. Believers thought it was time to rebuild the church. A church restoration committee was soon established. The chairman of the committee had just returned from Saudi Arabia where he had worked in construction. He was moved by the religious zeal of the Muslims in the Middle East, and wanted a modernized as well as a localized home church. He persuaded other fellow workers to donate generously as he did.

The restoration provided a chance of indigenizing the church. The first thing considered for replacement was the cross. Reverend Egli asked Tjinuai which image was the most popular among the Paiwan. Tjinuai remembered she had seen the image on the central post of the Patjalinuk chiefly house, and drew some snakes and human heads from memory. Reverend Egli showed her a book written by a Taiwanese ethnologist (Chen, 1968), *Material Culture of the Formosan Aborigines*, with some pictures of Paiwan traditional carvings. In a meeting, in order to stimulate imagination, Reverend Egli asked Sapari to pose his body as Christ being crucified. It occurred to Tjinuai that Christ could be represented by the 'Paiwan totem' shown on the book, so she designed a cross according to the image of a chiefly ancestor in life size.

Figures 1 and 2 and are from two collections of carved images on the central posts of chiefly houses recorded in Chen's book (1968: 295), from which Tjinuai drew her inspirations. These images are 'said to represent their ancestors'; some suggested they are representations of deified chiefly ancestors (Chen, 1968: 297). Juxtaposing the Paiwan Cross with Figure 1, we can identify many similarities, including: the two raised hands, the standing pose, two little snakes on the breast, and two animals beneath the feet. A two-headed snake, in the shape of an arch in the cross, is similar to two snakes stretching from the toes in Figure 1. Also, the head decoration in the cross is similar to that in Figure 2, which Tjinuai liked. But she disliked the outstretched genital in Figure 1, so she deleted it. She added an anchor at the bottom to symbolize the firmness and stability the Church provides for believers.

Her design was approved by Reverend Egli and fellow Catholics. The problem was where to find suitable carvers. In Tjaubar the tradition of carving had declined and there was only one carver available. He belonged to the Radan, the chiefly house of the third rank in Tjaubar. But his style,

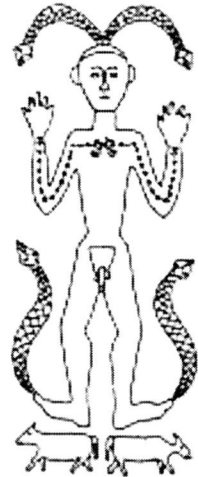 

Figure 1 The image on the central post (with snakes).
From Chen, 1968: 295

Figure 2 The image on the central post (with a feather crown).
From Chen, 1968: 295

like his mentality, was very conservative, and Tjinuai guessed he would not be interested in carving unconventional images. By contrast, the tradition of carving was flourishing in Kulalau, the home village of Tjinuai's parents, and carvers there were more experimental. So she went there to find two professional carvers. None of them were Christians, and one was even a traditional priest. When Tjinuai collected the cross, to her big surprise, she found a two-headed snake had replaced the anchor. Carvers explained that they were too accustomed to carving two-headed snakes so they mistook the anchor for yet another one. Tjinuai felt the snake was pretty, and she found some interesting meanings emerged from this mistake, so she did not ask them to correct it.

Interestingly, Tjinuai identifies this cross as a part of her body. She often tells the story that the two hands on the cross are in the real shape of her hands. When she designed it, she was not a good painter, and she felt drawing hands was difficult; she lay down on the ground to draw the shape of one hand holding a pencil in the other hand. Jesus's nailed hands are thus her own hands.

This cross is an externalized form of Tjinuai's thoughts and feelings. Many people heard about this special cross and come to see it out of curiosity. On these occasions, she often stands beside this cross and delivers a speech to explain the meaning of this cross and express her ideas about Christ. On 9 February 1998 a group of Protestant children from a neighboring village came to visit the Tjaubar Catholic Church as a summer camp activity. They were of Paiwan origin but knew very little about Paiwan traditions because their living environment was much influenced by dominant Han Chinese culture. A female pastor of the local Presbyterian church led them; she organized the trip in order for them to directly encounter their traditions. Tjinuai welcomed their visit and asked them all to sit in front of the cross, saying,

> This cross is an authentic Paiwan totem. It is an image of Jesus with localized traits. The carvers are non-Catholics, without any knowledge of Christianity. They carved it for three months. After they finished, they told me: 'It felt very painful when we carved the wound on this man's heart. We carved the wound and added red paint with tears. It is too painful for a man to have such a big wound on his heart, and being nailed on the wood. I never heard any Paiwan died in this horrible way. . . .'

Tjinuai wanted to emphasize that even non-Christians were moved by the suffering of this carved figure. The two carvers were Kulalau villagers with distinct traditional mentality. Tjinuai was at first surprised that even they had an emotional involvement in this image of Christ. She then realized that their reaction and words were an excellent testimony to this cross's capacity to move viewers' sensibilities. For her, the cross is first and foremost a devotional object which can evoke fellow Catholics' sympathy for Christ's passion, and enable them to develop a deeper relationship with Christ. By using images which are familiar to the Paiwan, she has made this cross appealing to non-Catholics.

This cross is also an objectification of her efforts to reconcile her past and present. She was born in Tjaubar in 1945. Her parents were former residents in Kulalau, a stronghold of traditionalism, and were baptized as Catholics in the 1960s after they migrated to Tjaubar. As an adolescent, Tjinuai left home and was taught by nuns, then studied in a girls' missionary school. In 1968, she returned to Tjaubar and began her service in the church. An American linguist, Raleigh Ferrell, went to Tjaubar to edit a Paiwan dictionary in 1970. Tjinuai was his assistant and interpreter, and through him became interested in studying mother tongue and folklore. Her association with Ferrell, unfortunately, led her to become a target of persecution by the secret police of the then authoritarian and communism-obsessed Nationalist Party. Under its reign the study of local language was suspected as being communist. In fear of becoming a burden to the Church, she left home and worked as a factory laborer in central Taiwan. She did not return until 1980 when her father was very ill. It was Reverend Hans Egli who encouraged her to restart her research. Since then she has continued her enthusiasm in studying the Paiwan culture and seeking her Paiwan origin.

It is against this background that we can recognize her design of the Paiwan Cross as a personal achievement. She tries to remain faithful to her Catholic identity and to be true to her Paiwan identity at the same time. In the past these two identities were thought to be contradictory, and many people still think in this way today. She persuades those people to change their thoughts; also, she fosters the awareness that tradition and Christianity are not necessarily exclusive; instead, they can co-exist in harmony and enrich each other.

Through incorporating artworks of carving into the church interior, the Tjaubar Catholic Church has contributed to the revival of the art of carving, and Sapari was an example of the product of Catholic revival of traditional art. For Sapari, carving was always his hobby; but he had to work in the city to raise his family. He joined in church reconstruction and was inspired by the Paiwan Cross made by the two Kulalau carvers. His potential was discovered by Reverend Egli, who encouraged him to express his belief through his work. According to custom, carving was an inherited or learned craft. He had no ancestral inheritance, and the only carver in Tjaubar was not inclined to teach others. But Sapari believes any Paiwan can carve. He often says, 'As long as I am born with the Paiwan blood, I must be endowed with the natural talent of carving.' Tjinuai also encouraged him to develop his talent, and in 1984, Tjinuai asked Sapari to carve a Eucharist Chest to hold bread and wine. Interestingly, this Chest, designed by Tjinuai, looked like an enlarged copy of shamans' boxes for holding offerings of pig bones. This Chest was the first piece Sapari made for the church. After this he began to find inspiration through listening to elders' stories of the past and oral traditions. The completion of 'the Paiwan Trinity' in 1989 proved him to be a carver with great potential. The design of this piece was a collective work among church officials, but Sapari insisted on endowing it with more Paiwan motifs, and was responsible for making it.

Today Sapari is a well-established indigenous artist. He converted part of his home into a studio and display room in 1998, and was busy working on commissions, taking part in exhibitions, as well as teaching. He was chosen by the local government to teach Paiwan school children how to carve. In his autobiography entitled 'The Cross and the Paiwan Carving Knife', Sapari describes himself as 'encountering the art of ancestors in the Catholic Church'. He recognizes his wish to become a serious carver stemmed from the experience of 'witnessing the Paiwan Cross'. Afterwards, his life unfolds as a chronicle of his works, events of exhibition and interviews. What Sapari represents in this autobiography is the progression of his fame, which grows as his artwork is distributed to more and more churches, exhibited in larger and larger events, and receives more and more recognition by media and officials. He likes to mention that his works are often requested by government officials who use his carvings as gifts to foreign friends when they go abroad.

What remains his favorite theme, above all, is Jesus's journey of passion (*Via Dolorosa*). In this kind of work, every human figure in the Bible story looks like a Paiwan, and is dressed like a Paiwan. No matter how famous he is, he remains a silent and humble Catholic. It is not surprising to find that he wants to identify with Jesus in his devotional life. Once in a Church memorial of Jesus's Passion, he played the character of Jesus. He imitated Christ by carrying a big cross, walking through the main road of the village, and pretending to be crucified in the church front yard. This experience of reenacting what happened in the *Via Dolorosa* helps him to inscribe this story on wooden boards with his carving knives.

Perhaps we can say Sapari is another example of a syncretic subject. Before making those syncretic objects, he was no more than an ordinary devout Catholic, but as I have shown, his life course has been changed by encountering these objects and later by actually creating these objects. His identity, more than Tjinuai, is built around the syncretic objects he made throughout his carving career. His story also suggests that, unlike Orta, we may go beyond the category of catechists and find other syncretic subjects among Catholics.

The house of syncretic objects

As I have mentioned, the chiefly house is a worship community built around sacred objects. In a similar way, the Tjaubar Catholic Church can be seen as a worship community built around syncretic objects. When I was in the church, I saw that every time believers entered the church, they knelt facing the Paiwan Cross. Christ, represented in the image of a paramount chief, is their divine king. During the Mass, they watched the priest standing behind the central altar protected by the carving of 'Twelve Apostles'. Each apostle, regarded as a chief, was represented as a human head surrounded by three snakes. This order of images resembles the carving on the beams of a traditional chiefly house. When a believer read the Bible, he or she placed the Bible on a wooden stand carved with four human figures in traditional style, called 'Four Evangelists'. When the Eucharist was started, the priest took the bread and wine from a chest engraved with human heads and curling snakes. When believers left the church, they looked up at 'the Paiwan Trinity' overlooking them.

We can see the Father, the Son, and the Holy Spirit are depicted as a standing person with one body and three connected faces sharing four eyes. Above the three faces is a big two-headed snake. In the middle of his breast is a sun, and beside his feet is the sky. Under the sky is a globe, upon which there is a pot with two curling snakes. The sun, the pot, and the snake are bound up with the Paiwan understanding of the creation of people. The design was based on a creation myth cited by Tjinuai,

> Once there was an egg in a pot. There were two one-hundred-pace snakes, one male and one female, which surrounded the pot and protected the egg. The pot was placed inside the house. The sun

penetrated the window and shed its light on the egg, which grew day by day. Eventually the egg was broken and a baby, the first person, came out.

The sun, the pot, and the snake are three Paiwan symbols of creation, called 'The Paiwan Trinity' by local Catholics. The central message of this carving, as Tjinuai explained, is to express a belief that the creation of the Paiwan is a part of God's project of creating the world and all other peoples. God thinks all his creation is good, so the Paiwan are blessed by the Trinity.

Reverend Egli often praised in Paiwan how these carvings beautified the church during Mass. Tjinuai constantly cited Bible texts to explain the meaning of the carvings, and used carvings as visual aids to illustrate Bible texts. The central message was that indigenous religion was not the worship of the Devil as early missionaries suggested; instead, indigenous religion deserved respect because it provided answers to life's fundamental problems. Indigenous rituals and symbols were not the reflection of a dark, backward mentality, but the expression of universal values such as beauty and holiness.

The introduction of one-hundred-pace snake imagery into church interior decoration provides stimulating thoughts about syncretism. This species of snake gets this popular name because it is so deadly that a bite will cause a person to die within one hundred paces. Its appearance is striking, with a triangular black and white design. Images of this snake are everywhere: on the cross, around the altar, on the Eucharist Chest, and on the Trinity. However, isn't the snake (serpent) the metamorphosis of the Devil who was responsible for the fall of humans? Indeed the once overwhelming presence of the snake imagery on the houses and personal belongings of chiefs and their bodies has led early missionaries to judge indigenous religion as 'the work of the Devil'. Contemporary Protestants have inherited this attitude, and still feel snakes are disgusting and see the representation of snakes as idolatry. By contrast, for traditionalists this snake is a sacred animal. It belongs to the category of spirits, but with positive rather than negative virtues, and is a human protector rather than enemy. They call it *vurung*, which means 'the eldest' among its kind, with the connotation of 'the greatest, the noblest'. In oral traditions, it is the ancestor of chiefs (Hsu, 1956). In pre-colonial times, chiefs identified strongly with *vurungs*,[8] and their bodies were tattooed with images of *vurung*. Tattooing was banned during colonialism, so today we can not find tattooed chiefs in Tjaubar. But the imagery of *vurung*, as mentioned, is still prominent in chiefly ritual houses.

Church leaders sympathized with the indigenous emotional and intellectual complex of *vurung*. It is based on a persistent mentality of old Catholics who have great respect for the one-hundred-pace snake and call it *ramaleng*, which is a term to address old and respected people. When Catholics call for God's mercy in a Mass, they call Him *Sa-ramaleng*, which literally means 'the old person'. Basically, *vurung* (or *ramaleng*) is treated as a sacred being with spiritual significance. In the carving of 'Twelve Apostles', snakes are interpreted by Reverend Egli and Tjinuai as protectors of the apostles. To strengthen this idea, they added a compatible view from a Bible text which is often quoted in Mass.[9] The snake is not always a symbol of evil; it is also a sign of healing power and salvation. This meaning is supported by the traditional meaning of the snake as a protector. Likewise, the traditional meaning is enriched by the biblical meaning.

It has to be pointed out that not every Catholic accepts the interpretations offered by Reverend Egli and Tjinuai, and not every Catholic is happy about these syncretic objects. The result of some informal interview shows that different responses can be discerned among believers in different age groups. The older Catholics (over 50) feel nostalgia because this imagery is familiar to them from their youth but then almost disappeared due to the confiscation and destruction of early missionaries and catechists. For young Catholics (under 25) it is a new and exciting visual experience. It is the middle-aged Catholics (25–40) who feel they are challenged. They were raised and educated in the Catholic way, and grew up during the period of intolerance of indigenous rites and symbols. But now these symbols are on the cross and the altar, the most sacred objects in the church. Some feel uneasy and eventually turn to Protestant churches nearby. From their viewpoint, pre-Christian life and its traditions are best forgotten because they represent their pagan past. Some, in contrast, begin to seriously reevaluate the past, and become interested in studying and learning traditional crafts and rituals. Some are absorbed in searching for traces of 'authentic' cultural origin, either in oral tradition or in material culture. The making of syncretic objects and the subsequent implementation of interpretation is thus simultaneously a process of selecting and shaping members in the church. Some support and stay, while some disapprove and leave.

We can conclude that the Tjaubar Catholic Church is a house of syncretic objects. It is a space where Catholicism and traditional religion are not treated as mutually exclusive and a dialogue between them is encouraged. In the historical process of the construction of the church, the ideas of syncretism are objectified and become concrete in syncretic objects.

Conclusion: from participation to reconciliation

I have taken valuable inspirations form Orta's study of 'syncretic subjects', yet moved beyond his concern and argued that syncretic subjects are constituted through the construction of syncretic objects. Through the making of religious objects combining Christian ideas and traditional symbols, the Paiwan Catholics develop and construct themselves as syncretic subjects. This study thus supports the theory of objectification which reminds us that we cannot take the existence of subjects for granted and that we should study the process of their becoming (Miller, 1987).

In the following I reflect upon the issue of how syncretic objects mediate the agency of designers or makers in a specific social milieu. Among all syncretic objects, the Paiwan Cross is primary, around which other objects are situated and given their meanings. Because of this I will use it as an example for the following discussion. Gell proposes the primordial artistic agency of 'captivation' (1998: 69); to trap spectators through technical excellence and let them feel inferior and defeated.[10] In a well-known interpretation of Trobriand canoe prow-boards, he argues that for their owners they serve as psychological weapons to demoralize exchange partners through the display of technical superiority. Unlike people in the western art world, Trobrianders see that artistic agency stems from the possession of magical resources rather than genius (Gell, 1998: 72).

Can we employ the notion of 'captivation' to explain the artistic agency invested in the Cross in the setting of the church? We should bear in mind that to represent 'the person of Christ' to spectators is the main concern of the designer, Tjinuai. Her intellectual or technical abilities are not intended to be the focus of a spectator's attention. Similarly, for spectators, the designer or carver is not significant. To identify who is on the cross is the main interest. This is a situation in which 'the activities of the artist are subordinate to the prototype' (Gell, 1998: 52). The prototype is Jesus Christ, who inspires the artist to produce the image, and is hence the ultimate agent causing the appearance of the cross rather than the artist. In Gell's terminology and framework, this relationship can be represented as follows (A: Agent; P: Patient):

[[[Prototype-A] → Artist-A] → Index-A] → Recipient-P
Jesus Christ   designer, carver   the cross   viewers

If technical ability is not an appropriate category for the attribution of the agency of the designer or carvers, how can we describe their agency and the efficacy of the cross? I propose the notion of 'participation' is a proper one. As I have suggested, the effect of the cross is primarily an emotional one, that is, to get viewers involved in the act of Christ's crucifixion, and to evoke sympathetic feelings for him. The artistic agency of the designer can be described as the capacity to draw viewers close to Christ and introduce them to participate in his emotional world. The final purpose can be described as being to motivate viewers to develop a fellowship with Christ. Two carvers, without knowing this intention, have become the first witnesses of the cross's efficacy in inviting participation.

For the designer, the effect of emotional participation is a crucial step to reach another dimension of participation, which can be called 'cultural participation'. The cross is a work of cultural synthesis which invites Christians to participate in non-Christian or traditional cultural worlds. For non-Christians, it is equally an invitation to participate in Christian cultural activities. And the aim of mutual participation is oriented toward the reconciliation between Catholics and traditionalists so that they can live together in peace.

Some traditional authorities do participate in Catholic activities, but with motivations which Catholics cannot control or predict. The chief of the Radan chiefly house mentioned earlier is a case in point. She had attended Mass for some time, under the influence of her shaman friend. In their eyes, the church was almost equivalent to a Paiwan chiefly ritual house, because they could see a central post with the image of a paramount chief, an altar protected by snakes and priests, and a chest like a shaman's box. Jesus for them was a foreigner with tremendous healing power. In this sense he is their predecessor and hero, a great shaman. What they are after is mainly to gain his power by copying his words and deeds.[11] Therefore, their reason for going to the church is less to participate in Christ's emotional world, but more to acquire his power.

This case also brings out the issue of power in religious synthesis. By incorporating elements of traditional religion into Catholicism, or by mixing elements of both religions, the Tjaubar Catholic Church has established itself as a religious community bearing the potential to encompass houses of both traditionalists and Catholics. For the paramount chiefly house, the Patjalinuk, the expansive potential of the Catholic Church constitutes a threat to their claim as a totalizing center of ancestor worship. This threat becomes more clear and present after the Radan chief, the peer rival of the Patjalinuk chief, joins the church and makes friends with church officials. This is one of the reasons why the Patjalinuk have been inclined to reject the invitation from the church officials to attend church activities.

As for Catholics, they recognize that their church has to live side-by-side with masters and followers of ancestral religion. Acknowledging this reality, the church is rather confident that ancestral religion is not a threatening force to Catholicism. So the church treats her relationship with chiefly houses and shamans as cooperative rather than competitive, and plays an active part in the revitalization of ancestral religion. Catholics are much encouraged to participate in rituals hosted by chiefly houses. For instance, they supported the Five-year-ceremony (*Maleveq*). This is the greatest traditional ritual which aims to glorify ancestors and chiefly power by impaling rattan balls with long bamboo poles (Tan, 2001).

In the early morning of the first rite of ball-impaling of the Five-year-ceremony, all of the bamboo poles were lined up beside the ball-impaling field to be consecrated by shamans. But nine of those belonging to Catholics were missing. They had been carried to the Catholic Church. After sprinkling the consecrated water on all bamboo poles, Catholics stood in front of the Paiwan Cross, saying rosary and prayers. Through consecrating the bamboo poles in their own way, Catholics maintained their identity when they participated in such a traditional ceremony. Chiefs allowed Catholics to have some autonomy if Catholics acknowledged their authorities. From Catholics' point of view, this does not constitute a dilemma. As long as they had carried out the devotional act to their heavenly King first, they had the right to live in harmony with their earthly king.

Acknowledgements

The fieldwork research was sponsored by the scholarship of Ministry of Education, Taiwan, and Institute of Ethnology, Academia Sinica. This article has been presented in a discussion group organized by Professor Daniel Miller. To all participants, including Danny, Kaori O'Conner, Mark Mullen, Alison Clarke, Inge Daniels, Jean-Sebastien Marcoux, Heather Horst, and Elia Petridou, I would like to say thanks for their helpful criticisms and comments.

Notes

1. These aborigines are different to the majority of Han Chinese people in Taiwan (of which there are about 22 million) in language and physical traits. Scholars now agree that their ancestors were earlier inhabitants in Taiwan than Han Chinese, whose mass migration to Taiwan took place in the 17th century. Based on archaeological and linguistic reconstruction, some scholars suggest that the ancestors of these aborigines were Proto-Austronesian speaking between 5–6000 years ago (see Jolly and Mosko, 1994: 4). In recent history, Taiwanese aborigines had been colonized by the Japanese government (from 1895–1945). Japanese colonialism provided a model for the Chinese Nationalist government in terms of aboriginal policies, which took over Taiwan after the Second World War.
2. For the Paiwan, gender is not an important factor in deciding who can become an ancestor, so ancestors can be either male or female. This point makes Paiwan ancestor worship different from Chinese ancestor worship. Freedman (1958) points out that Chinese ancestor worship is bound up with the structure of patrilineal lineage. The ancestral tablets are those of 'the deceased father, grandfather, and great-grandfather' (Freedman, 1958: 81–91).
3. Paiwan society is best described as a 'house-based society' (Lévi-Strauss, 1987; Carsten and Hugh-Jones, 1995). In Paiwan kinship, there is no organization like clan, lineage, or family. The house (*umaq*), including the building, the inhabitants and the name, is the basic and enduring social unit (Chiang, 1993).
4. This ritual house was once inhabited by the chief family. After it became too old, the chief converted it into a ritual house dedicated to storing heirlooms and worshipping ancestors.
5. Paiwan ancestor worship bears strong resemblance to other house societies in insular Southeast Asia. Errington (1987) suggests that groupings of this area often trace themselves to an ancestral point of origin, and the house serves as a material and symbolic construction which encompasses members with the same ancestral origin.
6. According to Luzbetak, Vatican II aimed to get rid of Europeanized Christianity by assuming 'the theological stand that the Church is in the most literal sense of the word a *world* Church, in nature *supra*cultural. In its very essence the Church is as Asian and African as European; it must be at home with every way of life

and every mentality' (Luzbetak, 1988: 112, italic in original). It follows that local churches have the right 'to self-determination in harmony with their own cultures and traditions' (p. 112).

7 Morphy defines frame as 'the encompassing set of cultural practices and understandings that defines the meaning of an object in a particular context' (1991: 21).

8 Hu (1999: 12) notes that Paiwan in Kulalau regard the *vurung* as the counterpart of the chief in the world of spirits. So traditionalists call the chief '*vurung*'.

9 According to the Old Testament, Moses has made a bronze figure of a snake and set it up on a pole, and rebellious Israelites bitten by snakes in the desert were cured by looking up at this bronze snake (Numbers, 21: 4–9).

10 In the western art world, Gell gives us an example of how he is captivated by Vermeer's artistic agency mediated by his paintings. As an amateur painter, Gell himself has some experience of the art-making process. He therefore is able to imagine a part of the process in which Vermeer produced his paintings. This is a world of artistic skills Gell can approach and know. There is a part of the process, however, that is impossible for Gell to access, and becomes an unknown world for him. In viewing Vermeer's painting such as *The Lacemaker*, Gell is trapped between these two worlds, and feels defeated by his artistic skill.

11 This reminds us of Cannell's (1995) study of local practices of Catholicism in Bicol, Philippines. Shamans there view the dead Christ as a shamanic exemplar, and manage relationships with spirits through 'the imitation of Christ'.

References

Cannell, F. (1995) 'The Imitation of Christ in Bicol, Philippines', *Journal of Royal Anthropological Institute* (NS)1: 377–94.

Carsten, J. and Hugh-Jones, S., eds (1995) *About the House: Levi-Strauss and Beyond.* Cambridge: Cambridge University Press.

Chen, Chi-Lu (1968) *Material Culture of the Formosan Aborigines.* Taipei: Southern Materials Center, Inc.

Chiang, Bien (1993) *House and Social Hierarchy of the Paiwan.* University of Pennsylvania (unpublished PhD thesis).

Errington, S. (1987) 'Incestuous Twins and the House Societies of Southeast Asia', *Cultural Anthropology* 2: 403–44.

Freedman, M. (1958) *Lineage Organization in Southeastern China.* London: The Athlone Press.

Gell, A. (1995) 'Vogel's Net: Traps as Artworks and Artworks as Traps', *Journal of Material Culture* 1(1): 15–38.

Gell, A. (1998) *Art and Agency: An Anthropological Theory.* Oxford: Oxford University Press.

Hu, Tai-Li (1999) 'One-hundred-pace Snake and Eagle: Cultural Identity and Representation of the Paiwan.' Paper presented at the International Conference on the Formosan Indigenous Peoples. Taipei: The Institute of Ethnology, Academia Sinica.

Hsu, Gong-Ming (1991) 'The Art and Society of the Paiwan from the Perspective of Collection'. Paper presented at the Art and Anthropology Conference, June 1991, Institute of Ethnology, Academia Sinica, Taipei.

Hsu, Shih-Tsen (1956) 'The Creation Myth of Taiwanese Aborigines', *Bulletin of the Institute of Ethnology* 2: 171–5. Taipei: Academia Sinica.

Jolly, M. and Mosko, M. (1994) 'Prologue' to 'Transformations of Hierarchy: Structure, History and Horizon in the Austronesian World', *History and Anthropology* 7(1–4): 1–18.

Lévi-Strauss, C. (1987) *Anthropology and Myth*. Oxford: Blackwell.

Luzbetak, L. (1988) *The Church and Cultures: New Perspective in Missiological Anthropology*. New York: Orbis.

Miller, D. (1987) *Material Culture and Mass Consumption*. Oxford: Blackwell.

Morphy, H. (1991) *Ancestral Connections: Art and an Aboriginal System of Knowledge*. Chicago: The University of Chicago Press.

Orta, A. (1999) 'Syncretic Subjects and Body Politics: Doubleness, Personhood, and Aymara Catechists', *American Ethnologists* 26(4): 864–89.

Stewart, C. (1999) 'Syncretism and its Synonyms: Reflection on Cultural Mixture', *Diacritics* 29: 40–62.

Stewart, C. and Shaw, R., eds (1994) *Syncretism/Anti-syncretism: The Politics of Religious Synthesis*. London: Routledge.

Tan, Chang-Kwo (2001) *Mediated Devotion: Tradition and Christianity among the Paiwan of Taiwan*. University of London (unpublished PhD Thesis).

Toren, C. (1988) 'Making the Present, Revealing the Past: The Mutability and Continuity of Tradition as Process', Man (NS) 23: 696–717.

96

INTRODUCTION TO *CHRISTIANITY IN INDIAN DANCE FORMS*

Francis Peter Barboza

Source: Francis Peter Barboza, *Christianity in Indian Dance Forms*, Delhi: Sri Satguru, 1991, pp. 1–7, 214–16.

> "And I came down from Heaven
> and I danced on the earth
> At Bethlehem I had my birth . . .
> . . . .
> They cut me down
> and I leap up high . . .
> I am the Lord of the Dance said he"

The sentiments of this popular Christian religious folk song give 'Dance' and 'Dancing' a special prominence in the life of Jesus. Of such importance in fact that dance figures both in his genesis and birth, as well as his crucifixion and death.

> Is this then a total contradiction of Christianity and the Spirit of the Gospel?

On the contrary, No.

It is an affirmation . . . a celebration of the joyousness and life that is at the core of the Christian religion. Here, in this song, the activity of 'Dance' refers figuratively to the growing moving embryo within Mary's womb . . . and finally to the same Jesus' rising in glorious triumph over despair and death on Easter Sunday.

The present study dwells upon dance in the Christian Scriptures and tradition in general and, Christianity and Indian Dance-Forms with special reference to the Southern Styles in particular. On the surface, one doesn't find a great deal of dance in practice among the Indian Christians, but a closer, critical and historical survey reveals that dance has been part and parcel of the Religious and social life of various groups of Christians in different regions of India. In fact, there are a few dance-forms exclusively practised by the Christians in India, which have a long-standing history of many centuries. Further, it is to be noted that Christian themes have also been introduced in many other Indian dance-forms. Efforts have been made here, first to delve deep into the various aspects of the dance-forms of Christians in different regions and communities. Then follows a critical evaluation of the attempts made at introducing Christian Themes in other dance-forms of India. This total presentation has been undertaken with a view to obtain and compile all possible information hitherto unavailable anywhere.

In order to properly evaluate, understand and interpret the origin and evolution of these above mentioned art-forms through time and space, I had to work out my research design, documentation method and methodologies required for the study.

The Methodology:

1. Personal visits to the different regions of India with special reference to the South to witness and study various dance-forms being actually performed by the various Christian communities and also to get acquainted with their life styles.
2. Interviews with scholars, teachers, performers and patrons of different dance-forms.
3. Analysis of the basic structure and form, and their variations.
4. Study of the depiction of dances in Christian sculpture and paintings with special reference to the South.
5. Data collection through the Research Questionnaire, especially in relation to contemporary attempts.
6. A survey of the Church history in India.
7. A critical compilation of all scriptural and historical references and details available in various Christian Sacred Books and Indian Christian tradition on dance.
8. Collection of data and information from the manuscripts written for the dance-forms by ancient authors on Christian Themes in India.
9. Study of the Indian Church documents and synods that affected the growth and development of performing art forms in the Indian Church.
10. Documentation through tape-recording, photography and choreographic line-drawings.
11. Analysis of all available data to arrive at the relevant conclusions.

According to the Christian Scriptures, dance has a very prominent and important function mainly in the religious and social life of the people. Both in the OLD and NEW TESTAMENT dance is referred to as an integral part of worship and it helped enliven the community spirit of the believers. The early Christians also used dance in their religious and social life. There are references to this effect in the writings of early Fathers and in Church history. The historical survey shows the development, growth and decline, use and misuse of dance down the centuries. The gnostic writers of the 2nd century consider Jesus Christ as the leader who leads his followers in the dance. In the thesis, a brief historical note up to the present time on the religious function and role of dance in the Church is discussed. Besides, the origin, growth and development and the present state of Sacred dance in the American, the European, the African and the Australian church is also presented, in brief.

Christianity and Indian dance-forms are presented under two categories and three phases:

- *Categories*:
    (a) Dance-forms exclusively practised by the Christians, that comprised mainly Christian Themes but at times included social and historical episodes.
    (b) The second category, where Christian Themes are depicted in the other dance-forms of India.
- *The Three Phases*:
    (a) Ancient or Traditional (52 A.D. to 1599)
    (b) Medieval to the Contemporary (1599–1947)
    (c) Post-Independece period (1947-onwards).

Introduction

Dance-forms in the first category are mostly found in the first two phases. Whereas the second category is found mostly in the third phase.

(a) Ancient and traditional

It is a commonly accepted fact that Christianity came to India in 52 A.D. through St. Thomas who landed at Maliankara, near Cranganore, Kerala. All those who embraced Christianity through him as well as their descendants are called 'Mar Thoma Syrian Christians'. In the year 345 A.D. a certain merchant Thomas of Cana (Kanai Thommen) migrated with 400 Syrian Christian families to Malabar and Cranganore. These are called Knanaya Syrian Christians. The worship pattern, art-forms, Church architecture etc. of the aforesaid groups of Christians were similar to those of the Hindu Bretheren of that time. Their art-forms were least affected by the foreign influence and were very much Indian in Form and Spirit. Dance-forms such as Mārgamkaḷi, Vaṭṭakaḷi and Pariśumuṭṭukaḷi practised by these Christians survive to the present day.

(b) Medieval onwards (II Phase)

On May 14, 1498 Vasco da Gama landed at Kappad near Calicut on the Malabar Coast. With the coming of the Portuguese a new group of believers called 'Latin Christians' came into existence. The Portuguese kept a strict control over the religious and social life of all Christians in Kerala. Their political dominance gave them a superior advantage over other groups of Christians already existing in Kerala. They made various attempts to Westernize the Church in India. The Westernization of the Church was intensified by the Synod of Diamper in 1599 which practically suppressed and forbade the existing art-forms of the Christians as superstitious and scandalous. However, the people couldn't suppress their artistic instinct to express religious experience in different art-forms. As a result, a number of new dance-forms came into existence since medieval times. Of course, they were greatly influenced by the western theatre especially in the aspect of theme, costume and presentation, though less affected in the technique. Caviṭṭunāṭakam and other art-forms of the Latin Christians in Kerala, and Mēl, Mando, Dēkhni etc. in Goa, are a few examples to be mentioned here.

(c) Post-Independence period

In the Post-Independence period many attempts have been made to depict Christian themes in the other dance-forms of India, i.e. Kathakali, Yakshgāna and other art-forms. Many institutions and individuals have tried to depict Christian themes borrowing and making use of one or more dance-styles for this purpose. Data has been collected on these attempts and a a critical evaluation has been presented. In this context, I have adopted a scientific approach in depicting Christian themes in Bharata Natyam. New Devahastas and postures for the Bible personalities have been invented on the basis of Christian Theology and study made on the different dance-treatises.

The major portion of the Thesis comprises the study and description of the dance-forms of the Indian Christians in different regions with special reference to the South as they are performed today with a historical background. Most of these dance-forms are found in Kerala and Goa. It is in Kerala that ancient art-forms like Mārgamkaḷi, Parisumuttukali and Vattakali, all practised by the Syrian Christians belonging to the Knanaya group are found. Caviṭṭunāṭakam and Pariśumuṭṭukali are prevalent among the Latin Christians in the Coastal area of Cochin, Alleppey etc. The Jacobite Syrian Christians also practise Parisumuttukali as their art-form: All the three sects have similarities and differences in their dance-form-Parisumuttukali.

In the district of Palghat the Tamil-speaking Christians have a theatre tradition of their own which originated in the 19th century. Kūthu (i.e. Mūnrurājakūthu) Nātakam (Allēsu Nātakam, Kunkunammal Nātakam etc.) and Kummiāttam are still in practice among these people. In Tamil Nadu, Pasca or passion play, at times called Siluvaimaranam, is in the style of Kūthu in some places and Nātakams at other places. In Goa, Mussal khel, Gauda Dhalo, Dekhni, Christian version of Jagar, Mando, Kumbi, Khēl, Mēl and Carnival are still practised by the different community of Christians. All these dance-forms have a tremendous tilt towards the social and entertainment aspect rather than purely religious. However, most of them are performed as per the religious calendar and feasts. Inspite of pressure tactics of the Portuguese the great influence they exerted and their way of life, these dance-forms have survived. Some of them may not retain the original nature and form yet they continue to be part of the fabric of life. In Andhra, efforts have been made to have Burrahkathas on Christian themes. However, Gumtanas of the Mangalore Christians is almost a story of the past. In the North, in many of the Ādivasi and Tribal dances, Christian themes have been introduced keeping the same format of their original dances. Dondo Nato of the Ganjam district in Orissa is the Christian version of the traditional Hindu Dondo Nato.

My knowledge and practice of classical dance helped me tremendously in comprehending and understanding the basis of physical movements, the rhythm and choreographic patterns of the above dance forms of the Christians. Though with limited resources, the attempt has been made to cover the maximum possible regions especially in the South among the different Christian communities to study dance in the religious and social context. The scope of the research is much wider and one hopes to continue further study. The dance-forms of the Christians can he studied in comparison to different regions and to other Indian dance-forms of the same area.

The urge for expression and communication is innate in every human being. All of us want to express our spiritual experience, our ideas, feelings and emotions to others, to ourselves and to God. Dance may be considered a mental projection of inner thoughts and feelings into movements, rhythm being the mould through which the creative life flows, giving it a meaningful form. To attain this as a meaningful art form the fusion of inner and outer form should take place. The unseen, inner form or dance is the organization of the mental attributes into content; the outer is the observed dance form, the movement which is the result of the organization and execution of the motor elements. The aesthetic quality or the value of the art form will depend on how perfectly the inner form (unseen dance) and the outer form (visual dance) is fused.

Art is ever the same, the efforts of man to interpret and represent life. Only the forms change. As art age or an individual accumulates more experience, new horizons of outlook and meanings are gained by the mind. The ideas, mode of life, principles, ideologies and religious experiences release new intellectual forces with the accompanying emotions. Hence, new forms have to be discovered and developed to express adequately the newly sensed emotions and experience.

Thus, to give expression to my experience of Christ and his message, I had to find new and adequate external forms (visual dance) to give life to the internal form (unseen dance). So, in Bharata Nātyam I have introduced new forms to give expression to the Christian experience. In other words it is an attempt to understand and comprehend Christian experience and express it in and through Bharata Nātyam.

Christian themes in Bharata Nātyam: an experiment

It was in the year 1979, after almost ten years of training in Bharata Nātyam under various gurus at Mangalore, Trichy and Baroda that I conceived the idea of introducing Christian themes into my dance recitals on an experimental basis. On 30th Dec. 1979 I accepted a performance in Indore where I requested the organisors whether I could dance on Christian themes? The organisors were only too happy with that novel idea.

I consulted Guru Kubernath Tanjorkar, one of my dance-teachers at the Dept. of Dance, M. S. University of Baroda, whether it was possible to compose music and do the choreography. He was very enthusiastic about this project and agreed to conduct the performance. Guruji and I selected a few good lyrics in Hindi and Sanskrit on Christian themes and proceeded with the composition of music and choreography. The music composition was easy for Guruji, but we had technical difficulties with regard to the choreography. The main problem that we encountered was concerning the Angika-Abhinaya which is unique in Indian Dance because of the gestures of the hands (hastas) and postures. In Abhinaya Darpanam, Nātya Shastra, Bharatārṇava and other treatises there are different categories of hastas namely, Nritta, Abhinaya. Dēva (Deities) etc. I could use all of them as they are, but *Dēva-hastās* I could not. Because the nature and significance of the Bible personalities are quite different and unique. Hence, when I wanted to depict Christ, the Christian Trinity (Father, Son and the Holy Spirit) etc. I was at a loss and had to invent new *Dēva-hastās* to suit the Divine personalities of the Christian Religion. However, with the knowledge of Christian theologoy and the studies made on our dance treatises, I introduced a number of *Dēva-hastās* to suit the personalities of the Bible in order to make the presentation genuinely Indian and Christian.

Key to the new hastās (hand gestures)

Gesture no. 1. *God the Father*

God the Father is the first person in the Christian Trinity. *The Right hand is held in Śikara (peak) to the right side of the body to denote 'father'*. God as Father is evident in the Old Testament. A large number of Hebrew personal names apply the title of father to deity such as Joab, Yahweh is "father". Abiel or Ehab, "El is father". Absalom, "the father i.e. the god is peace". These Israelite names do not differ in number of type from similar names in Mesopotamia and Canaan, Yahweh is called the father of Israel. The title of father of Israel is a theological metaphor which expresses the love of father for his son (Ho 11 : 1). This love exhibits itself in His paternal care of Israel (Ex 4 : 22 f; Dt. 1 : 31; 8 : s; Is 43 : 6 f.) in his compassion and forgiveness (s 103 : 13f; Je 3 : 19; 20; Ho 2 : 1). In the New Testament the same concept—God as the father of His people is continued. The concept of God as father includes the notion of paternal love and care (Mt 6 : 5–8, 26 ff; 7 : 11, 10 : 29–31; 18 : 14; Lk 11 : 13). Perhapas the supreme statement of God's paternal forgiveness appears in the parable of the prodigal son (Lk 15 : 11–32).

The Left hand is held in Tripatāka (a flag with three) to denote a crown signifying king, the greatest. In the Gospel according to St. John, the Father appears almost entirely as the Father of Jesus in contrast to the Father of the disciples. Jesus has a unique relationship with the Father, who communicates himself to men through His son Jesus and confers upon Him power and authority to execute His mission.

The Father is greater than Jesus (Jn 14 : 28) as the father is always superior to his son, and the sender to the one sent (Jn 16 : 23) Jesus is sent by the Father and lives through the Father (Jn 6 : 57 and thus is able to communicate life to those who believe in Him; and He can send His disciples with the fullness of power as He Himself was sent by the Father (Jn 20 : 21).

Gesture no. 2. *The Son of God*

The son of God is the second person of the Christian Trinity. *The right hand is held in Ardhapatāka (half flag) to denote the second person of the Trinity.*

The left hand opens in Alapadma in front of the abdomen and moves to the right side and held below the right Ardhapatāka to denote the birth of the son only by the Father. The son is the only begotten of the Father (Jn : 35; 5 : 20; 10 : 17). The creative aspect of the Son of God is clearly defined in the Nicene Creed. "We believe in one Lord, Jesus Christ, the only Son of God, eternally begotten of the Father, God from true God begotten not made, one in Being with the Father, Through him all things were made. For us men and for our salvation he came down from Heaven".

The gesture is shown in the right side because it is said that "Son is sitting at the right hand of the Father" (From the Apostles Creed).

Gesture no. 3. *The Holy Spirit*

He is the Third person of the Trinity. *The right hand is held in Hamsāsya used to denote Holy or Blessing.* Holy is the 'Numinous', the mysterious quality or the divine (1 S. 2 : 2 f). "The Son came down from heaven: by the power of the Holy Spirit". (Apostles Creed). *The left hand is held in Tripatāka—symbolising raising flame,* here used for the Spirit. Spirit in the Scriptures is conceived as dynamic entity by fall under this category. However, the Psalms, the Old Testement, the life and preaching of Christ give ample scope and subject matter for *Bhakti-Sringāra,* which in a strict and deeper sense is the characteristic of any temple art like Bharata Nātyam. Here, the mode of recitals is mostly dominated by *Bhakti-Śringāra,* of course, all the nine *rasas* have their role in the compositions. This trend is quite in line with the traditions and purpose of Indian classical dance as it is mentioned in our *śastras,* where dancing was considered to be the highest form of worship. *Visṇudharmoṭṭara Purānam* tells us that "to worship God by *Nriṭṭa* (dance) is to fulfill all desire, and to him who dances the paths of salvation are unfolded".

For the last 5 years I have been regularly performing Christian themes in my dance recitals both in and out of the country. I must however, admit that it took me quite sometime to get into the spirit of the Christian items though a Christian myself. Only repeated performances on Christian themes, long reflection and continual efforts have made it easy and spontaneous for me to dance Christian items. Yet I must affirm that I have not compromised with the *technique* and other requirements of the dance-form in order to incorporate the Christian themes into my dance recitals. These are a few technical difficulties that I faced in my new venture. However, there were countless social problems that I faced from the conservative church-corners.

Social problems

Besides the technical difficulties, initially, I had to face social problems—the opposition adverse criticism from many corners especially, the Indian Catholic press both Vernacular and English who wrote and passed judgements on my attempts without even attending my performance. 'The Laity', a magazine that stresses traditional Christian Values commented in its column; "It is nauseating to think a young Catholic priest could not find any other way to keep himself busy .... than in an art-form like Bharata Nātyam". They also denounced me as 'Half naked priest', 'Devadasi Priest' and accused me to have brought 'paganism' into the church. Oh, it was an agonizing and painful period! But by the dawn of 1984 most of the criticism died out and now the critics do not condemn me anymore about my dancing to Christ's story. I have performed in Tamilnadu, Kerala, Mangalore and many other places for a record number of times and before audiences where I was expected to be stoned according to some of my staunch critics!

Fortunately all my Gurus especially Guru Kubernath Tanjorekar, Prof. C. V. Chandrasekhar, Mrs. Anjali Mehr, Miss. Nargis K, and Shri. Pradeep Baruah encouraged me in every way possible, dance critics and the secular press have given me wide coverage, praised and commented on my innovations. A few of the views expressed in the press by the critics are mentioned below to substantiate this point:

"His attempts at depicting Christian themes through authentic Bharata Nātyam technique have been highly praised" (Indian Express Magazine Section, 6th June 1982).

"Francis has successfully experimented with intricate movements of Bharata Natyam to present the poignancy of Christ's story. Nātya Shastra experts, critics and exponents of the classical dance have acclaimed his efforts saying that the symbolism employed by Francis is original and shows his deep insight into Indian hasta language and as well as Christian Theology. One critic commented that it is a rare phenomenon for an artist to give form to lyrics of other religion through Bharata Nātyam". (Illustrated Weekly of India, Dec. 19–25, 1982.

"Francis Barboza is the latest in the chain of 'East meets West' of which Ravi Shanker and Uday Shanker have excelled . . . . . one could have never believed that a traditional Indian dance could merge so well with stories of the Bible until one saw it. . . . . The signs and symbols mostly came from classical Bharata Nātyam but some were definitely his own creation, and they went well into the performance". (Hitavada, Nagpur, Dec. 30th, 1982).

"Francis danced with dedication to potray the stories of Christ's life using the norms of the Nātyasastra. . . . . There was nothing artificial about this, because the sahitya (lyrics) was meaningful and Bharata Nātyam lent itself as naturally to this theme as it does to other themes of Bhakti". (Mid-Day, Bombay, April 28th, 1982).

". . . . . and in the realm of dance itself, Francis Barboza is evoking a great deal of interest with his experiments to move the classical art from the auditorium and the stage back to the Temples and Churches". (The Times of India, Ahmedabad, Dec. 10, 1980)

"Understanding Christian themes through Indian Classical music and dance has finally paid off in his quest of life. And one could easily see that in the spectacular performance of the Easter story last night". (The Afternoon, Bombay, April 8, 1985, page 2).

"In his unique recital, Gospel ideas were brilliantly portrayed with meaningful abhinaya by the dancer" (Newstimes, Hyderabad, 31 July, 1985 p. 4).

"His Bharata Nātyam set to Christian themes revealed the truth that the Indian Classical Dance is an excellent medium through which people communicate what lies beyond ordinary speech". (New Leader, 18th Aug, 1985, Bangalore).

"Barboza has tried to establish, and succeeded to a great extent, that cultural forms are independent and they can be used to express anything one wants to". (Indian Express Hyderabad, 4th Aug. 1, 1985).

"He gave Hindu audiences wonderful Christian themes while to the Christians he gave a taste of Bharata Nātyam. . . . . The entire exercise was indeed a lovely experience, polarising the two religions into a single fusion depicting that God is one". (The Hindu, Hyderabad, Aug. 2nd, 1985).

These above and many other reviews and articles on and about the innovations commented favourably and praising the attempts and experiments, have given me a lot more strength and encouragement in the new experience.

Dance in the churches

One of my childhood dreams had been to dance in Temples and Churches. I have danced in many temples and in Chidambaram at the Nātyanjali festival in 1985. Many times I have danced in Churches, sometimes alone and sometimes in the presence of a big congregation. On Good Fridays in different churches on the Passion, Death and Resurrection of Christ. During my dance-tour to Europe I danced in 1983 out of the 46 performances I gave 22 were conducted in Churches. When you dance in a place of worship it is a sublime and unique feeling. In the year 1984, on Sept. 7th I danced at the Shrine of Our Lady of Vellankanni before more than a lakh of pilgrims. That has been the record participation for a single recital of mine.

Today, in 1985 many Christians in India have accepted me as a dancer. But there are very few of them who will approve of my dancing in a Church. Some say, "it is not in our tradition," some others fear the reaction of other people. Some argue, "the temples themselves have discontinued dance in the places of worship, then why do you want to bring back the tradition which is proved wrong". Yet some others ask me, "how can it be a prayer?" and so on and on. . . . . [. . .]

Conclusion

[. . .] The study on the Christian Scriptures, both Old and New Testament has clearly shown that Dance has a very prominent and important function in Christianity. The frequent references to dance in the life of the people, explanation and description of the type of dance performed at religious and social occasions are some of the compelling proofs which further strengthen the prominent position that dance occupies in the Christian Scriptures. The existence and practice of dance throughout the Church history further stresses the functional value of dance in the religious and social life of the Christians. However, the history of the Religious dance in the Church is marked by misuse, the degradation, degeneration, and finally in its revival. This phenomenon is common to the Religious Dance of India too. If the early Church elevated, dance to the spiritual heights, the medieval and the subsequent period brought it down to the low level of misuse and disfavour. But in the late 19th and 20th centuries one finds the spirit of revivalism in the form of Sacred Dance groups in the Church especially, in America,

Europe, Australia and to some extent in India too after the first half of this century. In all these above development of dance, one finds continually the emphasis laid on the group dances. The individual or solo dances, if not totally absent are found minimum in practice.

It was very revealing to observe that in India too all the early dance forms of the Christians were performed in groups and no individual dance is to be found. Mārgamkaḷi and Pariśumuṭṭukaḷi of the Syrian Christians which are still practised, are all performed in groups. The same tendency can be observed in the middle ages and the contemporary period too. This is keeping in line with the Christian Scriptures and the early traditions of the Church where congregational or group dancing is encouraged and individual dances are not so common. This feature is also the reflection of the Christian theology where God is mainly encountered in group and people worship and praise him as group and in a congregation. The worship pattern, art-forms, Church architecture etc. of the early Syrian and Knanaya Syrian Christians in Kerala were similar to those of the native Hindus. The remnants of the old church architecture and a closer look at the form, style, mode of presentation, music etc. of the early art-forms like Mārgamkaḷi and Pariśumuṭṭukaḷi substantiate this contention.

It takes a long time for any performing art-form like dance to be expressed in visual forms like sculpture. The works of this kind do furnish us with the missing links in art-history and supply us with the needed information to the past. Unfortunately with regard to the Kerala Church most of these have been destroyed due to the suppressive attitude and decrees of the Synod of Diamper (1599). However, the dance sculptures of Mārgamkaḷi and pariśumuṭṭukaḷi on the basement of the granite Cross at Kaduthuruthy Valiapalli, erected in 1597 are some of the silent witnesses of the existence and practice of these art-forms among the early Christians for many centuries. The style and form of these sculptures is very Indian and not at all influenced by the west. While studying Mārgamkaḷi and Pariśumuṭṭukaḷi of the Syrian Christians as they are practised today, it can be seen that they are least affected by the western influence and the European Theatre. With the coming of the Portuguese to India, a Church that was very much indigenous was forced to be westernized. This process was intensified by the Synod of Diamper in 1599 which practically forbade the existing art-forms of the Christians as superstitious and scandalous. However, the people couldn't suppress their artistic instinct to express religious, spiritual and joyous experience in different art-forms. The outcome of this strange situation gave birth to a number of new art-forms mainly in Goa and Kerala. These art-forms are greatly influenced by the western theatre. The western influence is clearly seen and felt especially in the aspect of theme, costume and presentation, though less affected in the technique and the system of training. Caviṭṭunāṭakam is one such example where compared to the other elements of this dance form, the technique is comparatively less affected by the western theatre.

In Kerala, the art-forms which came into existence after the coming of the Portuguese, were based on the earlier art-forms of the Christians and Hindus. Pariśumuṭṭukaḷi of the Latin Christians and Orthodox Jacobite Syrian Christians is based on the Parisumuṭṭukaḷi of the Syrian Christians both in technique and the mode of presentation. However, one notices that the emphasis laid on the choice of the themes differs. In the technique and training system, Caviṭṭunāṭakam has been immensely influenced by Kathakaḷi, Mohiniāṭṭam and other local art forms. In Goa some of the art-forms of the Christians like the Mando are adapted to the local situation, though the origin could be traced back to the European opera. Others like Mussal Khel, Dekhni, Mēll etc. have a strong Hindu influence and background. The Hindu influence is maintained inspite of the vigorous suppression of the local customs, norms, language etc. by the Portuguese and the Church authorities. In the course of time, most of them tended to assume more social and less religious significance except for the occasion and time when they are performed. Whereas in Kerala the religious connotation and significance of these art-forms in their performance and practice is easily felt and observed.

Another feature can be observed is that the dance forms practised in the coastal line are relatively more influenced by the West and the European theatre than the interior regions. Caviṭṭunāṭakam, Mūnrurājākūthu, Nāṭakams, Kummiāṭṭam of Palghat area and the dance forms of the Christians in Goa, all originated after the coming of the portuguese to India. Here, it can be observed that Caviṭṭunāṭakam and the art-forms of Goa are comparatively more influenced by the European theatre than the art-forms of the Palghat area, a relatively interior region.

While the early dance forms of the Syrian Christians have their themes on the lives of the Saints who lived in Kerala and the geographical locations connected with the local Churches, the later forms take their themes from European history or the enactment of the outstanding lives of the Saints of the Western Church. However, at times the story content is found to be modified and adapted to the local situation. The main themes of Mārgamkaḷi and Pariśumuṭṭukaḷi are on the life of St. Thomas, the Apostle, and on the development and construction of some local church. But the Pariśumuṭṭukaḷi of the Latin Christians, Caviṭṭunāṭakam, Nāṭakams of Palghat region and many other contemporary art-forms of this period have to a great extent borrowed themes from European history and from the lives of the Western Church. This must have been a conscious dual effort by the Portuguese rulers and the Church to alienate the people and to teach them European history, customs, norms etc. to their own advantage. Even in the sphere of costume and decor the same trend carried On. It is believed that even Kathakaḷi is influenced to some extent by the Western theatre, here i.e. headgear of Hanuman.

Each community, depending on its social, regional and professional background, has developed its own dance movements, gestures, choreographic patterns etc. However, the basic choreographic patterns always remain a circle and two parallel lines. Dancing in the circle pattern and in circles is common and popular in all parts of India and the world. The couple formations and circular patterns accompanied by rhythmic and other movements and songs is common to all Indian group dances. It is interesting to note that the traditional dance forms of the Christians are all done in a circular pattern, keeping a lighted lamp or an idol of a deity in the centre. This symbolizes the micro and macro cosmos, relation of man to God, etc. It is interesting to note that the traditional dance forms of the Christians have a lighted lamp in the centre symbolizing Christ. The circle pattern is common to all the dance forms of the Christians whether they are ancient, medieval, modern or contemporary in their origin.

However, in the second phase which starts from the medieval period, a striking choreographic pattern in two parallel lines is developed without giving up or minimizing the importance of the circular pattern. This is clearly seen in Caviṭṭunāṭakam, Pariśumuṭṭukaḷi of the Latin Christians, Kummiāṭṭam and other forms which had their origin in the medieval and subsequent period. The pattern of two parallel lines must be the result of dance during the religious processions of the Christians, which are normally well-organized in two parallel lines.

The post Independence period has ushered in an innovative phase in the history of dance. Many attempts have been made by various people to depict the Christian message in Indian dance forms. Most of these attempts have not followed a particular form or style. Hence, hardly any form or tradition has developed in this direction. As a result the continuity and follow-up of these efforts has not been attempted. Again, the new trends have over stressed the themes to such an extent that technique has been neglected, if not completely lost. The primary purpose and aim of these attempts according to a survey and a question naire conducted by me is for the proclamation of the Gospel, preaching, adaptation, adoption, inculturation etc. Some use phrases like 'presenting the Gospel through Dance forms', others proudly talk about promoting the use of indigenous art-forms for the proclamation of the Gospel. This idea is somehow in contrast to the earlier dance forms of the Christians. Mārgamkaḷi, Pariśumuṭṭukaḷi, Nātakams etc. were developed in the Christian community to understand, experience and comprehend Christian message. But the present trend tends to be utilitarian, using art-forms for delivering Christ's message. Further this sort of understanding also gives the impression that the Gospel is a ready made product, neatly bound and packaged. Commenting on this point Rev. P. Nirmal says "art-forms are not primarily meant to propagate, proclaim or communicate a static and well-formulated Gospel. Their primary value lies in the fact that they enable us to understand and grasp the Gospel in a new way. They offer us fresh, new insights into the Gospel. They offer us new visions of the Gospel. Art and art-forms, therefore, have a tremendous hermeneutical and heuristic value.

They make possible new understandings, and formulations of the Gospel. They make the Gospel an 'event' a 'happening', and an 'emergence'. Art and art-forms unfold new Gospel mysteries, new Gospel dimensions and new Gospel of God in Jesus confessed to be the Christ is inexhaustibly rich. All art-forms and culture are not merely means and media for proclamation and communication of the Gospel. Rather they are an integral part of that process through which the Gospel is understood, comprehended and appropriated, nay, realised in ever new ways". (Abstract from the keynote address of Rev. P Nirmal, The Festival of Performing Arts and Literature, Jabalpur, Oct. 1982).

Part 24

ISSUES FOR CHRISTIANITY IN THE TWENTY-FIRST CENTURY

97

BEYOND CHRISTENDOM

Protestant–Catholic distinctions in coming global Christianity

D. Paul Sullins

Source: *Religion*, 36 (2006), 197–213.

Introduction

Over the next generation, the preponderance of the population of the world will shift to the continents of what is now known as the developing world, principally Africa and Asia. On a planet that is rapidly globalising, it is inevitable that this shift will be accompanied by global political and economic realignments. Cultural historians have predicted an attendant shift in world culture, a decline of the West, or clash of civilisations. Recently, Philip Jenkins has proposed that global demographic realignments will lead to a fundamental reorientation and revitalisation of Christianity. Jenkins notes that the Christian religion in traditional forms is being rapidly adopted in the developing world, while remaining stagnant or declining in the developed world. In a generation or two the majority of Christians will be non-white, traditional, and not of European origin. There will be a realignment of the centre of Christian culture from the global North (developed world) to the global South (developing world). As in the Middle Ages, when Christianity formed an 'overarching unity and focus of loyalty transcending mere kingdoms' (Jenkins, 2002a, p. 10), so the growth of Christianity in the South will lead to the rise of a powerful global Christian culture and identity and to the corresponding decline of national loyalties. There will arise what Jenkins calls 'The Next Christendom'.

But Christianity comes with a number of competing doctrinal and institutional divisions, principally though by no means solely that between Protestant and Catholic. I argue that these differences call Jenkins' thesis into question. His thesis must at least be qualified and specified in ways that are consequential for its accuracy. The effect of the global restructuring of the population of the world will be different for Catholics than for Protestants. In general, population shifts will be both more complicated and less transforming for the Catholic Church than Jenkins suggests. The shift from North to South will be much less extreme, with a countervailing shift from South to North. The Africanisation of the Church will be much less pronounced than its Latinisation. While the Catholic Church will grow in the South, it will not decline, as will Protestantism in the North.

Moreover, the conservative/liberal divide among Catholics is much less aligned with a South/North axis than holds for Protestants. Because of their divergent relations to the nation-state as a social form, Protestantism is much less likely to develop a centralised authority consistent with a new Christendom than is Catholicism. These differences also call into question Jenkins' predictions about the global dominance of Christianity and the development of a transnational Christian identity. Taken together, Protestant/Catholic differences in the coming population shifts suggest that, rather than renewing a common Christian culture or church order, church–state relations around the globe are more likely to reflect new, more complex, articulations of civil and religious realities that will move even further beyond the old arrangement of Christendom altogether.

Data

The primary data source for this analysis is the World Christian Database (WCD) (Johnson *et al.*, 2004), an exhaustive repository of demographic and institutional indicators on world religions maintained by the Centre for the Study of Global Christianity at Gordon-Conwell Theological Seminary. The WCD provides almost 400 variables on 238 countries, all major and minor world religions, including over 9000 separate Christian denominations, for six points in time from 1900 and projected to 2050.

Population projections are always perilous, subject as they are to unforeseen changes. For this reason this study, like Jenkins', can reasonably examine only broad general trends. But because this caution applies to all demographic projections, the WCD database is the most pertinent resource for this study, for it is the source of information for the World Christian Encyclopaedia (see Barrett, 2001), upon which Jenkins (2002b) bases his argument. Thus it allows us to examine Jenkins' claims on the basis of the same evidence that he analyses. For the purpose of examining broad trends, the WCD is the best source of information on world religions currently available. Its main weakness is that it must rely on institutionally derived information, and it applies estimates or interpolates when the information is missing. The quality of the data is therefore uneven. Still, aggressive attempts are made to be thorough and accurate in obtaining institutional measures, and estimation procedures, when used, are conservative and thoroughly documented. A comparison of summary information for three US denominations that independently publish institutional data—the Roman Catholic Church, the Southern Baptist Convention and the Episcopal Church—found no significant variance on numbers of parishioners, parishes or pastors reported for the year 2000.

Distinguishing Protestants from Catholics

For Jenkins, Christianity in the global North is 'headed South' in both a literal and a figurative sense: literally, as the centre of the Christian population shifts to Africa and Latin America; figuratively, as the formerly dominant North enters a secularised post-Christian era. Crucial to his thesis of a coming Christendom is the prediction that Latin American and African Christianity will align themselves in a common Christian culture. Although currently 'the two continents belong almost to different planets', Jenkins argues that 'a period of mutual discovery is inevitable' as Christianity grows rapidly in both. 'Once that axis is established', he concludes, 'we really would be speaking of a new Christendom, based in the Southern Hemisphere' (Jenkins, 2002a, p. 12). However, in both the literal and the figurative senses, the shifts in population will be quite different for Catholics than for Protestants.

African Protestants, Latino Catholics

While the Catholic demographic centre is, like that of Protestantism, moving from North to South, for Catholics the move is from a different North to a different South. In broad terms, the Protestant centre is shifting from North America to Africa, whereas the Catholic population centre is shifting, somewhat less radically, from Europe to Latin America.

Jenkins accurately notes that 'by 2025, Africans and Latin Americans combined will make up about 60 percent of Catholics' (Jenkins, 2002a, p. 195), but it is the Latin Americans who make up the bulk (73%) of that combination. Figure 1A,B shows the trends for Catholics and Protestants, respectively. These figures compare, for Protestants and Catholics, the proportion of adherents by continent in 1900, in 2000 and projected for 2050. Today, 43% of all Catholics are Latin American. By 2025, Africa will have added 108 million Catholics, almost doubling its Catholic population. But Latin American Catholics will have increased by 145 million, to almost 45% of world Catholics. If we include the populations outside of Latin America that are also generally defined as ethnically Hispanic—those of Spain, Portugal and Latino immigrants in North America—by 2025 or shortly thereafter a full half of the world's Catholics will be Latino. This milestone will be short-lived, slowly eroded by the burgeoning population of Asia, but the difference in Catholic and Protestant demographic trajectories will persist in broad terms. By 2050, about half (47%) of the world's Catholics will be

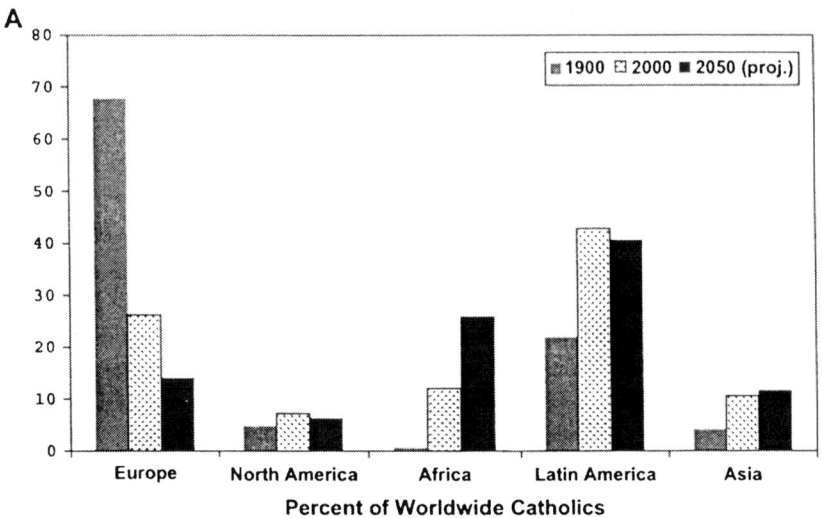
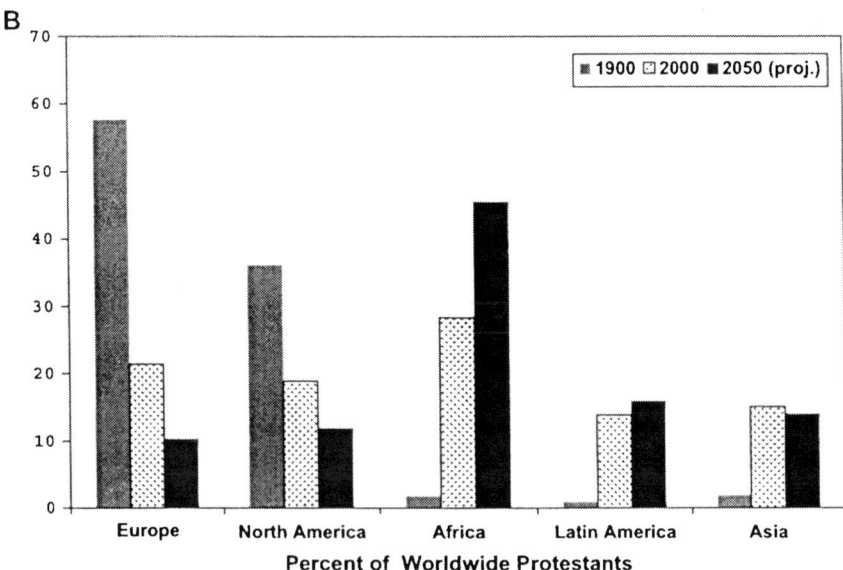

Figure 1 (A) Global shifts in the Catholic population 1900–2050. *Source*: WCD, 2003 (Johnson *et al.*, 2004). (B) Global shifts in the Protestant population 1900–2050. *Source*: WCD, 2003 (Johnson *et al.*, 2004).

Latino, but about half (51%) of the world's Protestants, including Anglicans, will be African.

Some question this claim of Catholic vitality in Latin America in light of the dramatic growth of Protestant groups observed there in recent years. But while a great deal of scholarly attention has focused on the growth of Protestant evangelical and Pentecostal groups in Latin America, the numerical effect of these inroads on the growth of the Catholic population of the continent has been quite small. While these non-Catholic groups are growing rapidly in percentage terms, the denominator for the percentages is many times smaller than the Catholic population. In raw numbers the relative growth is much smaller than it appears as a percentage. At the same time the Latin American population as a whole is growing rapidly. Too, the growth of non-Catholic groups in Latin America has already slowed dramatically from just a decade ago and will continue to decline through the next several decades. The result is that, while the Catholic proportion of the population will decline by single digits, the size of the Catholic population will grow by double digits.

Brazil, the typical and largest case, offers a good example. The Catholic proportion of the Brazilian population is projected to decline by 6% (from 86% to 80%) between 2000 and 2050. But during the same period the number of Catholics in Brazil will increase by 35%, from 147 million in 2000 to 198 million in 2050, for the total population of Brazil will increase by almost half. The proportional decline of Catholics in Brazil, moreover, is petering out (see Figure 2). After dropping by 4% during the 1990s, it is now projected to take until 2025 to decline another 4%, and then will decrease by only 2% between 2025 and 2050. The rate of decline today, then, is less than half of what it was during the 1990s, and will halve again in another twenty years.

For Protestants the South may be evangelising the North, but for US Catholics, the South is moving North, as the American Catholic Church is becoming home to increasing millions of Latino immigrants. Today about two-thirds of Hispanic immigrants report a Catholic affiliation (see Kosmin et al., 2001),[1] a proportion that, despite much publicised Protestant defections, has remained stable for over twenty years. The US Census projects that in the next forty-five years the US Hispanic population will triple, to over 100 million persons. Barring a dramatic change in Hispanic religious practices, then, the number of Hispanic Catholics in the United States can be projected to grow to about 66 million persons. Thus by 2050 there will be more Hispanic Catholics in the United States than there are total Catholics today.

For Protestants, the rise of a new African centre is being accompanied by a decline of the old Euro-American dominance, but this is not the case for Catholics. The proportion of Protestants in both Europe and North American has declined by about half since 1900 and will continue to decline in the future. This is true for Catholics in Europe, but not for those in North America. The proportion of Catholics in North America has never been large and will

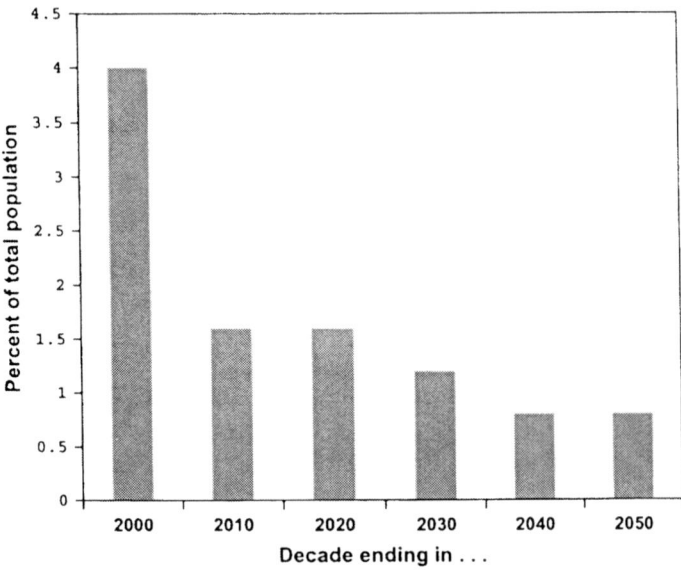

Figure 2 Current and projected decadal rate of decline of Catholics in Brazil, 1990–2050. *Source*: WCD, 2003 (Johnson *et al.*, 2004).

change only slightly. Today only 7% of the world's Catholics are in North America, a proportion that has remained relatively stable since 1900.

The overall population shifts, however, can be somewhat misleading when referring to the cultural or religious 'centre' of the Christian world. For a large part of these population shifts stems not from religious growth or decline but from an overall shift in the world population. In 1900, 25% of the population of the planet was European, and only 7% was in Africa. By 2050, those proportions will be largely reversed: Europe will comprise only 6% of the world population, and Africa almost 22%. The growth of Christians in Africa is therefore a result of both the Christianisation of Africa and the growth of African population. Likewise the numerical drop in the proportion of Christians in Europe is a result of both de-Christianisation—a shrinking proportion of Christians in Europe—and a relative decline in the European population.

Figure 3A,B shows the respective relative concentrations of Catholics and Protestants net of overall shifts in population. The statistic reported is the ratio of the proportion of Catholics or Protestants to the overall proportion of the world population for each continent. This analysis can best be thought of as an index of concentration for each group. If all group members (Catholics in Fig. 3A, Protestants in Fig. 3B) were distributed equally in the world population, all areas would have a value of 1.0 for this index. In Fig. 3A, for example, values greater than one indicate that the concentration

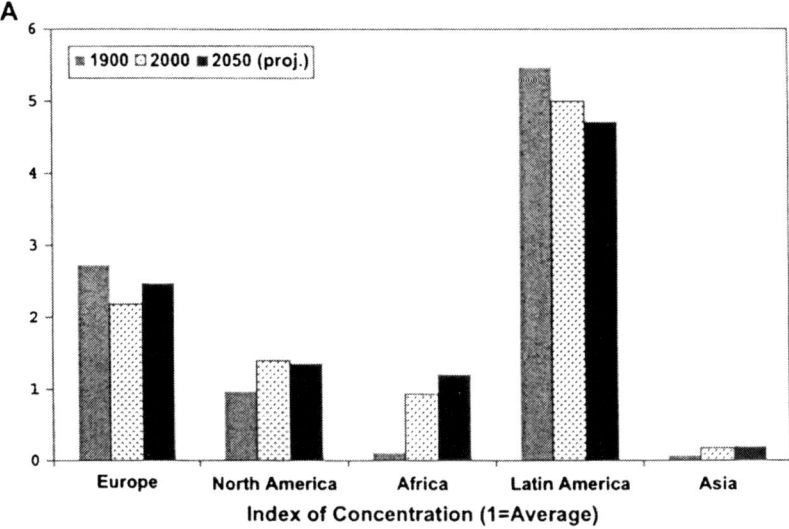

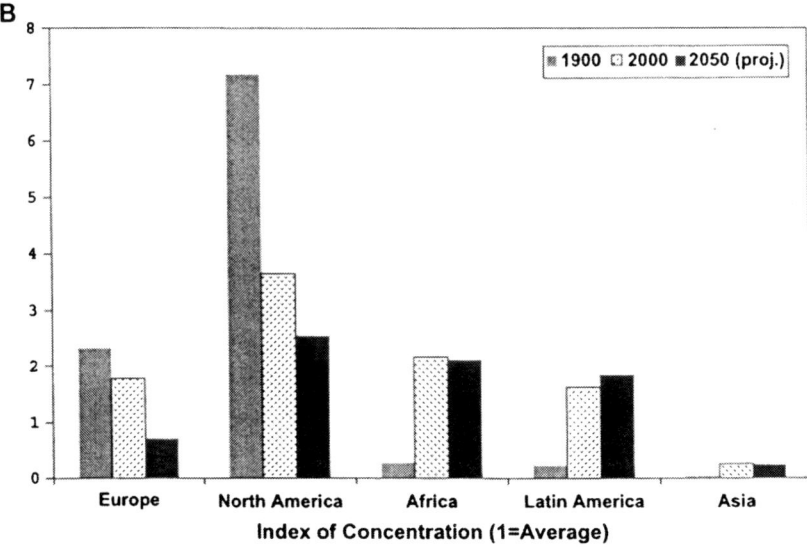

Figure 3 (A) Global cultural concentration of Catholics, 1900–2050. *Source*: WCD, 2003 (Johnson *et al.*, 2004). (B) Global cultural concentration of Protestants, 1900–2050. *Source*: WCD, 2003 (Johnson *et al.*, 2004).

of Catholics is greater than that of overall population in that area and that area is more pervasively Catholic than the norm. A value less than one indicates that Catholics are more sparse in that area than in the world as a whole. Fig. 3B shows the corresponding indices for Protestants. These figures show, then, the concentration of Catholics and Protestants that can be attributed to cultural dominance or continued evangelisation rather than simply to population growth.

These figures show that, while there will be some dramatic shifts in the Protestant centre, changes in the relative concentration of Catholics in the near future will be modest. The figures bring three trends into sharp focus. First, they show clearly that the growth of Christian concentration due to evangelisation in the global South—Africa, Asia and Latin America—has already occurred. The increased concentration in these areas in the next fifty years will stem entirely from population growth, not from any particular affinity of Christianity to the culture of these continents or from any general global advance of Christianity in relation to other religions. In fact, the cultural concentration of Catholics in Latin America and of Protestants in Africa will decrease slightly over the next five decades. (The concentration of Anglicans in Africa will drop the most, from 4.0 today to 3.6 in 2050.) Second, Latin America will continue to be several times more dominant for Catholics than is Africa, or than either Latin America or Africa is for Protestants. Catholics will remain about five times more concentrated in Latin America than they are worldwide, including Africa and North America, which are both just at the world average. Both Catholics and Protestants will remain marginal in Asia. Third, the changing centre of Protestantism will stem entirely from decline in the first world, not from cultural increase in the third world, as their relative dominance in Europe and North America continues to plummet. By contrast, the Catholic concentration in North America will remain virtually unchanged, and is projected to increase slightly in Europe. Despite this decline, by 2050 Protestants will still be slightly more concentrated in North America than they are in either Africa or Latin America.

The predominance of Latin America in the global Catholic population is not new. Although Latinos are still growing in their numerical dominance in the Church, Latin American culture was already more pervasively Catholic than was Europe a hundred years ago. Catholics have consistently been about five times as concentrated in Latin America as in the world population, and about double their concentration in Europe.

Liberal North versus conservative South?

How will these shifts affect religious practice and global society? For Jenkins, 'the most significant point [regarding the implications of demographic changes in Christian populations] is that in terms of both theology and moral teaching, Southern Christianity is more conservative than the Northern

—especially the American—version' (Jenkins, 2002b, p. 56). Compared with the democratised, secularised faith of European and American Christians, the churches of the global South are 'stalwartly traditional or even reactionary' in their literal adoption of the ancient world view of the New Testament.

However, just as Catholic demographic changes do not neatly align themselves with a global North to South shift, so the simple identification of liberalism (or dissent) with the North and of conservatism (or orthodoxy) with the South does not easily fit the Catholic reality. A case could be made that the opposite is more accurate. On issues of sexuality, for example, the liberal dissent of the North over contraception or even gay marriage is relatively mild compared with the bitter debate in Africa over polygamy, which requires the ongoing restructuring of families who become Catholic (see Gbonigi, 2002; Chama, 2004) and contravenes international ideals of women's rights (see Oloka-Onyango, 2002). Jenkins points out that there are now more Jesuits in India than in the United States, but he fails to note that in both the United States and India the Jesuits are among the most liberal of Catholics. In 1998, the writings of the Indian Jesuit Anthony De Mello were proscribed by the Church as heretical, as an assimilation to Buddhist teachings, in probably the most theologically serious such action of recent decades (see Congregation for the Doctrine of the Faith, 1998). Latin America has given rise to some of the most progressive, functionally Marxist theology and ecclesial movements in any age of the Church. Its theologians and bishops have been duly and repeatedly rebuked by the Holy See.[2] Priests in Europe or North America may question the rule of celibacy, but at least a third of rural priests in Latin America live in thinly hidden concubinage.

Despite the pretensions of some in the liberal Catholic media, which Jenkins takes at face value (see Jenkins, 2002a, pp. 194–198), the United States and Europe, not the global South, are the source of some of the most conservative movements in the Catholic Church (see Weaver and Appleby, 1995). In the past decade a half-dozen new Catholic colleges, which are among the most explicitly orthodox, even reactionary, in the world, have been founded in the United States (see Bollag, 2004). Numerous indications suggest that younger Americans, including Catholics, are growing more religious. The massive annual youth survey *Monitoring the Future* reports that the percentage of eighth graders who report that religion plays a very important role in their lives increased by 8% during the 1990s.[3] A 1999 study by pollster George Barna found that Americans under age 35 are more likely than their parents to attend church, to read the Bible and to pray (see Winner, 2000). A Gallup poll on 'The Spiritual Life of Young Americans' in the same year found that almost 90% of teenagers, including Catholics, said that they believed in the divinity of Jesus (see Gallup and Lindsay, 1999). The 2002 General Social Survey (see Davis *et al.*, 2002) reports that a higher proportion of Catholics under 30 than those over 45 reported that they believed the Bible to be the 'actual Word of God, to be taken literally, word for word' (23% vs. 16%), and that they had 'a great deal' of confidence in organised religion (29% vs. 24%). In a study of young adult Catholics, Dean Hoge and others reported that the faith of young Catholics was centred in three core elements which are all traditional, orthodox components of the faith: Marian devotion, God's presence in the sacraments, and concern for the poor (see Hoge *et al.*, 1998). These trends are suggestive, but still too new and too weak to be compelling. Colleen Carroll, in a book subtitled 'Why Young Adults are Embracing Christian Orthodoxy', argues that young adult traditionalists, while numerically small, have a disproportionately powerful cultural influence in reshaping American Christianity, including Catholicism (see Carroll, 2002). Whether this claim in fact turns out to be the case remains to be seen.

While the evidence is not yet conclusive for Catholic laity, among priests the trend is clear: younger, newly ordained priests today in the Catholic West are far more traditional than those of the preceding generation. Periodic surveys of American priests going back to 1970 have shown that newer ordinands have been growing more conservative since the early 1980s, to the point that the most recently ordained priests today express levels of belief and devotion that are comparable with those of priests ordained during the 1950s, when traditionalism was at its height. Dean Hoge and Jacqueline Wenger's recent interviews with priests found that, in contrast to priests ordained in past decades, today's new ordinands express a less reformist and more traditional view of the Church and the priesthood, centred in personal piety and in touch with the ancient roots of Catholic life, and yearn for a restoration of traditional elements in the liturgy (see Hoge and Wenger, 2003). A spate of surveys of Catholic priests during 2002 (commissioned by media organisations for background on the sexual abuse scandal) has provided a wealth of documentation on the growth of traditional, orthodox beliefs among younger clergy. In a July 2002 survey by the *Los Angeles Times*, 72% of Catholic priests agreed that 'younger clergy in America are more theologically conservative– that is, more religiously orthodox—than their older counterparts', and 76% believed that 'younger priests today are more theologically conservative than they were in the 1970s or 1980s'. The *Los Angeles Times* (Watanabe, October 21, 2002, p. A1) summarised these findings:

> Clerics under age 41 expressed more allegiance to the clerical hierarchy, less dissent against traditional church teachings, and more certainty about the sinfulness of homosexuality, abortion, artificial birth control, and other moral issues than did their elders, the poll found. Those attitudes place the younger priests at odds with many priests who were shaped by the liberal reforms of the Second Vatican Council in the 1960s and who tend to support further changes in the church—including women priests, optional celibacy, more lay empowerment, and the direct election of bishops.

These shifts in attitudes are confirmed by recruitment trends. US dioceses in which bishops are outspokenly orthodox have seen an influx of priestly aspirants, as have several relatively new orders of priests that emphasise fidelity rather than reform. Of current seminarians in the United States, 15% are members of just one of these orders, the Legionaries of Christ.[4] Conservatism is also clearly on the rise among Catholic nuns and monks in the West. In the last twenty years a new group of Catholic religious orders that have emphasised orthodox fidelity and have reinstated the traditional disciplines of communal living and prayer and wearing distinctive garb have attracted thousands of young new postulants in Europe and North America, while orders that discontinued such practices in the 1960s in favour a liberal theology of social justice have seen scant new vocations. This evidence directly contradicts Jenkins' claim that 'much of the liberal dissidence within Catholicism stems not from the laity but from clergy themselves . . . [who] are much more likely to be located in the North than the South' (Jenkins, 2002a, p. 198).

In sum, it appears that the reports of the demise of traditional Catholicism in the West and of its rise in the South have been greatly exaggerated. Anglican scholar Ian Douglas, pointing out that some of the Southern Anglican bishops are quite liberal, argues that this is also the case for Protestantism: 'To say that there is a normative Third World Christianity that speaks with a unified conservative voice committed to chastising the errant West over issues of human sexuality does not give full credit to the many diverse voices in this new Christianity'. (Douglas, 2003, p. 223) For global Catholicism, it is clear *a fortiori* that the distribution of orthodox and progressive elements is far more complex and diverse than the picture of a liberal North versus a conservative South would suggest.

From national to global

Jenkins' claims for the political implications of the shifts in global Christianity are sweeping. They portend a fundamental change in church–state relations that will alter the balance of political, religious and social forces that has been in place since the sixteenth century: 'We are at a moment as epochal as the Reformation itself—a Reformation moment not only for Catholics but for the entire Christian world' (Jenkins, 2002b, p. 53). He argues that the Counter-Reformation is a better referent for today's changes because what is occurring is the re-emergence of a religious dominance over the authority and legitimacy of political structures that is comparable with that in medieval Christendom. Resurgent global Christianity, corresponding to a decline of national identities, is leading to a rejection of Enlightenment secularity in political affairs in favour of 'a new transnational order in which political, social, and personal identities are defined chiefly by religious loyalties' (Jenkins, 2002b, p. 53).

It is, of course, widely recognised that nationalism has receded during the second half of the twentieth century and that the forces of globalisation, post-modernity and multinational capitalism, among others, pose ongoing challenges today to the legitimacy and autonomy of nation-states. It is not at all clear, however, that these challenges will result in an erosion of national identity or that religion will contribute to this erosion. Jenkins' depiction of resurgent religious salience in world affairs follows in many respects that of Samuel Huntington, who has famously argued that the coming fault lines in world affairs will be dominated by ethnic and religious concerns. Yet Huntington does not propose that the rise of civilisational conflict means the decline of nations. On the contrary, he predicts that 'Nation states will remain the most powerful actors in world affairs, but the principal conflicts of global politics will occur between nations and groups of different civilisations' (Huntington, 1993, p. 22).

Mark Juergensmeyer presents a similar alternative to Jenkins' vision of a reconstituted Christendom. He, with Jenkins, recognizes the corrosive effect of globalisation on the Enlightenment notion of the state. He also details the worldwide resurgence of traditional religion, not only in Christianity but also among all other major religions. However, he argues that traditional religion, as well as ethnicity and cultural traditions, has provided a new lease on life for outworn secular national identities. Far from further delegitimising the nation-state, 'traditional forms of social identity [religion and ethnicity] have helped to rescue one of modernity's central themes: the idea of nationhood' (Juergensmeyer, 2004, p. 37). Like Jenkins, Juergensmeyer notes that today's resurgent religious movements are, to Western eyes, conservative, intolerant and repressive. However, although they 'have reached back into history for ancient images and concepts that will give them credibility, theirs are not simply efforts to resuscitate old ideas form the past. These are contemporary ideologies that meet present-day social and political needs' (Juergensmeyer, 2004, p. 38). Like Jenkins, Juergensmeyer concludes that 'religious visions of moral order will continue to appear as attractive... solutions to the problems of authority, identity, and belonging in a globalise world' (Juergensmeyer, 2004, p. 38). Instead of reconstituting a premodern past that leaves nations behind, these religious visions have become carriers of renewed national identities.

Although the rise of religious nationalism has been noted among Muslim nations, it is too early to tell whether there will also be a rise in the resurgent Christian South. This outcome, to be sure, would be neither implausible nor unprecedented. In the United States a Christian *civil* religion that affirms the moral legitimacy and goodness of the American nation has long provided a religious penumbra for national ideals. Proper submission to political authority, moreover, is an explicit feature of traditional biblical Christian belief.

There is, however, a more serious problem with Jenkins' thesis than that resurgent Christianity will undermine national identities. Jenkins

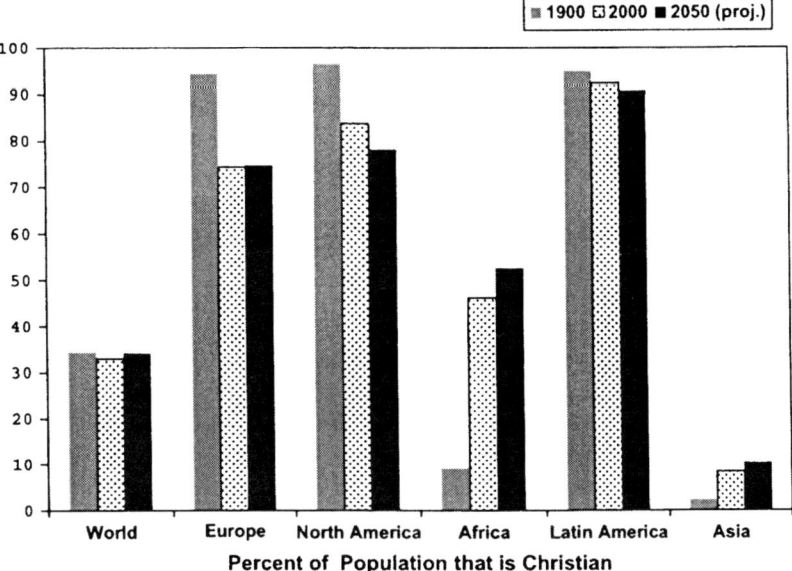

Figure 4 Population proportion of Christians by continent, 1900–2050. *Source*: WCD, 2003 (Johnson *et al.*, 2004).

counters Huntington's claim that 'In the long run . . . Muhammad wins out' (Huntington, 1996, p. 65) with the argument that Christianity will develop a 'massive lead' over Islam (Jenkins, 2002a, p. 6). But according to current projections, he is wrong. Although the shift in the Christian population has prompted a certain triumphalism regarding the growing global South, and corresponding despair or criticism regarding the declining global North, the net effect of these on the worldwide Christian population, for both Protestants and Catholics, has been zero. Figure 4 reports the proportion of the population that is Christian for the world and its major continents from 1900 to 2050, according to the same WCD and UN projections used by Jenkins. In 1900, 34.6% of the world's population was Christian. By 2000, after a century that saw the vigorous expansion of Christian missions, that proportion had declined slightly, to 33.0%. By 2050, it is projected to grow slightly, to 34.2%—still *below* what it had been one hundred and fifty years earlier. Moreover, this small variation is well within the range of uncertainty of measurement and projection in these data. Thus, despite large realignments of the Christian population by continent, there is no trend towards growing Christian dominance in the world. Generally speaking, the Christian share appears to be stable at about a third of world population.

Moreover, with only minor exceptions, Christianity is presently growing only in those parts of the world where the population itself is growing. Furthermore, those nations affected by growing Christianity will also be affected by rapid overall population growth, which is likely to induce its own unique stresses on political structures, independent of religious identities. Whatever effect a growing Christianity has on national structures, growing Christianity is not a global phenomenon. It will not have an effect on the nation as such, on the idea of a nation, or on the general legitimacy of the nation as form of political association. It will have an effect only on those that are affected by the locally resurgent, traditional Christianity. If this effect is taken as something like Christendom, it is, at minimum, an odd form of local, selective Christendom.

Although it is not possible to know for sure, it appears likely that the variety and growth of traditional religions, including Christianity, rather than reasserting a premodern religious order that dominates nations, will recast church–state relations in a multiplicity of forms that are only selectively modern. This situation would be better described not as a new Christendom but as a further loss of Christendom—likely, a movement beyond Christendom altogether.

Protestant particularity versus Catholic centrality

The differences between Protestants and Catholics suggest different outcomes regarding the possibility of a renewed Christendom. In the focus on the political implications of religious population change, the implications for religious institutions are often given relatively little attentions—a reflection, no doubt, of our secularised culture. Jenkins reflects this general imbalance. In his book-length treatment of the topic, there is no chapter on the implications of global change for religious institutions themselves. Yet while the global shifts in Christian population will surely affect political structures, they will likely to have a more direct effect on the institutional structures and arrangements of religion. These effects are not inconsequential for the notion of a new Christendom. I argue that the demographic changes in Christianity will encourage opposing trends—towards greater decentralisation in Protestantism but towards greater centralisation in Catholicism—with the result that a renewed sense of Christendom, as Jenkins conceives it, is more likely to occur for Catholicism than for Protestantism.

Understanding the current changes in Christianity, as Jenkins notes, requires understanding the Reformation, when Protestantism and the modern nation-state emerged together. During this era Protestant religions, I suggest, became identified with the nascent national entities, and to the benefit of both, in a way that Catholicism did not. Luther's revolt against Rome was famously abetted and made effective by the political support of local princes feeling their way towards a German national identity, on which Lutheranism in turn bestowed legitimacy. In a similar way the Church *in* England' (*ecclesia anglicana*) became the Church *of* England (*ecclesia anglicanae*) during the sixteenth century, so assimilated to national identity that the King, who was understood to rule by divine right, was in turn declared the head of the church, which by the nineteenth century was being described as merely 'the nation of England at prayer'. This congruence between national and religious identity inhibited both the inherently fractive tendencies of the new Protestantism and the inherently cohesive inclinations in Catholicism. Within a generation after Luther, both England and Germany were preoccupied with limiting internal religious dissent, while the so-called Catholic nations addressed themselves to asserting greater independence from Rome.

Jenkins notes that by 1600 the Catholic Church had become the first institution to operate on a global scale (see Jenkins, 2002b, p. 55). Indeed, the Catholic Church had expanded to the perimeters of the known world a thousand years earlier. For sixteenth-century Catholicism it was the nation, not the church, that was an innovation. The development of the institutional structures of Catholicism—the structures that persist to this day—predate the development of the nation–state, with the effect that the Catholic Church remains the only truly global Christian institution. Unlike all Protestant denominations and arguably any other modern institution, the centre of the Catholic Church today is not in any nation. Although its ruling structures are in Italy, it is not in any constitutive sense the Italian Catholic Church. The offices of the Pope in fact technically form a separate nation to itself (Vatican City), a sign of the Church's independence from all nations. To underscore this unique independence, Vatican City is the only universally recognised national entity that is not a member of the United Nations.

These structural differences suggest different institutional outcomes for Protestant and Catholic groups as nations change. In the face of the current and predicted decline of national autonomy, Protestant church order, aligned with political entities, will tend to lead either to localised certainty (in its more conservative forms) or to collegial relativism (in its more liberal forms). The Catholic Church, by contrast, as a kind of multinational religious corporation, would be led by the same forces to constrain local—that is, national—variation in the service of global coherence. If the projected decline in the strength of nation-states occurs, it will lead Protestant denominations to fracture further while spurring the Catholic Church to become more centralised. Increasingly deprived (or free) of national support, the strength of Protestantism will lie in its increasing adaptation to a diverse array of particular communities. The strength of Catholicism will lie in the further concentration of authority in a single person, with care for every member of the faithful on the entire planet. While there are many qualifications and exceptions to be noted, the most distinct institutional trends observed in these religions today strongly bear out this analysis. These trends are the rise of postdenominationalism among Protestants and, for Catholics, the increasing centralisation of church authority in the Pope.

David Barrett and Todd Johnson chronicle the further splintering of Protestantism. In a further consideration of the data these authors of the

World Christian Encyclopaedia make the case that the newest, rapidly emerging 'global megabloc' of alignments in Christianity is a phenomenon they term 'postdenominationalism'

> Contemporary postdenominationalism is a movement sweeping throughout the churches worldwide. It is a vast, scattered movement of many distinct and separate protests, revolts, schisms, secessions, rebellions, independencies, reformations, and renewals. Today it includes over 20,000 movements, networks, or new denominations with 394 million church members. . . . Basically it stands for a rejection of historic denominationalism. . . . At origin these new groups unilaterally adopt a markedly different church lifestyle from that of their parent bodies, rejecting the authority of existing parent denominations and many established aspects of denominationalist faith and life, and putting in their place new authority, new structures, new names, new beliefs, new solutions, and new forms of church life. . . . These churches are among the fastest-growing in the world. By A.D. 2025 the independents, who numbered less than half the size of Protestants in 1970, will have nearly 115 million more members than Protestants.
> (Barrett, 2001, p. 24)

The 'parent bodies' involved here, of course, are overwhelmingly the established Reformation and post-Reformation Protestant denominations. In this sense the rise of postdenominationalism is but a further extension of the fissiparous tendency of Protestantism.

At the same time the Catholic Church has not only resisted splintering but even become more centralised. Two relatively recent factors in the Church's life have paved the way for this result: the recognition of the development of doctrine, and the establishment of papal infallibility. Strikingly, both of these developments are fewer than one hundred and fifty years old. They are 'postmodern' developments, in the strict sense that they emerged subsequent to the birth of modernity. Together, they have uniquely positioned the Catholic Church to engage the twin forces of globalisation and postmodernity by allowing a balance of continuity and change, of variation within limits. In recent times the emphasis in the Catholic Church has clearly been on continuity and limits, by regularising the rapidly diversifying global Church under the unifying central authority of the Pope.

The Catholic Church today is rapidly centralising and regularising every aspect of Church life. Ironically, while progressive Catholics received the Second Vatican Council of the 1960s as a manifesto for local autonomy, the net effect of the Council has been as much to direct as to promote and legitimate local variation in the Church. In the period following the Council, assertions of centralised regulation occurred at a pace seldom, if ever, matched in the history of the Church. In the last forty years the Catholic Church has issued, as universal and new (or updated), a lectionary, a code of canon law, a catechism (the first in four hundred years), a general instruction for the liturgy, a general directory for catechesis, and norms for Catholic universities and schools, to mention only the most significant regulative documents. During the same period the Pope has issued more universal teaching documents, not just slightly more often but several times more often, than at any previous time in the history of the Church. By some measures more doctrine and discipline has been promulgated from Rome during the last forty years than in all the previous ages of the Church combined.

The likelihood is that centralisation will continue. It is common today to think of the Catholic Church as having always been a steeply hierarchical institution, but the level of centralisation and worldwide integration of authority that exists in the Church today is a fairly recent development. Throughout most of the Church's history the kind of pre-eminent authority the Pope exercises today has been challenged by the centrifugal forces of conciliarism (rule by church councils) and gallicanism (rule by national assemblies of bishops). Eight hundred years ago conciliarism was at its height. During most of the twelfth century there were two rival popes supported by competing councils. Gallicanism was in ascendancy just two centuries ago, when the prerogatives of the Pope were severely circumscribed following the French Revolution. The doctrine popularly known as papal infallibility, which establishes that the Pope's interpretation of doctrine cannot be overridden by a council or national assembly, was declared only in 1870. In historical terms, we may well be at only the beginning of a period of growing centralisation in the Catholic Church.

Conclusion

Jenkins' thesis that the global realignment of Christian populations will lead to a renewed Christendom in the emerging South must be qualified and even partly rejected by consideration of the differences between Protestant and Catholics in the projected population shifts. Over the next fifty years, as their centres of population are flung from their common origins in Europe, Protestants and Catholics will find divergent new centres of concentration in Africa and South America, respectively. Protestants, more closely allied to nations to begin with, will experience a greater decline of dominance in the North. The liberal/orthodox (or progressive/traditional) doctrinal responses to modernity will, for Catholics, be much less aligned with a global North/South tension. With the decline of the European style nation-state, religious authority will become more dispersed in Protestantism and more concentrated in Catholicism.

The effect of these changes, I have argued, will be more than just a transfer of venue of Christian dominance from North to South. Christianity is in fact not experiencing net global growth or increasing in population share in non-Christian regions. Protestant regions are experiencing a fragmentation, not a concentration, of church authority. The set of these realignments, I predict, should not be generalised as a 'new Christendom'. Rather, church–state relations around the globe are more likely to reflect new, more complex articulations of civil and religious realities that will move beyond the old arrangement of Christendom.

Acknowledgments

I wish to thank the Centre for Christian Studies at the University of Virginia for the speaking invitation that prompted this study, and to Dean Hoge, Philip Jenkins, Rhys Williams, James Youniss and anonymous reviewers for helpful comments on earlier drafts.

Notes

1 According to the ARIS 2001 survey, twenty-nine percent of surveyed Catholics identified themselves as Hispanic–a proportion acknowledged to be low, since the survey was administered only in English. This computes to about 20 million of the 65 million US Catholics, or about two-thirds of the 35 million US Hispanics.
2 Jenkins claims that 'Liberal criticism derives especially from only selected regions of the world—and moreover, the very regions in which Catholic numbers are stagnant, or worse [i.e., the global North]' (Jenkins, 2002a, p. 198). He duly chronicles the radical Marxist tendency of Latin American Catholicism as evidence of the Church's political participation in Latin America, but he misinterprets the imposition of orthodox bishops by Rome as an indigenous rightward turn, and he fails to see the implications of this obvious counter-example for his overall thesis. With similar confusion he argues in one place that Brazilian Catholicism instantiates increasing nationalism in the global South, and in another that it is questionable whether Brazil will even remain 'a major Catholic state' (Jenkins, 2002a, p. 92).
3 As reported by Child Trends, an independent youth research organisation, January 2002.
4 The Legionaries of Christ report 'almost 700' in formation to become priests, out of a reported population of seminarians of 4826.

References

Barrett, D. B., Johnson, T. M., 2001. Annual statistical table on global mission: 2001. International Bulletin of Missionary Research 25, 24–25.

Bollag, B., 2004. Who is Catholic? New conservative Catholic colleges say existing institutions lead students away from the true faith. Chronicle of Higher Education 50 (4 September), 31 ff.

Carroll, C., 2002. The New Faithful: Why Young Adults are Embracing Christian Orthodoxy. Loyola University Press, Chicago.

Chama, E., 2004. The Christian cost of rooting out polygamy. National Catholic Reporter 40 (17 September), 22.

Congregation for the Doctrine of the Faith, 1998. Notification Concerning the Writings of Father Anthony De Mello, S. J., Zenit News Agency (23 August) Electronically archived at. http://www.vatican.va/roman_curia/congregations/cfaith/documents/rc_con_cfaith_doc_19980624_demello_en.html. Davis, J. A., Smith, T. W., Marsden, P. V., 2002. General Social Surveys, 1972–2002: [Cumulative File] [Computer File]. 2nd ICPSR version. National Opinion Research Centre [producer], Chicago, IL, 2003, Roper Centre for Public Opinion Research, Storrs, CT, University of Connecticut/Inter-university Consortium for Political and Social Research [distributors], Ann Arbor, MI, 2003.

Douglas, L. T., 2003. The clash of global christianity. The world and I 18 (2), 222–224.

Gallup, G., Lindsay, W., 1999. Surveying the Religious Landscape: Trends in U.S. Beliefs. Morehouse Publishing, New York.

Gbonigi, E., 2002. Christian ethics versus African cultural values. Transformation 19, 79–81.

Hoge, D., Dinges, W., Gonzalez, J., Johnson Sr., M., 1998. Young Adult Catholics: Religion in the Culture of Choice. University of Notre Dame Press, Notre Dame, IN.

Hoge, D., Wenger, J. E., 2003. Evolving Visions of the Priesthood: Changes from Vatican II to the Turn of the New Century. Liturgical Press, Collegeville, MN.

Huntington, S. P., 1993. The clash of civilizations? Foreign Affairs 72 (3), 22–28.

Huntington, S. P., 1996. The Clash of Civilisations and the Remaking of World Order. Simon and Schuster, New York.

Jenkins, P., 2002a. The Next Christendom: The Coming of Global Christianity. Oxford University Press, New York.

Jenkins, P., 2002b. The next Christianity. Atlantic Monthly 290 (October), 53–68.

Johnson, T., et al., 2004. World Christian Database [Computer File]. Centre for the Study of Global Christianity, Gordon-Conwell Theological Seminary [producers], South Hamilton, MA. As updated March 2004 at. http://www.worldchristiandatabase.org.

Juergensmeyer, M., 2004. Holy orders: religious opposition to modern states. Harvard International Review 25 (4), 34–38.

Kosmin, B., Mayer, E., Keysar, A., 2001. American Religious Identification Survey (ARIS). Graduate Centre of the City University of New York [producers], New York. Findings report as updated March 2004 at http://www.gc.cuny.edu/studies/aris_index.htm.

Oloka-Onyango, J. O., 2002. Modern-day missionaries or misguided miscreants? NGOs, the women's movement and the promotion of human rights in Africa. In: Benedek, W., Kisaakye, E., Oberleitner, E. (Eds.), The Human Rights of Women: International Instruments and African Experiences. Zed Books, London, pp. 286–294.

Watanabe, T., 2002. Young priests hold old values. Los Angeles Times (21 October), A1.

Weaver, M. J., Appleby, S. (Eds.), 1995. Being Right: Conservative Catholics in America. Indiana University Press, Bloomington.

Winner, L., 2000. Gen X revisited: a return to tradition? Christian Century 117 (8 November), 1146–1147.

98

RELIGION AND THE AWAKENING OF INDIGENOUS PEOPLE IN LATIN AMERICA

Cristián Parker Gumucio

Source: *Social Compass*, 49(1) (2002), 67–81.

The "awakening" of the indigenous people of Latin America raises the following question: is it accompanied by a religious revitalization and a return to ancestral beliefs and rituals? Religion is, indeed, present in protests and visible movements such as those in Mexico or Ecuador, but religion does not appear to be the principal factor or the deepest source of these movements. Thus, alongside the rapid expansion of evangelicals (especially Pentecostals) among the indigenous communities, we also observe the higher profile and the increased respect achieved by ancestral indigenous religious traditions. Elsewhere, intense missionary activity by various churches has contributed to the emergence of new indigenous leaders, and shamanic rituals function as a means of reaffirmation of ethnic identity and in support of the struggle to recover ancestral lands, a struggle which is acquiring a sacred character. The battle is political and ethnic; it is fought for recognition of indigenous rights, for the specificity of people and their communities, for their ancestral lands, and for their cultural expression. Belief is by no means uniform among indigenous peoples. But there is no doubt that religion is a part of the process of recovery of ethnic identity, even though it is under threat from globalization.

Emergence of the indigenous population

An increasingly globalized society is experiencing the re-emergence of ethnic groups, which is bringing about and/or exacerbating a number of conflicts (including armed conflicts) partly or wholly caused by ethnic issues. This has occurred on all continents; East Timor, the former Yugoslavia, Chechnya,

Afghanistan, the Middle East, Sri Lanka, the Punjab, Rwanda, Sudan, the Congo, South Africa and Ireland have seen serious conflict, and cases of serious latent conflict exist in Belgium, the Basque region, East Germany and in vast regions of the former Soviet Union. This phenomenon has also found expression in Latin America (Stavenhagen, 2000).

In the Latin American case we are not dealing with a simple imitation, but with an authentic regional movement, with its own themes and characteristics, begun before the political changeover in Eastern Europe.

The unique aspect of this movement, especially since the end of the 1960s, is the awakening of a claim from indigenous people, oppressed by the secular state, and involved in confrontation with all the Latin American nation-states which have colluded since the 19th century in the exclusion and marginalization of the indigenous population in various ways. This awakening of the voice of the indigenous, over time, and with some variation of focal points, has now occurred in almost every country of the continent.

The awakening of the Latin American indigenous has taken place over several decades, but has occupied a higher profile since the early 1990s. We can trace the phenomenon's roots back to the 1980s, when many new indigenous organizations appeared, linked to non-governmental organizations and churches. But the voice of the indigenous people rang out most clearly upon the 500th anniversary of the coming of the Conquerors to America (Columbus' landing). The entire Ibero-American world was organizing celebrations, led by Spain, which had decided to make the event a showpiece for its new foreign policy; but the indigenous movements raised their voices to proclaim "500 years of indigenous resistance" (Bengoa, 2000), spoiling some of the gaiety of "parties" "celebrating" the "Discovery of America".

Ethnic movements in Guatemala and Nicaragua began to rise in those countries along with political revolutionary processes. Mexico was on center stage as a result of the armed uprising in Chiapas. Colombia saw the rise of a guerrilla movement named after Quintin Lame, an indigenous Paez leader from the early 20th century. Two massive indigenous risings of national scope have taken place in Ecuador in the last two years (2000–2001). Bolivia gave birth to several important social movements, including the Aymara, the Quechua and the Guarani. These groups shook the government of their country, and managed to modify the ideas of the political parties regarding the indigenous question. Peru in recent years has been the site of annual assemblies of the Permanent Conference of the Indigenous People of Peru. In Chile, the Mapuche managed to reclaim hundreds of thousands of hectares of land, and in Brazil a strong movement has arisen on behalf of black and mulatto people, a population of many millions. And even though indigenous people are only 1 percent of the total population of Brazil, the recognition they have gained has helped the defense of their threatened territories in Amazonia.

The question which the sociology of religion now poses is this: have these major movements toward greater ethnic consciousness among aboriginal people in Indian America been accompanied by a religious awakening and a restoration of the ancient rituals and beliefs of Indian America?

Without pretending to furnish the results of an exhaustive investigation, it is possible nonetheless to attempt a response to the question, based upon a number of hypothetical assumptions regarding some of the empirical and historical evidence that has accumulated in recent years.

The indigenous uprising and religion

The powerful entrance onto the political scene of the indigenous movement in various Latin American countries during the 1990s marked a definitive turning point in the general debate concerning the State and democracy, and the indigenous assumed new roles of importance in the social and political life of those countries (Lee Van Cott, 1994). But they also introduced a new factor with regard to the religious groups of the continent.

The eruption of the indigenous movement in the region had very important underlying social and political causes. However, as we consider a sequence of events from the EZLN uprising in Chiapas in 1994, to the indigenous work stoppages which caused the government of Mahuad to fall in Ecuador (2000), religion appears as a profound source of strength, wielding undeniably great influence upon the reconstitution of ethnic identities and the formulation of ethnic claims and principles for the 21st century.

Greater visibility and greater respect gained for indigenous religious traditions has obviously made public opinion more aware of these matters. In March 2001, the sixth anniversary of the peace accords that had put an end to a drawn-out and genocidal civil war in Guatemala was observed. These accords had included a special agreement dealing with indigenous people, and in the commemorative gatherings, right beside high civil and religious authorities, Mayan priests appeared in a distinguished role. Nor is it strange any longer to see bulletins broadcast by national television networks concerning the activities of shamans and indigenous priests on the occasion of great celebrations and rituals such as those of Inti Raymi (Ecuador, Bolivia and Peru) or We Tripantu (Chile).

This new conferring of value upon indigenous religions is certainly accepted in the indigenous communities themselves. Despite the Conquest, despite cultural and religious domination, and despite the syncretism that still characterizes their religious expressions, these religions have begun to shake loose from various prejudices introduced by Christian missionaries, intended to cast aspersions upon their rituals and traditions, these last often characterized as "pagan" in the best of cases, or in the worst as "idolatrous" or "demonic".

During the first half of 2001 I undertook an inquiry among the Mapuche communities in southern Chile, in the Lafquenche communities of Tirúa,

Table 1 Religious group membership among the Mapuche.

Religious affiliation	No.	%
Catholic	144	40.9
Catholic/Mapuche	11	3.1
Mapuche	28	8.0
Evangelical	83	23.6
Adventist	34	9.7
Anglican	10	2.8
Believer, no religion	33	9.4
Non-believer	7	2.0
Atheist	2	0.6
Total	352	100.0

Source: Inquiry 2001—Tirúa/Chol-Chol/San Juan de la Costa VIII, IX and X Regions of Chile.

the Nagche communities of Chol-Chol, and the Huiliche communities of San Juan de la Costa. Table 1 sets out the findings as regards religious self-identification.

The smaller current percentage of Catholics will immediately be remarked as important (44 percent if we include those who admit that their Catholicism is syncretic) within a national population in which 76.7 percent of residents identified themselves as Catholics in the most recent (1992) census. But this is not really so surprising, since the same phenomenon is occurring frequently indeed in all the indigenous populations on the continent. What is interesting is that if we add up those who identify themselves as belonging to "the Mapuche religion" and then add further those who identify themselves as "Catholic and Mapuche", we get to 11 percent, a figure that is surprisingly high in view of the fact that the Mapuche religion is of the shamanic type, and is not institutional in character.

We are dealing here with regions that have been "evangelized" by Catholic and Anglican missions, as well as by pentecostal and adventist missionaries, areas where only 20 years ago no one would have dared admit in public that he or she belonged to the "Mapuche" religion.

In general, the higher visibility of indigenous rituals among the diverse religious practices found in towns and villages is a qualitative phenomenon, which indicates a new climate of respect and recognition for older traditions in many indigenous areas and regions, where we also encounter ways of expressing aboriginal faith and religion, which are in danger of extinction, if not already completely forgotten. Indigenous shamanism, at least, is being valued more highly because of its healing powers, and for its spiritual dimension amid new magico-religious currents, which recognize forms of action that no longer obey Western models.

The religious situation: between churches and indigenous people

The same range of problems—of social, economic and cultural marginalization of indigenous people—can be found today affecting every country of the Latin American continent. There are mappings of statistical information from various countries (Mexico, Guatemala, Colombia, Ecuador, Peru, Bolivia, Chile, Argentina) that show the areas in which the highest number of people in poverty (defined by a minimum income) is located, and which also show areas with the highest number of people of indigenous origin. Is it really surprising that these two mappings tend to coincide (Bengoa, 2000; Bastida, 2001)?

Similar situations persist in all regions. Indigenous people have had territories usurped by colonists and landholders, and recently by narcotics traffickers. The quality of the land for farming has deteriorated. Basic necessities are not obtainable: health, education, food and shelter. Finally the indigenous face constant physical and cultural aggression from various institutions, often aided by the State itself. In many cases they are victims of armed conflict carried on by regular army and paramilitary troops, as in Guatemala, Chiapas, Amazonia, Colombia and Peru, and then even their very survival is at stake.

In such a context, another phenomenon issuing from the religious point of view seems relevant: evangelical group membership has grown explosively, among pentecostalists, neo-pentecostalists and new churches. This has happened in areas in which Catholic influence was traditionally very great, but also in areas in which the earlier process of missions and evangelization had had less effect, or had been only superficial.

Most States have maintained a "pro-indigenous" policy which only sought the assimilation of the indigenous into the official culture. This unenlightened attitude was modified under pressure from the "Indianismo" of the 1990s, and during that period almost all Latin American nations recognized, legally and in constitutional terms, the rights of indigenous people.

The church and other international religious missions have also maintained an attitude which during many years could be characterized as wavering between paternalism and colonialism. However, this attitude has undergone change since the end of the 1960s, and the changes have been more marked toward the end of the 20th century.

During the 1970s, in the context of the renewal of the churches—especially following the stimulus provided by the Medellin (1968) and Puebla (1979) Conferences in favor of the "liberating" activities of Catholic missionaries in indigenous communities—respect for these activities increased, and soon after new efforts began at gaining entry into the heart of aboriginal indigenous movements. Notable cases include that of Monsignor Proaño in Riobamba, in Ecuador, and that of Monsignor Samuel Ruiz in the diocese of San Cristobal de las Casas (Chiapas). Also, at a very early stage, progressive Catholic leaders had organized the Guarani Farmers' Leagues in Paraguay.

Internationally based religious missions, including many of those whose mother church was in the US, penetrated into indigenous territories as if these were "mission lands", pagan lands that needed to be converted to the Gospel. Usually the methods of teaching and catechizing employed up until quite recent times—with marked ethnocentric bias—were not respectful of the unique character, habits and dress of the indigenous population. They acted as if "Christianization" were equivalent to "civilization", following a *tabula rasa* policy, which also in recent times has been violently rejected by the ethnic and indigenous movements.

In many cases Catholic missions resorted to such practices, justifying them with statements that were strongly biased in favor of "nationalism", and justifying their own positions as defenders of the traditional, "hispanic" Catholicism of the indigenous, which accordingly needed to be respected and defended against the menace of "foreign-izing protestantism" promoted by North American missionaries.

Along these lines indigenous communities have been both target and battlefield in the religious battle being fought today in a pluralized Latin American religious context (see *Social Compass* 45/3 [1998]), which is more and more distorted by a conflict between a Catholic Church which does not wish to lose its secular hegemony, and the evangelists who for several decades have been trying to steal it away from them.

All in all, the Churches did contribute to the organization of the indigenous, providing some training, and eventually training a cadre of capable leaders. It is also significant that in some cases Church mediation has helped settle armed conflicts in which the indigenous populations were the principal victims. The case of Guatemala is the best example of this; the actions of churches, especially the Catholic Church, were directed toward peaceful intervention, and the defense of human rights under attack in indigenous territories that had been turned into war zones.

New leadership—and a role for religion?

The activities of the churches contributed, in decisive fashion in all contexts and in all the indigenous territories of Latin America, to the training of new leaders. Missions to the indigenous territories are a phenomenon of long standing: they were part of the process of conquest from the very beginning, but became entangled in the early polemics regarding the kind of treatment that was to be given to the conquered indigenous people. Father Bartolomeo de las Casas (Bishop of Chiapas in the 16th century) and many followers even managed to bring their protest before the King, arguing in favor of just treatment for these creatures of God and subjects of the King who did not merit being enslaved or mistreated by the *encomenderos* (grant-holders of forced indigenous labor), and who shared with the Spanish the benefit of an equal dignity conferred by baptism.

Following the line of Las Casas and other defenders of Indians, the Catholic Church altered its policy with regard to missionaries under the influence of Vatican II (1962–1965). In fact, this development of policy had been in the works since the end of the 1960s, but during the decade of the 1970s it was realized with greater clarity that neo-colonial and ethnocentric principles had to be abandoned; those who based themselves on Liberation Theology were leaders in this effort.

The training of indigenous leaders in schools, convents and parishes of the Catholic Church—and also in protestant missions—would have important and surprising consequences for the development of ethnic consciousness.

Better schooling for young leaders makes them more aware, but at the same time fosters fundamentalist attitudes with regard to ethnic consciousness. Many young leaders become quite intolerant of Christian churches (Catholic, protestant, evangelical), accusing them of working to prolong the "religious and cultural colonialism of the West", and viewing evangelical activity as a weapon of colonialism. The parents of these leaders, on the other hand, tend to be more satisfied with things, accepting their own syncretic beliefs—mixtures of popular Catholicism, old rituals and ancestral beliefs—as the source of their identity, traditional and authentic.

The indigenous leadership has taken its lead from traditional political points of reference, and has taken upon itself greater autonomy. This is an alternative style of leadership, which does not seek personal power, but collective power, in order to empower the people, so that the leadership that arises would be focused on the community and in full solidarity with it. A significant percentage of indigenous leaders was trained, as we said, in the churches during the decades of the 1970s and 1980s, and now, in an effort toward achieving autonomy, they are working independently of religious institutions, although they know how to make use of their network of contacts when certain kinds of assistance or access to the power structure are strategic necessities.

The search for alternative leadership takes place outside any explicit religious inspiration, but oftentimes the influence of traditional religious authorities upon these leaders is not any less for all that.

During the second week of January 2000, some 25,000 indigenous people took over the city of Quito. Antonio Vargas was the indigenous leader thrust suddenly into the limelight, the President of the Triumvirate which led the uprising of military personnel and indigenous people on 21 January 2000, which deposed Jamil Mahuad in Ecuador. Vargas considered himself to be "spiritually" inspired in the performance of his mission.

Just as in the historic indigenous uprisings of the colonial epoch, in which shamans played an exemplary role in inspiring messianic anticolonial fervor, at the beginning of the 21st century once again the shamans and the religious are inspiring uprisings, though clearly in an effort to improve and to perfect democracy. Vargas, swarthy, short, with a sparse beard and bright black little eyes, was in the forefront in taking this responsibility, drawing strength from what he called his "spirituality". In an interview which took place during the year of his successes, he observed

> One must pay attention to the spiritual part, because sometimes we only focus on the folkloric part. The spiritual part let us know six months before what was going to happen. It told us, for example, that no one would die and that everything would be peaceful. And our discourse was always without violence. A wise man among my companions told me: "Antonio, when you take control, the leadership, you keep it until the end." I relaxed, I realized that I had relaxed when I went to talk to the generals. That was when I lost control of the movement, when I gave up a little power to the army, trusting them.

The military–indigenous alliance gathered in forces within civil society, among which were included those on the religious side. In fact, many religiously inspired indigenous groups supported the struggle of popular uprisings, as was the case with the Indigenous Church Association of Chimborazo, an evangelical church which distanced itself from its original North American mission and preaching, and began to reinterpret indigenous cosmologies in the light of a new reading of the Christian tradition. This group also took up a position in favor of political compromise, and recognition of the rights of indigenous people (Andrade, 2001).

All this indicates to us that the schooling and training given by the Churches have begun a process of maturation on behalf of an autonomous leadership which has in some cases has gone so far as to separate from original relationships with particular churches.

Ritual healing, the role of shamans, and the reaffirmation of ethnic identity

Despite the emergence of new leadership, it is important to underline that traditional indigenous authorities continue in power, and chief among them are the shamans and priests of the ancestral religion.

Ritual cures and healing in indigenous communities are basically employed not so much as a direct means of cultural resistance, but more as a means of reaffirmation of ethnic identity. Studies carried out among the Navajo of North America make it possible to affirm that ritual healing, considered as a form of political identity-creation, acts on three levels: it makes possible a representation of the indigenous identity in relation to Euro-American society; it permits communication among the various traditions of religious healing in Navajo society itself; and it transforms individual experience, reaffirming the dignity and self-respect proper to the Navajo (Csordas, 1999).

That which was observed among the Navajo may also be found in a large number of types of religious healing and cures among the indigenous communities of South America—for example among the Mapuche in Chile and Argentina. There, magico-religious techniques of shaman cures have been essentially based on syncretic versions of Christian rituals, both Catholic and evangelical. Ritual healing has presented an alternative to the limitations of Western professional medicine; it has given rise to a common ground of reaffirmation for shamanic power—the *machi*—in a ritual context. And it has made it possible for members of these communities to recognize themselves anew as Mapuche, in the sense that they now recognize these healing rituals as an authentic expression of their ethnic identities.

Studies carried out among the Mapuche who have migrated to a large metropolis such as Santiago de Chile (Curivil, 1999) show us that the ritual activities that are central to a Mapuche community, such as the "nguillatún", a ritual that must be performed in a consecrated space, or the "nguillatuwe", which must be carried out by a *machi* (Mapuche shaman) in a field in the middle of a city, constitute a fundamental part of the process of re-ethnification, that is the recovery of an ethnic identity even in the face of marginalization and social, racial and workplace segregation in the big city. In this way indigenous shamanism is renewed, even under unfavorable sociological conditions, and as far as possible from the original conditions under which the ritual was first performed, in rural communities in the south. But with this renewal, there comes also a possibility of renewing the path toward ethnic authenticity for people who have abandoned those rural communities, and who live under adverse conditions, though in the center of the highly modernized urban capitalist society.

Defense of shamanic activity confronted with global society

Shamanic activity in many indigenous towns, insofar as this activity is a focus of ethnocultural self-identification, is being threatened by many aspects of contemporary global culture. In this context, the market economy and religion appear as primary loci of conflict.

On one side, there are problems that arise within the religious camp, inasmuch as the vast majority of pentecostal–evangelical groups fan out into indigenous communities denouncing "witchcraft" and "superstition" involved in aboriginal shamanic activity, attacking in particular their "demonic" practices, which must be overcome by a "conversion to the Gospel" and to its official cult, administered by the evangelical pastor.

But loss of prestige for the shamans can also come from the "commercialization" of their cures and spells, produced by a market that has no fear of converting ancient traditional rituals into "brand-new" products for "magical and post-modern healing" in the typical style of New Age syncretisms, which will attempt to incorporate these traditions into their counter-culture of symbolic consumption.

It is a matter of the cultural politics of "folklorization" of the "indigenous" in order to sell them in a globalized tourist market. First one builds up the "grandeur of pre-Columbian culture", while at the same time one attempts to mask the reality of the indigenous people of the present day (which is less interesting). This allows Latin American countries to reconcile their celebration of the pre-Hispanic patrimony with continuing discrimination against Indians today. The guided tours of the "Maya Circuit" are offered to North Americans and Europeans as a stroll past beautiful beaches, up to ancient Mayan ruins, followed by a tequila margarita in a typical bar. One is invited to "plunge into the ancestral magico-religious traditions of the Indian people which have survived down through the centuries" (Duterme, 1998: 27–29).

In recent times shamans of the communes of the indigenous Tsachila nation, descended from the Chibchas, which inhabits the subtropical region of the Ecuadorian coast, decided to reclaim the culture they had had before experiencing a loss of prestige (Kintto, 1999). At the end of the 1990s, there appeared men called *chimberos* (in the popular dialect of that country this means "the false ones") who acted as go-betweens for tourists, introducing them to a number of indigenous shamans (something of which the Tsachila disapproved). The chimberos marketed the curative powers of a few shamans, receiving in return a percentage of the price of the cures. The shamans were even led to advertise themselves as "vegetalists" for marketing-related reasons.

In 1999, dozens of Tsachilas protested to local authorities, claiming that the practices of the chimberos were "misrepresenting the cultural roots of shamanism". Faced with these protests, the governor issued a personal appeal to those shamans who were commercializing their powers instead of providing spiritual leadership for the Tsachila nation, 1403 persons in all.

Governor Manuel Calazacon states that the attitude of the townspeople toward the chimberos is due to the fact that their culture is being threatened severely. "Western culture penetrates our society easily, because our territory is not on top of a mountain or deep in the forest, but is easily accessible", he explained.

Territories/lands, development and spiritual values

The problem of lands and aboriginal development rights has been transformed at the beginning of the 21st century into a key question as regards the mobilization of indigenous people.

Even today, indigenous people are confronted with a host of problems caused by the application of various development models—usually in accordance with a neo-liberal paradigm—which are alien to their vision of the world, to their values, and to their habits of self-government. Most of the conflicts that occur in the territories where indigenous people live are in reality struggles for control of natural resources, such as wood, minerals, petroleum and biodiversity.

The struggle of indigenous people to reconquer lands that in history were usurped through Western colonization (and which they pursue in order to preserve the quality of the environment, ecological quality and rich biodiversity within their habitat), is being carried on, in many cases, upon the basis of a profound world-view through which lands and nature itself possess sacred significance.

On the occasion of the Third World Trade Conference at the beginning of the year 2000 in Seattle (USA), a united front of indigenous organizations published a declaration as follows:

> We, the indigenous people of many regions of the world, have come to Seattle to express our concern at the way the World Trade Organization (WTO) is destroying *Mother Earth* and the cultural and biological diversity of which we are a part. Liberalization of commercial activity and export-oriented development, the dominant principles and policies promoted by the WTO, are having an extremely negative impact on the lives of indigenous people.
> (Seattle Declaration of Indigenous People, 2000; italics added)

Faced with the menace of non-sustainable investment in indigenous lands, commercialization of products and patents, of natural resources, both biological and genetic, within indigenous territories and communities, as well as possible abuses and manipulation of biotechnology, the declaration concluded

> The indigenous people, undoubtedly, are the ones most harmed by globalization and the policies of the WTO. Nonetheless, we believe we are the ones capable of offering viable alternatives to the dominant policy of economic growth, and to the export-oriented development model. Our lifestyles and our sustainable cultures, our *traditional wisdom*, our *cosmogonies*, our *spirituality*, our *principles of solidarity*, *neighborliness*, and *respect and reverence toward Mother Earth*, all of these are crucial in the search for a transformed society in which justice, equality, and sustainability may prevail.
> (Seattle Declaration of Indigenous People, 2000; italics added)

It is well known that Indo-American world-views are deeply rooted in a soil both sacred and mythic. Despite the prejudices of the West and of Western historical and scientific analysis, South American cultures continue living through peoples involved in meaningful processes which surged forth in the beginning from sacred events and beings (cf. Sullivan, 1988).

The concept of "earth" or "land" in the indigenous way of thinking is interwoven with mythic and sacred meanings. Starting from the various indigenous world-views, it is possible to experience multiple levels of existence in the world and multiple qualities of space. The richness of existence in these interconnected worlds cannot be captured in simple images. The most important thing is the fact that this multiplicity of spaces is in essence a manifestation of the path toward the meaning of existence in all its forms. In consequence, in this variety of spaces, human consciousness, enriched by the imagination, can enter into contact with many kinds of beings in their various forms. From this point of view, the world is "inhabited" by beings of many natures, with whom human beings can enter into contact. Nature is alive, and is far from being able to be considered as an inert "thing" which can be put on sale and purchased in a market.

The convergence of the indigenous movement and ecological movements (cf. Toledo, 1997) has to do with the ecological significance of the indigenous vision of the territories in which they live. But this very significance stems precisely from the sacred character which they attribute to nature, and to the beings who live within it (Davis and Ebbe, 1993).

In this respect some recent examples should be mentioned. In Imbabura a "sacred lake" lends strength to the indigenous organizations, and supports them as they struggle to defend their rights. In fact, one of the ecological projects promoted by the Ecuadorian indigenous people has to do with the cleanup and protection of Lake San Pablo, located in the province of Imbabura, some 50 km from Quito, Ecuador's capital. Indigenous groups converged on this place—Quechua and Cayambe, those who had venerated the lake as a mythical and religious site, where planting and harvest rites have been celebrated since before the time of the Incas.

In the vicinity of Lake San Pablo today there are 38 indigenous communities, comprising about 20,000 people, all dependent upon the lake for irrigation and domestic water use. Despite the cultural and economic importance of Lake San Pablo, its waters—which since time immemorial have given birth to many legends—have suffered from increasing contamination, and the level of lake water has even gone down. The causes are multiple: the woodlands around the lake have been destroyed; pasture land near the lake has been damaged by overgrazing, by burning of uncultivated land, by cultivation of land that is too steeply sloping, and by the indiscriminate use of agricultural chemicals; waste water and solid waste from too many residences, tourist attractions and factories have completed the process of contamination of the lake.

Faced with such problems, in October 2000 a Committee for the Defense and Sustainable Development of Lake San Pablo was established, counting among its members "green" organizations, and other social and cultural organizations of the region, including the Federation of Indigenous People and Farmers of Imbabura (FICI). The Committee is promoting a project for the Conservation and Sustainable Development of the Lake San Pablo Basin, which is intended to support the communities and organizations of the region, as they attempt to become active fighters for the preservation and rational development of Lake San Pablo. "We of the indigenous communities are pushing for a complete rehabilitation of the lake, because for us, ecology means an improvement in our quality of life, and of course we wish to save our traditional values", an indigenous leader has declared.

In Colombia, the U'wa achieved an important victory in 2001 over the management of Occidental Petroleum and the government of Colombia, when legal recognition was won of their rights over an important tract of land in the northeast of the country, traditionally held to be theirs. A recent resolution passed by the Colombian government, part of an agreement with U'wa leaders, increased the size of their legally recognized territory by 120,000 hectares. The total now comprises 220,275 hectares in the administrative regions of Boyacá, Norte de Santander, Santander and Arauca.

The negative environmental and social impact caused by these investment projects, aimed at lands that the indigenous people consider sacred, constitutes a serious threat to the physical and cultural survival of the people. In many countries in the region, prospecting and drilling for oil are accompanied by violations of human rights, and by corruption and violence.

> Upon the occasion of the recovery of a part of our lands, which you are formally granting to us today, we demand absolute respect for our decision to forbid absolutely any prospecting or drilling for oil in our traditional territories, whether this is inside or outside the area which has been legally recognized as ours,

declared Roberto Perez, president of the governing council of the U'wa, during the ceremony held to celebrate the creation of the Reserva (a preserve of indigenous territories).

In Chile large investments in hydroelectric dams on the Bio Bio River by the ENDESA company are now affecting many communities. Members of the Pehuenche indigenous group who live in the foothills area, and who have been resisting the flooding of their ancestral lands, are objecting to the project on the grounds that there are sacred cemeteries and sites necessary for the performance of religious rituals in the areas that would be affected—only one of many weighty reasons to oppose the project. Even though the company succeeded in creating a program of displacement of residents and resettlement elsewhere, there is still a section of the project that remains paralyzed because of the opposition of various families who refuse to abandon their sacred lands.

Perspectives on Indian syncretism

The central cultural question of today is located between two contradictory but mutually necessary tendencies: globalization and the persistence of local identities. The indigenous people, more than any other, are subjected to the full force of the tension that this contradiction produces.

However, when cultures have been deeply anchored in their regional and local contexts, it may be difficult to accept when the traditions do not survive completely intact (Portella, 2000). The correct concept of what is considered "authentic" is not the simple reproduction of elements from the past, but rather calls for a new interpretation of past and present elements, using as starting point the codes and requirements of the culture that belongs to the people we are dealing with. Our society has never known such a pace of change, or such major modifications to traditions. These have a great impact upon the process of social construction of ethnic identity and ethnic traditions.

Such has been the fate of religious codes in indigenous towns. As a result it is very difficult to find, today, traditional indigenous religionists who are "pure", in the sense of unaltered nuclei of the traditional pre-Columbian religions. What is more likely to be found is the result of processes of reinterpretation and syncretization, carried on over centuries, having sunk deeply into consciousness and constituting a basis for the working out of new syncretic religious models within indigenous cultures that are strongly influenced by processes of acculturation and modernization.

In other historical and sociopolitical contexts the relation between ethnic groups and religion has been articulated in various forms: in many cases American indigenous resistance against Spanish conquerors took on a pronounced messianic or even millenarian aspect (see Parker, 1996: 10–12); in other cases the relation has been one of a struggle for fundamental legitimation by extremist movements opposed to the West, as is the case with various Islamic fundamentalist movements.

Nothing indicates that as regards the current role that religion plays in the awakening of the indigenous towns of Latin America, we stand before a resurgence of millenarianism or fundamentalism. The processes of recovery of the ancient rituals and beliefs, occurring within a framework of new syncretisms connected to Christianity, appear to occur upon the basis of a process of rationalization related to the reconquest of an indigenous American sociological logic, not Western, but not necessarily anti-Western. The battle is political and ethnic, fought for the recognition of the rights of indigenous peoples, for the autonomy of their towns and their ancestral lands, and for their authentic cultural forms. This struggle attempts to resist the domination of global capitalism, which does not respect ethnic minorities. We are concerned here with a constructive project which points toward a multiethnic and multicultural democracy, in which religion forms a part of the global project without being the center of the interpretation of reality. It is not a matter of the recovery of a traditionalism at bottom deeply nostalgic, for which autochthonous religion would constitute a central component of pre-modern legitimation.

The diversity of religious forms found among the indigenous movements is also contradictory, and the religious camp is divided. Catholics, evangelicals, protestants, adventists and other movements compete for adherents in many communities. But priests of the ancient religion and indigenous shamans, in numbers that have been slowly but steadily increasing, still perform the rituals and sustain the magico-religious beliefs that are to some extent able to contribute to the reaffirmation of an authentic ethnic identity. But the old religions of the high pre-Columbian cultures (Andean or Mesoamerican), possessing esoteric, complex and paradoxical mythical, ritual and liturgical systems, can never be resuscitated. Still, in the collective imagination of Latin American indigenous peoples of the 21st century, a part of the teachings, beliefs and wisdom of their ancestors will continue to offer a path, an embracing vision, a form for understanding the nature of society, and the nature of a kind of healing and salvation that is different from the rationality of the Christian West. In all probability we stand before a slowly developing new syncretization of beliefs and rituals, and out of this process a variety of forms of expression of indigenous religiosity will emerge, sharing one characteristic: the discounting of aboriginal religions ridiculed as "pagan" or "demonic" will no longer be easily accepted, and in turn a tendency will arise toward their re-validation, each time in clearer form for new generations to come. In this manner religion will form a part of the process of recovery of an indigenous identity that is certainly menaced by the processes of globalization.

References

Andrade, Susana (2001) "Le réveil politique des Indiens protestants de l'Equateur". Paper delivered to the XXVI International Conference of the International Society for the Sociology of Religion ISSR, Ixtapan de la Sal, México, 20–24 August.

Bastida Muñoz, Mindahi C. (2001) *500 años de resistencia de los pueblos indios de México en la actualidad.* Toluca: Universidad Autónoma del Estado de México.

Bengoa, José (2000) *La emergencia indígena en América Latina.* Santiago: Fondo de Cultura Económica.

Csordas, Thomas J. (1999) "Ritual Healing and the Politics of Identity in Contemporary Navajo Society", *American Ethnologist* 26(1): 3–5.

Curivil, Ramón (1999) "Procesos de reetnificación de los Mapuches en Santiago", Tesis de Maestría en Ciencias Sociales, Universidad Academia de Humanismo Cristiano, Santiago, Chile.

Davis, Shelton H. and Ebbe, Katrinka (eds) (1993) *Traditional Knowledge and Sustainable Development*, Proceedings of a Conference held at the World Bank. Washington, DC: World Bank.

Duterme, Bernard (1998) *Indiens et Zapatistes, Mythes et réalités d'une rébellion en sursis*. Brussels: Luc Pire.

Kintto, Lucas (1999) "Ecuador. Los chamanes Tschilas reivindican su cultura", *Noticias en Espanol* (Global Information Network) 3 September.

Lee Van Cott, Donna (ed.) (1994) *Indigenous Peoples and Democracy in Latin America*. New York: St. Martin Press.

Parker, Cristián (1996) *Popular Religion and Modernization in Latin America: A Different Logic*. New York: Orbis.

Portella, Eduardo (2000) "Cultural Cloning or Hybrid Cultures?", *UNESCO Courrier* (April): 9.

Seattle Declaration of Indigenous People (2000) "La Declaración de Seattle de los Pueblos Indígenas. Tercera conferencia ministerial de la OMC", *Revista del Sur* 99–100 (January/February): 1–3.

Social Compass (1998) Issue entitled "Les transformations du champ religieux en Amérique latine/Religious Transformation in Latin America", Vol. 45(3).

Stavenhagen, Rodolfo (2000) "Les organisations indigènes: des acteurs émergents en Amérique latine", *Alternatives Sud* 7(2): 53–59.

Sullivan, Lawrence E. (1988) *Icanchu's Drum: An Orientation to Meaning in South American Religions*. New York and London: Macmillan.

Toledo, Victor (1997) "Todas las aguas. El subsuelo, las riberas, las tierras: Notas acerca de la (des) protección de to derechos indígenas sobre sus recursos naturales y contribución a una política pública de defensa", in *Anuario LIWEN*, Año 7, No. 4, pp. 36–79. Temuco, Chile: Centro de Estudios y Documentación Mapuche LIWEN.

99

HALF A CENTURY OF AFRICAN CHRISTIAN THEOLOGIES

Elements of the emerging agenda for the twenty-first century

Tinyiko Sam Maluleke

Source: *Journal of Theology for Southern Africa*, 99 (1997), 4–23.

The topic of this essay is an ambitious one; I cannot and do not mean to satisfy it. Proceeding topically rather than chronologically, I wish to highlight certain themes and sub-themes with which African theology has been occupied in the twentieth century. From these, I hope to sketch an outline of the emerging face of African Christian theologies in the next century.

I. Dynamism and innovation

From the early 1980s, calls for African theologies and African churches to either recognize the "paradigm shifts"[679]—which are occurring before their own eyes—or to effect some "paradigm shifts" themselves, have increased.[680]

More significantly, major works on African theology during the 1990s indicate that African Christian Theology will not be allowed to degenerate into an immutable museum ornament. It is a dynamic, growing, multifaceted and dialectic movement built diachronically and synchronically upon contextualization and constant introspection. Rightfully, the All Africa Conference of Churches (AACC) has taken a leading role in providing direction to the burgeoning suggestions for new forms of African theology and Christianity.[681]

One of my operating assumptions is that, in order for African theology to grow and effect meaningful paradigm shifts, a careful note of the ground already captured must be made. This may prevent an unbridled manufacturing of an infinite number of supposedly "new" and "projective" African theologies that are not thoroughly informed by what has been done before. Kwesi Dickson[682] makes the same point:

> "... the present stagnation may be accounted for by reference to the fact that recent discussants often seem to be unaware of past discussions on the subject. Again and again contributions made at conferences have not been such as to build upon the insights which have already been gained into the subject...."

Construction, innovation and contextualization in African theology/Christianity should not be left entirely in the hands of each generation of African theologians as if African theology was a frivolous and merely cerebral activity that is unconnected either to African Christian life or previous African theologies.[683]

For nearly half a century, Africans have attempted to articulate their own brands of Christian theologies consciously and deliberately. Generally this production has been ecumenical in nature, consultative, and in written form. Before the 1950s, African Christian theologies (henceforth referred to only as African theologies) had existed largely in less deliberate, consultative, ecumenical, organized, and written forms. Without discounting or doubting the value of unwritten forms of African Christian expressions prior to the 1950s, we shall focus on those articulations of African theologies since the 1950s.[684] Most of these have either been expressed as self-conscious theologies, or at least been documented as ecclesiastical, ecumenical or theological events. Yet even this apparently well-delimited focus on consciously constructed and written forms of African theology has become a vast and dynamic field that defies easy classification and simplistic analysis.

II. "Africa", "Africa Christianity" and "African theology"

I assume that the phenomena of African Christianity and African theology are so closely related that the two terms may be used interchangeably. African theologies exist because of African Christianities, and without African theologies we would not have any sustainable African Christianities. African Christianities are therefore expressions of African theology.

However, while these terms have become common today, their meaning (or even the fact that they have meaning) has not always been taken for granted. Oduyoye speaks of those who still question whether there ever can be "such an animal as African Christianity".[685] During our own times, African philosophers such as Anthony Appiah and Mudimbe also appear to be questioning the usefulness of the concept "Africa" beyond a reductionist conceptual level. Appiah seems to argue that while Africa is a physical and geographical reality with some shared experiences (such as slavery and colonialism), it is still precarious to believe that expressions such as "African

Christianity", "African philosophy", "African literature", or even simply "African", have intrinsic meaning. He also points out the irony of the fact that African intellectuals need the languages of their former colonial masters in order to construct "African literature", "African philosophy"—and, we may add, "African theology". However, as Oduyoye says, while African intellectuals debate whether "African Christianity" or "African theology" either exist or make sense at all, Africans everywhere are fashioning theologies and Christian forms with which they can identify.

It is important to be conscious of the vastness, divisions, affinities, and diversities of Africa. To that extent, there is some truth in the suggestion that "Africa" does not exist as such, but rather to the extent that people articulate a shape and form for the Africa they desire.[686] There are several other possible reasons why it took so long for the phrases "African Christianity" and "African theology" to be accepted as valid expressions. The most basic is simply the strong grip of the West's tutelage of African Christianities in the twentieth century. Neither westerners nor Africans risked a hasty qualification of the term "Christian" with "African". This was part of the reason why Africa was at one time full of "missions" as opposed to churches. The adjective "African" would only gradually and with care be placed alongside terms such as "church", "Christian", "Christian", or "theology".

"From 1854 onwards", we may confidently say, "West African Christian leaders, lay and clerical had felt and indeed initiated schemes to indigenize the Christian faith."[687] However, among many African theologians, the idea of African theology or an African Indigenous Theology[688] started rather tentatively.[689]

Less tentative was Bolaji Idowu's call for an indigenous African church with its own theology.[690] John Mbiti expresses concern over the use of the term "African theology" as a big banner under which could be placed "all sorts of articles and references . . . the substance [of which] often turns out to be advice on how African theology should be done. . . ."[691] For himself, however, Mbiti[692] confidently declares that "I will use the term 'African theology' . . . without apology or embarrassment, to mean theological reflection and expression by African Christians."[693] According to Mbiti, the chief yardstick for determining the validity of any Christian theology purporting to be African is its "Biblical basis".[694] For him "nothing can substitute for the Bible". For this reason, Mbiti has tended to be suspicious (to say the least) of what he sees as "theological debates. . . . propagated without full or clear grounding". Such theologies would include "theologies of liberation", the moratorium debate of the 1970s, and South African Black theology—which he sees as "primarily [a] ready-made European theology turned into a consumption commodity for Africans."[695]

We can thus see that even after the term "African theology" and/or "African Christianity" had found general acceptance, the debate on the sources and criteria for truly African and truly Christian theology has continued to our times. Henry Okullu attempts to cut through the arduous process of debate about the criteria and sources of African theology:[696]

"... when we are looking for African theology we should go first to the fields, to the village church, to the village church, to Christian homes to listen to those spontaneously uttered prayers before people go to bed. We should go to the schools, to the frontiers where traditional religions meet with Christianity. We must listen to the throbbing drumbeats and the clapping of hands accompanying the impromptu singing in the independent churches ... Everywhere in Africa things are happening. Christians are talking, singing, preaching, writing, arguing, praying, discussing. Can it be that all this is an empty show? It is impossible. This then is African theology."

III. The wide-ranging agenda and tasks of African theology: enabling the church, articulating African Christianity

The more basic issue that caused differences in degrees of acceptance of the term "African theology" was and still is the use for which African theology is constructed. That African Christian theology ought to be at the service of the church in Africa is seldom in doubt. In other words, its chief task is that of enabling the church to develop her own theologies so that she may cease depending on "prefabricated theology, liturgies and traditions,"[697] to be "not an exotic but a plant become indigenous to the soil."[698] Thus from the earliest times, written African theology was inspired by the conviction that "the opportunity for evangelism has never been greater ... but it will take a church which is alive and vigorous"[699] to muse of such an opportunity. While this basic church-enabling task of African theology has never been seriously disputed, other voices within African theology, at least in recent times, have called for theologies that are more critical of both received traditions within the church and of the church itself—enabling the church to be both prophetic and self-critical. One of the early criticisms leveled against the then emerging African theology was that it threatened the catholicity of both the global church and Christian theology. The response of Kwesi Dickson[700] to this criticism is one of the most lucid offered by an African theologian in defense of African theology.[701] Yet, as indicated above, African theology has from the 1950s on always been connected to the (African) church. To that extent, we could say that it has largely been church theology done by church people for the sake of the church and its missionary task. It was by no accident, therefore, that issues of selfhood and the moratorium have loomed large in the African theological agenda. Incidentally, the questions of (in)dependence and ownership inherent in the moratorium debates do connect to issues of negritude, "African identity", and inculturation.

In connection with African theology's church-enabling task, we can and should inquire about the form and shape of the African church or African Christianities which African theology was meant to enable and bring about. Was it (and is it) the whole Christian church in Africa? What visions of the church should and do inspire African theology? The church is not the sole and primary subject of God's mission. It is itself a product of God's mission and that mission encompasses more than the churches we see and dream about. African theology may therefore need to explore ways in which to speak not only to, about, and for the church, but for the larger African society. After all, the church, in some parts of Africa at least, has grown to be one of the important players in society—sometimes too important a player. The Christian theology of Africa does, therefore, almost by definition, have a public function beyond its magisterial one. This means that it may have to do and articulate things that are not always comforting or acceptable to (sections of) the African church. South African Black theology has certainly fulfilled this particular task, because, according to Mosala:[702]

> "... it [Black theology] has never been co-opted by the Establishment. No church has ever officially affirmed black theology as a legitimate and correct way of doing theology in South Africa. Not even the South African Council of Churches has given official recognition to black theology."

What cannot be denied, however, is that by and large, church and theology have been related in Africa. Even South African Black theology originated and flourished in church caucuses, movements, and organizations.[703] Indeed, the bulk of Africa's ecumenical and theological consultations have been initiated by churches or church organizations and Christian councils.[704] However, all is not well in the "African church" itself. It faces challenges such as "denominationalism and religious competitiveness,"[705] the reduction of Africa into a "dumping ground" for curious forms of North-American Charismatic and Pentecostal groups, the rise of church independentism and the concomitant decline in "historic mission church membership",[706] growing urbanization,[707] as well the cultural, political, economic, sexual, and ecclesiastical oppression of African women.[708]

IV. Inculturation issues

African culture and African Traditional religions (ATRs) have long been acknowledged as the womb out of which African Christian theology must be born. From various fronts, African Christians insisted that the church of Africa and its theology must bear an African stamp. This insistence went beyond theological and ecclesiastical matters as other African thinkers also attempted to construct "African philosophy", "African literature", "African art", and "African architecture". The question we asked earlier about Africa, African Christianity, and African theology can and has indeed been asked of African culture and ATRs, namely: "are there such animals?" Given the vastness and diversity of the continent's peoples, this is justifiable. However, African church leaders and theologians have not allowed this question to dampen their spirits. Unlike European imperial historians, explorers, and missionaries of the previous centuries, African theologians have generally been wary of generalizations about "Africa" and African culture. Special efforts have been made to speak in contextualized and specified terms, such as "the Akan Doctrine of God", "the image of God among the Sotho-Tswana", "Oludumare", and "West African Christianity". In her book on African women and patriarchy, Oduyoye[709] is at pains to demonstrate that the primary context of her reflections is the Akan of Ghana and the Yoruba of Nigeria. Even Mbiti, who has been accused of making generalizations and reductions about "Africa", is careful to contextualize his research and findings in terms of tribes—at least in his work *Concepts of God in Africa*. Generalizations are still made, but mostly on the basis of well-focused contexts of research. In that way, therefore, serious attempts have been made to ensure that the terms ATRs have not been allowed to degenerate into meaningless generalizations and clichés.

However, references to both African Traditional Religions and to African culture remained a hazardous exercise in African theological construction. It has been the source of much tension, both within and without African theology. The central bone of contention may be summarized this way: African Christian theology needs to decide not only how to refer to African culture and ATRs but to carefully weigh the objectives of such references. Various proposals have been made. Those who advocate the position that both African culture and ATRs are part of the *praeparatio evangelica* have been highly critical of the two. Many missionary councils have wholly condemned ATRs as something to be converted from.[710]

Scholars like Bediako and Turner actually argue that the "phenomenal growth" of Christianity in Africa cannot be understood without reference to ATRs as an excellent preparation for the gospel. However, the granting of *praeparatio evangelica* status to ATRs and African culture may be a veiled refusal to accept the latter on its own terms.[711] This is the theological practice which Okot p'Bitek characterized in 1970 as "intellectual smuggling". Thus, other African theologians, such as Setiloane, Christian Gaba, Bolaji Idowu, and Samuel Kibicho, have called for the suspension of any evangelical or "missionary" motives when African theology refers to ATRs. In any case, it is probably bad research methodology to mix what purports to be objective research with a hidden proselytizing agenda. If ATRs are such a fertile ground waiting to be "fulfilled" by Christianity, other African theologians have asked, why are ATRs so resilient? Indeed, some African thinkers, both Christian and non-Christian, have argued that, not only has Christianity brought nothing "new", but that ATRs are "superior" to Christianity. These types of assertions have greatly troubled some African Christian theologians—especially Evangelicals, who tend to feel that if the theology being constructed intends to be Christian theology, ATRs should not be viewed as equal to Christianity, let alone "superior".[712]

What this debate demonstrates rather clearly, however, is that theological reference to ATRs and African culture comes at a price—as with other religions, ATRs must be taken seriously in their own right, beyond the *praeparatio evangelica* framework. Some among the first generation of African theological writers made admirable attempts to take ATRs seriously, in their own terms, without relinquishing their own belief in the "superiority" of Christianity. These are examples worthy of being followed. In fact, it is possible to argue that the increasingly pluralistic context in Africa demands that we "listen" to other religions more carefully and more respectfully, without ceasing to be committed Christians ourselves and yet without a hidden evangelistic motive. We should, in the words of the late David Bosch:[713]

> "... Regard our involvement in dialogue and mission as an adventure [and be] prepared to take risks... Anticipating surprises as the Spirit guides us into fuller understanding. This is not opting for agnosticism, but for humility. It is, however, a bold humility—or a humble boldness. We know only in part, but we do know. And we believe that the faith we profess is both true and just, and should be proclaimed. We do this, however, not as judges or lawyers, but as witnesses; not as soldiers, but as envoys of peace; not as high-pressure salespersons, but as ambassadors of the Servant Lord."

1. Christianisation or Africanisation?

Kwame Bediako has identified as a distinct but no longer crucial emphasis in African theology what he calls "the Christianisation of the African past". This task, he argues, served its valuable purpose of providing Africans with "cultural continuity", which in turn helps to clarify African Christian identity. But it is now a task whose time has passed. Therefore, Bediako is concerned when African theologians appear unable to transcend their African past, so that it continues to dictate an agenda for the present. Bediako (1992) almost blames African theologians' preoccupation with identity issues on eighteenth and nineteenth century European perceptions of Africans, based on the slave-trade. It is to this legacy that African theologians are supposed to be reacting when they harp on past traditions and religions. My feeling is that this may be a simplistic view of African theology's reference to African traditions and the African past. To view it as a "tendency" from which African theology is supposed to graduate may be shortsighted.

What is needed now, Bediako argues, is the Africanization of Africa's Christian present.[714] Without unquestioningly accepting Bediako's reduction of decades of African theologies into a "quest for Christianizing the African past", he puts his finger on an element that provides a fruitful angle into the wide-ranging agenda of African theology during the past forty years. But, "Christianizing the African past" is only one perspective on the agenda of African theology, and it is therefore reductionistic to analyze, evaluate, and classify African theologians mainly and only on this criteria—which is virtually what Bediako does.[715] Juxtaposing Christianization and Africanization appears to rest on too rigid a separation between that which is Christian and that which is African. Besides, many African theologians understood and still understand themselves to be "Africanizing" Christianity when they appear to be "Christianizing" their past and vice versa! To posit the Africanization of Christianity as the new task facing African theology may not, in reality, be as groundbreaking as it appears. For African Christian theologians, the two processes—Christianization and Africanization—have not and cannot be artificially separated.

2. Beyond Christian theology

There is a deep sense in which African theology has never been just Christian theology. From its earliest times, written African theology has always sought, not merely to dialogue with ATRs and African culture, but also to make sense of the complex world of ATRs.[716] Strictly speaking, therefore, there has been, up to now, no such thing as a purely "African Christian theology". Therefore, the majority of African theologians have not been highly concerned with a specifically "African Christian identity" either for themselves or for the church. Is this a weakness? Bediako and probably other evangelical theologians seem to think so. Therefore, a significant concern in his theology is the quest for a truly Christian African identity. However, it is possible to see the non-Christian concern as a sign of realism and maturity. African theology has always been inter-religious, seeking to be more than a proselytizing theology without denigrating Christianity. In other words, it is with good reason that African Christian theologians have had to ask themselves and to be asked by others "why do we continue to seek to convert to Christianity the devotees of African traditional religion?"[717] This is a crucial question for all African theologies as we move into the twenty-first century. It seems to me that we will have to redefine the role of our theologies beyond seeking either to "convert" unreached Africans or support those who carry out such a task. For himself, Setiloane answers this question thus:[718]

> "I am like someone who has been bewitched, and I find it difficult to shake off the Christian witchcraft with which I have been

captivated. I cannot say I necessarily like where I am. Second, I rationalize my position by taking the view that to be Christian I do not have to endorse every detail of western theology."

There may be some leads for African theology to follow in our times from this. Will it be possible to do exclusively Christian African theology—anymore than it was possible for the first generation of African theologians? I doubt it. If anything, the growing plural situation in Africa demands an even broader and more rigorous inter-religious approach. African Christian theologians and their churches have to learn new ways of speaking to and relating to other religious people. We have to listen anew to the critiques that have been leveled against African Christian theology by (apparently) non-Christian Africans such as P'Bitek and others.[719] This listening and dialogue must not be done on a basis of a rigid separation between "African Christian" theologians/intellectuals as opposed to "non-Christian African" intellectuals—as Bediako sometimes seems to imply.[720] In reality, such a distinction is, strictly speaking, very difficult to sustain. There is, therefore, a sense in which African theology, even African Christian theology can only be truly African if it abandons artificial identity boundaries—including the tag "Christian" when and where it is used merely as a boundary marker.

3. The Bible

As with ATRs and other aspects of African culture, the Bible has enjoyed a respected status and place in African theology. "Any viable theology must and should have a biblical basis,"[721] Mbiti declares. Similarly, Fashole-Luke declares that "the Bible is the basic and a primary source for the development of African Christian Theology."[722] To underscore the significance of the Bible in the construction of African theology, Mbiti also says:[723]

> "Nothing can substitute for the Bible. However much African cultural-religious background may be close to the biblical world, we have to guard against references like "the hitherto unwritten African Old Testament" or sentiments that see final revelation of God in the African religious heritage."

We have already mentioned that Mbiti's basic criticism of Black and Latin American liberation theologies has been that these "theological debates have been propagated without full Biblical grounding." However, even those who, according to Mbiti, made exaggerated connections between the Bible and African heritage still underscore the significance of the Bible in African theology. The very fact that theologians felt the need to make such outrageous connections between the world of the Bible and the African world is proof of the esteem with which the Bible was held. The emerging African

Feminist or Womanist theology has also underscored the importance of the Bible. The very titles of some of the books on African Feminism emphasize this reality: *Talitha, qumi, Who Will Roll Away the Stone* and *The will to Arise*.

What has, in my opinion, been lacking is a vigorous debate on biblical hermeneutics akin to the vigorous debate that African (and non-African) theologians have held on culture, politics, and ATRs. In fact, for a long time the very notion of "biblical hermeneutics" would not be mentioned even by trained biblical scholars such as Mbiti. Instead, it is the authority of the vernacular Bibles that seems to be emphasized.[724] It was almost as if some of these theologians were afraid to alert African Christians to the fact that the Bible can and needs to be interpreted. Those who attempted to interpret the Bible creatively and boldly would be accused of extravagance, as we have illustrated above. Indeed, "fidelity to the Bible" or "biblical grounding" have remained the chief control mechanisms with which to regulate the pace and scope of African theology particularly in its reference to socio-political liberation and to ATRs.

Unfortunately, this has led to a situation in which, throughout Africa, the Bible has been and continues to be absolutized: it is one of the oracles that we consult for instant solutions and responses.[725] What makes the situation worse is that any unconventional reading of the Bible quickly earns one the charge of not being respectful of the authority of scripture. There are other socio-religious reasons for the almost fanatical attachment to the Bible—especially in Protestant Africa. Bereft of the rituals and symbols of ATRs, Roman Catholicism, and African Independentism, African Protestants have nothing but the Bible—*sola scriptura*. Once their attachment to "the big black book" is attacked they have nothing else to hold onto. However, on the whole, and in actual practice, African Christians are far more innovative and subversive in their appropriation of the Bible that they appear. Developments within South African Black theology, Latin American-type liberation theologies and African theology in the area of Biblical hermeneutics since the early eighties give us hope.[726] Here attempts are being made not only to develop creative Biblical hermeneutic methods, but also to observe and analyze the manner in which African Christians "read" and view the Bible.

In an illuminating article, Nthamburi and Waruta propose a set of common themes that would characterize the Biblical hermeneutics of African Christians:[727] a quest for salvation/healing and wholeness, a keen awareness of human alienation, an appreciation of God's promise to "put things right", a desire to know how to deal with the spirit world, attaching importance to initiation rites, an awareness of God's advocacy for the down-trodden, a sense of belonging in and to a visible community, commitment to social morality, and an intense concern for death and life beyond it. The biblical hermeneutical "principles" of South African Black theology could be summarized in this way: a "suspicious" and critical view of the status, contents, and use of the Bible, a commitment to a materialist reading of the Bible ("behind the text"), a commitment to the cultural struggles of black workers and women, and finally a view of the Bible as (or a need for it to become) a "weapon of struggle" in the hands of blacks, workers, and women.

4. Rethinking distinctions within African theologies

As with the Bible and African Culture, socio-economic and political issues have been on the agenda of African theology, especially what has been termed the African theology of liberation and South African Black theology. However, as we shall see in the next section, the conventional distinctions of "Black" from "African" theologies as "siblings", "distant cousins", "old guard", or "new guard",[728] "soul mates or antagonists",[729] theologies of "inculturation and liberation"[730] are no longer adequate. They do not sufficiently account for either the supposed similarities, or differences between the various, dynamic, and emerging strands of African theologies. With the changing ideological map of the world and the sweeping changes on the African continent itself, the agendas of what has been termed "African theologies of inculturation" as opposed to "African theologies of liberation" plus South African Black theology are moving closer together.[731] Having been cautious to speak about "African culture"—due probably to the apartheid state's manipulation of African culture into the Bantustan system—South African Black theologians are now beginning to speak more freely about culture.[732] This is illustrated by the increasing references being made to the concept of ubuntu (African personhood) in numerous South African intellectual debates.

The coming together of agendas of African theologies does not, and should not, be interpreted to mean that some forms of these theologies are becoming redundant and are about to be phase out. This is a common, hasty judgment often made in the zeal to construct ever and more definitive African theologies or theological paradigms. First generation African theologians responded to the charge that African theology—and calls for the selfhood of the African Church—were a threat to Christian catholicity, by debunking the myth of a uniform and universal theology. In like manner, we must respond to those who are either trying to exaggerate similarities between various African theologies, or to replace all previous African theologies with one all-encompassing theological paradigm, by indicating that African Christianity need not have "one" Christian theology in order to be valid and authentic.

What the coming together of different agendas does mean is that we can no longer rigidly separate the various African theologies from one another. The established "cleavages" of African theologies are, furthermore, no longer an adequate indication of the variety and lively ferment that is taking place within African Christianity and between African Christian theologies. So we have to begin to "speak" and "do" African theology differently; in more dialogical, consultative, and open-ended ways. I now sketch a few emerging models of African theology. These merely illustrate some new currents, and are by no means comprehensive. I regard these new currents as indicators of the possible directions into which African theologies will move in future.

V. Emerging theologies

1. Theologies of the AICs

A few scholars deserve special mention for their pioneering role in the irruption of AIC studies and the subsequent exposure of the significance of these churches for African Christianity and African theology: Bengt Sundkler, who wrote one of the earliest in-depth studies of AICs,[733] Christian Baeta,[734] David Barrett,[735] Martinus Daneel,[736] and Harold Turner.[737] Following the work of these scholars, a flood of theses and books on AICs has occurred.[738] The basic proposal of many AIC "theologians" is that the praxis of these churches must now be regarded not only as the best illustration of African Christianity, but also as "enacted", "oral", or "narrative" African theology—a type of theology that is no less valid than written African theologies, they would add. In this way, AICs are adding to and becoming a facet of African theology at one and the same time. Furthermore, the numerical growth of these churches[739] means that they have, in many parts of Africa, become, the mainline churches.

These churches, together with similar Christian movements among other primal societies may indeed be seen as the fifth major Christian church type, after the Eastern Orthodox Churches, the Roman Catholic Church, the Protestant Reformation, and the Pentecostal Churches.[740]

African theologies will no longer be able to ignore or dismiss the theological significance of the AICs in African Christianity. However, these churches must neither be romanticized nor studied in isolation from other African churches—including the so-called "mainline churches". In the same way that an African theology based only on a reference to mainline churches is inadequate, so too will any African theology based exclusively on African independent churches.

The tendency to regard AICs as the most authentic, if not as the only authentic African churches, has often created some unhealthy theological rivalry—notably between theologians rather than African Christians—wherein AIC praxis is supposed to be more African, more grassroots-based, more local, and more genuine than so-called written African theologies. I have found such distinctions and theological rivalries to be generally unreliable and artificial—at least in the South African context.[741] The issues are further complicated by the fact that, by and large, authoritative AIC scholars in the twentieth century have been overwhelmingly white (missionaries), with

Africans themselves taking a back seat. But African silence on AICs may be a loaded and eloquent one, needing to be decoded and reflected upon. The white missionary domination of AIC studies may be attributable to the fact that the emergence of AICs, almost without exception, was initially viewed as a "problem", "reflection", or "failure" of missionary work. In many colonial African countries, AICs were supposed to either be political movements (Ethiopianism) or ecclesiastical movements with a political agenda. The call for a distinction between African Christianity, on the one hand, and literature on African Christianity on the other,[742] may help clarify here. Reflection and research on AICs, however excellent and authoritative, must never be equated with the actual praxis of AICs. Yet at the end of the day no serious African theology can ignore either the studies mentioned or the African Christianities displayed in AICs—for research and reality always mirror one another, albeit imperfectly.

2. *African charismatic/evangelical theology*

Not only is African Christianity generally evangelical, if not Pentecostalist in orientation, but there is a sizable body of literature and events that could be said to be representative of a theological strand of African theology. We remember, without necessarily discussing it, the debate between Byang Kato's evangelical and "biblical" theology and John Mbiti's alleged "universalist" theology in the 1970s.[743]

Without joining this debate we need to recognize that it demonstrated the existence of a different theological orientation from that which we normally assume when we speak of African theology. All over Africa, evangelicals exist in organized and confessional communities. They are, of course, no less heterogeneous in theological outlook than "ecumenical" African Christians. Within South Africa, one may think of Ray McCauley's Rhema Church and its affiliates, Michael Cassidy's Africa Enterprise, and a grouping which has until recently been called "the Concerned Evangelicals". We must take note of a movement such as the Pan African Leadership Assembly (PACLA).[744] Indeed, there have been tensions and probably justifiable suspicions between PACLA and the AACC,[745] and tensions remain between many sectors of evangelicalism and ecumenism all over Africa. But the twenty-first century will not allow us to either ignore or smooth these over. One of the challenges we face, is to seek out all expressions of African theology and Christianity, however inadequate and suspicious, so that we may expose them to serious and dialogical theological reflection. I am not calling for superficial confessional and theological unities. We are better off without those, even if we suffer the terrible situation of denominationalism. My feeling is that in as much as we have seen tensions between evangelicals and ecumenicals in Africa, there are also cases of solidarity in action and theological dialogue between these groups in many African countries. These may serve as a framework for further theological dialogue and partnership. At the end of the day, African theology may be the richer for it.

3. *Translation theologies*

Elsewhere,[746] I have linked translation theologies to the names of Lamin Sanneh[747] and Kwame Bediako.[748] This, however, must not be taken to mean that Sanneh and Bediako present us with exactly the same agenda. Both of them are important, innovative voices whose thinking bear significant implications for African theology. In a series of works spanning a decade and culminating in his *Translating the Message*, Lamin Sanneh has mounted a passionate argument in defense of both African Christianity and the twentieth century missionary enterprise.[749] The gist of his argument is that the clue to the tremendous growth of African Christianity during this century was the logic of the translatability of the Christian message or gospel into African vernacular languages. This is signified most potently in the historic necessity of translating the Bible into vernacular languages. It is this translatability of the Gospel rather than the agency of missionaries that accounts for African Christianity. Therefore, focus must shift from a preoccupation with missionary omissions and the supposed link between Christianity and colonialism to the "heart of the matter", namely gospel translatability.

Bediako shares with Sanneh the conviction that it is the translatability of the gospel more than anything else that made large parts of Africa so vastly Christian. He therefore argues that African Christians and theologians alike must let the gospel speak to the African situation, "in its own right". For this reason Bediako is highly critical of a section of African theologians who insist on assuming that Christianity is foreign to Africa almost as a fundamental datum. Since the gospel is essentially translatable, it no longer makes sense to speak of Christianity as "foreign"; hence he confidently calls African Christianity a "non-western" religion. Bediako admits that the task of African theology is not finished simply because the gospel is translatable. But its essential task is to assist African Christians, theologians, and non-Christian intellectuals alike to exorcise the phantom foreignness of Christianity. While understanding it, Bediako sees African theology's decadeslong preoccupation with both the foreignness of Christianity and the African past as ultimately no longer necessary.

The boldness and projectiveness of Bediako and Sanneh's proposals are indisputable. But their reliance on dubious distinctions (e.g. gospel versus Christianity) and equations (e.g. Bible equals Word of God) are a serious drawback.[750] Also, the translatability of the gospel does not eliminate the significance of the role of the missionary enterprise or colonialism. While the gospel may indeed be eminently translatable, human intervention can affect the pace and quality of such translation—even arresting it into all sorts of orthodoxies.

4. *African feminist/womanist theologies*

We have seen an explosion of African women's theological events, organizations and publications since the mid-eighties. In reality, women's issues have been on the agenda of such organizations as the Ecumenical Association of Third World Theologians (EATWOT), the AACC, local Christian councils, and in para-church organizations since the early 1980s. However, it is a serious indictment of African male theologies that women's issues have not received immediate and unreserved acceptance.

Within South Africa, the first feminist conference that was predominantly black, was held at Hammanskraal in 1984; immediately followed by a predominantly white feminist conference at the University of South Africa. The Hammanskraal conference noted that, "whereas women form the majority of the oppressed, we note with regret that Black theology has not taken women seriously, but has seen theology as a male domain."[751] Participants in a Black theology conference held in Cape Town that same year concurred, albeit cautiously, in their final statement: "There are evidently structures oppressive of women inherent in both the Black community and the Church."[752] From these tentative beginnings African Feminist/Womanist theology has grown in South Africa.[753] Continentally and internationally one of the significant catalysts for African Feminist/Womanist theology was EATWOT. From its inception, EATWOT has always had a strong contingent of women in its ranks. But the women felt that "our voices were not being heard, although we were visible enough . . . We demanded to be heard." The result was the creation within EATWOT of a Women's Commission.[754] Within the World Council of Churches (WCC), Oduyoye[755] notes that "it took seven years from its founding for the WCC to establish a department to deal with the issue of cooperation of women and men in church and society"—in the establishment of a Department of Cooperation of Men and Women in Church and Society. Special note must be taken of the WCC's "Decade of Churches in Solidarity with Women", which officially ended in August 1998. Some of the "target areas agreed upon [for the Decade] in 1987 were church teachings about women, women and poverty, women and racism, and violence against women."[756] These ecumenical conferences and events have resulted in chains of local consultations, events, and publications all over the world. A significant consultation of Third World Women took place under the auspices of EATWOT in 1986 at Oaxtepec, Mexico. One of the results of this event was the publication of *With Passion and Compassion*. On the African continent, the Circle of Concerned Women in Theology, as well as its Biennial Institute of African Women in Religion and Culture, was established in 1989 in Accra, Ghana.[757] Some of the papers read at the Accra meeting were published in the book *The Will to Arise*. Since then several regional circles have been formed. One specific objective of the circles has been the production of African feminist literature. More recently, the circle has produced the book *Groaning in Faith*.[758] However, it would be a mistake to limit the influence of the Circles, EATWOT, the WCC, or local Christian councils to publications linked directly to their consultations. What these organizations have managed to do is to create space for Feminist/Womanist theology to grow and blossom, not only in Africa but in the wider Third World.

One of the most peculiarly African publications on Feminist theology is Mercy Oduyoye's recent work *Daughters of Anowa*. Whereas Black and African theologies have for the past half-century argued for the validity of African Christianities and the legitimacy of African culture, African Feminist/Womanist theology is charting a new way. This theology is mounting a critique of both African culture and African Christianity in ways that previous African theologies have not been able to do. From these theologies, we may learn how to be truly African and yet critical of aspects of African culture. African womanist theologians are teaching us how to criticize African culture without denigrating it, showing us that the one does and should not necessarily lead to the other. My prediction is that the twenty-first century is going to produce an even more gendered African theology. All theologians and African churches will be well advised to begin to take heed.

5. *Theologies of reconstruction*

Leading the pack in the theologies of reconstruction are Kenya's Jesse Mugambi[759] and South Africa's Charles Villa-Vicencio.[760] Although Villa-Vicencio's work was published first,[761] Mugambi had already been propagating the idea of a Theology of Reconstruction in 1990 in the context of AACC consultations.[762] It was, of course, Gorbachev's "*perestroika*" (reconstruction), which led to the break-up of the old USSR, which helped to popularize the notion of "reconstruction". For Mugambi, both the inculturation and liberation paradigms within which African theologies had been undertaken were no longer adequate frameworks for doing African theology after the cold war. Both inculturation and liberation responded to a situation of ecclesiastical and colonial bondage. In the place of the inculturation-liberation paradigm, which was, according to Mugambi, mainly "reactive", we should install a "pro-active" theology of reconstruction. Mugambi's originality lies in that, instead of calling for the ascendancy of liberation over inculturation or vice-versa (a "game" well-rehearsed in African theologies), he calls for an innovative transcendence of both. For this part, Villa-Vicencio appeals for a post cold-war (African) theology to engage in serious dialogue with democracy, human rights, lawmaking, nation-building, and economics in order to ensure that these do indeed improve the quality of human life.

My main critique of both Mugambi and Villa-Vicencio is in their assumption that the end of the "cold war" has immediate significance for ordinary Africans and that the so-called "New World Order" is truly "new" and truly "orderly" for Africans. Yet, as Mugambi himself rightly points out, Africa's problems of poverty, war, dictatorships, and American bully-boy tactics are unlikely to decrease. In fact, the New World Order is not only likely to relegate Africa into a "fourth world" but it will also impose its own prescriptions on African countries. One such prescription is "democracy" or its semblance. I am also critical of the fact that both Mugambi and Villa-Vicencio appear to minimize the value of previous African theologies of inculturation and liberation. Formations such as EATWOT and l'Association oecuménique des théologiens africains (AOTA) in Francophone Africa have done a tremendous amount of theological reflection and construction. Weaknesses notwithstanding, twenty-first century African theologies cannot afford to simply abandon them. We must look for ways in which to move on without despising what has already been achieved. Otherwise we might think we have progressed forward when in reality we have moved backwards.

Concluding remarks

Firstly, I want to restate my basic thesis, the contours of the emerging face of the twenty-first century African theologies must be sought in a thorough grasp of the ground captured so far, plus a keen awareness of new and emerging currents. African theologies are already reassessing their objectives and redefining their agendas. I have tried to indicate some of the ways in which the "traditional agendas" of African theologies may need to be altered. I have also indicated how many of the tags and categories used to describe and differentiate African theologies have become dated. Finally, new African theologies, capable of dealing with the New World Order can only be fashioned out of a vigorous interrogation of such emerging theologies as I have sketched above. What about previous theologies? Am I suggesting that their usefulness consist only in terms of "the ground that they have captured" so that they are of no direct relevance now? No. The issues that were being addressed by these theologies are far from finished. South African Black theology needs to continue its anti-racist critique of African Christianity. It must also develop its tremendous strides in biblical hermeneutics further. Nor have issues of Africanization, enculturation, and identity expired. African theology needs to continue addressing these issues. What I am saying is that in addressing these established and still relevant agendas, Black and African theologies will need to do so in consultation with insights from such emerging theologies as I have sketched above.

Notes

679 David J. BOSCH, *Transforming Mission: Paradigm Shifts in Mission Theology* (Maryknoll: Orbis Books, 1991), uses the idea of paradigm shifts to explain the manner in which theologies of mission have changed over the centuries. It is an idea borrowed from the scientist Thomas Kuhn.

680 Cf. e.g. David B. BARRETT *et al*, *World Christian Encyclopedia: A Comparative Survey of Churches and Religions in the Modern World AD 1900–2000* (New York: Oxford University Press, 1982); John S. MBITI, *The Bible in African Christianity* (Nairobi: Oxford University Press, 1986); Charles VILLA-VICENCIO, *A Theology of Reconstruction: Nation-Building and Human Rights* (Cape Town, Cambridge: David Philip, Cambridge University Press, 1992); Lamin SANNEH, *Translating the Message: The Missionary Impact on Culture* (Maryknoll: Orbis Books, 1989); J. N. K. MUGAMBI, *From Liberation to Reconstruction: African Christian Theology After the Cold War* (Nairobi: East African Educational Publishers, 1995); Kwame BEDIAKO, *Christianity in Africa: The Renewal of a Non-Western Religion* (Maryknoll: Orbis Books, 1995); A. KARAMAGA, *Problems and Promises of Africa: Towards and Beyond the Year 2000* (Nairobi: All Africa Conference of Churches, 1991); Mercy Amba ODUYOYE, *Daughters of Anowa: African Women and Patriarchy* (Marynoll: Orbis Books, 1995); M. A. ODUYOYE "Christianity and African Culture", in *International Review of Mission*, 84, 332/333 (January/April 1995), 77–90; Allan ANDERSON & Samuel OTWANG, *Tumelo: The Faith of African Pentecostals in South Africa* (Pretoria: University of South Africa Press, 1993).

681 KARAMAGA, *Problems and Promises*; José CHIPENDA, "The Church of the Future in Africa", in Douglas WARUTA (ed.), *African Church in the 21St Century: Challenges and Promises* (Nairobi: AACC, 1995), 16–36.

682 Kwesi A. DICKSON, *Theology in Africa* (Maryknoll: Orbis Books, 1984), 8.

683 Cf. Tinyiko Sam MALULEKE, "Black and African Theologies in the New World Order: A Time to Drink From Our Own Wells", in *Journal of Theology for Southern Africa*, 96 (November 1996), 3–19; T. S. MALULEKE, "Recent Developments in the Christian Theologies of Africa: Towards the 21st Century", in *Journal of Constructive Theology*, 2, 2 (December 1996), 33–60.

684 In this recent work on African theology, Josiah U. YOUNG, *African Theology: A Critical Analysis and Annotated Bibliography* (Westport: Greenwood Press, 1993), 6f., identifies those whom he calls "the ancestors of African Theology" such as Clement of Alexandria, Origen, Athanasius, Tertullian, Cyprian, Augustine of Hippo and Kimpa Vita or Dona Beatrice. See also John PARRATT, *Reinventing Christianity: African Theology Today* (Grand Rapids: Eerdmans, 1995); Marie-Louise MARTIN, *Kimbangu, an African Prophet and His Church* (Oxford: Oxford University Press, 1975); David J. Bosch, "Currents and Crosscurrents in South African Black Theology", in Gayraud S. WILMORE & James H. CONE (eds), *Black Theology: A Documentary History, 1966–1979* (Maryknoll: Orbis Books, 1979); Kwame BEDIAKO, *Theology and Identity: The Impact of Culture Upon Christian Thought in the Second Century and Modern Africa* (Oxford: Regnum Books, 1992).

685 ODUYOYE, "Christianity and African Culture", p. 8.

686 The same could be said of places like Jerusalem or Israel.

687 Harry SAWYERR, *The Practice of Presence: Shorter Writings of Harry Sawyerr*, John PARRATT (ed.), (Grand Rapids: Eerdmans, 1996), 87.

688 Edward W. Fashole-Luke, *An African Indigenous Theology: Fact or Fiction?* (Aberdeen: University of Aberdeen Press).

689 Both Sawyerr (SAWYERR, *The Practice of Presence*, pp. 93–99) and Fashole-Luke— in heavily qualified terms. Indeed they use it almost reluctantly. See, Edward W. FASHOLÉ-LUKE, "An African Indigenous Theology: Fact or Fiction?", in *Sierra Leone Bulletin of Religion* 11 (1971).

690 Bolaji IDOWU, *Towards an Indigenous Church* (London: Oxford University Press, 1965).

691 John S. MBITI. "The Biblical Basis for Present Trends in African Theology", in Kofi APPIAH-KUBI & Sergio TORRES, *African Theology en Route: Papers from*

the Pan-African Conference of Third World Theologians. Accra. December 17–23, 1977 (Maryknoll: Orbis Books, 1977), 90.
692 MBITI, "The Biblical Basis", p. 83.
693 The approach of Kwesi A. DICKSON, "The African Theological Task", in Sergio TORRES & Virginia M. M. FABELLA (eds), *The Emergent Gospel: Theology from the Underside of History: Papers from the Ecumenical Dialogue of Third World Theologians, Dar es Salam, August 5–12* (Maryknoll: Orbis Books, 1978), 46, is similar if not slightly more radical in that he rejects the notion of universal theology and thus argues for the validity of African Theology. For a fuller discussion of the merits of an 'African Theology' see one of his other works: DICKSON, *Theology in Africa*, 1–10.
694 MBITI, "The Biblical Basis", p. 90. Cf. MBITI, *The Bible in African Christianity*.
695 MBITI, "The Biblical Basis", p. 90.
696 Henry OKULU, *Church and Politics in East Africa* (Nairobi: Uzima Press, 1974), 54.
697 Idowu quoted by SAWYERR, *The Practice of Presence*, p. 85.
698 James Johnson quoted by SAWYERR, *The Practice of Presence*, p. 86.
699 SAWYERR, *The Practice of Presence*, p. 85.
700 DICKSON, *Theology in Africa*, pp. 1–10.
701 See also Ngidi MUSHETE, "Unity of Faith and Pluralism in Theology", in TORRES & FABELLA, *The Emergent Gospel*, pp. 50–75.
702 Itumeleng J. MOSALA, "Spirituality and Struggle: African and Black Theologies" in TORRES & FABELLA, *The Emergent Gospel*.
703 Tinyiko Sam MALULEKE, *"A Morula Tree Between Two Fields": The Commentary of Selected Tsonga Writers on Missionary Christianity* (DTh dissertation, University of South Africa, 1995).
704 Cf. J. N. K. MUGAMBI, "The Ecumenical Movement and the Future of the Church in Africa", in J. N. K. MUGAMBI & Laurenti MAGESA, *The Church in African Christianity: Innovative Essays in Ecclesiology* (Nairobi: Initiatives, 1990), 14–20; Margaret S. LAROM (ed.), *Claiming the Promise: African Churches Speak* (New York: Friendship Press, 1994).
705 D. W. WARUTA, "Towards an African Church: A Critical Assessment of Alternative Forms and Structures", in MUGAMBI & MAGESA, *The Church in African Christianity*, p. 33.
706 BARRETT, *World Christian Encyclopedia*; ANDERSON & OTWANG, *Tumelo*.
707 Aylward Shorter, *The Church in the African City* (London: Geoffrey Chapman, 1991).
708 Cf. Virginia M. M. FABELLA & Mercy Amba ODUYOYE (eds), *With Passion and Compassion: Third World Women Doing Theology* (Maryknoll: Orbis Books, 1988); Mercy Amba ODUYOYE & Musimbi R. A. KANYORO (eds), *Talitha, Qumi!: Proceedings of the Convocation of African Women Theologians 1989* (Ibadan: Daystar Press, 1990); Mercy Amba ODUYOYE & Musimbi R. A. KANYORO (eds), *The Will to Arise: Women, Tradition and the Church in Africa* (Maryknoll: Orbis Books, 1992); ODUYOYE, "Christianity and African Culture", pp. 77–90; Aruna GNANADASON, Musimbi R. A. KANYORO & Lucia Ann MCSPADDEN (eds), *Daughters of Anowa: African Women and Patriarchy: Women, Violence and Non-Violent Change* (Geneva: World Council of Churches Publications, 1996); Denise ACKERMANN, Jonathan A. DRAPER & Emma MASHININI (eds), *Women Hold up Half the Sky: Women in the Church in Southern Africa* (Pietermaritzburg: Cluster Publications, 1991).
709 ODUYOYE, "Christianity and African Culture", pp. 77–90; ODUYOYE, *Daughters of Anowa*.

710 Cf. BEDIAKO, *Theology and Identity*. For a contrary view, see J. S. FRIESEN, *Missionary Responses to Tribal Religions at Edinburgh, 1910* (Frankfurt: Peter Lang, 1996).
711 MALULEKE, "Black and African Theologies".
712 K. BEDIAKO, "Understanding African Theology in the 20th Century", in *Themelios*, 20, 1 (October 1994), 14–20; K. BEDIAKO, "Five Theses on the Significance of Modern African Christianity: A Manefesto", in *Transformation*, 13 (1996), 21–29.
713 Quoted on the title page: Willem SAAYMAN & Klippies (J. J.) KRITZINGER (eds), *Mission in Bold Humility: David Bosch'Work Considered* (Maryknoll: Orbis Books, 1996).
714 Cf. BEDIAKO, *Theology and Identity*.
715 BEDIAKO, *Theology and Identity*.
716 Bolaji IDOWU, *African Traditional Religion: A Definition* (London: SCM Press, 1973); SAWYERR, *The Practice of Presence*.
717 Gabriel SETILOANE, "Where Are We in African Theology?", in K. APPIAH-KUBI & S. TORRES, *African Theology en Route: Papers from the Pan-African Conference of Third World Theologians. Accra. December 17–23, 1977* (Maryknoll: Orbis Books 1977), 64.
718 Cf. J. N. K. MUGAMBI, *Critiques of Christianity in African Literature* (Nairobi: East African Educational Publishers, 1992).
719 Cf. MUGAMBI. *Critiques of Christianity*.
720 BEDIAKO, *Theology and Identity*.
721 John S. MBITI, *Concepts of God in Africa* (London: SPCK, 1979), 90.
722 Edward W. FAHOLE-LUKE, "The Quest for African Christian Theologies", in G. H. ANDERSON & T. F. STRANSKY (eds), *Mission Trends No 3: Third World Theologies* (Grand Rapids: Eerdmans, 1976), 141.
723 MBITI, *Concepts of God in Africa*, p. 90.
724 Cf. SANNEH, *Translating the Message*; MBITI, *The Bible in African Christianity*.
725 ODUYOYE, *Daughters of Anowa*, p. 174.
726 Here attempts are being made not only to develop creative biblical hermeneutic methods, but also to observe and analyze the manner in which African Christians "read" and view the Bible.
727 Zablon NTHAMBURI & Douglas WARUTA, "Biblical Hermeneutics in African Instituted Churches", in J. S. MBITI (ed.), *The Bible in African Christianity* (Nairobi: Oxford University Press, 1986), 40.
728 Josiah U. YOUNG, *Black and African Theologies: Siblings or Distant Cousins?* (Maryknoll: Orbis Books, 1986); YOUNG, *African Theology*.
729 Desmond TUTU, "Black Theology and African Theology: Soulmates or Antagonists?", in Dean William FERM (ed.), *Third World Liberation Theologies: A Reader* (Maryknoll: Orbis Books, 1986), 256–264.
730 Emmanuel MARTEY, *African Theology: Inculturation and Liberation* (Maryknoll: Orbis Books, 1993).
731 Mokgethi G. MOTLHABI, "Black or African Theology? Toward and Integral African Theology", in *Journal of Black Theology in South Africa*, 8, 2 (November 1994), 113–141.
732 Tinyiko Sam MALULEKE, "African Culture, African Intellectuals and the White Academy in South Africa", in *Religion and Theology*, 3, 1 (1996), 19–42.
733 Bengt G. M. SUNDKLER, M., *Bantu Prophets in South Africa* (Oxford: Oxford University Press, 1948); B. G. M. SUNDKLER, *The Christian Ministry in Africa* (Liverpool: Charles Birchal, 1962); B. G. M. SUNDKLER, *Zulu Zion and Some Swazi Zionists* (Oxford: Oxford University Press, 1976).

734 C. G. BAËTA, *Prophetism in Ghana* (London: SCM Press, 1962).
735 David B. BARRETT, *Schism and Renewal in Africa: An Analysis of Six Thousand Contemporary Religious Movements* (Nairobi: Oxford University Press, 1968); BARRETT, *World Christian Encyclopedia.*
736 M. L. DANEEL, *Old and New in Southern Shona Independent Churches* (New York: Mouton Publishers, 1971); M. L. DANEEL, *Quest for Belonging: Introduction to a Study of African Independent Churches*, (Gweru: Mambo Press, 1987).
737 H. W. TURNER, *History of an African Independent Church* (Oxford: Clarendon Press, 1967).
738 Cf. Tinyiko Sam MALULEKE, "Theological Interest in African Independent Churches and Other Grass-Root Communities in South Africa: A Review of Methodologies", in *Journal of Black Theology in South Africa*, 10, 1 (May 1996), 18–48.
739 Cf. BARRETT, *World Christian Encyclopedia*; ANDERSON & OTWANG, *Tumelo.*
740 Bosch in DANEEL, *Quest for Belonging*, p. 9.
741 MALULEKE, "Theological Interest", pp. 18–48.
742 Bediako, "Five Thesis", p. 264.
743 Cf. Byang KATO, *Theological Pitfalls in Africa* (Kisimu: Kenya Evangelical Publishing House, 1975); MBITI, *The Bible in African Christianity*, 48f; BEDIAKO, *Theology and Identity*, 386f.
744 Michael CASSIDY & Gottfried OSEI-MENSAH, *Together in One Place: The Story of PACLA, December 9–19, 1976* (Nairobi: Evangel Publishing House, 1978).
745 CASSIDY & OSEI-MENSAH, *Together in One Place*, p. 31.
746 MALULEKE, "Black and African Theologies", pp. 3–19; MALULEKE, "Recent Developments", pp. 33–60.
747 SANNEH, *Translating the Message.*
748 BEDIAKO, *Theology and Identity*; BEDIAKO, *Christianity in Africa.*
749 Cf. MALULEKE, "Black and African Theologies", pp. 3–19.
750 See MALULEKE, "Black and African Theologies", pp. 3–19.
751 D. RAMODIBE, "Women and Men Building Together the Church in Africa", in FABELLA & ODUYOYE, *With Passion and Compassion.*
752 RAMODIBE, "Women and Men", p. 20.
753 A recent issue of the *Bulletin for Contextual Theology in Southern Africa & Africa*, 4, 2 (July 1997) has been devoted to Feminist/Womanist theology in South Africa. It also contains an annotated bibliography on South African Feminist/Womanist works. Cf. also Christina LANDMAN, *The Piety of Afrikaans Women: Diaries of Guilt* (Pretoria: University of South Africa Press, 1994); ACKERMANN et al, *Women Hold Up Half the Sky.*
754 FABELLA & ODUYOYE, *With Passion and Compassion*, p. x.
755 Mercy Amba ODUYOYE, *Who Will Roll the Stone Away? The Ecumenical Decade of the Churches in Solidarity with Women* (Geneva: World Council of Churches Publications, 1988), 3.
756 ODUYOYE, *Daughters of Anowa*, p. 187.
757 Cf. Mercy Amba Oduyoye, "The Circle", in ODUYOYE & KANYORO, *Talitha.*
758 Musimbi R. A. KANYORO & Nyambura J. NJOROGE (eds), *Groaning in Faith: African Women in the Household of God* (Nairobi: Acton Publishers, 1996).
759 MUGAMBI, *From Liberation to Reconstruction.*
760 MALULEKE, "Recent Developments"; T. S. MALULEKE, "Review Mugambi, J N K 1995. From Liberation to Reconstruction: African Christian Theology After the Cold War. Nairobi: East African Educational Publishers", in *Missionalia*, 24, 3 (November 1996), 472–473; "African Culture, African Intellectuals and the White Academy in South Africa". MALULEKE, "Recent Developments".

761 VILLA-VICENCIO, *A Theology of Reconstruction*.
762 Cf. KARAMAGA, *Problems and Promises*; J. N. K. MUGAMBI, "The Future of the Church and the Church of the Future Africa", in J. CHIPENDA, A. KARAMAGA, J. N. K. MUGAMBI & C. K. OMARI (eds), *The Church of Africa: Toward a Theology of Reconstruction* (Nairobi: AACC, 1991); Tinyiko Sam MALULEKE, "The Proposal for a Theology of Reconstruction: A Critical Appraisal", in *Missionalia*, 22, 3 (November 1994), 245–258.

INDEX

Abgar VIII I 199, 214–15
Aborginal Australians
  ancestral practice **III** 166, 168–71, 173–8
  Arrernte people **IV** 14–22
  assimilation **IV** 20
  baptismal clothing **IV** 17, 19
  bodily decoration **IV** 16–17
  Central Australia **IV** 14
  clothes **IV** 13–24
  codes of behaviour **III** 167–9
  colonization **III** 165
  cultural relativism **IV** 13–14
  dancing **III** 172–3, 176–7
  Dhuwa and Yirritja **III** 170
  discipline **III** 167, 173
  disclosure and non-disclosure **III** 170
  doctrinal mode **III** 166–7, 171–3, 177–8
  feet, covering of **IV** 15
  free will **III** 166–7
  funerals **III** 170, 174, 177
  hair **IV** 16
  imagistic mode **III** 166, 171–3
  indigenous expressions of Christianity **III** 167
  interaction **III** 165–80
  knowledge transmission **III** 166–71, 176
  language **III** 168
  Little Flower Catholic Mission **IV** 19
  Lutheran missionaries **IV** 14, 16–19
  memory **III** 171–3
  missionaries **III** 165–9, **III** 171, 177–8, **IV** 13–24
  nakedness **IV** 13–24
  Pomio Kivung of New Guinea **III** 170
  power **III** 167
  Presbyterians **IV** 14
  religiosity **III** 165–7, 171, 176–8
  rituals **III** 170, 172–4, 177
  routinization **III** 167–8
  self-harm **III** 172
  songs **III** 170, 172–4, 177
  spirits, white men as **IV** 15
  translation of Bible **I** 71, **III** 168, 169
  unification **III** 165–80
  washing **IV** 16
  welfare **III** 169
  work ethic **III** 169
  Yolngu Christianity **III** 165–78
abortions I 324, **III** 280–1
Abraham the solitary I 241–2
Abraim, Abuna II 377
Adas, Michael II 118
Adejobi, Adekele III 111–14
Adeshir I 215
Adetunji, J III 282
admonition I 129, 130, 131, 133
Adrian I 245
Aedesius I 201
Aethelstan I 221
Africa *see also* **Africa, Orthodox mission in tropical; African Christian theologies; individual countries**
  African Immigrant Religion (AIR) **III** 108–10, 122, 123
  African Instituted/Initiated Churches (AICs) **I** 113, **III** 110, 113, 124
  Aksum, Christianization of **I** 198–212

Barwe refuees from Portuguese East Africa **II** 385
Berbers **I** 181–4
Bible **I** 70, 72–5, 94–5, 112–13
Bushmen, Christ as trickster in religion of contemporary **III** 298–316
Catholics **I** 348–66, **IV** 299–303, 313
Christian Marching Church of Central Africa **III** 368
Church of the Lord (Aladura) in United States **III** 106–26
Colenso, John William. *Commentary of Romans* **I** 101–10
colonialism **I** 70, 72–5, 94–5
gender, translation of Bible and **I** 74–6
hegemony **I** 97, 99
Latin American Christianity **IV** 299–304, 313
'long conversation' **I** 95, 96–7
missionaries **I** 94–100, **IV** 156–7
Numidia **I** 181–3, 186, 189–92
Pentecostal movement, spread of **II** 400
Phrygian language **I** 187
population projections **IV** 299–301
Punic culture **I** 181–6, 191
Roman Africa, Christianity and local culture in **I** 181–97
Southern Tswana, cultivation and colonialism in **II** 28–50
Soyo, Capuchins and rulers of **I** 348–66
translation of Bible **I** 72–5, 112–13
Tswana people of Africa **I** 97
United States **III** 106–26
Universities Mission to Central Africa **II** 66, 68, 73
Vandals, arrival of **I** 189, 191
white church leaders **III** 366–7
white-led churches before independence **III** 357–9
Zulus **I** 96–7, 99–110

Africa, Orthodox mission in tropical II 368–82
African Orthodox Church (AOC) **II** 370–1, 372, 375, 377
Alexandrian Christianity **II** 369, 371–4
approaches and characteristics **II** 378
Arian controversy **II** 369
Byzantine Patriarchate **II** 369

Cameroun **II** 377
Central Africa **II** 377
Chad **II** 377
colonialism **II** 368, 371–3, 380
Constantinople **II** 369, 370
Coptic Patriarchate **II** 369, 371
Council of Chalcedon **II** 369
education **II** 375, 379–80
Greek communities **II** 370, **II** 372, 375–7
Greek Orthodox Church **II** 372, 377
Ethiopian Church **II** 370
Ghana **II** 376–7
gossiping the gospel **II** 378
Kenya **II** 371–5, 377, 379–80
language **II** 377, 379
literature evangelism **II** 379
Madagascar **II** 376, 379
medical services **II** 379–80
monasticism **II** 369, 379
Nicene Creed **II** 369
Nigeria **II** 376–7
paganism **II** 368
Pan African movement **II** 370–1, 377
Pope and Patriarch of Alexandria and All Africa **II** 369–73, 377–8
reading about the Church **II** 378–9
Russian Orthodox Church **II** 370–1
seminaries **II** 375, 379
slave trade **II** 369–70
South Africa **II** 370–1, 372
Southern Africa **II** 369–71
Tanzania **II** 375, 379
Uganda **II** 373–5, 377, 379–80
West Africa **II** 376–7, 378
Zaire **II** 374, 376, 379
Zimbabwe **II** 375–6

African Christian theologies IV 332–53
Africa, concept of **IV** 333–4, 337
'African Christianity' use of term **IV** 333–4
African culture **IV** 336–8
'African theology', use of term **IV** 333–4
agenda of African theology **IV** 335–6
All Africa Conference of Churches **IV** 332–3, 344, 346
Bible **IV** 340–3
charismatic theology **IV** 344–5
Christianisation or Africanisation of past **IV** 338–9
Cold War, end of **IV** 347–8

INDEX

colonialism **IV** 345, 347
denominationalism **IV** 336
distinctions within African theology, rethinking **IV** 342–3
dynamism **IV** 332–3
Ecumenical Association of Third World Theologians (EATWOT) **IV** 346–7, 348
ecumenicals **IV** 344, 346
emerging theologies **IV** 343–8
evangelicalism **IV** 337–9, 344–5
feminist/womanist theologies **IV** 346–7
hermeneutics **IV** 341–2
identity **IV** 338
inculturation issues **IV** 336–43, 347
innovation **IV** 332–3
liberation theology **IV** 340–2, 347
missionaries **IV** 345
oral theology **IV** 343
Pan African Leadership Assembly **IV** 344–5
paradigm shifts **IV** 332
reconstruction, theologies of **IV** 347–8
South Africa **IV** 336, 341, 342, 344, 346
terminology **IV** 333
traditional religions **IV** 332–53
translation theologies **IV** 345
West **IV** 334
after-death I 4
Aglukark, David III 217, 219
agriculture
  aesthetics **II** 31–5
  cattle **II** 30
  Chile, Pentacostalism in **II** 297
  God as farmer **IV** 250, 251
  India
    Parsis of Bombay and Christian conversion **II** 16
    Tarangambadi (Tranquebar), missionaries in **I** 441–69
  Parsis of Bombay and Christian conversion **II** 16
  pastoralism **II** 30
  ploughs, use of **II** 41
  rice production **I** 443
  Southern Tswana, Africa, cultivation and colonialism in **II** 28–50
  Tarangambadi (Tranquebar), India, missionaries in **I** 441–69

Zimbabwe, missionaries in Northern Nyaga District **II** 385
AIDs III 255
Ajayi, Joel III 283–4
Akpahatak, Maggie III 214
Aksum, Christianization of I 198–212
  church, construction of principal **I** 203–4
  coinage with cross, issue of **I** 198–9
  comparative approach **I** 200–1
  conversion **I** 201, 203
  countryside, Christianization of the **I** 204–7
  culture **I** 207–8
  indigenous Christians **I** 203
  Jewish communities **I** 202–3
  Nine Saints **I** 204–5
  phases **I** 208
  Roman Empire **I** 198–208
  royal conversion **I** 201, 203
  Sassanian Empire **I** 200–1
  trade routes **I** 200–3
Albrecht, FW IV 19
Alderson, Cecil IV 159
Alexander II II 184
Alexander, Charles IV 208–16, 220, 221
Alexander, Daniel William II 370–2, 374
Alexandrian Christianity II 369, 371–4
Alfonso I I 260–2, 348–9
Algonquian Indians I 379, **IV** 181–9
All Africa Conference of Churches IV 332–3, 344, 346
Allen, Roland II 291
Allende, Salvador II 298–9
Alleyne, Mervyn III 188
Alloloo, J III 219–20
Alopen I 200
Althanasius of Alexandria I 24, 167
Alvaro II I 262
American Baptist Missionary Society II 323–4, 334–6
Americas *see also* **particular countries**
  Inuit Pentecostalism and Evangelicalism in Canadian and Eastern Arctic **III** 201–29
  Latin America, awakening of indigenous people in **IV** 316–31
  Nanrantsouak, church at **I** 379–93
  Native American missionaries **I** 470–82
  Navajo, healing and **IV** 323–4
  Prairie Indians, pilgrimages of **IV** 140–53

356

INDEX

Tupi and European women in eyes of Claude d'Abbeville I 295–308
Yaqui and southwest and central American literature III 310
Amjad Ali, Christine I 79, 81
Ammerman, NJ III 448
amulets I 242
anarchism II 278, III 342–3
Anastasius I 205
Anatolia, conversion from paganism in 6th century rural I 233–54
ancestor worship and practices
  Aborginal Australians III 166, 168–71, 173–8
  China
    Catholic women of Congregation of Sisters in IV 70
    sectarian violence II 328
    Western cultural communication at end of Ming dynasty I 281–5, 290
  Decalogue in Tagalog, Oliver's manuscript of I 313
  Inuit Pentecostalism and Evangelicalism in Canadian and Eastern Arctic III 221–2
  Merina traditional religion and the Bible in Madagascar I 113–14
  Norddeutsche Missiongesellschaft, role of Devil in preaching of III 415–16
  sectarian violence II 328
  Soyo, Capuchins and rulers of I 361
  syncretism IV 264, 276
  Taiwan
    conversion to Protestantism amongst urban immigrants in III 318
    syncretism among Paiwan Catholics in IV 264, 276
    Western–sino cultural communication at end of Ming dynasty I 280–94
Anchieta, José de I 373–4
Ancient Greece, glossolalia in II 307
Anderson, Karen I 297
Andersson, Efraim II 253–4, 262
André, Louis IV 185–6, 188
angels III 469, 475–6
Angirõ (Sante Fe, Paulo de) I 269–70, 272, 275

Anglican Church
  Jamaican peasant life, religion as resistance in III 181
  missionaries II 66–75
  Mizeki, Bernard IV 156–65
  Nigeria, young converts in Onitsha II 95–111
  Zimbabwe, American Evangelicalism in III 358, 371–2
  Walsingham, United Kingdom, pilgrimage to IV 121–3, 125–8, 132
animal leaders I 242
animism
  Decalogue in Tagalog, Oliver's manuscript of I 312–13
  paganism in rural Anatolia and Greece from 6th century, conversion from I 240–1
  Philippines, trial of Seberine Candelaria in II 120, 129
  priestesses II 120, 129
  Sumatra, Karo Batak Protestant Church in II 149–50
  witchcraft and devils II 119–20
  women II 120
Anthrakitis, Methodios II 212
anticlericalism II 209 *see* **Aracena, Andalusia, anticlericalism in**
anti-structure and structure III 307–13
Antonio I, ruler of Soyo I 358, 362–3
Aphrates I 216
apostasy
  Russian Orthodox Church II 179–200
  Seventh–day Adventism III 386
  Tatars II 179–200
apostles I 55–6, 162, 479–80
Apostles' Creed I 263
App, Urs I 270
Appavoo, Theophilus IV 242–6, 249–57
Appiah, Anthony IV 333–4
Aquinas, St Thomas I 18, 337, II 119
Aracena, Andalusia, anticlericalism in II 340–67
  1936, August III 340–61
  anarchism III 342–3
  anti-institutional, as II 344
  blasphemy II 354–6
  Catholic mutualism II 349–50, 357, 359–60
  churches, burning III 341–7, 351–61

357

INDEX

Civil War **III** 341, 344
class divisions **III** 340–1, 344–60
conservatism and gentry, clerics' alliance with **II** 348–9
corruption and moral lapses of clergy **II** 352–3
culture **II** 343–4
disentailment **II** 348
domination and resistance **II** 344, 352–3, 361
ecclesiastical land, sale of **II** 348
gender **II** 354
hegemony **II** 344–5, 352–3, 357–8
hierarchy **II** 351–2
ideological polarization **II** 347–51, 357–8
instrumentalism **II** 344–5, 360
irreligious expression, forms of **II** 354–6
leftist radicals **III** 341–61
long run, structures of the **II** 351–8
millenarian theory **II** 343, 344–5, 358–61
modernity and tradition, dialectics of **II** 358–61
mutualism **II** 349–50, 357, 359–60
nuns, treatment of **III** 341–2
popular anticlericalism **II** 352–8
rituals **II** 352
scapegoating **II** 344
social justice **II** 359–60
socio-political movements **II** 358–61
spirit and the flesh **II** 351
tradition and modernity, dialectics of **II** 358–61
violence **III** 341–7, 350–61
Aragon, Louis **II** 360
architecture **II** 385
Aregawi **I** 206–7
Arensen, Jon **IV** 205
Argentina **III** 428
Arian controversy **I** 215, **II** 369
Aries, Philippe **III** 144
Aristotle **I** 337
Arlotto, Piovano **III** 311–12
Armbruster, Marje **III** 221–3
Armbruster, Roger **III** 214–16, 218, 221–6
Armstrong, C **III** 364
Arreak, James **III** 219
art, sales of **IV** 267
Artemis cult **I** 237–8

Arthur, John **II** 372
As'ad, Gamal **III** 18
Asbury, Francis **IV** 173–4
Ashmore, William **II** 324, 328, 330, 331–2, 335
Asia *see also* **individual countries**
   Catholic beliefs **I** 57–65
   Dominus Iesus declaration **I** 57–65
   Martha and Mary from Asian perspective, story of **I** 79–84
Aslanidis, Yannis **II** 376
assimilation
   Aboriginal Australians **IV** 20
   California, breakdown of Spanish mission system in **II** 227
   Latin America, indigenous people in **IV** 320
   Native American missionaries **I** 471–2, 477
   New Zealand, Irish Catholics in 19th century Christchurch in **II** 171–2
   syncretism **II** 256
   Tatars and apostasy **II** 181
   Zaïre, Kimbanguism and syncretism in **II** 253–70
Assisi, St Francis of **III** 91–2
Athanasius **I** 201
atheists **III** 233
attendance at church **I** 17
Augustine of Canterbury **I** 200
Augustine of Hippo, St **I** 4, 167, 181, 184–90, 193, **II** 118–19, **IV** 91
Austin, JL **I** 125
Australia **II** 84 *see also* **Aboriginal Australians**
Austria, folk songs from **IV** 187
Awakening movements **II** 244–5
Awdry, JW **II** 17, 22
Ayliff, J **II** 41
Axtell, James **I** 472
Azariah, M **IV** 243
Azevedo, Agostinho de **I** 276
Azpilcueta, João **I** 369–70
Azpilcueta Navarro, Martin de **I** 369–70

Baeta, Christian **IV** 343
Bagin, S **II** 192
Bagnall, Roger **I** 167
Bahai **III** 471, 474–6
Bainbridge, William **III** 340, 352, 375
Bairong, Stephanus Tang **I** 431
Bairos, Antonio de **I** 372–3

INDEX

Baiyu, Li III 40–1
Baker, Moses III 188
Bakhtin, MM III 458
Balandier, G I 360
Banana, Canaan III 357–8, 372
Bancroft, Hubert Howe II 226
Banda, Hastings IV 229
baptism
  Aboriginal Australians IV 17, 19
  American Baptist Missionary Society II 323–4, 334–6
  analogy I 138
  anointing I 135
  apostasy II 180–2
  Chile
    pentacostalism II 287
    young women as apostles to the poor II 276, 279
  China,
    Christian sectarian violence in late 19th century II 323–36
    Christian Virgins in 18th century China I 432
  clothing IV 17, 19
  confession I 135–6, 139
  death of death, as I 138
  Didache I 134
  dying and rising with Christ I 138–40
  dying children I 432
  Eleusinian mysteries I 136
  French Antilles, Catholic missions to slaves in I 394–403
  glossolalia I 135
  Gnostics I 168, 170–1
  Greece, religion and modernization in 19th century II 205
  heresy II 205
  immersion I 134–7
  interpretation 133–4, 136
  Japan, indigenous movements in III 339
  Judaism, water rites of I 136–7
  Kongo, church in I 258
  Li lineage, Baptist and Catholic elements of II 323–36
  living water I 133–4
  Lord's Supper I 144–5
  Mexico, native evangelism in central III 394, 398–9
  Mezzogiorno, glossolalia and possession amongst Pentecostal groups of the II 308, 311
  mikveh I 134–5, 137
  miming Jesus' death I 138–40
  motifs I 138–40
  nakedness I 135, 138–40
  'new human', characteristics of I 138–9
  Norddeutsche Missiongesellschaft, role of Devil in preaching of III 412–14
  opposites I 139–40
  paradisiac motifs I 139
  paraenetic reminders I 138
  participation, language of I 138
  Pauline baptism I 133–40
  purity I 136–7
  ritual and early church in Eastern Mediterranean I 125, 133–41, 146
  sexual matters I 137
  Soyo, Capuchins and rulers of I 360–1
  Stephanas, household of I 133–4
  Sumatra, Karo Batak Protestant Church in II 140
  Tatars and apostasy II 180–2
  United States, gender and change in Church of the Lord (Aladura) in III 112
  washing I 136–7
Baptists
  conversions III 317, IV 64–5
  court use I 36–42
  hats as symbol of women's position in Evangelical churches in Edinburgh, Scotland IV 26, 27–8, 32–4, 37–9
  ideology I 35–42
  Jamaican peasant life, religion as resistance in III 187 III 181–93
  millenarianism IV 64
  missionaries in Jamaica III 181–4, 188
  reframing life IV 64
  Revival Cults III 189–93
  ruptures and discontinuities IV 64–5
  salvation IV 64
  Taiwan, conversion to Protestantism amongst urban immigrants in III 317
  United States I 36–42, IV 64
  Zaïre, Kimbanguism and syncretism in II 255

INDEX

Bar Sabbae, Simon I 215
Baraga, Friedrich IV 187, 188, 189
Barker, John III 168
Barna, George IV 305
Barnabas I 158, 160, 187
Barnard, Alan III 301
Barnhouse, Donald Grey III 378, 386
barrenness III 285–9
Barrett, CK I 127
Barrett, David IV 343
Barretto, Adalberto IV 98–9
Barrios Valdes, Marciano II 280–1
Barrows, Cliff IV 207
Barsum the Naked III 15
Bartels, Dieter II 126, 127
Bascio, Matteo de I 296
base communities *see* **Brazil, base communities (CEBs) in**
Basil I I 244
Basil, St III 15
Bassajjikitalo, Obadiah II 371, 372–3
Bastide, Roger IV 92
Baxter, Joseph I 390
Bayle, Pierre I 285
Bayly, Susan I 450
Bear Nicholas, Andrea I 381
Bediako, Kwame IV 337, 338–9, 345
Bekker, Balthazar III 410
Belgium II 257–8
Bell, C IV 52, 123
Benjamin, Walter I 71
Benjaminites I 88–90
Bentley, Jerry I 130
Berber culture I 181–4
Berdiaev, N III 349
Berger, Peter I 125, III 330–1
Berthier, A I 182
Beti I 48–50, 52
Beutah, James II 371–2
Beyer, Peter III 423
Bhabha, Homi I 69–72, 472
Bible *see also* **translations of the Bible**
 Africa
  African Christian theologies IV 340–3
  colonialism I 70, 72–5, 94–5
  Ethiopian Orthodox Church I 24
  Merina traditional religion in Madagascar I 112–20
 agreed text, as I 24–5
 closed book, as I 114–18

Colenso, John William
 Commentary on the Pentateuch I 95, 97
 Commentary on Romans I 101–10
colonialism I 69–78
Colossians I 127–9
Corinthians I 127–8, 133
creation account I 99
cultic purification, used for I 115
decolonization I 77
elites I 74–5
Ephesians I 127–9
Ethiopian Orthodox Church I 24
exegesis, societal changes and I 25
glossolalia II 307
hats as symbol of women's position in Evangelical churches in Edinburgh, Scotland IV 25, 27–31, 33–7
hegemony I 94–7
hermeneutics IV 341
Hindi I 69
hybridity I 70–2
inclusion I 24
India I 69–70, 72, 75–7
John, Gospel of I 169–70, 172
Judges I 85–93
languages I 24–5
Latin, recital in I 24–5
liberation movements I 95
literacy I 74–5
literalists I 24
Merina traditional religion in Madagascar I 112–20
missionaries I 70–4, 94–7, 112
morals, Bible used as reference book for I 116–17
nationalism I 74
native agency I 70–1
New Testament I 24, II 307
Norddeutsche Missionsgesellschaft, role of Devil in preaching of III 417
Old Testament
 date I 24
 glossolalia II 307
 reading of the I 129–30
Oliver's manuscript of Decalogue in Tagalog I 311–27
patriarchal attitudes I 75
Pentateuch I 95, 97
Philip, Gospel of I 170–1

360

protection, Bible used for **I** 115–16
psalms **I** 127–8
purification, Bible used for **I** 115
reading aloud **I** 116
recognition **I** 69–70
Romans **I** 101–10
Sarah and Hannah, story of **III** 277, 285–90
subalterns **I** 74–6
Syrian Orthodox Church **I** 24
Tamils **I** 70
Ten Commandments **I** 311–27
textual interpretation **I** 25
translations **I** 24–5
Truth, Gospel of **I** 169–70
witchcraft or evil spirits **I** 115–16, **III** 291
Bice, Charles II 75
Bicol, Philippines, imitation of Christ in III 61–80
Bigot, Jacques I 380
Bigot, Vincent I 380
Bilar, Catalina Villanueva I 269
Birmingham, David I 257
bishops
China, beliefs of Zhouzi village people in Catholic diocese in **III** 40
control, disputes over **II** 172–3
governance in the early church **I** 156–7, 158–9, 161–3
Kongo, church in **I** 261
New Zealand, Irish Catholics in 19th century Christchurch in **II** 172–3
Blackfoot IV 142–3, 145
Blasi, Anthony III 336
blasphemy II 354–6, **III** 307
Blazennyi, Vasilij III 311
Bloom, Harold I 280, 283–4
Blume, Bernhard I 409–10, 414
Blumhardt, Johann Christoph III 410–11, 417–18
bodily decoration IV 16–17, 273–4
Boer, Roland I 71–2
Boim, Michael I 333–4
Bolivia, catechists of Aymara Indians in IV 263–4
Bomaseen of the Wabanakis, chief I 389
Bombay, India, conversion of Parsis of II 13–27
Bonnke, Reinhard III 362, 370

Boomer, William II 292
Boris I I 247
Botswana III 298–300
Bott, Elizabeth III 140, 143–4
Boudon, Raymond III 196
Boulton, ECW II 392
boundaries, futility of marking I 5
Boutrous-Ghali, Boutrous III 19
Bouvet, Joachim I 285
Bowman, M IV 137
Brahmins I 444, 449, 459, **II** 56, **IV** 248, 254, 255
Brancati, Francesco I 334
Brazil *see also* **Brazil, base communities (CEBs) in; Brazil, women and religion in colonial**
Catholic-Protestant distinctions in coming global Christianity **IV** 301
missionaries **III** 424–5
Pentecostalism **III** 424–5
pilgrimage **IV** 87–103
population projection **IV** 301
syncretism **III** 463–79
Tupi and European women in eyes of Claude d'Abbeville **I** 295–308
Universal Church of the Kingdom of God of Brazil **III** 423–42
Brazil, base communities (CEBs) in III 195–211
A Folha publication **III** 204–5
community councils **III** 206
democracy **III** 195
disempowerment **III** 206–7
economic crisis **III** 196, 202–4, 206–7
elitism **III** 208
evangelism **III** 197, 199
failure to mobilize communities **III** 195–6
French priests **III** 201–2, 205–6
grupo de reflexão **III** 197
Irish priests **III** 201–2, 204–5, 207
liturgical innovations **III** 197–8, 205–6
liturgy, standardisation of **III** 204–5, 207
military rule **III** 199
neighbourhood associations **III** 199
overbureaucratization **III** 206
pastoral–pedagogical method **III** 197, 208
Pedro Bonita case study **III** 196–209

perverse unintended consequences III 196, 202–3
political activism III 198–202, 208
popular church III 195
poverty III 195–6
radicalization III 198–9
Romanization III 204
saints, cult of III 200
see-judge-act method III 198–9
social outreach III 200–2, 206–7
spontaneity III 197–8
Vatican conservative pressure III 203–5, 207
Vicentino practice III 200–1, 205–8
women III 197–8, 202
Workers' Catholic Action (ACO) III 198–202, 205–8
Brazil, pilgrimage and patronage in IV 87–103
Francis of Assisi in Canindé, shrine of IV 88–98
healing IV 99–100
industrialization IV 87
luminal state IV 90
merchandise 93–4
modernity IV 100
modernization IV 87
popular Catholicism IV 87
potential devotees IV 87
preparation for pilgrims IV 93–4
saints, cult of IV 91–3
social relations IV 87–8
Brazil, women and religion in colonial I 367–78
1550–1750 I 367–76
adultery I 369, 370
autonomy I 370
Brazilindians women I 373–6
Catholic Church I 367
control over women, need for I 372
education I 368, 374
European women I 368–73
idealized elite role and responses I 368–73, 375
lower class women I 373–6
marriage I 368–74
mixed-race women I 373–6
religious duties I 368–72, 375
servitude and slavery of native women I 374–5
virginity before marriage I 368, 373–4
witchcraft I 375

Brenan, Gerald III 342
bricolage IV 263
Brien, Cecil II 385, 388–92, 396, 398, 399–400
Brien, Mary II 385, 389–92, 396, 398, 399
Bright, Bill III 359
British East India Company I 464, II 59–60
Broadbent, Samuel II 36–8
Brook, Peter IV 124
Brothers I 155–6, 158–9, 162
Brown, CP I 455
Brown, J II 33
Brown, Judith K I 297
Brown, Peter I 240
Budala, Paul II 375
Buddhism
Japan, indigenous movements in III 329, 334, 338, 339–40
monasticism I 268–9, 271–2
poetry I 329, 332
sino-Western cultural communication at end of Ming dynasty I 287, 290
Suma Ching Hai International Association III 319
Wu Li and first Chinese Christian poetry I 337–8
Xavier, Francisco, Japanese in letters of I 268–9, 271–2
buffoon-clerics III 311–12
Bultmann, Rudolf I 130, II 71
Bunuel, Luis II 360
Burchell, Thomas III 182
Burdick, John III 208
burial *see also* **funerals**
Eastern Mediterranean, early church in I 145–6
graveyards, transfer of corpses from I 409, 413–15
India, Orthodox Christian Pilgrim Centre in Kerala IV 111–12
Jamaican peasant life, religion as resistance in III 192–3
Lübeck, Germany I 409, 413–15
Philippines, imitation of Christ in III 68
tombs
intercession, theology of IV 111–12
India, Orthodox Christian Pilgrim Centre in Kerala IV 111–12

INDEX

Ulster Pentecostals **II** 392
Zimbabwe, missionaries in Northern Nyaga District in **II** 392
Burkino Faso, faith-healers of Assemblies of God in III 253-72
AIDs **III** 255
collective deliverance ceremonies **III** 257-61, 267-70
confessions, provoking **III** 257-8
conversions **III** 256, 260-1
definition of faith-healers **III** 253
deliverance
   collective deliverance, prayers for **III** 257, **III** 261-70
   conversion, as **III** 261
   private exorcism **III** 257-61, 263, 267-70
demonization of ancient customs **III** 256-7
demons, detecting **III** 262-5
diseases, devil and **III** 256
economic crisis **III** 254-5
effectiveness of dual therapeutic arrangements **III** 267-70
eternal life **III** 256
exorcisms **III** 257-67
first miracles **III** 257
genies **III** 259-60
guilt, third person who erases **III** 259-61
impure, unmasking the **III** 262-5
initiation, steps in **III** 257
insight, gift of **III** 258-9
interpreter of God **III** 253
legitimation, processes of **III** 257
millenarianism **III** 256, 257, 269
missionaries **III** 253-4
modernity **III** 255-7, 260, 268
mossi **III** 253-4, 259-61
multiple identity **III** 256-7
other, genie as **III** 260
Pentecostal Movement **III** 254, 256, 270
possession **III** 255, 256-61
praise **III** 266-7
prayers **III** 253
private exorcism by faith-healers **III** 257-61, 263, 267-70
professionals **III** 253-4
prophets, healers as **III** 253
proselytization **III** 253
social upheavals **III** 254-5

sorcery **III** 255
spirits, presence of **III** 265-6
testimony **III** 266-7
thanks **III** 266-7
therapeutic attitudes and techniques **III** 255-6, 257-70
thought, categories of **III** 256-7
burning churches III 341-7, 351-61
Burrhys I 155, 157
Bushmen, Christ as trickster in religion of contemporary III 298-316
anti-structure and structure **III** 307-13
blasphemy **III** 307
Botswana **III** 298-300
communitas festivals **III** 308-13
earnestness of mainstream Christianity **III** 308-10
//Gauwa/veld-god **III** 298-307
//Gauwassa **III** 302
healing **III** 300, 306-7
Heitsi-aibib **III** 301
laugh, Christ being able to **III** 307
mediator, Gauwa and Christ as **III** 306-7
miracles **III** 304
mission Bushmen **III** 298
Namibia **III** 300
passion, resurrection and ascension **III** 304, 306-7, 309
rebellion **III** 307-8
Satan **III** 298, 302-3, 310-11
Simon Peter as trickster **III** 310
supernatural **III** 298-301
Butler, Joseph II 71-2
Byron, George II 210, 212-13
Byzantium
Byzantine Patriarchate **II** 369
Greece, religion and modernization in 19th century **II** 201-8, 211, 213, 217

Calazacon, Manuel IV 325
Caldwell, Patricia I 474
California, breakdown of Spanish mission system in II 225-36
assimilation **II** 227
birth rate **II** 231
character of Californian Indians **II** 225
cultural sections **II** 227
decolonization **II** 232

INDEX

disease **II** 231
fugitivism **II** 230, 231
heterogeneous societies **II** 227
land **II** $228, 232–3, 234
Mexican War of Independence **II** 231–2
minorities **II** 227
mixed ethnicity Spaniards **II** 228–9
neophytes **II** 225–34
Native Americans **II** 225–34
plural institution, mission as **II** 228–31, 234
plural society **II** 226–8
Proclamation of Emancipation **II** 232
punishments **II** 229–30
sectional inequalities **II** 227, 234
secularization of missions **II** 226, 232–3
total institutions **II** 226–8
Calvinists III 137
Cameron, J II 40
Cameroun
  Beti **I** 48–50, 52
  Catholic mass, presentation of **I** 52–5
  communion meal **I** 52–5
  cultural model **I** 52
  dance **I** 50, 53–4
  Future of the Universal **I** 56
  historical background **I** 48–50
  Incarnation, mystery of the **I** 50–1
  indigenization, theological and Biblical foundations of **I** 50–2, 55
  Judaization of the Christian **I** 51
  kissing of cross or altar, offensiveness of **I** 48–9
  Latin **I** 49
  liturgical adaptation in St Paul de Ndzon-Melen **I** 48–56
  Melen liturgy **I** 53
  Orthodox Mission **II** 377
  sacraments **I** 51
  singing **I** 49–50, 53–5
  universality **I** 50, 52, 56
Campbell, J II 29, 35
Campus Crusade III 359, 363
Canada
  bathing in clothes **IV** 146
  Blackfoot **IV** 142–3, 145
  Catholic shrines **IV** 141, 143–9
  confessions, language of **IV** 145
  continuity in ritual **IV** 151
  Cree **IV** 142, 150–1
  divergence, points of **IV** 147–8
  healing **IV** 146
  identity **IV** 150
  information exchange **IV** 148
  Inuit Pentecostalism and Evangelicalism in Canadian and Eastern Arctic **III** 201–29
  merger of traditions **IV** 147–8
  missionaries **IV** 143–5, 147
  Oblates of Mary Immaculate **IV** 141
  persistent peregrination **IV** 149–52
  physical and cultural stress **IV** 143–4
  pow-wows **IV** 148–9
  Prairie Indians, pilgrimages of **IV** 140–53
  relaxation/holidays **IV** 148
  rituals and ceremonies **IV** 143, 145–52
  social interaction **IV** 148, 149–51
  summer gatherings
    abandonment of traditional gatherings **IV** 141
    pre-missionary gatherings **IV** 142–3, 150–1
  Ste-Anne d'Auray shrine **IV** 141, 143–51
  Sun Dance **IV** 143, 148–52
  Tea Dance **IV** 147
  trading **IV** 148
  Way of the Cross procession **IV** 146–7
Candelaria, Seberine, trial in Philippines of II 117–33
  19th century **II** 117–30
  avoidance protest **II** 118
  bandits as social avengers **II** 118
  Christianity, incorporation of **II** 126–30
  colonialism, latent hostility to **II** 118, 129
  defiance, acts of **II** 118, 129
  Devil, accusations of associating with **II** 117–18, 122–9
  diviners **II** 125
  dissonant political culture **II** 118
  effigies **II** 120
  Enlightenment **II** 118, 129–30
  gender **II** 127, 129
  hidden transcripts **II** 118, 129
  indigenous religion, hybrid cosmology with **II** 129–30
  men, competition with **II** 127, 129

music, role of **II** 125–6
power, access to **II** 127–8
priestesses of animism **II** 120, 129
priests, Catholics **II** 124–8
resistance **II** 118
supernatural **II** 117–18, 122–9
transcultural association **II** 126
village, supernatural world of the **II** 124–9
weapons of the weak **II** 118
women celebrants **II** 120, 129
cannibalism I 299
Cão, Gaspar I 261
Capuchins
French Antilles, Catholic missions to slaves in **I** 395, 398, 401–3
India, lower-caste Catholics in Madras **II** 53, 55–6, 59–60
Kongo, church in **I** 259–60, 262–3
Soyo, Capuchins and rulers of **I** 348–66
Tupi and European women in eyes of Claude d'Abbeville **I** 296
Cardoso, Mateus I 258–9
Cardoso, Renato III 433–4
Carey, Henry IV 188
Carey, William I 72, **II** 14
Caribbean *see* **French Antilles, Catholic missions to slaves in; Jamaican peasant life, religion as resistance in**
Carlyle, Thomas I 98
Carmelites
French Antilles, Catholic missions to slaves in **I** 402
Irish Carmelites **II** 384, 385–8, 394–401
Ulster Pentecostals **II** 398–400
Zimbabwe, missionaries in Northern Nyaga District **II** 384, 385–8, 394–101
Carnegie, David IV 156–7
Carpegna, Gaspare I 362
Carr, MW I 455
Carroll, Colleen IV 306
Carter, JJ III 363–4
Carter, William E II 292–3
carving IV 266–73
Cassidy, Michael III 365, **IV** 344
caste *see also* **dalits**
Brahmins **I** 444, 449, 459, **II** 56, **IV** 248, 254, 255

Catholics **II** 51–64
Paraiyar caste **II** 52–3, 55, 60–1, **IV** 244–5, 256
Southists **I** 222
Tarangambadi (Tranquebar), missionaries in **I** 444, 449, 459
Thomas Christians and the Thomas tradition **I** 222
catechism
Bolivia, catechists of Aymara Indians in **IV** 263–4
Chile, young women as apostles to the poor in **II** 277–8, 280–1
Catholic beliefs in Asia I 57–65
Catholicos IV 108–10, 113–14, 116, 119
Catholics *see also* **Jesuits; mass; Protestant-Catholic distinctions in coming global Christianity**
Africa
Cameroun, liturgical adaptation in St Paul de Ndzon-Melen in **I** 52–5
Kongo, church in **I** 257, 259–61
Nigeria, young converts in Onitsha **II** 107
Roman Africa, Christianity and local culture in **I** 183, 186–7, 191
Soyo, Capuchins and rulers of **I** 348–66
Zimbabwe **II** 385–6, 394–101, **III** 358, 363
Avila mission **II** 385–6, 395, 397, 399
Brazil
pilgrimage and patronage **IV** 87–103
Universal Church of the Kingdom of God **III** 436
women **I** 367
Cameroun, liturgical adaptation in St Paul de Ndzon-Melen in **I** 52–5
Canadian Prairie Indians, pilgrimages of **IV** 140–53
caste **II** 51–64
Catholic Action **II** 273–4, 280–2
centrality **IV** 310–13
Chile
Pentecostalism **II** 286–7, 293–4, 300–1
young women as apostles to the poor **II** 273–82

INDEX

China
  Catholic women of Congregation of Sisters in **IV** 68–83
  Christian Virgins in 18th century China **I** 425–37
  sectarian violence **II** 323–36
  Shaanxi Province, Catholic community in **IV** 69–70
  Western cultural communication at end of Ming dynasty **I** 286–9
  Zhouzi village people, beliefs of **III** 38–60
Church Mission Society **II** 107
cloisters **I** 296
colonialism **I** 394–408, **II** 52, 81–94, 161, 164–5, 170, 397, **IV** 266–7, 273
convent in Mexico, immediacy and eternity in a **IV** 45–67
Donatism **I** 183, 186–7, 191
faith and works, balance between **I** 6–7
folk Catholicism **II** 275, 395–6
France, faith, family and fashion in Strasbourg **III** 127–31, 133, 135–8
French Antilles, Catholic missions to slaves in **I** 394–408
gender **I** 296–7
Greece, religion and modernization in 19th century **II** 203–5
identity, Irish **II** 161, 167–8, 171–2
idolatory **IV** 171
imitation of Christ in Philippines **III** 61–80
India
  caste **II** 51–64
  Parsis of Bombay and Christian conversion **II** 15
  Tarangambadi (Tranquebar), missionaries in **I** 443
intercession, theology of **IV** 112
Irish Catholics in 19th century New Zealand **II** 160–78
jagar rituals in Goa, India **III** 21–37
Kongo, church in **I** 257, 259–61
Latin America, awakening of indigenous people in **IV** 319–22
Li lineage, Baptist and Catholic elements of **II** 323–36
Lübeck prophet in local and Lutheran context **I** 414

Mexico
  immediacy and eternity in a Catholic convent in **IV** 45–67
  native evangelism **III** 389, 390–3, 395–8, 401–3
Mezzogiorno, glossolalia and possession amongst Pentecostal groups of the **II** 308, 315
Michigan Indians, Catholic hymns of **IV** 181–90
missionary work **I** 297, **II** 81–94 385–6, 395–7, 399
mutualism **II** 349–50, 357, 359–60
New Guinea, gendered images of Holy Spirit Sisters (SSpS) in colonial **II** 81–94
New Zealand, Irish Catholics in 19th century Christchurch **II** 160–78
Nigeria, young converts in Onitsha **II** 107
pagan Catholicism **II** 275
Paiwan Catholics **IV** 252–80
Parsis of Bombay and Christian conversion **II** 15
pilgrimage **IV** 90–1
Philippines
  imitation of Christ in **III** 61–80
  Candelaria, Seberine, trial of **II** 124–8
popular Catholicism **II** 287, 293–4
purgatory **I** 414
Reformation **I** 296–7
Regina Coeli mission **II** 395–7
Roman Africa, Christianity and local culture in **I** 183, 186–7, 191
saints **IV** 171
Second Vatican Council **IV** 312–13, 265–6
sectarian violence **II** 323–36
Shaanxi Province, Catholic community in **IV** 69–70
shrines **IV** 122–3, 125–31, 141, 143–9, 169, 171, 173–5
slavery **I** 394–408
Social Catholicism **II** 275
Soyo, Capuchins and rulers of **I** 348–66
Spain, anticlericalism in Aracena in **II** 349–50, 357, 359–60
Sri Lanka **III** 458
syncretism **III** 469–71, 375, **IV** 262–80

366

Taiwan, syncretism among Paiwan
   Catholics in **IV** 262–80
Tarangambadi (Tranquebar), India,
   missionaries in **I** 443
women
   Brazil **I** 367
   Chile, young women as apostles to
      the poor **II** 273–82
   China, Congregation of Sisters in
      IV 68–83
   Zaïre **II** 266–7
   Zimbabwe
      American Evangelicalism **III** 358,
         371
      missionaries in Northern Nyaga
         District **II** 384–8, 394–401
**Catholicos, Christian patriarch of
   Georgia I** 206, 215
Caughey, John I 225
**Cavazzi, Giovanni Antonio da
   Montecuccolo I** 356–7, 359, 361
celibacy **I** 216–17
cell groups **III** 318, 321–3
censorship **III** 25
ceremonies *see also* **baptism; funerals;
   rituals**
   Burkino Faso, faith-healers of
      Assemblies of God in
      III 257–61, 263, 267–70
   Canadian Prairie Indians,
      pilgrimages of **IV** 143,
      145–52
   circumcision **III** 230–1
   deliverance **III** 257–61, 263, 267–70
   India, lower-caste Catholics in
      Madras **II** 53
   Kyrgyzstan, missionaries in
      post-Soviet **III** 230–1
   marriage **III** 112
Cerullo, Maurice III 363
Chad II 377
Chaka, king of the Zulus I 100
Chakrabarty, Dipesh I 441
Chan, Albert I 328
Chandaru, Nowroji Dorabji II 16
Chadwick, D II 201–2
Chang Hsing-yao I 329
Ch'an-yüeh I 329
chants **I** 127–9
Chapman, J Wilbur IV 212–13, 221
**charisma in early Christian Ephesus
   I** 153–64

charismatic movements
   African Christian theologies
      IV 344–5
   Japan, indigenous movements in
      III 335–8, 339
   India
      Madras, fundamentalism in
         III 451–6
      Orthodox Christian Pilgrim Centre
         in Kerala **IV** 110–13
   Leningrad, independent religious
      communities in **III** 353
   New Zealand, gospel songs in **IV** 216
   Taiwan, conversion to Protestantism
      amongst urban immigrants in
      III 321–3, 323–4
   Third Wave Charismatic Movement
      III 320
Chen Aming II 323, 328, 330–6
Chen, Chi-Lu IV 268
Chen Houguang I 292–3
Ch'en Hu I 336–7, 342
Ch'en Yüan I 338
Chenani I 185–6
Ch'ien Ch'ien-i I 335, 336
children and young people
   apostates **II** 186–9
   China, beliefs of Zhouzi village
      people in Catholic diocese in
      III 55
   Decalogue in Tagalog, Oliver's
      manuscript of **I** 313–14, 320,
      323–4
   natives as children, treating **I** 320–1
   Nigeria, young converts in Onitsha
      II 95–116
   Tatars and apostasy **II** 186–9
   witchcraft, denouncing by children of
      II 121
   Youth With a Mission **III** 359–60
Chile *see also* **Chile, pentacostalism in;
   Chile, young women as apostles
   to the poor in**
   healing **IV** 234
   indigenous people **IV** 328
   land rights **IV** 328
   Mapuchu **IV** 318–19, 324
   Universal Church of the Kingdom of
      God of Brazil **III** 428
Chile, pentacostalism in II 285–306
   1910–1930 **II** 295–6
   1932–1934 **II** 295–6

367

INDEX

1930–1964 **II** 296
1960–1970 **II** 296
1973 **II** 297–301
agrarian sector, organizing labour in **II** 297
bajo pueblo **II** 285, 286–301
baptism **II** 287
Catholicism **II** 286–7, 293–4, 300–1
Chilenization **II** 294
conflicts in national religious field **II** 285, 289–92
co-optation **II** 297
coup d'etat **II** 296, 300
cultures or mentalities, clash between **II** 289–92, 296
discrimination **II** 301
healing **II** 292–3
housing **II** 297–8
human rights **II** 300
identity **II** 293, 301
indigenization **II** 291, 293–4, 301
institutionalization **II** 296
labour organizations **II** 297
Methodist Church **II** 287–92, 295–6
militancy **II** 298–9
military rule **II** 300–1
missionaries **II** 286, 289–93
music **II** 294–5
nationalism **II** 291
Pentecostal explosion **II** 296
political parties **II** 297–9
politics **II** 285, 295–301
popular Catholicism **II** 287, 293–4
poverty **II** 286–301
Presbyterian Church **II** 289–92, 295–6
Protestantism **II** 286–90
relief organizations **II** 299–300
religious discrimination **II** 301
social organizations **II** 297–9
social participation **II** 297–9
socio-cultural changes **II** 285
stabilization **II** 296
Unidad Popular **II** 296, 298–300
Chile, young women as apostles to the poor in II 273–84
1922–1932 **II** 273–82
anarchism **II** 278
Asociacion de la Juventud Catolica Feminana de Chile (AJCFCh) **II** 273–82

baptism **II** 276, 279
catechism **II** 277–8, 280–1
Catholic Action **II** 273–4, 280–2
Catholics **II** 273–82
confirmation **II** 276
Eucharist **II** 276, 282
folk/pagan Catholicism **II** 275
gender **II** 274
Liberation Theology **II** 274
marriages **II** 279
Mary, mother of Jesus **II** 279–80
Mass **II** 275–6, 278–9, 281
men **II** 2746
missionaries **II** 276
models and rituals of female spirituality **II** 275–6
modernization **II** 278, 280–1
paganism **II** 275, 278
priests, shortage of **II** 273, 281
procession **II** 276
Protestantism **II** 278, 281
Social Catholicism **II** 275
socialism **II** 278, 281
teaching **II** 277–8
writings **II** 279–80, 282
China *see also* **China, Catholic women of Congregation of Sisters in**
Ch'ing-tsing **I** 227–32
Confucianism
  Japan, indigenous movements in **III** 333, 334, 340
  Neo-Confucianism **I** 337
  Western cultural communication at end of Ming dynasty **I** 281–6, 290–3
  Wu Li and first Chinese Christian poetry **I** 336–7, 338, 342–3
Cultural Revolution **III** 45
Macau **I** 339–40, 342
Neo-Confucianism **I** 337
Nestorian tablet **I** 227–32
poetry **I** 328–47
sectarian violence in late 19th century **II** 323–39
Sichuan, Christian Virgins in 18th century **I** 425–40
translation of Bible **I** 71
Western–sino cultural communication at end of Ming dynasty **I** 280–94
Wu Li and first Chinese Christian poetry **I** 330–47

368

INDEX

China, Catholic women of Congregation of Sisters in IV 68–83
  ancestor worship IV 70
  divorce IV 70
  education IV 79
  employment IV 69–70
  gender ideologies IV 68–9, 75–9
  kindergartens IV 74, 75–6
  marriages IV 70
  Mary, cult of IV 69–70
  money IV 75–7
  obedience IV 78–82
  politics IV 73
  priests, relationship with IV 75–80
  rituals IV 70
  Shaanxi Province, Catholic community in IV 69–70
  Society of the Sacred Heart of Jesus IV 72–3
  state, relationship with IV 68, 71–2, 73–5, 82
  vocation IV 71
  Western Church, relationship with IV 71–3, 81–2
China, Christian sectarian violence in late 19th century II 323–39
  American Baptist Missionary Society II 323–4, 334–6
  ancestral worship II 328
  Baptists II 323–36
  Catholics II 323–36
  colonialism II 324, 329–30
  conversions II 327, 330–1, 334
  French Catholic Missions II 324, 325–6, 329–30, 334–6
  intervention by external forces II 334–6
  intralineage disputes II 323–36
  kinship networks II 327
  Kuxi II 323–4
  Li lineage, Baptist and Catholic elements of II 323–36
  marginal members of society II 331
  missionaries II 323–4, 325–6, 329–30, 334–6
  Paris Foreign Missions II 324
  power II 323–4, 326
  Protestantism II 323–36
  surnames II 326
  territorial division II 326–7
Chinese Christian poetry I 328–47
  Book of Songs (Shih ching) I 328
  Buddhist poetry I 329, 332
  Confucianism I 328, 332, 336–7
  converts I 343
  criticism I 332
  eulogies (*tsan*) I 329
  'iron cross' I 333–5
  missionaries I 328
  paintings I 329
  Sung dynasty I 332, 335
Ch'ing–tsing I 227–32
Chiniquy, Charles II 169
Chola kingdom, persecution of I 217
Cholenec, Pierre IV 185–6
Chombart de Lauwe, Paul-Henri III 143
chosenness III 275–7
Christ for All Seasons III 362, 365, 367
Christ for the Nations in Dallas, United States III 364
Christchurch, New Zealand, Irish Catholics in 19th century II 160–78
Christian Marching Church of Central Africa III 368
Christmas, importance of I 6
Christodoulos of Athens, archbishop III 97–8
Christopherous II of Alexandria II 373
Chrysopolis I 198–9
Chrysostom, John I 204
Chu Hsi I 336
Chu I-tsun I 333
Ch'ü Yu-chung I 336, 342
Chung-Ok Yun I 86
Chung Sook Ja I 82–3
Church of the East I 213–17
Church of the Lord (Aladura) in United States, gender and change in III 106–26
  African Immigrant Religion (AIR) III 108–10, 122, 123
  African Instituted/Initiated Churches (AICs) III 110, 113, 124
  arbitration of doctrine III 112
  baptism ceremonies III 112
  categories III 110–11
  challenges to CLA III 117–19
  clergy, experiential and communication gap with III 118, 119
  communion III 112
  concepts III 110–11
  culture III 120

INDEX

funerals **III** 112
gender rules and structures **III** 111–12
Germany **III** 107
immigration enforcement, fear of **III** 118–19
language **III** 110–11
Liberia **III** 107, 116
local authorities, interaction with **III** 118
Lutheran Church in United States **III** 123, 124
male clergy, relationship with **III** 119
marriage ceremonies **III** 112
menstrual blood taboo **III** 109, 110–12, 119, 120–2
mission in reverse **III** 112–13
negotiation of gender practices in United States **III** 119–20
Nigeria **III** 107, 110, 113–14, 118, 123
offices **III** 110–11
ordination of women **III** 107, 110, 113
primacy **III** 111–12
professionals as members of Church **III** 109
Sierra Leone **III** 107, 108, 113–18, 120–1
slavery **III** 106
stereotyping **III** 109
Togo **III** 107
tradition **III** 120
United Kingdom **III** 107, 120
utilitarian approach **III** 118
website **III** 107–9, 112–13
witchcraft **III** 110
Yoruba people **III** 107, 110
Cipriani, R II 205
circumcision III 230–1
Civavaakiyar I 456–7, 459–60, 463–4
civilisation
  clash of civilizations **IV** 297, 308
  missionaries **II** 29–31, 65, 67
  Southern Tswana, Africa, cultivation and colonialism in **II** 29–31
clairvoyance III 475
Clark, John III 189–90
Clarke, Tony II 394–5, 399
class see also **elites**
  attendance at church **I** 17
  Brazil
    women in colonial Brazil **I** 373–6
    Universal Church of the Kingdom of God **III** 430
  Chile, Pentecostalism in **II** 285, 286–301
  Coptic cultural nationalism **III** 19–20
  Dalit theology in Tamil Christian folk music **IV** 248–9, 257
  Decalogue in Tagalog, Oliver's manuscript of **I** 321–2
  India, status of Christian women in Kerala **III** 85
  Southern Tswana, Africa, cultivation and colonialism in **II** 40–5
  Spain, anticlericalism in Aracena in **II** 340–1, 344–50
  Sumatra, Karo Batak Protestant Church in **II** 148
  Sunday School Movement **III** 16, **III** 18
  Zaïre, Kimbanguism and syncretism in **II** 269
Claúdio, Father III 197–8
Cleland, Robert Glass II 226
Clemens, VI I 290
clergy see also **bishops**
  animism **II** 120, 129
  Brazil, French priests in **III** 201–2, 204–6, 207
  buffoon-clerics **III** 311–12
  Chile, young women as apostles to the poor in **II** 273, 281
  China, Catholic women of Congregation of Sisters in **IV** 75–80
  conservatism and gentry, clerics' alliance with **II** 348–9
  corruption and moral lapses of clergy **II** 352–3
  episcopal control, disputes over **II** 172–3
  French Polynesia, women in ordained ministry in Mô'ohi Protestant Church in **III** 149–61
  French priests
    Brazil **III** 201–2, 205–6
    New Zealand, Irish Catholics in 19th century Christchurch in **II** 173
  Greece
    contested masculine spaces in Greek Orthodoxy **III** 94, 95–100

370

religion and modernization in 19th century **II** 208–9, 213
illiteracy **II** 213
Irish priests
Brazil **III** 201–2, 204–5, 207
New Zealand, Irish Catholics in 19th century Christchurch in **II** 171–2
Kongo, church in **I** 259–60
Malawi, women as religious and political praise singers and dancers in **IV** 224–41
Malo cult in Torres Straits Islands **I** 45–6
Melanesian Mission **II** 66–75
Mezzogiorno, glossolalia and possession amongst Pentecostal groups of the **II** 309
Nanrantsouak, church at **I** 383–4
New Zealand, Irish Catholics in 19th century Christchurch in **II** 171–3
Nigeria, young converts in Onitsha **II** 95–6, 99
ordination of women
French Polynesia, Mô'ohi Protestant Church in **III** 149–61
United States, Church of the Lord (Aladura) in **III** 107, 110, 113
Philippines, trial of Seberine Candelaria in **II** 124–8
Seventh–day Adventism **III** 381
shortage **II** 273, 281
Spain, anticlericalism in Aracena in **II** 352–3
United States
gender and change in Church of the Lord (Aladura) in **III** 118, 119
Zimbabwe, American Evangelicalism in **III** 369
unmarried women in ministry, role of **I** 81–2
white church leaders **III** 366–7
white-led churches before African independence **III** 357–9
Zimbabwe, American Evangelicalism in **III** 369
Cline-Smythe, Gloria Malake III 108–10, 113–17, 119–25
Clogg, R II 209, 212, 216–17
clothing *see* dress
Cockspur Island, United States IV 169

Codrington, Robert H II 68, 69, 72–4
cognitive dissonance II 256
coinage I 198–9
Colbert, Jean-Baptiste I 402
Cold War IV 347–8
Cole, Ed Louis III 363
Colenso, John William
Africa **I** 95–110
background **I** 98
Bishop of Natal, as **I** 98, 109
Commentary on Romans **I** 101–10
context of the text **I** 101–9
Greek **I** 101
Jewish prejudices, letter as addressed to **I** 101–2
outline **I** 102–9
Commentary on the Pentateuch **I** 95, 97
creation account in Bible **I** 99
double nature of man **I** 106–7
hegemony **I** 97, 107–9
heresy **I** 95
hermeneutics **I** 97, 101–2, 109
ignorance **I** 102–3
Lambeth Conference 1868 **I** 95
'long conversation' **I** 95, 96–7, 109
Jewish prejudices, *Romans* as addressed to **I** 101–2
marriage **I** 98
missionary, as **I** 95–9, 109
Original Sin **I** 103–5
sin **I** 102–6
translation of Bible **I** 101
universality **I** 102, 104
Zulus **I** 99–110
Coleridge, Samuel Taylor I 98
Colin, John Claude II 173
Colombia, land rights in IV 328
colonialism
Aboriginal Australians **III** 165
Africa
African Christian theologies **IV** 345, 347
Barwe refugees from Portuguese East Africa **II** 385
Bible **I** 70, 72–5, 94–5
Orthodox Mission in **II** 368, 371–3, 380
Southern Tswana, cultivation and colonialism in **II** 28–50
Zimbabwe **II** 383–5, 397, **III** 357–9

INDEX

Barwe refugees from Portuguese East Africa **II** 385
Bible **I** 69–78, 112
Brazil, women in **I** 295–308, 367–78
Catholics **I** 394–408, **II** 52, 81–94, 161, 164–5, 170, 397, **IV** 266–7, 273
China, Christian sectarian violence in late 19th century **II** 324, 329–30
chosennesss **III** 275–7
conversions **I** 10–11
Cyprus **II** 373
Dalit theology in Tamil Christian folk music **IV** 245
decolonization **I** 77, **II** 232, **III** 150, **IV** 160
elites **I** 74–7
feminist theory **I** 297
French Antilles, Catholic missions to slaves in **I** 394–408
gender **I** 295–308
hegemony **I** 94–7
hybridity **I** 70–2
India **I** 69–70, 72, 75–7, **III** 443, **IV** 245
Irish Carmelites **II** 397
Jamaican peasant life, religion as resistance in **III** 181–7, 191
Japan **IV** 266–7, 273
Kenya, Orthodox Mission in **II** 371–2, 373–4
Korean military 'comfort women' **I** 91–2
Latin America, awakening of indigenous people in **IV** 320–2, 326
liberation movements **I** 95
literacy **I** 74–5
Madras
  Catholics **II** 52
  global fundamentalism and local Christianity in **III** 443
missionaries **I** 15, 7–4, 94–7, **IV** 154
Mizeki, Bernard **IV** 156–65
nationalism **I** 74
native agency **I** 70–1
New Guinea, gendered images of Holy Spirit Sisters (SSpS) in colonial **II** 81–94
New Zealand, Irish Catholics in 19th century Christchurch in **II** 161, 164–5, 170

Orthodox Mission **II** 368, 371–3, 380
patriarchy **I** 75, 297
Philippines
  Candelaria, Seberine, trial of **II** 118, 129
  imitation of Christ in **III** 62, 76
Portugal **II** 385, **III** 23–5, **IV** 283–4, 293–4
recognition, ruse of **I** 69–70
Southern Tswana, Africa, cultivation and colonialism in **II** 28–50
subalterns **I** 74–6
subversion **I** 69–70
Sumatra, Karo Batak Protestant Church in **II** 141, 144–6, 150–1, 153
syncretism **II** 257, **IV** 266–7, 273
Taiwan, syncretism among Paiwan Catholics in **IV** 266–7, 273
Tamils **I** 70
translations **I** 70–7, 112
Tupi and European women in eyes of Claude d'Abbeville **I** 295–308
United Kingdom **III** 181
United States **III** 357–9
white-led churches before African independence **III** 357–9
women
  Brazil **I** 295–308, 367–78
  Tupi and European women in eyes of Claude d'Abbeville **I** 295–308
  Zaïre, Kimbanguism and syncretism in **II** 257–9, 269
Zimbabwe
  American Evangelicalism **III** 357–9
  Northern Nyaga District, missionaries in **II** 383–5, 397
Colossians **I** 127–9
Columbanus, St I 205
Comaroff, Jean I 95–7, 99, 441, **II** 141
Comaroff, John I 95–7, 99, 441, **II** 141
comfort women *see* **Korean military 'comfort women'**
Comins, Richard B II 72–3
Commentary of Romans. **Colenso, John William I** 101–10
context of the text **I** 101–9
Greek **I** 101
Jewish prejudices, letter as addressed to **I** 101–2
outline **I** 102–9
Compassion Ministries III 371

INDEX

communion
  Cameroun, liturgical adaptation in St Paul de Ndzon-Melen in **I** 52–5
  United States, gender and change in Church of the Lord (Aladura) in **III** 112
  Zaïre, Kimbanguism and syncretism in **II** 262
communism
  anti-communism **III** 367, 370
  India, global fundamentalism and local Christianity in **III** 447–8
  Sumatra, Karo Batak Protestant Church in **II** 148–9
  Zimbabwe, American Evangelicalism in **III** 367, 370
communitarianism III 393
communitas-style movements III 312–13
connectionism III 465
confessions
  baptism **I** 135–6, 139
  Burkino Faso, faith-healers of Assemblies of God in **III** 257–8
  Canadian Prairie Indians, pilgrimages of **IV** 145
  Soyo, Capuchins and rulers of **I** 356, 360–2
confirmation II 276
Confucianism
  Chinese
    Christian poetry **I** 328, 332, 336–7
    Neo-Confucianism **I** 337
    Western cultural communication at end of Ming dynasty **I** 281–6, 290–3
    Wu Li and first Chinese Christian poetry **I** 336–7, 338, 342–3
  Japan, indigenous movements in **III** 333, 334, 340
  missionaries, misinterpretation by **I** 281–6
  Neo-Confucianism **I** 337
Congregation of Sisters in China IV 68–83
conservatism
  Brazil, base communities (CEBs) in **III** 203–5, 207
  conservative/liberal divide **IV** 298, 304–7
  New Zealand, gospel songs in **IV** 216
  Spain, anticlericalism in Aracena in **II** 348–9

  United States **IV** 305–7
consolation I 129, 130
consolidation I 28–9
Constantine, emperor I 11–12, 198–9, 201, 208, 215, **II** 206–7
Constantine VII Porphyrogenitus, emperor I 244
Constantinople Orthodox Church II 213–14, 217–18, 369, 370
Constantius I 219
context I 23–4
  ethnic other **I** 12
  hierarchy, replication of **I** 11–12
  language **I** 11
  local traditions **I** 18
  particularity **I** 18
  sociology **I** 11–12
  specificity **I** 17–18
  uniformity **I** 18
  universalism **I** 18
convent in Mexico, immediacy and eternity in a Catholic IV 45–67
  Congregation, description of **IV** 49–50
  continuity and discontinuity **IV** 45–6, 48, 64–5
  conversions **IV** 64–5
  evangelizing the self **IV** 63–5
  fundamentalism **IV** 46
  future into the past, reading the **IV** 53–4
  globalization **IV** 50
  millenarianism **IV** 46
  modernization **IV** 49–50
  narratives
    identity **IV** 50–1
    vocations **IV** 5–63
  political commitment **IV** 50
  preciousness of time **IV** 45
  recollecting and rearranging personal history into new narrative of self **IV** 46, 53–4
  ritualization of everyday life **IV** 52–3, 65
  rituals **IV** 52–3, 65
  sacred and profane, time as **IV** 46–8, 65
  self, religious vocation as story of **IV** 50–2, 63–5
  social commitment **IV** 50
  stages of transformation **IV** 46, 49, 53–4, 65

373

INDEX

time **IV** 46–51, 65–6
  commodification and personalization **IV** 46
  framing **IV** 46–7
  precious, as **IV** 45
  sacred and profane, time as **IV** 46–9, 65
  transformation **IV** 46, 48–9, 53–4, 63–6
  vocation **IV** 48–9, 50–66

conversions
  Aksum, Christianization of **I** 201, 203
  anthropology **I** 10
  apostasy **II** 179–82, 187, 190
  Baptists **IV** 64–5
  Burkino Faso, faith-healers of Assemblies of God in **III** 256, 260–1
  China, Christian sectarian violence in late 19th century **II** 327, 330–1, 334
  Chinese Christian poetry **I** 337, 343
  colonial or neo-colonial subjects **I** 10–11
  ethnic or national identity, formation of **I** 200
  forced conversions **I** 470
  French Antilles, Catholic missions to slaves in **I** 394–5
  Iberia, Christianization of **I** 201, 203
  immigrants **III** 317–29
  India
    jagar rituals in Goa, India **III** 23
    lower-caste Catholics in Madras **II** 51, 58, 62
    Parsis of Bombay **II** 13–27
    Tarangambadi (Tranquebar), missionaries in **I** 441–3, 448–9, 453–62
  jagar rituals in Goa, India **III** 23
  Japan **I** 269–72, 274–5
  Karo Batak Protestant Church, Sumatra, conversion and **II** 137–59
  Kyrgyzstan, missionaries in post-Soviet **III** 240–3
  Leningrad, independent religious communities in **III** 346, 352–4
  marginal people **II** 97–8
  mass conversions **II** 148, **III** 23
  Methodist shrines **IV** 173
  Mexico
    immediacy and eternity in a Catholic convent in **IV** 64–5
    native evangelism **III** 389–90, 392–4, 398
  Mezzogiorno, glossolalia and possession amongst Pentecostal groups of the **II** 308–11
  Native American missionaries **I** 470–82
  New Guinea, gendered images of Holy Spirit Sisters (SSpS) in colonial **II** 83
  Nigeria, fertility in Itapa-Ekiti in **III** 276–8, 284
  paganism in rural Anatolia and Greece from 6th century, conversion from **I** 233–54
  Parsis of Bombay **II** 13–27
  Pentecostalism
    Sumatra, Karo Batak Protestant Church in **II** 139–40
  political phenomenon, conversion as a **II** 141, 143–4
  process, as **I** 10
  Protestants
    Taiwan, immigrants to **III** 317–29
  psychological models **II** 142–3
  representation **I** 17
  Roman Empire, Christianization of **I** 200
  royal conversions **I** 201–2, 203
  self, conversion as care of **I** 453–62
  shrines **IV** 173
  sociology **I** 10–11, **II** 141–3
  support, acts of **III** 323, 324–6
  Taiwan, conversion to Protestantism amongst urban immigrants in **III** 317–29
  Tarangambadi (Tranquebar), India, missionaries in **I** 441–3, 448–9, 453–62
  Tupi and European women in eyes of Claude d'Abbeville **I** 298–9, 301–5
  United States, shrines in **IV** 173
  urban immigrants **III** 317–29
  usefulness **I** 441
  volition **I** 10–11
  Xavier, Francisco, Japanese in letters of **I** 269–72, 274–5
  Zulus **I** 99–101

Cook, Sherburne II 230
Cooley, Frank L II 147–8
Cooty, Cauden II 53, 59
Copeland, Gloria III 362
Copeland, Kenneth III 362
Coptics
  Africa, mission in II 369, 371
  cultural nationalism III 13–20
  language, resurrection of Coptic III 16–17
  music III 14–15
  Orthodox Church II 369, 371
  Patriarchate II 369, 371
  political ramifications III 18
  printing workshops III 16
  secularization III 14, 18
  socialization III 14
  Sunday School Movement III 16, III 18
  university, endowment of III 18
  upper middle-class, attraction of III 19–20
Corbin, John II 343
Corinthians I 127–8, 133
corruption of clergy II 352–3
Cosmos Indicopleustes I 207–8
Council of Chalcedon I 204–5, II 369
Council of Ephesus I 215
Couplet, Philippe I 339
Courage, Sarah Amelia II 169
court use by Baptists in United States I 35–43
Courtois, C I 182, 192
Cowle, CE IV 17
Cox, Harvey III 307
Crane, Edwin IV 158
Cree IV 142, 150–1
creation I 99, III 278–9
Croke, Thomas II 172
Crowther, Samuel II 96–7
Crumbley, Deidre Helen III 108–10, 112–13, 119–23
crusades III 362–4, 448–9, 454, IV 214
Csordas, TJ IV 47
Cullen, Paul II 172
cultivation and colonialism in Southern Tswana, Africa II 28–50
  agrarian aesthetics II 31–5
  cattle II 30
  civilising mission II 29–31
  class II 40–5
  division of labour II 33–4

  exports II 41–2
  gender II 33–4, 38–9, 42
  missionaries II 28–9
  moralism II 31
  pastoralism II 30
  ploughs, use of II 41
  production, patterns of II 29
  salvation II 29
  slavery II 31
  socialism II 31–5
  superstition II 31–5
  taboos II 33
  transformation II 41
culture
  Aboriginal Australians IV 13–14
  Africa
    African Christian theologies IV 336–8
    Berbers I 181–4
    Cameroun, liturgical adaptation in St Paul de Ndzon-Melen in I 52
    Malawi, women as praise singers and dancers in IV 224–7, 238
    Roman Africa I 181–97
    Zimbabwe, American Evangelicalism in III 366
  Aksum, Christianization of I 207–8
  Berbers I 181–4
  Brazil, Universal Church of the Kingdom of God in III 426–7
  California, breakdown of Spanish mission system in II 227
  Cameroun, liturgical adaptation in St Paul de Ndzon-Melen in I 52
  Chile, Pentacostalism in II 289–92, 296
  China-Western cultural communication at end of Ming dynasty I 280–94
  continuity III 319
  Coptic cultural nationalism III 13–20
  conversions III 319
  Dalit theology in Tamil Christian folk music IV 242, 244–7, 256
  French Antilles, Catholic missions to slaves in I 451–3
  French Polynesia, women in ordained ministry in Mô'ohi Protestant Church in III 157–8
  Greece, religion and modernization in 19th century II 202–6, 216–18

INDEX

hybridity **III** 22–3
Iberia, Christianization of **I** 207–8
imitative and derivative, culture as **III** 63
inculturation **II** 396, **IV** 336–43, 347
India,
    Madras, global fundamentalism and local Christianity in **III** 443–62
    Parsis of Bombay and Christian conversion **II** 14–16, 18, 20, 24
jagar rituals in Goa, India **III** 22–3
Jamaican peasant life, religion as resistance in **III** 187–93
Kyrgyzstan, missionaries in post-Soviet **III** 231–3, 237–9, 243–9
Malawi, women as religious and political praise singers and dancers in **IV** 224–7, 238
mentalities and culture, clash between **II** 289–92, 296
merchandising **IV** 324–5
Mezzogiorno, glossolalia and possession amongst Pentecostal groups of the **II** 316
missionaries **II** 65–6, 67–8, 74
nationalism **III** 13–20
Parsis of Bombay and Christian conversion **II** 14–16, 18, 20, 24
Philippines, imitation of Christ in **III** 62, 76
pilgrimage **IV** 141–2, 151
Punics **I** 181–6, 191
relativism **IV** 13–14
ritual and early church in Eastern Mediterranean **I** 125
Roman Africa, local culture in **I** 181–97
Spain, anticlericalism in Aracena in **II** 343–4
syncretism **IV** 263, 266–7, 274
Taiwan
    conversion to Protestantism amongst urban immigrants in **III** 319
    syncretism among Paiwan Catholics in **IV** 263, 266–7, 274
Tamils **I** 451–3, **IV** 242, 244–7, 256
United States
    gender and change in Church of the Lord (Aladura) in **III** 120
Zimbabwe, Evangelicalism in **III** 366
Zimbabwe, American Evangelicalism in **III** 366
Curley, Tagak III 217, 219
Cyprus, fight against colonial rule in II 373
Cyril, Bishop of Alexandria I 215
Cyril, St III 15

Dababhoy, Heerjeebhoy II 17–18
d'Abbeville, Claude I 295–308
Dahl, Nils I 130
Dalit theology in Tamil Christian folk music IV 242–61
    Appavoo, Theophilus **IV** 242–6, 249–57
    Brahmins **IV** 248, 254, 255
    Carnatic music **IV** 244, 246, 248
    caste **IV** 242–5, 248, 254–5
    Church of South India **IV** 243, 247, 252
    class **IV** 248–9, 257
    colonization **IV** 245
    culture **IV** 242, 244–7, 256
    drumming **IV** 245–6, 256
    Eucharist **IV** 245, 250–1, 254, 256–7
    farmer, God as **IV** 250, 251
    feminine and masculine, God as **IV** 250, 251, 253–4
    gender 250, 251, 253–4
    Giramiya Isai Varipadu **IV** 251–2, 256
    Greetings and Praise of God **IV** 253–6
    hegemony **IV** 244, 245, 247, 251, 254, 256
    Hindu dalits **IV** 243
    Hinduization **IV** 248
    indigenization of Christianity **IV** 242, 245–51, 255–7
    indigenized Tamil Christian music, history and context of **IV** 246–9
    indigenous classical, folk and popular songs **IV** 247
    karugippona **IV** 256
    kirtanai **IV** 248, 249
    language **IV** 246–7, 249–51
    liberation **IV** 242, 245, 246, 249–51, 255–6
    Lutherans **IV** 247–8
    missionaries **IV** 245, 247–8
    nanappattu **IV** 247

oppari **IV** 251–2
oru olai **IV** 245, **IV** 250–1, 254, 256–7
pamalai **IV** 247
Paraiyar caste **IV** 244–5, 256
pohhum **IV** 254
pop music **IV** 249
possession by village deity **IV** 245–6
prejudice **IV** 243–4, 249
Protestants **IV** 243–4, 247–8
reversal, strategy of **IV** 250, 251
rights for Christian Dalits, lack of **IV** 243
rural symbols **IV** 254
salvation **IV** 256
Samiya Vananguradu **IV** 252–3
Sanskritization **IV** 246–7
Sankritized Tamil music **IV** 247, 248–9
social change **IV** 256–7
tamil isai vari pattu **IV** 248–50
Tamil Nadu Theological Seminary **IV** 244
theology **IV** 244–5, 253
translation **IV** 246–7
Trinity, qualities of **IV** 253–4
use of word 'Dalit' **IV** 243
universal family **IV** 250, 253
Vellala **IV** 248
Western hymns sung in European languages **IV** 247
Western hymns translated into Sanskritized Tamil **IV** 247
Westernization **IV** 246–7
'Worship in Folk Music' **IV** 249–57
dalits *see also* **Dalit theology in Tamil Christian folk music**
Catholics **I** 444, **II** 57–8
Manu, Laws of **I** 12
Tarangambadi (Tranquebar), missionaries in **I** 444
Thomas Christians and the Thomas tradition **I** 212
dance
Aboriginal Australians **III** 172–3, 176–7
Cameroun, liturgical adaptation in St Paul de Ndzon-Melen in **I** 50, 53–4
Canadian Prairie Indians, pilgrimages of **IV** 143, 147–52
Gnostics **IV** 282

hastas (hand gestures) **IV** 285–7
India
 Christianity in Indian dance forms **IV** 280–93
 hastas (hand gestures) **IV** 285–7
 jagar rituals in Goa **III** 32–3
 Tarangambadi (Tranquebar), missionaries in **I** 460
Malawi, women as religious and political praise singers and dancers in **IV** 228–31
Norddeutsche Missionsgesellschaft, role of Devil in preaching of **III** 416–17
Sun Dance **IV** 143, 148–52
Tea Dance **IV** 147
trance dances **III** 416–17
women **I** 460, **IV** 228–31
worship, as integral part of **IV** 281–2
Dandekar, Mora Bhat II 16
D'Andrade, Roy III 466
Daneel, ML IV 163, 343
Daniel the Stylite I 205
***dar-al-Islam*, refugees from I** 220–3
Darwin, Charles I 99
Das, Veena III 86
David, king I 240
David of Garedji I 206
Day of Judgment IV 191–2
de la Touche, Daniel I 296
De Mello, Anthony IV 305
de Paul, Vincent, St I 430
de Rougemont, François I 330–1, 339, 343
de Saint-Loû, Alexis I 395
de Saint-Martin, Jean-Didier I 433–4
de Saussure, Ferdinand IV 33
deacons I 157–8, 159, **III** 96, 98–9
death *see* **burial; funerals**
Decalogue in Tagalog, Oliver's manuscript of I 311–27
decolonization I 77, **II** 232, **III** 150
decor III 128–9, 130, 132–3, 137–9
definition of religion I 124
Deiros, PA III 451
Delia, Tiang III 72–3
deliverance ceremonies III 257–61, 263, 267–70
democracy I 112–13, **III** 195
demons *see* **spirits and demons**
Dennis, Frances II 102–3
denominationalism IV 336

INDEX

Deuterius I 235-6
Devens, Carol I 297
Devil *see also* **spirits and demons; witchcraft, sorcery and devils**
  Bushmen, Christ as trickster in religion of contemporary III 298, 302-3, 310-11
  image of Satan III 410-15
  Norddeutsche Missiongesellschaft, role of Devil in preaching of III 409-22
devotional objects IV 263-4
Dewang, Fang III 40
Dewar, Veronica III 215
Dexter, Benjamin III 182
Dharampal-Frick, Gita I 444-5
diaspora
  Greece, religion and modernization in 19th century II 218
  Kongo, church in I 257-8
  Pentecostalism III 424
Díaz del Moral, Juan III 342
Didache I 134, 142
Diehl, C III 446
Dickson, Kwesi IV 333, 335
diseases
  AIDs III 255
  Burkino Faso, faith-healers of Assemblies of God in III 256
  California, breakdown of Spanish mission system in II 231
  devils III 256
Djilas, Milovan I 190-1
Dimaras, CT II 209
Diogo I I 260-1, 262
Dioscorus I 205
Disciples I 155-6, 161-2
discrimination and prejudice *see also* **gender**
  Chile, pentacostalism in II 301
  Colenso, John William. *Commentary of Romans* I 101-2
  Dalit theology in Tamil Christian folk music IV 243-4, 249
  Latin America, awakening of indigenous people in IV 325
  Native American missionaries I 471-2, 478-9
  New Zealand, Irish Catholics in 19th century Christchurch in II 168-71
  racism I 269, 275, 471-2, 478-9
  Xavier, Francisco, Japanese in letters of I 269, 275
dispensationalism IV 215
diviners
  Candelaria, Seberine, trial in Philippines of II 125
  Nigeria, fertility in Itapa-Ekiti in III 277-8
  paganism in rural Anatolia and Greece from 6th century, conversion from I 239, 242, 243, 245
divorce IV 70
domestic servants, women as II 165-6, 169
Dominicans I 402-3, 430
***Dominus Iesus* declaration in Asia** I 57-65
  belief I 57-65
  one and only saviour, Jesus as I 57-65
  relativism I 62-3
  salvation, necessity of Church for I 60-3
  sensus fidelium I 57-8
  surveys I 57-65
Donatism I 183, 185-92
Donatus I 192
Dorsey, George IV 143
double nature of man I 106-7
Douglas, Ian IV 307
Douglas, Mary I 125
Dowd, Berthold II 396
Down to Earth outreach program III 366-7
dowries III 86, 87
dress
  Aboriginal Australians III 14-24
  baptismal clothing III 17, 19
  feet, covering of IV 15
  France, faith, family and fashion in Strasbourg III 128, 130, 132-3, 135-8
  Greek Orthodoxy, contested masculine spaces in III 97-8
  hair IV 16
  Lübeck prophet in local and Lutheran context I 416-17
  Malawi, women as religious and political praise singers and dancers in IV 226-8
  missionaries III 14-24

378

INDEX

nakedness **III** 14–24
pride **I** 416–17
Strasbourg, France, faith, family and fashion in **III** 127–48
Droogers, André I 13
Druillettes, Gabriel I 379, 388
dualism **I** 168–70, **III** 410
Dudink, Ad I 329, 330–1
Dudko, Dmitrii III 354
Duff, Alexander II 14
Dufresse, Gabriel-Taurin I 435–6
Duguid, Charles IV 19–20
Duncan, Carol IV 125
Durkheim, Emile I 124–5, **III** 247–8, **IV** 30, 47
Dutch East India Company I 442
Dzobo, NK III 417

Eade, J IV 124
Earhart, HB III 335, 340
Eastern Mediterranean
  early church **I** 25–7, 155–64, 165–78
  Gnostics **I** 166, 167–75
  governance **I** 155–63
  heretics **I** 165–78
  office charisma in early Christian Ephesus **I** 153–64
  paganism in rural Anatolia and Greece from 6th century, conversion from **I** 233–54
  rituals **I** 123–52
Eberts, Harry W I 155–6
ecclesiology I 14–15
ecological movements IV 327–8
economic conditions
  Brazil, base communities in **III** 196, 202–4, 206–7
  Burkino Faso, faith-healers of Assemblies of God in **III** 254–5
  jagar rituals in Goa, India **III** 23
ecumenicalism
  African Christian theologies **IV** 344, 346
  Ecumenical Association of Third World Theologians (EATWOT) **IV** 346–7, 348
  French Polynesia, women in ordained ministry in Mô'ohi Protestant Church in **III** 150–1
  Greek Orthodoxy, contested masculine spaces in shrines **IV** 170

Edessa, Osrhoene I 199, 214–15
Edict of Constantine I 215
Edinburgh *see* hats as symbol of women's position in Evangelical churches in Edinburgh, Scotland
education and teaching
  Africa
    Orthodox Mission in **II** 375, 379–80
    Zimbabwe, American Evangelicalism in **III** 369
  apostasy **II** 188
  Brazil, women in colonial **I** 368, 374
  Chile, young women as apostles to the poor in **II** 277–8
  China
    Catholic women of Congregation of Sisters in **IV** 79
    Zhouzi village people, beliefs of **III** 40
  Coptic cultural nationalism **III** 18
  French Polynesia, women in ordained ministry in Mô'ohi Protestant Church in **III** 153–4, 157–8
  Greece, religion and modernization in 19th century **II** 204
  Irish Carmelites **II** 399–400
  Korean Protestantism, contribution of Biblewomen to **II** 239–40, 242, 245, 248
  New Guinea, gendered images of Holy Spirit Sisters (SSpS) in colonial **II** 82–3, 91
  New Zealand, Irish Catholics in 19th century Christchurch in **II** 171
  Nigeria, young converts in Onitsha **II** 95–6, 98–104
  Parsis of Bombay and Christian conversion **II** 14, 23–5
  schools, disputes over number and location of **II** 399–400
  Taiwan, syncretism among Paiwan Catholics in **IV** 265
  Tatars and apostasy **II** 188
  Zimbabwe **II** 399–400, **III** 369
Edwards Salas, Rafael II 273–4, 276
effigies II 120
egalitarianism
  Greek Orthodoxy, contested masculine spaces in **III** 96

Korean Protestantism, contribution
of Biblewomen to **II** 239–40
spiritual egalitarianism **I** 399–400
Egan, Peter II 396
Egli, Hans IV 265–6, 268, 270, 274
Egypt *see* **Coptic Orthodox Church**
ekklesia
admonition **I** 129, 130, 131, 133
chants **I** 127–9
Colossians **I** 127–9
conformity pattern **I** 130
consolation **I** 129, 130
Corinthians **I** 127–8, 133
Ephesians **I** 127–9
exhortation **I** 129, 130–3
hymns **I** 127–8
instruction **I** 129, 130
Old Testament, reading of the
I 129–30
prayer **I** 131–2, 133
psalms **I** 127–8
reading **I** 129–30
revelation pattern **I** 130
rituals **I** 126, 127–33, 141
singing **I** 127–9
social cohesion **I** 129
soteriological pattern **I** 130
spiritual odes **I** 128–9
teleological pattern **I** 130
Eleusinian mysteries I 136
Eliade, Mircea I 342, **III** 70
Elias, Norbert I 451–2
Elim movement II 385–6, 388–93,
397–401
elites
Bible **I** 74–5
Brazil
base communities in **III** 208
women **I** 368–73, 375
colonialism **I** 74–5, 368–73, 375
India, status of Christian women in
Kerala **III** 84, 89
Korean Protestantism, contribution
of Biblewomen to **II** 247–9
Kyrgyzstan, missionaries in post-
Soviet **III** 231
lay agency **I** 29–30
literacy **I** 74–5
Persia **I** 216–17
Soyo, Capuchins and rulers of
I 355–7
Elizalde, Ignacio I 269

Ella Amidas I 205
Ellis, Francis Whyte I 453
Ellul, Jacques III 438–9
Elphick, Robert II 289
emotionalism IV 221
employment *see* **labour**
endogamy II 167
Endubis, King I 199
Engelhardt, Zephrin I 225
Engels, Friedrich I 297
Engelstein, Laura II 187
Enlightenment
Greece, religion and modernization
in 19th century **II** 205, 209,
211–13
inter-continental Enlightenment
I 31–2
Philippines, trial of Seberine
Candelaria in **II** 118, 129–30
sino-Western cultural communication
at end of Ming dynasty **I** 285–6
witchcraft and devils **II** 119
Epaphras I 158
Ephesians **I** 127–9
**Ephesus, office charisma in early
Christian I** 153–64
Epiphanius I 168
episcopacy *see* **bishops**
Erickson, Carolly III 127
Ernle, Lord (Prothero, Rowland) II 35
Errazuriz, Amalia II 276, 279–80
eschatology
Lord's Supper **I** 142–4
New Zealand, gospel songs in
IV 214–15
Seventh–day Adventism **III** 376,
377–84
essentialism I 13
eternal life
Burkino Faso, faith-healers of
Assemblies of God in **III** 256
Mexico, immediacy and eternity in a
Catholic convent in **IV** 45–67
Ethelbert of Kent, King I 200
Ethiopia I 24, **II** 370
ethnicity
ethnic other **I** 12
France, faith, family and fashion
in Strasbourg **III** 128, 133,
139–40
French Antilles, Catholic missions
to slaves in **I** 397–8

INDEX

Greece, religion and modernization in 19th century **II** 206–12
interracial marriages, promotion of 402
Latin America, awakening of indigenous people in **IV** 316–18
New Zealand, Irish Catholics in 19th century Christchurch in **II** 161, 163–4, 167–8, 170–5
racism **I** 269, 275, 471–2, 478–9
ethnocentrism II 65
ethnography I 311–17, **III** 62, 245–7, **IV** 25, 321–2
Ettawageshik, Fred IV 182–3, 187
Eucharist
  Chile, young women as apostles to the poor in **II** 276, 282
  Dalit theology in Tamil Christian folk music **IV** 245, 250–1, 254, 256–7
EuroAmerica *see* **West and Westernization**
eulogies I 329
European Union III 94–5, 100–4
Eusebius of Caesarea I 199, 201, 214
evangelism
  Africa
    African Christian theologies **IV** 337–9, 344–5
    Malawi, women as religious and political praise singers and dancers in **IV** 226
    Zimbabwe, American Evangelicalism in **III** 357–73
  Brazil, base communities in **III** 197, 199
  China, Christian Virgins in 18th century **I** 426, 431, 437
  Decalogue in Tagalog, Oliver's manuscript of **I** 317–22
  Evangelistic Explosion **III** 364
  Explo '85 **III** 363
  India, global fundamentalism and local Christianity in Madras **III** 445–56
  Inuit Pentecostalism and Evangelicalism in Canadian and Eastern Arctic **III** 201–29
  Japan, indigenous movements in **III** 331
  Kongo, church in **I** 260–4
  Korean Protestantism, contribution of Biblewomen to **II** 237–49
  Kyrgyzstan, missionaries in post-Soviet **III** 232–40, 244–5, 248–9
  Latin America, awakening of indigenous people in **IV** 320
  literature **II** 379
  Malawi, women as religious and political praise singers and dancers in **IV** 226
  Mexico, native evangelism in central **III** 389–405
  Mezzogiorno, glossolalia and possession amongst Pentecostal groups of the **II** 309–10
  New Zealand, gospel songs in **IV** 207–21
  Norddeutsche Missionsgesellschaft, role of Devil in preaching of **III** 409, 415–20
  Orthodox Mission **II** 379
  self **IV** 63–5
  Seventh–day Adventism **III** 376, 380–1
  United States
    New Zealand, gospel songs in **IV** 207–10
    Zimbabwe **III** 357–73
  Zimbabwe, American Evangelicalism in **III** 357–73
evil, meaning of I 4
evolution III 219
Ewe people III 409–10
exclusivity
  exclusive truth claims **III** 332, 444
  institutional expression **I** 5
  Lord's Supper **I** 143–4
excommunication II 52
execution of prisoners I 300–1
exegesis I 25
exhortation I 129, 130–3
exorcisms
  Burkino Faso, faith-healers of Assemblies of God in **III** 257–67
  Norddeutsche Missionsgesellschaft, role of Devil in preaching of **III** 415, 418, 49–20
Ezana I of Aksum I 199, 200

Fabri, Friedrich II 82–3
fairy tales III 410
faith
  grace **I** 7

INDEX

India, global fundamentalism and local Christianity in Madras III 443–62
Leningrad, independent religious communities in III 347, 352–4
Strasbourg, France, faith, family and fashion in III 127–48
syncretism III 475
works and faith, balance between I 6–7
faith healing *see* **healing**
Falashas Jewish community of Ethiopia I 202
Falmerayer, J P II 217
families
  Decalogue in Tagalog, Oliver's manuscript of I 313–14
  France, faith, family and fashion in Strasbourg III 127–48
  Inuit Pentecostalism and Evangelicalism in Canadian and Eastern Arctic III 219–20
  Jamaica, family land in III 186–7
  Mexico, native evangelism in central III 394–5
  modernization III 143–4, 145
  New Zealand, Irish Catholics in 19th century Christchurch in II 164–6
  nuclear families III 144
  values III 394–5
  visiting and interaction with families III 140–1
famine I 432, II 385
Farantos, Megas III 100
Farrant, Jean IV 159
Fashole-Luke, Edward W IV 340
Fátima Batista, Maria de IV 88–90, 92, 94–8
Faustus of Milevis I 189
Feast of Fools III 309
feet, covering of IV 15
female circumcision II 372
feminism
  African Christian theologies IV 346–7
  Greek Orthodoxy, contested masculine spaces in III 94, 96, 100, 103
  Martha and Mary from Asian perspective, story of I 81–2
  Native Americans I 297

  patriarchal structures, imposition on colonial subjects on I 297
  Tupi and European women in eyes of Claude d'Abbeville I 297–8
Ferguson, J III 231
Ferrell, Raleigh IV 270
fertility in Itapa–Ekiti, Nigeria III 275–97
festivals
  Bushmen, Christ as trickster in religion of contemporary III 308–13
  India, lower-caste Catholics in Madras II 55–6
  Philippines, imitation of Christ in III 65
  Soyo, Capuchins and rulers of I 354–5
feudalism II 240
Fiji
  Inuit Pentecostalism and Evangelicalism in Canadian and Eastern Arctic III 211, 213–19, 221–5
  Last Supper tapestries IV 262
Finke, H III 318
Firmus I 183
Firth, Raymond III 143
Flögel, Friedrich III 309
folk Catholicism II 275
Fools for Christ's Sake III 311
Ford, Leighton IV 208, 216–21
forgiveness of sins I 6
Forsberg, Malcolm IV 194
Foucault, Michel I 451, 457, 462, II 361
Fox, George II 390
France
  Brazil, French priests in III 201–2, 205–6
  China
    Christian sectarian violence in late 19th century II 324, II 325–6, 329–30, 334–6
    Christian Virgins in 18th century China I 426
  French Antilles, Catholic missions to slaves in I 394–408
  French Polynesia, women in ordained ministry in Mô'ohi Protestant Church in III 149–61

INDEX

Nanrantsouak, church at I 379–80
New Zealand, Irish Catholics in 19th century Christchurch in II 173
secularization I 14
Strasbourg, France, faith, family and fashion in III 127–48
Francis of Assisi in Canindé, shrine of IV 88–98
Franco, Francisco III 341, 345
Frankiel, T I 16
Franklin, Benjamin I 474
Frazee, A II 213
free will III 166–7, 468–9
freedom of conscience II 181
Frei, Hans II 71
Freire, Paulo III 198
French Antilles, Catholic missions to slaves in I 394–408
baptism I 398–403
Capuchins I 395, 398, 401–3
Caribs I 396
Carmelites I 402
Code Noir 402
conversions I 394–5
culture I 451–3
Dominicans I 402–3
Guadeloupe I 395–6, 402
Haiti I 394–5
indigenous religion I 395
interracial marriages, promotion of I 402
Islam I 395
Jesuits I 398, 401–3
land I 451–3
language I 397, 399
local site, Tamil land and culture as a I 451–3
marriage I 400–2
Martinique I 402
racial lines, organization of parishes on I 397–8
revolts in Saint-Dominique and Haiti I 394–5
Saint-Christophe I 396, 398, 400
Saint-Dominique I 394–5
sexual abuse I 402
socialization I 397
spiritual egalitarianism I 399–400
voodoo (*Vaudou*) I 394
French Polynesia, women in ordained ministry in Mô'ohi Protestant Church in III 149–61
acceptance by parishioners III 156–7, 159
autonomy of Church III 150
baccalauréat requirement III 153–4, 158
culture III 157–8
debates on ordination of women III 151
decolonization III 150
derived ministries III 151, 152
differentialists versus egalitarians III 155–6
ecumenical movement III 150–1
educational requirements for ministers III 153–4, 157–8
employment for women III 150
feminization of ministry III 152–5, 157–8
higher education III 151, 152, 153–4, 157–8
husband's ministries, wives involvement in III 151, 152, 156, 158–9
incomplete process, feminization as III 155–8
institutional marginalization III 156–7, 158
institutionalization of women's activities at parish level III 152
language III 157
London Missionary Society III 149, 152
marry, obligation of missionaries to III 152, 159
missionaries III 149–50, 152, 159
non-parish ministry as ideally feminine III 154–5, 156
pastoral couples III 151, 152, 156, 158–9
pastoral training III 153–4
pluralism III 157
political and religious spheres, separation of III 155
professionalization of ordained ministry III 152–5, 158
regional and international context III 150–1
theological tensions III 157–8
translation of the Bible III 157
Frend, W H C I 182–4
Frese, David I 409–18

INDEX

Frumentius I 201, 203
Frye, N III 285
fugitivism II 230, 231
Full Gospel Businessmen's Fellowship International III 360
fundamentalism
  Madras, India, global fundamentalism and local Christianity in III 443–62
  Mexico, immediacy and eternity in a Catholic convent in IV 45
  New Zealand, gospel songs in IV 207
  Sudan, Uduk faith in five-note scale in IV 192–3
funerals
  Aboriginal Australians III 170, 174, 177
  Jamaican peasant life, religion as resistance in III 188, 192–3
  Philippines, imitation of Christ in III 65–9
  United States, gender and change in Church of the Lord (Aladura) in III 112
  wakes III 65
Fuze, Magema Magwaza I 100

Gaba, Christian IV 337
Gabiani, Giandomenico I 339
Gabra Maskel I 207
Gadamer, H–G I 3, 15
Gaillard, Louis I 334–5
Gaius's house, *ekklesia* in I 126, 130
Gama, Vasco de IV 283
Ganda, Raphael II 375–6
Gandhi, Indira III 84
Gandhi, Mahatma III 25
Gao Qizheng III 40
Gao Ying I 82
Gao Zhengyi III 40
Garcia II I 260, 349, 351, 352–4
Garvey, Marcus II 370, 377
Gathuna, Arthur Gatungu II 372, 374
Gautier, EF I 182
Geertz, Clifford I 1, 125, II 204, III 128
Geffcken, Johannes I 237
Gelfand, Michael II 396
Gell, A IV 264, 275
Gellner, Ernest I 125
Gendall, Stephen IV 161

gender *see also* **patriarchy; women**
  Africa
    African Christian theologies IV 346–7
    translation of Bible I 75
  Bible I 75
  Catholic Reformation I 296–7
  Chile, young women as apostles to the poor in II 274
  China, Catholic women of Congregation of Sisters in IV 68–9, 75–9
  colonialism I 75, 295–308
  comfort women I 85–93
  Dalit theology in Tamil Christian folk music IV 250, 251, 253–4
  deacons I 157–8, 159
  differentialists versus egalitarians III 155–6
  discipleship, equality in I 83
  domestic training of girls II 99–101, 105–7
  female circumcision II 372
  feminist theory I 81–2, 297–8, III 94, 96, 100, 103
  French Polynesia, women in ordained ministry in Mô'ohi Protestant Church in III 149–61
  God IV 250, 251, 253–4
  Greek Orthodoxy, contested masculine spaces in III 94–105
  hats as symbol of women's position in Evangelical churches in Edinburgh, Scotland IV 25–41
  ideologies IV 68–9, 75–9
  India I 75–6
  Korean military 'comfort women' I 85–93
  Malawi, women as religious and political praise singers and dancers in IV 224–7, 237–9
  Martha and Mary from Asian perspective, story of I 79–84
  menstrual blood taboo III 109, 110–12, 119, 120–2
  missionaries
    Catholic Reformation I 297
    Tupi and European women in eyes of Claude d'Abbeville I 295–308
  motherhood II 110–11
  misogyny I 302

384

INDEX

negotiation of gender practices in United States **III** 119–20
New Guinea, gendered images of Holy Spirit Sisters (SSpS) in colonial **II** 81–94
Nigeria, young converts in Onitsha **II** 95–111
Philippines
  translation of Bible **I** 74–5
  trial of Seberine Candelaria in **II** 127, 129
polygyny **II** 98–9, 106–7
Reformation **I** 297
Southern Tswana, Africa, cultivation and colonialism in **II** 33–4, 38–9, 42
Spain, anticlericalism in Aracena in **II** 354
speaking in church, women **IV** 26–7, 36–7
spiritual inequality **IV** 30, 32, 35
subordination **IV** 29, 30, 32, 35–8
syncretism **III** 463–79
tradition **IV** 224–7, 238–9
translation of Bible **I** 74–6
Tupi and European women in eyes of Claude d'Abbeville **I** 295–308
United States
  Church of the Lord (Aladura) **III** 106–26
  negotiation of gender practices in United States **III** 119–20
  unmarried women in ministry, role of **I** 81–2
  witchcraft accusations **II** 97–8
Genesios, Joseph I 245
genies *see* **spirits and demons**
genocide I 89
George I, king of Greece II 218
George the Hagiorite I 246–7
Gergen, K IV 46
Germany
  Lübeck prophet in local and Lutheran context **I** 409–19
  New Guinea **II** 82–5, 91
  Norddeutsche Missiongesellschaft, role of Devil in preaching of **III** 409–22
  United States, gender and change in Church of the Lord (Aladura) in **III** 107
Gernet, Jacques I 341

Ghana
  Ewe people **III** 409–20
  Norddeutsche Missiongesellschaft, role of Devil in preaching of **III** 409–20
Gibeah I 87–9
Giddens, Anthony II 143, **IV** 46
Gildo I 183
Gilhus, Ingvild I 171, 173
Gilman, Lisa IV 233–4
Glastonbury, United Kingdom IV 137
Gleyo, Jean-François I 431, 432–4
globalization
  Catholic-Protestant distinctions in coming global Christianity **IV** 297–315
  Inuit Pentecostalism and Evangelicalism in Canadian and Eastern Arctic **III** 213–18
  Latin America, awakening of indigenous people in **IV** 316–17, 324–5, 329–30
  Madras, global fundamentalism and local Christianity in **III** 443–62
  Mexico, immediacy and eternity in a Catholic convent in **IV** 50
  Pentecostalism **II** 423–33
glossolalia
  Accadia group, glossolalic practice of **II** 312–15
  adversity and oppression, as response to **II** 317
  Ancient Greece **II** 307
  anthropological interpretations 315–18
  baptism **I** 135
  definition **II** 307
  dissidents **II** 308
  exhortation **I** 129, 132–3
  interpretation **II** 310–18
  Jamaican peasant life, religion as resistance in **III** 191
  Mezzogiorno, glossolalia and possession amongst Pentecostal groups of the **II** 307–19
  New Testament **II** 307
  Old Testament **II** 307
  shamanism **II** 307
  Taiwan, conversion to Protestantism amongst urban immigrants in **III** 322
  United States **II** 308

Zaïre, Kimbanguism and syncretism in **II** 262–6
Gluckman, M III 308
Gnostics
  apologists **I** 167–8
  baptism **I** 168, 170–1
  dance **IV** 282
  demonization **I** 168
  dualism **I** 168–70
  heresy **I** 166, 167–75
  hierarchy **I** 171, 173
  institutionalization, threat of **I** 172–3
  Jesus, nature of **I** 170
  John, Gospel of **I** 169–70, 172
  mainstream groups **I** 170–2
  Manichaeans **I** 167
  marginalization **I** 173
  origins **I** 168–9
  orthodoxy **I** 171–2
  Pauline tradition **I** 171–2
  Philip, Gospel of **I** 170–1
  rituals **I** 170–1
  slander **I** 167–8
  students **I** 174
  Truth, Gospel of **I** 169–70
Goa, India, *jagar* rituals in III 21–37
  Arya Samaj **III** 26
  autos-da-fe **III** 24
  Catholics **III** 21–6, 33
  censorship **III** 25
  colonialism **III** 23–5
  constitution, secular and democratic **III** 24
  cultural hybridity **III** 22–3
  dancing **III** 32–3
  economic crisis **III** 23
  Goan Gaude **III** 26–8, 31–2
  hegemony **III** 23
  Hinduism **III** 21–2, 24–35
  historical narrative **III** 23–4
  hybrid features **III** 21–2
  hymns **III** 29–30, 32
  iconic embodiments **III** 30–2
  languages **III** 21–2
  liberalization **III** 24
  mass conversions **III** 23
  mass emigration **III** 23–4
  nationalism **III** 25
  night vigils **III** 21
  performance of rituals **III** 27–35
  plays **III** 32–3

  pluralism **III** 24
  political reforms **III** 24
  Portuguese colonialism **III** 23–5
  prayers **III** 27–9
  reconversion to Hinduism **III** 26–7, 30
  singing **III** 29–30, 31–2
  Siolim *zagor* **III** 26, 27
  social worlds, relationship of ritual with **III** 34–5
  syncretism **III** 22–3, 27
  varieties of *jagar* **III** 21–2
  wakefulness **III** 21
  zagor **III** 24–33
God
  farmer, as **IV** 250, 251
  fear of God **I** 116–17
  gender **IV** 250, 251, 253–4
  Malo cult in Torres Straits Islands **I** 46
  separation from God **I** 4
  sino-Western cultural communication at end of Ming dynasty **I** 284–5, 290
  Sudan, Uduk faith in five-note scale in **IV** 194–5
Goddard, Pliny IV 142, 150–1
Goffman, Erving II 227–8
Goldsmith O II 36
Golvers, Noël I 330–1, 343
Gondarra, Djiniyini III 175–6
Good Friday III 65, **III** 66–9
Goodman, Felicitas I 132
Goody, Jack I 73, 124, **II** 256
Gorbachev, Mikhail IV 347
Goricheva, Tatiana III 351
Gott, Richard II 285
governance in the early church I 155–63
  Apostles **I** 155–6, 162
  bishop, office of **I** 156–7, 158–9, 161–3
  Brothers **I** 155–6, 158–9, 162
  deacons **I** 157–8, 159
  Disciples **I** 155–6, 161–2
  Hellenists **I** 155–6
  Pauline tradition **I** 156–9
  presbyters and presbytery **I** 157–60, 161–3
  subgroupings **I** 162
grace I 7
Graham, Billy III 363, **IV** 208, 213, 215–16, 218, 220–1

Gramsci, Antonio I 8, 15, 464–5,
  II 274, 281
Grant, Robert I 175
Gray, Robert I 95
Greece *see also* **Greek Orthodox Church**
  19th century II 201–21
  anti-clericalism II 209
  Bavarian administration II 213–16
  Byzantium II 207–8, 211, 213, 217
  Catholics II 203–5
  clergy
    illiteracy II 213
    interaction with the II 208–9
    war of independence II 209
  constitution, secularization of
    II 210–11
  culture II 202–6, 216–18
  diaspora II 218
  education II 204
  Enlightenment II 205, 209, 211–13
  ethnic character of Greek Orthodoxy
    II 206–12
  future of national aspirations and
    religious culture II 216–18
  Hellenism II 202, 206–7, 210–11,
    217–18
  hellenochristianikos II 217
  heretics, baptism of II 205
  identity II 202
  independence of church from
    Patriarch of Constantinople
    II 213–14, 217–18
  individual and Church, relationship
    between II 205–6
  individualism II 201
  intellectuals II 209, 211, 218
  land II 208, 213
  missionaries II 215
  modernization II 201–21
  monarchy II 213, 216, 218
  national aspirations, future of
    II 216–18
  Ottoman occupation II 202, 204–5,
    207–9, 217–18
  paganism in rural Anatolia and
    Greece from 6th century,
    conversion from I 233–54
  pluralism II 201
  political context II 202–3, 209, 216
  Protestants II 202, 204
  rationalism II 202
  Reformation II 201, 203–4

  saints, declaration of II 206
  secularization
    constitution II 210–11
    definition II 201
    intellectuals II 211
  separation of church and state II 210
  social control II 203–5
  war of independence II 209
Greek Orthodox Church
  Africa II 370, 372, 375–7
  deaconess, revival of office of III 96,
    98–9
  devilizing women III 103
  dress III 97–8
  Ecumenical Movement III 94, 95
  egalitarianism III 96
  European Union III 94–5, 100–4
  feminism III 94, 96, 100, 103
  gender III 94–105
  Hellenism II 202
  iconism III 99
  India, Orthodox Christian Pilgrim
    Centre in Kerala IV 104–20
  masculine spaces, contested
    III 94–105
  ministry, women excluded from
    III 94, 95–100
  menstruation III 97
  modernity and tradition III 95, 96–7,
    100, 102
  Mother of God III 96
  Mount Athos, exclusion from
    III 94–5, 100–4
    devilizing women III 103
    European Union III 94–5, 100–4
    mythology III 102
    national identity III 102, 103
    tradition III 100–3
    Virgin Mary III 102–3
  mythology III 102
  national identity III 102, 103
  nationalization of women III 95
  Nigeria II 377
  ordination of nuns III 98–9
  ritual impurity III 97
  spiritual mothers III 98
  theology, women studying III 95
Gregorias, Mar IV 105–7, 108–9,
  112–19
Gregory of Nyssa I 127
Gregory of Tours I 221
Gregory the Great I 192

INDEX

Greier, Franciscus I 410
Greundler, Ernest I 446, 448, 453, 462
Grigoriatis, Cosmas II 376
Grimaldi, C F I 285
Grimes, John Joseph II 174
Gross, Daniel IV 87–8, 100
Gross, S O IV 20
Grosz, George II 360
Grothier, William III 386
Gsell, S I 182
Guadeloupe I 395–6, 402
Guest, Florian F II 226
Gunning, J H II 140
Gunson, Neil II 70
Gupta, A III 231

habeas corpus II 17, 22
Habermas, Jürgen II 359, IV 46
Hackett, Cecil IV 21
Hagin, Kenneth III 361, 362
hagiography III 311
hair IV 16
Haiti I 265, 394–5
Hall, Stuart II 344
Hall, W J II 246–7
Halloween III 309
Hammer of Witches (*Malleus Maleficarum*) II 119
Hammond, Peter III 372
Han Shan I 329
hun (wounded heart) I 86, 90 2
Handelman, D IV 136
Hannah and Sarah, story of III 277, 285–90
Hardacre, Helen III 340
Harding, Susan F III 240, IV 63–5
Hardy, Thomas II 32
Hare, Julius Charles I 98
Harris, Charles I 464
Harris, Grace IV 33
Harris, Stephen III 169
Harrison, R M I 239
Harvey, D IV 46
Hassius, J S I 443
Hastings, Adrian II 383, 386–7
Hastrup, K IV 135–6
hats and women's position in evangelical churches in Edinburgh, Scotland IV 25–41
age 34, 37–8
authority, exclusions of women from positions of IV 26–7
Baptist church IV 26, 27–8, 32–4, 37–9
Bible IV 25, 26, 27–31, 33–7
complementarity principle IV 36
core meaning IV 26, 29–32, 37, 39
dignity or modesty IV 29, 30–1, 39
ethnography of communication IV 25
factionalism IV 34–6
formality IV 29, 31, 37–8
individuals, use of symbols by IV 25–6
modesty IV 29, 30–1, 36
offence, causing IV 38
Open Brethren assembly IV 26–7, 31, 38–9
Pauline tradition, hats and IV 28–9, 30, 34–5
Seventh Day Adventist church IV 26, 32, 36–7
signifiers, attaching importance to IV 33
situational meaning IV 26, 32–9
social position of women IV 26–9, 32–3, 36–7
speaking in church, women IV 26–7, 36–7
spiritual inequality IV 30, 32, 35
subordination IV 29, 30, 32, 35–8
symbols
  analysis IV 25
  core meanings IV 26, 29–32, 37, 39
  individuals, use by IV 25–6
  nature IV 25
  situational meanings IV 26, 32–9
  types IV 25
  women 25–6, 29–39
Women's Meeting of Open Brethren IV 26–7
Haydn, Joseph IV 187
healing
AIDs III 255
Bible I 115
Brazil, pilgrimage and patronage in IV 99–100
Burkino Faso, faith-healers of Assemblies of God in III 253–72
Canadian Prairie Indians, pilgrimages of IV 146
Chile, pentacostalism in II 292–3
identity creation IV 323–4

INDEX

Inuit Pentecostalism and
    Evangelicalism in Canadian and
    Eastern Arctic **III** 218–19, 221–6
Irish Carmelites **II** 396
land, healing the **III** 212–19, 221–6
Mapuche people of Chile **IV** 234
Merina traditional religion and the
    Bible in Madagascar **I** 115
Nigeria, fertility in Itapa-Ekiti in
    III 282
Norddeutsche Missionsgesellschaft,
    role of Devil in preaching of
    III 415, 416
Pentecostalism **II** 386
Philippines, imitation of Christ in
    III 61–2, 63–5, 70–3
prophets **III** 253
rituals **IV** 323–4
shamanism **IV** 323–4
spirits **III** 69–71
Zaïre, Kimbanguism and syncretism
    in **II** 262–6
Zimbabwe, missionaries in Northern
    Nyaga District in **II** 390–1, 396
health *see also* **medical services**
    AIDs **III** 255
    Burkino Faso, faith-healers of
        Assemblies of God in **III** 256
    California, breakdown of Spanish
        mission system in **II** 231
    devils **III** 256
    Tarangambadi (Tranquebar), India,
        missionaries in **I** 450–1, 459,
        461, 464
Hefner, Robert **II** 141–2, **III** 276
hegemony
    Africa **I** 97, 99
    Bible **I** 94–7
    Colenso, John William **I** 97, 107–9
    colonialism **I** 94–7
    Dalit theology in Tamil Christian
        folk music **IV** 244, 245, 247, 251,
        254, 256
    ideology **I** 95–6, 99
    liminal space **I** 96, 108
    jagar rituals in Goa, India **III** 23
    missionaries **II** 65
    power **I** 8
    resistance **I** 96
    Spain, anticlericalism in Aracena in
        II 344–5, 352–3, 357–8
    Zulus **I** 107–8

Hein, Norvin **III** 33
Heinrich, H **IV** 18
Hellenists **I** 155–6, **II** 202, 206–7,
    210–11, 217–18
hellenochristianikos **II** 217
Helliwell, David **I** 331
Henderson, Clara **IV** 233
Henry IV, king of France **I** 295–6
heresy
    baptism **II** 205
    Brazil, Universal Church of the
        Kingdom of God in **III** 432
    early Christianity in Eastern
        Mediterranean **I** 165–78
    Colenso, John William. *Commentary
        of Romans* **I** 95
    Gnostics **I** 166, 167–75
    Greece, religion and modernization
        in 19th century **II** 205
    heterodoxy **I** 166
    Japan, indigenous movements in
        III 330–1
    Jesus, experiences of **I** 174
    Leningrad, independent religious
        communities in **III** 354
    mainstream groups **I** 166–7, 170
    orthodoxy **I** 165–7, **I** 174
    personal belief **I** 174
    political power **I** 167
heritage landmarks **IV** 174
hermeneutics
    African Christian theologies **IV** 341–2
    Colenso, John William. *Commentary
        of Romans* **I** 97, 101–2, 109
    Korean military 'comfort women'
        I 85–6, 90–1
Hervieu-Léger, Danièle **III** 346, 347,
    353–4
heterodoxy **I** 166
Hexham, I **III** 318
hierarchy
    Gnostics **I** 171, 173
    Mexico, native evangelism in central
        III 391, 397
    Mezzogiorno, glossolalia and
        possession amongst Pentecostal
        groups of the **II** 311
    power **I** 8–9
    replication **I** 11–12
    Spain, anticlericalism in Aracena in
        II 351–2
    syncretism **III** 466, 475

INDEX

Hilda, Abbess of Whitby **I** 7
Hill, Mel **II** 397
Hilliard, David **II** 67
Hilton, Anne **I** 257
Hindus
  Bible in Hindi **I** 69
  BJP Party **IV** 116
  Catholics **II** 55, 60
  colonialism **I** 69
  dancer forms, Christianity in **IV** 282–3
  Dalit theology in Tamil Christian folk music **IV** 243, 248
  Hindu Brethren **IV** 282–3
  hinduization **IV** 248
  jagar rituals in Goa, India **III** 21–2, 24–35
  militants **IV** 115–16, 119
  nationalism **III** 25
  Orthodox Christian Pilgrim Centre in Kerala **IV** 111, 112, 115–17, 119
  reconversions **III** 26–7, 30
  Tarangambadi (Tranquebar), missionaries in **I** 455–6
Hippolytus **I** 134–5
historical context **I** 2, 16
Hobsbawm, Eric **III** 342–3
Hocart, A M **III** 277
Hodgson, Janet **IV** 159
Hoge, Dean **IV** 306
Hollenweger, Walter **II** 287
Holy Week **III** 65, 66–9
Hoover, Willis **II** 287–92, 294, 296
Hopkins, Arthur Innes **II** 68
Houguang, Chen **I** 291–2
House Church movement **III** 368
household assemblies **I** 126, 130–1
housing **II** 297–8
Howells, Rees **II** 390–1
Hsü Kuang-ch'i **I** 329, 333–4
Huang Zhen **I** 292
human rights **II** 300
Humperdinck, Engelbert **IV** 187
Huntington, Samuel **IV** 308–9
Hurtado Cruchaga, Alberto **II** 273–5, 281
Huxley, Aldous **II** 38
Hwal-ran, Kim Helen **II** 248–9
Hwesa people **II** 384–5, 388–90
hymns
  Catholics **IV** 181–90

  Dalit theology in Tamil Christian folk music **IV** 247
  exhortation **I** 127–8
  jagar rituals in Goa, India **III** 29–30, 32
  lyrics **IV** 194–203
  Michigan Indians, Catholic hymns of **IV** 181–90
  New Zealand, gospel songs in **IV** 207–21
  Sudan, Uduk faith in five-note scale in **IV** 191–205
  translated hymns **IV** 196–9, 204–5
Hynes, William **III** 308, **III** 310, 312
Hypatius, St **I** 237, 238–9

Iachevskii, ME **II** 190
Iberia, Christianization of I 198–212
  church, construction of principal **I** 203–4
  comparative approach **I** 200–1
  conversion **I** 201, 203
  countryside, Christianization of the **I** 204–7
  culture **I** 207–8
  indigenous Christians **I** 203
  Jewish communities **I** 202–3
  phases **I** 208
  Roman Empire **I** 200–8
  royal conversion **I** 201–2, 203
  Sassanian Empire **I** 200–1
  Thirteen Syrian Fathers **I** 204–7
  trade routes **I** 200–3
identity
  attendance at church **I** 19
  Burkino Faso, faith-healers of Assemblies of God in **III** 256–7
  Canadian Prairie Indians, pilgrimages of **IV** 150
  Christian identity **I** 18–20
  definition **I** 18–20
  ethnic or national identity, formation of **I** 200
  exclusion, criteria for **I** 19–20
  Greece, religion and modernization in 19th century **II** 202
  healings **IV** 323–4
  Irish Catholics in New Zealand **II** 161, 167–8, 171–2
  Kongo, church in **I** 257–8

Kyrgyzstan, missionaries in post-Soviet III 232–3, 237–48
Mizeki, Bernard IV 160–1, 165
Mount Athos, exclusion of women from III 102, 103
national and religious identity, congruence between IV 310–11
nationalism III 102, 103
Native American missionaries I 470–82
Navajo IV 323–4
Patrick, St IV 155–6, 165
power I 18–20
'proper' Christians I 19
shamanism IV 323–4
shrines IV 171, 173
syncretism IV 263–4, 270–1, 276–7
Taiwan, syncretism among Paiwan Catholics in IV 263–4, 270–1, 276–7
icons III 30–2, 99
ideology
    Baptists in United States I 35–42
    China, Catholic women of Congregation of Sisters in IV 68–9, 75–9
    France, faith, family and fashion in Strasbourg III 128
    gender ideologies IV 68–9, 75–9
    hegemony I 95–6, 99
    Spain, anticlericalism in Aracena in II 347–51, 357–8
idol worship I 312, 317–18, 325–6, IV 171
Idowu, Bolaji IV 334, 337
Igbo II 95–111
Ignatius Elias III IV 110
Ignatius of Antioch I 154–7, 159–63
Ileto, V III 75–6
Il'minskii, N I II 188
immediacy and eternity in a convent in Mexico IV 45–67
imitation of Christ in Bicol, Philippines III 61–80
immigration
    African Immigrant Religion (AIR) III 108–10, 122, 123
    enforcement, fear of III 118–19
    jagar rituals in Goa, India III 23–4
    New Zealand, Irish Catholics in 19th century Christchurch in II 160–78
    Northern Ireland II 163
    Protestantism, conversion to III 317–29
    Taiwan, conversion of urban immigrants in III 317–29
    United States, gender and change in Church of the Lord (Aladura) in III 106–26
    urban immigrants, conversion of III 317–29
imperialism *see* **colonialism**
incarnation, mystery o the I 50–1
inculturation II 396, IV 336–43, 347
India *see also* **caste; Hindus; Thomas Christians and the Thomas tradition**
    Bible I 69–70, 72, 75–7
    British East India Company II 59–60
    dar-al-Islam, refugees from I 220–1
    Dalit theology in Tamil Christian folk music IV 242–61
    Catholics II 51–64
    Church of South India IV 243, 247, 252
    colonialism I 69–70, 72, 75–7
    conversions II 13–27
    dance forms IV 280–93
    fundamentalism III 443–62
    gender, translation of Bible and I 74–6
    Goa, India, *jagar* rituals in III 21–37
    Hindi, Bible in I 69
    Jacobite Christians IV 283
    Kerala
        dance, IV 283, 293–4
        Orthodox Christian Pilgrim Centre IV 104–20
        women, status of III 83–93
    language I 216
    Madras
        Catholics, lower-caste II 51–64
        global fundamentalism and local Christianity in III 443–62
    Manu, Laws of I 12
    missionaries I 441–69
    Orthodox Christian Pilgrim Centre in Kerala IV 104–20
    Parsis of Bombay and Christian conversion II 13–27
    Persia I 216
    Sanskritization IV 246–7
    Sankritized Tamil music IV 247, 248–9

science **I** 77
siddhars **I** 449–51, 458–61
Syrian Orthodox church **I** 12
Tarangambadi (Tranquebar), India, missionaries in **I** 441–69
translation of Bible **I** 72, 75–7
Vedanta-based practices **I** 12
women in Kerala, status of Christian **III** 83–93
Indian dance forms, Christianity in IV 280–93
ancient and traditional phase **IV** 282–3
Bharata Natyam, Christian themes in **IV** 285–90
Goa **IV** 283–4, 293
God the Father hand gesture **IV** 285–6
hastas (hand gestures) **IV** 285–7
Hindu Brethren **IV** 282–3
Holy Spirit hand gesture **IV** 286–7
Jacobite Christians **IV** 283
Kerala **IV** 283, 293–4
Knanaya Syrian Christians **IV** 282–3, 290
Latin Christians **IV** 283
Mar Thoma Syrian Christians **IV** 282–3, 290–1
medieval phase **IV** 283, 292
Portuguese colonists **IV** 283–4, 293–4
post-independence phase **IV** 283–4
social problems **IV** 287–9
Son of God hand gesture **IV** 286
Southern Styles **IV** 280–1
Synod of Diamper **IV** 283, 293
Tamil Nadu **IV** 284
Westernization **IV** 283, 291
Indian (Native American) missionaries, conversion, identity and I 470–82
assimilation **I** 471–2, 477
forced conversions **I** 470
individualism **I** 474
language **I** 477, 478–9
Mohegans **I** 471, 472, 475–6, 481
Protestants **I** 471
racism **I** 471–2, 478–9
resistance **I** 470
Indians *see* **indigenization of Christianity; indigenous people; traditional or indigenous religions**

indigenization of Christianity
African Immigrant Religion (AIR) **III** 108–10, 122, 123
African Instituted/Initiated Churches (AICs) **III** 110, 113, 124
Catholicism **II** 275, 395–6
Chile, Pentacostalism in **II** 291, 293–4, 301
Dalit theology in Tamil Christian folk music **IV** 242, 245–51, 255–7
Japan, indigenous movements in **III** 329–41
Korean Protestantism, contribution of Biblewomen to **II** 238
Mexico, native evangelism in central **III** 389–405
Philippines
Candelaria, Seberine, trial of **II** 126–30
imitation of Christ in **III** 67
rituals of paganism **I** 242
indigenous people *see also* **Aboriginal Australians; paganism; traditional or indigenous religions**
African Christian theologies **IV** 332–53
Aksum, Christianization of **I** 203
Algonquian Indians **I** 379, **IV** 181–9
art, sales of **IV** 267
Barwe refugees from Portuguese East Africa **II** 385
Bolivia, catechists of Aymara Indians in **IV** 263–4
Brazil, women in colonial **I** 373–6
Brazilindians **I** 373–6
California, breakdown of Spanish mission system in **II** 225–36
Canadian Prairie Indians, pilgrimages of **IV** 140–53
Christian Virgins in 18th century China **I** 426
feminist theory **I** 297
French Antilles, Catholic missions to slaves in **I** 396
Hwesa people **II** 384–5, 388–90
Igbo **II** 96–111
Inuit Pentecostalism and Evangelicalism in Canadian and Eastern Arctic **III** 201–29
Kennebec Wabanaki **I** 379–86, 390
land **IV** 325–8

INDEX

Latin America, awakening of indigenous people in **IV** 316–31
Manyika people **II** 384–5, 395–6, 401
Michigan Indians, Catholic hymns of **IV** 181–90
missionaries
  California, breakdown of Spanish mission system in **II** 225–36
  Native American **I** 470–82
  Nanrantsouak, church at **I** 379–93
  Native American missionaries **I** 470–82
  Pomio Kivung of New Guinea **III** 170
  translation of Bible into indigenous languages and dialects **I** 70–7, 112
  Wabanaki people **I** 379–90
  Yaqui and southwest and central American literature **III** 310
Indikopleustes, Cosmas I 215
individualism I 474, **II** 201
Indonesia *see* **Karo Batak Protestant Church, Sumatra, conversion and industrialization IV** 87
infanticide II 89–90
Ingram, Philip II 168
instruction I 129, 130
instrumentalism II 344–5, 360
Inuit Pentecostalism and evangelicalism in Canadian and Eastern Arctic III 201–29
  ancestral spirits **III** 221–2
  Canadian Awakening Ministries **III** 212–19, 221–6
  evangelical movements **III** 212–14
  evolution, teaching of **III** 219
  Fiji connection **III** 211, 213–19, 221–5
  globalisation **III** 213–18
  healing circles **III** 218–19, 225–6
  healing the land **III** 212–19, 221–6
  Kekerten **III** 223–5
  land rituals of Canadian Awakening Ministries **III** 212–19, 221–5
  Marble Island **III** 221–2
  marriage and family, protection of **III** 219–20
  moral reform **III** 219–25
  networks **III** 213–18
  Pangnirtung, healing at **III** 218–19

  past, redefining connections to the **III** 220–5
  Pentecostal movement **III** 212–14
  politics **III** 214–15
  Rankin Inlet, reconciliation at **III** 215–18
  rituals **III** 213–19, 221–7
  sexual orientation **III** 219
  shamanism **III** 213, 222–4
  sins of previous generations **III** 220–1
  taboos **III** 221
  traditional beliefs, integration of Christianity with **III** 213
  women **III** 220
Ioannikios, St I 243
Iran *see* **Persia**
Ireland
  Brazil, clergy in **III** 201–2, 204–5, 207
  Carmelites **II** 384, 385–8, 394–401
  Catholic identity **II** 161, 167–8, 171–2
  Croagh Patrick **IV** 155, 165
  Irish Question **II** 398
  national identity **IV** 155–6, 165
  New Zealand, Irish Catholics in 19th century Christchurch in **II** 160–78
  pilgrimages **IV** 155
  snakes, banishment of **IV** 155
  St Patrick **IV** 155–6, 165
  Zimbabwe **II** 384, 385–8, 394–401
Irenaeus, St I 342
Isidore of Seville I 185
Islam *see* **Muslims**
Italy *see* **Mezzogiorno, glossolalia and possession amongst Pentecostal groups of the**

Jabesh-gilead massacre I 88–9, 91
Jackson, Andrew I 40
Jackson, Michael III 171–2
Jacobite Christians IV 106–11, 115, 117–18, 283
***jagar* rituals in Goa, India III** 21–37
Jamaican peasant life, religion as resistance in III 181–94
  Afro-Caribbean cultural resistance **III** 187–93
  Anglican Church **III** 181
  Baptist Church

missionaries III 181–4, 188
Native Baptist beliefs III 189–93
paradox of resistance III 184–6
resistance III 181–7
Revival Cults III 189–92
Baptist war III 182, 188, 191–2
British rule III 181
burials III 192–3
colonialism III 181–7, 191
cultural resistance III 187–93
customary system of tenure III 186–7
dual spirits III 188
emancipation III 188–9
family land III 186–7
free villages III 182–7, 189, 193
funerals III 188, 192–3
glossolalia III 191
land III 182, 186–7
missionaries III 181–4, 188
Myalist traditions III 187–9, 191–2
Obeah cult III 187–90
Old Families III 186–7
Pukimina III 189
reservoirs of labour, free villages as III 184
Revival Cult III 187–93
rituals III 187–8, 190–3
slavery III 181–91
spirit possession III 187–8, 191
witchcraft and sorcery III 187–8
women III 187, 190–1
James, Williams II 141, IV 53
Jansen, Guy IV 216
Jansen, Marius III 333
Janssen, Arnold II 86
Janzen, J M I 360
Japan *see also* **Japan, indigenous movements in**
colonialism III 266–7, 273
comfort women I 85–93
Korea
  military 'comfort women' I 85–93
  Protestantism, contribution of Biblewomen to 2
samurai I 272
syncretism IV 266–7, 273
Taiwan, syncretism among Paiwan Catholics in IV 266–7, 273
Xavier, Francisco, Japanese in letters of I 268–79
Japan, indigenous movements in III 329–41
authority III 335–9
baptism III 339
basic orientation III 330
Buddhism III 329, 334, 338, 339–40
charismatic authority III 335–8, 339
Church-sect theory III 330–2
Confucianism III 333, 334, 340
degree of indigenization III 330
de-Westernization III 333
enabling factor III 334–5
evangelicalism III 331
exclusive truth claims III 332
foreign-oriented churches III 331
future directions III 338–40
heresy III 330–1
imported and native elements III 334–5
indigenization III 330–2
innovation III 335–8
institutionalization III 337
legitimacy III 331–2
minor founders III 334, 335–8
missionaries III 329, 331, 332–3, 335
modernization III 333
nationalism III 333, 335
New Religions, Christian-related movements as a III 329
number of members III 339–40
orthodoxy III 331, 338
over-indigenization III 340
restorationist explanations III 338
sects III 332
self-definition III 330
Shinto III 333, 334, 340
social background III 332–5
succession to leadership III 339
typology III 330–1
Jeffreys, George II 388, 390, 392
Jeffreys, Stephen II 388
Jen, Françoise I 432–3
Jenkins, Philip IV 297–9, 304–5, 307–11, 313–14
Jenkyns, Richard II 211
Jerome I 214
Jerusalem, status of III 386
jestes III 309
Jesuits
Catholic-Protestants distinctions in coming global Christianity IV 305
French Antilles, Catholic missions to slaves in I 398, 401–3

Nanrantsouak, church at I 379–80
Tarangambadi (Tranquebar), India, missionaries in I 452, 460
Jesus Christ
  Bushmen, Christ as trickster in religion of contemporary III 298–316
  Dominus Iesus declaration in Asia I 57–65
  European features III 63–4
  experiences of Jesus I 174
  France, faith, family and fashion in Strasbourg III 138
  Gnostics I 170
  heresy I 174
  imitation of Christ III 61–80
  Philippines, imitation of Christ in III 61–80
Jewish people
  Aksum, Christianization of I 202–3
  Iberia, Christianization of I 202–3
  mikveh I 134–5, 137
  Romans as addressed to Jewish prejudices I 101–2
  Thomas Christians and the Thomas tradition I 214
  water rites I 136–7
Jimmy Swaggart Ministries III 360, 365–6, III 371
Jirjis, Habib III 15
João I Nzinga Nkuwu I 260
Joaquin, Arón III 397
Joaquin, Samuel III 397
Jogues, Isaac, St IV 188
John of Ephesus I 204, 234–8, 243–4, 248
John of Zedazeni I 206
John Paul II II 274, III 380, IV 148
John, St I 160, 169–70, 172
Johnson, Todd IV 311–12
Jolly, Margaret II 88
Jones, A H M I 184
Joseph, T K I 219
Josephus I 130
Jowett, Benjamin I 98
Judge, E A I 123–4
Judges I 85–93
Juergensmeyer, Mark IV 308
Julliard, Étienne III 127
Justinian, emperor I 203, 234, 236

Kailasapathy, K I 450, 459
Kaimal, Padma I 450

Kaiseki, Matsumara III 339
Kak-kyong, Ryu II 249
Kaleb I I 203, 207
Kamara, Christine III 120, 121
Kamstra, J H II 253
Kanelli, Liana III 102
Kang Xi, emperor I 290
Kant, Immanuel I 125
Kaplan, Temma II 343
Karaka, Dosabhoy Framjee II 15
Karamanou, Anna III 102
Kardecist-Spiritist belief III 470–1, 474
Karo Batak Protestant Church, Sumatra, conversion and II 137–59
  affiliation, change of II 141, 145, 152
  animists II 149–50
  baptism II 140
  class consciousness II 148
  colonial domination II 141, 144–6, 150–1, 153
  Communism II 148–9
  community, Christendom as a II 140, 147–8, 150–1
  conceptualizing conversion II 141–4
  differences, reforming or enhancing II 142
  Dutch Missionary Society (NZG) II 140, 145–6, 153
  economic advantages II 144–5
  ethnicity of Karo II 144, 146–9
  evangelical strategies II 139–40
  folk churches II 146
  growth of Christianity II 144–53
  historical perspective II 143, 153
  identity politics II 143–4, 146
  indigenization II 143
  literacy II 138–9, 144, 147
  mass conversions II 148
  migration II 149–50
  missionaries II 137–47
  Muslims II 147, 148–9, 153
  nationalism II 148
  nominal adherents II 144, 152
  organized religion, pressure of animists to adopt an II 149
  Pentecostal Church II 137, 139–40
  PKI party, crushing of II 140
  pluralism II 137
  political phenomenon, conversion as a II 141, 143–4
  practice theory II 152

psychological models **II** 142–3
reference group theory **II** 141–2
religious transformation **II** 138, **II** 140–3, 145, 153
sociology of conversion **II** 141–3
syncretism **II** 143
synthetic vision of change **II** 143
Karp, Ivan III 171–2
Karpat, Kemal III 233
Kashish, bishop of Chios I 235–6
Kato, Byang IV 344
Keane, W III 235–6
Kellis, Nectarios II 376
Kellner, Hansfried III 330–1
Kelly, Dean III 322
Kempe, AH IV 16–17
Kempis, Thomas á IV 172
Kennebec Wabanaki I 379–86, 390
Kennedy, JF III 379
Kenosha, David IV 182–4, 186–9
Kenya
  colonialism **II** 371–2, 373–4
  female circumcision **II** 372
  independence **II** 373–4, 377
  Kikuyu **II** 371–2
  language **II** 379
  Mau Mau **II** 373
  Orthodox Mission **II** 371–2, 373–4, 377, 379
  Patriarchate of Alexandria **II** 372–3
  seminary in Nairobi **II** 375, 379, 380
Kenyatta, Jomo II 372, 373–4
Kerala, India I 199 see also **Kerala, India, Orthodox Christian Pilgrim Centre in; Kerala, status of Christian women in**
Kerala, India, Orthodox Christian Pilgrim Centre in IV 104–20
  BJP Party **IV** 116
  Catholicos **IV** 108–10, 113–14, 116, 119
  changes **IV** 104
  charismatics **IV** 110–13
  demolition at Parumala **IV** 117–18
  divisions in 20th century **IV** 107–9
  evolving character of the pilgrimage **IV** 113–14
  Gregorios, tomb of Mar **IV** 105, 107, 108–9, 112–19
  historical background **IV** 105–7
  Hindus **IV** 111, 112, 115–17, 119

Indianness of Indian Orthodoxy **IV** 114–17
  intercession, theology of **IV** 111–13
  Jacobite Christians **IV** 106–11, 115, 117–18
  loyalty to groups, pilgrimages as display of **IV** 113–14
  Manjinikara **IV** 109–10, 117
  Mar Thoma Church **IV** 107, 115
  Mary, St **IV** 111
  Metropolitan, quarrels between Patriarch and **IV** 108
  Nilackal issue **IV** 116–17
  Pampa River **IV** 104–5
  Parumala **IV** 105, 107–10, 112–19
  Patriarch of Antioch **IV** 107–9, 114
  politicisation **IV** 116, 119
  status of Parumala and its rivals **IV** 109–10, 114–17
  Syrian Christians **IV** 105–7, 108, 114–15, 118
  Thomas, St **IV** 106, **IV** 115–18
  walking pilgrimages **IV** 113
Kerala, status of Christian women in III 83–93
  class **III** 85
  coir rope **III** 91–2
  dowry **III** 86, 87
  elites **III** 84, 89
  emotional relationships **III** 86
  fishermen, wives of **III** 88, 89–91
  intimacy **III** 86
  Mar Thoma movement **III** 84
  marriage and marriage service **III** 87–9
  mother-in-law and daughters-in-law, relationship between **III** 86–7
  passivity **III** 88
  patriarchy **III** 85–7, 92
  poverty **III** 91
  sexuality **III** 88
  social constructs, rules as **III** 83
  St Thomas tradition **III** 85
  stridhan **III** 86, 87
  Syrian Christians **III** 83–92
Kessler, JBA II 288–90, 296
Keswick movement IV 212–13
Khrushchev, Nikita III 347
Khusro I I 207
Kibicho, Samuel IV 337
Kikuyu II 371–2
Kim, Sadie II 246–7

INDEX

Kimbanguism and syncretism in Zaïre II 253–70
  affliction, freedom from II 262
  assimilation II 259
  Baptist Missionary Society II 255
  Belgium II 257–8
  bureaucratic institutions II 257–61, 268
  Church of Jesus Christ on the Earth by the Prophet Simon Kimbangu (EJCSK) II 253–5, 259–63, 269
  class II 269
  colonialism II 257–9, 269
  communion II 262
  customary institutions II 257–9, 268
  DMN churches II 254–5, 265
  ecstatic practices II 262–6
  glossolalia II 264–6
  healing practices II 262–6
  Kongo II 253, 255, 257–8, 264–5
  language II 258–9
  Ngunzism II 254, 255, 263–6
  orthodox churches II 254
  pluralism II 259, 268–9
  political discrimination II 254–5
  prophecy II 254, 255, 263–6
  retreats II 262–3
  rituals II 262, 264–6
  rules of church II 260
  Swedish mission church II 255
  taboo food II 260, 261
  taxation II 260–1
  whiteness II 266
  witchcraft II 264–6, 268
Kinanyi, Thomas I 219
Kingsley, Charles I 98
kinship networks
  China, Christian sectarian violence in late 19th century II 327
  Mexico, native evangelism in central III 395–6
  New Zealand, Irish Catholics in 19th century Christchurch in II 164–7
Kircher, Althanasius I 333
Kitagawa, JN III 332
Kiyonga, Sosthenes II 378
Knanaya Syrian Christians IV 282–3, 290
Knibb, William III 182–7
Knight, James III 222

Knight-Bruce, George Wyndham IV 157, 165
Knitter, Paul I 57, 65
knowledge transmission III 166–71, 176
Kocherry, Tom III 90–1
Kollaparambil, Jacob I 217–18
Kongo, church in I 257–67, 395 *see also* Soyo, Capuchins and rulers of
  AfroAmerican diaspora I 257–8
  Apostles' Creed I 263
  baptism I 258
  bishops I 261
  Capuchins I 259–60, 262–3, 350–1
  Catholics I 257, 259–61, 350–1
  chapel boys I 260
  Christian identity I 257–8
  clergy, role of I 259–60
  definition of Christianity I 258
  extinction of Christianity I 348–9
  Haiti I 265
  Kimbanguism and syncretism II 253, 255, 257–8, 264–5
  Kimbundu religion I 263–4
  language I 264
  lay evangelization I 260–4
  Mary I 264
  missionaries I 258–64, 348–9
  pre-existing religion, compromise with I 259
  real Christianity, as I 258–60
  royal cult I 257
  rural areas I 257–65
  saviour, concept of I 264
  Soyo, Capuchins and rulers of I 350–1
  superstitions I 263
  syncretism II 253, 255, 257–8, 264–5
  virgin birth I 264
Korais, Adamantios II 205, 212
Korea *see* Korean military 'comfort women'; Korean Protestantism, contribution of Biblewomen to
Korean military 'comfort women'
  anonymity I 87, 89
  Beijing women's conference 1995 I 85
  Benjaminites I 88–90
  betrayal I 91
  consolation I 91
  genocide I 89
  Gibeah, old man in I 87–9
  gifts, women as I 90
  han (wounded heart) I 86, 90–2

hermeneutics **I** 85–6, 90–1
imperialism **I** 91–2
Jabesh-gilead massacre **I** 88–9, 91
Japanese military **I** 85–93
Judges 19–21 **I** 85–93
Levite's concubine **I** 87–90
names **I** 89
patriarchal culture **I** 87, 91–2
scapegoats, women as **I** 90
secrecy and silence **I** 85, 90–1
state-ordered violence **I** 89
Korean Protestantism, contribution of Biblewomen to II 237–52
19th century **II** 237–50
American missionaries **II** 238–41, 244
Awakening movements **II** 244–5
Bible, existence of vernacular **II** 241–2
education **II** 239–40, 242, 245, 248
egalitarianism **II** 239–40
elite, Biblewomen as new **II** 247–9
equal pay **II** 245–6
evangelism **II** 237–49
feudalism **II** 240
indigenisation of Bible knowledge **II** 238
Japan **II** 248–9
persecution of churches **II** 248
social reformers, Biblewomen as **II** 247–9
submissive assistants or essential leaders, Biblewomen as **II** 244–7
training in Bible **II** 242, 245, 247
Korias, Adamandios II 211
Kourappos, Theodotos I 240
Krupat, Arnold I 474–5
Kuan Yü I 338
Kunonga, Nolbert IV 164
Kuxi II 323–4
Kybele, cult of I 242–3
Kyrgyzstan, missionaries in post-Soviet III 230–52
atheist Muslims **III** 233
Bishkek, church in **III** 239–40, 243–6
circumcision festivals **III** 230–1
conversion **III** 240–3
cultural objectification **III** 245–7
culture **III** 231–3, 237–9, 243–9
deception **III** 237, 243–5
elites **III** 231
ethnocentrism **III** 245–7
ethno-nationalist identity **III** 232–5, 237–48

evangelicalism **III** 232–40, 244–5, 248–9
folk Islam **III** 241
folklorization **III** 243–5
independence **III** 233–4
independent churches **III** 239–40
Kyrgyz church, emergence of **III** 235, 237–9
language **III** 236–8
lost tribes of Israel, Kyrgyz people as one of **III** 245–7
Manas epic **III** 245–7
Muslims **III** 231, 232–7, 241–2, 244, 248
national categories in Soviet Kyrgyzstan **III** 232–4
nationalism **III** 231
objectification **III** 245–7
religious categories in Soviet Kyrgyzstan **III** 232–4
Russian, Christianity seen as **III** 236, 245, 247
self, constructing a Christian **III** 240–3
socio-economic disruptions **III** 232
speech, importance of **III** 240–1

Labat, Jean-Baptiste I 400
Labi, Joseph Kwame II 377
labour
Chile, labour organizations in **II** 297
French Polynesia, women in ordained ministry in Mô'ohi Protestant Church in **III** 150
mobility **II** 165, 385
New Zealand, Irish Catholics in 19th century Christchurch in **II** 165–6, 169
servants **II** 165–6, 169
Southern Tswana, Africa, cultivation and colonialism in **II** 33–4
wages **II** 165–6
women
domestic servants **II** 165–6, 169
New Zealand, Irish Catholics in 19th century Christchurch in **II** 165–6, 169
work ethic **III** 169
Lactantius I 193
lakes IV 327
Lalive d'Epinay, Christian II 297
Lambek, Michael III 458

INDEX

Lambert, Margaret IV 188
Lambert, Pierre I 430
Lambeth Conference 1868 I 95
Lamont, Donal II 398, 399
land
  California, breakdown of Spanish mission system in II 228, 232–3, 234
  Chile IV 328
  China, beliefs of Zhouzi village people in Catholic diocese in III 41–2
  Colombia IV 328
  French Antilles, Catholic missions to slaves in I 451–3
  Greece, religion and modernization in 19th century II 208, 213
  healing the land III 212–19, 221–6
  India, lower-caste Catholics in Madras II 58
  indigenous people IV 325–8
  Inuit Pentecostalism and Evangelicalism in Canadian and Eastern Arctic III 212–19, 221–6
  Jamaican peasant life, religion as resistance in III 182, 186–7
  lakes IV 327
  re-sacralising the landscape II 392–3, 401
  rituals III 212–19, 221–5
  sale of ecclesiastical land II 348
  Spain, anticlericalism in Aracena in II 348
  Tamils I 451–3
  trees and groves, destruction of sacred I 234–7
  Ulster Pentecostals II 392
  Zimbabwe, missionaries in Northern Nyaga District in II 385, 392–3
landmarks or shrines IV 174–6
language *see also* **translations of the Bible**
  Aboriginal Australians III 168
  Africa
    Orthodox Mission in II 377, 379
    Roman Africa, Christianity and local culture in I 182, 184–93
  Berbers I 182, 184
  Bible I 24–5
  Chad II 377
  context I 11
  Coptic III 16–17
  Dalit theology in Tamil Christian folk music IV 246–7, 249–51
  France, faith, family and fashion in Strasbourg III 128, 137–40
  French Antilles, Catholic missions to slaves in I 397, 399
  French Polynesia, women in ordained ministry in Mô'ohi Protestant Church in III 157
  India I 216
  jagar rituals in Goa, India III 21–2
  Kongo, church in I 264
  Kyrgyzstan, missionaries in post-Soviet III 236–8
  Latin I 24–5, 49
  Lübeck prophet in local and Lutheran context I 410
  Malawi, women as religious and political praise singers and dancers in IV 231–2
  misreading I 280–1
  Mizeki, Bernard IV 157
  Nanrantsouak, church at I 380–1, 383–5
  Native American missionaries I 477, 478–9
  Nigeria, young converts in Onitsha II 107
  Numidia I 182
  Oliver's manuscript of Decalogue in Tagalog I 311–27
  paganism I 187, 238–9
  Persia I 216
  Phrygian language I 187
  Punic culture I 182, 194–6, 191
  ritual and early church in Eastern Mediterranean I 124–5
  Roman Africa, Christianity and local culture in I 182, 184–93
  Sudan, Uduk faith in five-note scale in IV 191–205
  syncretism IV 265–6
  Syriac language I 214–16, 219
  Taiwan, syncretism among Paiwan Catholics in IV 265–6
  United States, gender and change in Church of the Lord (Aladura) in III 110–11
  Vandals I 189, 191
  Zaïre, Kimbanguism and syncretism in II 258–9
  Zulus I 96–7, 99

las Casas, Bartolomeo de **IV** 321–2
Lasine, Stuart **I** 87
Laslett, Peter **III** 143
Lasley's memorandum **IV** 174
Latin
  Bible, recital of the **I** 24–5
  Cameroun, liturgical adaptation in St Paul de Ndzon-Melen in **I** 49
  Roman Africa, Christianity and local culture in **I** 181–93
Latin America *see also* **individual countries; Latin America, awakening of indigenous people in**
  Catholic-Protestants distinctions in coming global Christianity **IV** 299–301, 313
  population projections **IV** 299–301, 313
  Universal Church of the Kingdom of God **III** 424–5
Latin America, awakening of indigenous people in IV 316–31
  aggression, religious and cultural **IV** 320
  assimilation **IV** 320
  Catholics **IV** 319–22
  Chile, land rights over Bio Bio River in **IV** 328
  Chile, Mapuche people in religious affiliation **IV** 318–19 ritual healing **IV** 324
  churches and indigenous people **IV** 320–1
  Colombia, land rights in **IV** 328
  colonialism **IV** 320–2, 326
  commercialization of cures and spells of shamans **IV** 324–5
  declaration at Third World Trade Conference **IV** 325
  development **IV** 325–8
  discrimination **IV** 325
  drugs **IV** 320
  ecological movements **IV** 327–8
  emergence of the indigenous population **IV** 316–18
  ethnic conflicts **IV** 316–17
  ethnic consciousness **IV** 316–18, 322–4
  ethnocentric bias **IV** 321–2
  evangelicalism, growth in **IV** 320
  folklorization **IV** 325
  globalisation **IV** 316–17, 324–5, 329–30
  Guatemala peace accords **IV** 318
  healing **IV** 323–4
  identity creation **IV** 323–4
  indigenous religion **IV** 318–19, 323–30
  Lake San Pablo **IV** 327–8
  lakes **IV** 327
  land rights **IV** 325–8
  leadership **IV** 321–3
  merchandising of culture **IV** 324–5
  missionaries **IV** 318–19, 321–2
  nationalism **IV** 321
  natural resources **IV** 326
  paternalism **IV** 320
  poverty **IV** 320
  pro-indigenous policies **IV** 320
  ritual healing **IV** 323–4
  role for religion **IV** 321–3
  sacred lakes **IV** 327
  shamanism **IV** 318, 319, 323–5, 330
  spiritual values **IV** 325–8
  syncretism **IV** 318, 329–30
  territories **IV** 325–8
  uprisings **IV** 317, 318–19, 322–3
Latin, recital of Bible in I 24–5
Latour, B III 275
Leach, Edmund II 257
Leacock, Eleanor Burke I 297
leadership and leaders
  chieftainship **IV** 265, 266, 276
  Latin America, awakening of indigenous people in **IV** 321–3
  Malawi, women as religious and political praise singers and dancers in **IV** 233–4
  Merina traditional religion and the Bible in Madagascar **I** 113–18
  Mezzogiorno, glossolalia and possession amongst Pentecostal groups of the **II** 317
  power **I** 8–9
  Taiwan, syncretism among Paiwan Catholics in **IV** 265, 266, 276
Lee, Robert III 339
Lehman, H III 275
Lemercier-Quelquejay, C III 233
Leningrad, independent religious communities in III 345–56
  1960–1970s **III** 345–56
  auto-validation of faith **III** 353–4

charismatic validation of faith
   III 353
chronological list of independent
   communities III 350
communal validation of faith III 353
conversions III 346, 352–4
Council for Religious Affairs
   III 347–8
dissident movements III 348–51
faith III 347, 352–4
heresy III 354
home circles or seminars III 351
institutional validation of faith
   III 353
integral space of information III 347
KGB III 348
literature III 354–5
mutual validation of faith III 353
nationalism III 349
Orthodox Church in Soviet years
   III 347–55
repression and persecution III 347
rituals III 347, 353
rupture of religious tradition III 347
seekers III 346, 352–3, 355
terminology III 346–7
tradition III 347
validation of faith III 353–4
Leo III I 244
Leo XIII II 280
Leontius the Presbyter I 235–6
Lestanc, Jean-Marie IV 141
Levi-Strauss, Claude IV 47
Levite's concubine I 87–90
Lewis, IM II 316–17
Leyel, Wöllum I 442
Li lineage, Baptist and Catholic
   elements of II 323–36
Li Tsu-po I 329, 330
Li Zheye II 330–1
Liang Qichao I 281
liberal/conservatives divide IV 298,
   304–7
liberation movements I 95
liberation theology
   African Christian theologies
      IV 340–2, 347
   Chile, young women as apostles to
      the poor in II 274
   Zimbabwe, American Evangelicalism
      in III 367–8
Liberia III 107, 116

Licinius I 198
Lieban, Richard II 121
Liebniz, Gottfried I 285–6
Lienhardt, Godfrey IV 194
Life Ministries III 359
Lightfoot, JB I 127, II 69
liminal space I 96, 108, 140–1, IV 90
Lin, PH III 319
Lin Xiaoping I 337
Lincoln, Bruce II 343–4
Lindsay, Gordon III 361, 362, 366
Liqanos I 205, 207
Lisle, George III 188
literacy
   Bible I 74–5
   China, beliefs of Zhouzi village
      people in Catholic diocese in
      III 42
   colonialism I 74–5
   elites I 74–5
   Mexico, native evangelism in central
      III 395, 399–400
   modernity III 275–6
   Nigeria, fertility in Itapa-Ekiti in
      III 276–7
   subalterns I 74–5
literalism I 24
literature
   Africa, Orthodox Mission in II 375
   evangelism II 379
   Coptic cultural nationalism III 16
   Leningrad, independent religious
      communities in III 354–5
   Mexico, native evangelism in central
      III 399
   Yaqui and southwest and central
      American literature III 310
   Zimbabwe, American Evangelicalism
      in III 365–6
liturgy
   Brazil, base communities (CEBs) in
      III 197–8, 204–7
   Cameroun, liturgical adaptation in St
      Paul de Ndzon-Melen in I 48–56
   Malo cult in Torres Straits Islands
      I 46
Liu Ch'ang I 332
Liu Sung I 333–4
Livingstone, David I 72, II 30, 35, 43
Lobengula, king IV 156–8
Locke, John II 71
London Missionary Society III 149, 152

INDEX

'long conversation' I 95, 96–7, 109
Longobardi, C I 288, 290
Loosemore, Winnie II 389, 392–3
Lorca, Federico Garcia II 360
Lord of Disorder III 309, 310–11
Lord's Supper
  baptismal reunification I 144–5
  coming together I 126
  commemoration I 142
  Didache I 142
  early Church I 125–6, 141–5, 146
  eschatological element I 142–4
  exclusivity, symbolism of I 143–4
  interpretation I 144
  Pauline tradition I 141–5
  re-presentation of Jesus' death I 142
  reunification I 144–5
  social intention I 142–3
  social status I 142–3
  solidarity, ritual of I 141–5
  syncretism IV 262
  unity, symbol of I 144–5
  vicarious death, meaning of I 142
Louis XIII, king of France I 295, 396
Loukaris, Kyrillos II 203
Lovely Lane Museum, Baltimore, United States IV 173–5
Lowie, RH IV 149
Loyola, Ignatius I 398, III 74
Lu Shih-i I 336–7
Lübeck prophet in local and Lutheran context I 409–19
  1629, Lübeck in April I 412–14
  apparitions I 411–14, 417–18
  Catholics I 414
  collective prayer I 417
  dress, pride in I 416–17
  graveyard, transfer of corpses from I 409, 413–15
  language I 410
  plague I 412
  prayer I 417–18
  pride, sin of I 416–17
  prophecy I 409–12, 418–19
  popular opinion, prophets as barometers of 418–19
  purgatory I 414
  repentance 416–18
  spirits of the dead I 409, 414–16
  St George, destruction of church of I 409, 412
  St Gertrude, destruction of chapel of I 413
  Thirty Years War I 412
Luckmann, Thomas I 125
Lucretius I 283–4
Lufuluabo, Mizeka II 267
Luhrmann, TM IV 137
Lukes, Stephen 8
Luther, Martin I 416–17, III 410, IV 310
Lutherans
  Dalit theology in Tamil Christian folk music IV 247–8
  faith and works, balance between I 6–7
  France, faith, family and fashion in Strasbourg III 137
  Lübeck prophet in local and Lutheran context I 409–19
  United States III 123, 124
Ly, Andreas I 427
Lycia I 239
Lyell, Charles I 99
Lykosoura, temple complex at I 244

Macau I 339–40, 342
MacCabe, Luke II 396
Macedo, Edir III 425, 427, 432, 436–7
MacGaffey, W I 351, 355, 360
MacGuire, George II 370–1
Mackenzie, John II 29–30, 32, 41–2
MacMullen, Ramsay I 118
Madagascar
  Merina traditional religion and the Bible in Madagascar I 112–20
  Orthodox Mission II 376, 379
Madras *see* **Madras, global fundamentalism and local Christianity in; Madras, India, lower-caste Catholics in**
Madras, global fundamentalism and local Christianity in III 443–62
  absolute truth, privileged access to III 444
  charismatic fundamentalism III 451–6
  Church of South India III 445, 449–50, 453
  colonialism III 443
  Communism III 447–8
  crusades III 448–9, 454
  culture III 443–4

INDEX

evangelism III 445–56
faith III 443–4
healing III 454–5
local religion, Christianity becoming
   a III 443
magic III 446–7, 456
migrations of Protestants III 445
missionaries III 443–8, 457–8
Pentecostalism III 452–6
pietism III 446
popular religiosities III 446–7
promotion of fundamentalism
   III 448–51
Protestantism III 443–58
sorcery III 446, 452–4
spirits III 446, 452–4
United States III 443, 447–8, 456–8
**Madras, India, lower-caste Catholics in
   II 51–64**
borrowing II 52
Brahmans II 56
British East India Company
   II 59–60
Capuchins II 53, 55–6, 59–60
ceremonial positions II 53
Church disputes in early 19th century
   II 52–4
colonialism II 52
conversions II 51, 58, 62
Dalits II 57–8
debate on religion II 59–60
excommunication II 52
festivals and ceremonies II 55–6
'Heathen' Paraiyars II 52–3, 55,
   60–1
Hinduism II 55, 60
land, importance of II 58
Muslims II 61–2
outcaste Paraiyar congregations
   II 51–62
Paracheri petitions II 58
Protestants II 51, 58, 62
San Thome church II 54–5, 59–61
self-expression II 51
self-perception II 51
urban space and lower castes II 56–9
Madziyire, Salathiel IV 159
Maggi, Luigi I 429
magic *see* **witchcraft, sorcery and devils**
Magimba, Irenaeus II 373, 377
Mahoney, Ralph III 362, 370
Mahuad, Jamil IV 322

Mailla, Joseph-Anna-Marie de I 334
Makwasha, Gift IV 162
**Malabar Christians I 215, 217, 219, 221,
   223–4**
Malankara Nazaranis I 219, 223
**Malawi, women as religious and political
   praise singers and dancers in
   IV 224–41**
African institutions, in IV 224–39
Alliance for Democracy IV 226
CCAP Blantyre Synod of Church
   of Central Africa Presbyterian
   IV 224–39
clergy IV 227
colours of political parties IV 227–8
culture IV 224–7, 238
dancing styles IV 228–31
dress IV 226–8
drumming IV 229
evangelism IV 226
function of women dancers and
   singers IV 235–7
gender IV 224–7, 237–9
languages IV 231–2
leadership IV 233–4
Malawi Congress Party IV 226, 234
meeting schedules IV 234–5
Mvano IV 225–6, 228–39
national dress IV 227–8
organizational structure IV 232–5
performance IV 226–32
political parties IV 224–39
praise poetry IV 230–1
proselytism IV 235–6
Scottish Presbyterianism IV 238–9
special occasions, dress for IV 228
traditional or African ways IV
   224–7, 238–9
uniforms IV 227–8
United Democratic Front IV 226,
   235
women's wings of political parties
   IV 224, 225–6, 233
West IV 224–7, 238
Mandelbaum, David IV 150–1
Maine, Henry II 69
Makarios III, Mihail II 373–4
Malalus I 203
Malleus Maleficarum **(Hammer of
   Witches) II 119**
**Malo cult in Torres Straits Islands
   I 44–5**

403

INDEX

bowing **I** 45
Christianity as fulfilment of cult
 I 44–5
discipline and law **I** 47
God, nature of **I** 46
hereditary power **I** 44–5
initiation of priests and Anglican
 ordination **I** 45–6
institutions **I** 46–7
liturgy **I** 46
missionaries **I** 44–6
modu **I** 44
sorcery **I** 46–7
traditional reverence **I** 46
Malov, EA II 188
Malula, Joseph II 267
Mananzan, Mary John I 74–5
Manas cult III 245–7
Mandelbaum, David G IV 150
Mangwende, Mungate IV 157–8
Manichaeans I 167, 189
Mann, James III 182
Manu, Laws of I 12
Manyika people II 384–5, 395–6, 401
Mapuche people of Chile IV 318–19, 324
Mar Thomas Christians *see* **Thomas Christians and the Thomas tradition**
Marcussen, A Jan III 384–5
marginalization
 China, Christian sectarian violence in late 19th century **II** 331
 conversions **II** 97–8
 Gnostics **I** 173
Mariah, Chong II 246
Mariz, Cecilia III 208
Mark, St II 369
marriage
 Brazil, women in colonial **I** 303–4, 368–74
 ceremonies **III** 112
 Chile, young women as apostles to the poor in **II** 279
 China, Catholic women of Congregation of Sisters in **IV** 70
 Colenso, John William **I** 98
 Decalogue in Tagalog, Oliver's manuscript of **I** 323–4, 326
 divorce **IV** 70
 endogamy **II** 167

French Antilles, Catholic missions to slaves in **I** 400–2
French Polynesia, women in ordained ministry in Mô'ohi Protestant Church in **III** 149, 152
India, status of Christian women in Kerala **III** 87–9
Inuit Pentecostalism and Evangelicalism in Canadian and Eastern Arctic **III** 219–20
interracial marriages, promotion of **I** 402
Irish Carmelites **II** 400
Merina traditional religion and the Bible in Madagascar **I** 117
Mexico, native evangelism in central **III** 394–5
Mezzogiorno, glossolalia and possession amongst Pentecostal groups of the **II** 310, 311
Nanrantsouak, church at **I** 383
New Guinea, gendered images of Holy Spirit Sisters (SSpS) in colonial **II** 90–2
New Zealand, Irish Catholics in 19th century Christchurch in **II** 166–8
Nigeria, young converts in Onitsha **II** 98–100, 102–9
Philippines **I** 323–4, 326
ritual and early church in Eastern Mediterranean **I** 146
Soyo, Capuchins and rulers of **I** 357–8
Tupi and European women in eyes of Claude d'Abbeville **I** 303–4
Ulster Pentecostals **II** 400
United States, gender and change in Church of the Lord (Aladura) in **III** 112
virginity **I** 368, 373–4
Zimbabwe, missionaries in Northern Nyaga District in **II** 400
Marry, Catherine III 151
Marsden, C III 449
Marshall, Lorna III 302
Martha and Mary from Asian perspective, story of I 79–84
 discipleship, equality in **I** 83
 feminist perspective **I** 81–2
 partnership **I** 83

INDEX

patriarchy I 83
unmarried women in ministry, role of I 81–2
Martiliat, Joachim Enjobert de I 427, 428–30, 434, 437
Martin, D II 201–2
Martin, David IV 207
Martin, François I 443
Martin, Mary Louise II 254–5
Martin, Walter R III 378, 386
Martinique I 402
martyr cults I 244
Mary, mother of Jesus
  Chile, young women as apostles to the poor in II 279–80
  China, Catholic women of Congregation of Sisters in IV 69–70
  Edessa, Osrhoene I 215
  Greek Orthodoxy, contested masculine spaces in III 96
  India, Orthodox Christian Pilgrim Centre in Kerala IV 111
  Kongo, church in I 264
  Mount Athos, exclusion of women from III 102–3
Maswanganyi, Elijah III 362
mass
  Cameroun, liturgical adaptation in St Paul de Ndzon-Melen in I 52–5
  Chile, young women as apostles to the poor in II 275–6, 278–9, 281
  Nanrantsouak, church at I 383–4
  Soyo, Capuchins and rulers of I 354, 356, 363
Mather, Cotton I 389
Matthew, St I 188, 214
Mau Mau II 373
Maurer, Ludwig von II 213–15
Maurice, Frederick Denison I 98, 107–8
Maximus of Turin I 204
May, Carlyle II 316
Mazoomdar, PC II 18
Mba, Isaac II 98
Mbanza Soyo I 351–2, 354–6, 358, 360
Mbiti, John IV 334, 337, 340–1, 344
Mbuwayesango, Dora I 75
McBrien, Richard I 57–8
McCauley, Ray III 362, 365, IV 344
McGavran, Donald II 379
McLean, James II 292
McLean, John IV 142–3

medical services *see also* **healing**
  China, beliefs of Zhouzi village people in Catholic diocese in III 43
  New Guinea, gendered images of Holy Spirit Sisters (SSpS) in colonial II 84, 87
  Orthodox Mission II 379–80
  Zimbabwe, missionaries in Northern Nyaga District in II 389
Medici, Marie de I 296
meditation III 319
Medlycott, AE I 219
Mei Yao-ch'en I 332
Melanesian Mission II 66–75
memory III 171–3
Menelik I 202
menstruation III 97, 109, 110–12, 119, 120–2
merchandise
  Brazil, pilgrimage and patronage in IV 93–4
  culture IV 324–5
  Latin America, awakening of indigenous people in IV 324–5
  shamanism IV 323–4
  shrines IV 126, 132–3, 174
Meredith, NC II 399–400
Merina traditional religion and the Bible in Madagascar I 112–20
  ancestors I 113–14
  closed book, Bible as I 114–16
  context I 113–14, 118
  cultic purification, Bible used for I 115
  fear of God I 116–17
  followers I 113–14
  healing, Bible used for I 115
  heritage, as part of Merina I 117
  inside perspective I 117
  leaders I 113–18
  legitimacy I 118
  marriage I 117
  Merina traditional religion I 113–19
  missionaries I 114
  morals, Bible used as reference book for I 116–17
  name of God I 118
  open book, Bible as I 116–17
  outside perspective I 117–18
  protection, Bible used for I 115–16
  purification, Bible used for I 115

INDEX

reading aloud **I** 116
sacrifices **I** 116, 118–19
traditio-practitioners (leaders)
  I 113–18
translation of the Bible **I** 114, 117, 118
universality **I** 117
use **I** 114–19
why Bible is used **I** 117–19
witchcraft or evil spirits, Bible used as protection against **I** 115–16
Zanahary **I** 113–16 **god**
Meletios of Alexandria **II** 372–3
Messeh, Anund **I** 69
Methodists
  Chile, pentecostalism in **II** 287–92, 295–6
  shrines **IV** 169–77
  United Methodist church **III** 358
  United States **IV** 169–77
Methodus of Philippi **III** 307
Mexico *see also* **Mexico, immediacy and eternity in a Catholic convent in; Mexico, native evangelism in central**
  California, breakdown of Spanish mission system in **II** 231–2
  convent in Mexico, immediacy and eternity in a **IV** 45–67
  War of Independence **II** 231–2
Mexico, immediacy and eternity in a Catholic convent in **IV** 45–67
  Congregation, description of **IV** 49–50
  continuity and discontinuity **IV** 45–6, 48, 64–5
  conversions **IV** 64–5
  evangelizing the self **IV** 63–5
  fundamentalism **IV** 46
  future into the past, reading the **IV** 53–4
  globalization **IV** 50
  millenarianism **IV** 46
  modernization **IV** 49–50
  narratives
    identity **IV** 50–1
    vocations **IV** 5–63
  political commitment **IV** 50
  preciousness of time **IV** 45
  recollecting and rearranging personal history into new narrative of self **IV** 46, 53–4

ritualization of everyday life **IV** 52–3, 65
rituals **IV** 52–3, 65
sacred and profane, time as **IV** 46–8, 65
self, religious vocation as story of **IV** 50–2, 63–5
social commitment **IV** 50
stages of transformation **IV** 46, 49, 53–4, 65
time **IV** 46–51, 65–6
  commodification and personalization **IV** 46
  framing **IV** 46–7
  precious, as **IV** 45
  sacred and profane, time as **IV** 46–9, 65
  transformation **IV** 46, 48–9, 53–4, 63–6
  vocation **IV** 48–9, 50–66
Mexico, native evangelism in central **III** 389–405
  Amistad y Vida AC (Cristianos) **III** 390–401
  baptism **III** 394, 398–9
  Catholicism **III** 389, 390–3, 395–8, 401–3
  class **III** 392, 398
  communitarianism **III** 393
  community service **III** 395, 399
  conversions **III** 389–90, 392–4, 398
  economic integration **III** 400–1
  family values **III** 394–5
  good works **III** 395, 399
  hierarchy **III** 391, 397
  kinship groups **III** 395–6
  La Luz del Mundo **III** 396–401
  literacy **III** 400
  liturgy **III** 395, 399–400
  marriage **III** 394–5
  moral principles **III** 394–5, 400
  Pentecostalism **III** 393–4
  prayer sessions **III** 391
  proselytism **III** 390, 393, 396, 397, 399, 401–2
  Protestantism **III** 389–92, 397–8, 401–3
  residential pattern **III** 398
  socio-psychological profile **III** 392
  Sunday schools **III** 400
  Trinitarianism **III** 398–9
  written material **III** 399

INDEX

Meyer, Birgit III 220
Mezzabarba, Jean Ambroise I 290
Mezzogiorno, glossolalia and possession amongst Pentecostal groups of the II 307–19
  Accadia group, glossolalic practice of II 312–15
  adversity and oppression, as response to II 317
  anthropological interpretations 315–18
  baptisms II 308, 311
  Catholics II 308, 315
  consolidation II 309
  conversions II 308–11
  creation and development of Pentecostal groups II 308–10
  culture II 316
  emotional intensity II 309
  evangelical churches, joining II 309–10
  geographic areas, confined to II 315–17
  hierarchy II 311
  institutionalization II 309–10
  integration II 317
  interpretation, gift of II 312
  interpretation of glossolalia II 310–18
  leaders, serving interests of II 317
  marriage II 310, 311
  missionaries II 309–11, 313–14, 317
  ostracism II 309
  pastors II 309
  rupture II 309
  rural areas II 308
  sainthood II 309, 310
  social function II 317
  stages II 308–10
  tarantate II 316
  translations 314–15
  women II 316–18
Michigan Indians, Catholic hymns of IV 181–90
  Algonquian Indians IV 181–9
  Austrian folk songs IV 187
  Dorian mode IV 186
  folk music IV 182, 187–9
  Jesuit Relations IV 184–5
  L'Arbe Croche IV 181–2, 187–8
  metre IV 183
  missionaries IV 181, 187
  native songs IV 183–4
  paganism IV 181
  plainsong IV 185, 186–7
  scales IV 184
  spirits IV 185
Mike, Loie III 219, 223
mikveh I 134–5, 137
military comfort women *see* **Korean military 'comfort women'**
millenarianism
  Baptists IV 64
  Burkino Faso, faith-healers of Assemblies of God in III 256, 257, 269
  Mexico, immediacy and eternity in a Catholic convent in IV 49–50
  Papua New Guinea IV 47
  Philippines, imitation of Christ in III 75–6
  postmillennialism IV 215
  Spain, anticlericalism in Aracena in II 343, 344–5, 358–61
  Urapmin IV 47–8
Miller, William III 374, 376
Milvian Bridge, Battle of I 199
Mingana, Alphonse I 219
Mint, Jerome II 343
Mintz, Jerome R II 343
Mintz, Sydney W III 185
miracles
  births III 285–91
  Bushmen, Christ as trickster in religion of contemporary III 304
  shrines IV 171, 172
Mirian III of Iberia I 201, 203–4
mirth and ribaldry III 308
missionaries
  19th century mission methodology II 65–77
  Aboriginal Australians III 165–9, III 171, 177–8, IV 13–24
  accommodation II 66
  Africa I 95–110, IV 156–7
    African Christian theologies IV 345
    African descent II 96–7, 100–1, 107–8
    Burkino Faso, faith-healers of Assemblies of God in III 253–4
    Bushmen, Christ as trickster in religion of contemporary III 298

INDEX

Kongo, church in I 258–64, 348–9
Niger Mission II 96–8, 108–10
Nigeria, young converts in Onitsha II 95–111
Orthodox Mission II 368–82
Southern Tswana, Africa, cultivation and colonialism in II 28–9
Sudan, Uduk faith in five-note scale in IV 191–205
Tswana people of Africa I 97, II 28–9
Zimbabwe II 384–402, III 357–73
American Baptist Missionary Society II 323–4, 334–6
Anglican Church II 66–75
Anglican Mission to Papua II 66, 73
Avila Mission II 385–6, 395, 397, 399
background I 97–8
Baptists III 181–4, 188
Bible I 70–4, 112
Brazil I 295–308, III 424–5
Burkino Faso, faith-healers of Assemblies of God in III 253–4
Bushmen, Christ as trickster in religion of contemporary III 298
California, breakdown of Spanish mission system in II 225–36
Canadian Prairie Indians, pilgrimages of IV 143–5, 147
Catholics
　Avila Mission II 385–6, 395, 397, 399
　gender I 297
　China, beliefs of Zhouzi village people in Catholic diocese in III 39–40
　Regina Coeli mission II 395–7
Chile
　Pentecostalism in II 286, 289–93
　young women as apostles to the poor II 276
China
　American Baptist Missionary Society II 323–4, 334–6
　Christian Virgins in 18th century I 426
　Confucianism, misinterpretation of I 281–6
　poetry I 328

sectarian violence II 324, 325–6, 329–30, 334–6
Zhouzi village people, beliefs of III 39–40
Western cultural communication at end of Ming dynasty I 281–6, 290–4
christianize and civilise mission II 65, 67
Church Mission Society II 96–111
civilisation II 29–31, 65, 67
clothing IV 13–24
Colenso, John William I 95–9, 109
colonialism I 15, 295–308, IV 154
Confucianism I 281–6
culture II 65–6, 67–8, 74
Dalit theology in Tamil Christian folk music IV 245, 247–8
discipline II 73–4
dress IV 13–24
Dutch Missionary Society (NZG) II 140, 145–6, 153
ecclesiology I 15
enemies, conflicts between missionaries creating II 400
ethnocentrism II 65
EuroAmerican I 15
French Catholic Missions II 324, II 325–6, 329–30, 334–6
gender I 297
Greece, religion and modernization in 19th century II 215
hegemony II 65
home control I 15
India
　global fundamentalism and local Christianity in Madras III 443–8, 457–8
　Parsis of Bombay and Christian conversion II 13–27
　Tarangambadi (Tranquebar), India, missionaries in I 441–69
Jamaican peasant life, religion as resistance in III 181–4, 188
Japan
　indigenous movements in III 329, 331, 332–3, 335
　Xavier, Francisco, Japanese in letters of I 268, 275–6
Kongo, church in I 258–64, 348–9
Kyrgyzstan, missionaries in post-Soviet III 230–52

408

INDEX

Latin America, awakening of indigenous people in **IV** 318–19, 321–2
London Missionary Society **III** 149–50, 152, 159
'long conversation' **I** 95
Lutherans **IV** 14, 16–19
Malo cult in Torres Straits Islands **I** 44–6
marginalization **I** 97–8
maternalism **II** 81–94
meanings invested in missionaries **IV** 154–5
Melanesian Mission **II** 66–75
　discipline **II** 73–4
　indigenous clergy **II** 74
Merina traditional religion and the Bible in Madagascar **I** 114
Mezzogiorno, glossolalia and possession amongst Pentecostal groups of the **II** 309–11, 313–14, 317
Michigan Indians, Catholic hymns of **IV** 181, 187
Mizeki, Bernard **IV** 154–8
moral consciousness **II** 72–3
nakedness **IV** 13–24
Native American missionaries **I** 470–82
New Guinea, gendered images of Holy Spirit Sisters (SSpS) in colonial **II** 81–94
New Zealand, gospel songs in **IV** 207–13
Niger Mission **II** 96–8, 108–10
Nigeria, young converts in Onitsha **II** 95–111
Norddeutsche Missiongesellschaft, role of Devil in preaching of **III** 409–22
Orthodox Mission **II** 368–82
otherness **II** 66
Oxford Movement **II** 74
paganism in rural Anatolia and Greece from 6th century, conversion from **I** 234
paternalism **II** 68
Patrick, St **IV** 155–6, 165
　Croagh Patrick **IV** 155, 165
　Irish national identity **IV** 155–6, 165
　pilgrimages **IV** 155
　snakes, banishment of **IV** 155

Pentecostalism **III** 424–5
Philippines, imitation of Christ in **III** 62
pluralism **II** 226–8
poetry **I** 328
recognition **II** 66
Regina Coeli mission **II** 395–7
resistance **I** 94–5
reverse, mission in **III** 112–13
sectarian violence **II** 324, 325–6, 329–30, 334–6
secularization **II** 226, 232–3
Seventh–day Adventism **III** 376–7
Southern Tswana, Africa, cultivation and colonialism in **II** 28–9
Sudan, Uduk faith in five-note scale in **IV** 191–205
Sumatra, Karo Batak Protestant Church in **II** 137–47
syncretism **IV** 265–6, 274
Taiwan, syncretism among Paiwan Catholics in **IV** 265–6, 274
Tarangambadi (Tranquebar), India, missionaries in **I** 441–69
translation of Bible **I** 70–4
Tupi and European women in eyes of Claude d'Abbeville **I** 295–308
Tswana people of Africa **I** 97, **II** 28–9
United States
　California, breakdown of Spanish mission system in **II** 225–36
　Church of the Lord (Aladura) **III** 112–13
　Korean Protestantism, contribution of Biblewomen to **II** 238–41, 244
　Zimbabwe, evangelicalism in **III** 357–73
Universities Mission to Central Africa **II** 66, 68, 73
women **I** 295–308
Xavier, Francisco, Japanese in letters of **I** 268, 275–6
Zimbabwe **II** 383–405, **III** 357–73, **IV** 156–8
Mitchell, Timothy **II** 111, 343–4
Mizeki, Bernard **IV** 154–68
　Anglican Church **IV** 156–65
　background **IV** 156
　Bernard Mizeki Guilds **IV** 160, 165

biography **IV** 159
civil war **IV** 159
colonialism **IV** 156–65
contested interpretations **IV** 163–5
decolonization **IV** 160
dramatizations of life **IV** 163
identity **IV** 160–1, 165
interpretations **IV** 159–65
language **IV** 157
martyrdom **IV** 158–9
memorials **IV** 159
missionaries
   Africa, struggles for influence in **IV** 156–7
   big man approach **IV** 154
   colonialism **IV** 154
   meanings invested in missionaries **IV** 154–5
   role **IV** 154
   Zimbabwe **IV** 156–8
mythification **IV** 154
nationalism **IV** 159
ngangas **IV** 157–8, 163
personality **IV** 157
pilgrimages **IV** 156, 160–5
popular appropriation **IV** 160–2
saint, as **IV** 156, 159, 163–4
Shona **IV** 157–9, 162–5
shrine **IV** 157–9
South Africa **IV** 160, 163–4
spirits **IV** 157–8, 163
traditional beliefs **IV** 162–4
Zimbabwe/Rhodesia **IV** 156–65
Mkhungo, son of Mpande I 99–100
modernity and modernization
   Brazil, pilgrimage and patronage in **IV** 87, 100
   Burkino Faso, faith-healers of Assemblies of God in **III** 255–7, 260, 268
   Chile, young women as apostles to the poor in **II** 278, 280–1
   China, beliefs of Zhouzi village people in Catholic diocese in **III** 38–9, 59–60
   families **III** 143–4, 145
   France, faith, family and fashion in Strasbourg **III** 143–4, 145
   Greece
      contested masculine spaces in **III** 95, 96–7, 100, 102
      religion and modernization in 19th century **II** 201–21
   Japan, indigenous movements in **III** 333
   literacy **III** 275–6
   Mexico, immediacy and eternity in a Catholic convent in **IV** 49–50
   Nigeria, fertility in Itapa-Ekiti in **III** 292–3
   secularism **III** 275
   Spain, anticlericalism in Aracena in **II** 358–61
   tradition and modernity **II** 358–61, **III** 95, 96–7, 100, 102
   Taiwan, conversion to Protestantism amongst urban immigrants in **III** 325
Moffat, Mary II 34, 36, 40
Moffat, Robert II 29–31, 39
Mohegans I 471, 472, 475–6, 481
Mo-jung I 338
Molema, SM II 37
Momba, Barbara IV 234
monasticism and monks *see also* **Capuchins**
   Africa, Orthodox Mission in **II** 369, 379
   Buddhism **I** 268–9, 271–2
   Dominicans **I** 402–3, 430
   East **I** 216–17
   paganism in rural Anatolia and Greece from 6th century, conversion from **I** 233, 235, 237, 243–4, 247–8
   Persia **I** 216–17
Mongin, Jean I 398–400
Mon-Lin Chung III 324–5
Moodeliar, Chinniah II 54
Moody, DL IV 209
moralism II 31
Moran, Patrick II 170–1, 172
Morán, Tulio II 292
Moreau, Guillaume I 400
Morphy, H IV 266
Morrison, Kenneth M I 386
Mosala, Itumeleng J IV 336
motherhood I 302, **II** 110–11, **III** 142–3
Mount Athos, exclusion of women from III 94–5, 100–4
   devilizing women **III** 103
   European Union **III** 94–5, 100–4
   mythology **III** 102
   national identity **III** 102, 103
   tradition **III** 100–3
   Virgin Mary **III** 102–3

INDEX

Mountford, CP **IV** 20–2
Moÿe, Jean-Martin **I** 431–3, 437
Mpinda **I** 349, 351, 353
Mudimbe, VY **IV** 333
Mueller, Friedrich Max **II** 69
Muftah, Raghib **III** 14–15
Mugabe, Robert **III** 357, 372, **IV** 164
Mugambi, Jesse **IV** 347–8
Mukasa, Reuben Sseseya (Spartas, Reuben) **II** 371, 372–3, 378–9
Mulago, Vincent **II** 267
Mungello, DE **I** 329
Muro y Cuesta, Juan Diego **IV** 49–50
Murray, Andrew **II** 390
music *see also* **songs and singing**
  chants **I** 127–9
  Chile, Pentacostalism in **II** 294–5
  Coptic cultural nationalism **III** 14–15
  Dalit theology in Tamil Christian folk music **IV** 242–61
  exhortation **I** 127–8
  jagar rituals in Goa, India **III** 29–30, 32
  Michigan Indians, Catholic hymns of **IV** 181–90
  Philippines, trial of Seberine Candelaria in **II** 125–6
  Sudan, Uduk faith in five-note scale in **IV** 191–206
  Wu Li and first Chinese Christian poetry **I** 332
Muslims
  apostasy **II** 179–93
  atheist Muslims **III** 233
  Brazil, attacks on Islam by Universal Church of the Kingdom of God in **III** 436
  burial practices **I** 12
  Catholic-Protestants distinctions in coming global Christianity **IV** 308–9
  Christian churches **I** 12
  dar-al-Islam, refugees from **I** 220–3
  folk Islam **III** 241
  French Antilles, Catholic missions to slaves in **I** 395
  India
    lower-caste Catholics in Madras **II** 61–2
    Tarangambadi (Tranquebar), missionaries in **I** 442, 454–5
    Thomas Christians and the Thomas tradition **I** 214

  Ottoman occupation **II** 202, 204–5, 207–9, 217–18
  Sumatra, Karo Batak Protestant Church in **II** 147, 148–9, 153
  Tatars and apostasy **II** 179–93
  Thomas Christians and the Thomas tradition **I** 214
mutualism **II** 349–50, 357, 359–60
Muyambi, Lazarus **IV** 161–2
Muzorewa, Abel **III** 358
Mvano **IV** 225–6, 228–39
Myalist traditions **III** 187–8, 191–2
Myongsong of Korea, queen **II** 239
myths
  Greek Orthodoxy, contested masculine spaces in **III** 102
  Mount Athos, exclusion of women from **III** 102

nakedness **I** 135, 138–40, 303, **III** 14–24
Nakumura Hajime **III** 338
Namatjira, Albert **IV** 21
names
  Brazil, Universal Church of the Kingdom of God in **III** 428–9
  God, name of **I** 118
  Korean military 'comfort women' **I** 89
  Tatars and apostasy **II** 186, 189
Namibia, Christ as trickster in religion of contemporary Bushmen of III 300
Nankyamas, Theodore **II** 373, 375
Nanrantsouak, church at I 379–93
  Algonkian natives **I** 379
  chapel-building by natives **I** 384–5
  clergy **I** 383–4
  customs **I** 388–9
  English **I** 379–80, 386–90
  French **I** 379–90
  Kennebec Wabanaki **I** 379–86, 390
  language **I** 380–1, 383–5
  marriage **I** 383
  Mass **I** 383–4
  Society of Jesus **I** 379–90
  Wabanaki people **I** 379–90
Nan–sa, Hahr II 248
Nardo, Leonardo da I 352
nationalism
  Bible **I** 74
  Catholic-Protestants distinctions in coming global Christianity **IV** 308

411

INDEX

Chile, pentacostalism in **II** 291
colonialism **I** 74
Coptic cultural nationalism **III** 13–20
ethnic or national identity, formation of **I** 200
Hindus **III** 25
identity **III** 102, 103
Irish Carmelites **II** 387, 397, 398
jagar rituals in Goa, India **III** 25
Japan, indigenous movements in **III** 333, 335
Kyrgyzstan, missionaries in post-Soviet **III** 231
Latin America, awakening of indigenous people in **IV** 321
Leningrad, independent religious communities in **III** 349
Mizeki, Bernard **IV** 159
Mount Athos, exclusion of women from **III** 102, 103
New Zealand, Irish Catholics in 19th century Christchurch in **II** 172
shrines **IV** 170
Sumatra, Karo Batak Protestant Church in **II** 148
Zimbabwe, missionaries in Northern Nyaga District in **II** 383, 387, 397, 398, 400
native people *see* **indigenous people; traditional or indigenous religions**
natural resources IV 326 *see also* **land**
Nauroji, Dhanjibhai II 13, 17–25
Nehru, Jawaharlal III 25
Nelson, Dana I 478–9
Nestorian tablet I 227–32
Nestorians Christians I 215–16
Nestorius, Bishop of Constantinople I 215
Netherlands
Dutch East India Company **I** 442
Dutch Missionary Society (NZG) **II** 140, 145–6, 153
Sumatra, Karo Batak Protestant Church in **II** 140, 145–6, 153
Tarangambadi (Tranquebar), India, missionaries in **I** 442
Neumann, JH II 151–2
New Guinea, gendered images of Holy Spirit Sisters (SSpS) in colonial II 81–94
Australians **II** 84
childbirth **II** 89–90
conversions **II** 83
custom **II** 89
division of labour **II** 83
education **II** 82–3, 91
external and internal education **II** 83
Germans in New Guinea **II** 82–5, 91
hegemony **II** 81–2
infanticide **II** 89–90
marriage **II** 90–2
maternal, meaning of **II** 81
missionary maternalism **II** 81–94
morality **II** 85
nurses **II** 84, 87
paternalism **II** 82
patriarchy **II** 83
plantations **II** 83–4
protection of women and girls **II** 90–2
reality versus rhetoric **II** 88–91
social motherhood **II** 84–5
socialization **II** 82–3
Society of the Divine Word **II** 82, 84, 91
teachers **II** 84, 87
New Guinea
knowledge transmission **III** 170
paganism **I** 187
Pomio Kivung **III** 170
Tangu **I** 187
New Testament
date **I** 24
glossolalia **II** 307
New Zealand *see* **New Zealand, Irish Catholics in 19th century Christchurch; New Zealand, gospel songs in**
New Zealand, Irish Catholics in 19th century Christchurch II 160–78
assimilation **II** 171–2
clergy, disputes between **II** 171–2
colonialism **II** 161, 171–5
culture **II** 161, 164–5, 170
domestic servants, women working as **II** 165–6, 169
education **II** 171
endogamy **II** 167
episcopal control, dispute over **II** 172–3
ethnic awareness **II** 161, 163–4, 167–8, 170–5
families **II** 164–6
French clerics **II** 173

INDEX

immigration policies II 162
Irish Catholic identity II 161, 167–8, 171–2
labour market II 165–6, 168
marriage II 166–8
mobile employment II 165
nationalism II 172
neighbourhood communities II 164–5
Northern Ireland, immigrants from II 163
prejudice and discrimination II 168–71
proportion of Irish immigrants in colony II 163
Protestants II 168–70, 175
regional origins II 163
rituals II 173–4
rural kinship communities II 164–7
sectarianism II 170
social unrest II 170
Society of Mary II 172–5
subsidies II 162
transience 165, 166
wages II 165–6
women, work of II 165–6, 169
New Zealand, gospel songs in IV 207–23
American evangelists IV 207–10
charismatic movements IV 216
conservatism IV 216
crusades IV 214
dispensationalism IV 215
emotionalism IV 221
eschatology IV 214–15
evangelical theology and practice IV 207–21
fundamentalists IV 207
hymns IV 207–21
Keswick movement IV 212–13
missionaries IV 207–13
Pentecostalism IV 216, 221
postmillennialism IV 215
Presbyterians IV 213
Protestantism IV 207–21
revivalism IV 213
Servant Songs IV 216–18
theology IV 214–21
Newlandsmith, Earnest III 14
Nfinda I 349
ngangas IV 157–8, 163
Ngidi, William I 96–7, 99, 100–1

Ngumi, Pie-Claude I 49–50
Ngunzism II 254, 255, 263–6
Nicene Creed II 369
Nicholas of Hagia Sion I 237, 239–40
Nida, Eugene II 301
Niebuhr, H Richard III 375
Niger II 96–8, 108–10
Nigeria *see also* **Nigeria, fertility in Itapa-Ekiti in**
Greek Orthodox Church II 377
Onitsha, Nigeria, young converts in II 95–116
Orthodox Mission II 376–7
United States, gender and change in Church of the Lord (Aladura) in III 107, 110, 113–14, 118, 123
Nigeria, fertility in Itapa-Ekiti in III 275–97
abiku III 280–1, 291
abortions III 280–1
barrenness III 285–9
clinics, giving birth at faith healing III 282
control of fertility III 284–5
conversions III 276–8, 284
co-wives, disputes between III 287–8
creation, ideas about III 278–9
divination III 277–8
faith healing revival services III 282
limits on fertility III 281, 284
literacy III 276–7
miraculous births III 285–91
modern hybrids III 276–7
modernity III 292–3
morality III 277–8, 282–4
rituals III 277–8, 292
Sarah and Hannah, story of III 277, 285–90
spirits III 280
streams III 277, 281–3, 292
traditional beliefs and practices III 276–8, 281–4
water, use of ritual III 280, 281–3, 292
witchcraft III 277–8, 291
Yoruba beliefs III 277–82, 287–8, 291–2
Nikodim, bishop of Cheboksary II 188–9
Nikon the Metanïte I 245
Nile river cults I 244
Nilsson, Martin I 241
Nine Saints of Aksum I 204–5

INDEX

Nirmal, AP IV 243, 292–3
Niu-lang I 331–2
Nobili, Robert de II 55–6, **IV** 248
Noble, Mattie II 246–7
Nóbrega, António de I 369–70
Nock, Arthur II 141
Norddeutsche Missiongesellschaft, role of Devil in preaching of III 409–22
  19th century **III** 409–20
  Agbelengor **III** 409, 415
  ancestor worship **III** 415–16
  baptism **III** 412–14
  Bible Study and Prayer Fellowship **III** 417
  deliverance meetings **III** 418
  dualism **III** 410
  evangelical Presbyterian Church **III** 409, 415–20
  Ewe people **III** 409–20
  exorcism **III** 415, 418, 419–20
  fairy tales **III** 410
  Ghana **III** 409–20
  healing **III** 415, 416
  image of Satan **III** 410–15
  libation to ancestors **III** 416
  Lord's Pentecostal Church **III** 415–16
  Pentescostalism **III** 415–20
  Pietism **III** 410–11, 415, 418–20
  prayer groups **III** 415
  traditional religions **III** 416–18
  trance dances **III** 416–17
  witchcraft **III** 410
Norman, E III 446
Northern Ireland
  Elim movement **II** 385–6, 388–9, 397–401
  New Zealand, immigrants to **II** 163
  secularization, opposition to **II** 388
  Ulster Pentecostals **II** 384, 385–92, 397–401
Nthamburi, Zablon IV 341
nuclear families III 144
nudity I 135, 138–40, 303, **III** 14–24
Numidia I 181–3, 186, 189–92
Nuñez, Juan II 121
nuns *see also* **Carmelites**
  Greek Orthodoxy, contested masculine spaces in **III** 98–9
  ordination **III** 98–9
  Mexico, immediacy and eternity in a Catholic convent in **IV** 45–67

New Guinea, gendered images of Holy Spirit Sisters (SSpS) in colonial **II** 81–94
Spain, anticlericalism in Aracena in **III** 341–2
Nympha's house in Laodicea, *ekklesia* in **I** 123

Obeah cult III 187–90
obedience IV 78–82
Oberoi, Harjot II 52
Occom, Samson I 470–80
Oduwale, Delicia III 116, 121
Oduwale, Samuel III 116, 121
Oduyoye, Mercy IV 333–4, 337, 347
office charisma in early Christian Ephesus I 153–64
  historical retention **I** 162–3
  hostility **I** 163
  Ignatius of Antioch's letter to the Ephesians **I** 154–5, 159, 160–3
  legitimacy **I** 154
  Paul **I** 157, 160–1
  routinized charisma **I** 162
  subgroup transactions **I** 163
Offspring of the Covenant I 216–17
Ojo, ORO III 281
Okullu, Henry IV 335
Old Testament
  date **I** 24
  exhortation **I** 129–30
  glossolalia **II** 307
Oliver, Juan de *see* **Oliver's manuscript of 10 Commandments in Tagalog**
Oliver's manuscript of Decalogue in Tagalog I 311–27
  abortion **I** 324
  ancestor worship **I** 313
  animism **I** 312–13
  audience **I** 320–2
  children **I** 313–14, 320, 323–4
  content of instruction **I** 322–7
  eight commandment **I** 325
  ethnological significance **I** 311–17
  evangelization **I** 317–22
  family life **I** 313–14
  fear **I** 326
  fifth commandment **I** 324
  first commandment **I** 322–3, 325–6
  fourth commandment **I** 323–4
  gods of natives **I** 312, 322–3
  homes **I** 314

husband-wife relationship I 323–4, 326
idol worship I 312, 317–18, 325–6
importance of manuscript I 311–27
Lacan Balingasay I 312, 323
local religion I 312, I 322–3
missiological significance I 317–22
natives as children, regarding I 320–1
ninth commandment I 325
psychology of natives I 315–17
respect 327
ruling class I 321–2
sacrifices I 312
second commandment I 323
seventh commandment I 324–5
sexual offences I 324, 326
sixth commandment I 324
slave institution I 312–13
Spanish occupation I 311
teacher and catechist, Oliver as I 317–20
tenth commandment I 325
third commandment I 323
trade I 324–5
way of live of natives I 311–15
Olwig, Karen Fog III 185
Omuroka, Charles II 378
Onesimus of Ephesus I 155, 160, 161–2
Ong, Walter J II 83
Onitsha, Nigeria, young converts in II 95–116
African descent, male missionaries of II 96–7, 100–1, 107–8
Anglican Church II 95–111
body/mind disciplines II 96
British priests and layworkers II 99
British women missionaries II 99
Catholics II 107
Church Mission Society II 96–111
constructing young converts II 96–102
domestic training of girls II 99–101, 105–7
education II 95–6, 98–104
fattening houses for girls II 105
female separation II 99, 105, 111
gender II 95–111
Igbo men and boys II 95–109
Igbo women and girls II 96–111
indigenous priests II 95–6
language II 107
marginal people, conversion of II 97–8

marriage II 98–100, 102–9
menstruation II 105
missionaries II 95–11
motherhood II 110–11
Niger Mission II 96–8, 108–10
Onitsha people II 97–9, 107–8
patriarchy II 101
polygyny II 98–9, 106–7
priests II 95–6, 99
role models, women as II 106
surveillance and control II 110
witchcraft accusations against women II 97–8
wives of male African missionaries II 107–8
Open Brethren assembly, Scotland IV 26–7, 31, 38–9
oral theology IV 343
ordination of women
French Polynesia, women in ordained ministry in Mô'ohi Protestant Church in III 149–61
nuns III 98–9
United States, gender and change in Church of the Lord (Aladura) in III 107, 110, 113
Original Sin I 4, 103–5
Origen I 193
Orta, A IV 263
Orthodox Christianity
Africa, mission in II 368–82
African Orthodox Church (AOC) II 370–1, 372, 375, 377
Alexandrian Christianity II 369, 371–4
apostasy II 179–200
approaches and characteristics II 378
Arian controversy II 369
Byzantine Patriarchate II 369
Cameroun II 377
Central Africa II 377
Chad II 377
colonialism II 368, 371–3, 380
Constantinople II 213–14, 217–18, 369, 370
Coptic church II 369, 371, III 13–20
Council of Chalcedon II 369
Eastern Orthodox Church III 311
education II 379–80
Ethiopia I 24
Fools for Christ's Sake III 311

Greek communities **II** 370, 372, 375–7
Greek Orthodox Church **II** 202, 372, 377, **III** 94–105
Ethiopian Church **II** 370
Ghana **II** 376–7
gossiping the gospel **II** 378
India, Orthodox Christian Pilgrim Centre in Kerala **IV** 104–20
Kenya **II** 371–5, 377, 379–80
language **II** 377, 379
Leningrad, independent religious communities in **III** 347–55
literature evangelism **II** 379
Madagascar **II** 376, 379
missionaries **II** 368–82
medical services **II** 379–80
monasticism **II** 369, 379
Nicene Creed **II** 369
Nigeria **II** 376–7
paganism **II** 368
Pan African movement **II** 370–1, 377
Pope and Patriarch of Alexandria and All Africa **II** 369–73, 377–8
reading about the Church **II** 378–9
Russian Orthodox Church **II** 179–200, 370–1, **III** 347–55
seminaries **II** 375, 379
slave trade **II** 369–70
South Africa **II** 370–1, 372
Southern Africa **II** 369–71
Soviet era **III** 347–55
Syrian Orthodox Church **I** 12, 24
Tanzania **II** 375, 379
Tatars and apostasy **II** 179–200
Uganda **II** 373–5, 377, 379–80
West Africa **II** 376–7, 378
Zaire **II** 374, 376, 379, 254
Zimbabwe **II** 375–6
orthodoxy
Gnostics **I** 171–2
heresy **I** 165–7, **I** 174
Japan, indigenous movements in **III** 331, 338
Ortiz, Tomás II 126
O'Shea, James Carmel II 399
Ositelu, Barbara III 113
Ositelu, Gabriel III 117
Ositelu, Olunowo III 107
Ositelu, Rufus Okikiolaolu Olubiyi III 107–10, 112

Osrhoëne, King of **I** 199
Ossandon, Teresa **II** 276–8, 280, 281–2
Ostow, M **III** 44
ostracism **II** 17–18, 309
Otto, king of Greece **II** 213, 218
Ottoman occupation **II** 202, 204–5, 207–9, 217–18
Ouen, Madeleine **I** 431
Oxford Movement **II** 74

paganism *see also* **paganism in rural Anatolia and Greece from 6th century, conversion**
Africa
Orthodox Mission in **II** 368
Roman Africa, Christianity and local culture in **I** 187
Catholicism **II** 275
Chile, young women as apostles to the poor in **II** 275, 278
Michigan Indians, Catholic hymns of **IV** 181
Phrygian culture **I** 187
Roman Africa, Christianity and local culture in **I** 187
Tangu in New Guinea **I** 187
paganism in rural Anatolia and Greece from 6th century, conversion from I 233–54
adaptation of Christianity to pagan culture **I** 240–1
amulets, purveyors of **I** 242
animal leaders **I** 242
animism **I** 240–1
Artemis cult **I** 237–8
churches, construction and furnishing of **I** 234–6
cult, survival of **I** 242–6
destruction of sacred trees and groves **I** 234–7
divining **I** 239, 242, 243, 245
genuine conversion **I** 234
Kybele, cult of **I** 242–3
language and dialects **I** 238–9
Lycia **I** 239
Lykosoura, temple complex at **I** 244
martyr cults **I** 244
missionaries **I** 234
monasteries and monks, implanting **I** 233, 235, 237, 243–4, 247–8
rituals, Christianization of **I** 242

sacrifice I 238, 239–40
self-castration I 243
Spartan plane, survival of cult on
    I 245–6
springs I 239
stone, agency of the I 243
surcharges on villages I 236
temples into churches, conversion of
    I 234–7
trees and groves, sacred I 237–8, 239
paintings I 329, 330, 337
**Paiwan Catholics in Taiwan, syncretism
    among IV 262–80**
**Paiwan Cross IV 262–4, 266, 268–72,
    275–6**
PaLani, Muddu I 460
Palau, Luis III 363, IV 208, 220–1
Pallas, Demetrios I 245–6
**Pan African Leadership Assembly
    IV 344–5**
Pan African Movement II 370–1, 377
Panikkar, KN II 17
Pantaenus I 214
Pantoja, Didaco de I 290
papal diplomacy I 352–3
Paparrigopoulos, K II 217
Papasarantopoulos, Chrysostom II 376
Papua New Guinea
    millenarianism IV 47
    Urapmin, millenarianism of IV 47–8
paraenetic reminders I 138
paradisiac motifs I 139
Park, Kim II 248
Parry, Benita I 71–2
**Parsis of Bombay and Christian
    conversion II 13–27**
    1839 case II 17–25
    Anti-Conversion Memorial II 23
    Catholics II 15
    children, conversion of II 13, 17–25
    colonialism II 13–14, 17, 20, 24–5
    culture II 14–16, 18, 20, 24
    education II 14, 23–5
    fertile land, concentration of II 45
    habeas corpus II 17, 22
    inter-faith dialogue II 15–16
    law courts, challenges in II 13, 17–25
    missionaries II 13–27
    ostracism II 17–18
    Parsi Panchayat II 18, 20
    proselytism II 14, 15, 24
    Protestants II 14
    reconversion II 18–19
    seizure of land II 45
    tenant farmers II 45
    Zoroastrianism II 16
Parson, J II 45
Parsons, Lin IV 161
Parsons, Liz IV 161
Parsons, T II 203, 207
particularity I 18
Paschal I II 279–80
Pashing, Eugenie III 354
passion players III 68–9, 73
pastoralism II 30
paternalism II 68, 82, IV 320
Patriarch
    Alexandria II 372–3
    Byzantine Patriarchate II 369
    Coptic Patriarchate II 369, 371
    Constantinople II 213–14, 217–18
    Greece, religion and modernization
        in 19th century II 213–14,
        217–18
    India, Orthodox Christian Pilgrim
        Centre in Kerala IV 107–9, 114
patriarchy
    Bible I 75
    China, beliefs of Zhouzi village
        people in Catholic diocese in
        III 59
    colonialism I 75, 297
    feminist theory I 297
    India, status of Christian women in
        Kerala III 85–7, 92
    intimacy III 86
    Korean military 'comfort women'
        I 87, 91–2
    Martha and Mary from Asian
        perspective, story of I 83
    New Guinea, gendered images of
        Holy Spirit Sisters (SSpS) in
        colonial II 83
    Nigeria, young converts in Onitsha
        II 101
    translation of Bible I 75
**Patrick, St I 187, 199–200, 205, IV
    155–6, 165**
Patteson, John Coleridge II 67–70, 72–5
**Paul, St I 4, 7, 51, 101–10, 123–47,
    156–61, 171–2, 479–80,
    II 307–8, III 112, 308, IV 28–9,
    30, 34–5**
Paul the Younger I 243

INDEX

Pavia, Andrea da **I** 359, 361–2
p'Bitek, Okot IV 337, 340
Peacock, JL IV 134
Peck, EJ III 226
Pedro I I 260–1, 349
Pelleprat, Pierre I 397
penances **I** 449, 453
Penny, Alfred II 73
Pentecostalism
  Adventism **II** 386–7
  African Pentecostal movement, spread of **II** 400
  Brazil
    missionaries **III** 424–5
    Universal Church of the Kingdom of God **III** 423–39
  Burkino Faso, faith-healers of Assemblies of God in **III** 254, 256, 270
  Chile **II** 285–306
  conversions **II** 139–40
  diasporas **III** 424
  Elim movement **II** 385–6, 388–93, 397–401
  globalisation **III** 423–33
  glossolalia **II** 307–19
  healing **II** 386
  India, global fundamentalism and local Christianity in Madras **III** 443–62
  Inuit Pentecostalism and Evangelicalism in Canadian and Eastern Arctic **III** 201–29
  Mexico, native evangelism in central **III** 393–4
  Mezzogiorno, glossolalia and possession amongst Pentecostal groups of the **II** 307–19
  missionaries **III** 424–5
  New Zealand, gospel songs in **IV** 216, 221
  Norddeutsche Missiongesellschaft, role of Devil in preaching of **III** 415–20
  possession **II** 307–19
  revivalism **II** 386
  salvation **II** 386
  sanctification **II** 386
  Sumatra, Karo Batak Protestant Church in **II** 137, 139–40
  Ulster Pentecostals **II** 384, 385–93, 397–401
  United States **III** 424
  Zimbabwe
    American Evangelicalism in **III** 359–60
    Northern Nyaga District **II** 384, 385–93, 397–400
Pentelewon I 205, 206
perception of Christianity, checklist on **I** 17
Perez, Roberto IV 328
Pergamum, bishop of I 243
persecution
  China, Christian Virgins in 18th century **I** 435–6
  Chola people **I** 217
  Korean Protestantism, contribution of Biblewomen to **II** 248
Persia
  celibacy **I** 216–17
  dar-al-Islam, refugees from **I** 220
  disappearance of Christianity **I** 216
  Edessa, Turkey, links of Christians with Christians in **I** 214–15
  elites and masses, divide between **I** 216–17
  language **I** 216
  monasticism **I** 216–17
  Offspring of the Covenant **I** 216–17
  Penitents **I** 216–17
  persecution of Christians **I** 199
  Persian, failure of elites to use **I** 216
  Syriac language **I** 216
  theological controversies **I** 214–15
  Thomas Christians and the Thomas tradition **I** 222
  Zoroastrians **I** 217
Peter, St I 161
Peterson, William J I 337
Petrides, Lela III 19
Pharmakides, Theoklitos II 217
Philemon I 145
Philip, Gospel of I 170–1
Philip, John II 33, 39–40
Philippines
  imitation of Christ in Bicol **III** 61–80
  Amang Hinulid **III** 61–9, 71–6
  Bicol, imitation of Christ **III** 61–80
  burial of Christ **III** 68
  Candelaria, Seberine, trial in Philippines of **II** 117–33
  colonialism **III** 62, 63, 75–6
  culture **III** 62, 76

INDEX

'dead Christ' **III** 61–9, 71–6
ethnography **III** 62
European features, Christ with
    III 63–4
festivals **III** 65
funerals **III** 65–9
Good Friday **III** 65, 66–9
healing **III** 61–2, 63–5, 70–3
Holy Week **III** 65, 66–9
identification, process of **III** 68, 74
imitation of Christ in Bicol **III** 61–80
imitative and derivative, culture as
    III 63
indigenization **III** 67
lowland culture **III** 63, 76
mediums **III** 61–2, 63
millenarian peasant uprisings
    III 75–6
missionaries **III** 62
Oliver's manuscript of Decalogue in
    Tagalog **I** 311–27
passion players **III** 68–9, 73
Passion text **III** 67–8
possession **III** 70
poverty **III** 62
ritual weeping **III** 65–6
rural area, Bicol as **III** 62
saints **III** 64
shamans **III** 71–2, 75, 76
Spanish rule **III** 62, 63, 75–6
spirits
    communication with **III** 61–2,
        75–6
    sickness and healing **III** 69–71
Tagalog
    Oliver's manuscript of Decalogue
        in Tagalog **I** 311–27
    translation of Bible **I** 73–5
translation of Bible into Tagalog
    I 73–5
United States **III** 62, 75–6
wakes **III** 65
Westernization **III** 61–2, 76
witchcraft and devils **II** 120–1
Phillippo, James III 182
Philo I 127, 130
Philostorgius I 219
Phoebe of Cenchreae I 157–8
Phrygian language I 187
pietism **III** 410–11, 415, 418–20, 446
pilgrimage
    Brazil **IV** 87–103

Canadian Prairie Indians,
    pilgrimages of **IV** 140–53
Catholics **IV** 90–1
cultural change **IV** 141–2, 151
Francis of Assisi in Canindé, shrine
    of **IV** 88–98
Glastonbury, United Kingdom
    IV 137
healing **IV** 99–100
India, Orthodox Christian Pilgrim
    Centre in Kerala **IV** 104–20
industrialization **IV** 87
intercession, theology of **IV** 111–13
liminal state **IV** 90
loyalty to groups, display of
    IV 113–14
magico-religious complex **IV** 90–1
merchandise **IV** 93–4
Mizeki, Bernard **IV** 156, 160–5
modernity **IV** 100
modernization **IV** 87
oppressive ideologies, pilgrimages as
    legitimatizing **IV** 124
pastiche **IV** 137
Patrick, St **IV** 155
performance **IV** 122–37, 151–2
popular Catholicism **IV** 87
potential devotees **IV** 87
preparation for pilgrims
    IV 93–4
pre-Reformation **IV** 90–1
saints, cult of **IV** 91–3
social relations **IV** 87–8
vows to saints **IV** 91
Walsingham, United Kingdom,
    pilgrimage to **IV** 121–39
Pilkinton, Ross IV 216–17
Pil-rye, Kim II 249
Pipili, Fotini III 102
Pius IX II 171
Pius XI II 386
plague **I** 412
plainsong **IV** 185, 186–7
plays **III** 32–3
Pleutschau, Heinrich I 442–3, 445–6,
    448
Pliny I 123–4, 127, 136, 141
Plotinus I 193
ploughs **II** 41
pluralism
    California, breakdown of Spanish
        mission system in **II** 226–8

419

INDEX

French Polynesia, women in ordained ministry in Mô'ohi Protestant Church in III 157
Greece, religion and modernization in 19th century II 201
jagar rituals in Goa, India III 24
Sumatra, Karo Batak Protestant Church in II 137
syncretism II 257–9
United States I 35–43
Zaïre, Kimbanguism and syncretism in II 259, 268–9
Pobedonostsev, KP II 188
poetry
  Book of Songs (Shih ching) I 328
  Buddhist poetry I 329, 332
  China I 328–47
  Confucianism I 328, 332, 336–7
  converts I 343
  criticism I 332
  eulogies (*tsan*) I 329
  'iron cross' I 333–5
  Malawi, women as religious and political praise singers and dancers in IV 230–1
  missionaries I 328
  paintings I 329
  spiritual odes I 128–9
  Sung dynasty I 332, 335
  Wu Li and first Chinese Christian poetry I 330–47
Poewe, K III 318
politics
  Brazil
    base communities (CEBs) III 198–202, 208
    Universal Church of the Kingdom of God III 431
  Chile
    pentacostalism II 285, 295–301
    young women as apostles to the poor II 278, 281
  China, Catholic women of Congregation of Sisters in IV 73
  communism II 148–9, III 367, 370, 447–8
  conservative/liberal divide IV 298, 304–7
  conversions II 141, 143–4
  Coptic cultural nationalism III 18
  French Polynesia, women in ordained ministry in Mô'ohi Protestant Church in III 155

Greece, religion and modernization in 19th century II 202–3, 209, 216
jagar rituals in Goa, India III 24
heresy I 167
India, Orthodox Christian Pilgrim Centre in Kerala IV 116, 119
Inuit Pentecostalism and Evangelicalism in Canadian and Eastern Arctic III 214–15
Malawi, women as religious and political praise singers and dancers in IV 224–41
Mexico, immediacy and eternity in a Catholic convent in IV 50
parties II 297–9
Philippines, trial of Seberine Candelaria in II 117–33
Protestants II 204
religico-political ritual II 204
socialism II 31–5, 278, 281
Spain, anticlericalism in Aracena in II 340–67
Sumatra, Karo Batak Protestant Church in II 141, 143–4
syncretism IV 263
Taiwan, syncretism among Paiwan Catholics in IV 263
Zaïre, Kimbanguism and syncretism in II 254–5
Zimbabwe, American Evangelicalism in III 369–70
Politis, N II 217
polygyny I 301–2, II 98–9, 106–7
Pomio Kivung of New Guinea III 170
Pompallier, Jean II 173
Pontchartrain, Jérome I 401
population projections IV 298–302, 309–10, 313
Portugal
  Brazil, Universal Church of the Kingdom of God in III 429–33, 438
  Barwe refugees from Portuguese East Africa II 385
  colonialism II 385, III 23–5, IV 283–4, 293–4
  Christianization of Iberia I 198–212
  dance IV 283–4, 293–4
  India
    dance IV 283–4, 293–4
    jagar rituals in Goa III 23–5
    Tarangambadi (Tranquebar), missionaries in I 442

INDEX

jagar rituals in Goa **III** 23–5
Macau **I** 339
Soyo, Capuchins and rulers of
   I 349–55, 363
Tarangambadi (Tranquebar), India,
   missionaries in **I** 442
Wu Li and first Chinese Christian
   poetry **I** 339
possession
   Burkino Faso, faith-healers of
      Assemblies of God in **III** 255,
      256–61
   exorcism **III** 257–67, 415, 418, 419–20
   Mezzogiorno, glossolalia and
      possession amongst Pentecostal
      groups of the **II** 307–19
postdenominationalism IV 312
postmillennialism IV 215
Pottier, François I 433–4
poverty
   Brazil, base communities (CEBs) in
      III 195–6
   Chile
      pentacostalism in **II** 286–301
      young women as apostles to the
         poor **II** 273–84
   India, status of Christian women in
      Kerala **III** 91
   Latin America, awakening of
      indigenous people in **IV** 320
   Philippines, imitation of Christ in
      III 62
   women in Chile **II** 273–84
power *see also* **hegemony**
   Aboriginal Australians **III** 167
   authority **I** 8
   Brazil, base communities in **III** 206–7
   China, Christian sectarian violence in
      late 19th century **II** 323–4, 326
   Christian identity **I** 18–20
   hierarchy, acceptance of **I** 8–9
   illegitimacy **I** 9
   internalization **I** 8
   leaders **I** 8–9
   Philippines, trial of Seberine
      Candelaria in **II** 127–8
   reflection **I** 9
   representation **I** 10
   sociology **I** 8–9
   Soyo, Capuchins and rulers of
      I 351
   syncretism **III** 466, 473, 477–8
   toleration **I** 13

pow-wows **IV** 148–9
Prakash, Gyan I 77
Pratt, Mary Louise I 475
prayers
   Burkino Faso, faith-healers of
      Assemblies of God in **III** 253
   China, beliefs of Zhouzi village
      people in Catholic diocese in
      III 55–6
   ekklesia **I** 131–2, 133
   intercession, theology of **IV** 111
   jagar rituals in Goa, India **III** 27–9
   Lübeck prophet in local and
      Lutheran context **I** 417–18
   Mexico, native evangelism in central
      III 391
   Norddeutsche Missiongesellschaft,
      role of Devil in preaching of
      III 415
prejudice *see* **discrimination and
   prejudice**
Prelatic fools III 309
Presbyterians
   Aboriginal Australians **IV** 14
   Chile, pentacostalism in **II** 289–92,
      295–6
   Malawi, women as religious and
      political praise singers and
      dancers in **IV** 238–9
   New Zealand, gospel songs in **IV** 213
   Scotland **IV** 238–9
   Taiwan, conversion to Protestantism
      amongst urban immigrants in
      III 317, 320–4
presbyters and presbytery I 157–60,
   161–3
pride I 416–17
priests *see* **clergy**
Procopius I 181, 234, 236
'proper' Christians I 19
prophets
   Burkino Faso, faith-healers of
      Assemblies of God in **III** 253
   healers **III** 253
   Lübeck prophet in local and
      Lutheran context **I** 409–12,
      418–19
   popular opinion **I** 418–19
   Zaïre, Kimbanguism and syncretism
      in **II** 254, 255, 263–6
proselytism
   Burkino Faso, faith-healers of
      Assemblies of God in **III** 253

Malawi, women as religious and political praise singers and dancers in **IV** 235–6
Mexico, native evangelism in central **III** 390, 393, 396, 397, 399, 401–2
Parsis of Bombay and Christian conversion **II** 14, 15, 24
Protestant-Catholic distinctions in coming global Christianity IV 297–315
  African Christianity **IV** 299–304, 313
  Latin American Christianity **IV** 299–304, 313
  population projections **IV** 299–301
  Brazil, population projection for **IV** 301
  centrality of Catholicism **IV** 310–13
  church-state relations **IV** 307
  clash of civilizations **IV** 297, 308
  conservative/liberal divide **IV** 298, 304–7
  data **IV** 298–9
  developing countries **IV** 297
  distinguishing Protestants from Catholics **IV** 299
  Euro-American dominance, decline in **IV** 301–2
  institutional outcomes **IV** 311
  Jesuits **IV** 305
  Latin American Christianity **IV** 299–304, 313
  liberal North versus conservative South **IV** 304–7
  Muslims **IV** 308–9
  national and religious identity, congruence between **IV** 310–11
  national to global, from **IV** 307–10
  nationalism **IV** 308
  nation-states **IV** 308
  'Next Christendom' **IV** 297
  population projections **IV** 298–302, 309–10, 313
  particularity of Protestantism **IV** 310–13
  postdenominationalism **IV** 312
  Reformation **IV** 307, 310, 312
  Second Vatican Council **IV** 312–13
  sexuality **IV** 305, 307
  South, shift from North to **IV** 297–307, 313
  transnational identity **IV** 298
  United States, conservatism in **IV** 305–7
  World Christian Database **IV** 298
  World Christian Encyclopaedia **IV** 298–9, 312
Protestants *see also* **Baptists; Lutherans; Pentecostalism; Presbyterians**
  Brazil, Universal Church of the Kingdom of God in **III** 431–3
  Catholic-Protestant distinctions in coming global Christianity **IV** 297–315
  Chile **II** 278, 281, 286–92, 295–6
  China, Christian sectarian violence in late 19th century **II** 323–36
  conversions **III** 317–29
  Dalit theology in Tamil Christian folk music **IV** 243–4, 247–8
  France, faith, family and fashion in Strasbourg **III** 127–9
  French Polynesia, women in ordained ministry in Mô'ohi Protestant Church in **III** 149–61
  Greece, religion and modernization in 19th century **II** 202, 204
  hats and women's position in evangelical churches in Edinburgh, Scotland **IV** 25–41
  immigrants, conversion of **III** 317–29
  India
    Catholics **II** 51, 58, 62
    global fundamentalism and local Christianity in Madras **III** 443–58
    Parsis of Bombay and Christian conversion **II** 14
    Tarangambadi (Tranquebar), missionaries in **I** 442
  Karo Batak Protestant Church, Sumatra, conversion and **II** 137–59
  Kimbanguism and syncretism in Zaïre **II** 253–70
  Korean Protestantism, contribution of Biblewomen to **II** 237–52
  magic and mysticism in UK, effect on **II** 204
  Methodists
    Chile, pentacostalism in **II** 287–92, 295–6
    shrines **IV** 169–77
    United Methodist church **III** 358

United States **IV** 169–77
Native American missionaries **I** 471
New Zealand
  gospel songs **IV** 207–21
  Irish Catholics in 19th century
    Christchurch in **II** 168–70, 175
Parsis of Bombay and Christian
  conversion **II** 14
particularity **IV** 310–13
rationalism **II** 202
religico-political ritual **II** 204
Seventh–day Adventism **III** 377
shrines **IV** 169–77
syncretism **II** 253–60
Taiwan, immigrants to **III** 317–29
Tarangambadi (Tranquebar), India,
  missionaries in **I** 442
United Methodist church **III** 358
United States **IV** 169–77
urban immigrants, conversion of
  III 317–29
women **II** 237–52
Zaire **II** 253–70
Prud'homme, Paul IV 182, 188
psalms I 127–8
Psomas, Al 213
Punic culture I 181–6, 191
purgatory I 414
Pye, Michael II 253, 256, 259

Quan Yan Method III 319
Queiroz, MEP de IV 91

Raapoto, Turo III 157
race *see* **ethnicity**
Racey, RL II 82
Rafael, R III 705
Rahner, Hugo III 308
Râle, Sébastien I 380–90
Ramalingaswami I 463–4
Rambo, L I 10
Ramsay, William Mitchell I 234–5
Ranger, Terry II 383–4, 389, 392,
  394, **III** 238–9, **IV** 159
Raphael, Vicente I 73–5
Rappaport, R IV 130–1
rationalism II 202
Razafindrakoto, Georges I 113
Reagan, Ronald III 360
rebellions and uprisings
  Bushmen, Christ as trickster in religion
    of contemporary **III** 307–8

French Antilles, Catholic missions
  to slaves in **I** 394–5
Latin America, awakening of
  indigenous people in **IV** 317,
  318–19, 322–3
Saint-Dominique and Haiti
  I 394–5
Soyo, Capuchins and rulers of
  I 349
Recabarren, Luis II 278
recognition, ruse of I 69
reconstruction, theology of IV 347–8
Reformation
  Catholics **I** 296–7, **IV** 307, 310, 312
  gender **I** 296–7
  Greece, religion and modernization
    in 19th century **II** 201, 203–4
  missionaries **I** 296–7
  nuclear families **III** 144
  shrines **IV** 172
Regina Coeli mission II 395–7
Reicke, Bo I 142
Reid, Anthony II 145
Reid, G Edward III 384
Reimarus, Albert I 410, 412–13
reincarnation, belief in III 470–2
Reisner, MA II 181–2
relief organizations II 299–300
Renaissance III 144
repentance I 414
representation I 9–10
retreats II 262–3
revelation I 130, **III** 385
Revivalism
  Jamaican peasant life, religion as
    resistance in **III** 187–93
  New Zealand, gospel songs in **IV** 213
  Pentecostalism **II** 386
  Zimbabwe, missionaries in Northern
    Nyaga District in **II** 401–2
Rey, Terry I 265
Rhodes, Cecil III 357, **IV** 156–8
Rhodes, Willard IV 181
Ricci, Matteo I 281–6, 288–92, 330
Richelieu, Armand, cardinal I 396
Richter, Christian Friedrich I 458
Ricoeur, P IV 50, 65
ritual *see* **ritual and early church in
  Eastern Mediterranean; rituals**
**ritual and early church in Eastern
  Mediterranean I** 123–52
  baptism **I** 125, 133–41, 146

burial **I** 145–6
coming together **I** 126–7, 146
communication, ritual as **I** 124–5
culture, transmission of **I** 125
ekklesia **I** 126, 127–33, 141
frequency of meetings **I** 127
Gaius's house, *ekklesia* in **I** 126, 130
household assemblies **I** 126, 130–1
language **I** 124–5
liminality **I** 140–1
Lord's Supper **I** 125–6, 141–5, 146
marriage **I** 146
minor ritual **I** 125–33
Nympha's house in Laodicea, *ekklesia* in **I** 123
Pauline tradition **I** 123–47
performative speech, as **I** 125
religion, whether early Christianity was a **I** 123–4
speech, ritual as **I** 124–5
superhuman beings, interaction with **I** 124
symbolism **I** 124–5
unknown and controverted rituals **I** 145–7

rituals I 123, 126–7 *see also* **baptism; ceremonies; funerals; mass**
Aboriginal Australians **III** 172–3
Canadian Prairie Indians, pilgrimages of **IV** 143, 145–52
China
  Catholic women of Congregation of Sisters in **IV** 70
  sino-Western cultural communication at end of Ming dynasty **I** 283, 285, 290
Christianization **I** 242
confirmation **II** 276
Eastern Mediterranean, early church in **I** 123–52
ekklesia **I** 126, 127–33
everyday life, ritualization of **IV** 52–3, 65
exhortation **I** 129, 132–3
female spirituality, models and rituals of **II** 275–6
Gnostics **I** 170–1
healing **IV** 323–4
identity creation **IV** 323–3
impurity **III** 97
Inuit Pentecostalism and Evangelicalism in Canadian and Eastern Arctic **III** 213–19, 221–7
jagar rituals in Goa, India **III** 21–37
Jamaican peasant life, religion as resistance in **III** 187–8, 190–3
land, healing the **III** 12–19, 221–5
Latin America, awakening of indigenous people in **IV** 323–4
Lord's Supper **I** 125–6, 141–5, 146
Mexico, immediacy and eternity in a Catholic convent in **IV** 52–3, 65
Navajo **IV** 323–3
New Zealand, Irish Catholics in 19th century Christchurch in **II** 173–4
Nigeria, fertility in Itapa-Ekiti in **III** 277–8, 292
paganism in rural Anatolia and Greece from 6th century, conversion from **I** 242
Philippines, imitation of Christ in **III** 65–6
social worlds **III** 34–5
Soyo, Capuchins and rulers of **I** 354–6, 360–2, 363
Spain, anticlericalism in Aracena in **II** 352
syncretism **II** 256–7, **IV** 264–7, 272–4, 276
Taiwan, syncretism among Paiwan Catholics in **IV** 264–7, 272–4, 276
Ulster Pentecostals **II** 389
Walsingham, United Kingdom, pilgrimage to **IV** 121–5, 132–7
water **III** 280, 281–3, 292
weeping **III** 65–6
Zaïre, Kimbanguism and syncretism in **II** 262, 264–6
Zimbabwe, missionaries in Northern Nyaga District in **II** 388

Rivers, William Halse II 67
Robert, Dana II 238
Robert, Louis I 237
Robertson, Pat III 361
Robertson, Roland III 423
Robbins, Joel III 213–14, **IV** 47, 64
Rodriguez, Simón I 276
Rogers, F II 59
Rolle, Andrew F II 226
Roman Catholics *see* **Catholics**

Roman Empire, Christianization of
I 198–212
Aksum, Christianization of I 198–208
comparative approach I 200
conversion I 200
countryside, Christianization of the I 204–7
Iberia, Christianization of I 200–8
Nile river cults I 244
Osrhoëne, King of I 199
Thomas Christians and the Thomas tradition I 213
Roman Africa, Christianity and local culture in late I 181–97
Berber (Libyan) culture I 181–4
Catholics I 183, 186–7, 191
Donatism I 183, 185–92
language I 182, 184–93
Latin I 187–93
Law I 186–7
Manichaean propaganda I 189
Numidia I 181–3, 186, 189–92
paganism I 187
Phrygian language I 187
Punic culture I 181–6, 191
social mobility I 189
teaching profession I 189
testimonia I 188–9
Vandals, arrival of I 189, 191
Romano, Giovanni da I 361
Romans *see* **Roman Empire, Christianization of; Roman Africa, Christianity and local culture in late**
Roosevelt, FD III 378
Rosaldo, Michelle III 86
Rosaldo, Renato III 75
Ross, John II 241
Row, Pamela II 99
Rowe, John III 181–2
Roy, Arundhati. *God of Small Things* III 83–5
Roy, Manisha I 80
Roy, Mary III 83–4
Roy, Raja Ram Mohan I 451
royal conversions I 201–2, 203
Rudder, John III 173–4
Rudolph, Kurt I 173
Rufinus of Aquileia I 201, 203
Ruggieri, Michele I 328–9, 343
rural areas
attendance at church I 17

China, beliefs of Zhouzi village people in Catholic diocese in III 38–60
Iberia, Christianization of I 204–7
Irish Carmelites from rural areas II 397
Jamaican peasant life, religion as resistance in III 181–94
Kongo, church in I 257–65
Mezzogiorno, glossolalia and possession amongst Pentecostal groups of the II 308
New Zealand, Irish kinship groups in II 164–7
paganism in rural Anatolia and Greece from 6th century, conversion from I 233–54
Philippines, imitation of Christ in III 62
Roman Empire, Christianization of I 204–7
uptake I 17
Zimbabwe, missionaries in Northern Nyaga District in II 383
Russia
Africa, Orthodox Mission in II 370–1
Kyrgyzstan, missionaries in post-Soviet III 236, 245, 247
Leningrad, independent religious communities in III 345–56
Tatars and apostasy II 179–200

sacraments
Cameroun, liturgical adaptation in St Paul de Ndzon-Melen in I 51
incarnation, mystery of the I 51
sacred lakes IV 327
sacred trees and groves, destruction of I 234–7
sacrifices
Decalogue in Tagalog, Oliver's manuscript of I 312
Merina traditional religion and the Bible in Madagascar I 116, 118–19
paganism in rural Anatolia and Greece from 6th century, conversion from I 238, 239–40
sino-Western cultural communication at end of Ming dynasty I 283
syncretism IV 266
Taiwan, syncretism among Paiwan Catholics in IV 266

INDEX

Sahlins, Marshall II 143, 344
Said, E III 457
Saint-Dominique, revolts in I 394–5
saints
  Brazil
    base communities (CEBs) III 200
    pilgrimage IV 91–3
  Greece, religion and modernization in 19th century II 206
  hagiography III 311
  intercession, theology of IV 113–14
  Mezzogiorno, glossolalia and possession amongst Pentecostal groups of the II 309, 310
  Mizeki, Bernard IV 156, 159, 163–4
  Philippines, imitation of Christ in III 64
  pilgrimage IV 91–3
  saints as tricksters III 311
  shrines IV 171
  syncretism III 469–70, 476
  vows to saints IV 91
Salazar, Gabriel II 286, 295
Sallnow, M IV 124
Sallualuk, E III 219–20
Salluviniq, Allie III 214
Salluviniq, Susan III 214
salvation
  Baptists IV 64
  Dalit theology in Tamil Christian folk music IV 256
  Dominus Iesus declaration in Asia I 60–3
  Pentecostalism II 386
  Southern Tswana, Africa, cultivation and colonialism in II 29
  Tarangambadi (Tranquebar), India, missionaries in I 453, 460
samurai I 272
Sánchez, José Maria III 342
Sanneh, Lamin I 72–4, IV 345
Sanskrit IV 246–9
Sanz, Leandro Tormo I 269
Sarah and Hannah, story of III 277, 285–90
Sarawia, George II 73, 75
Sargeant, John I 477
Sarikas, Nicodemus II 370, 373, 374, 375
Sassanian Empire I 200–1
Sastriar, Vedanayagam IV 248
Satan *see* Devil; spirits and demons; witchcraft, sorcery and devils

scapegoating II 344
Schaaf, Thomas III 367
Schall von Bell, Adam I 330
Schechner, R IV 136
Schell, Edwin IV 175
Schleiermacher, Ernest II 71
Schleiermacher, Friedrich III 410
Schuler, Monica III 188, 191
science I 77
Scotland *see* hats as symbol of women's position in Evangelical churches in Edinburgh, Scotland
Scott, James II 118, 129
Scott, WH III 75
Scranton, Mary F II 239
Scranton, WB II 242
Searle, John R II 257
Sebastian, Mrinalini I 75–6
Second Vatican Council IV 312–13, 265–6
sectarianism
  China, Christian sectarian violence in late 19th century II 323–39
  New Zealand, Irish Catholics in 19th century Christchurch in II 170
secularization
  California, breakdown of Spanish mission system in II 226, 232–3
  Coptic cultural nationalism III 14, 18
  definition II 201
  ethical ideas I 282–3
  France I 14
  Greece, religion and modernization in 19th century II 210–11
  intellectuals II 211
  modernity III 275
  separation of church and state II 210
  sino-Western cultural communication at end of Ming dynasty I 282–3
  sociology I 13–14
  Ulster Pentecostals II 388
  United States I 14
Sedode, Theodor III 414
Seeley, John II 69
self
  conversion as care of self I 453–62
  evangelising the self IV 63–5
  Kyrgyzstan, missionaries in post-Soviet III 240–3
  Mexico, immediacy and eternity in a Catholic convent in IV 50–2, 63–5

INDEX

recollecting and rearranging personal history into new narrative of self **IV** 46, 53–4
vocation as story of self **IV** 50–2, 635
self-castration **I** 243
self-harm **I** 243, **III** 172
Selwyn, George Augustus **II** 66, 68
Sen, Lucie **I** 431
Sen, Monique **I** 431, 432–3
sensus fidelium **I** 57–8
separation from God **I** 4
Seratwa-Ntloedibe-Kuswani, Gomang **I** 75
servants, women as domestic **II** 165–6, 169
Setiliane, G **IV** 337
Seventh–day Adventism **III** 374–88
  6,000 year umbrella time prophecy **III** 38
  apostasy of Church, those who sigh and cry over **III** 386
  church administrators **III** 379–80
  church-sect theory **III** 375
  colleges, accreditation for **III** 378
  Daniel, timeline prophecies of **III** 385
  denominations **III** 375
  departments of religion **III** 382
  early Adventists, apocalyptic urgency among **III** 376
  eschatology **III** 376, 377–84
  evangelism **III** 376, 380–1
  expectancy and delay **III** 378–9
  extending the time **III** 376–8
  fragmenting of Adventist apocalyptic **III** 379–83
  fringes of Adventism, movements on **III** 383–6
  Great Disappointment **III** 374
  hats as symbol of women's position in Evangelical churches in Edinburgh, Scotland **IV** 26, 32, 36–7
  institutions **III** 376–7
  Jerusalem, status of **III** 386
  Jubilee Cycle **III** 385
  laypersons **III** 382–3
  Millerite Movement **III** 374
  missionaries **III** 376–7
  multimedia **III** 380
  origins **III** 374–5
  pastors **III** 381
  premillennialists **III** 384

  Protestantism, attitude to **III** 377
  Revelation **III** 385
  seminars **III** 382
  spiritualism **III** 380
  states of tension **III** 375, 376–7
  United States **III** 375–80
Severinus, St **I** 206
Severus, Septimus **I** 185–6
sexual abuse **I** 402
sexuality
  baptism **I** 137
  celibacy **I** 216–17, 434
  India, status of Christian women in Kerala **III** 88
  Inuit Pentecostalism and Evangelicalism in Canadian and Eastern Arctic **III** 219
  male homoeroticism **I** 272
  sodomy **I** 269, 271–2
  Tupi and European women in eyes of Claude d'Abbeville **I** 303–4
  Xavier, Francisco, Japanese in letters of **I** 272
Shaanxi Province, China, Catholic community in **IV** 69–70
Shagonaby, Susan **IV** 182
Shahji, king of Tanjavur **I** 443
Shahrani, M **III** 233
Shakarian, Demos **III** 360
Shalifoe, Thomas **IV** 184, 186
shamans
  glossolalia **II** 307
  healing **IV** 323–4
  Inuit Pentecostalism and Evangelicalism in Canadian and Eastern Arctic **III** 213, 222–4
  Latin America, awakening of indigenous people in **IV** 318, 319, 323–5, 330
  merchandising **IV** 324–5
  Philippines, imitation of Christ in **III** 71–2, 75, 76
Shapur II **I** 199, 215
Sharpe, Sam **III** 188
Shastri, Laxman **II** 16
Shaw, R **IV** 263
Sheba, Queen of **I** 202
Shekinah Ministries **III** 364, 367, 372
Shen Que **I** 290–1
Shenuda **III** 13, 15, 18, 19–20
Shepherdson, Ella **III** 167–8
Shepherdson, Harold **III** 167–9
Shepstone, Theophilus **I** 100, 109

Shillington, K II 40
Shimazono, Susimu III 330
Shin, Maria II 242
Shinshu, Kawai III 337–8
Shinto II 256, III 333, 334, 340
Shona IV 157–9, 162–5
shrines
  Anglican shrine IV 121–3, 125–8, 132
  Brazil IV 88–98
  built or found object shrines IV 171, 172
  Canadian Prairie Indians, pilgrimages of IV 141, 143–9
  Catholics IV 122–3, 125–31, 141, 143–9, 169, 171, 173–5
  classification IV 170–2
  commemorative shrines IV 170–1, 173
  domestic and civic space IV 170
  ecumenical shrines IV 170
  ex voto shrines IV 171, 172
  Francis of Assisi in Canindé, shrine of IV 88–98
  geographical classification IV 170
  homes IV 170
  identity shrines IV 171, 173
  imitative shrines IV 171, 172
  Methodists IV 169–77
  Mizeki, Bernard IV 157–9
  miraculous shrines IV 171, 172
  nationalism IV 170
  native Americans IV 171
  origin and function 170–1
  pilgrimages IV 88–98
  Protestants IV 169–77
  quasi-religious shrines IV 170
  religious traditions, classification by IV 170
  saints IV 171
  secular shrines IV 170
  Ste-Anne d'Auray shrine IV 141, 143–51
  United States IV 169–77
  Walsingham, United Kingdom, pilgrimage to IV 121–39
Shulman, David I 450
Sichuan, Christian Virgins in 18th century I 425–40
  1784, after I 434–6
  age I 433–5
  Amantes de la Croix I 430
  assault, risk of I 433–4
  baptism of dying children I 432
  Catholics I 425–37
  christendoms or *chrétientés* I 426–7, 432–4
  Daughters of Charity I 430
  decline in 20th century I 436
  Dominicans I 430
  duties I 426, 429–35
  famine work I 432
  French missionaries I 426
  indigenous leadership, role of I 426
  Institute of Christian Virgins I 425, 429–33
    establishment I 429–31
    reorganization of I 431–3
    tensions between Church and Institute I 433–4
  lay evangelism I 426, 431, 437
  missionaries I 426
  origins I 426–9
  persecution I 435–6
  preaching I 434
  priests I 426
  sexual license, Christians as behaving with I 428
  teaching I 432–5, 437
  three dependencies I 430
  vows of chastity I 434
  White Lotus sect I 425, 428, 436–7
siddhars I 449–51, 458–61
Sierra Leone III 107, 108, 113–16, 120–1
Sigehelm I 221
signification III 465–6, 473
Silva, Giovanni Barreto da I 356, 358, 359
Silva, Manuel III 438
Simon, Marcel I 182
Simon of Cyrene I 185–6, IV 133–4
Simon Peter III 310
Simpson, Ernest IV 158
sin I 4, 6, 102–6, III 220–1
sins of previous generations III 220–1
singing *see* **songs and singing**
sino-Western cultural communication at end of Ming dynasty I 280–94
  ancestor worship I 281–5, 290
  Catholicism, scholar-officials' interpretation and adoption of I 286–9
  Celestial Emperor I 282, 284–5, 290

Chinese Buddhism (Zenism) **I** 287, 290
Confucianism **I** 281–6, 290–3
differentiation **I** 290–3
Disputation on Rite and Ritual **I** 285, 290
Enlightenment **I** 285–6
God **I** 284–5, 290
heaven and human nature **I** 293
misreading **I** 280–93
missionaries **I** 281–6, 290–3
Qing dynasty **I** 293
Riccian rules **I** 290
rite **I** 283, 285, 290
sacrifice **I** 283
secularised ethical ideas **I** 282–3
teachings and codes **I** 287
Xia dynasty, supreme deity in **I** 284
Yin dynasty **I** 282, 284
Zhou dynasty **I** 282
Siolim *zagor* **III** 26, 27
Siqueira, Paula de I 372–3
Siurot, Manuel II 346–7
Skinner, G William II 325
slavery
Brazil, women in colonial **I** 374–5
Decalogue in Tagalog, Oliver's manuscript of **I** 312–13
French Antilles, Catholic missions to slaves in **I** 394–408
Jamaican peasant life, religion as resistance in **III** 181–91
Orthodox Mission **II** 370–1, 372
Southern Tswana, Africa, cultivation and colonialism in **II** 31
Soyo, Capuchins and rulers of **I** 359, 362–3, 364
Sudan, Uduk faith in five-note scale in **IV** 192
Tarangambadi (Tranquebar), India, missionaries in **I** 443, 448
Tupi and European women in eyes of Claude d'Abbeville **I** 299–300
United States, gender and change in Church of the Lord (Aladura) in **III** 106
Smith, Anthony III 437
Smith, Christian III 207
Smith, Edwin II 36
Smith, Florence II 288–9
Smith, Ian III 357–8, **IV** 159
Smith, MG II 226–8

Smith, Robertson I 123
Social Catholicism II 275
social change
Dalit theology in Tamil Christian folk music **IV** 256–7
Korean Protestantism, contribution of Biblewomen to **II** 247–9
social context I 2
social justice
Indian dance forms, Christianity in **IV** 287–9
Spain, anticlericalism in Aracena in **II** 359–60
social outreach in Brazil III 200–2, 206–7
socialism
Chile, young women as apostles to the poor in **II** 278, 281
Southern Tswana, Africa, cultivation and colonialism in **II** 31–5
Society of the Sacred Heart of Jesus IV 72–3
sociology
basic sociological plank **I** 7–14
contextualization **I** 11–12
conversion **I** 10–11
power **I** 8–9
representation **I** 9–10
secularization **I** 13–14
syncretism **I** 12–13
Solomon I 202
songs and singing *see also* **music**
Aboriginal Australians **III** 170, 172–4, 177
Austrian folk songs **IV** 187
Cameroun, liturgical adaptation in St Paul de Ndzon-Melen in **I** 49–50, 53–5
ekklesia **I** 127–9
jagar rituals in Goa, India **III** 29–30, 31–2
Malawi, women as religious and political praise singers and dancers in **IV** 224–41
New Zealand, gospel songs in **IV** 207–23
plainsong **IV** 185, 186–7
sorcery *see* **witchcraft, sorcery and devils**
Sorrento, Girolamo da I 354–5, 359, 361–2
soteriology I 130
Sousa, Clarice Magalhães de IV 95

INDEX

South Africa
  Brazil, Universal Church of the Kingdom of God in **III** 427–8
  Greek Orthodox Church **II** 372
  Mizeki, Bernard **IV** 160, 163–4
  Orthodox Mission **III** 370–1, 372
Souto, Sebastião I 262
Soviet Union
  Leningrad, independent religious communities in **III** 347–55
  Orthodox Church **III** 347–55
Soyo, Capuchins and rulers of I 348–66
  advantages possessed by Capuchins **I** 351–2
  ancestors **I** 361
  authorities, relationship with **I** 353–60, 362–4
  baptism **I** 360–1
  Christian festivals **I** 354–5
  Come vero Prencipe Catolico **I** 353
  confessions **I** 356, 360–2
  confraternities and congregations, use of **I** 356–7
  diplomatic role of Capuchins **I** 352–3, 357
  discipline of ruling elite **I** 355–7
  economic and strategic importance **I** 349
  indigenous religion, interaction of Christianity with **I** 358–62
  interpreters **I** 356–7, 362, 363
  Kongo, battles with **I** 350–1
  legitimacy of rulers **I** 355–7, 363
  marriage **I** 357–8
  Mass **I** 354, 356, 363
  Mbanza Soyo **I** 351–2, 354–6, 358, 360
  Mpinda **I** 349, 351, 353
  Nfinda **I** 349
  nganga **I** 359
  papal diplomacy **I** 352–3
  Portugal **I** 349–55, 363
  power, centre of **I** 351
  public rituals **I** 354–5
  rebellion **I** 349
  ritual **I** 354–6, 360–2, 363
  rulers and court **I** 351, 353–60, 362–3
  San Salvador **I** 350–2, 356
  slaves and slave trade **I** 359, 362–3, 364
  trade **I** 349–50, 362–3, 364

Spain *see also* **Aracena, Andalusia, anticlericalism in**
  California, breakdown of Spanish mission system in **II** 225–36
  Christianization of Iberia **I** 198–212
  Decalogue in Tagalog, Oliver's manuscript of **I** 312–13
  Xavier, Francisco, Japanese in letters of **I** 275–6
Sparta plane, survival of cult on I 245–6
speaking in tongues *see* **glossolalia**
specificity I 17–18
Speer, Robert II 288–9
Spencer, Baldwin IV 17, 18–19
Spenser, Edmund II 30
Spieth, Jacob III 413
Spinoza, Benedict IV 45
spirits and demons *see also* **witchcraft, sorcery and devils**
  Aboriginal Australians **IV** 15
  angels **III** 469, 475–6
  Burkino Faso, faith-healers of Assemblies of God in **III** 259–60, 262–6
  deliverance **III** 257–61, 263, 267–70
  diseases **III** 256
  Gnostics **I** 168
  healing **III** 69–71
  Jamaican peasant life, religion as resistance in **III** 187–8, 191
  Kardecist-Spiritist belief **III** 470–1, 474
  Lübeck prophet in local and Lutheran context **I** 409, 414–16
  Michigan Indians, Catholic hymns of **IV** 185
  Mizeki, Bernard **IV** 157–8, 163
  Nigeria, fertility in Itapa-Ekiti in **III** 280
  Philippines, imitation of Christ in **III** 61–2, 69–71, 75–6
  syncretism **IV** 264
  Taiwan
    conversion to Protestantism amongst urban immigrants in **III** 321
    syncretism among Paiwan Catholics **IV** 264
  Zimbabwe, missionaries in Northern Nyaga District in **II** 393
spiritualists III 312–13, 380

430

INDEX

spirituality
  Chile, young women as apostles to the poor in **II** 275–6
  China, beliefs of Zhouzi village people in Catholic diocese in **III** 42–4
  female spirituality, models and rituals of **II** 275–6
  Latin America, awakening of indigenous people in **IV** 325–6
Spiro, Melford E I 124
Spivak, GC I 10
Sri Lanka III 458
Stanley, Arthur Penrhyn I 98
Stark, Rodney III 318, 375
Stark, Werner III 335–6, 340
Starkey, D II 204
state
  China, Catholic women of Congregation of Sisters in **IV** 68, 71–2, 73–5, 82
  church-state relations **IV** 307
  Korean military 'comfort women' **I** 89
  separation of church and state **II** 210
Steele, Thomas III 308, 310, 312
Steiner, Jean I 433
Stenmanns, Hendrina II 86
Stephanas, household of I 133–4
stereotyping **III** 109
Stewart, C IV 263
Stirrat, RL III 458
Stollenwerk, Helena II 86
stone, agency of the I 243
Strabo I 234
Strasbourg, France, faith, family and fashion in III 127–48
  accents **III** 140
  aesthetics **III** 128, 137–40
  Alsace **III** 127, 128–9, 140
    accents **III** 140
    ethnic identity **III** 128
  Calvinists **III** 137
  Catholics **III** 127–31, 133, 135–8
    Christ, representation of **III** 138
    church interiors **III** 138
    decor **III** 130, 133
    dress **III** 130, 135–6
    imagery **III** 138
    mothers **III** 142
    Protestant in Catholic family **III** 132–3
    social interactions **III** 129–30, 134
    social networks **III** 140
    visiting and interaction with families **III** 140–2
    voluntarism **III** 144
  Christ, representation of **III** 138
  church interiors **III** 137–9
  City styles **III** 136
  decor **III** 128–9, 130, 132–3, 137–9
  dress **III** 128, 130, 132–3, 135–8
  economic activities **III** 127–8
  ethnic identity **III** 128, 133, 139–40
  family social organization **III** 140–5
  homes, interiors of **III** 128–9, 130, 132–3
  husbands **III** 142–3
  ideology to social action, relationship of **III** 128
  imagery **III** 138
  language **III** 139–40
  lay aesthetics **III** 128, 137–40
  Lutherans **III** 137
  modernization on family, effect of **III** 143–4, 145
  mothers **III** 142–3
  networks **III** 140
  Protestants **III** 127–9, 131–8
    Catholic family, Protestant in a **III** 132–4
    Christ, representation of **III** 138
    church interiors **III** 138
    decor **III** 132
    dress **III** 132, 135–6
    social interactions **III** 129, 131, 134
    social networks **III** 140
    visiting and interaction with families **III** 140–1
  religious affiliation **III** 128–9
  social action and interaction **III** 127–31, 134, 140, 145
  social identity and style **III** 129
  style **III** 128, 130, 132–3, 135–6
  traditional dress **III** 135–6
  visiting and interaction with families **III** 140–1
  voluntarism **III** 144
  wives **III** 142–3
streams III 277, 281–3, 292
Strehlow, Carl IV 16
structure and anti-structure III 307–13
Sturge, Joseph III 182
Su Shih I 329

INDEX

subordination of women IV 29, 30, 32, 35–8
Subramaniam, KR I 464–5
subversion I 69–70
Sudan, Uduk faith in five-note scale in IV 191–206
Suetonius I 123
Sultan, Tippu IV 106
Suma Ching Hai International Association (SCHIA) III 319
Sumatra *see* **Karo Batak Protestant Church, Sumatra, conversion and**
Sun, Benedictus I 431
Sun, Clara I 427–8, 430
Sun Dance IV 143, 148–52
Sunday schools III 400
Sundkler, Bengt II 401, **IV** 343
Sung dynasty I 332, 335
supernatural *see also* **Devil; spirits and demons; witchcraft, sorcery and devils**
   Bushmen, Christ as trickster in religion of contemporary **III** 298–301
   Philippines, trial of Seberine Candelaria in **II** 117–18, 122–9
   syncretism **III** 464–5, 474
   Ulster Pentecostals **II** 390, 401
   Zimbabwe, missionaries in Northern Nyaga District in **II** 390, 401
superstition *see also* **Devil; spirits and demons; witchcraft, sorcery and devils**
   Kongo, church in **I** 264
   reincarnation, belief in **III** 470–2
   Southern Tswana, Africa, cultivation and colonialism in **II** 31–5
support, acts of III 56–7, 323, 324–6
Svoronos, N II 208–9, 215, 218
Swaggart, Jimmy III 360, 362, 365–6, **III** 371
Swanepoel, Dominie III 300
Swedish Mission Church II 255
symbols
   hats as symbol of women's position in Evangelical churches in Edinburgh, Scotland
   core meanings **IV** 26, 29–32, 37, 39
   individuals, use by **IV** 25–6
   ritual and early church in Eastern Mediterranean **I** 124–5
   situational meanings **IV** 26, 32–9

Taiwan, syncretism among Paiwan Catholics in **IV** 263
   types **IV** 25
   women 25–6, 29–39
Symeon of Emesa III 311
Symphorianus of Augustodunum, St I 238
syncretism
   actor's level, at **III** 463–79
   agency, exercise of **I** 13
   assimilation **II** 256
   Bahai **III** 471, 474–6
   Bolivia, catechists of Aymara Indians in **IV** 263–4
   Brazil **III** 425, 463–79
   bricolage **IV** 263
   Catholics **III** 469–71, 475, **IV** 252–80
   clairvoyance **III** 475
   cognitive dissonance **II** 256
   colonialism **II** 257, **IV** 266–7, 273
   connectionism **III** 465
   essentialism **I** 13
   external dimension **III** 464
   faith **III** 475
   Fiji, Last Supper tapestries in **IV** 262
   free will **III** 468–9
   gender **III** 463–79
   guardian angels, belief in **III** 469, 475–6
   hierarchy of motives **III** 466, 475
   identity **IV** 263–4, 270–1, 276–7
   institutionalized religion, non-participation in **III** 464, 474–5
   inter-dimensional approach **III** 464–5
   internal dimension **III** 464
   intermediate goals **III** 466
   jagar rituals in Goa, India **III** 22–3, 27
   Kardecist-Spiritist belief **III** 470–1, 474
   Kimbanguism and syncretism in Zaïre **II** 253–70
   Latin America, awakening of indigenous people in **IV** 318, 329–30
   master motives **III** 466
   meaning **I** 12–13, **II** 253, **IV** 263
   missionaries **IV** 265–6, 274
   Paiwan Catholics **IV** 252–80
   politics **IV** 263
   power **III** 466, 473, 477–8
   reincarnation, belief in **III** 470–2

ritual **II** 256–7, **IV** 264–7, 272–4, 276
saints **III** 469–70, 476
schemas **III** 466, 473, 475–8
Shinto-Buddhism **II** 256
signification **III** 465–6, 473
social pluralism **II** 257–9
social relations **III** 464
sociology **I** 12–13
structure and agency, relationship between **III** 465
Sumatra, Karo Batak Protestant Church in **II** 143
supernatural **III** 464–5, 474
syncretic objects **IV** 264, 268–74
syncretic subjects **IV** 263–4, 268–72, 274–5
Taiwan
  conversion to Protestantism amongst urban immigrants in **III** 319
  Paiwan Catholics **IV** 252–80
tattooing **IV** 273–4
traditional or indigenous religion **IV** 263–8, 273–4, 276
translation of the Bible **IV** 265
women **III** 463–79
Zaïre **II** 253–70
Syrian Christians I 216, 219, **III** 83–92; **IV** 105–7, 108, 114–15, 118
Syrian Orthodox Church I 24

taboos
  Inuit Pentecostalism and Evangelicalism in Canadian and Eastern Arctic **III** 221
  menstrual blood taboo **III** 109, 110–12, 119, 120–2
  Southern Tswana, Africa, cultivation and colonialism in **II** 33
  Zaïre, Kimbanguism and syncretism in **II** 260, 261
Tac, Pablo II 229
Tacitus I 123
Tagalog
  Oliver's manuscript of Decalogue in Tagalog **I** 311–27
  translation of the Bible **I** 73–5, 311–27
Taiwan *see also* **Taiwan, conversion to Protestantism amongst urban immigrants in; Taiwan, syncretism among Paiwan Catholics in**

conversions **III** 319
Quan Yan Method **III** 319
Suma Ching Hai International Association (SCHIA) **III** 319
Taiwan, conversion to Protestantism amongst urban immigrants in III 317–29
  ancestor worship **III** 318
  attachments **III** 318–19, 322–3
  Baptists **III** 317
  cell groups **III** 318, 321–3
  charismatic signs and wonders **III** 321–2, 323–4
  community service centres **III** 321
  Confucianism **III** 318–19
  cultural continuity **III** 319
  demons **III** 321
  deviants, converts as **III** 318
  foreign or Western religion, Christianity as **III** 318
  glossolalia **III** 322
  institutional factors **III** 319
  mechanisms of conversion **III** 319, 322–3
  meditation groups **III** 319
  modernity **III** 325
  norms, violation of **III** 318
  Pan-Tin Presbyterian Church **III** 320–5
  Presbyterians **III** 317, 320–4
  profile of churches **III** 320–2
  religious experience **III** 319
  support, acts of **III** 323, 324–6
  syncretism **III** 319
  theological approach **III** 325
  Third Wave Charismatic Movement **III** 320
  Tunghai Bread of Life Christian Church **III** 317, 320–5
Taiwan, syncretism among Paiwan Catholics in IV 262–80
  agency **IV** 275
  ancestor worship **IV** 264, 276
  animal sacrifice **IV** 266
  captivation **IV** 275
  carving **IV** 266–73
  chieftainship **IV** 265, 266, 276
  Christian symbolism **IV** 263
  colonialism **IV** 266–7, 273
  culture **IV** 263, 266–7, 274
  devotional objects **IV** 263–4
  discourse of syncretism **IV** 263

education **IV** 265
emotional participation **IV** 275–6
Five-year ceremony of ball impaling **IV** 276–7
identity **IV** 263–4, 270–1, 276–7
indigenous art, sales of **IV** 267
indigenous religion **IV** 263–8, 273–4, 276
Japanese colonialism **IV** 266–7, 273
language **IV** 265–6
making of syncretic objects and subjects **IV** 268–72
material culture of chieftainship **IV** 266
millet reaping, disputes over **IV** 265
missionaries **IV** 265–6, 274
Paiwan Cross **IV** 262–4, 266, 268–72, 275–6
politics of religious synthesis **IV** 263
process of synthesis **IV** 263
religious synthesis **IV** 263, 276
ritual houses for collective worship **IV** 264–5, 272–4, 276
rituals **IV** 264–7, 272–4, 276
Second Vatican Council **IV** 265–6
snake imagery **IV** 273
social agency of syncretic objects **IV** 264
spirits **IV** 264
syncretic objects **IV** 264, 268–74
syncretic subjects **IV** 263–4, 268–72, 274–5
tattooing **IV** 273–4
tradition and Catholicism in Tjaubar **IV** 264–77
translation of the Bible **IV** 265
Taizong, Emperor I 200, 208
Talbot, Cynthia I 445
Tamaz, Pastor III 239–40, 245–7, 249
Tamils
   Bible **I** 70
   colonialism **I** 70
   culture **I** 451–3
   Dalit theology in Tamil Christian folk music **IV** 242–61
   dance **IV** 284
   land **I** 451–3
   Tarangambadi (Tranquebar), India, missionaries in **I** 441–4
T'ang Pin I 338
Tanjorkar, Kubernath IV 285
Tanzania II 375, 379

Tarangambadi (Tranquebar), India, missionaries in
   18th century, early **I** 441–69
   agriculture **I** 444–5
   behaviour of European Christians **I** 446–51
   Brahmins **I** 444, 449, 459
   British **I** 443, 464
   British East India Company **I** 464
   care of self, conversion as **I** 453–62
   caste **I** 444, 449, 459
   Catholics **I** 443
   conversions **I** 441–3, 448–9, 453–62
   Dalits **I** 444
   dancers, women as **I** 460
   discipline **I** 449–50
   Dutch East India Company **I** 442
   exclusion **I** 446
   health and body **I** 450–1, 459, 461, 464
   Hinduism **I** 455–6
   Jesuits **I** 443
   language **I** 452, 460
   moral behaviour **I** 446–62
   Muslims **I** 442, 454–5
   mutual dependence **I** 444
   penances **I** 449, 453
   Portugal **I** 442
   Protestants **I** 442
   rice production **I** 443
   salvation **I** 453, 460
   siddhars **I** 449–51, 458–61
   slave trade **I** 443, 448
   social system **I** 444–5
   Tamils **I** 441–4
   women **I** 460–1
Tarasoff, Koozma IV 148
Tatars and apostasy II 179–200
   1840–1905 **II** 179–93
   assimilation **II** 181
   baptism **II** 180–2
   children and grandchildren of apostates **II** 186–9
   conversions **II** 179–82, 187, 190
   court cases **II** 183–4
   decentralization **II** 180–1
   Department of Religious Affairs of Foreign Faiths **II** 190
   distribution of power **II** 185
   education **II** 188
   freedom of conscience **II** 181
   generational shift **II** 187

instigators II 183
Law of 1905 II 189-92
material advantages II 180
Muslims II 179-93
names II 186, 189
religious toleration II 181-2, 187-8, 189, 193
resettlement II 183-4
Russian Orthodox Church II 179-93
seducers II 183, 185, 188
self-ascription II 186-93
Tatian (Addai) I 214-15
tattooing IV 273-4
Taylor, W I 463
Taylor, William II 290-1
Tea Dance IV 147
temples into churches, conversion of I 234-7
Ten Commandments, Oliver's manuscript in Tagalog of I 311-27
Tengström, Emil I 184
Teresa of the Andes, St II 274
Tertullian I 146, 171-2
Theben, Wigand von III 312
Theissen, Gerd I 142-3
Theodore of Sykeon I 237-42
Theodosius I, Emperor I 201
theology
  Africa
    African Christian theologies IV 332-53
    Zimbabwe, American Evangelicalism in III 368-9
  basic plank of theology I 6-7
  Dalit theology in Tamil Christian folk music IV 242-61
  Edessa, Osrhoene I 214-15
  French Polynesia, women in ordained ministry in Mô'ohi Protestant Church in III 157-8
  Greek Orthodoxy, women studying in III 95
  intercession IV 111-13
  liberation theology II 274, IV 340-2, 347
  New Zealand, gospel songs in IV 214-21
  oral theology IV 343
  Persia I 214-15
  reconstruction, theologies of IV 347-8
  specific theology I 2
  Taiwan, conversion to Protestantism amongst urban immigrants in III 325
  traditional religions IV 332-53
  women III 95
  Zimbabwe, American Evangelicalism in III 368-9
Theophanes the Confessor I 242
Theophilus I 219
Thirteen Syrian Fathers, Georgia I 204-7
Thirty Years War I 412
Thomas Christians and the Thomas tradition I 213-26
  caste I 222, II 54-5, 59-61
  Chola kingdom, persecution within the I 217
  Church of the East I 213-17
  dalits I 212
  dance IV 283-3, 290-1
  dar-al-Islam, refugees from I 220-3
  Jewish communities I 214
  Kerala,
    early communities in I 199
    women III 84-5
  Malabar Christians I 215, 217, 219, 221, 223-4
  Malankara Nazaranis I 219, 223
  martial sciences, training in I 222-3
  Muslim communities I 214
  Nestorians Christians I 215-16
  Northists I 222
  Orthodox Christian Pilgrim Centre in Kerala IV 107, 115
  Persia I 222
  refugees I 217-20
  Roman peace I 213
  Southists I 222-4
  Syriac language I 219
  traders I 213
  Udayamperur I 223
  women III 84
Thomas, Keith II 204, III 447, 456
Thomas of Cana IV 282
Thomas, St IV 106, 115-18
Thomas, Sabu III 83
Thomma, Knayil I 222
Thompson, George II 36
Thornton, John I 398-9
Thurn, Everard im II 67
Tibetts, Janice III 219

435

INDEX

time
  commodification and personalization **IV** 46
  framing **IV** 46–7
  Mexico, immediacy and eternity in a Catholic convent in **IV** 46–51, 65–6
  precious, as **IV** 45
  sacred and profane, time as **IV** 46–9, 65
Timothy **I** 157, 159–60
Tindale, Norman **IV** 21–2
Tiridates IV **I** 199
Tirumuular **I** 459
TiruvaLLUvar **I** 456
Titus **I** 157, 159–60
Tjalkabota. Moses **IV** 14–17
Togo **III** 107
tombs
  intercession, theology of **IV** 111–12
  India, Orthodox Christian Pilgrim Centre in Kerala **IV** 111–12
tongues, speaking in *see* **glossolalia**
Tookaluk, Q **III** 219–20
Topping, Eva C **III** 96
Toren, C **IV** 262
Torres Strait Islands *see* **Malo cult in Torres Straits Islands**
Torrey, Reuben Archer **IV** 208, 209, 213, 221
Tournon, Carlo de **I** 290
Towler, R **III** 443–4
tradition *see also* **traditional or indigenous religions**
  context **I** 18
  gender **IV** 224–7, 238–9
  Leningrad, independent religious communities in **III** 347
  Malawi, women as religious and political praise singers and dancers in **IV** 224–7, 238–9
  Malo cult in Torres Straits Islands **I** 46
  Mizeki, Bernard **IV** 162–4
  modernity and tradition **II** 358–61, **III** 95, 96–7, 100, 102
  Mount Athos, exclusion of women from **III** 100–3
  shrines **IV** 170
  Spain, anticlericalism in Aracena in **II** 358–61
  syncretism **IV** 264–77
  Taiwan, syncretism among Paiwan Catholics in **IV** 264–77
  United States, gender and change in Church of the Lord (Aladura) in **III** 120
traditional or indigenous religions *see also* **animism; healing; paganism; spirits**
  Aboriginal Australians **III** 165–80
  African Christian theologies **IV** 336–7, 339–40
  Bushmen, Christ as trickster in religion of contemporary **III** 298–316
  Chile, young women as apostles to the poor in **II** 275
  Dalit theology in Tamil Christian folk music **IV** 245–6
  Decalogue in Tagalog, Oliver's manuscript of **I** 312, 322–3
  diviners **I** 239, 242, 243, 245, **II** 125, **III** 277–8
  French Antilles, Catholic missions to slaves in **I** 395
  Inuit Pentecostalism and Evangelicalism in Canadian and Eastern Arctic **III** 213
  Kongo, church in **I** 259
  Merina traditional religion and the Bible in Madagascar **I** 112–20
  Nigeria, fertility in Itapa-Ekiti in **III** 276–8, 281–4
  Norddeutsche Missionsgesellschaft, role of Devil in preaching of **III** 416–18
  Philippines, trial of Seberine Candelaria in **II** 129–30
  siddhars **I** 449–51, 458–61
  Soyo, Capuchins and rulers of **I** 358–62
  Sudan, Uduk faith in five-note scale in **IV** 191–206
  syncretism **IV** 263–8, 273–4, 276
  Taiwan, syncretism among Paiwan Catholics in **IV** 263–8, 273–4, 276
  Thomas Christians and the Thomas tradition in India **I** 213–26
  Zaïre **II** 266–8
Trajan **I** 123, 141, 154
Tranquebar, India *see* **Tarangambadi (Tranquebar), India, missionaries in**

translations of the Bible I 24–5
  Aboriginal Australians III 168, 169
  Africa I 72–5, 112–13, IV 345
  African Initiated Churches I 113
  Australian aboriginals I 71
  China I 71
  colonialism I 70–1
  democratisation I 112–13
  French Polynesia, women in ordained ministry in Mô'ohi Protestant Church in III 157
  gender I 74–6
  India I 72, 75–7
  indigenous languages and dialects I 70–7, 112
  interpretation I 112–13
  Korean Protestantism, contribution of Biblewomen to II 241–2
  Merina traditional religion and the Bible in Madagascar I 114, 117, 118
  missionaries I 70–4
  native agency I 70–1
  Oliver's manuscript of Decalogue in Tagalog I 311–27
  patriarchal attitudes I 75
  Sudan, Uduk faith in five-note scale in IV 192–3
  syncretism II 265
  Tagalog language, Philippines I 73–5
  Taiwan, syncretism among Paiwan Catholics in II 265
  Zulus I 96–7, 101
trees and groves, destruction of sacred I 234–7
Trible, Phyliis I 88, 91
trickster, Christ as *see* Bushmen, Christ as trickster in religion of contemporary
Trinity
  Dalit theology in Tamil Christian folk music IV 253–4
  Trinitarianism III 398–9
  Wu Li and first Chinese Christian poetry I 338–9
Trumbull, David II 290
Truth, Gospel of I 169–70
Tryphon, St I 235
Tupi and European women in eyes of Claude d'Abbeville I 295–308
  cannibalism I 299
  Capuchins I 296
  colonization I 295–308
  conversion I 298–9, 301–5
  execution of prisoners, involvement in I 300–1
  feminist scholarship I 297–8
  gender and colonization I 295–308
  marriage I 303–4
  military assistance, need for I 299
  misogyny I 302
  motherhood I 302
  nudity I 303
  polygyny I 301–2
  productivity I 300–1
  sexuality I 303–4
  slavery I 299–300
  war I 299–300
  witchcraft I 304–5
Turkey, Edessa in I 214–15
Turner, E IV 124
Turner, Harold IV 337, 343
Turner, Victor I 140–1, 173, III 308, 312, IV 47, 90, 124, 137
Tuti, Desmond III 367
Tswana people of Africa I 97
Tychicus I 158
Tyconius I 191
Tylor, Edward B II 69

Uchimura Kanzo III 333, 336–7
Uduk faith in five-note scale IV 191–206
  Day of Judgment IV 191–2
  fundamentalism IV 192–3
  'God', word for IV 194–5
  hymns IV 191–205
  language IV 191–205
  lyrics IV 194–203
  missionaries IV 191–205
  neologisms IV 194–5
  new lyrics to old tunes IV 199–203
  new songs IV 203–5
  slavery IV 192
  songs of praise, composition of IV 193
  Sudan Interior Mission IV 192–4, 205
  translated hymns IV 196–9, 204–5
  translation of the Bible IV 192–3
  words of hymns IV 194–203
Uganda II 373–5, 377, 379–80
Ulster Pentecostals II 384, 385–92
  Elim movement II 385–6, 388–9

INDEX

secularization, opposition to **II** 388
Zimbabwe, missionaries in Northern Nyaga District in **II** 384, 385–93, 397–4, 401
Umana, Manuel II 294
Underhill, EB III 189–90
Underwood, Kenneth III 127
United Kingdom *see also* **Anglican Church; Northern Ireland**
Brazil, Universal Church of the Kingdom of God in **III** 433–7, 439
British East India Company **I** 464, **II** 59–60
colonialism **III** 181
Glastonbury, United Kingdom **IV** 137
hats as symbol of women's position in Evangelical churches in Edinburgh, Scotland **IV** 25–41
House Church Movement **III** 368
India
 British East India Company **I** 464, **II** 59–60
 Tarangambadi (Tranquebar), missionaries in **I** 443, 464
Jamaican peasant life, religion as resistance in **III** 181
magic and mysticism **II** 204
Nanrantsouak, church at **I** 379–80, 386–90
United States, gender and change in Church of the Lord (Aladura) in **III** 107, 120
Walsingham, pilgrimage to **IV** 121–39
United States *see also* **United States, Methodist shrines in**
Baptists **I** 35–43, **IV** 64
Brazil, Universal Church of the Kingdom of God in **III** 427
California, breakdown of Spanish mission system in **II** 225–36
Catholic-Protestants distinctions in coming global Christianity **IV** 305–7
Christ for the Nations in Dallas **III** 364
Church of the Lord (Aladura), gender in **III** 106–26
conservatism **IV** 3–7
court use **I** 35–42
evangelists
 New Zealand, gospel songs in **IV** 216
 Zimbabwe, in **III** 357–73
glossolalia **II** 308
India, global fundamentalism and local Christianity in Madras **III** 443, 447–8, 456–8
Korean Protestantism, contribution of Biblewomen to **II** 238–41, 244
missionaries
 California, breakdown of Spanish mission system in **II** 225–36
 Korean Protestantism, contribution of Biblewomen to **II** 244–5
Pentecostalism **III** 424
secularization **I** 14
Seventh–day Adventism **III** 375–80
shrines **IV** 170
suburbs, legal pluralism in **I** 35–43
Zimbabwe, American Evangelicalism in **III** 357–73
United States, Methodist shrines in IV 169–77
Book of Discipline **IV** 173, 175
Catholics **IV** 169, 171, 174–5
Christmas Conference **IV** 174
classification of shrines **IV** 172
Cockspur Island **IV** 169
commemorative shrines **IV** 173
Commission on Archives and History **IV** 174
conversions **IV** 173
death mask of John Wesley **IV** 172
heritage landmarks **IV** 174
historical self-consciousness **IV** 173
identity shrines **IV** 173
idolatory **IV** 170
landmarks or shrines **IV** 174–6
Lasley's memorandum **IV** 174
Lovely Lane Museum, Baltimore **IV** 173–5
merchandise **IV** 174
miracles **IV** 172
number of pilgrims **IV** 173–4
Protestants **IV** 169–71, 175
Reformation **IV** 172
Robert Strawbridge House **IV** 174–5
Shrines and Landmarks Committee **IV** 174
St George's Church, Philadelphia **IV** 173
Trinity United Methodist Church **IV** 173

INDEX

United Methodists **IV** 169–70, 172–3, 175
Universal Church of the Kingdom of God of Brazil III 423–42
  Argentina **III** 428
  Catholics, attacks on **III** 436
  Chile **III** 428
  class **III** 430
  cultural blocs **III** 426–7
  embargoes **III** 428–9
  England, as a black church in **III** 433–7, 439
  global expansion **III** 425–9
  heretical ideas **III** 432
  Islam, attacks on **III** 436
  Latin America **III** 424–5
  magic-sacramental methods **III** 432
  media **III** 430–1
  missionaries **III** 425
  names, use of different **III** 428–9
  negative image **III** 425–6, 428–9, 438
  number of branches abroad **III** 426–9
  parliamentary elections **III** 431
  Pentecostalism **III** 423–39
  Portugal **III** 429–33, 438
  Protestantism, conflicts with **III** 431–3
  social composition **III** 425
  social work **III** 429
  South Africa **III** 427–8
  syncretism **III** 425
  transnationalisation **III** 423–39
  United States **III** 427
universalism
  Cameroun, liturgical adaptation in St Paul de Ndzon-Melen in **I** 450, 52, 56
  Colenso, John William. *Commentary of Romans* **I** 102, 104
  context **I** 18
  Dalit theology in Tamil Christian folk music **IV** 250, 253
  horizontal **I** 7
  Merina traditional religion and the Bible in Madagascar **I** 117
untouchables *see* **dalits**
Urapmin, millenarianism of IV 47–8
Urban VIII I 352
urban areas
  attendance at church **I** 17
  Chile, pentacostalism in **II** 285, 286–301
  Taiwan, conversion of immigrants in **III** 317–29
  uptake **I** 17
Usener, Hermann I 243
Ussher, James III 384

Valerian I 215
Valerius I 185
Valuev, PA II 183
van der Veer, P III 275–6
Van Lonkhuyzen, Harold W I 470
Vandals I 189, 191
Vanhee, Hein I 265
Vargas, Antonio IV 322–3
Varikas, Eleni III 155–6
Vattaseril, Geevarghese IV 109
Vaz, Jorge I 261–2
Vedanta-based practices I 12
Vellapally, Markose III 83–4
Vellapally, Susan III 83–4
Venizelos, Evangelos III 101
vernacular colonialism I 70–7, 112
Viard, Philip II 173
vicarious death, meaning of I 142
Vieira, Antonio I 369, 370–1
Vilatte, Joseph II 371, 377
Villa-Vicencio, Charles IV 347–8
violence *see also* **war**
  China, Christian sectarian violence in late 19th century **II** 323–39
  churches, burning **III** 341–7, 351–61
  Spain, anticlericalism in Aracena in **III** 341–7, 350–61
virgin birth I 264
virginity I 368, 373–4
Viswanathan, Gauri I 470
Vladimir of Kiev, prince II 378
vocations IV 48–9, 50–66, 71
voluntarism III 144
voodoo (*Vaudou*) I 394
Voulgaris, Eugenios II 212

Wabanaki people I 379–90
wages II 165–6
Wahba, Magdi III 18
wakes III 65
Waldron, Peter II 187
Walsh, Thomas II 160
Walsingham, United Kingdom, pilgrimage to IV 121–39
  Anglican shrine **IV** 121–3, 125–8, 132
  canonical enactments **IV** 127–37

Catholic shrine **IV** 122–3, 125–31
  genre of pilgrimage, as **IV** 123–5
  Holy House **IV** 126–7
  innovation **IV** 122
  irony, performance of **IV** 130–5, 137
  merchandise **IV** 126, 132–3
  official or controlled pilgrimages
    IV 122, 127–8
  oppressive ideologies, pilgrimages as
    legitimatizing **IV** 124
  pastiche **IV** 137
  performance
    cultivation of creativity in
      IV 122–3
    dimensions of performance
      IV 127–8
    irony **IV** 130–5
    rituals **IV** 121–5, 132–7
  ritual performance **IV** 121–5, 132–7
  ritualization **IV** 123–4
  self-consciousness **IV** 132
  sets and props **IV** 126–7
  Slipper Chapel **IV** 126–7
  social relations **IV** 122–3
  stage, Walsingham as a **IV** 125–7
  vulgarity **IV** 132–3
Wan Li, emperor I 290–1, 333
Wang Ch'iu-kuei I 332
Wang Shih-chen I 335, 342
war
  Civil War **III** 341, 344
  Cold War **IV** 347–8
  Greek war of independence **II** 209
  Mexican war of independence
    II 231–2
  Thirty Years War **I** 412
  Tupi and European women in
    eyes of Claude d'Abbeville
    I 299–300
Ware, Kallistos II 377
Warner, Lloyd W III 84
Waruta, Douglas IV 341
washing I 136–7, **IV** 16
water see also **baptism**
  Judaism **I** 136–7
  Nigeria, fertility in Itapa-Ekiti in
    III 280, 281–3, 292
  Nile river cults **I** 244
  paganism in rural Anatolia and
    Greece from 6th century,
    conversion from **I** 239
  rituals **III** 280, 281–3, 292
  streams **III** 277, 281–3, 292

Waters, Malcolm III 423–4
Way of the Cross procession
  IV 146–7
Webb, Theodor III 167
Weber, Max I 8, 153–4, 163, **II** 202,
  III 127–9, 137, 213, 335, **IV** 47
Weiss, HL II 292
Wenger, Jacqueline IV 306
Werbner, Pnina III 23, 458
Wesley, John II 390, **IV** 169, 171–5
West and Westernization
  African Christian theologies **IV** 334
  China
    Catholic women of Congregation
      of Sisters in **IV** 71–3, 81–2
    sino-Western cultural
      communication at end of Ming
      dynasty **I** 280–94
  Christianity as foreign or Western
    religion **III** 318
  Dalit theology in Tamil Christian
    folk music **IV** 247
  dominance, decline in **IV** 301–2
  focus on West **I** 2
  Indian dance forms, Christianity in
    IV 283, 291
  Malawi, women as religious and
    political praise singers and
    dancers in **IV** 224–7, 238
  missionaries **I** 15
  nuclear families **III** 144
  Philippines, imitation of Christ in
    III 61–2, 76
  Protestant-Catholic distinctions in
    coming global Christianity
    IV 301–2
Westcott, Brooke II 69
Wheeling, Charles III 385
Wheelock, Eleazer I 471–2
White, Ellen III 376, 377–9, 380,
  384–6, **IV** 37
White Lotus sect I 425, 428, 436–7
Whitefield, George I 473–4, 477
Whitehouse, Harvey III 165, 168, 170,
  171–3
Whiteman, Daniel II 67
Wiest, Jean-Paul I 385
Wilberforce, William III 183
Williame, Jean-Paul III 151, 152–3
Williams, Glanmor I 11
Williams, Jesse II 397, 399
Williams, R I 16
Willis, Paul II 110

INDEX

Willoughby, WC **II** 30, 32–3
Wilson, B **II** 201
Wilson, Bryan **II** 386–7, 398
Wilson, John **II** 14–17, 20, 22
Wilson, Kottapalli **IV** 242
Wilson, Larry **III** 385
Wilson, R **II** 95, 104
Wilson, Stephen **IV** 91
Wimber, John **III** 363
Wimbush, Vincent **I** 70
Wissler, Clark **IV** 143
witchcraft, sorcery and devils *see also* **spirits and demons**
   20th century **II** 121
   animism **I** 120, **II** 119–20
   Augustinian doctrine **II** 118–19
   Bible **III** 291
   Brazil
      Universal Church of the Kingdom of God **IV** 432
      women in colonial Brazil **I** 304–5, 375
   Burkino Faso, faith-healers of Assemblies of God in **III** 255
   Bushmen, Christ as trickster in religion of contemporary **III** 298, 302–3, 310–11
   children, denouncing by **II** 121
   China, beliefs of Zhouzi village people in Catholic diocese in **III** 38–9
   covenants and pacts **II** 119
   denouncing **II** 121
   Enlightenment **II** 119
   India, global fundamentalism and local Christianity in Madras **III** 446–7, 452–4, 456
   Jamaican peasant life, religion as resistance in **III** 187–8
   Malleus Maleficarum (Hammer of Witches) **II** 119
   Malo cult in Torres Straits Islands **I** 46–7
   Merina traditional religion and the Bible in Madagascar **I** 115–18
   Nigeria, fertility in Itapa-Ekiti in **III** 277–8, 291
   Norddeutsche Missiongesellschaft, role of Devil in preaching of **III** 410
   Philippines **II** 117–18, 120–9
   pilgrimage **IV** 90–1
   priestesses **II** 120
   prosecutions **II** 119
   Protestants **II** 204
   reporting **II** 121
   Tupi and European women in eyes of Claude d'Abbeville **I** 304–5
   United Kingdom **II** 204
   United States, gender and change in Church of the Lord (Aladura) in **III** 110
   voodoo (*Vaudou*) **I** 394
   witch-hunts **II** 119
   women **II** 118–21
      accusation **II** 97–8
      Brazil **I** 304–5, 375
      Zaïre, Kimbanguism and syncretism in **II** 264–6, 268
Wolff, Christian **I** 285–6
women *see also* **gender**
   animism **II** 120
   Brazil
      base communities (CEBs) in **III** 197–8, 202
      colonialism **I** 367–78
      Tupi and European women in eyes of Claude d'Abbeville **I** 295–308
   Chile, young women as apostles to the poor in **II** 273–84
   China, Catholic women of Congregation of Sisters in **IV** 68–83
   colonialism **I** 367–78
   comfort women **I** 85–93
   dance **I** 460
   domestic servants, as **II** 165–6, 169
   French Polynesia, women in ordained ministry in Mô'ohi Protestant Church in **III** 149–61
   Inuit Pentecostalism and Evangelicalism in Canadian and Eastern Arctic **III** 220
   Jamaican peasant life, religion as resistance in **III** 187, 190–1
   India
      Kerala, status of Christian women in **III** 83–93
      Tarangambadi (Tranquebar), missionaries in **I** 460–1
   Korea
      military 'comfort women' **I** 85–93
      Protestantism, contribution of Biblewomen to **II** 237–52

liturgical leadership **I** 7
Malawi, women as religious and political praise singers and dancers in **IV** 224–41
Mezzogiorno, glossolalia and possession amongst Pentecostal groups of the **II** 316–18
models and rituals of female spirituality **II** 275–6
Mount Athos, exclusion of women from **III** 94–5, 100–4
nationalization **III** 95
New Zealand, Irish Catholics in 19th century Christchurch in **II** 165–6, 169
Nigeria, fertility in Itapa-Ekiti in **III** 275–97
ordination of women **III** 107, 110, 113, 149–61
Paul, St **III** 112
role models **II** 106
syncretism **III** 463–79
Tarangambadi (Tranquebar), India, missionaries in **I** 460–1
theology, studying **III** 95
Tupi and European women in eyes of Claude d'Abbeville **I** 295–308
witchcraft and devils **II** 118–21
Zimbabwe, missionaries in Northern Nyaga District in **II** 385
Won, Tabitha II 243
Wookey, AJ II 34, 44–5
work *see* **labour**
World Christian Database IV 298
World Christian Encyclopaedia IV 298–9, 312
Wu Li and first Chinese Christian poetry I 330–47
aria (*ch'ü*) **I** 336, 339, 342–3
Buddhism **I** 337–8
Ch'ing dynasty **I** 335
Confucianism **I** 336–7, 338, 342–3
conventional *shih* poems **I** 339
conversion **I** 337
cults **I** 337–8
folk material **I** 331–2, 343
Hakka love-songs **I** 331–2
Heaven **I** 336–7
heavenly ladders **I** 341–2
lyric (*tz'u*) **I** 335–6
Macau **I** 339–40, 342
Moses Admonishes the People **I** 344

musical performances **I** 332
Neo-Confucianism **I** 337
Occupation of the Months **I** 332
painting **I** 330, 337
Portuguese community, customs and festivals of Macau **I** 339
shih poetry **I** 335–6, 339–42
Singing of the Source and Course of Holy Church **I** 338–9
Song of the Fisherman **I** 340–1
Sorrow of Ten Thousand Ages (Kuei Chuang) **I** 342
Sung dynasty **I** 335
Tea-Gathering Songs **I** 331
Trinity **I** 338–9
Wurmbrand, R II 299–300
Wutawanashe, Andrew III 365
Wylie, Alexander I 331
Wyss, Hilary I 470

Xavier de Medeiros, Francisco IV 92–3
Xavier, Francisco I 340, III 31
Xavier, Francisco, Japanese in letters of I 268–79
bonzes **I** 268–9, 271–2
Buddhist monasticism, attacks on **I** 268–9, 271–2
conversion **I** 269–72, 274–5
cultural identity **I** 270
hostility to Spain **I** 275–6
male homoeroticism **I** 272
missionaries **I** 268, 275–6
racism **I** 269, 275
samurai **I** 272
sodomy **I** 269, 271–2
Xu Dashou **I** 291, 293
Xu Guangqi **I** 287–91
Xun Zi **I** 282–3

Yang, Agnes **I** 427, 429–30
Yang, Fenggang **III** 318–19
Yang Guangxian **I** 293
Yang Kuang-hsien **I** 329–30
Yang Tingjun **I** 291
Yannoulatos, Anastasios **II** 374
Yaqui and southwest and central American literature III 310
Yazdgard I I 208
Ye Xianggao I 286
Yezdgerd's Edict of Toleration I 215
Yi, Maria **II** 242

INDEX

Yi U-jong II 238
Yinger, JM III 340
Yolngu Christianity III 165-78
Yong Zhen, emperor I 293
Yoruba people III 107, 110, 277-82, 287-8, 291-2
Young, LL II 243
Young, Richard Fox II 15
Yusuf, Akil III 20

Zachariah, Mathai III 85
zagor III 24-33
Zaïre
    Catholicism II 266-7
    colonialism II 269
    indigenous religion II 266-8
    institutional pluralism II 268-9
    Kimbanguism and syncretism in Zaïre II 253-70
    Kongo Christians II 266
    Orthodox Mission II 374, 376, 379
    Protestantism II 267-8
    social pluralism II 268
    syncretism II 253-70
    witchcraft II 267, 268
Zampelios, Spyridon II 217
Ze-Mikael (Aregawi the Elder) I 205
Zhang Zhinan III 40
Zhouzi, China, beliefs of village people in Catholic diocese in III 38-60
    bishops III 40
    citizenship courses III 43
    companion in support of lonely and distressed, acting as III 58-60
    Cultural Revolution III 45
    economy III 41-2
    education III 42-3
    ethical standards III 38-9, 43, 56, 57-9
    literacy III 42
    medical treatment and health III 43
    missionaries III 39-40
    Ming period III 40
    modernization III 38-9, 59-60
    natural environment III 41-2
    oral enquiry III 38-60
    patriarchal clan system III 59
    prayer III 55-6
    Qing period III 40
    society III 39-44
    spiritual civilization III 42-4
    support, providing III 56-7
    witchcraft III 38-9
    Wugong County III 44-7
    Yangling District III 47-55
    young people III 43-4
    Yuan Mongol dynasty III 41
    Zhouzhi County III 55
Zhu Xi I 284
Zialcita, FN III 69
Ziegenbalg, Bartholmäus I 442-63
Zimbabwe *see also* Zimbabwe, American evangelicalism in; Zimbabwe, missionaries in Northern Nyaga District in
    missionaries IV 156-8
    Mizeki, Bernard IV 156-65
    Orthodox Mission II 375-6
    Rhodesia IV 156-65
Zimbabwe, American evangelicalism in III 357-73
    Anglican Church III 358, 371-2
    anti-communism III 367, 370
    awareness, level of III 366-73
    bans III 371, 372
    Campus Crusade III 359, 363
    Carter Report III 363-4
    Catholic Church III 358, 371
    Christ for All Seasons III 362, 365, 367
    Christ for the Nations in Dallas III 364
    Christian Marching Church of Central Africa III 368
    colonization III 357-9
    Compassion Ministries III 371
    crusades and conferences III 362-4, 370
    culture III 366
    Down to Earth outreach program III 366-7
    education of local pastors III 369
    Evangelistic Explosion III 364
    Explo '85 III 363
    foreign currency III 365-6
    Full Gospel Businessmen's Fellowship International III 360
    funding III 366-7
    House Church movement III 368
    Jimmy Swaggart Ministries III 360, 365-6, III 371
    liberation theology III 367-8
    Life Ministries III 359
    literature III 365-6

INDEX

local ministries **III** 364
media **III** 365–6
Northside Community Church **III** 366
Pentecostalism **III** 359–60
political agenda **III** 369–70
Rhema Bible Church **III** 361, 362, 364–5
Rhodesia to Zimbabwe, from **III** 357–9
Shekinah Ministries **III** 364, 367, 372
significance **III** 364–6
sociopolitical issues **III** 371–3
theological awareness, lack of **III** 368–9
transnationals **III** 359–61
United Methodist church **III** 358
white church leaders **III** 366–7
white-led churches before independence **III** 357–9
World Vision International **III** 360–1, 371
Youth With a Mission **III** 359–60
Zimbabwe, missionaries in Northern Nyaga District in II 383–405
Adventism **II** 387
African Pentecostal movement, spread of **II** 400
agriculture **II** 385
architecture **II** 396
Avila mission **II** 385–6, 395, 397, 399
Barwe refugees from Portuguese East Africa **II** 385
Carmelites **II** 384, 385–8, 394–401
Catholics **II** 384, 385–8, 394–401
cemeteries **II** 392
Chikumbirike spirit **II** 393
colonialism **II** 383–5, 397
conflict between Ulster Pentecostalists and Carmelites **II** 398–400
Elim movement **II** 385–6, 388–93, 397–401
enemies, conflicts between missionaries creating **II** 400
famines **II** 385
folk Catholicism **II** 395–6
healing **II** 390–1, 396
Hwesa people **II** 384–5, 388–90
inculturation **II** 396

Irish Carmelites **II** 384, 385–8, 394–401
  architecture **II** 396
  colonialism **II** 397
  healing **II** 396
  inculturation **II** 396
  Irish Question **II** 398
  marriage, interference with **II** 400
  nationalism **II** 387, 397, 398
  rural background **II** 397
  schools, disputes over number and location of **II** 399–400
  veneration **II** 394
Irish Question **II** 398
land **II** 385, 392–3
localism **II** 384, 388–90
Manyika people **II** 384–5, 395–6, 401
marriage, interference with **II** 400
medical work **II** 389
migrant labour, absences due to **II** 385
missionaries **II** 384–402
nationalism **II** 383, 387, 397, 398, 400
native commissioners **II** 385
Pentecostals **II** 384, 385–93, 397–400
popular Christianity **II** 383–4
Regina Coeli mission **II** 395–7
re-sacralising the landscape **II** 392–3, 401
reserves **II** 385
revivalism **II** 401–2
rituals **II** 388
rural politics and consciousness **II** 383
schools, disputes over number and location of **II** 399–400
socio-economic context of missionisation **II** 384–5
Southern Irish Catholicism **II** 385–8
spirits **II** 393
supernatural **II** 390, 401
Ulster Pentecostals **II** 384, 385–93, 397–401
  cemeteries **II** 392
  Irish Carmelites, conflict with **II** 398–400
  Irish Question **II** 398
  land **II** 392
  localisation **II** 388–90

marriage, interference with **II** 400
medical science **II** 390–2
re-sacralising the landscape
 II 392–3, 401
rituals **II** 389
schools, disputes over number and
 location of **II** 399–400
supernatural **II** 390, 401
veneration **II** 394, 396
women, work of **II** 385
Zoa, Jean I 50–1
Zoroastrianism I 217, **II** 16

Zucker, W III 307–8, 309
Zulus
 Colenso, John William **I** 96–7,
  99–110
 consciousness **I** 99
 converts of Ekukhanyeni **I** 99–101
 double nature of man **I** 107
 hegemony **I** 107–8
 language **I** 96–7, 99
 translation of Bible **I** 96–7, 101
Zuo Baihao III 41
Zvelebil, Kamil I 450, 455, 459–60